James Woodress is Professor of English, University of California, Davis. In addition to editing seven volumes of *American Literary Scholarship*, he has written and edited many books, among them *Willa Cather: Her Life and Art*, *Eight American Authors: A Review of Research and Criticism*, and *Essays Mostly on Periodical Publishing in America: A Collection in Honor of Clarence Gohdes*.

American Literary Scholarship

1974

American Literary Scholarship

An Annual / 1974

Edited by James Woodress

Essays by Lawrence Buell, Nina Baym, G. R. Thompson, Hershel Parker, Bernice Slote, Hamlin Hill, William T. Stafford, Richard M. Ludwig, Karl F. Zender, Jackson R. Bryer, Robert D. Arner, Warren French, David Stouck, Margaret Anne O'Connor, James H. Justus, Richard Crowder, Linda Welshimer Wagner, Jordan Y. Miller, John T. Flanagan, Michael J. Hoffman, Jean Rivière, Hans Galinsky, Rolando Anzilotti, Keiko Beppu, Rolf Lundén

Duke University Press, Durham, North Carolina, 1976

© 1976. Duke University Press. Library of Congress Catalogue Card number 65–19450. I.S.B.N. 0–8223–0362–0. Printed in the United States of America by Heritage Printers, Inc.

Foreword

This is the twelfth volume of *American Literary Scholarship* to appear since the series was begun in 1965. It continues to grow in size each year like a healthy adolescent despite the editor's efforts to stunt its growth. This is not surprising, as there are more and more places to publish literary scholarship than ever before. The 164 journals listed in the table of abbreviations in the first *ALS* have grown to 247 listed here. In addition, as teaching positions become scarcer and the competition for tenure and promotion grows more and more intense, the pressures to publish increase. Unfortunately, the complaints of the contributors to this volume in recent years still are valid: much of the ore assayed in these chapters contains only a small amount of gold. The annual production of literary scholarship still is often padded, repetitious, and trivial.

In an effort to keep up with changing trends and interests in American literary scholarship, I have made some innovations in this year's volume. For the first time there is a chapter devoted exclusively to Pound and Eliot. This perhaps was a logical step after we reclaimed Eliot last year from British bibliography where he had been comfortably ensconced for many years. In addition, the present volume divides 20th-century fiction into three segments instead of the previous two. This was done to save the sanity of those intrepid contributors willing to undertake a review of the scholarship in this vast area. Scholarship abroad in American literature continues to flourish, and the section on foreign contributions begun last year has been continued. One foreign scholar, however, has objected to this segregation of overseas scholarship, but I have continued it as the only practical way of drawing attention to the large amount of research and criticism going on outside of the United States. In some instances, however, when the American contributors to this volume have known of foreign scholarship, they have included it in their essays. Foreign authors are invited to send their books and offprints to the appropriate *ALS* contributors.

I have continued the separate Poe chapter, as in last year's volume, and moved the minor 19th-century poets to the 19th-century general chapter, which has been retitled "19th-Century Literature." The chapter on black writers, which was promised for this volume, did not materialize due to circumstances beyond the control either of the editor or the contributor, but there is every expectation that this innovation will begin appearing in the volume for 1975. Meanwhile, coverage of black writers, as in the past, is distributed among the various chapters.

The present volume, it seems to me, is an excellent survey of American literary scholarship for 1974. The old contributors have maintained their high standards, and the new ones have equalled their predecessors. Newcomers this year are Lawrence Buell, Richard M. Ludwig, Karl F. Zender, Robert D. Arner, David Stouck, Margaret O'Connor, Jordan Miller, and Keiko Beppu. I welcome them aboard and am grateful for their essays. I also am deeply grateful to the four who are leaving the volume with this issue: Nina Baym, G. R. Thompson, Bernice Slote, and John T. Flanagan. And to those who have contributed before this year and will be back again next year I also offer thanks: Hershel Parker, Hamlin Hill, William T. Stafford, Jackson Bryer, Warren French, James Justus, Richard Crowder, Linda Wagner, Michael Hoffman, Jean Rivière, Hans Galinsky, Rolando Anzilotti, and Rolf Lundén.

I also wish to thank Jackson Bryer and his research assistant, Nancy Prothro, for sending bibliographical items from the master files of the MLA International Bibliography to the contributors to this volume. And finally I am very grateful to Warren French for making the index to ALS 1973 when I was teaching in France; Mark Morgan, my present research assistant, who compiled this index; and the Research Committee of the University of California at Davis for a grant to help in the preparation of this volume.

James Woodress

University of California, Davis

Table of Contents

Key to Abbreviations

ABC / *American Book Collector*
ABR / *American Benedictine Review*
AFS / *Asian Folklore Studies*
AI / *American Imago*
AION-SG / *Annali Istituto Universitario Orientale, Napoli, Sezione Germanica*
AL / *American Literature*
ALR / *American Literary Realism*
ALS / *American Literary Scholarship*
America-Austriaca / *America-Austriaca: Beiträge zur Amerikakunde* 3 (Wien and Stuttgart: Wilhelm Branmüller)
AmerS / *American Studies*
AN / *Acta Neophilologica* (Ljubljana)
AN&Q / *American Notes and Queries*
AntigR / *Antigonish Review*
Approdo / *L'Approdo Letterario* (Rome)
AQ / *American Quarterly*
ArmD / *Armchair Detective* (White Bear Lake, Minn.)
ArQ / *Arizona Quarterly*
AtM / *Atlantic Monthly*
ATQ / *American Transcendental Quarterly*
AusLS / *Australian Literary Studies*
BB / *Bulletin of Bibliography*
BC / *Book Collector*
BMHS / *Bulletin of the Missouri Historical Society*
BMWMLA / *Bulletin of the Mid-West Modern Language Association*
BNYPL / *Bulletin of the New York Public Library*
Boundary 2 / *Boundary 2: A Journal of Postmodern Literature*
BP / *Banasthali Patrika*
BSUF / *Ball State University Forum*
BuR / *Bucknell Review*
CarolinaQ / *Carolina Quarterly*

CE / *College English*
CEA / *CEA Critic*
CEAA / Center for Editions of American Authors
CentR / *The Centennial Review*
ChR / *Chicago Review*
CL / *Comparative Literature*
CLAJ / *College Language Association Journal*
ClioW / *Clio: An Interdisciplinary Journal of Literature, History, and the Philosophy of History* (Univ. of Wisc.)
CLQ / *Colby Library Quarterly*
ColL / *College Literature* (West Chester, Pa., State College)
ColQ / *Colorado Quarterly*
CompD / *Comparative Drama*
ConL / *Contemporary Literature*
ConnR / *Connecticut Review*
Costerus / *Costerus: Essays in English and American Language and Literature*
CP / *Concerning Poetry*
CR / *Critical Review* (Australia)
CRevAS / *Canadian Review of American Studies*
CritI / *Critical Inquiry*
CritQ / *Critical Quarterly*
DAI / *Dissertation Abstracts International*
DHLR / *D. H. Lawrence Review*
DLR / *Delaware Literary Review*
DN / *Dreiser Newsletter*
DQR / *Dutch Quarterly Review of Anglo-American Letters*
DR / *Dalhousie Review*
DVLG / *Deutsche Vierteljahrsschrift für Literatur Wissenschaft und Geistesgeschichte*
EA / *Etudes Anglaises*
EAL / *Early American Literature*

ECS / *Eighteenth-Century Studies*
EDB / *Emily Dickinson Bulletin*
EIC / *Essays in Criticism*
EIHC / *Essex Institute Historical Collections*
EIL / *Essays in Literature* (Western Illinois University)
ELH / *English Literary History*
ELN / *English Language Notes*
ES / *English Studies*
ESA / *English Studies in Africa* (Johannesburg)
ESP / *English Symposium Papers*
ESQ / *Emerson Society Quarterly*
ETC. / *ETC.: A Review of General Semantics*
ETJ / *Educational Theatre Journal*
Expl / *Explicator*
FCN / *Faulkner Concordance Newsletter*
FForum / *Folklore Forum*
FHA / *Fitzgerald-Hemingway Annual*
FI / *Forum Italicum*
FOB / *Flannery O'Connor Bulletin*
Frost: *Centennial Essays* / Jac Thorpe, ed., *Frost: Centennial Essays*, (Hattiesburg, Miss.: Univ. Press of Miss.)
GaR / *Georgia Review*
Gohdes Festschrift / James Woodress, ed., *Essays Mostly on Periodical Publishing in America: A Collection in Honor of Clarence Gohdes* (Durham, N. C.: Duke Univ. Press, 1973)
GSlav / *Germano-Slavica*
HC / *The Hollins Critic*
HLB / *Harvard Library Bulletin*
HLQ / *Huntington Library Quarterly*
HSL / *Hartford Studies in Literature*
HTR / *Harvard Theological Review*
ICarbS
IEY / *Iowa English Bulletin: Yearbook*
IFR / *International Fiction Review*
IJAS / *Indian Journal of American Studies*
IllQ / *Illinois Quarterly*
InR / *Intercollegiate Review* (Bryn Mawr)
IndF / *Indiana Folklore*
IR / *Iliff Review*

JA / *Jahrbuch für Amerikastudien* (now *Amerikastudien*)
JAAC / *Journal of Aesthetics and Art Criticism*
JAAR / *Journal of the American Academy of Religion*
JAF / *Journal of American Folklore*
JAH / *Journal of American History*
JAmS / *Journal of American Studies*
JASAT / *Journal of the American Studies Association of Texas*
JBlS / *Journal of Black Studies*
JEMFQ / *John Edwards Memorial Foundation Quarterly*
JEthS / *Journal of Ethnic Studies*
JFI / *Journal of the Folklore Institute*
JHI / *Journal of the History of Ideas*
JGE / *Journal of General Education*
JLN / *Jack London Newsletter*
JLS / *Journal of Literary Semantics*
JML / *Journal of Modern Literature*
JNT / *Journal of Narrative Technique*
JPC / *Journal of Popular Culture*
JSR / *Jackson State Review*
KF / *Keystone Folklore*
KFR / *Kentucky Folklore Record*
KN / *Kwartalnik Neofilogiczny* (Warsaw)
L&P / *Literature and Psychology*
LaS / *Louisiana Studies*
LCrit / *Literary Criterion* (Univ. of Mysore, India)
LFQ / *Literature/Film Quarterly*
LHY / *Literary Half-Yearly*
LitR / *Literary Review* (Farleigh Dickinson Univ.)
LJ / *Library Journal*
LWU / *Literatur in Wissenschaft und Unterricht* (Kiel)
MAPS / *Memoirs of the American Philosophical Society*
MarkhamR / *Markham Review*
MD / *Modern Drama*
MDAC / *Mystery and Detection Annual*
MichA / *Michigan Academician* (formerly *PMASAL*)
MidSF / *Mid-South Folklore*
MFS / *Modern Fiction Studies*
MHRev / *Malahat Review*
MinnH / *Minnesota History*

MissFR / Mississippi Folklore Register
MissQ / Mississippi Quarterly
MLN / Modern Language Notes
MLQ / Modern Language Quarterly
ModA / Modern Age
Mosaic / Mosaic: A Journal for the
    Comparative Study of Literature
    and Ideas
MPS / Modern Poetry Studies
MQ / Midwest Quarterly
MQR / Michigan Quarterly Review
MR / Massachusetts Review
MTJ / Mark Twain Journal
N&Q / Notes and Queries
NCarF / North Carolina Folklore
NCF / Nineteenth-Century Fiction
NConL / Notes on Contemporary
    Literature
NCHR / North Carolina Historical
    Review
NCTR / Nineteenth Century Theatre
    Research
NDQ / North Dakota Quarterly
NEQ / New England Quarterly
NHJ / Nathaniel Hawthorne Journal
NM / Neuphilologische Mitteilungen
NMexFR / New Mexico Folklore
    Record
NMW / Notes on Mississippi Writers
NN / Northwestern Univ. Press—
    Newberry Library
NS / Die Neueren Sprachen
NYFQ / New York Folklore Quarterly
NYT / New York Times
NYTBR / New York Times Book
    Review
NYTM / New York Times Magazine
OhR / Ohio Review
PAAS / Papers of the American Anti-
    quarian Society
Paideuma / Paideuma: A Journal
    Devoted to Ezra Pound Scholarship
Papajewski Festschrift / Paul Buchloh,
    et al., eds., Studien zur englischen
    und amerikanischen Sprache und
    Literatur: Festschrift für Helmut
    Papajewski (Newmünster:
    Wachholz)
PBSA / Papers of the Bibliographical
    Society of America
Person / The Personalist

PF / Pennsylvania Folklife
PLL / Papers in Language and
    Literature
PMLA / Publications of the Modern
    Language Association
PNJHS / Proceedings of the New
    Jersey Historical Society
PoeS / Poe Studies
PolR / Polish Review
PQ / Philological Quarterly
PR / Partisan Review
Proof / Proof: Yearbook of American
    Bibliographical and Textual
    Studies
PrS / Prairie Schooner
QJLC / Quarterly Journal of the
    Library of Congress
QJS / Quarterly Journal of Speech
RALS / Resources for American
    Literary Study
RANAM / Recherches Anglaises et
    Américaines (Strasbourg)
RES / Review of English Studies
RJN / Robinson Jeffers Newsletter
RLC / Revue de Littérature Com-
    parée
RLV / Revue des Langues Vivantes
SAB / South Atlantic Bulletin
SAF / Studies in American Fiction
SAmH / Studies in American Humor
S&S / Science and Society
SAQ / South Atlantic Quarterly
SB / Studies in Bibliography
SBL / Studies in Black Literature
SCB / South Central Bulletin
SCN / Seventeenth-Century News
SCR / South Carolina Review
SDR / South Dakota Review
SEL / Studies in English Literature,
    1500–1900
SELit / Studies in English Literature
    (Japan)
SFQ / Southern Folklore Quarterly
ShawR / Shaw Review
SHR / Southern Humanities Review
SIL / Studies in Linguistics
SIR / Studies in Romanticism
SLitI / Studies in the Literary
    Imagination
SLJ / Southern Literary Journal
SLN / Sinclair Lewis Newsletter

SN / *Studia Neophilologica*
SNNTS / *Studies in the Novel*
  (North Tex. State Univ.)
SoQ / *The Southern Quarterly*
SoR / *Southern Review*
SR / *Sewanee Review*
SSF / *Studies in Short Fiction*
StQ / *Steinbeck Quarterly*
SwAL / *Southwestern American
  Literature*
SwHQ / *Southwestern Historical
  Quarterly*
SwR / *Southwest Review*
TamR / *Tamarack Review*
TCL / *Twentieth-Century Literature*
TFSB / *Tennessee Folklore Society
  Bulletin*
ThS / *Theatre Survey*
TJQ / *Thoreau Journal Quarterly*
TkR / *Tamkang Review*
TLS / *Times Literary Supplement*
TQ / *Texas Quarterly*
TriQ / *Tri-Quarterly*
TSB / *Thoreau Society Bulletin*
TSEN / *T. S. Eliot Newsletter*
TSL / *Tennessee Studies in Literature*
TSLL / *Texas Studies in Literature
  and Language*

TUSAS / *Twayne United States
  Authors Series*
UDR / *University of Dayton Review*
UWR / *University of Windsor Review*
Versions of the Past / Harry B. Hen-
  derson, *Versions of the Past: The
  Historical Imagination in American
  Fiction* (New York: Oxford)
Viebrock Festschrift / Klaus Schuh-
  mann, et al., eds., *Miscellanea
  Anglo-Americana: Festschrift für
  Helmut Viebrock* (Munich:
  Pressler)
VQR / *Virginia Quarterly Review*
WAL / *Western American Literature*
WCR / *West Coast Review*
WF / *Western Folklore*
WHR / *Western Humanities Review*
WMQ / *William and Mary Quarterly*
WSCL / *Wisconsin Studies in Con-
  temporary Literature* (now ConL)
WWR / *Walt Whitman Review*
WWS / *Western Writers Series*
  (Boise State College)
YR / *Yale Review*
YULG / *Yale University Library
  Gazette*

Part I

1. Emerson, Thoreau, and Transcendentalism

Lawrence Buell

i. Books

The year's one book on Transcendentalism in general is Paul F. Boller, Jr., *American Transcendentalism, 1830–1860: An Intellectual Inquiry* (New York: Putnam's), an overview of the religious, philosophical, and social aspects of the movement. Surprisingly broadranging for a work of 227 pages, it manages to touch on most major developments and to portray and compare all the prominent Transcendentalists. For the specialist, its value is limited: it is written mainly for a lay audience, without footnotes and in an impressionistic style; and it contains little information which has not been long available. But it may prove a useful pedagogical tool—*if* used with caution. Unfortunately the book happens to be quite deficient on the subject of Transcendentalist aesthetics, and it is not always to be trusted in matters of detail.

The two full-length studies of Emerson published in 1974 differ markedly in almost every respect. Edward Wagenknecht, *Ralph Waldo Emerson: Portrait of a Balanced Soul* (New York: Oxford Univ. Press), is a highly readable, succinct introduction to Emerson as thinker, writer, and person, based on a solid grasp of Emerson scholarship. Like Wagenknecht's previous "psychographs" of American writers, this book proceeds by topic ("Biography," "Self-Reliance," "Nature," "Art," "Friendship," "Love," "Politics," "The Oversoul"— some rubrics proving more coherent than others), rather than by tracing Emerson's thought as it developed. This format reflects Wagenknecht's preference for stressing the constant elements running throughout Emerson's life and writing, in dissent from Stephen Whicher's conception of Emerson's career as a brief flowering and long decline. What naturally emerges is a sympathetic portrait of Emerson as the conservative sage—the balancer of opposites—rather than the radical seer who later lapsed. In this respect, Wagenknecht's study reinforces the growing trend of interest in the later Emerson. But for the most part Wagenknecht's aim is to articulate scholarly consensus and not to revolutionize the field—another reason why the image of "balance" is an apt choice for the book's dominant metaphor.

In contrast, Erik I. Thurin, *The Universal Autobiography of Ralph Waldo Emerson* (Lund, Sweden: C. W. K. Gleerup), is very much a young man's book, an impetuous attempt to take the field by storm. It is disorganized, redundant, polemical, often tedious and self-indulgent, yet at the same time a fresh approach to Emerson. Roughly speaking, Thurin tries to do for Emerson what Leslie Fiedler has done for the American novel. For Thurin, at the heart of Emerson's bipolar vision is the dichotomy of the sexes; the spirit is identified with the male principle, physical nature and the body with the female; and the explanation for Emerson's desire for the first to control the second lies in a preference for male friendship to heterosexual love, this proclivity also finding a somewhat more direct form of expression in what Thurin calls an ethos of "spiritual androgyny." To validate his claims, Thurin resorts not only to Emerson's life and writings but also to those of his intellectual mentors, particularly Plato, Plotinus, Dante, Michelangelo, Montaigne, Shakespeare, Milton, and Swedenborg. Altogether Thurin brings to bear upon his subject a greater array of erudition than any previous Emerson critic, although he does not always use his learning wisely. His psychological-archetypal approach to Emerson deserves to be taken seriously notwithstanding the defects of his study.

Turning to books on Thoreau, by far the most impressive is a bibliographical work, William L. Howarth, *The Literary Manuscripts of Henry David Thoreau* (Columbus: Ohio State Univ. Press), which lists and describes all known manuscripts. The listings are organized chronologically according to type of work (e.g., "Poems and Translations," "The *Journal*") and prefaced by a brief account of the history of the manuscripts and Thoreau's habits of composition. The product of very careful research, Howarth's calendar is an indispensable guide for scholars seeking to work with Thoreau's manuscripts.

All three books of Thoreau criticism on which I should report try in their own ways to combine analysis of certain aspects of Thoreau's world-view and life-style with an appraisal of his relevance today. The best of the three, William J. Wolf, *Thoreau: Mystic, Prophet, Ecologist* (Philadelphia: Pilgrim), seems designed primarily to convince a Christian readership that despite his anticlericalism Thoreau is one of America's "creative religious thinkers." Wolf has little really new to say about Thoreau's thought; but his knowledge of modern theology enables him to put Thoreau in that context more authoritatively than has yet been done.

Michelene Flak, *Henry-David* [sic] *Thoreau: ou la Sagesse au service de l'Action* (Paris: Éditions Seghers, 1973), presents a sympathetic although somewhat stereotypical portrait of Thoreau as a practical mystic who, with the aid of Emersonian and Oriental wisdom, escaped the confines of American materialism in order to cultivate a rich interior spiritual life without losing touch with the mundane world. Flak tends to be rhapsodic rather than factual, but she is accurate in her major generalizations about Thoreau except for an overemphasis on the influence of Oriental religion upon his development.

Robert S. Dickens, *Thoreau: the Complete Individualist: His Relevance—and Lack of It—for Our Time* (New York: Exposition), attempts a critique of Thoreau's philosophy from a radical point of view. Dickens admires Thoreau's individualism but finds him lacking in awareness of "communal (real democratic-social) solutions" to the problems he diagnoses. The subject is absorbing, but unfortunately the book is crudely written and argued.

No new CEAA texts of Emerson and Thoreau were published during 1974, but Princeton University Press has published a handsome edition of *The Illustrated Maine Woods*, in which Joseph Moldenhauer's definitive text is accompanied by 48 photographs from the Gleason Collection. A less satisfactory edition is Richard F. Fleck, ed., *The Indians of Thoreau: Selections from the Indian Notebooks* (Albuquerque: Hummingbird), which consists of a "representative sampling" from all eleven volumes. In an effort to provide organization according to Thoreau's topical outline, Fleck is forced to take the excerpts out of chronological order and tie them together with transitional comments which in some sections threaten to become longer than the Thoreau passages themselves. The typesetting often makes it hard to tell whether the editor or the author is speaking, and the number of excerpts is too small to give a distinct picture of the original notebooks.

Two other Transcendentalist compilations are Kenneth W. Cameron, ed., *Response to Transcendental Concord: The Last Decades of the Era of Emerson, Thoreau and the Concord School as Recorded in Newspapers* (Hartford, Conn.: Transcendental Books); and Robert E. Collins, *Theodore Parker: American Transcendentalist: A Critical Essay and a Collection of His Writings* (Metuchen, N.J.: Scarecrow, 1973). Cameron's collection of newspaper clippings, covering the years 1879–87, is the latest of the many goldmines of information which he has provided for students of Transcendentalism. Collins reprints in full six significant Parker discourses (including "A Discourse of the Transient and Permanent in Christianity"), which have the added advantage of paralleling various works by Emerson. Unfortunately this useful text is introduced by a one-sided polemic praising Parker at Emerson's expense.

Among the books which deal with Transcendentalism in part, there are several items that deserve notice. To begin with literary criticism, Laurence Stapleton, *The Elected Circle: Studies in the Art of Prose* (Princeton, N.J.: Princeton Univ. Press, 1973), devotes a chapter apiece to Emerson (pp. 166–94) and Thoreau (pp. 195–232). The discussion of Thoreau is rather desultory and unoriginal, but on Emerson Stapleton argues provocatively for a redefinition of Emerson's best work as including such previously neglected efforts as "Works and Days," "The Fugitive Slave Law," and "Natural History of Intellect." Donald B. Stauffer surveys the poetry of Transcendentalism in one chapter of *A Short History of American Poetry* (New York: Dutton, pp. 93–113), concentrating on Emerson, Thoreau, Very, and Cranch. Stauffer's analysis is brisk, concise, and predictable in its assessment of Transcendentalist verse as largely second-rate but important as a stage in the evolution of American poetry.

Two essays on Transcendentalist writing by Joel Porte appear in successive volumes of Harvard English Studies: "Transcendental Antics," in *Veins of Humor*, ed. Harry Levin (Cambridge, Mass.: Harvard Univ. Press, 1972, pp. 167–83), and "The Problem of Emerson," in *Uses of Literature*, ed. Monroe Engel (Cambridge, Mass.: Harvard Univ. Press, 1973, pp. 85–114). The latter presents what is by now an unnecessary argument that Emerson's writing should be studied with the same critical scrutiny accorded other major literary figures of the American Renaissance, followed by a perceptive reading of *English Traits*. The former essay is a very fine job of work—a real breakthrough in Transcendentalist criticism—in which Porte makes a persuasive case for the importance of "the comic impulse" among the Transcendentalists. Yet another Porte essay, "Henry Thoreau and the Reverend Poluphloisbois Thalassa," appears in Matthew J. Bruccoli, ed., *The Chief Glory of Every People: Essays on Classic American Writers* (Carbondale: So. Ill. Univ. Press, 1973, pp. 191–210). This is a rather thin and derivative attempt to trace Thoreau's fondness for water imagery in the manner of Gaston Bachelard.

Turning to biography and intellectual history, the same volume contains an essay by Eleanor Tilton, "Mr. Emerson—of Boston" (pp. 77–95), which claims a bit too much for the influence of David Hume upon Emerson. Perry Westbrook's study of *John Burroughs* (New York: Twayne), summarizes Burroughs's personal and intellectual relations with Emerson and Thoreau (pp. 50–63). Richard Slotkin's chapter on Thoreau in *Regeneration Through Violence: The Mythology of the American Frontier, 1600–1860* (Middletown: Wesleyan Univ. Press, 1973, pp. 518–38), gives a competent though predictable account of Thoreau's career as manifesting "an ethical system based on Deerslayer's experience of the wilderness." Wilson Carey McWilliams's ambitious history of *The Idea of Fraternity in America* (Berkeley and Los Angeles: Univ. of California Press, 1973), contains a chapter on Emerson and Thoreau (pp. 280–300) which compares them on the subjects of friendship and politics, arguing that Thoreau attached more value to both. Although McWilliams is not entirely convincing, his discussion—and his book as a whole—merit close study.

ii. Periodicals

Let me begin with articles on Emerson that deal with significant general aspects of his life and thought. Evelyn B. Greensberger, "The Phoenix on the Wall: Consciousness in Emerson's Early and Late Journals" (*ATQ* 21:45–56), is a thoughtful psychological study which detects a movement from fear to acceptance of social interaction in the journals between 1820 and the late 1840s. Maurice Gonnaud, "The Humane Seer and Its Avatars in Emerson" (*ATQ* 22:79–85), defines and traces the development of comic elements in Emerson's work. This article should be read in conjunction with Porte's "Transcendental Antics." Jeffrey Steinbrink, "Novels of Circumstance and Novels of Character: Emerson's View of Fiction" (*ESQ* 20:101–10), the best review of the subject to date, contends that Emerson did not so much dislike prose fiction itself as the direction which the genre had taken thus far. Gay Wilson Allen's lecture, "Emerson and the Establishment" (*UWR* 9,i[1973]:5–27, finds Emerson to have been more social reform–minded than is generally accepted. Two studies which rediscover the "dark" side of Emerson without advancing notably beyond Stephen Whicher and Newton Arvin are Joseph F. Doherty, "Emerson and the Loneliness of the Gods" (*TSLL* 16:65–75), and Louis B. Salomon, "A Walk with Emerson on the Dark Side" (*Costerus* 6[1972]:121–35).

Turning to studies of Emerson's relation to individual figures ancient and modern, Stanley Brodwin, "Emerson's Version of Plotinus: the Flight to Beauty" (*JHI* 35:465–83), identifies Emerson's reluctance to accept the risk of total self-denial involved in the Plotinian quest for ideal beauty as a crucial difference between the two thinkers and as a source of conflict in Emerson's thought. Sheldon W. Liebman retells with a few amplifications the twice-told tale of "Emerson's Discovery of the English Romantics, 1818–1836" (*ATQ* 21:36–44). Frank Lentricchia compares "Coleridge and Emerson: Prophets of Silence, Prophets of Language" (*JAAC* 32[1973]: 37–46), in order to show how the romantic organicism of both differs fundamentally from New Critical formalism. Christopher W. Sten, "Bartleby the Transcendentalist: Melville's Dead Letter to Emerson" (*MLQ* 35:30–44), gives a sophisticated reading of Melville's story as a representation of the conflict between materialism and Transcendental idealism. Richard DiMaggio, "A Note on *Sons and Lovers* and Emerson's 'Experience' " (*DHLR* 6[1973]:214–16), notes that Lawrence may have taken his title from Emerson, but the affinities between the novel and the essay are charted in a more searching and extensive article, James N. Wise, "Emerson's 'Experience' and *Sons and Lovers*" (*Costerus* 6[1972]:179–221). Carl Lindner finds "Newtonianism in Emerson's *Nature*" (*ESQ* 20:260–69); R. A. Yoder sees Emerson and Hawthorne as sharing a similar "conservative" philosophy of cosmic optimism in "Transcendental Conservatism and *House of the Seven Gables*" (*GaR* 28:33–51); Elizabeth Perkins,

"Emerson and Charles Harpur" (*AusLS* 6[1973]:82–88), describes the Australian poet's marginalia in his copy of Emerson; James E. Mulqueen gives a negative answer to the question, "Is Emerson's Work Central to the Poetry of Emily Dickinson" (*EDB* 24[1973]: 211–20).

Harold Bloom, "The Freshness of Transformation: or Emerson on Influence" (*ATQ* 21:59–63), meditates insightfully on the conflict in Emersonian—and American—aesthetics between the desire for independence and the desire to be mastered by a supreme influence. David Bromwich, "Suburbs and Extremities" (*Prose* 8:25–38), proceeds from Bloom's conviction that Emerson is the Milton of American poetry—its father/oppressor, so to speak—but goes further than Bloom in identifying Emerson's dualistic tendency as the specific source of a profound ambivalence in American nature poetry from Whitman on down.

Alfred F. Rosa, "Emerson and the Salem Lyceum (*EIHC* 110: 75–85); Joel Myerson, "An Unpublished Interview with Emerson in 1867" (*SAB* 39,ii:89–94); and David Sowd, "Peter Kaufmann's Correspondence with Emerson" (*ESQ* 20:91–100), add somewhat to our knowledge of how Emerson interacted with his contemporaries.

Critical studies of Emerson's writings include Leonard N. Neufeldt, "The Law of Permutation—Emerson's Mode (*ATQ* 21:20–30), which traces the process of image-transformation in Emerson's prose; Martha Banta, "Gymnasts of Faith, Fate, and Hazard" (*ATQ* 21: 6–20), which views the gymnastic metaphor as indicative of a striving after the balance of opposites in both thought and technique; Brian M. Barbour, "Emerson's 'Poetic' Prose" (*MLQ* 35:157–72), an unsympathetic and reductive indictment of Emerson's prose style as capable of nothing but rhapsodic lyrical abstraction; Richard Lee Francis, "The Evolution of Emerson's Second 'Nature'" (*ATQ* 21:33–35), a brief account of how the second essay serves to modify the first. Kenneth W. Cameron collects Charles Malloy's 19th-century papers on Emerson as poet in " 'A Study of Emerson's Major Poems' " (*ATQ* 23:1–121).

In a careful job of textual analysis, Joel Myerson, "Practical Editions: Ralph Waldo Emerson's 'The American Scholar'" (*Proof* 3 [1973]:379–94), surveys 27 recent editions of the discourse and finds varying degrees of inaccuracy in each.

By way of transition from Emerson to Thoreau, we should note

Donald Ross, Jr., "Emerson and Thoreau: A Comparison of Prose Styles" (*Lang&S* 6[1973]:185–95). By means of an intensive linguistic analysis of "Discipline" as compared with the sandbank passage in *Walden,* Ross succeeds in speaking more minutely about the stylistic differences between the two writers than has yet been done. Michael Orth, "The Prose Style of Henry Thoreau (*Lang&S* 7:36–52), subjects the sandbank passage to even more detailed scrutiny. Given the ease with which Emerson and Thoreau can be cited to support almost any proposition, there may be some real promise to the objectivity of a linguistic approach, although its results so far seem microscopic.

Among the year's short critical studies of Thoreau, the most provocative is Michael West, "Scatology and Eschatology: The Heroic Dimensions of Thoreau's Wordplay" (*PMLA* 89:1043–64), which unearths a large amount of scatological punning in Thoreau and relates it to his lifelong concern for personal hygiene, and in particular for maintaining his health against the threat of consumption. Thoreau's emphasis on a disciplined life is thus seen to have a psychophysiological as well as an epic-heroic side. Sometimes West's ingenuity gets the better of him, as can be seen more clearly in a second, much less substantial article, "*Walden*'s Dirty Language: Thoreau and Walter Whiter's Geocentric Etymological Theories" (*HLB* 22:117–28); nevertheless his work contributes significantly to our understanding of Thoreau.

Other studies of the general aspects of Thoreau's thought and work include Kenneth W. Rhoads, "Thoreau: The Ear and the Music" (*AL* 46:313–28), which will surely be accepted as the best short analysis of what music meant to Thoreau; Brian R. Harding, "Swedenborgian Spirit and Thoreauvian Sense: Another Look at Correspondence" (*JAmS* 8:65–79), which demonstrates that correspondential vision is more basic to Thoreau's approach to nature than has been realized; Lewis Leary, "Beyond the Brink of Fear: Thoreau's Wildness" (*SLitI* 7,i:67–76), which reviews Thoreau's mixed feelings about the wilderness; Jason Marks, "Thoreau's Literary Style" (*LitR* 17:227–37), which adds little to what is already known about Thoreau's development as a writer; and Rolandas Pavilionis, "H. D. Toro ir asmenybes apsisprendimas" ["Thoreau and Self-Determination of Personality"] (*Problemos* [Vilnius] 2[1973]:40–49), an intellectual portrait (abstract in English).

Two studies which try with partial success to make a case for Thoreau as poet are Richard Tuerk, "The One World of Thoreau's Verse (*TJQ* 6,iv:3–14), and especially H. Grant Sampson, "Structure in the Poetry of Thoreau" (*Costerus* 6[1972]:137–54), which places Thoreau in the tradition of meditative poetry as defined by Louis Martz.

As might be expected, *Walden* continues to be the most dissected of any individual Thoreau work. In addition to articles already cited, the following deserve mention. Of special value are Thomas Werge, "The Idea and Significance of 'Economy' Before *Walden*" (*ESQ* 20: 270–74), which outlines the theological origins of that term; and Barbara H. Carson, "An Orphic Hymn in *Walden*" (*ESQ* 20:125–30), a deft and knowledgeable exegesis of "Smoke" as an orphic. Martin Bickman, "Flawed Words and Stubborn Sounds: Another Look at Structure and Meaning in *Walden*" (*SHR* 8:153–62), identifies the principle of continuous transition as central to Thoreau's style and vision; Douglas B. Hill, Jr., "Getting to *Walden*: The Strategies of Thoreau's Thought" (*BSUF* 15,ii:14–26), argues interestingly but inconclusively that *Walden*, "Ktaadn," and "Civil Disobedience" must be approached as a single unit; Robert Kettler, "The Quest for Harmony: A Unifying Approach to *Walden*" (*BSUF* 15,ii:3–13), restates the view that the work is not nature essay, social criticism, or art so much as the expression of an ethic or value system; Gordon V. Boudreau, "Thoreau and Richard C. Trench: Conjectures on the Pickerel Passage of *Walden*" (*ESQ* 20:117–24), claims a possible influence or affinity. Finally, Jeffrey M. Jeske, "*Walden* and the Confucian *Four Books*" (*ATQ* 24, suppl. 1:29–33), contends that Thoreau was more affected by Confucianism than has been realized, while Chung-nam Chang takes much the opposite position in an article in Korean, "Confucian Influences on Thoreau's *Walden*" (*The English Language and Literature* 50:47–68, abstract in English).

Regarding "Civil Disobedience," William A. Herr, "Thoreau: A Civil Disobedient?" (*Ethics* 85:87–91), argues persuasively that in modern terminology Thoreau should rather be labeled a conscientious objector. Christopher L. Johnstone, "Thoreau and Civil Disobedience: A Rhetorical Paradox" (*QJS* 60:313–22), expounds laboriously on the notion that Thoreau's discourse threatens to undermine itself by presenting "a political doctrine that requires the rejection of rhetoric as a form of strategic political activity."

Discussions of other Thoreau works are, as usual, distressingly sparse. The only three of note are Mario L. D'Avanzo, "Fortitude and Nature in Thoreau's *Cape Cod*" (*ESQ* 20:131–38), which finds in the book a view of nature different from that of *Walden*; Kerry Ahearn, "Thoreau and John Brown: What to Do About Evil" (*TJQ* 6,iii:24–28), which shows that both "assertive and retiring impulses" are interwoven in Thoreau's response to Brown and to slavery in general; and William J. Scheik, "The House of Nature in Thoreau's *A Week*" (*ESQ* 20:111–16), a motif study.

Discussions of Thoreau's legacy include Richard F. Fleck, "A Report on Irish Interest in Thoreau" (*TJQ* 6,iv:21–27); Edward C. Jacobs, "Thoreau and Modern Psychology" (*TSB* 127:4–5); and Raymond H. Geselbracht, "The Ghosts of Andrew Wyeth: The Meaning of Death in the Transcendentalist Myth of America" (*NEQ* 47:13–29).

Turning now to short studies of Transcendentalism in general, we find several items of considerable significance. R. A. Yoder, "The Equilibrist Perspective: Toward a Theory of American Romanticism" (*SIR* 12[1973]:705–40), is a brilliant critique that deals in part with Transcendentalist aesthetics. Yoder explains the relative brevity of American Romanticism in terms of its tendency to retreat from a radical prophetic stance to one of cautious mediation between the visionary and the practical. Emerson is his chief exhibit. Duane E. Smith, "Romanticism in America: The Transcendentalists" (*Review of Politics* 35[1973]:302–25), charts a similar tendency in the area of social theory and with it in mind makes some useful distinctions between American vs. German Transcendentalists with respect to political philosophy. Sacvan Bercovitch, "The Image of America: From Hermeneutics to Symbolism" (*BuR* 20[1973]:3–12), argues provocatively if not conclusively that the visions of America expressed by the Transcendentalists and their contemporaries derive from the Puritan settlers' view of American destiny.

Two thoughtful and well-researched discussions of the Fruitlands experience are Richard Francis, "Circumstances and Salvation: The Ideology of the Fruitlands Utopia" (*AQ* 25[1973]:202–34); and Taylor Stoehr, "Transcendentalist Attitudes Toward Communitism and Individualism" (*ESQ* 20:65–90). Both tend in some measure to rehabilitate the reputation of Charles Lane. Stoehr also compares three major Transcendentalists' political attitudes in a less focused and original article, " 'Eloquence Needs No Constable'—Alcott, Emerson and Thoreau" (*CRevAS* 5:81–100). John T. Irwin has much to say about Emerson and Thoreau in "The Symbol of the Hieroglyphics in the American Renaissance" (*AQ* 26:103–26), although this article is more valuable for its background information about Egyptology than for its discussion of the Transcendentalists.

Articles on individual Transcendentalists other than Emerson and Thoreau include Michael Fellman, "Theodore Parker and the Abolitionist Role in the 1850s" (*JAH* 61:666–84), a biased attempt to unmask the racism and pent-up violence in Parker's character which nonetheless contains a good measure of truth and reminds one of the pressing need for a new full-scale biography; Sheldon Peterfreund, "George Ripley: Forerunner of Twentieth Century Ethical Intuitionalism" (*Person* 55:298–302), which accords Ripley an honorable if minor niche in the history of American philosophy; and Richard F. Fleck, "Jones Very—Another White Indian" (*Concord Saunterer* 9,iii:6–12), a superficial treatment of Very's interest in the Indian, which may, however, point the way for further study. Joel Myerson presents excerpts from two important Transcendentalist manuscripts in "Bronson Alcott's 'Scripture for 1840' " (*ESQ* 20:237–59) and "Caroline Dall's Reminiscences of Margaret Fuller" (*HLB* 22:414–28).

Finally, serious students of Transcendentalism in general and Thoreau in particular should not fail to make a full review of the five specialized periodicals in the field: *ESQ*, *ATQ*, *TSB*, *TJQ* and the *Concord Saunterer*. Limitation of space has kept me from discussing a number of articles in these publications, especially the latter three.

iii. Dissertations

In 1974 five dissertations were reported that were devoted to Emerson, four more to Emerson in part, seven to Thoreau, two to Margaret Fuller and Orestes Brownson, and one apiece to F. H. Hedge, F. B. Sanborn, and *The Harbinger*. On the basis of the *DAI* abstracts, the most original contributions would appear to be the following. On Emerson: Leonard G. Gougeon, "The Forgotten God: A Study of Ralph Waldo Emerson as Man and Myth" (*DAI* 35:2940A–41A, Mass.), a psychological-archetypal study; and Suzanne Marrs, "Ralph Waldo Emerson and the Eighteenth-Century English Moralists" (*DAI* 34:5920A–21A, Okla., 1973), which traces Emerson's ideas of self-reliance, correspondence, and compensation back to the Enlightenment. On Thoreau, Joan S. Gimlin, "Henry Thoreau and the American Indian" (*DAI* 35:2221A–22A, Geo. Washington), a study of both the published works and the Indian Notebooks; and Michael C. Meyer "Several More Lives to Live: Thoreau's Political Reputation in America, 1920–1970" (*DAI* 35:1113A, Conn.). On other Transcendentalist topics: John W. Clarkson, Jr., "An Annotated Checklist of the Letters of Franklin Benjamin Sanborn" (*DAI* 34: 6584A, Columbia, 1971), which describes 1,449 letters covering the period 1880–1917; and Sterling F. Delano, "*The Harbinger*: A Portrait of Associationism in America" (*DAI* 35:1043A–44A, So. Ill.), which appears to be a comprehensive account of that periodical's history, contents, and relation to the Association movement in America. For the information of those who would like to look further, here are citations for the other abstracts: *DAI* 34:5047A, 5157A, 5929A, 5963A, 6558A, 6668A, 7204A, 7241A, 7246A; and 35:417A, 1065A, 1632A, 1636A, 2270A, 2935A, 3108A, 3672A.

iv. Conclusion

Not surprisingly, the majority of the year's work on Transcendentalism is more workmanlike than brilliant, less original than dependent upon prior scholarship. Nevertheless in several areas important advances have been made which no serious student should overlook. I would cite especially accomplishments in bibliography (Howarth), psychological and/or archetypal criticism (Greensberger; West, *PMLA*; and—with strong reservations—Thurin); Emersonian humor (Porte, Gonnaud); the Fruitlands experiment (Francis, Stoehr); and the concept of Transcendentalist "conservatism" (Yoder, Smith). Let us hope, however, that it will not be necessary to wait indefinitely for the completion of the many major projects of which the field has need: e.g., the remaining CEAA texts, up-to-date biographies of Parker, Cranch, Dwight, Sanborn, and other neglected figures; a history of Transcendentalism as a social reform movement; and of course the "definitive" account of Transcendentalism as a whole.

Oberlin College

2. Hawthorne

Nina Baym

In 1974 fewer articles were published on Hawthorne than in the previous two years, and no book-length studies. The articles, though mostly not of major scholarly or critical importance, attained a higher general level of interest and competence than at any time since I began to write this yearly review. If there is a trend toward fewer and better publications on Hawthorne, it is something to be grateful for. Sixteen dissertations listed in *DAI* (but not discussed in this essay) testify to Hawthorne's continuing importance in the graduate schools, while the formation late in 1974 of the Nathaniel Hawthorne Society suggests the emergence of a community of scholars and interested persons. The hard-covered annual *Nathaniel Hawthorne Journal*, handsomely designed and richly illustrated with photographs of items from C. E. Frazer Clark, Jr.'s superb collection, continued its announced function of elucidating less-known areas of Hawthorne's life and works.

The review that follows is meant to be comprehensive. I omit from the survey of articles read only a few valueless notes, although doubtless some publications have been unintentionally missed.

i. Texts, Life, Reputation, Bibliography

Three volumes of the Centenary Edition, published by the Ohio State University Press, appeared in 1974: vol. 9, *Twice-told Tales*; vol. 10, *Mosses from an Old Manse*; and vol. 11, *"The Snow-Image" and Uncollected Tales*. The volumes have excellent historical commentary by J. Donald Crowley, who is a leading authority on Hawthorne's short works, and a somewhat less satisfactory textual commentary by Fredson Bowers. Crowley, in 1968, wrote a fine essay explaining the rationale of Hawthorne's revisions and arguing convincingly that the writer and not his wife was responsible for the changes. (See "The Artist as Mediator: The Rationale of Hawthorne's Large-Scale Revisions in his Collected Tales and Sketches," *Hawthorne and Melville in the Berkshires*, ed. Howard P. Vincent [Kent, O.: Kent State Univ. Press, 1968], pp. 79–88, 156–57.) It is amusing therefore to find Bowers blithely attributing one change after another to Sophia Hawthorne's overwrought sensibilities, for all the world as if he were unaware of his colleague's scholarship. In fact, the Bowers textual method is designed to rescue a text from mistakes committed by others, and cannot really make sense out of changing authorial intentions. Happily, the Centenary volumes contain excellent tables showing all variants, and one can study Hawthorne's revisions as well as unauthoritative departures from the text. It was an error in judgment to print the contents of *Twice-Told Tales* and *Mosses* without any indication, except in the apparatus, of the original two-volume divisions. It is at least possible that the arrangement of works within each volume was intended by the author; the present printing gives no sense of the collections as units.

Textual scholars continue to assess the merits and flaws of the Centenary Edition. Hershel Parker, in "Regularizing Accidentals: The Latest Form of Infidelity," *Proof* 3(1973):1–20, singles out the Centenary for especially severe censure. He says that the practice of regularizing accidentals in Hawthorne's case has led to "demonstrable infidelities" to Hawthorne's text and on occasion "flagrant misrepresentation of his practices." Parker and Bruce Bebb in "The 'CEAA': An Interim Assessment," *PBSA* 68:129–48, criticize the Centenary additionally for poor volume design, too much textual material, and historical introductions that "draw back from serious engagement with their materials." On the other side of the debate, G. Thomas Tanselle praises the Centenary in "The New Editions of Hawthorne and Crane," *BC* 23:214–29. The texts, he says, are suitable both for scholars and general readers, and the apparatus provides all the information necessary for examining the editors' decisions. The editors themselves, then, have given us the basis on which to accept or reject their practice.

John J. McDonald has edited "A Sophia Hawthorne Journal, 1843–1844," *NHJ* 4:1–30. Fragments of this journal have been printed before but not the whole, and it is a remarkable contribution to understanding the relation between Hawthorne and his wife. Apart from this personal interest, the journal displays a mental set in Sophia Hawthorne that is altogether incompatible with textual tampering: "Apollo boiled some potatoes for breakfast. Imagine him with that magnificent head bent over a cooking stove & those star-eyes watching the pot! There never were such good potatoes before in consequence." Interestingly, Sophia objected strongly to a reviewer's characterization of her husband as "gentle." " 'Gentle' surely he is," she wrote, "but such an epithet does not comprehend him & gives a false idea." McDonald, in a footnote, finds it "difficult to understand Sophia's strenuous objection to the characterization," but the entire journal testifies to her sense of his basic strength as well as sweetness. From a different period in Hawthorne's life, Patrick Brancaccio's "Hawthorne and the English Working Class," *NHJ* 4:135–49, fleshes out Hawthorne's own account in his notebooks and *Our Old Home* with other sources, while Raymona E. Hull's "Bennoch and Hawthorne," *NHJ* 4:48–74, chronicles one of Hawthorne's two close English associations and follows Francis Bennoch's relationship with the Hawthorne family until his death in 1874.

Scholars are also at work turning up more evidence, in the form of reprints and reviews, of Hawthorne's wide reputation in his lifetime. Wayne Allen Jones has done a good job of scholarship in "New Light on Hawthorne and the *Southern Rose*," *NHJ* 4:31–46. He publishes a newly found letter from Hawthorne showing that he sent Caroline Gilman, editor of the periodical, his story "The Lily's Quest" in gratitude for one of the earliest favorable reviews of the 1837 volume of *Twice-told Tales*. Gilman also reprinted three other Hawthorne pieces, enlarging his readership if not his bank balance. Arlin Turner, "Elizabeth Peabody Reviews *Twice-told Tales*," *NHJ* 4:75–84, reprints a long, unsigned review by Peabody in Park Benjamin's *New-Yorker* for March 24, 1838, one of many of Peabody's efforts to encourage and assist Hawthorne. The review is rhapsodic and overwritten but is a good lesson in 19th-century taste, for Peabody praises such saccharine works as "Sunday at Home" and "Little Annie's Ramble" while sternly warning the author to avoid the meretricious attractions of the grotesque and horrible. Admitting that the fantastic tales are probably the most effective in the volume, she prophesies nevertheless that they will have no lasting fame. Turning from this to Turner's second contribution, "Park Benjamin on the Author and Illustrator of 'The Gentle Boy,' " *NHJ* 4:85–91, one gets the sense of an interested conspiracy to puff Hawthorne's reputation as a means of puffing those who published him.

Richard Tuerk, " 'An Exceedingly Pleasant Mention': *The Scarlet Letter* and *Holden's Dollar Magazine*," *NHJ* 4:209–30, reprints a long, unsigned review of the romance by the Rev. Henry Giles that appeared in June 1850. Giles later republished his review—with no mention of the earlier printing—in his *Illustrations of Genius* (1854). The laudatory review is old-fashioned in its sermonlike structure and rhetoric, but quite modern in its analysis of *The Scarlet Letter* as a story concerned with social and personal interrelations. George Monteiro, "Hawthorne in the English Press," *NHJ* 4:162–78, surveys one English magazine, *The Ladies Companion and Monthly Magazine*, for 16 of its 20 volumes (1849–66; why the complete set was not studied is left unexplained), and finds two printings, four notices and reviews, and a long essay on the occasion of Hawthorne's death. The article reprints these last five items. In the area of bibliography, Jerome Klinkowitz published "The Hawthorne-Fields Letterbook: A Census and Description," *NHJ* 4:93–103. The letterbook, now at Harvard, is a transcription, executed by Fields's copyists in June 1867, of all the letters from Hawthorne to Fields that the publisher still had. The number of letters is 68, dating from January 15, 1850, to April 9, 1864. George Monteiro, "Hawthorne in Portuguese (3)," *NHJ* 4:280–81, adds seven items to his earlier checklists published in the *Nathaniel Hawthorne Journal*.

ii. General Studies

Although no books on Hawthorne came out during the year, there were several short studies of a general nature. Joseph F. Doherty studies Hawthorne in a broad context in "Hawthorne's Communal Paradigm: The American Novel Reconsidered," *Genre* 7:30–53. Doherty points out, in contradistinction to the American romance of isolation, a different pattern of narratives devoting themselves to a sympathetic study of the human urge for community. He considers *The Scarlet Letter* a paradigm, in its search for a basis of community founded on an acceptance of man's "compromised, mortal imperfection." In "Love Among the Ruins: Hawthorne's Surrogate Religion," *SoR* 10:535–65, Otis B. Wheeler traces the theme of sacramental love through Hawthorne's work from "Rappaccini's Daughter" and

"The Birthmark" through the long romances. In the two tales Hawthorne opposes science and love as surrogate religions; then in the romances he tries but fails to realize an effective sacramental love. Hawthorne's life testified to the redemptive quality of love, Wheeler says, but his art showed love failing to redeem.

Two pieces concerned themselves with Hawthorne and history. "Hawthorne and the Limits of the Holist Imagination," a chapter in *Versions of the Past* by Harry B. Henderson, pp. 91–126, cuts and shapes Hawthorne's historical writing to fit a thesis. Hawthorne's work embodies a "holist" view of history, the idea that the nature of historical events is determined within each society by the definitions and rules of the group. Glancing at Hawthorne's historical fiction before *The Scarlet Letter*, Henderson concentrates on that romance with only partial success. For as he himself admits, the stories of both Hester and Dimmesdale show precisely that society's terms are inadequate explanations for events. My chief objection to this essay is its inaccurate representation of Hawthorne's canon, for according to Henderson *all* of Hawthorne's good work is both historical in setting and concerned with history as its subject. Patricia A. Carlson's "National Typology and Hawthorne's Historical Allegory," *CEA* 37,i: ii–13 [*sic*] is a general survey, too brief for its broad topic.

Four studies looked at Hawthorne's imagery. The least interesting of these is Richard Harter Fogel's "Hawthorne's Variegated Lighting," *BuR* 21,ii(1973):83–88, a short article about Hawthorne's attempts to be a balanced writer as reflected in his imagery of light and dark and different kinds of light. Its points are well taken but Fogel has made them all before. David B. Kesterson in "Nature and Hawthorne's Religious Isolationists," *NHJ* 4:196–208, studies the kinds of nature imagery that Hawthorne uses to define his religious extremists. His point, that Hawthorne uses images of disease in nature for these types (e.g., weeds, barren landscapes) in contrast to healthy natural images for virtuously pious people, works very well for several short stories. But the argument falters when Kesterson tries to demonstrate through the natural images associated with Hilda that she too is a religious extremist, because the image cluster around her is not easily classified.

Harry C. West, "Hawthorne's Magic Circle: The Artist as Magician," *Criticism* 16:311–25, studies the image complex of circles, magic, and the artist. The work of art is akin to the magic circle created by a sorcerer within which he conjures up the "semblance of life." A long article by Taylor Stoehr, "Physiognomy and Phrenology in Hawthorne," *HLQ* 37:355–400, shows that although Hawthorne looked on phrenology as a fraud he used physiognomy (reading character from the face) throughout his fiction. The implication of physiognomy—that character does not change in time, but merely works itself out—underlies Hawthorne's handling of personal psychology and human relations and hence affects his plots and structures.

Two general articles by important Hawthorne scholars present opposing views of a basic aspect of Hawthorne's work. J. Donald Crowley in "Hawthorne and Frost: The Making of a Poem," *Frost: Centennial Essays*, pp. 288–309, argues that there is a basic condition of "homelessness" in Hawthorne's writing owing to the absence of civilization, in a Jamesian sense, in his native land. But Terence Martin, "Hawthorne's Public Decade and the Values of Home," *AL* 46:141–52, argues the reverse: that Hawthorne was oppressed by dense civilization, and that his imagination was at home in the rarified social atmosphere of America. In fact, he "deliberately courts in his own work a thinness and sparseness far greater than that in his own day," going back to earlier historical periods precisely to achieve "iconic sparseness." I side with Martin on this issue, feeling that Crowley has too quickly equated James's values with Hawthorne's, when actually Hawthorne responded to Europe more like Mark Twain. On the other hand, Martin's analysis is unable to show why Hawthorne was able to do so little with his English, and so much with his Italian, experience; he has not seen any distinctions among responses Hawthorne had to Europe. And Martin is surely wrong when he asserts that "only in *The Marble Faun* does a past loom thick *behind* the setting of a Hawthorne story." One thinks immediately of works from "Roger Malvin's Burial" to *The House of the Seven Gables* as counterexamples.

iii. Long Romances

Arne Axelsson, *The Links in the Chain: Isolation and Interdependence in Hawthorne's Fictional Characters*, Studia Anglistica Upsaliensis 17 (Uppsala: Universitets-Biblioteket), is the dissertation from which his fine 1973 *SN* article was derived (see *ALS* 1973, pp. 21, 454–55). It is a study of the structure of personal relationships in the four major romances, and the only work published in 1974 to look at all of them (See also p. 456). Nina Baym's "Hawthorne's Gothic Discards: *Fanshawe* and 'Alice Doane,'" *NHJ* 4:105–15, is a study of the beginnings of Hawthorne's career and of his first attempts to reproduce the gothic in an American context. *Fanshawe* tries to "Americanize" the gothic by toning down its characteristic excesses but in so doing it loses the essence of gothic and therefore fails in its intention. A scattering of articles (in addition to those discussed in section *ii* of this review) dealt in minor ways with *The Scarlet Letter*. John T. Irwin in "The Symbol of the Heiroglyphics in the American Renaissance," *AQ* 26:103–26, relates the recurrent motif of interpretation from multiple perspectives in *The Scarlet Letter* to the surge of interest in the hieroglyph generated by the decoding of the Rosetta stone. Hieroglyphic symbolism is noted in other writers of the time, including Melville and Thoreau, and the article provides a fine account of the "Egyptian revival." Allan Lefcowitz offers a Freudian analysis of Roger Chillingworth in "*Apologia* pro Roger Prynne: A Psychological Study," *L&P* 24:34–44. Behind the diabolic veneer that is projected onto him by the self-serving rationalizations of Hester and Dimmesdale, and the unexplained falsifying of the narrator, Chillingworth is a realistic character suffering from an unresolved oedipal dilemma. He has sublimated his need for love into a search for knowledge, but he remains an emotional child. Louis Owens's "Paulding's 'The Dumb Girl,' a Source of *The Scarlet Letter*," *NHJ* 4:240–49, closely compares the two plots and finds in Paulding's story a simpler version of Hawthorne's story.

R. A. Yoder, "Transcendental Conservatism and *The House of the Seven Gables*," *GaR* 28:33–51, discusses a set of conservative political ideas in Emerson and the historian Bancroft and identifies them in Hawthorne's romance. He sees the end of the story, the union of Maule and Pyncheon, as symbolizing a proper social balance of permanence and progression, a conciliatory gradualism. Frank Kermode's "Hawthorne's Modernity," *PR* 41:428–41, is a silly article trying to squeeze a case for Hawthorne's modern world-view from the evidence of punning on ideas of "types" implicit in the names Holgrave, Pyncheon, and Maule. Louis Aggasiz, phrenology, mesmerism, and Puritan typology are thrown in for good measure; it looks very scholarly but is quite unsound. Richard F. Fleck pursues "Industrial Imagery in *The House of the Seven Gables*," *NHJ* 4:273–

76, to note that images of machines, electricity, and gaslight are used to represent mental states.

Kent Bales wrote two articles modifying Nina Baym's reading of *The Blithedale Romance* (see *ALS 1968*, p. 27). In *"The Blithedale Romance*: Coverdale's Mean and Subversive Egotism," *BuR* 21, ii(1973):60–82, he attacks the reliability of Coverdale's narrative primarily as a means of revaluing Hollingsworth, who is treated in Baym's article as the truly "covert" character at Blithedale, ostensibly libertarian but in fact rigidly authoritarian. In arguing for the moral worth of Hollingsworth's reform project, and insisting that Coverdale's denigration of Hollingsworth is self-serving, Bales overlooks two important facts: first, that Coverdale does not denigrate Hollingsworth but that the criticism is implied in a comparison of his project with that of the Blithedalers; and second, that in attaching himself to Zenobia and Blithedale for the ulterior purposes of gaining possession of their property, Hollingsworth is extraordinarily dishonest. In "The Allegory and the Radical Romantic Ethic of *The Blithedale Romance*," *AL* 46:41–53, Bales discovers an underlying allegory represented by various character dichotomies: Zenobia and Priscilla as flesh and spirit, Coverdale and Hollingsworth as intellect and will. From this he derives an ideal of wholeness according to which, he argues, the incomplete personalities in the romance are judged. Joan Magretta in "The Coverdale Translation: *Blithedale* and the Bible," *NHJ* 4:250–56, reminds us that one Miles Coverdale produced the first complete translation of the Bible, but her quasi-religious interpretation of *The Blithedale Romance* offers no new insights.

Dennis Berthold discusses "Hawthorne, Ruskin, and the Gothic Revival: Transcendent Gothic in *The Marble Faun*," *ESQ* 20:15–32, pointing out many images of gothic architecture in the romance and arguing that Hawthorne's use of those images was controlled by Ruskin's theory. In "The Reluctant Yankee in Hawthorne's Abortive Gothic Romances," *NHJ* 4:179–94, Ronald T. Curran points out similarities in the theme of *The House of the Seven Gables* and the various unfinished versions of an English romance that Hawthorne wrote late in his career. The story, Curran says, was intended to endorse democracy but because of his doubts about America Hawthorne could not carry this theme through. The Civil War, in fact, produced a "national identity crisis" in Hawthorne (whatever that might mean) such that he was unable to write a coherent work. He took refuge from his problems in gothic embellishments that overgrew and destroyed his original intentions in the English romance. A somewhat different approach to the last phase is seen in Donald Kay's "English Fruits, Yankee Turnips: Another Look at Hawthorne and England," *NHJ* 4:150–61, which relies mostly on *Dr. Grimshawe's Secret* for its discussion of Hawthorne's mixed reaction to England. In effect this article follows Davidson in applying to the late romances Randall Stewart's thesis regarding the *English Notebooks*: that Hawthorne was agonizingly caught between his patriotism and his attraction to England. A fresh rereading of the *English Notebooks* has convinced me that Stewart was wrong on two counts: first, he greatly overstated the extent to which Hawthorne was attracted to England and second, he radically misunderstood Hawthorne's actual impressions of the country. Hawthorne's England was not James's England, and until this is clearly seen there will be serious shortcomings in the criticism of the English years and the English romances.

iv. Short Works

James W. Mathews, "Hawthorne and the Periodical Tale: From Popular Lore to Art," *PBSA* 68:149–62, makes a very important general point. Mathews says that in length, subject matter, and sentiment, Hawthorne's short works were written for the popular taste as it expressed itself in periodical readership. Hawthorne's short works may have been better in quality but they were not different in kind from standard magazine fare. He points out evidence of this in many of Hawthorne's short stories in a systematic and convincing manner. I would very much like to see a piece of scholarship that treated this thesis in reverse: that studied such publications as *The Token* to show how contributions by other authors were similar to Hawthorne's. We need a fresh and less prejudiced study of popular 19th-century authors to put Hawthorne in proper context.

Three articles looked at "Alice Doane's Appeal." Nina Baym's article (discussed in part above) studies the original "Alice Doane" as an early attempt to be gothic by using the whole bag of gothic tricks. The revision, "Alice Doane's Appeal," shows Hawthorne achieving his own kind of American Gothic, derived from American history. Baym believes that Hawthorne used history for literary purposes, in contrast to the usual view that he used literature for historical purposes.

She also discounts any personal dimension to "Alice Doane's Appeal," treating incest and parricide motifs as part of the standard gothic repertoire, rather than as revelation of Hawthorne's pathology. Stanley Brodwin's "Hawthorne and the Function of History: A Reading of 'Alice Doane's Appeal,'" *NHJ* 4:116–28, is a good example of the other historical approach, for it says that the story shows how fiction is better at conveying history than "history" itself, and that the purpose of historical writing for Hawthorne was to achieve a change of heart in readers through confrontation with forgotten, repressed, or ignored material. John Shroeder's well-written "Alice Doane's Story: An Essay on Hawthorne and Spenser," *NHJ* 4:129–34, represents yet another approach to this tale, through the medium of Hawthorne's concealed borrowings from Spenser. Like many other Hawthorne works, says Shroeder, "Alice Doane's Appeal" is a paraphrase of, and elaboration on, the Archimago episode in *The Faerie Queene*. To the question, Why did Hawthorne borrow so much from Spenser? (for Spenser has been cited by one or another critic as a source for almost everything in the canon), Shroeder proposes two answers. First, Hawthorne learned how to write psychological romance from Spenser, and second, because no one read Spenser any more in Hawthorne's day, he thought he could get away with wholesale borrowing. I would like to put a different question: what is the attraction of Spenser-hunting for so many critics of Hawthorne? My answer is the critics' literary training: they are strong in the English Renaissance and much less so in the late 18th and early 19th centuries. Missing therefore the obvious ways in which Hawthorne was swimming in the literary currents of his own time, they have exaggerated his genuine indebtedness to Spenser out of all proportion.

Sheldon W. Liebman has published several superfluous articles on Hawthorne's tales and this year added another, "Moral Choice in 'The Maypole of Merry Mount,'" *SSF* 11:173–80. This repeats a standard reading of the story as representing a choice between pagan and Christian viewpoints and urging the Christian as necessarily right in view of man's fallen but redeemable nature. The argument is not only old-hat; in Liebman's version it is also circular, assuming a Christian view of human nature that by rights it should demonstrate. James Quinn and Ross Baldessarini, "Literary Technique and Psychological Effect in Hawthorne's 'The Minister's Black Veil,'" *L&P* 24:115–23, assumes a Freudian reading of the story and undertakes to investigate the literary techniques by which this meaning is achieved. However, the techniques—symbolism, imagery, ambiguity, indirection, and equivocation—are precisely those that critics agree on regardless of the particular interpretation of a story's theme, so the article makes no contribution.

In "'Young Goodman Brown' and Puritan Justification," *SSF* 11:200–203, Claudia G. Johnson judges Brown's experience by Puritan criteria and finds it a mockery of regeneration. Michael J. Colacurcio wrote a lengthy and important article on this story, "Visible Sanctity and Specter Evidence: The Moral World of Hawthorne's 'Young Goodman Brown,'" *EIHC* 110:259–99. This is a historical reading of the story in terms of a thorough and precise application of Puritan doctrine and religious controversy at exactly the time in which Hawthorne sets the story. Colacurcio does not deny the general psychological import of the tale, but insists that this import is there because Hawthorne discovered it in the historical record; he took on "the task of creating a doctrinally adequate and dramatically believable version of 'how it might have felt' to live in the moral climate of Puritanism's most troubled years." Of the many critics who have written about Hawthorne and Puritanism, Colarcurcio is the most knowledgeable about the Puritans themselves, and if he says that "Young Goodman Brown" is compatible with the finest points of Puritan doctrine and psychology, we must believe him. But when he goes on to say that Hawthorne cannot be understood or appreciated without reference to these fine points, that "the reader of 'Young Goodman Brown' needs to keep constantly in mind the first theological premises and the latter-day ecclesiological practices of the Puritan economy of salvation," I cannot agree. Hawthorne wrote to an audience that would assuredly not have such premises and practices in mind, and he himself could not abide theological disputation and doctrinal hair-splitting. Every reference he ever made to theological controversy was contemptuous. Let us compromise by saying that as he read the Puritans, Hawthorne read past their dogma and grasped, like the great psychologist he was, their essential anxiety and distress, which he reproduced, like the great artist he was, without detailed reference to their own particular formulation of their malaise. Thus he recast the Puritans in terms immediately comprehensible to his own day and to ours.

Another rising critic in the Hawthorne sky is John J. McDonald, whose article " 'The Old Manse' and its Mosses: The Inception and Development of *Mosses from an Old Manse*," *TSLL* 16:77–108, is one of the most important to appear this year. McDonald is interested in the work of the Manse Period as coherent in itself and different from Hawthorne's earlier writing. He is also interested in the collected tales as an integrated whole. This article traces the development of the idea of the collection, and studies "The Old Manse" with reference to its role as a partial frame and unifier of *Mosses from an Old Manse*. His work is both scholarly and imaginative. A note by Thomas Werge, "Thomas Shepard and Crèvecoeur: Two Uses of the Image of the Bosom Serpent before Hawthorne," *NHJ* 4:236–39, delivers what its title promises, and demonstrates again that "Egotism" draws on a stock metaphor for its central symbol. Jane Chambers's "Two Legends of Temperance: Spenser's and Hawthorne's," *ESQ* 20:275–79, adds "The Birthmark" to the list of works Hawthorne owed to Spenser.

Richard Clark Sterne, "A Mexican Flower in Rappaccini's Garden: Madame Calderon de la Barca's *Life in Mexico* Revisited," *NHJ* 4:277–79, finds a new source for Hawthorne's poisonous shrub. So many sources for the flower have been discovered that it is time to agree that, like the bosom serpent, it is a folk-motif. Deiter Shulz wrote an ambitious piece called " 'Ethan Brand' and the Structure of the American Quest Romance," *Genre* 7:233–49, in which he explicates "Ethan Brand" as the final episode in a quest-romance. But the article merely yokes conventional statements about quest-romances with conventional analysis of "Ethan Brand." A ground-breaking article is James A. Hijiya, "Nathaniel Hawthorne's *Our Old Home*," *AL* 46:363–73, the first attempt that I know of studying Hawthorne's last collection as a whole. Hijiya interprets it as a dramatization of Hawthorne's ambivalences toward England. Beginning with paradisical landscapes and an idealized sense of the past, the work progresses to scenes of poverty and corruption and thus represents a "regretful repudiation of England."

v. Hawthorne and Others

I detect a growing interest in Hawthorne's influence on other writers of his time, both American and English, as well as his likeness to later American authors. Jerome M. Loving, "Melville's Pardonable

Sin," *NEQ* 47:262–78, is the inevitable yearly work on the Melville connection. Loving argues, for a surprise, that Hawthorne may *not* have influenced the writing of *Moby-Dick* as much as has been suspected; less originally, he points out that Melville misunderstood Hawthorne. D. M. McKeithan, "Poe and the Second Edition of Hawthorne's *Twice-Told Tales*," *NHJ* 4:257–69, assesses the influence of that collection on Poe's work and concludes that it affected Poe's theory of fiction and also inspired "The Masque of the Red Death." McKeithan seems not to know Regan's brilliant article on the same subject (*ALS 1971*, p. 38), which insists that Poe plagiarized Hawthorne's "Legends of the Province House" in "The Masque of the Red Death" and that his attack on Hawthorne for plagiarizing him was a cover.

Thaddeo Kitasimbwa Babukia, "James' *Washington Square*: More on the Hawthorne Relation," *NHJ* 4:270–72, pursues Robert Emmet Long's thesis of Hawthorne influence on that novel (see *ALS 1973*, p. 123). He proposes interesting parallels between Catherine Sloper and Hester Prynne as older women, angels of mercy, and confidantes of the young. Jonathan R. Quick studied Hawthorne's influence on George Eliot in "*Silas Marner* as Romance: The Example of Hawthorne," *NCF* 29:287–98, and David W. Jarrett did likewise for Hardy in "Hawthorne and Hardy as Modern Romancers," *NCF* 28:458–71. Two articles in *Frost: Centennial Essays* (cited above), draw parallels between Frost and Hawthorne. J. Donald Crowley's article (discussed partly in Section *ii*) and Edward Stone's "Other 'Desert Places': Frost and Hawthorne," pp. 275–87, stress the bleaker Frost rather than the cracker-barrel philosopher and relate that poet of empty space to Hawthorne.

University of Illinois, Urbana

3. Poe

G. R. Thompson

The volume of Poe studies declined somewhat in 1974, and almost nothing appeared on the poems, which have not been the subject of much critical interest for years. The most important contributions include John Ward Ostrom's fourth supplement to his edition of the letters, *two* book-length bibliographies aiming at "completeness," and Roger Forclaz's attempt at a "complete" picture of Poe the man and artist in a closely printed 600-page study. The most controversial works of the year will be easily recognized: Barton Levi St. Armand's continuing examination of Poe's esoteric knowledge of occult lore in his most famous tales; and Bernard Rosenthal's attempt to reestablish the notorious *Southern Literary Messenger* review of J. K. Paulding's *Slavery in the United States* and William Drayton's *The South Vindicated* firmly in the Poe canon.

i. Biography and Contemporary Relations

Work in this area was comparatively thin. Charles Haines's *Edgar Allan Poe: His Writings and Influence* (New York: Franklin Watts) is an introduction for young people. Phillip Van Doren Stern's *Edgar Allan Poe: Visitor from the Night of Time* (New York: Crowell, 1973) is a romanticized sketch. Barry Perowne's *A Singular Conspiracy* (Indianapolis, Ind.: Bobbs-Merrill) is a fictionalized version of what happened to Poe in 1844. Seymour Adelman's *Poe: Philadelphia—A Keepsake* (Philadelphia: Friends of the Free Library, 1972) is a small pamphlet memorializing Poe's years in that city. Kenneth W. Cameron lists Poe's borrowings from the University of Virginia library in "Notes on Young Poe's Reading" (*ATQ* 24 Suppl.: 33–34). Mukhtar Ali Isani, in "A Further Word on Poe and Alexander Crane" (*PoeS* 7:48), clears up some textual and factual ambiguities in his previous article on the memory of Poe's onetime office boy

(see *ALS* 1973, p. 38). The most important contribution to Poe biography, simply for putting more facts before us, has to be John
Ward Ostrom's "Fourth Supplement to *The Letters of Poe*" (*AL*
45:513–36), which augments the expanded 1966 edition of Ostrom's
collection, originally published in 1941, even though the new letters
do not seem at first glance to contain much of first importance in
themselves.

Burton R. Pollin, in "Poe, Freeman Hunt, and Four Unrecorded
Reviews of Poe's Works" (*TSLL* 16:305–13), notes that Poe's friend
Hunt was careful to review Poe's works favorably. In a similar vein
Pollin, in "More on Lippard and Poe" (*PoeS* 7:22–23), supplements
two recent articles on the two authors by Emilio DeGrazia (see *ALS*
1973, p. 38) by presenting a review of a Poe book by Lippard and the
full text of Lippard's obituary notice of Poe. Pollin's "Poe's *Narrative
of Arthur Gordon Pym* and the Contemporary Reviewers" (*SAF*
2:37–56) begins characteristically: "Almost without exception the
biographies and commentaries concerning Edgar Allan Poe have repeated several errors made by James A. Harrison, George Wood-
berry, and Killis Campbell . . . on the subject of the contemporary
reception of . . . *Pym*." Pollin proceeds, by a close look at the reviews,
to correct the three major misconceptions about the reception of the
book: that it was treated as true or authentic; that it was virtually
ignored; that the only three American reviews condemned the book
unequivocally. David K. Jackson, in "A Poe Hoax Comes Before the
U.S. Senate" (*PoeS* 7:47–48), reproduces a paragraph and a footnote
from the records of the first session of the 26th Congress (1839–40),
in which "The Journal of Julius Rodman" is cited as a factual description of an actual journey of Westward exploration.

Two essays look again at Poe's assessment of Hawthorne, neither
coming to very startling conclusions. Walter Evans, in "Poe's Revisions in His Review of Hawthorne's *Twice-Told Tales*" (*PBSA*
66[1972]:407–09), notes that in his second review, five years after
the first, Poe criticizes Hawthorne's tendency toward allegory while
still praising his artistry. D. M. McKeithan, in "Poe and the Second
Edition of Hawthorne's *Twice-Told Tales*" (*NHJ* 4:257–69), rehearses the parallels between Hawthorne's fiction and Poe's and suggests that in his review we can see Poe's "confession that before he
began reading the second edition he had never read enough of Hawthorne to form an opinion of his worth," that he was amazed to dis-

cover that such an artist was at work in America, and that "the immediate effect" upon Poe was the inspiration to write "The Oval Portrait" and "The Masque of the Red Death"; moreover, his study of Hawthorne probably helped him formulate his theory of the short story.

The most suggestive comparison of Poe and another author is Benjamin Lease's "John Neal and Edgar Allan Poe" (*PoeS* 7:38–41). Lease notes that Poe and Neal spoke of American subserviency to British criticism in similar terms of outrage at the same time that they similarly attacked uncritical praise of American writing by Americans. Neal gave Poe his first critical recognition (in 1829), and, Lease argues, Neal exerted influence on Poe's critical ideas, especially in his acceptance of the Schlegels's conceptions of unity or totality of effect and their theories of irony. Moreover, Neal's fiction, which Poe read, is "charged with romantic irony." Neal "struggled to combine this ironic vision—this intense serio-comic emphasis on self and the uncertitude of self—with his persistent quest for authentic nationality in literature," to which Poe responded positively. Lease concludes with a brief comparison of horror and humor in the two authors. Related is a recovered 19th-century essay by the Italian scholar, Pasquale Jannaccone. Peter Mitilineos has translated his "The Aesthetics of Edgar Poe" (*PoeS* 7:1–13), which was first published in the *Nuova Antologia* in 1895. Jannaccone develops a set of ideas about Poe's aesthetic theories from an international perspective, focusing on Poe's use of Coleridge's synthesis of the scattered ideas of the German romantics. He deals with Poe's counterdefinitions of fancy and imagination and the allied theories of Jean Paul, the Schlegels, Tieck, Novalis, Schelling, and Fichte. Poe's major difference from the German aestheticians, according to Jannaccone, is his conception of poetic effect based on quantitative calculation, mathematical proportion, geometry; but Poe is like the Germans in his blending of the ideal and the mundane, of poetry and calculation, of seriousness and humor and irony.

W. T. Bandy, in "Taine on Poe: Additions and Corrections" (*PoeS* 7:48), notes that a letter from Baudelaire dated October 6, 1863, was not addressed to Taine, as Thomas H. Goetz claims (see *ALS 1973*, p. 62), but to Jacques Babinet. John L. Idol, Jr., in "William Cowper Brann on Edgar Allan Poe" (*PoeS* 7:24–25), extracts "all of Brann's remarks concerning Poe," which are few, brief, and unfavorable.

John C. Miller notes the curious fact that one of Poe's early biographers changed his birthdate to the day and year of Poe's death: "The Birthdate of John Henry Ingram" (*PoeS* 7:24). Miller also recounts "The Exhumations and Reburials of Edgar and Virginia Poe and Mrs. Clemm" (*PoeS* 7:46–47) from Poe's funeral to 1885, when the three bodies were "brought . . . together at last."

ii. Sources, Texts, and Bibliography

Burton R. Pollin, in "Another Source of 'The Bells' by Poe: A *Broadway Journal* Essay" (*MissQ* 27:467–73) claims that "The Broadway Carnival," a short filler piece in Poe's magazine provided key words and ideas for a revision of "The Bells." In his "Names Used for Humor in Poe's Fiction" (*Love and Wrestling, Butch and O.K.* [Commerce, Tex.: Pub. of So. Central Names Inst., 1973], pp. 51–57), Pollin lists the names of characters in 21 selected tales of "clearly humorous implication," with a brief account of Poe's humorous plots.

Evidencing Pollin's characteristic interests and thoroughness is the 85-page pamphlet, *Poe, Creator of Words* (Baltimore, Md.: Enoch Pratt Free Library, Edgar Allan Poe Society, and the Library of the Univ. of Baltimore). Pollin writes: "In presenting this list of over nine hundred words, either coined by Edgar Allan Poe or rightfully to be ascribed to him as first instances in print [*sic*], I wish to open up a field of study for further investigation which has been virtually uncharted, untapped, and even unimagined." He observes that in 1942–43, only 27 words and compounds were given as Poe's total contribution to the English language. Reading through the three alphabetical lists ("I. Single Words First Used or Coined by Poe"; "II. Compound Words Coined by Poe"; "III. Proper Noun Coinages") is interesting and amusing; and certainly Pollin is right to call attention to Poe's undervalued or unrecognized wordplay. But many, if not most, of the compounds (such as "art-product," "beast-like") do not suggest originality in language so much as bad-spelling.

Bernard Rosenthal, in "Poe, Slavery, and the *Southern Literary Messenger*: A Reexamination" (*PoeS* 7:29–38), reopens the entire question of Poe's authorship of the April 1836 *Southern Literary Messenger* review of two books defending slavery. At first attributed to Poe and printed in the Harrison edition of the *Complete Works*, the review has been generally excluded from the Poe canon since 1941 on the basis of William Doyle Hull's argument (in his doctoral dissertation at the University of Virginia) that it is the work of Nathaniel Beverley Tucker. The significance of establishing Poe's authorship goes beyond the goal of accuracy per se, for the proslavery sentiments in the review have provided the basis for racial interpretations of Poe's fiction, especially *Arthur Gordon Pym*. Although Rosenthal in part is defending his inclusion of the review as Poe's in his collection (with Vincent Freimark), *Race and the American Romantics* (New York: Schocken, 1971), and although his argument depends on a number of ambiguities and a few improbabilities, he does a good job of showing greater improbability that the review is Tucker's. In addition to a careful examination of the historical facts and bibliographical data, Rosenthal surveys Poe's statements about slavery and race and shows a consistency between them and those in the review.

Although the Dameron-Cauthen project of a "complete" bibliography has been in progress for more than a decade, has had an initial list published supplementing an earlier M.A. thesis by Cauthen, and has been underwritten by a grant from the National Endowment for the Humanities, a duplicative dissertation was accepted at Columbia in 1968. As a result, in 1974 we were presented with two massive bibliographies covering much of the same material; and the dedicated Poe scholar who wants "completeness" will have to pay $40 to obtain the two volumes. *Edgar Allan Poe: A Bibliography of Criticism, 1827–1967* (Charlottesville: Univ. Press of Va.) by J. Lasley Dameron and Irby B. Cauthen runs to nearly 400 pages altogether and contains more than 4,000 items in English and foreign languages. Esther K. Hyneman's *Edgar Allan Poe: An Annotated Bibliography of Books and Articles in English, 1827–1973* (Boston: G. K. Hall) is something over 300 pages and contains some 2,300 items—about 400 fewer English-language citations than Dameron-Cauthen despite six years extra coverage. The organization of Hyneman's volume is slightly more complex than that of the other volume. Hyneman arranges 19th-century items alphabetically by author; the 20th-century items by subject categories, and then by author. Dameron and Cauthen have two straight alphabetical lists, one for the English-language items, one for foreign-language items. The annotations in Dameron-Cauthen are for the English-language items only and are frequently so laconic as merely to repeat the title of the article in almost the same words. The annotations in Hyneman are much fuller,

though, as J. Albert Robbins points out in a detailed comparison of
the coverage, methodology, usefulness, and accuracy of the two
volumes (*PoeS* 8:26–27), Hyneman is also more error-prone than
Dameron and Cauthen.

iii. General Studies and the Short Fiction

One wonders if Roger Forclaz had not consumed both of the fore-
going bibliographies in manuscript with fanatical care before producing *Le monde d'Edgar Poe* (Berne: Herbert Lang; Frankfort:
Peter Lang), a volume in the Europäische Hochschulschriften, Series
14 (Anglo-Saxon Language and Literature), Vol. 17. Forclaz attempts to comprehend the entire "universe" of Poe as embodied in
his prose by an examination of, first, the "world" in which the "real"
Poe lived and worked, and, second, of the ideational world which he
created out of that first world. The second world, that created by Poe
in his writings, is the result of the interpenetration of the mind of the
artist, the everyday world he worked in, and the intellectual world
he came to possess as a literate member of the Western intelligentsia.
In the process of examining Poe's consciousness, Forclaz cites just
about every article and book ever published on Poe (in nearly 200
pages of notes and bibliography printed in tiny type). The overwhelming documentation is doubtless the result of the book's origin
as a dissertation in the European style.

The study has three main parts, each with three subdivisions. The
first, titled "The Writer," initiates what seems to be the central thesis
of the book. Here, in three introductory chapters, Forclaz deals with
Poe as journalist, as a poet working out an aesthetic, and as a man
living in 19th-century America. The two sides of Poe's daily working
life, the pragmatic and the visionary, the journalistic and the poetic,
are seen not as providing a schizophrenic division in Poe but as two
sides of a complex synthesis that is characteristically American.
Forclaz is also insistent that Poe was not schizoid in his personal
life—and that scholars who have tried to make him out as an alcoholic,
drug addict, necrophiliac, and the rest, are themselves guilty of
insanities.

The second major part of the book, titled "The Writer and his
Universe," is composed of three sections of three chapters each.

Forclaz first examines "The Context" of Poe's literary inheritance, the intellectual climate which played a greater role in the genesis of Poe's work than did the journalistic, the poetic, or the social contexts discussed in part one. Forclaz deals with Poe's affinities with European romantic writers, Poe's sources in the gothic tradition, and Poe's relations with American writers and thinkers. The next group of three chapters comprises a section called "The Theories," followed by another group of three called "The Practice"; in these six chapters Forclaz deals with the application of Poe's ideas about art and imagination to his practice in his tales in terms of the development of his literary career.

The third major part of the book, titled "The World," is likewise divided into three groups of three chapters each. In the first group, called "The Exterior World and the Narrative Structures," Forclaz discusses the Poe narrator, the Poe hero, and the Poe world described by the narratives. He next takes up "The Interior World" of Poe's fictive universe, focusing on the themes of intuition and dream, reason and analysis, and terror. The final grouping of three chapters deals with what Forclaz calls Poe's "Grand Themes" and brings full circle the argument that Poe is not schizophrenically divided against himself. In separate chapters Forclaz deals with beauty, death, and truth in Poe's fictive world, arguing that Poe achieved a synthesis of seemingly disparate elements in *Eureka*. He takes *Eureka* to be the "fundamental work for the comprehension of the writer," for it is the continuation of the cosmological dialogues, "Eiros and Charmion," "Monos and Una," "Power of Words," "Mesmeric Revelation"—all of which represent Poe's attempt to arrive at a philosophy of life. He identifies Poe's quest for unity as the motivating impulse in his life, in his criticism, in his aesthetic theory, in his poetry, in his tales, and in his philosophical writings. In this obsessive quest for cosmic unity, Poe is at one with the American romantic movement.

Although it is an impressive piece of scholarship, the book as a whole is nevertheless unwieldy. The mass of material frequently blurs the central thesis suggested above, and much of the book seems principally a defense of Poe against all other critics. Moreover, the overall argument has been anticipated recently by Joseph Moldenhauer, John F. Lynen, David Halliburton, and Stuart Levine (see *ALS 1968*, pp. 159–60, *ALS 1969*, pp. 185–87, *ALS 1972*, pp. 215–16, *ALS*

1973, pp. 41–44). It is Forclaz's details, his treatment of Poe's gothic sources, for example, or Poe's revisions, that the scholar will find most rewarding, rather than the large shape of the book.

Unity is the topic of two rather different articles on Poe's imagination. T. J. Reiss, in "The Universe and the Dialectic of Imagination in Edgar Allan Poe" (*EA* 27:16–25), argues that the search for unity represents an attempt to transcend the mere intellect (cf. Flory below). Patricia C. Smith, in Poe's "Arabesque" (*PoeS* 7:42–45), at first argues that the two terms, *grotesque* and *arabesque*, in the 19th century "really were not as slippery as they seem in 1974" but are distinguishable styles of decoration. Arabesques are properly flower-pieces; grotesques mingle flowers, genii, men, beasts, and buildings. Much of the rest of her article, however, is devoted to showing the historical blending of the two terms, especially in literature: ". . . both represent forms melting into one another." Smith concludes that the arabesque in Poe has to do with a perception of harmoniously blended overall design and Poe's "conception of the universal human inclination to struggle in the direction of the lost memories of unity."

Arthur Voss's chapter on Poe, "Terror, Mystery, and Ratiocination," in his *The American Short Story: A Critical Survey* (Norman: Univ. of Okla., 1973) is an uncritical survey. Robert F. Marler, in "From Tale to Short Story: The Emergence of a New Genre in the 1850's" (*AL* 46:153–69), makes several questionable assumptions in concluding that Poe's characters do not inhabit "short stories" but rather "tales" because they are not "realistic." This article may be profitably read in conjunction with Bruce I. Weiner's "Poe's Subversion of Verisimilitude" (*ATQ* 24 Suppl.:2–8), which argues that the sensation tale as a genre allowed Poe to use "verisimilitude to attain an idealized realm of the imagination." Another article that may be relevant here is Allan Smith's "The Psychological Context of Three Tales by Poe" (*JAmS* 7:279–92), which deals with Poe's "realism" in terms of how well Poe's conception of the morbid mind corresponds to the theories of his day.

The gothic tradition with regard to Poe continues to stimulate interest. Patricia Merivale, in "The Raven and the Bust of Pallas: Classical Artifacts and the Gothic Tale" (*PMLA* 89:960–66), surveys the use of busts and statues in gothic writings as image, symbol, plot element, character. She asks what "the real interloper" (the bust of Pallas) in Poe's poem "is doing in a world whose imagery comes almost exclusively from Christian and pre-Christian Teutonic mythology and folklore . . . ." In Poe and Hawthorne the function of serene, white, chiseled marble is to keep at bay or hold in tension the gothic darkness, suggesting some sort of "deliberate antithesis of 'classical' and 'Gothic.'" In continental writers, however, the statue, especially of Venus, becomes the focus of gothic horror and a central 19th-century image. *The Gothic Imagination: Essays in Dark Romanticism*, ed. G. R. Thompson (Pullman, Wash.: Wash. State Univ. Press), brings together eight original essays and an introduction on "Romanticism and the Gothic Tradition" in an effort to delineate the recurrent concerns and images of gothic literature. Collectively, the essays suggest that the gothic is the embodiment of the demonic quest romance, the imagery of which employs an iconography tracing an unbroken tradition from ancient times, through the medieval world, to the 19th century.

One of the essays is focused on Poe's knowledge and use of the occult. Barton Levi St. Armand, in "The 'Mysteries' of Edgar Poe: The Quest for a Monomyth in Gothic Literature" (pp. 65–93), examines early 19th-century taste for Egyptian lore; Poe, he argues, consciously worked with the non-Western tradition behind Christian myth. "The Fall of the House of Usher" presents a Faustian quest for initiation into the occult mysteries of forbidden knowledge derived from the rites of Isis as described in classical and Renaissance writings. The novitiate becomes victim when he profanes such mysteries by his presence at the rites. The development in the Middle Ages of the pseudoscience of alchemy represented in part a merging of Egyptian and Christian myth; as the hierarchy of metals became codified in a mystic science representing a quest for ultimate illumination, there developed an iconography suitable for a richly implicative substratum of meaning in the gothic romance as it matured in the Romantic period. The Isis figure is transmuted into a sinister supernatural presence, the high priest into a mysterious monk or archvillain, and the novitiate into a trembling and stupefied victim—while the theater for this rite, the temple, becomes a cathedral or castle. Although the general reader is likely to feel an initial resistance to the application of this transformed gnosticism, alchemy, and associated mysteries to "Usher," and to Poe's conscious awareness in general, the evidence St. Armand presents is beginning to be of such mass that it cannot be easily dismissed; and the present essay should be read in conjunction with his others on Poe and alchemy, which together now form almost a small monograph (see *ALS 1971*, pp. 199–200, *ALS 1972*, pp. 220–21).

Wendy Stallard Flory's "Usher's Fear and the Flaw in Poe's Theories of the Metamorphosis of the Senses" (*PoeS* 7:17–19) somewhat elliptically argues that the tottering of Usher's reason is a sign not of insanity but of his approach to a state of superior perception. Poe's use of the word *intellect* in several works suggests that ultimate knowledge comes through "the almost entirely *passive* state of receiving sense impressions without the mediation and interference of reason—a state precisely like Usher's." The tale is a "dramatization of a dilemma . . . at the heart of Poe's theories about the experience of dying." The ultimate horror Usher faces is the possibility that the senses will persist after death, as in "Monos and Una," "Valdemar," and other works. What exactly the "flaw" is in Poe's "theory of the senses" is never made clear. Robert Reeder, in " 'The Black Cat' as a Study in Repression" (*PoeS* 7:20–21), examines the tale in terms of Jungian psychology. The cat symbolically functions as the narrator's *anima*, defined by Jung in *Alchemical Studies* "as a personification of the unconscious in general." As the narrator loses touch with his *anima* and identifies only with his *animus* (reason), he provokes increasingly violent emotions within himself as his being loses harmony with itself; his cruelties to the cat are stages in his unsuccessful attempt to control and repress his *anima*. Shannon Burns, in " 'The Cask of Amontillado': Montresor's Revenge" (*PoeS* 7:25), contends that by "placing the tale in the tradition of Italian revenge" we can "better understand the nature of Fortunato's insult and, consequently, identify the 'you' Montresor address." The Protestant Fortunato must have directed his insult against the religion and honor of the Catholic Montresor's family; having completed his revenge, Montresor is standing in the catacombs addressing the bones of his ancestors.

iv. The Narrative of Arthur Gordon Pym

J. V. Ridgely surveys the recent critical attention given to *The Narrative of Arthur Gordon Pym*, of which there has been considerable, in "Tragical-Mythical-Satirical-Hoaxical: Problems of Genre in *Pym*" (*ATQ* 24,i:4–9). Richard Wilbur's introduction to an impressively illustrated edition of *The Narrative of Arthur Gordon Pym* (Boston, Mass.: David R. Godine, 1973), is heavily biographical in its interpretation of the novel as a spiritual quest and is not as provocative as his earlier, seminal considerations of the work of Poe. In "The Mythic Initiation of Arthur Gordon Pym" (*PoeS* 7:14–16), Kathleen Sands argues that the initiation motif provides the work with unity, throws light on many narrative details, and accounts for its power. The two main narratives (the *Grampus* and the *Jane Guy* adventures) "form a logical progression in the formation of the mythic hero" in his advance toward a higher level of understanding of the "oneness" of the universe. Sands amplifies some of Grace Farrell Lee's speculation about the mythic quality of the death and rebirth motifs (see *ALS 1972*, p. 223).

Robert L. Carringer, in "Circumscription of Space and the Form of Poe's *Arthur Gordon Pym*" (*PMLA* 89:506–16), presents the old argument that the unity and purpose of the work falter midway through, but he argues the case on somewhat new grounds. He begins familiarly enough. "Besides physical disintegration and psychological terror," he writes, "the third identifying characteristic of a story by Poe [is] a strong impulse to delimit space." Most of Poe's works employ obvious restrictive enclosures (rooms, tombs, secret compartments, pits, caves), but in several there is a paradoxical tension between open space and enclosure. In "Ms. Found in a Bottle" and "A Descent into the Maelström," for example, "in reversal of all conventional associations, Poe manages to have his narrator delimited by space *on the ocean.*" So also William Wilson's travels all over Europe are simultaneously within enclosed structures, never in the open. This circumscription involves the Poe character "in some form of violent destructiveness" that in part derives from the character's own internal "penchant for disaster." It is the "possibility of being further circumscribed," the "threat of being confronted with diminishing space" that is the "compelling motive" of Poe's narrators in their self-destructive quest to discover "some unknown and irresistable thing that lurks at the point where space ends." In a somewhat muddled discussion of the quest for ideal beauty and the central threat of sexuality in Poe, Carringer claims that Poe's works are "Romantic allegories of withdrawal into self." Having set up this tension between outer and inner, both of which lead to the same thing, Carringer then, rather incredibly, criticizes *Pym* as failing because it embodies these two contradictory impulses.

Detailing the increasing contrasts of opposites at the end of the narrative, Carringer concludes that there is "no more inherent justification for having Pym perish in a white fog rather than in a blackened tomb," so that "the book simply stops at one of the extremes"; and this, he feels, constitutes an "evasion." Having shown how Poe reverses all conventional associations of open space and light to mean the same as enclosure and darkness, and further, having shown that Poe's theme is infinite regression (the impulse toward further and further circumscription), Carringer criticizes Poe for withholding the final revelation in the same way that Paul Eakin concludes *Pym* is an "invalid" Lazarus pattern (see *ALS 1973*, p. 53). Carringer's article ends with a somewhat irrelevant expansion of his comments to include American fiction in general, the American Adam, racial motifs in 19th-century American literature, and other matters obviously designed to conform to *PMLA*'s new "breadth of interest" editorial policy. Actually, a more narrowly argued essay, with greater attention to recent Poe criticism, would have provided a more consistent essay and a more satisfactory conclusion.

The conclusion of *Pym*, in fact, is not composed of unremitting whiteness but a chiaroscuro. The depths of the ocean have a "milky" and "luminous glare," but just above hovers "a sullen darkness." Moreover, as any reader of "Benito Cereno" knows, the symbolic import of black mingled with white in American romantic fiction is the grayness of Void. In *Pym*, the white cataract is of an "ashy material," and the atmosphere near the pole is composed of "light gray vapour." The images of the absorption of black into white are observed more precisely than in Carringer in Victor J. Vitanza's "Edgar Allan Poe's *The Narrative of Arthur Gordon Pym*: An Anatomy of Perverseness" (*EA* 27:26–37), where a "distinct balance between black and white" is seen as supporting the central theme of perversity. Although Vitanza cites most of the pertinent scholarship, he is quite wrong to claim that until his essay Joseph Moldenhauer was "the only critic to discuss Perverseness in relation to *Pym*"; both Edward H. Davidson and Patrick F. Quinn have a good deal to say about it, as do two critics cited by Vitanza, along with two recent books on Poe he does not cite. Nevertheless Vitanza's essay is useful for its

close examination of patterns of *Pym*. Two three-part structures are
first identified: Pym moves from (1) a conscious state of mind to
(2) a preconscious state of mind, to (3) a collective subconscious
[*sic*] state that is one with the "basic principle of the universe." Pym
descends to this perverse depth of mind as he moves through three
corresponding voyages that shape the narrative: a regression from
(1) civilization, to (2) barbarism, to (3) the brink of original unity,
during a nine-month period. (This is an extension of Davidson's
argument.) A third three-part pattern is found in what Vitanza calls
the "mechanics of Perverseness," which take the form of thesis-
antithesis-synthesis. In "The Imp of the Perverse," for example, the
thought of falling is by itself harmless; but when it is consciously
opposed (antithesis), it becomes an uncontrollable urge. (This is an
extension of Quinn's argument.) This pattern he relates to a fourth
three-part design (also suggested by Quinn): there are three levels of
deception—by nature, by others, and by self. "Poe has Pym, as the
Imp of the Perverse and a symbol for a Perverse 'mode of consciousness,' voyage into the internal abyss of his mind to explore Perverseness, the impulse for self-destruction. In this way, the narrative
becomes an anatomy of Perverseness."

John P. Hussey, in "'Mr. Pym' and 'Mr. Poe': The Two Narrators
of 'Arthur Gordon Pym'" (*SAB* 39:22–32), attempts to show that
Pym is "neither particularly passive nor perverse, even though the
"larger meanings of the novel" elude him. Pym is a Romantic hero,
who, through "tenacious though calm gathering up of the mental
forces of sensitive observation and induction as well as such moral
qualities as patience, fortitude, and courage," masters himself and
survives briefly in a capricious world. But all these virtues are not
enough; Pym also needs "the blessings of *chance*." At the end Peters,
representing a poetic, visionary, "guide to eternity," is fused into one
with Pym, "the master of mortality." Yet there is no transfiguration of
Pym into a wise Ishmael or a Marlow meditating the meaning of his
experience. Pym is merely attracted by novel experiences; it is "Poe,"
the intruder "editor" of Pym's narrative, who has shaped events into
a "design which can be made to enclose them all." The arithmetical
symmetry of its nine episodes (1½ pp., 3½ pp., 29 pp., 16 pp., 27 pp.,
16 pp., 29 pp., 3½ pp., 1½ pp.), its nine months' duration, the fact that
the narrative moves from the last day of spring to the first day of

spring on the succeeding year, and other symbolic implications, are all the "fabrication" of the "editor," who simultaneously mocks the genre of the travel journal and shows what it could become "if transformed by a true poet." And *Pym* thus represents "one of the most sophisticated experiments in narrative technique in all the nineteenth century."

Purdue University

4. Melville

Hershel Parker

i. Edition

After two decades and more in limbo (the first preface is dated 1951) the Hendricks House *Omoo*, edited by Harrison Hayford and Walter Blair, has become available for purchase. As users of the page proofs have known for many years, it is one of the best volumes in that edition. The introduction advances an elaborate and plausible hypothesis about the composition of *Omoo* and the explanatory notes are unusually full. An appendix prints the consular documents (surviving in an Australian library) of the *Lucy Ann* revolt, the basis for Melville's comic opera revolt in *Omoo*. Very little is out of date in this plum pudding of a book, a valuable companion volume to the NN *Omoo*. On a few points newer information has been incorporated into the NN volume, but for serious—and joyous—study of *Omoo* this edition is essential.

ii. Bibliography, Biography, and Reputation

Strong factual ballast comes in G. Thomas Tanselle's "Bibliographical Problems in Melville" (*SAF* 2:57–74). As Tanselle says, the range and character of bibliographical problems raised by 19th-century American fiction "can be better understood as more specific examples from individual writers are brought together." Admitting that there are special circumstances in the publication history of Melville's books, Tanselle shows that many of the problems are the same "raised by other 19th-century authors." What makes this survey most valuable is the twin point of view, that of descriptive bibliographer as well as bibliographical editor of the NN Edition: as Tanselle rightly says, "the CEAA editions have furnished ample evidence of the inseparability of descriptive bibliography and editing." Something of a companion piece is a contribution to the history of recent scholarship,

"The CEAA: An Interim Assessment," by Hershel Parker with Bruce Bebb (*PBSA* 68:129–48), which makes scattered references to the NN Edition.

The year's best study is *The Early Lives of Melville: Nineteenth-Century Biographical Sketches and Their Authors*, by Merton M. Sealts, Jr. (Madison: Univ. of Wisc. Press). As the dust jacket says, at the core of the book are the primary documents, "four significant articles from biographical reference works published between 1852 and 1890, six retrospective essays of 1891–1892, and further reminiscences of Melville by his wife and two of his granddaughters. . . . Sealts has established the texts of these documents, surveyed their basis and reliability, and provided accompanying notes and commentary that identify persons and places and trace allusions and sources." This is a highly significant contribution, a long-needed work which is a model of responsible scholarship, both meticulous and far-ranging, a reproach and an inspiration to the dozens who regularly publish on Melville with none of the respect for truth which pervades this study. The illustrations, mainly contemporary portraits of Melville and his family and friends but also some interesting manuscript leaves, are sharply reproduced. Wisconsin has done well by Sealts in this handsome presentation of a loving and learned study.

Franklin Walker's *Irreverent Pilgrims: Melville, Browne, and Mark Twain in the Holy Land* (Seattle: Univ. of Wash. Press) belongs to a venerable 19th-century genre, the reverent pilgrimage "in the footsteps of [author's name to be supplied]." Walker's wayfaring after these irreverent pilgrims is pretty much on the right track but of no use to a scholar. In the section on *Clarel*, rather than examining the development from journal entry to poem (as the dust jacket promises) Walker merely gives us his pilgrimage in the tracks of the fictional pilgrims, reverent and irreverent. All in all, a book for 19th-century readers.

Most critics will ignore the next item (as indeed they will ignore Sealts's new book), but Charles Olson's ghost will rejoice at the materials and weights in Wilson Heflin's "New Light on Herman Melville's Cruise in the *Charles and Henry*" (*Historic Nantucket* 22:6–27). Edouard A. Stackpole recently found what Heflin fairly calls "a treasure trove of documents," including the itemized ship's library for the voyage of the *Charles and Henry* on which Melville sailed, as well as the shipping paper (with names of the original ship's company), bills for provisions, purchases for the "slop-chest," and a letter from Captain Coleman to the owners written shortly after Melville left the whaler. This valuable supplement to Sealts's *Melville's Reading* deserves wider dissemination: can the Melville Society strike a bargain with the Nantucket Historical Association for a reprinting of two or three hundred copies?

Another solid contribution is "Melville's Education in Science" (*TSLL* 16:411–25), in which Tyrus Hillway demonstrates science's importance in shaping Melville's ideas and attitudes: "Its teachings challenged, weakened, and for a time at least nearly destroyed his religious beliefs, and its tendency to view nature not as benevolent and peaceful but as 'a thing of tooth and claw' helped in turning him against the prevailing romanticism of his day." To the Olson issue of *Boundary 2* (2:55–84), Martin L. Pops contributed "Melville: To Him, Olson," a revision of his article in *MPS* (2:[1971]61–96). This is a sympathetic and perceptive analysis of what Melville meant to Olson and what Olson meant by the typography of *Call Me Ishmael.* Although tantalized by the thought of the unpublished first version of that book, which he has not seen, Pops does not seem to realize that the redoing of the *Twice a Year* essay into *Call Me Ishmael* affords proof of just how good a reviser of his Melville work Olson was.

A big handsome book, exorbitantly priced, is Watson G. Branch's *Melville: The Critical Heritage* (London and Boston: Routledge & Kegan Paul), which holds to the familiar format of the series. As Branch says, "The selection of reviews, essays, and other documents in this volume is intended to present a broad and accurate picture of the contemporary critical response to Melville's works and his own reaction to that criticism. The period covered begins with a review of his first book, *Typee,* in 1846 and ends with another review of *Typee* (and three other books) in 1892, the year after Melville died." Of special interest is a lavish, responsible 49-page introduction. Behind Branch's collection lies Hugh W. Hetherington's error-ridden but invaluable *Melville's Reviewers,* and companion volumes are *The Recognition of Herman Melville,* the Norton *Moby-Dick* and *The Confidence-Man,* the paperback reprint of Kaplan's facsimile of *Battle-Pieces,* and *"Moby-Dick" as Doubloon.* What with the forthcoming *Checklist of Melville Reviews* (see section *xii* below), this may strike some readers as more reviews than they want to read or know about. But having a large number of reviews in print may not only create new respect for the reviewers and new interest in their critical assumptions and practices, it may also shed light on Melville's works: revelations still await the scholar who will painstakingly work back and forth between Melville's writings and the reviewers' writings about him. Therefore Branch's book is heartily welcome, though in these depression days most readers will have to consult it in library copies.

George Monteiro's "Melville Reviews in *The Independent*" (PBSA 68:434–39) reprints from that New York weekly the reviews of *Typee*, *White-Jacket*, *Moby-Dick*, *The Confidence-Man*, and *Battle-Pieces*. Hershel Parker had already printed the one on *Moby-Dick* (*ELN* 9:182–85), but the others are new, and the one on *Battle-Pieces* is remarkably long and interesting. (See section *xii* below.) A related contribution is made by Hennig Cohen in "The 'Famous Tales' Anthologies: Recognition of Melville, 1899" (*PBSA* 68:179–80). Cohen shows that a turn-of-the-century New York publisher condensed *Moby-Dick* in *Famous Tales of the Sea*, printed "The Bell-Tower" in *Famous Tales of Enchantment*, and incorporated "a pastiche of selections from *Typee*" in *Famous Tales of Barbarians and Savages*. The series, Cohen informs us, was reprinted between 1902 and 1905 by the Bodleian Society of New York as *Classic Tales by Famous Authors*, with a new synopsis of *Moby-Dick* and a biographical note on Melville. Thomas Woodson's " 'Oblivion Lingers in the Neighborhood': The Loss and Recovery of 19th Century American Literature" (*BMWMLA* 7:26–39) contains comments on Melville's reputation, though it lacks the zest for gossip Hubbell displayed in *Who Are the Major American Writers?* and is weakened by a tendency to denounce rather than analyze the 19th-century failure to appreciate writers like Melville, Thoreau, and Dickinson.

iii. General

The best of the general studies is Tyrus Hillway's "Melville and the Young Revolutionaries" (*Americana-Austriaca*, pp. 43–58), an avuncular reaction to the New Left in the United States and corresponding impulses in Europe: the young people of the title are Hillway's "academic friends, both colleagues and students," who want to know how " 'Melville can be used to teach revolution.' " After a survey of recent writing on Melville's treatment of the individual and society, Hillway provides a salutary reminder that Melville regarded "specific social evils" as "rooted firmly in the foundations of human nature and not merely in the social or political superstructure." He concludes that "finding appropriate fuel for social revolution in Melville's prose works and the bulk of his poetry after 1850 requires highly individualized interpretations or distortions of meaning." Far less thoughtful is "Melville: Rebellion, Tragedy, and Historical Judgment," Harry B. Henderson, III's very long chapter in *Versions of the Past* (New York; Oxford Univ. Press), pp. 127–74. According to Henderson, violent revolution for Melville "was the significant historical event and he was preoccupied with questions of change rather than the limitations of roles." Nothing significant gets said about Melville's historical imagination, and there is not even any fresh grappling with major issues. Too much emphasis is placed on the hypothetical effect of the Astor Place Riot on Melville; details are distractingly wrong (Melville wrote no book called *His Fifty Years of Exile,* although the Sagamore Press published one with that title, there never was an authorial preface to *Billy Budd, Sailor,* etc.); and the general level of literary and historical sophistication is not high.

Two books provoke a question: Whatever happened to the promises that the new economic straits would at least force the presses to publish only superior books? The first, Edward S. Grejda's *The Common Continent of Men: Racial Equality in the Writings of Herman Melville* (Port Washington, N.Y.: Kennikat Press), explores, says the dust jacket, how Melville's "fiction and multi-racial characters" reflect his "deep commitment to the ideal of the brotherhood of man." The naïveté of the argument invites fanciful rebuttals ("All together now for bigotry!"). There is nothing here to interest a genuine scholar or critic. A comparable volume, Joseph Flibbert's paperback *Melville and the Art of Burlesque* (Amsterdam: Rodopi) has a handsome cream cover but little of interest inside it. This was not thoroughly researched when it was accepted as a dissertation back in 1970 and has not been brought up to date beyond the futile gesture of citing NN texts from 1970 and 1971 (though not the "Historical Notes" in them). *Nothing* else from 1970 onwards is mentioned, not even Browne's *Melville's Drive to Humanism* (1971), which deals extensively with Melville and the art of burlesque. If anyone asks you to read this, reply with the ineffable formula Flibbert attributes to Bartleby: " 'I would rather not.' " Then flee the foul fiend who hisses puns from *King Lear* into your ear.

In "Elements of Anatomy in Melville's Fiction" (*SNNTS* 6:38–61) Paul McCarthy admits that the "anatomy is not a new form to students of Melville, for elements of the genre appear throughout the fiction, and a few studies have directly or indirectly discussed the relationship or influence." McCarthy's own survey of the anatomy in *Mardi, White-Jacket, Moby-Dick*, and *The Confidence-Man* is never strenuously analytical; as he rightly says, his study of *Moby-Dick* "can do little more than summarize familiar views" and "offer a few hardly original opinions." "Melville's Use of Mysticism" (*PQ* 53:413–24) by Joel J. Thomas is amateurish (garbling quotations, citing the Constable texts, *not* citing the *Letters*, citing a major passage from "The Symphony" without knowing that it may be corrupt, twice referring to "Lawrence Thompson") but the basic argument is of potential interest—that mysticism in *Mardi, Moby-Dick*, and *Pierre* "represents a mode of noesis."

iv. The Early Books

In "*Redburn*: The Psychological Pattern" (*SAF* 2:133–44) Charles Haberstroh rather simplistically calls *Redburn* "probably as much the end product" of Melville's "suicidal crisis" as of his "economic necessity." He concludes that in this book Melville "for a time made successful use of his fiction to quiet his rage, to tell himself that endurance and control were still possible." Maybe what Charles Lionel Regan says in "Dilemma of Melville's Horned Woman" (*AN&Q* 12:133–34) is news to him, but Vincent's *The Tailoring of Melville's "White-Jacket"* (1970) had covered the same ground.

v. Moby-Dick

Morton L. Ross's "*Moby-Dick* as an Education" (*SNNTS* 6:62–75) is an original and responsible engagement of a major problem, the nature of the experience of reading the book right. As Ross says, "a proper appreciation of the novel begins with the unmediated experience of its remarkably intricate play of pedagogy" in which much depends "on the reader's willingness to be informed," especially his willingness to recognize that his "capacity for the awesome needs training." Ross is excellent on the narration, particularly on Ishmael's way of animating mere facts, "transforming them from discrete items in objective inventory into the play of stimuli within specific human experience." He is best of all in emphasizing the educative function of Melville's kinetic appeals, "the part they play in creating for us the illusion of experiential knowledge." Like Wadlington's recent essay (*ELH* 39:309–31), Ross's article promises to be of permanent value.

Also of value is Jerome M. Loving's "Melville's Pardonable Sin" (*NEQ* 47:262–78), perhaps not the classic refutation of the "two *Moby-Dicks* theory" which some of us have been waiting for but an admirably cogent presentation of evidence that "Melville was well on his way to writing his 'wicked book' before he met Hawthorne." Loving's mildly argued essay is slightly weakened by a casualness about the contemporary American literary milieu and about the history of scholarship on both Hawthorne and Melville, but it deserves everyone's attention. Now maybe someone will responsibly take up the larger topic, overworked but underthought, of the effects Melville and Hawthorne may have had on all of each other's writing in the years after they began reading each other.

Nathalia Wright's "The Tale of Moby Dick" (*Phi Kappa Phi Journal* 54:42–58) is an evocative and sophisticated introduction of the book to an intelligent and well-educated audience. Maybe every would-be critic ought to set himself the task of writing this sort of general account now and then: he might learn something from it, and teach and write about the book better. In a time when most of us see things shakily and in part, this sort of essay is refreshing. A slightly modified version of Leo Marx's " 'Noble Shit': The Uncivil Response of American Writers to Civil Religion in America" (*MR* 14[1973]: 709–39) appears in this year's *American Civil Religion*, eds. Russell E. Richey and Donald G. Jones (New York: Harper & Row), pp. 222–51, with the original subtitle chastely serving as the new title. This is a lucid discussion of the American civil religion (in Robert Bellah's sense of "a body of beliefs, symbols, and rituals which provides a religious dimension for the whole fabric of American life, including the political realm") and how "certain of our most distinguished writers" have reacted "to this strain of nationalistic religiosity." Marx uses the "great democratic God" passage from *Moby-Dick* as a climactic illustration, calling it probably "the most affecting, and the most explicitly religious, evocation of this egalitarian commitment in our literature—one that forms the basis of a prophetic judgment." Richard K. Cross in "*Moby-Dick* and *Under the Volcano*: Poetry from the Abyss" (*MFS* 20:149–56) sometimes fails to distinguish between Melville and his characters and seems (like Malcolm Lowry) a little shaky about the facts of Melville's life, but his ways of defining the strategies of the two novelists are suggestive. While full assessment of the relationship awaits the use of more of Lowry's letters about Melville, this essay is a good interim report. There were two slight but interesting notes. In the first, "Whodunit? *Moby Dick!*" (*JPC* 8:280–85), Edward Stone amusingly recollects his adolescent reading of Tiffany Thayer, whose *Thirteen Men* contains references to *Moby-Dick*. The second, Rodelle and Stanley Weintraub's "*Moby-Dick* and *Seven Pillars of Wisdom*" (*SAF* 2:238–40), is thin, but sensitive to Melville's influence on T. E. Lawrence, and the mention of E. M. Forster's comparison of the writers was news to me.

Everything else was downhill. In "Ishmael's Nightmare and the American Eve" (*AI* 30[1973]:274–93) Mark Hennelly sets out "to provide a psychoallegorical reading" of *Moby-Dick*, "not in terms of the mind that produced it, but rather in terms of the uniquely American consciousness and unconsciousness" that it dramatizes, "especially with regard to the American male's 'flight from woman.'" Well, right this way, folks, read all about postcoital depression, masturbation anxiety, and such like in Melville. But don't share Hennelly's ridicule of Bezanson for being scandalized by Melville's sexual metaphors: Hennelly is missing Bezanson's humor, a failing which raises the larger possibility that he may also be missing Melville's. I doubt that any Melvillean will profit from Dan Vogel's *The Three Masks of American Tragedy* (Baton Rouge: La. State Univ. Press). Vogel is simplistic toward *Moby-Dick* ("We pity Ahab for his suffering, we are awed by the dimensions of his tragedy, but we also take pride in the fact that an American hero dies in defiance of limitation") and toward *Billy Budd, Sailor* (a rigid "theological allegory"). Vogel cites the Mansfield-Vincent text of *Moby-Dick*, the Rinehart (!) text of *Billy Budd*, quotes "same madness" from the *Mosses* essay, declares that in August 1850 Melville himself described his whaling manuscript as "mostly done," and in general shows that he has not dipped into much Melville scholarship and criticism since the 1950s. Similarly old hat with its fifties-like treatment of Ishmael and Ahab as opposites is Walter L. Reed's chapter, "Melville: The Extended Hero and Expanded Meditation," in his *Meditations on the Hero: A Study of the Romantic Hero in Nineteenth-Century Fiction* (New Haven, Conn.: Yale Univ. Press). Through most of this rather rambling chapter Reed seems to have been reading a *Moby-Dick* in which there was no Moby Dick.

John Idol's "Ahab and the 'Siamese Connection'" (*SCB* 34:156–59) at least reminds us of a pervasive image pattern in trying to show "how Ahab as the chief of isolatoes led thirty or more other isolatoes to accept his quest as their own, and how Melville, through narrative elements, imagery, and commentary, strung together a variety of ligatures to indicate the bonds linking Ahab to humanity and to nature." Carl G. Vaught's "Religion as a Quest for Wholeness: Melville's *Moby-Dick*" (*JGE* 26:9–35) is an attempt "to indicate the ways in which the novel may be understood as a concrete embodiment of the religious quest, and as a set of clues about ways in which the language of a quest may finally be transcended." The result is of little or no value to literary critics. It is hard to guess why any editor accepted Garth McCann's "Circumstance and the Publication of *Moby Dick*" (*Serif* 11:58–60), since it adds nothing to the familiar story told in the *Log* and other works, none of which is cited.

vi. Pierre

Perhaps the most trivial of Mildred K. Travis's string of trivial notes is her "Relevant Digressions in *Pierre*" (*ATQ* 24:7–8). Paul Baender's weary "Reflections Upon the CEAA by a Departing Editor" (*RALS* 4:131–44) condemns the disproportion in the NN "Historical Note" (especially the "exhaustive résumé of critical opinion from the first reviews to the present day"), scorns the "excrescences in the 'Note on the Text,'" and denounces the novel itself as "absurd" and as "turgid, pretentious, and boring." By contrast, Robert Milder's "Melville's 'Intentions' in *Pierre*" (*SNNTS* 6:186–99) raises significant questions. Challenging some of Leon Howard's assumptions (especially the notion that the novel Melville began was a simple one designed only to captivate the female book-buyers), Milder insists that "Whatever its excesses, *Pierre* is an intensely deliberate book," and that the "book Melville published, 'loathsome' as it seemed to many of its first readers, is the book he set out to write." Good as Milder's questions are, his answers are unsatisfactory. Rather than elaborate here, I refer the reader to my study of the writing of *Pierre* which will appear in the spring 1976 issue of *SNNTS*. There I present new documentary evidence which redates the drawing up of the contract and Melville's decision to enlarge his manuscript. The *Pierre* Melville published is demonstrably *not* the book he set out to write.

vii. "Bartleby"

There were two economic readings. In "Bartleby as Alienated Worker" (*SSF* 11:379–85) Louise K. Barnett reductively contends that Bartleby is Melville's portrait of a worker alienated under a capitalistic society who, "realizing that his work is meaningless and without a future, can only protest his humanity by a negative assertion." Better is Marvin Fisher's " 'Bartleby,' Melville's Circumscribed Scrivener" (*SoR* 10:59–79), which intelligently but without force or originality sees the story as exploring the "stony impersonality of urban America." Fisher's belief in the narrator's capacity for moral growth is most open to challenge: Is the emotion of the lawyer at the end the "overpowering stinging melancholy" which earlier he momentarily felt but quickly rationalized out of, or is it nearer to "a not-unpleasing sadness"?

   Three other articles in one way or another relate "Bartleby" to the contemporary scene. In "Melville, the Colt-Adams Murder, and 'Bartleby'" (*SAF* 2:123–32), T. H. Giddings takes several pages before making his most interesting point, that for the lawyer to get to his law office on Wall Street from the corner of Broadway and Canal he might well have passed Broadway and Chambers, the location of the murder, and thereupon have had it brought into his mind. I find unconvincing Christopher W. Sten's contention in "Bartleby the Transcendentalist: Melville's Dead Letter to Emerson" (*MLQ* 35:30–44) that the story is based upon Emerson's essay "The Transcendentalist." Hershel Parker's "Dead Letters and Melville's 'Bartleby'" (*RALS* 4:90–99) consists mainly of a reprinting of an article on dead letters from the Albany *Daily State Register* for September 23, 1852. The document is not presented as a specific source for "Bartleby," but it begins very evocatively with an allusion to Dickens, and is not without "a certain strange suggestive interest."

viii. Later Stories

In "Melville's 'The Encantadas': The Deceptive Enchantment of the Absolute" (*PLL* 10:58–69) Nicholas Canaday, Jr., promisingly suggests that "geography, history, and legend are the broad topics through which Melville transmuted his view of the Galapagos Islands into art." But like Margaret Yarina and Arlene Jackson (*ALS 1973*, pp. 77–78), Canaday seems unaware "that cautious study of the way the sketches were composed and published must precede any meaningful discussion of their unity." Marvin Fisher offers a disappointing analysis in "Melville's 'The Fiddler': Succumbing to the Drummer" (*SSF* 11:153–60). Right about the narrator's foolish pride in his awful pseudoclassical tragic poem, Fisher fumblingly belabors the possible meanings of the characters' "tag names," blunderingly applies "Hawthorne and His Mosses" to "The Fiddler" as if Melville had not undergone a profound shift of attitude between *Pierre* and "Bartleby," and grimly closes his eyes to the wise humor that brightens the poignance of the sketch. (If Fisher had consulted Thorp's edition of the *Mosses* essay instead of that in the Constable he would have known for sure that Irving was the imitative author Melville had in mind.) Beryl Rowland in "Melville Answers the Theologians: The Ladder of Charity in 'The Two Temples'" (*Mosaic* 7:1–13) usefully reminds us that much of the imagery of these sketches might have derived from the writings of Sheridan Knowles, the actor-preacher to whom it was dedicated, but Rowland's allegorical reading is strained.

Slave-revolt buffs will be pleased to see the facsimile reprinting of John W. Barber's *History of the Amistad Captives* (*ATQ* 22:109–20). In Joyce Adler's "Melville's *Benito Cereno*: Slavery and Violence in the Americas" (*S&S* 38:19–48) the ratio of summary to argument is 8:22, well outside the tolerable limits for modern criticism. This is a simplistic, modish (or maybe no longer modish) reduction of Melville's story to one about slavery in the United States, his warning to the nation "of a tragic fate if it did not eliminate slavery, its tragic flaw." Bernard Rosenthal in "Melville's Island" (*SSF* 11:1–9) insists that the "politics of 'Benito Cereno' are no doubt interesting but finally not the main subject of the story." The island referred to is Santa Maria, a name that Rosenthal takes as a clue to a "Marian motif," seeing significance in the fact that "Melville's exploration of a theologically dead world, set around the island of Saint Mary, was written almost simultaneously with the Papal decree in 1854 making the doctrine of the Immaculate Conception church dogma." I remain a skeptic, unintimidated by some aggressive writing, such as Rosenthal's implying that anyone disagreeing with him on one point must have "absolute contempt for probability theory." Another anti-antislavery reading, John Harmon McElroy's "Cannibalism in Melville's *Benito Cereno*" (*EIL* 1:206–18), holds that the evil of Negro slavery in America was not the "paramount theme," despite the date the story was written. In this attempt to put together the two parts of the story, the regular narrative and the deposition, McElroy may place too much stress on the cannibalism itself and too little on the cruelty of using cannibalism (and threats of emasculation) in the psychological torture Babo inflicts on Benito Cereno. Ignoring the sexual significance of the scabbard, artificially stiffened, McElroy too readily assumes that the reason Cereno will not testify about the cannibalism is that he has forgiven Babo—not that it is too painful for him to mention. McElroy thinks the deposition continues "the experience of half-lights and half-truths that enveloped Delano in the early part of the story"; others might think that the straightforwardness of the deposition was designed to provide relief after the all but intolerable ambiguity of the early part. The classic essay on the deposition remains to be written.

Only cranks will find much of interest in Charles E. Nnolim's *Melville's "Benito Cereno": A Study in Meaning of Name Symbolism* (New York: New Voices) but at least it affords conclusive proof that being a West African doesn't help you understand Babo.

Marvin Fisher's "Prospect and Perspective in Melville's 'Piazza'" (*Criticism* 16:203–16) fails to mention or improve upon earlier critics such as Hyatt H. Waggoner, who had anticipated his suggestion that "in stories like 'The Piazza' Melville is indebted to his recurring encounters with Hawthorne in person and on the page, using Hawthorne's earlier work to clarify his own meaning and shape his own means, adapting Hawthorne's strategy to his own artistic ends." As well as not being original, Fisher's analysis is simply not rigorous enough. It is a mistake to slight the "quest" theme as being "so reduced in scale as to seem almost a comic parody of the remote or fantastic adventures in *Typee* or *Mardi*." After all, in "The Piazza" the narrator, a veteran of physical adventuring in remote places, embarks on a yet more daring sort of internal adventuring into aesthetics and philosophy. Fisher's respectful and cautious essay ends by minimizing one of Melville's finest achievements.

ix. The Confidence-Man

Little new light was shed this year. The longest article, Helen P. Trimpi's "Harlequin-Confidence-Man: The Satirical Tradition of Commedia Dell'Arte and Pantomime in Melville's *The Confidence-Man*" (*TSLL* 16:147–93), tells much more about the *commedia dell'arte* and pantomime than it does about Melville's book. Enthusiastic about her thesis, Trimpi slights more obvious influences and strains too hard at associating Melville's characters with specific type-characters in the *commedia dell'arte*. Jane Donahue Eberwein in "Joel Barlow and *The Confidence-Man*" (*ATQ* 24:28–29) fails to make any case for Barlow's influence on Melville. In *The Poetry of Melville's Late Years* (1970) William Bysshe Stein described his approach as "Freudian, Jungian, and sometimes plainly Steinian." In "Melville's *The Confidence-Man*: Quicksands of the Word (*ATQ* 24:38–50), a breathtaking fantasia apparently begotten by H. Bruce Franklin's footnotes to the Bobbs-Merrill text upon a dictionary of cognates, the approach is quintessentially Steinian. Stein holds that (mainly inspired by Swift, Sterne, Descartes, and St. Paul) "Melville manipulates the language of the novel to illustrate how the body makes (or writes) the mind"; in instance after instance, "the theological and sexual bifurcations of meaning provide the artist-narrator with the verbal artifice to orchestrate the discordant flow of his controlled legerdemain." First to disappear in the quicksand are Melville's immediate literary, political, and cultural contexts. John Seelye and I protested against Stein's making the older Melville a dirty old man; in this essay Stein makes Melville such a dirty middle-aged man that only the diehard textual scholar will suspect a typo in a passage such as this: "In days of yore the barber's sign, a standing pole and two wash balls, stood for the genitals."

In "Melville and 'Romance': Literary Nationalism and Fictional Form" (*ATQ* 24:56–62) Michael Davitt Bell uses *The Confidence-Man* as test case for his argument that "the central 'subject' of Melville's fiction became the relationship, and ultimately the conflict," between "the demands and 'truths' of Romantic literary nationalism" and "the nature of his literary form, 'romance.'" Rather than zeroing in on his topic, Bell moves about it in turgid circles, repeating himself distractingly and straining the sense of the text. Somewhere in all this is a fine topic waiting to be defined and explored. Christopher W. Sten's "The Dialogue of Crisis in *The Confidence-Man*: Melville's 'New Novel'" (*SNNTS* 6:165–85) is a well-written but cheerless essay which exemplifies the seemingly willful blindness critics develop out of a need to publish and an unwillingness to go at a text with the aid of the best that has already been written about it. It also exemplifies a tendency of critics not steeped in literary tradition to find arbitrary modern correspondences, in this case a close resemblance to French "new novels." What Sten argues is that readers have no way of being sure that the title character is a confidence man. John G. Blair's "Puns and Equivocation in Melville's *The Confidence-Man*" (*ATQ* 22:91–95) attempts to distinguish between the circular puns which in the first half of the book reflect, "on the level of verbal play, the narrator's global strategy of ambiguity," and the puns in the second half, which "no longer play between word and word, but between word and action." Blair aligns himself with those critics who believe that the book is "intentionally inconclusive." It would be good to see someone of this persuasion pay serious attention to Elizabeth S. Foster's discussion of Melville's satiric targets in her Hendricks House edition of this book (1954). Tom Quick's note on "Saint Paul's Types of the Faithful and Melville's Confidence Man" (*NCF* 28:472–77) makes an intriguing if ultimately unpersuasive case for taking the types of the faithful in I Corinthians 12 as "the disguises that Melville provided for his confidence man's masquerade." This note winsomely testifies to our urge to make Melville's book as complexly unified as any New Critic could wish.

x. The Poetry

Five pieces are slight. In "Melville's *Battle-Pieces* and Whitman's *Drum-Taps*: A Comparison" (*WWR* 19[1973]:81–92), Vaughan Hudson does not mention some of the best criticism and is not especially informative on Melville's techniques or meanings; furthermore, his distaste for Melville's poetry leads him into some embarrassing rewritings in the manner of T. B. Aldrich improving Dickinson. Best ignored is Donald Barlow Stauffer's derivative and superficial survey in *A Short History of American Poetry* (New York: Dutton), pp. 131–37. George Monteiro's note on "Melville's 'America'" (*Expl* 32: item 72) suggests (unconvincingly, it strikes me) that "Brazilian" ("As rolled Brazilian billows go") might carry the contemporary meaning of "red." I would like to think that C. N. Srinath's "A Note on Melville's Poetry" (*LCrit* 11[1973]:33–40) would not have been published in this country, but to shake that notion comes Lynn W. Denton's trivial "Melville's Jerusalem—'Wreck Ho—the wreck!'" (*HTR* 67:184–86).

In "The Erotic Motif in Melville's *Clarel*" (*TSLL* 16:315–28) Nina Baym brilliantly makes a major original point. Taking *Clarel* as one of Melville's works which set out "with a combined erotic and philosophical situation" (though unlike either *Mardi* or *Pierre* it "carries the erotic theme all the way through to the conclusion"), she argues that "Melville has dramatized the way in which his [Clarel's] understanding of Christianity makes it impossible for Clarel to accept his own sexuality, and incapacitates him for relationships with the opposite sex"; Melville "has shown, conversely, how the protagonist's heterosexual drives make him incapable of living up to his Christian ideals." There are problems with this essay. Baym needlessly scorns *Clarel* as poetry and once or twice slights Bezanson's work when he is fuller and better on a particular point than she is. *Clarel* is complexly political, theological, and psychological as well as erotic and philosophical, and one becomes uneasy at the rigorous focus on the title character alone, even to overuse of formulas like "two pilgrims" when two other prominent characters are meant: it *is* an oversimplification to say that the "action of *Clarel*, then, is Clarel's meeting with, rejection of, and final—futile—return to Ruth." There are misreadings: in "The Celibate" Clarel does not accept "the idea of a physical dimension to homosexual love"; and I see no grounds for anyone's thinking that what kills Ruth and Agar is Clarel's desertion. The worst page is on "Vine and Clarel," where Baym seriously misrepresents an important passage in her text, only to make partial reparation in a footnote. The fact is that we do not know what Vine's "rebukeful dusking" implies, and the interpretations given in the canto are not even definitely ascribed to Clarel—they are conceits "such" as could cling to his dream of vain surmise and imputation full of sting. Furthermore, Baym misreads the "negatives of flesh" passage, which merely asserts that a man's not having a natural sexual organ to receive another man's sexual organ should be taken as an analogical argument against the notion of male unity of spirit. The whole canto is much more complex psychologically than Baym makes it. But better than Bezanson (and, needless to say, any other writer on *Clarel*), Baym shows that though Clarel is strongly drawn to women, he "feels that sexual love is inherently impure and that his erotic feelings must therefore necessarily separate him from God." Baym is good enough, I'll wager, to drive even Bezanson back to certain passages to make sure he understood them aright.

xi. Billy Budd, Sailor

In arguing that "Billy in the Darbies" embodies "the meaning implicit in the narrator's activity," Robert T. Eberwein's "The Impure Fiction of *Billy Budd*" (*SNNTS* 6:318–26) naïvely quotes from the Chicago edition without understanding the aesthetic implications of the textual evidence there presented. Theo Steinmann's "The Perverted Pattern of *Billy Budd* in *The Nigger of the 'Narcissus'*" (*ES* 55:239–46) makes routine comparisons which are vitiated by the author's apparent belief that Conrad had read *Billy Budd* before writing *Nigger*. Unlike Steinmann, John B. Humma in "Melville's *Billy Budd* and Lawrence's 'The Prussian Officer': Old Adams and New" (*EIL* 1:83–88) knows that Lawrence could not have read Melville's story before writing his own. What he offers is a study of the correspondences (e.g., "both subalterns are unconscious types," both officers "are acutely *conscious* individuals who repress their instincts").

xii. Miscellaneous

Another, perhaps final, review essay appeared on (or mainly on) the 1970 outpouring of books on Melville, Charles N. Watson, Jr.'s "Melville's Fiction in the Early 1970's" (*ESQ* 20:291–97). This year I continue the policy of not discussing the many notes and short articles printed in *Extracts: An Occasional Newsletter of the Melville Society* unless they have clear biographical or bibliographical significance. (The way things are going, it will soon make sense to ignore *ATQ* and review *Extracts*.) But anyone writing on Melville ought to subscribe by sending five dollars to the treasurer, Donald Yannella, at Glassboro State College, Glassboro, N.J.; Hennig Cohen, University of Pennsylvania, is the editor. One item requires mention here, Arthur H. Miller, Jr.'s "Melville Dissertations: An Annotated Directory" (*Extracts* 20 sup.:1–11), which brings the Myerson-Miller pamphlet of 1972 up to date. Well before this volume of *ALS* appears, the Melville Society will have printed Steven Mailloux's and Hershel Parker's *Checklist of Melville Reviews* so that (among other benefits) new reviews can more easily be flushed out and duplication of effort avoided. Scholars can help with this clearinghouse effort by publishing any new reviews they find in *Extracts*, which will then include them in supplements to the *Checklist*. Reporting on Beatrice Ricks's and Joseph D. Adams's *Herman Melville: A Reference Bibliography* (*ALS 1973*, p. 66), I concluded that little good could be said of it, although its badness should not reflect on works done after G. K. Hall hired Joseph Katz to supervise its bibliographical and textual series. Now G. K. Hall has demonstrated its good faith in the best possible way, by commissioning a Melville scholar, Brian Higgins, to do a new book, *Herman Melville: A Reference Guide*, a full-scale annotated secondary bibliography.

University of Southern California

5. Whitman and Dickinson

Bernice Slote

Whitman studies in 1974 remain quantitatively about the same as in 1973, though published work on Dickinson has increased. It is particularly enhanced by the appearance of Richard B. Sewall's excellent two-volume biography of Dickinson; other writing, too, seems to have more depth and sharper focus. Ten dissertations on Whitman turn primarily to his place in American literature or his relationship with other writers; only one deals directly with the poetics of *Leaves of Grass*. The three dissertations on Dickinson all bear on the nature of her poetry. Both Whitman and Dickinson are about equal in Donald Barlow Stauffer's *A Short History of American Poetry* (New York: E. P. Dutton), pp. 137–58. But Stauffer links them acutely in their merging of "poetry with experience until both are one," and their forging of language "into a highly personal instrument" to make a new reality.

i. Whitman

a. **Bibliography, Collections, Editing.** One of the most interesting of recent bibliographical notes on Whitman is a list of his poetry which appeared in periodicals from 1838 on, including posthumous printings from manuscripts as late as the 1960s. William White has 151 entries in "Walt Whitman's Poetry in Periodicals: A Bibliography" (*Serif* 11,ii:31–38), printed, he says, "in the hope that readers will inform me of omissions or errors." See also White's continuing Whitman bibliography in the *Walt Whitman Review*.

Five new letters are noted. The text of a letter from Whitman to an unnamed book collector (October 17, 1871) indicates where a copy of the 1855 edition of *Leaves of Grass* might be purchased (E. Earle Stibitz, "Walt Whitman Answers a Collector," *ICarbS* 1:141–44). Two unpublished letters recently obtained by the Feinberg

Collection are addressed to the English poet and critic Roden Noel. One of June 29, 1886, is reproduced with a note by William White ("Whitman to Roden Noel: A New Letter," *WWR* 20:117). White also cites another note of August 30, 1886, to Carlyle, in which Whitman thanks him for "Notes on America" ("Whitman to Carlyle: A New Letter," *WWR* 20:74). The text of a March 21, 1891, letter from Whitman to Richard M. Bucke, one formerly thought lost, is given by the owner, Charles L. Batten, Jr. ("Unpublished Letter to Dr. Bucke," *WWR* 20:115–16).

Two additional newspaper articles of early 1865 have been assigned to Whitman, with cogent reasons, by Jerome M. Loving. Both are about Whitman's soldier brother, George Washington Whitman, and show particular family knowledge: " 'A Brooklyn Soldier, and a Noble One': A Brooklyn *Daily Union* Article by Whitman" (*WWR* 20:27–30) and " 'Our Veterans Mustering Out'—Another Newspaper Article by Whitman about His Soldier Brother" (*YULG* 49:217–24).

In an interesting bibliographical note Peter Van Egmond discusses briefly the collection of Whitman's own books and others on or to him in the Canaday Library at Bryn Mawr College, and gives a descriptive listing of the books including inscriptions and notations ("Bryn Mawr College Library Holdings of Whitman Books," *WWR* 20:41–50). Most of the 41 books in the collection were given to the library by Professor Herbert G. Harned; several were added by Charles E. Feinberg.

William White in "Textual Editing: A Whitman Note" (*AN&Q* 12:15–16) usefully comments on confusions arising from errors in Whitman's handling of "Salut Au Monde" and the perpetuation of error by editing which adheres slavishly to an author's original marred by such chance mistakes.

b. **Biography.** The most substantial contribution to our understanding of Whitman the man—and perhaps of the poet—is Floyd Stovall's *The Foreground of Leaves of Grass* (Charlottesville: Univ. Press of Va.), a meticulously detailed review of the context of Whitman's world before 1855, not only his family and his personal life but the influences that aided in the metamorphosis of journalist to poet. Stovall discusses popular literature (Scott was important), the New York stage, opera, current science and pseudoscience, philosophy, and the influence of other writers—Heine, Goethe, Tennyson, Emerson. The flowering of Whitman's poetic imagination, says Stovall, was less a sudden illumination than "the gradual opening of latent faculties under the stimulation of his reading combined with a growing confidence in himself" (p. 14). There was also the fortunate circumstance that he happened to grow up in the very moment of America's growing energy, the "decades of westward expansion, national pride, and general prosperity." Throughout Whitman's life, as Stovall admirably shows, he was engaged in the search, the storing, the uses of knowledge.

A short chapter (pp. 39–58) in *The "Eagle" and Brooklyn* by Raymond A. Schroth, S.J. (Westport, Conn.: Greenwood Press) summarizes Whitman's journalistic years on that newspaper with some good primary details. Whitman's career with the *Eagle* is viewed as important to Brooklyn and the paper and also as "a high point in a journalistic career that spanned sixty-one years and that would merit the attention of journalism historians even if he had not written *Leaves of Grass*" (p. 39).

Whitman's relationship with the Civil War and his attitudes toward slavery continue to interest scholars. Somewhat peripheral to Whitman's own career but of interest biographically are the Civil War letters of his brother, George Washington Whitman, eight of which are presented with notes and commentary by Jerome M. Loving in "Civil War Letters of George Washington Whitman from North Carolina" (*NCHR* 50[1973]:73–92). On slavery itself, Ken Peeples, Jr., has a well-reasoned presentation in "The Paradox of the 'Good Gray Poet' (Walt Whitman on Slavery and the Black Man)" (*Phylon* 35:22–32). His conclusion is that Whitman disliked slavery as an institution but that in line with the political and social pressures of his age he did not consider the slave himself as equal to the white man in American democracy. Another article in general agreement is Mary-Emma Graham's "Politics in Black and White: A View of Walt Whitman's Career as a Political Journalist" (*CLAJ* 17 [1973]:263–70), which shows Whitman, especially in his journalism, as theoretically opposing slavery because it blurred the American dream but never quite accepting "the free Black Man."

c. **Criticism: General.** *Walt Whitman* (New York: McGraw-Hill), ed. Arthur Golden, is a useful collection of criticism containing nine reprinted essays by Gay Wilson Allen, Roger Asselineau, and others, and a compact introduction by Golden on the making of *Leaves of Grass*. It includes a chronology and a selected bibliography. A handsome, useful, but strangely organized book is called *Walt Whitman*, subtitled *Walt Whitman's Autograph Revision of the Analysis of "Leaves of Grass"* (New York: New York Univ. Press). It is primarily a valuable facsimile printing of the final two chapters and appendix from part 2 of *Walt Whitman*, by Richard Maurice Bucke, with Whitman's holograph notes for revision reproduced. This major part of the book is presented in a foreword by Daniel Maggin, who owns the original manuscript, and who credits Stephen Railton for the editing. Between Maggin's note and the facsimile pages, however, are an essay by Quentin Anderson, "Whitman's New Man" (pp. 11–52), and one by Galway Kinnell, "Whitman's Indicative Words," reprinted from *American Poetry Magazine*. These are worth reading but seem irrelevant to the "Autograph Revision," which every scholar will want to see.

There are several substantial general essays on Whitman this year. A carefully worked-out discussion of his relationship to tradition is in Sam B. Girgus, "Culture and Post-Culture in Walt Whitman" (*CentR* 18:392–410). Whitman looked both ways, says Girgus—to the "traditional concept of culture as a set of beliefs, ideals and symbols" for the American experience, and to a "new transcendence" that would shape a distinctive American personality. "The revolutionary and traditional impulses engaged each other in a dialectical relationship out of which he hoped a newer and healthier cultural environment would emerge." Whitman prefigured the contemporary world as modern humanists see it by his attack on "the hierarchical value structure," yet it was in the interest of "the religious democracy based upon a commitment to culture," in the full sense of the word *culture*. He attempted "to find a structure for continual change."

A fine essay by Robin P. Hoople, "Walt Whitman and the City of Friends" (*ATQ* 18[1973]:45–51), traces the garden-city dualities through the "Children of Adam" and "Calamus" poems. Here is first "the predominant shape of the garden of natural process, against which, parallel but subtly opposed, is that very urban world in which comradeship develops." The city's compression "results in man en masse, the matrix from which the individual must arise." Hoople suggests that "Crossing Brooklyn Ferry" comes out of Whitman's "struggle for a reconciliation between nature and city," and that both that poem and "Chants Democratic" are "particularizations of the generic principle embodied in 'Calamus.'" Whitman's reference is to the conciliatory Quaker idiom of a "city of friends."

Arthur Wrobel's "Whitman and the Phrenologists: The Divine Body and the Sensuous Soul" (*PMLA* 89:17–23) is a knowledgeable discussion of the link between Whitman's interest in phrenology and his concept of the physical and spiritual oneness of experience. As the phrenologist saw the physical man identified with his spiritual health, each acting on the other, so Whitman combined body and soul, seeing the universe as one organic whole with nature the instrument "to provide intuitive insights of an immanent God and to be used by man in his quest for truth." This view of Whitman's philosophy (and poetic theory) is not new, but Wrobel makes the further case that Whitman "found in phrenology a scientific confirmation of the merely intuitive truths offered by the Transcendentalists."

An essay by Roger Asselineau, "Walt Whitman's Humor" (*ATQ* 22:86–91), traces Whitman from his youthful attitudes of literary mimicry in his journalistic prose to his more serious stance as the poet of *Leaves of Grass* who, like Dickens and Carlyle, used humor as a means to an end. Asselineau cites ways in which the mature Whitman in *Leaves of Grass* became a humorist of wit and love in the 18th-century sense of the term. In "Walt Whitman: The Pedagogue as Poet" (*WWR* 20:140–46) Bert Hitchcock traces the effects of Whitman's experience as a schoolmaster on his writings. By subject, phraseology, and theme Whitman continued to affirm the importance of education and to see his poetic function as that of a teacher. Although I am rarely impressed with psychoanalytic studies of art, those interested in psychology and literature will want to see Stephen A. Black's "Journeys into Chaos: A Psychoanalytic Study of Whitman, His Literary Processes and His Poems" (*L&P* 24:47–54).

A helpful article on Whitman's language is P. Z. Rosenthal's "'Dilation' in Whitman's Early Writing" (*WWR* 20:3–15). Here all of the uses of *dilation* are carefully studied, with the conclusion that the chief impulse in Whitman's meaning is toward the idea of "beyond"; Whitman is attempting "to make the word dramatize his immense faith in the expansive possibilities of the human soul.' Gerald F. Amyot in "Walt Whitman's 'Language Experiment'" (*WWR* 20:97–103) also stresses the importance of Whitman's concern for words, for language; he sees *Leaves of Grass* as both a "language experiment" and an experiment in living. A dynamic poetic language for Whitman was developed only by an immersion in life. Carl Nelson in "Whitman's Dynamic Form: The Image of the Divine" (*WWR* 20:121–32) reviews a number of images and metaphors that embody a dynamic, organic cosmos—some from Eastern iconography, others from music or from the evolving life of nature.

d. **Criticism: Individual Works.** Dealing with the "Calamus" poems as a unit, Leland Krauth in "Whitman and His Readers: The Comradeship Theme" (*WWR* 20:147–51) sees a change through the section from "a groping exploration of the meaning of comradeship to a joyful celebration of the fact of comradeship." The pattern can be seen in three poems, "Scented Herbage of My Breast," "States!," and "Of the Terrible Doubt of Appearances," through which Whitman links comradeship to death, to democracy, and finally to the universe. Comradeship, involving the reader, then becomes the "encompassing metaphor" of Whitman's book. Two articles consider the poems of "Drum-Taps." Agnes Dicken Cannon analyses with good detail the elements of Whitman's life—emotional as well as factual—which have reverberations in these poems ("Fervid Atmosphere and Typical Events: Autobiography in *Drum-Taps*," *WWR* 20:79–96). In a perceptive article by John Snyder, "The Irony of National Union: Violence and Compassion in 'Drum-Taps'" (*CRevAS* 4[1973]: 169–83), this group of poems is related to "Calamus," in which communion emerges from violence (which is the result of love) and compassion. In the war poems warriors "appear to Whitman as violent lovers, ready to sacrifice themselves for the mystical ideal of Union." Violence in the war is "an ironic metaphor: men killing one another are bound together." There are some good readings of individual poems in the essay.

"Song of Myself" has yet another structural analysis—but why not? Alfred S. Reid ("The Structure of 'Song of Myself' Reconsidered," *SHR* 8:507–14) offers a five-part division: an initial definition of the Self (1–7); a first catalogue of Self-identities (8–19); a second and more exact definition of Self (20–25); a second and more complex catalogue, stressing expansion through four senses (26–47); and a concluding "re-definition of Self as divine, eternal, progressing, 'untranslatable,' and fulfilled." An appendix outlines five earlier analyses by Carl Strauch, Gay Wilson Allen, James E. Miller, Jr., Malcolm Cowley, and Roy Harvey Pearce. David Robinson considers the reciprocal relations of poet and reader in a well-argued piece, "The Poetry of Dialogue in 'Song of Myself'" (*American Poetry and Poetics* 1,i:34–50). If the poem begins with "I," it ends with "you"; but in the course of the dialogue the poet "I" moves through several attitudes and tones in relation to the reader and his response. It ends with a gesture toward beginnings, "I stop somewhere waiting for you." Whitman's poem is discussed in relation to the Freudian concept of libido, the force of sexual instinct which unifies all of life, by James E. Mulqueen in "'Song of Myself': Whitman's Hymn to Eros" (*WWR* 20:60–67). Related mythic elements involve Dionysus, Narcissus, and Orpheus. Other notes on passages of the poem include Grace Pow Simpson, "Susannah and the Elders: A Source for 'Song of Myself,' Section 11" (*WWR* 20:109–11); and Sholom J. Kahn, "Whitman's 'Overstaid Fraction' Again" (*WWR* 20:67–73).

John Ditsky suggests that the best approach to the "whole" Whitman for teacher and students may be through "When Lilacs Last in the Dooryard Bloom'd," for in that poem we find the dramatic conflict between the darker and the more optimistic sides of the poet ("'Retrievements Out of the Night': Approaching Whitman Through the 'Lilacs' Elegy" (*Calamus* 7[1973]:27–37). He stresses the music, or the oral qualities of the poetry, as a first appeal, followed by images and usage of a kind of "existential experience" which is also process and movement. Robert E. Morsberger considers the bird of "Lilacs" in "Whitman's Hermit Thrush: An Ornithological Note" (*WWR* 20:111–13). A helpful prosodic analysis of "Song of the Broad-Axe" is contributed by Linda S. Peavy ("'Wooded Flesh and Metal Bone': A Look at the Riddle of the Broad-Axe," *WWR* 20:152–54). A note by Robert K. Martin, "Whitman's 'The Sleepers,' 33–35" (*Expl* 33: Item 13) cites the sexual allusions of the French terms in "The Sleepers" as relating appropriately to Whitman's "more general theme of hiding" in the poem.

e. **Relationships, Influences.** The most important study in relationships this year is Diane Wood Middlebrook's thoughtfully considered and well-written book, *Walt Whitman and Wallace Stevens* (Ithaca, N.Y.: Cornell Univ. Press), which centers the likeness of the

two poets in their belief in the supreme fiction of the creative imagination. In *Leaves of Grass* the imagination is a character—the Real
Me. In Stevens the myth is more impersonal. Though different in
style, Whitman and Stevens share the same tradition in their celebration of the physical, concrete world; in their sense of America and
the common man. Yet Stevens's man is the fallen, rather than the
original, Adam; process is in seasonal cycles rather than in Whitman's physical growth and decline. *Notes Toward a Supreme Fiction*
is seen as Stevens's version of "Song of Myself," and numerous other
individual works are compared throughout, concluding with Stevens's "The Auroras of Autumn" and Whitman's "As I Ebb'd with
the Ocean of Life." Both describe, in Whitman's terms, the relin-
quishment of the persona of the "Real Me" and the possible end of
action.

A revealing essay is Henry B. Rule's "Walt Whitman and Thomas
Eakins: Variations in Some Common Themes" (*TQ* 17,iv:7–57),
which gives in comprehensive detail the story of the poet's relationship with "his ideal artist-comrade" Eakins, who painted a number
of the Whitman portraits. They were "remarkably alike," says Rule,
"in their backgrounds, careers, and aesthetic vision." Eakins was
unconventional, masculine, honest, direct, and independent—somewhat the ideal American Whitman celebrated. They were also
"unique in their age in their passion to recreate the near, the commonplace, without false sentiment or ornamentation," in their belief
in the body, in their American sense of life. In other, more indirect,
ways than portraiture, the work of Eakins can also illuminate Whitman. Eakins is also discussed in an earlier note by Claire McGlinchie
—"Three Indigenous Americans (Whitman, Eakins, Gilbert)," in
Proceedings of the Sixth International Congress of Aesthetics (Uppsala, Sweden:[1972]), pp. 709–13—in which she cites Eakins as
Whitmanesque but adds as also uniquely American the composer
Henry F. Gilbert, who was called "the Walt Whitman of American
music." Other brief articles on writers with related interests are
James E. Quinn, "Yeats and Whitman, 1887–1925" (*WWR* 20:106–
09), and John D. Baker, "Whitman and Dos Passos: A Sense of Communion" (*WWR* 20:30–33). Turning in a different direction, Larry
Gregg summarizes the work of Whitman's propagandist and translator in Russia, Kornei Chukovsky, whose translations of Whitman
"have had a great and diverse impact on the Russian world of letters

in this century," not only as revelations of Whitman but as models for the Soviet art of translation ("Kornei Chukovsky's Whitman," *WWR* 20:50–60). There is also a good discussion of Chukovsky's *My Whitman*, published in Moscow in 1966.

Very few suggestions of influence on Whitman have appeared this year, and none on what has recently been an interest—Whitman's debt to Indian philosophy and literature. One article by Monica R. Tisiker deals effectively with the possible relationship of the writings of the 17th-century mystic Jacob Boehme (*WWR* 20:15–27). The connection is somewhat through Boehme's influence on Quaker beliefs, but according to Richard Maurice Bucke, is seen also in parallel passages from Boehme and from *Leaves of Grass*. The most direct relationship seems to be in "Chanting the Square Deific" and in some of the "Calamus" themes. Another 17th-century antecedent is suggested in Ida Fasel's "Whitman and Marvell's 'The Garden'" (*WWR* 20:114–15).

The two public roles of Whitman as barbarian or messiah are reflected in his mixed reception in Canada for many years, according to S. E. McMullin in "Whitman and the Canadian Press, 1872–1919: A Brief Survey" (*WWR* 20:132–40). Reactions were either "high praise or outright damnation." Although McMullin gives both sides of the critical response in Canada, the conclusion is that "to admire Whitman in late nineteenth-century Canada was to be radical," though by 1919 in the celebration of the first centenary of Whitman's birth the critical response was more favorable, responding to the image of teacher and prophet in Whitman.

ii. Dickinson

a. **Bibliography.** The wealth of bibliographical information and notes in Dickinson studies this year indicates that a long-needed ordering of the field may be at hand. One must begin by reading Willis J. Buckingham's invaluable review of the current scene, "The Bibliographical Study of Emily Dickinson" (*RALS* 4:57–71), in which he gives complete and detailed evaluations of numerous Dickinson bibliographies, including even the partial listings of scholarship and criticism. Buckingham's conclusions are that we need, among other thngs, "a detailed census of Dickinson collections in major libraries," "a full-length review of scholarship which will discuss

special problems in Dickinson studies and critically survey the existing research," and, most of all, "a complete descriptive bibliography"
and "a full-length handbook to Dickinson studies that will winnow
and appraise the mass of accumulating materials."

In current bibliographical information one should also consult
the *Emily Dickinson Bulletin* (No. 26), which includes a number
of helpful items: Willis J. Buckingham's addition of 227 items to his
1970 volume, *Emily Dickinson: A Bibliography* ("1880–1968 Addenda to the Buckingham Bibliography," pp. 103–28); other additions to Buckingham by George Monteiro in "Re MS Dickinson" (pp.
73–75); Sheila Taylor's "Emily Dickinson: Annual Bibliography for
1973" (pp. 93–101); and Frederick L. Morey's "ED Treasures in
Amherst" (pp. 65–71), analyses of seven unpublished papers done at
Amherst College and the University of Massachusetts. William White
in "Emily Dickinson's *An Amazing Sense*: Addendum to Buckingham" (*PBSA* 68:66–67) notes a previously unlisted Dickinson collection published in India. And a helpful checklist of 58 recent items
is given by Inder Nath Kher in "Emily Dickinson Scholarship: Some
Fugitive References 1969–70" (*Higginson Journal of Poetry* 8:11–12).

b. **Biography.**   A biography for which readers are indeed grateful
is Richard B. Sewall's *The Life of Emily Dickinson* (New York:
Farrar, Straus and Giroux), a full, detailed, and meticulously handled story of the Amherst family whose mark on American literature
is unmistakable. Sewall handles the various slants of light on Emily
Dickinson through successive narratives of her relationships with
individual members of her family and her friends; the result is a
portrait with dimensions. Sewall's intention, he says, is to enable the
reader to share the central theme of the poet—the experience of "survival and its demands." To keep the work in readable bounds, his
task was to contain the material, even as he entered deeply into the
Dickinson world. For this reason, much has been omitted; and
Sewall is careful not to make final judgments under the guise of
opinion. For example, he does not settle the question of Emily Dickinson's major love influence, though he leans to Samuel Bowles. He
does discount theories of an emotional triangle involving Emily
Dickinson, her brother, Austin, and his wife, Susan. Some of the new
material incorporated into the work is of Austin's long love affair
with Mabel Todd, and of the lasting effects of the entangled family

affairs in the publication of the poems. This is a rich, fascinating, and lucid biography, with complexities judiciously handled and a living image of Emily Dickinson achieved—not only of the poet but of the elements of life which touched her. The experience is unique, for, as Emily Dickinson once said of herself and Austin—"we're all unlike most everyone."

Only two articles refer to biographical matters. Francis J. Molson in "Emily Dickinson's Rejection of the Heavenly Father" (*NEQ* 47:404–26) takes the position that Dickinson's rejection of orthodox Christianity was not from a dislike of dogma but from a more complicated attitude which he analyses through statements in both her letters and her poems. She was at first willing to accept the orthodox God, "provided that He would grant her certain promises she felt He had made as the Heavenly Father"; rejection came after these promises were not kept—promises such as the reward of "spiritual joy and consolation" for giving up the world and accepting Jesus as savior. Dorys C. Grover suggests that the person Hamlin Garland met in 1902 and thought was Emily Dickinson was in fact Martha Gilbert Dickinson ("Garland's 'Emily Dickinson'—A Case of Mistaken Identity," *AL* 46:219–20).

c. **Criticism: General.** Since scholars generally look for sound introductions in the *Literary History of the United States*, ed. Robert Spiller *et al.* (New York: Macmillan), it is good to have the Dickinson section in "Experiments in Poetry: Emily Dickinson and Sidney Lanier" rewritten both intelligently and eloquently by William M. Gibson in the revised fourth edition (pp. 903–16). The account relates life and work judiciously, gives a vivid sense of Dickinson's personal presence, and, most important, gives a fine review of the nature of the poetry with much detail and many references to individual poems. Gibson's essay does much to show that Dickinson's place in American literature was not as an eccentric but as a force.

A review of Dickinson scholarship and criticism might begin with George Monteiro's "The One and Many Emily Dickinsons" (*ALR* 7:137–41). We have had too many fragmented Dickinsons, suggests Monteiro; each "poacher" takes from the field what he wishes to fit his thesis, picking out categories as if they were entities. "We need," he says, "to see the poetry as a whole without sacrificing the individual poem." An overview of the poems to suggest judgments is presented in "The Fifty Best Poems of Emily Dickinson" by Frederick L. Morey (*EDB* 25:5–52), in which selections by various critics are collated and classified. The top five in his listing include "Because I could not stop for Death," "There's a certain Slant of light," "Safe in their Alabaster Chambers," "I heard a Fly buzz—when I died," and "After great pain." A major effort to order and understand Dickinson's work without reference to her more external biography is Inder Nath Kher's *The Landscape of Absence: Emily Dickinson's Poetry* (New Haven and London: Yale Univ. Press). This is a book with depth, not easy to read (the style needs lightening) but containing many perceptive comments on the poems and outlining some valid general themes in the poetry as a whole. Numerous primary patterns are discussed, such as the "myth of the eternal return" through cyclic images in time, or as delineated in chapters such as "Love: The Garment of Fire," "Death: The Cosmic Dance," or "Self: The Quest for Identity." The existential nature of her poetry is emphasized, just as Kher states his intention to make possible "an encounter and dialogue with the creative mind of Dickinson." This he does with intensity and seriousness. I find it difficult to consider poetry, as he does, without consideration for its youth or maturity, its placement in the writer's canon, for subtle gradations of changing light may in time remold a metaphor. Still, this book usefully directs the reader to the page, and to a long look at the poem.

Several substantial articles this year do attempt to find a cohesive pattern in the works or in the reading of the poems. David Porter, in "The Crucial Experience in Emily Dickinson's Poetry" (*ESQ* 20:280–90), suggests that it is not the "inaccessible lovers" who were central to her imagination but the crucial affair of "living after things happen." The perspective for many poems is "from afterward, from behind the 'soft Eclipse,' " such as "After great pain." There are excellent examples in the essay. Roland Hagenbückle turns to her manner of thinking in contradiction and ambivalence, giving good explications of poems in his "Precision and Indeterminacy in the Poetry of Emily Dickinson" (*ESQ* 20:33–56). He suggests that the real difficulties come not "from metaphorical but metonymical references," in which the cause is inferred from the effect; other extended discussions consider symbols and other language elements. This is a complicated but helpful study. In "Emily Dickinson's Literary Allusions" (*EIL* 1:54–58) Vivian R. Pollack reviews one use of

sources, "allusions to literature that are signaled by the use of quotations and proper names." Most, if not all, aim to obliterate "any
significant difference between literature and life." The Bible turns
out to be the only literary source used continuously. The subjects of
a few other useful articles can be determined from their titles: John
Wheatcroft, " 'Holy Ghosts in Cages'—A serious View of Humor in
Emily Dickinson's Poetry" (*ATQ* 22:95–104); Andrea Goudie, "Another Path to Reality: Emily Dickinson's Birds" (*CP* 7,i:31–38);
Vivian R. Pollak, "Emily Dickinson's Valentines" (*AQ* 26:60–78);
and Frederick L. Morey, "Emily Dickinson as a Modern" (*EDB* 26:
83–86).

Two other articles look briefly at particular problems in Dickinson. Considerations of the poetry according to modern linguistic
techniques have developed, but not to every scholar's satisfaction.
J. Noël in "A Critique of S. R. Levin's 'Analyses of Compression in
Poetry' " (*RLV* 39[1973]:231–38) reviews an earlier linguistic analysis (see *ALS 1971*, p. 73) and presents his objections and arguments.
The many problems of dating the Dickinson poems are touched on
again in a note by Rebecca Patterson ("On Dating Dickinson's
Poems," *AN&Q* 12:84–86), in which variously timed sources for
imagery in "I like to see it lap the Miles" are cited. Patterson sees it as
a youthful poem, earlier than the 1862 date given by Johnson.

d. **Criticism: Individual works.** Only a few explications appeared
this year. Archibald Hill has an interesting discussion of his own interpretation in relation to others of "The Soul selects her own Society"
and "It dropped so low—in my Regard" in "Figurative Structure and
Meaning: Two Poems by Emily Dickinson" (*TSLL* 16:195–209). His
own interpretation of the first poem is that in the central metaphor
the soul is an oyster, the chosen one a pearl. The tightly knit organization of this poem is unlike the looser structure of "It dropped so
low." His judgment that the first poem is the superior is thus taken
from an "intellectual analysis" and verifiable evidence. Along with
Hill's discussion of the "Plated wares" in this poem see a note by
Ted-Larry Pebworth, "The Lusterware on Dickinson's Silver Shelf"
(*AN&Q* 12[1973]:18). In "Dickinson's 'Summer has two Beginnings' " (*Expl* 33:Item 16), Lawrence A. Walz shows that the two
summers are those of the seasonal June and of the mind "which is
brought to life in October." As in Keats's "Ode on a Grecian Urn,"

there is the final affirmation of "the real world over the construct of the mind." Laurence Perrine analyses "The Robin is the One" as organized on the principle of progression, stanzas developing through parallel movements of sound, of time, and of activity. He suggests also that "An" in line four is a mistake for "And."

In a skirmish on the metaphor of "She sweeps with many-colored Brooms," Laurence Perrine obviously has the right on his side. The central metaphor is sunset, not fall ("Dickinson's 'She sweeps with many-colored brooms,'" *EDB* 26:72), nor the unliberated woman ("Dickinson Distorted," *CE* 36:212–13). The latter interpretation in the sense of "containment" (see *ALS 1973*, pp. 96–97) is defended by Linda Mizejewski ("Reply to Laurence Perrine," *CE* 36:213).

e. **Relationships.**   In spite of differences in style and form, Poe and Dickinson are kindred spirits, says Wendy Flory in "Rehearsals for Dying in Poe and Emily Dickinson" (*ATQ* 18[1973]:13–18). Dickinson's poems "can present in small compass dizzying flights of speculation, defiant assertions of will, and overwhelming testimony of anguish comparable to any in Poe" (see *ALS 1973*, p. 56). A slight but interesting allusion to Dickinson places her as "a real-life 'provincial heroine'" (like Austen's Emma Woodhouse or Flaubert's Emma Bovary) with her poem "I took my Power in my Hand" as a motif for this kind of fictional character (Elizabeth Sabiston, "The Prison of Womanhood," *CL*[1973]:336–51). And a continuing interest in Dickinson in other countries may be represented by a general article in Norwegian by Inger Hagerup, "Emily Dickinson" (*Vinduet* [Oslo] 28:43–46), and a group of poems translated into German by Kurt J. Fickert ("14 ED Poems," *EDB* 26:77–82). There, in other accents, are both the seldom-quoted poems, such as "I went to Heaven" or "I reason, Earth is short," and the familiar ones whose lines have come into our language, like "My life closed twice before its close," or the Dickinson signature of "This is my letter to the World."

University of Nebraska, Lincoln

6. Mark Twain

Hamlin Hill

Last year Huck was the neglected character in the Mark Twain pantheon; this year neither Tom Sawyer nor Pudd'nhead Wilson attracted any attention in scholarly journals and Huck is back at center stage. A delay in printing postponed the issue of the first two volumes of the *Notebooks & Journals* until 1975; but Arthur G. Pettit's *Mark Twain and the South* and an article or two made substantial contributions to Mark Twain scholarship in a year otherwise distinguished only for its ineptness and insipidity.

i. Textual and Bibliographical

Rodelle Weintraub, ed., " 'Mental Telegraphy?': Mark Twain on G.B.S." (*ShawR* 17:68–70) reprints "here for the first time" Twain's manuscript describing the similarities in Shaw's "Aerial Football" and his own "The Late Rev. Sam Jones's Reception in Heaven" as due to thought transference in 1907 while the two lunched together. In fact, the text of "Mental Telegraphy?" was published in 1970 in Ray B. Browne's *Mark Twain's Quarrel with Heaven*. George Monteiro nominates "Such as Mother Used to Make," a short essay extolling in mock-heroic language the advantages of adding pork to vegetables, as Mark Twain's anonymous contribution to the January 1903 *Atlantic* "Contributors' Club" and reprints the essay in its entirety in " 'Such as Mother Used to Make': An Addition to the Mark Twain Canon" (*PBSA* 67[1973]:450–52). In fact, to my own ears, another item in that month's "Club," "A Song Composed in a Dream," sounds like a more probable candidate.

Louis J. Budd's "Mark Twain Talks Mostly about Humor and Humorists" (*SAmH* 1:4–22) is an overview of commentary and a reprinting of three newspaper interviews (New York *Sun*, January 27, 1895; Sydney *Morning Herald*, September 17, 1895; and Auckland

New Zealand Herald, November 21, 1895) which touched on the aspects of American humor. The Sydney interview is especially useful in its extended discussion of the seriousness underlying humor: "Behind the broadest grins, the most exquisitely ludicrous situations," Mark Twain said, "they [humorists] know there is the grinning skull, and that all roads lead along the dusty road to death." Timothy Long's "Mark Twain's Speeches on Billiards" (*MTJ* 17,ii:1–3) provides the biographical background for two separate speeches—April 17 and April 24, 1906—that Twain delivered to the audience at a billiards tournament.

The "Hitherto Unpublished Letter" gambit has reached the point that even hitherto published letters are fair game—at least in the *Mark Twain Journal*. Without even attempting to discover the contexts of a single letter by inquiring of Frederick Anderson at the Mark Twain Papers, much less looking at published research, the following writers have produced dubious scholarship: Without consulting Ellen Ballou's *The Building of the House* or *Mark Twain's Letters to His Publishers*, George Monteiro has printed three "New Mark Twain Letters" (*MTJ* 17,ii:9) which, in fact, have been in print since the late 1960s and for which there is ample documentation of the Hurd & Houghton "plan" which Monteiro says is not "now identifiable"; E. F. Briden in "Samuel L. Clemens and Elizabeth Jordan: An Unpublished Letter" (*MTJ* 17,ii:11–13) provides an admirable thumbnail biography of the editor of *Harper's Bazar* and prints a December 4, 1908, letter from Twain to Jordan, declining an invitation to comment in print about "that (to me) utterly unimportant subject," but Briden has not apparently bothered to use the extensive collection of letters from Jordan to Clemens in the Mark Twain Papers to identify that subject; and William Weaver reprints a letter from Clemens to Kate Field that was written in 1886 and published in 1899 in "Mark Twain and Kate Field Differ on Constitutional Rights" (*MTJ* 17, ii:16–17).

Sidney Berger has managed (where many others failed) to obtain access to the Chatto & Windus records; and, in "New Mark Twain Items" (*PBSA* 68:331–35), has used that publisher's copies of letters to show conclusively that the British edition of *Pudd'nhead Wilson* was set predominantly from the text of *The Century* serialization rather than the American Publishing Company edition. Lewis Leary's provocative "Troubles with Mark Twain: Some Considerations on

Consistency" (*SAF* 2:89–103) looks closely at the textual problems of *Innocents Abroad* and the raftsmen's passage from *Huckleberry Finn*. In both cases, Mark Twain's "final intention" seems to Leary to bear a problematic relationship to good sense.

Mark Twain, A Collection of Criticism, ed. Dean Morgan Schmitter (New York: McGraw-Hill) contains 13 selections of reprinted criticism, divided into sections on "Biography and General Criticism," and "Criticism of the Major Works," with an introduction by Schmitter on "Mark Twain and the Pleasures of Pessimism" (that promises more in its title than it delivers) and an extensive, up-to-date bibliography of criticism. Hamlin Hill's survey of the current state of Mark Twain scholarship and the future possibilities for research turns into an assault on dull, trivial, and repetitious scholarship, the unimaginativeness of contemporary bibliography, and the hostility of the Mark Twain Establishment toward unconventional and untraditional ideas. "Who Killed Mark Twain?" (*ALR* 7:119–24), Hill insists, was the boring state of secondary materials.

Finally, "The Appert Collection of Mark Twain" (*Bancroftiana* 57[Jan.]:5–6) describes the acquisition by the University of California of a collection of letters and memorabilia about Twain from the collection of Mr. and Mrs. Kurt Appert.

ii. Biographical

T. H. Watkins's *Mark Twain's Mississippi* (Palo Alto: American West) is one of those sumptuous picture-books of the type ballyhooed one Christmas and remaindered by Marboro the next. There is a lot more Mississippi than Mark Twain between its covers—from the Mound Builders to modern grain elevators—but nestled in the middle is the text of parts of *Life on the Mississippi* and a magnificent collection of woodcuts and photographs of the river during Clemens's day. Justin Kaplan's *Mark Twain and His World* (New York: Simon and Schuster) is also a picture-book—with a text that retreads much of *Mr. Clemens and Mark Twain* by adding an opening section on Clemens's biography to 1869 and stringently paring the earlier book to its most objective and least controversial essentials. As a one-volume biography, it might have rivalled DeLancey Ferguson's 30-year-old *Mark Twain: Man and Legend*; but its lavish illustrations inflate the price to $19.95, and occasionally they bear only a surreal relationship to the text: two full pages showing a South African diamond field in operation because Twain once contemplated a book on that subject; full color reproductions of paintings by Monet, de Feure, Lenz, and Whistler; plates of Madison Square Garden, Hornellsville (New York), and the Philadelphia City Hall seem both tangential and prodigal.

Mark K. Wilson's "Mr. Clemens and Madame Blanc: Mark Twain's First French Critic" (AL 45:537–56) is a thorough sketch of Marie-Thérèse Blanc, who championed the Genteel Tradition writers in her long career as critic for the Revue des Deux Mondes and deprecated Mark Twain's brand of western humor. Unable to understand the deadpan humor of "The Jumping Frog," the fictional first-person narration of Innocents Abroad, or the comic personality of Colonel Sellers in The Gilded Age, she engendered an antagonism in Mark Twain that Wilson believes "surely contributed significantly to the angry store of loathing for the French."

Two articles fill in details on Mark Twain lectures: William Weaver, "Samuel Clemens Lectures in Kentucky" (MTJ 17,ii:20–21) prints some commentary from the Paris Kentuckian, the Louisville Evening Post, and the Louisville Courier-Journal concerning the Twain-Cable lectures at those cities on January 1 and 5, 1885; and I. N. Agrawal, "Mark Twain's Visit to Allahabad" (IJAS 3,i[1973]: 104–08) has assembled a few quotations from Allahabad newspapers puffing the lecture there on February 3, 1896.

And Lewis Leary straightens out some business and real-estate details concerning the Casey house at Tarrytown which Olivia Clemens purchased in 1902. But "Mark Twain Did Not Sleep Here: Tarrytown, 1902–1904" (MTJ 17,ii:13–17), Leary points out, having leased and then sold the estate after Olivia's death.

Robert Bray's "Mark Twain Biography Entering a New Phase" (MQ 15:286–301) is an essay-review of Mark Twain: God's Fool, which surveys the Brooks-DeVoto controversy and proposes that "America's will-to-believe has supported this institution called Mark Twain, and just as surely we will now be called upon to give at least a part of him up." Howard O. Brogan, "Early Experience and Scientific Determinism in Twain and Hardy" (Mosaic 7,iii:4–22), notes biographical parallels—both grew up in a "primitive rural region" and were nurtured by a "rich folk culture." Their "grim Protestant religious background" was the common denominator that produced a belief in innate human depravity and pervasive evil, for which a form of scientific determinism "was for both a blessed escape."

And John W. Crowley's "The Sacerdotal Cult and the Sealskin Coat: W. D. Howells in *My Mark Twain*" (*ELN* 11:287–92), although it is concerned with Howells's biography of Twain, offers some intriguing insights into the relationship of the two writers when it suggests that Howells consciously adopted the Gentleman-Clown axis of southwestern humor when he rendered himself more fastidiously prim and Mark Twain more raucously unpredictable than might have been completely accurate.

iii. General Criticism

There was only one study of a general nature in 1974, but it was rewarding enough to make up for its solitary position. Arthur G. Pettit's *Mark Twain and the South* (Lexington: Univ. Press of Ky.) is a comprehensive appraisal of Clemens's attitudes toward the South, slavery, and the black man, as they affected both his attitudes and his literature. Clemens moved "from Southerner to anti-Southerner to one who longed for a South he finally realized had never existed; from conscious bigot to unconscious bigot to one who became fully aware of his bigotry, fought it, and largely overcame it." If this sounds like a whitewashing of the Geismar tint, nothing could be further from the truth. Documenting Clemens's prejudices, noting his sublimated attraction to black women, and understanding his essential contradictions with keen perception, Pettit has traced Clemens's confused reactions not just to the literal and geographical South, but also to the more subtle ramifications of the Southern Curse—aristocracy, sexuality, and genealogy included. Substantial examinations of Jim, Roxy, and Jasper (in "Which Was It?") support Pettit's thesis that Twain the writer "began his career as a segregationist, turned himself into a champion of interracial brotherhood, and ended his life as a prophet of racial war."

iv. Earlier Works

The final third of Franklin Walker's *Irreverent Pilgrims, Melville, Browne, and Mark Twain in the Holy Land* (Seattle: Univ. of Washington Press) deals with the *Quaker City* trip and its conversion into

Innocents Abroad. While that section of the study will be familiar ground, Twainians will paradoxically find the other two-thirds significant and useful. For Walker documents, in those portions dealing with Melville and *Clarel* and J. Ross Browne and *Yusef*, an impressive tradition of irreverence, skepticism, and mockery which antedates Twain's book and foreshadows its significant virtues.

John Rachal proposes that a mutual "lack of communication between the speakers, and . . . clergymen [who] fail to understand the card metaphor used by their counterparts" unites the "Buck Fanshaw's Funeral" anecdote from *Roughing It* with Johnson J. Hooper's "Simon Plays the Snatch Game" and "Simon Attends a Camp-Meeting." "Scotty Briggs and the Minister: An Idea from Hooper's Simon Suggs?" (*MTJ* 17,ii:10–11) fails to note that Twain actually wrote down Simon's comment that he "went in on nary a pair" in his Notebooks or that Walter Blair called attention to the similarity of Simon and Scotty Briggs fifteen years ago in *Mark Twain and Huck Finn* (p. 280). A substantial interpretation of *Roughing It*, by contrast, is Tom H. Towers, " 'Hateful Reality': The Failure of the Territory in *Roughing It*" (*WAL* 9:3–15). Looking at the entire book rather than the Overland journey only, Towers argues convincingly that "disillusion, more truly than growth or initiation, is the prevailing pattern of *Roughing It*, and the cynical assurance of the old-timer is only another of the illusions which the hero must cast off in his constantly frustrated quest for a life of freedom and significance." Just as the tenderfoot's visions of a pastoral West and great fortune are undercut by the real geography and hard work of Nevada, so the European elegance of San Francisco is a veneer and the Hawaiian Eden, with its barbarities of both the native rulers and the Christian settlers, proves "that there is no scheme in myth or science which will account for the awful facts of human life."

Leland Krauth, "Mark Twain: At Home in the Gilded Age" (*GaR* 28:105–13), also provides some new insights: "Domesticity is . . . the heart of *The Gilded Age*," he argues, and in order to preserve the family, we readers hope for the acquittal of Laura, the passage of the Knobs University Bill, and (because it will aid that passage) the re-election of Senator Dilworthy. The loss of family becomes Mark Twain's version of the Fall of Man. But Krauth's focus on *The Gilded Age* diffuses into broad generalizations.

Thomas H. Pauly's brief "The 'Science of Piloting' in Twain's 'Old

Times': The Cub's Lesson on Industrialization" (*ArQ* 30:229–38) argues that the "Old Times on the Mississippi" series reaches beyond the immediate issues of the cub's education, "first to a larger consideration of the 'science of piloting' and ultimately to Twain's artistic intentions." But "industrialization" here is limited to the Pilots' Association; and Pettit (see above) has a fine consideration of the industrialization of the river as it is contained in *Life on the Mississippi*.

Tom Sawyer was ostracized in 1974 (execpt as he appears in *Huckleberry Finn*) and silence could not surround a more deserving kid.

v. *Huckleberry Finn*

Until a few years ago, *American Quarterly* was an important and exciting journal for students of American literature; and then it donned its gray-flannel cover and, if Beverly R. David's "The Pictorial *Huck Finn*: Mark Twain and His Illustrator, E. W. Kemble" (*AQ* 26:331–51) is valid evidence, lost its right to be taken seriously. The thesis of the article is that Twain "controlled" Kemble's illustrations so that vicious passages were illustrated with comic drawings (or not illustrated at all), diverting readers' attentions from the death and brutality of the text itself. But it is almost impossible to pay attention to that thesis because of the sloppy, unprofessional, and incomprehensible quality of the article. It uses a 1948 Grosset & Dunlap *Huck* for documentation; it prefers the spellings *Shepardson* and *Wilkes* to Mark Twain's choices; it contains one footnote which is positively surreal: "[6] E. W. Kemble, letter of June 2, 1884, *Mark Twain Papers* (Berkeley: Mark Twain Co., 1960)." Now there is no volume called *Mark Twain Papers*, published in 1960 or any other year. There is no publisher in Berkeley, or anywhere else, called The Mark Twain Co. Then there is the opaque logic of some of the conclusions: Mark Twain objected to an "Irishy" mouth which Kemble had drawn on one of the illustrations of Huck; what do you suppose that meant? Well, as someone once said, "It would take you thirty years to guess, and even then you would have to give it up, I believe." Removing that ugly mouth proves that "there would be little sense, in his [Twain's] mind, to limiting the appeal of Huck Finn to the increasing but unpopular urban Irish." Now, mull that over for a while: one ugly Irish mouth would limit the appeal of the book to "the increasing but unpopular urban Irish"? Leaving one ugly Irish mouth in would restrict the sales of the book (and of course subscription books did not sell to unpopular urban Irish, whatever kind of mouth the illustrations had) to the very audience that ought to be offended by that mouth? Finally there is the Great Issue of the hair on Jim's chest, which is never shown in the illustrations because Jim is always wearing a shirt. Why did Mark Twain not allow a picture of a topless Jim? "After all, he knew Negro characteristics well and realized that hair or lack of it would make his Nigger Jim different from the usual Negro." Well, I don't believe that Mark Twain for a minute grouped his black characters into "hairy" or "slick" categories, or that he would find "hair or lack of it" (I keep wondering which) made one black man different from others, or that the whole issue is anything more than a black-red-herring. (In fact, except for two illustrations of the King performing the Royal Nonesuch and being tarred and feathered no one in the entire novel is shown shirtless—not Huck, Jim, or the Widow Douglas!)

Back to the right side of the Looking Glass again, several articles continue to gnaw at the Evasion sequence. Edward H. Cohen, "The Return to St. Petersburg" (*IEY* 23[1973]:50–55), argues that Huck returns to the "mood" of the town in the Evasion, to the "sham and cruelty and slavery of civilization," and in *Huck Finn and Tom Sawyer among the Indians* and *Tom Sawyer Abroad*, Huck proves that he cannot escape the efforts to "sivilize him." At greater length but along the same lines is David F. Burg's "Another View of *Huckleberry Finn*" (*NCF* 29:299–319). In the pugnacious tone of a bull-terrier barking at a herd of elephants, Burg attacks those "moralistically oriented critics" (Henry Nash Smith and Leo Marx), by arguing that "the final chapters . . . are a confirmation of Mark Twain's belief that systematic philosophies are obsolete, that value systems are malign shams." Adopting Robert Scholes's discussion of black humor and much of Camus to his argument, Burg suggests that Huck's, Jim's, and Mark Twain's acceptance of the circumstances of the Evasion confirms that Huck's decision in chapter 31 is "easier" than to write Miss Watson, that revolt and rootlessness are the only defenses in a world in which "neither Huck nor Jim has any illusions. . . . They cannot change the order of things; all that they can do is endure."

Georg Meri-Akri Gaston, "The Function of Tom Sawyer in *Huck-*

leberry Finn" (*MissQ* 27:33–39), proposes that Tom's "sinister" spirit pervades the middle sections of the book (when Huck remembers how Tom might manipulate various adventures), but that Huck has "developed to the point where he can assert his independence and superiority" to Tom. And James D. Wilson's "*Adventures of Huckleberry Finn*: From Abstraction to Humanity" (*SoR* 10:80–94) catalogs the abstract moral codes symbolized in Miss Watson and the Widow Douglas (Christianity), Tom (romanticism), Pap (hedonism), and the Grangerfords and Colonel Sherburn (aristocracy). But each of these theoretical codes "when applied to human situations proves woefully perverted and inadequate." Jim, as natural man, represents a workable system, to which Huck aligns himself. His acceptance of Jim's values results in his lighting out, though, for "the morally liberated individual can never hope for integration into the existing social structure."

By far the most "radical" interpretation of *Huck* in 1974, or in many years, though, is Harold Beaver, "Run, Nigger, Run: *Adventures of Huckleberry Finn* as a Fugitive Slave Narrative" (*JAmS* 8:339–61). In spite of some syntactical confusion that results from Beaver's liberal scattering of quotations in mid-sentence, his article is possibly provocative enough to allow for some thorough reevaluations of *Huck*, if only to challenge his thesis. Which is, startlingly enough, that Jim is a crafty manipulator, who acts the minstrel darky in order to gain Huck's help in escaping. "Whether Jim manipulated Huck's behavior," by shuffling and playing Brer Rabbit, "out of ecstasy or guile hardly matters," Beaver says. "This story of escapes and escapades is essentially one of status and power-play—a book of controls. As Huck apparently takes charge of Jim's escape—guiding and controlling that fatal journey—so Tom, in the end, takes charge of Huck. But the ultimate guiding factor of the whole journey, after all, is Jim. As soon as Jim is left to his own devices, notice, he is quite capable of seizing the initiative." And Huck, all the way through the novel, "had been an unconscious hostage not only to Tom's idea of 'fun' but Jim's flight from slavery. The quick-witted, quick-change boy-artist, who can fool almost everybody, is also everybody's fool." And Huck's "recognition is never really of Jim . . . but only of some self-satisfied projection of his own boyish sentiments—converging on that ultimate delusion: 'I knowed he was white inside.'" Beaver may be extreme and distorted; but his article is challenging, innovative, and thought-provoking in ways that little else in the past six years of Mark Twain scholarship and criticism has been.

vi. Later Works

Joseph R. McElrath, Jr.'s grandiose title, "Mark Twain's America and the Protestant Work Ethic" (*CEA* 36,iii:42–43) camouflages the observation that Hank Morgan's manipulation of St. Simeon Stylite in *A Connecticut Yankee in King Arthur's Court* allegorizes "the mentality that embraced and cultivated the Protestant work ethic." Philip Klass's blithely written "An Innocent in Time: Mark Twain in King Arthur's Court" (*Extrapolation* 16:17–32) focuses on the insight that *A Connecticut Yankee* was "perhaps the first genuine time-travel story ever written"—in blissful ignorance of H. Bruce Franklin's *Future Perfect* or David Ketterer's "Epoch-Eclipse and Apocalypse: Special 'Effects' in *A Connecticut Yankee*" (reprinted, incidentally, along with a discussion of "The Great Dark" in his *New Worlds for Old: The Apocalyptic Imagination, Science Fiction, and American Literature* [Bloomington: Univ. of Ind. Press]).

Sydney J. Krause, in "The Pearl and 'Hadleyburg': From Desire to Renunciation" (*StQ* 7:3–18), compares Steinbeck's short novel with "The Man That Corrupted Hadleyburg"—"that work in the pessimistic-naturalistic tradition to which it bears the closest affinities." They "are both stories of consuming greed, in which we follow the helpless entanglement of decently inclined but wrong-minded protagonists who cast aside their better instincts in the crass pursuit of wealth." But wealth proves worthless, and both Kino and the Richardses must be isolated from communal values and pressures (through flight and insanity) before their moral recovery is feasible through their renunciation of the pearl and the checks for $38,500.

L. W. Denton's "Mark Twain on Patriotism, Treason, and War" (*MTJ* 17,ii:4–7) is a cursory examination of a number of antiimperialist writings of the humorist's last decade: "As Regards Patriotism," "Glances at History," "The Czar's Soliloquy," and "The War Prayer"; and Joan Baum's "Mark Twain on the Congo" (*MTJ* 17,ii:7–9) is a strangely belated review of *King Leopold's Soliloquy* in an edition published in 1961. Antonio Illiano, in "'Italian Without A Master': A Note for the Appreciation of Mark Twain's Undictionarial Translation as Exercise in Humor" (*MTJ* 17,ii:17–20), provides accurate translations of some of the Italian phrases which Mark Twain butchered by mistakenly identifying cognates, as he had done with French and German earlier in his career.

James L. Livingston's "Names in Mark Twain's *The Mysterious Stranger*" (*AN&Q* 12:108–09) is one of those curious identifications (Bauman—workman, Seppi Wohlmeyer—Good Steward, Philip in Eseldorf—A lover of horses in Ass Village) that never quite enlighten as much as they portend.

I can still remember when, years ago, I enjoyed the delusion that scholarship and criticism were an act of discovery for both the author and the reader. New data, original insights, scrupulous command of prior scholarship were, I thought, the hallmarks of published research. A fraternity of scholars, I believed, shared a mutual subject which their collective efforts enlightened and elucidated. And then, six years ago, I began writing the "Mark Twain" chapter for *American Literary Scholarship*.

What is increasingly clear—and 1974 was simply the worst of the past six years—is that the shock of recognition comes a lot less frequently than the shock at the deformities paraded into view as "scholarship." Sloppy, unresearched, poorly documented articles are the rule rather than the exception; and even the appearance of their names above their efforts does not engender enough self-respect to stifle the braying of asses in public. And editors of scholarly journals continue to serve as wagon-masters for mule trains.

University of New Mexico

7. Henry James

William T. Stafford

Items of note during this year stand out in splendid isolation among this comparatively small total gathering of attention to Henry James: Edel's first volume of letters, Richard A. Hocks's book on the James brothers, a sensitive, brief overview of James from India (by Darshan Singh Maini), and three or four articles, Adeline Tintner's perspective on Jamesian criticism, Denis Donoghue's uses of James in his fine essay "The American Style of Failure," Mildred Hartsock's quarrel with the criticism of *The Golden Bowl*, and possibly one or two others. Most Jamesians will probably want to own Harry T. Moore's beautifully produced pictorial biography of the Master. And, generally speaking, one can only continue to applaud increased attention to broad comprehensive aspects of James's work and the consequent continued decrease of explications of already overly explicated tales and novels. Perhaps nothing more needs to be said.

i. Letters, Biography, Travel Essays, and Bibliography

Few surprises, in content or format, are to be found in the first volume of Leon Edel's long-awaited *Henry James Letters, 1843–1875* (Cambridge: Harvard Univ. Press)—which is not to say that various satisfactions are not evident in finally having the selection available. Little is here of the young James and the family milieu that is unfamiliar to most Jamesians, much of it indeed from as long ago as Matthiessen's *The James Family* of 1947. And its paucity of documentation is as evident here as elsewhere in Edel's work. (How useful would have been an addendum listing and locating *all* of the known letters Edel has unearthed from this period!) The letters he does include are gathered into six groups—"Boyhood and Youth," "Beginnings," "The Grand Tour," "A Season in Cambridge," "Travel and Opportunity," and "The Choice"—each prefaced by a succinct and pithy introduction setting forth the major events of James's life. But few, I suppose, will quarrel with his stated principles of selection, first, "literary content"; second, letters that have "documentary" value, "throw light on character or personality, or furnish a picture of family background," with especial "importance [given] to James's 'working' letters—the correspondence of the artist and the 'professional.'" Probably, however, some will quarrel with Edel's persistent attention in many of his explicatory footnotes to those letters to the family which support his thesis in the *Life* about psychic rivalries within the family; and some, no doubt, with his admitted textual practice of silently correcting only *some* of the spelling or syntactical errors resulting from haste. The apparatus is otherwise at its best in Edel's introductory account of the "history" of the 1920 selection of letters, the ins and outs of the ultimate choice of Percy Lubbock as editor, and the various reactions of various heirs to it and to subsequent selections. Withal, the "epistolary James" here introduced is "representative" and "useful," Edel's expressed intentions "showing . . . [James's] evolution in a literary form which is at once 'interpersonal' and also in a certain sense self-exhibiting." Our earliest view of this James is through a note of 1856 expressing a juvenile interest in the theater. The James we leave in London in November of 1875 (on his way to Paris and in fact to expatriation) is an established author of ten years' professional experience, now ready, as he himself puts it, "to take possession of the old world . . . [to] inhale it . . . [to] appropriate it."

The text of Harry T. Moore's pictorial biography, *Henry James and His World* (New York: Viking) also has few surprises, slavishly agreeable, as it is, to Edel's view of James. Its some 130 illustrations (no two pages are without at least one), however, are a visual delight, with reproductions of various pictures of James himself, his family, his friends, of letters and manuscripts and book covers, of sketches and cartoons and caricatures, and of many, many places. The brief life itself, moreover, is beautifully lucid, concise, informed, with nothing more pretentious as a "thesis" than the ties between James's fiction and many of the people and events of his life, a life that is said to appropriate the world rather than withdraw from it. Obviously published for the coffee table (in Viking's Studio Book Series), it is, at only $7.95, a coffee-table bargain. I recommend it highly.

Additional attention to James's life appears in S. Gorley Putt's "Henry James Haggles over Terms for 'Guy Domville'" (*TLS* 11 Jan.:35–36), wherein are published four letters from James to Isaac Austen Henderson (between December 1892 and September 1893), seeking advice about how to get the best financial terms possible from George Alexander for producing *Guy Domville*. F. G. Atkinson's "Henry James and 'The Sign of Sympathy'" (*N&Q* 21:363–65) establishes James's acquaintance with A. T. Quiller-Couch and his nouvelle *The Westcotes* (which was dedicated to James) through a letter from James about the dedicatory preface dated October 1901. And Franciszek Lyra's "A Note to 'Correspondence of Helena Modrzejewska (Modjeska) to Henry James'" (*KN* 19,iii[1972]:325–26) corrects her previous identification (*ALS 1972*, p. 98) of seven letters from Modjeska to James to accommodate the later-discovered fact that only the sixth and seventh of those were to the Master. The first five had been addressed to Longfellow!

The extended attention Stephen Spender devotes to the novelist in "Henry James as Centre of the English-American Language" (in his *Love-Hate Relations: English and American Sensibilities* [New York: Random House], pp. 53–100) is only moderately and sporadically provocative. The fiction is given only scant attention, but James's contrastive views of the French and English, of the English and the American, of the European and American are emphasized. Whitman is said to be James's great American contrast, Henry Miller symbolically the son of both, and Norman Mailer somehow as having thereby been predicted! The insights are thus alternately discreet and discursive, banal and audacious—except for extended attention to *The American Scene* and James's turn-of-the-century visit to his homeland, especially to James's ambition "to fuse Anglo-American literature into a single whole in which the observer could not trace the line that marked the 'join.'" Alas, the language, James's language, that was to serve as model and in which the plea was made was totally incomprehensible to the audience for which it was written! Yet, concludes Spender, *The American Scene* is "a masterpiece in James's late manner. . . . [combining] despair, hysteria and a kind of exuberance reflecting the overwhelming vigour, and quantity of the phenomenon attacked." Much more narrow and even less satisfying is W. D. Sterner's attempt, in "Henry James and the Idea of Culture in 'The American Scene'" (*ModA* 18:283–90), to define James's complex ideas on this complex subject and apply them to his homeland; but in failing to attend to the "how" of this complex experience, the result is disappointing in the extreme. My choice among this year's essays on James as travel writer thus rests with Mary Ann Hoberman's "Henry James: On a Tour of the Provinces" (*NYT* 24 Nov:xx,1, 16–17), a charming account of a trip the author and her husband took to the Midi with *A Little Tour in France* as their guide, contrasting and comparing James's views and observations (of October 1882) with theirs (of October 1973) as to hotels, museums, cathedrals, wines, ruins, etc. Of no great moment, to be sure, but obviously "fun" nonetheless.

Among various bibliographical items of the year, by far the most significant is Adeline R. Tintner's "Henry James Criticism: A Current Perspective" (*ALR* 7:155–68), which must stand by Robert Gale's chapter in *Eight American Authors* (*ALS 1971*, pp. 86–87) among indispensable overviews of criticism on James, even as it stands apart from Gale's in its attention to directions the author feels Jamesian criticism should take. I have no quarrels with her "Cursory Glance" at the history of this subject, and only a quibble or three with her assessment of "Current Trends: The Last Decade." It seems to me somewhat overarching in its emphasis on the whole complex problem of influences on James, her own distinguished work in this field and her citation of Harold Bloom's *The Anxiety of Influence* notwithstanding. But I can only applaud her pleas in "Further Directions" for giving more attention to the tales in the context of the collections in which they appeared, for seeing James as Edwardian and Georgian as well as Victorian and Modernist, for examining his knowledge and uses of historians, journalists, and fellow expatriates, and for paying close, close attention to every discoverable clue. Ms. Tintner is surely right in her eloquent final plea that all we can discover about James, his friends, his travels, his reading, and his picture-viewing will meaningfully enhance our understanding of his art.

Other attention to this subject is not so important, although S. Gorley Putt's "James," in A. E. Dyson's *The English Novel: Select Bibliographical Guides* (London: Oxford), pp. 280–99, should be cited for its succinct and breezy account of textual problems, critical studies (mostly books), bibliographies, background readings, and the Jamesian canon itself, even if prepared primarily for students. Much more specialized is Mary Lee Field's "Henry James's Criticism of French Literature: A Bibliography and a Checklist" (*ALR* 7: 379–94), an extraction, in effect, from the Edel/Laurence *Bibliography*, with the added virtue of an index to French authors and titles mentioned by James with distinctions made between mere allusions and more extended comments. George Monteiro's "Addendum to Edel and Laurence: Henry James's 'Two Old Houses and Three Young Women'" (*PBSA* 68,iii:331) locates the first printing of the essay in *The Independent*, 51 (7 Sept. 1899):2406–12. And most Jamesians will probably want to see the 1973 annual survey of James studies in *JML*, 4:358–67.

ii. Sources, Influences, Parallels

Source studies are again swamped by the indefatigable Adeline R. Tintner. Her "The Countess and Scholastica: Henry James's 'L'Allegro' and 'Il Penseroso'" (*SSF* 11:267–78) is a somewhat overburdened demonstration of James's knowledge and uses of Milton, poor "Benvolio" almost inevitably sinking under the erudite weight of the attributed allegorical cargo. Her "James's Monologue for Ruth Draper and *The Tragic Muse*: A Parody of the 'Usurping Consciousness'" (*SELit* [English number]:149–54) is for me a somewhat more persuasive piece in its description of the monologue James wrote for Ruth Draper (in 1913) as a kind of self-conscious parody of his concept of "the enveloping personal consciousness." Ms. Tintner discovered the source of the monologue in a scene from *The Tragic Muse* and its ties to the "usurping consciousness" in his preface to that novel. Of far less importance is her "Sir Sidney Colvin in *The Golden Bowl*: Mr. Chrichton Identified" (*CLQ* Series 10, 7:428–31), which identifies Sir Sidney as possibly Mr. Chrichton, and his wife, Fanny Sitwell, as perhaps the source for the name of Fanny Assingham. And her "Henry James and a Watteau Fan" (*Apollo*, June 1974:488) posits Balzac and a Watteau design James might have seen near Ascot as the source for the allusion in "A New England Winter." Probably the best of her source studies this year is "Octave Feuillet, *La Petite Comtesse* and Henry James" (*RLC* 48:218–32), which gives a detailed account of allusions to Feuillet in letters, journals, conversations, and elsewhere and consequent echoes, especially of *La Petite Comtesse*, everywhere in his writings, early and late. Her reverse tactic, in "'The Hermit and the Wild Woman': Edith

Wharton's 'Fictioning' of Henry James" (*JML* 4:32–42), is a highly speculative reading of "The Hermit . . ." and of her medieval imitation "Ogrin . . ." as disguised pictures of Henry James and his relation to her and her relation to Edward Wharton and Walter Berry. This is a long way to go to deposit much interest in either the story or the poem.

Much more significant in this vein, for me, is Lydia Rivlin Gabbay's "The Four Square Coterie: A Comparison of Ford Madox Ford and Henry James" (*SNNTS* 6:439–53). It is a knowledgeably intricate account of Ford/Jamesian antagonisms, even if finally not fully persuasive in its fascinating central thesis that *The Good Soldier* is a "vehicle" exposing "the absurdity of James's values, the amorality and stupidity of his protagonists, [and] the falsity of James's belief in the delicacy and restraint of the aristocratic soul . . . [all thereby permitting Ford] to kill his own Jamesian passion."

The remaining source study I saw for 1974, James J. Kirschke's "Henry James's Use of Impressionist Painting Techniques in *The Sacred Fount* and *The Ambassadors*" (*Studies in the Twentieth Century*, 13:83–116), is a discursive, pedantic, and ultimately only partially successful attempt to establish ties between the narrative techniques of the two novels, on the one hand, and the techniques and philosophy of impressionistic painting on the other.

The case is quite different in parallel studies, however, especially in Richard A. Hock's *Henry James and Pragmatistic Thought: A Study in the Relationship between the Philosophy of William James and the Literary Art of Henry James* (Chapel Hill: Univ. of N.C. Press), clearly the most provocative work of the year. Hocks's thesis is put succinctly: "William James's pragmatistic thought is literally actualized as the literary art and idiom of his brother Henry James, especially so in the later work." There is no case made here for influence, although Hocks faithfully recounts all that the brothers are known to have said about one another's work. Neither is this a biographical nor psychological study, although the contentions of Edel and others about sibling rivalry are comprehended, even if ultimately dismissed. It is more centrally concerned with the many ways William's "pragmatistic" thought—his radical empiricism, his consequent distinctions between "saltatory" and "ambulatory" relations and their epistemological, ethical, and religious consequences—are amazingly acute rubrics by which to "read" the major fiction of Henry James.

The readings themselves (of "The Real Thing" with *The Spoils of Poynton*, of "The Beast in the Jungle" with *The Ambassadors*, and of what he calls the "quasi-supernatural" work of later years, all within obviously demonstrated knowledge of the entire corpus), although they are finely discriminated and persuasive, do not ultimately provide analyses with which most dedicated Jamesians are unfamiliar. (That "the real thing" is finally located in the Monarchs is hardly news.) This is nevertheless an extremely important book, for nowhere else I know is there a better demonstration of how in the works of both famous brothers are such ideas articulated as the self-consciousness of consciousness and its consequent inseparateness from the world (or indeed from the body), the "polarity" that enclosed the brothers, or the final intimated realization *by both* that this was all true. More needs to be said than I have space for about the book's method (sometimes repetitious or discursive), its expression (only occasionally turgid or obscure), its historical perspective (possibly misleading). If, finally, the book eventually comes to be more influential for its lucid exposition of William's thinking than it does for Henry's practice—as I somehow perversely suspect it will, however opposite to what its author intended and indeed unfair to the real virtues of the book—that ironic result would not have gone unappreciated, one feels, *by both*.

Almost equally important, in much briefer scope, is Denis Donoghue's "The American Style of Failure" (*SR* 82:407–32) and its complex thesis of the transformation of "the mere state of failure into the artistic success of forms and pageants." James is his great exemplar, his "hyperbole" placed first and most extensively against the "irony" of Henry Adams, that contrast then moved to such figures as Wallace Stevens, Veblen, Lionel Trilling, and others, and finally a definition of style proposed that is spectacularly "warm[ing]" to Europeans such as himself who know that "its desperate metaphysic lives by will, risk, and every kind of exorbitance." Very Good.

Other parallel studies of 1974 are comparatively thin. Caroline Gordon's "Rebels and Revolutionaries: The New American Scene" (*FOB* 3:40–56) is a mere assertion of how such qualities of "illusionism," professionalism, and esthetic dedication are said to mark the careers of both James and Ms. O'Connor and of how her ties are much closer to James than to Hawthorne. Gary Lemco's "Henry James and Richard Wagner: *The American*" (*HSL* 6,ii:147–58) purports to see Newman as a reflection of Lohengrin, a "man apart" reaffirming the "true myth" of "the death and rebirth of a god"! My own essay, "An 'Easy Ride' for Henry James; or, Is Captain America Christopher Newman(?)—The Master and Pop Kultur, a Note from the Midwest" (*JPC* 8:320–27), sees, with only a modicum of facetiousness, parallel myths in *The American* and the Dennis Hopper film, *Easy Rider*, and finds Jamesian themes contemporaneously reflected in other popular media sources as disparate as Jules Feiffer cartoons and Bertolucci's *Last Tango in Paris*. Another article by me, "A Whale, an Heiress, and a Southern Demigod: Three Symbolic Americas" (*ColL* 1:100–12), purports to be a contextual study linking *Moby-Dick*, *The Wings of the Dove*, and *Absalom, Absalom!* as collective prophecy through imagistic ties of whiteness.

Two excellent studies attest to Jamesian influence on experimental fiction. H. A. Bouraoui's "Henry James's *The Sacred Fount*: Nouveau Roman avant la lettre?" (*IFR* 1:96–105) sees all kinds of Jamesian echoes in Nathalie Sarraute's *Portrait d'un inconnu* and consequently a James who anticipated "not only the experiments of the French 'noveau roman,' but also their greatest problem: their creation of hermetic private consciousness" and its accompanying problems of credulity. Arnold Weinstein's "Enclosed Vision: Conrad, Ford, and James," in his *Vision and Response in Modern Fiction* (Ithaca: Cornell Univ. Press), pp. 50–90, also with special attention to *The Sacred Fount* and, more extendedly, to "The Turn of the Screw," sees a James always aware of "the biases and dangers that may beset an unswerving commitment to imagination at the expense of visible surfaces." Hence later fiction—from such novelists as Faulkner, Bernanos, Kafka, Joyce, Butor, Proust, Borges, Simon, Robbe-Grillet—is said to owe James's fiction a good deal, even as it is occasionally able to "transcend its ambiguities and limitations."

iii. Criticism: General

Two remaining book-length studies of James under review were both published abroad, and one of them, at least, Darshan Singh Maini's *Henry James: The Indirect Vision, Studies in Themes and Techniques* (Bombay-New Delhi: Tate McGraw Hill [1973]) is very good indeed. Although prepared as an introduction to the Master in the Indian Major American Authors Series, it is anything but introductory in its knowledge of James, in its candid, lucid, and common-sensical understanding of the dubious need for another "general" book on the subject, of the specialized appeal of James (the appeal to that "secret sharer" in all of us that yearns for "the uncovenanted consciousness, owing allegiance to nothing outside of its own earned insights"), and of how, in Clifton Fadiman's phrase, James's "insight was so tireless that it was bound to comprehend his own prejudices." Divided into twelve topical and only occasionally overlapping chapters—on such subjects as the theory of the novel, American women, irony, style, ethics, point of view, etc.—the book is an amazingly comprehensive coverage of at least the fiction, especially the novels; but it also is everywhere demonstrably conscious of all that James has written and of much more that has been written about him than is usually the case. Critics will inevitably quarrel with parts here and there (I, for example, see as quite otherwise the distinctions he draws between such pairs as Milly and Kate, Maggie and Charlotte). But the book is finely written (James's style is described as "an ambassadorial prose having patrician moorings"). And overall it may just be the best brief overview of James since F. W. Dupee's back in the early 1950s.

Hildegard Domaniecki's *Zum Problem literarischer Ökonomie— Henry James' Erzählungen zwischen Markt und Kunst* (Stuttgart: J. B. Metzlersche) is (1) an examination of how the exigencies of the ever-changing short-story marketplace affected James's practice and (2) an analysis of the demonstrated consequences of those exigencies in the short fiction itself. (See also p. 439.)

Of much less importance is Lisa Appignanesi's *Femininity and the Creative Imagination: A Study of Henry James, Robert Musil and Marcel Proust* (New York: Barnes and Nobles [1973]), a book whose 60 pages on James (pp. 20–80) strike me as arbitrary and simplistic. Its strategy is direct. Qualities of mystification and interiorization, those aspects of being which turn one inward and have a spiritual rather than an intellectual quality and admit the possibility for attaining "consciousness," are all said to be "feminine." Opposite qualities are of course "masculine" (and of course destructive), those aspects that turn one outward toward social norms or other people or absolutes. Characters are then categorized, the canon schematized, and everyone put in his/her perfectly predictable and proper place: good people (male *and* female, not to be sexist) are

said to be feminine; bad people, masculine. This account is hardly fair
—and yet, I cannot help saying, not basically inaccurate either, in
spite of some sensitive applications here and there of her dichotomy,
in spite of the much more fruitful and concomitant rubric she applies
in seeing the Cinderella tale as substructure to the major novels.

In a way I am not much happier with two additional and complimentary overviews of James, one by a structuralist, the other employing psychology. Tzvetan Todorov's "The Structural Analysis of
Literature: The Tales of Henry James" (in David Robey's *Structuralism: An Introduction* [Oxford: Clarendon Press, 1973], pp. 73–
103) focuses mostly on the tales between about 1892 and 1903 and
cleanly sets forth his clearly discerned pattern: "the quest for an
absolute and absent cause," with of course "absence as the essential
element," for the fundamental precept is "the affirmation of the
absence, [that is] of the impossibility of describing the truth by its
name." The resolution is said to be at one with the proper function of
criticism: "the search for truth, not its revelation—the quest for the
treasure rather than the treasure itself, for the treasure can only be
absent." The major exemplum becomes, somewhat predictably, "The
Figure in the Carpet" and, to be sure, the ghostly tales where the
absolute absence literally appears, but only (!) as a "presence."
Manfred Mackenzie, in "A Theory of Henry James's Psychology"
(*YR* 63:347–71), describes his prototype as a Jamesian "self," who is
"shocked by a rival, a competitor . . . a *double*," the latter coming in
various guises, strongly or faintly, but almost always seeming to
have some clear superiority, almost always reminding the protagonist of "what he might have been." This is accurate concerning "The
Jolly Corner," his hardly surprising example, but as guide to the
canon it leaves much to be desired in spite of felicitous application
of it in unexpected places, in spite of its laudable ambition (as with
Todorov) to schematize the canon.

The remaining essays in this gathering of general studies move all
over the Jamesian map. Patrick Swinden, in "Registration" (in his
Unofficial Selves: Character in the Novel from Dickens to the Present
[New York: Harper & Row, 1973], pp. 100–119), reverses the
method, provoking my reservations to the preceding, and sees James
himself, especially in the later work, as so exclusively interested in
pattern, with relation, with what one simply *sees*, that pattern is all
the reader himself *can* see, not motive, not even meaningful meaning.

Raymond Thorberg's "Henry James and the Sense of the Past" (*ModA* 18:272–82) covers all-too-familiar ground in his attention to how the international tales develop "a relation between past and present [and the process] of . . . 'manipulating a continuous parallel' between the two." Shizue Ebine's "The Central Theme of Henry James" (*SELit* [English number]:53–60), according to a synopsis in English appended to its Japanese original, is still another study of the last three novels and their concerns with consciousness, freedom, and social relationships. Pamela Jacobs Sheldon's "Jamesian Gothicism: The Haunted Castle of the Mind" (*SLitI* 7:121–34) surveys once more the gothic in James, especially in "The Jolly Corner" as "a peregrination into self." W. R. Macnaughton's "The First-Person Narrators of Henry James" (*SAF* 2:145–64) calls attention to the number of tales employing first-person narrators (some fifty of them) and then deftly demonstrates how the use of an unreliable narrator throws new light on such often discussed tales as "A Passionate Pilgrim" or "The Author of Beltraffio" no less than on such relatively undiscussed ones as "The Special Type" or "The Tone of Time." Christoph K. Lohmann's "Jamesian Irony and the American Sense of Mission" (*TSLL* 16:329–47) is another good article that sees James possessed of a penetrating political insight into the American "mission" to save the world, especially in *The American* and *The Ambassadors*, which ironically depict "national idealism that is always on the verge of turning into jingoistic braggadocio." Granville H. Jones's "Henry James's 'Georgina's Reasons': The Underside of *Washington Square*" (*SSF* 11:189–94) sees the tale as an almost exact "reverse mirror image" of the novel via a contrastive view of Georgina and Catherine Sloper. The former is a kind of Hedda Gabler, to be admired, however dire the eventual consequences of her rebelliousness. John Halperin's long analysis of *The Portrait of a Lady* (in his *Egoism and Self-Discovery in the Victorian Novel* [New York: Burt Franklin], pp. 247–76) tells us nothing about the novel we did not know before except that it is a perfect "fit" among those Victorian novels whose theme "is that of the moral and psychological expansion of protagonists who begin in self-absorption and move, through the course of a tortuous ordeal of education, to more complete self-knowledge." And Harry B. Henderson, III's brief attention to the nouvelle, in his "James's Sense of the Past and *The Europeans*" (*Versions of the Past: The Historical Imagination in American Fiction* [New York, Oxford

Univ. Press], pp. 209–13), finds James's place in historical fiction restricted to this single example of "the tendency of the holist historical novel . . . to become pure surface, with no effort to represent historical forces or movements."

iv. Criticism: Individual Tales

Most of the important criticism of the tales this year is in material already cited. The five studies remaining provide slim pickings indeed. William E. Grant's " 'Daisy Miller': A Study of a Study" (SSF 11:17–25) is an overblown analysis by way of seeing the tale focused as a "study of Winterbourne studying Daisy," the loss of his innocence thereby bringing "him from moral blindness into the full golden light of day." Paul Rodgers, in "Motive, Agency, and Act in James's *The Aspern Papers*" (SAQ 73:377–87), makes the not totally persuasive case that it is Juliana who "sets up" Tina's condition of marriage as the price for the papers by controlling the action to the very end. Arthur Boardman, in "Mrs. Grose's Reading of *The Turn of the Screw*" (SEL 14:619–35), brings no startling new news about the tale in his elaborate analysis of the housekeeper as a "kind of first reader" to the governess's story, a "rhetorical element and a character" who corroborates her story and thus provides a touchstone to its meaning. And the two studies by Allen F. Stein make essentially the same kind of point: his "The Beast in 'The Jolly Corner': Spencer Brydon's Ironic Rebirth" (SSF 11:61–66), argues that the ghost is not of what Brydon might have been but of what he is, "a selfish and isolated old man . . . who has never been able to feel a mature emotional attachment to anyone but himself" and who is thus "reborn" only into "old conceits and new self-delusions"; his "The Hack's Progress: A Reading of James's 'The Velvet Glove' " (EIL 1:219–26) maintains that Berridge is finally seen to be a "self-deluding hack who, unable to cope with the humiliation into which his romantic yearnings lead him, attempts to re-establish his self-esteem by assuming a pose of artistic integrity."

v. Criticism: Individual Novels

Studies of individual novels, although more numerous than those of the tales, are not of marked better quality. Larry J. Reynolds's "Henry James's New Christopher Newman" (*SNNT* 5[1973]:457–68), for example, is still another defense of the revisions. And Mary Jane King's "The Touch of the Earth: A Word and a Theme in *The Portrait of a Lady*" (*NCF* 29:345–47) is a mere explicatory note on the variety of ways the word *touch* is used in the novel to relate theme and action.

Three studies of *The Bostonians* are only moderately more significant. Lee Ann Johnson, in "The Psychology of Characterization: James's Portraits of Verena Tarrant and Olive Chancellor" (*SNNT* 6:295–303), covers some old ground in her speculation that the superior characterization of Olive, in contrast to that of Verena, may have resulted from James's close observations of the relationship between his sister Alice and her companion Katherine Loring. In contrast, Howard Pearce, in "Witchcraft Imagery and Allusion in James's *Bostonians*" (*SNNT* 6:236–47), denigrates Olive in defense of Basil by tracing the novel's witchcraft imagery and literary allusions (especially to *Faust* and "Christabel"). Somewhat more original than either of these is Philip Page's attention, in "The Curious Narration of *The Bostonians*" (*AL* 46:374–83), to the failures of the narrative voice in the work in attempting to engage the reader in an active role in the novel's life. But the best article of the year on the novels of the late 1880s is Daniel J. Schneider's "The Theme of Freedom in James's *The Tragic Muse*" (*ConnR* 7,ii:5–15) for its insight into parallel attitudes in the novel toward both art and politics and the way in which Gabriel Nash is set both above and below the rest, above because of his representing the ideal, below because he is of an "other world."

Lee Ann Johnson's "James's Mrs. Wix: The 'Dim, Crooked Reflector'" (*NCF* 29:164–72) poses Maisie's old nurse as an important part of the satiric thrust of the novel. Better is A. E. Davidson's "James's Dramatic Method in *The Awkward Age*" (*NCF* 29:320–35) and its insistence that the strategy of the novel demands that the reader focus less on what characters say than on what they do and view with special distrust those characters who themselves appear to be interpreting others. But best of all is Josephine Harris's "*The Sacred Fount*: The Geometry in the Jungle" (*MQR* 13:57–73), a witty and penetrating reading of the novel as replicating through the modes of comedy, romance, and irony various modes any artist might take toward his material (and as James himself was to take in his

three great last novels). This essay is also very good in some suggested ties it makes between the narrator of this novel and Gabriel
Nash of *The Tragic Muse*.

Sarah Blacher Cohen's "*The Ambassadors*: A Comedy of Musing
and Manners" (*SAmH* 1:79–90) is a totally predictable piece on the
variety of ways high comedy is evidenced in the novel. Also hardly
new is Pauline Fletcher's view, in "The Sense of Society in *The
Ambassadors*" (*ESA* 17:79–88), that when Strether "is most fully
inside the consciousness of his characters . . . he is also most fully
aware of their social conditions" or that it is the societies of Woollett
and Paris that condition what James lets one "see." Easily the best
study of this novel in 1974 is T. B. Tomlinson's "An American
Strength: James's *The Ambassadors*" (*CR* 17:38–58) for its account of the various triumphs of the work, its comedy, its familiarity
and distance, its "moral earnestness," and, in spite of style and technique, its "strait-forwardness"—all said to be peculiarly American—
and nowhere more so than in its effective joining in imagination what
cannot be joined in fact, "the raw directness of Woollett and the
experienced duplicity of Paris."

Mildred E. Hartsock's "Unintentional Fallacy: Critics and *The
Golden Bowl*" (*MLQ* 35:272–88) is full of marvelous common sense
in its elaborate chronicle of biased or mistaken criticism of this
novel—by those who insist that no "good" American capitalist can
exist, those who cry "ambiguity" at what is perfectly clear, those who
for some reason cannot accept the novel's central and clear concerns:
"the human mandate to mature through a full consciousness and the
human responsibility to solve common and difficult marital problems
in a civilized way." And my last citation this year, Amy Ling's "The
Pagoda Image in Henry James' *The Golden Bowl*" (*AL* 46:383–88),
locates a probable source but more importantly elucidates the function of the extended pagoda image in the novel as a "visual, auditory
and tactile" clarification of Maggie's situation on the edge of discovering the truth about the Prince and Charlotte.

Purdue University

8. Pound and Eliot

Richard M. Ludwig

Debate still continues on whether T. S. Eliot is a British or an American poet, but the question is academic. We welcome him to these pages quite apart from his citizenship and find the linkage with Ezra Pound, here for the first time in a chapter of their own, both fitting and natural.

The number of completed dissertations on these two poets is exactly the same as last year: seven on Pound, six on Eliot. All of them are not devoted exclusively to their work; several, it is to be hoped, might become books: a study of the American aspects of the *Cantos*, a comparative treatment of Pound and Cavalcanti, a placing of Eliot in the English critical tradition.

The books and articles on both poets continue to proliferate to such a degree that it will be difficult to do justice in brief notices to the quality of certain of them; the quantity is another matter. Far too many of the critical articles range from dull and redundant to unreadable. Michael Millgate said the final word on this subject in *ALS 1971*: "The trouble with so many of the items is that we simply do not need them." Anything but unreadable is a new book by Cyrena N. Pondrom, which touches closely on the young Pound and Eliot: *The Road from Paris: French Influence on English Poetry, 1900–1920* (Cambridge: Cambridge University Press). Pondrom begins her 50-page survey of the period by reminding us that in *The Criterion* in 1934 Eliot observed that "younger generations can hardly realize the intellectual desert of England and America during the first decade and more of this century" and thus set about explaining why "the predominance of Paris was incontestable." She then reprints contemporaneous essays by Flint, Murry, Hulme, Tristan Derème, and others, including Pound's series of essays in *The New Age* (1931) with the general title "The Approach to Paris." Pound praised the *unanimistes* for their "efforts at 'simplification of

structure' and risked the opinion that 'the next great work may be
written' in the fashion of Henri-Martin Barzun's 'poems like or-
chestral scores.'" Among individual poets he extolled are Remy de
Gourmont, Henri de Régnier and the less well-known Francis Jammes
and Laurent Tailhade. Pound, she argues, was one of the heralds of
the new French poetry; Eliot was absorbing it. This is an important
book, ingeniously organized, but no introduction for novice readers.
Bernard I. Duffey's "The Experimental Lyric in Modern Poetry:
Eliot, Pound, Williams" (*JML* 3:1085–1103) concentrates on Eliot's
dissertation on F. H. Bradley and its relevance to the lyrical passages
in *The Waste Land*, followed by too brief a look at "the untiring and
wide-weaving voice of the *Cantos*" as the "containing element" of
Pound's lyricism. Provocative ideas are here, but they are too tightly
compressed.

i. Pound

a. **Collections, Letters, Bibliography.**   Not everyone will be happy
with William Cookson's choices, but his edition of *Ezra Pound:
Selected Prose, 1909–1965* (New York: New Directions, 1973) has
at least a reasonable intention: "to gather the core of Pound's writing
on religious, Confucian, historical, economic and monetary subjects
together with some previously uncollected literary essays." It was
assembled in 1971 with Pound's help; the order within the eight parts
is chronological; and it offers about 175 pages of first reprints otherwise unavailable. The serious student, however, still needs the
Literary Essays (ed. T. S. Eliot) and *Impact: Ideas on Ignorance and
the Decline of American Civilization* (ed. Noel Stock) as well as
Pound's full-length prose books.

Stray letters will continue to surface for many years. F. G. Atkinson prints a rare early letter to Sir Arthur T. Quiller-Couch (October 1912) in "Ezra Pound's Reply to an 'Old-World' Letter" (*AL*
46:357–59). Four letters (1939) to Joseph Brewster, former president
of Olivet College, and an earlier note to Ford Madox Ford are printed
by Maurice Hungiville in "Ezra Pound's Letters to Olivet" (*TQ* 16
[1973]:77–87). His correspondence in 1956 with a young Indian
printer (Pound was still in St. Elizabeths) is the substance of Debra
P. Patnaik's "Only the Quality of the Affection Endures" (*Paideuma*
3:313–18).

"Corrections and Additions to the Pound Bibliography (Part 3)" by Donald Gallup (*Paideuma* 3:403–04) lists notes and additional entries based upon issues of *Il Popolo di Alessandria* and *Marina Repubblicana* that have recently become available in the Pound Archive at Yale. Gary Lane edited *A Concordance to "Personae": The Shorter Poems of Ezra Pound* (New York: Haskell House, 1972), part one of a complete concordance to the collected poetry.

b. **Biography.** More than a dozen articles, of varying quality, give us glimpses of Pound between 1907 and the year of his death, 1972. It is wisest to survey them in terms of the calendar. Ernest L. Boyd's "Ezra Pound at Wabash College" (*JML* 4:43–54) uses first-, second-, and third-hand information to explain Pound's "forced resignation" from his instructorship. Whether he was a rebel, victim, misfit, eccentric, or young genius, Boyd cannot decide. Eric Homberger discusses briefly Arundel del Re's "A Glimpse of Pound in 1912" (*Paideuma* 3:85–88) and the quarrel del Re may have precipitated between Pound and Harold Monro over *The Sonnets and Ballate of Guido Cavalcanti*. In "Allan Upward and Ezra Pound" (*Paideuma* 3:71–83), Bryant Knox offers a fascinating portrait of a man who began to change Pound's theories of the Divine Man or Genius about 1913; there are five references to Upward in the *Cantos*. Patricia Hutchins's "Young Pound in London, Friends and Acquaintances" (*ConnR* 7:87–93) reminds us that in *Patria Mia* he confessed to knowing hardly anything of England apart from the metropolis; Miss Hutchins then elaborates on Pound's social life, his acquaintance with Luke Alexander Ionides, Margot Asquith and her stepdaughter Violet, C. F. G. and Lucy Masterman, May Sinclair, and Michael Arlen among others.

Four memoirs by young scholars, all in *Paideuma* 3, add important details to our knowledge of Pound's confinement (1945–58) at St. Elizabeths. Carroll F. Terrell's reminiscence, "St. Elizabeths" (pp. 363–79), is by far the most ambitious in its attempt to combine notes on Pound's daily routine, his visitors, his mental health, his contributions to "a series of small, short-lived publications [which] were created, edited and promoted by some of EP's dedicated young followers" (*Strike, Four Pages, Academia Bulletin*) and other publishing concerns like the Square Dollar Series, *Edge*, and *Voice*. Bill MacNaughton recalls Pound's conversations on the Chinese language, on governments, religion, and poetics during the years 1950–53 in "Pound, A Brief Memoir: 'Chi Lavora, Ora'" (pp. 319–24). Angela Palandri's memoir, "Homage to a Confucian Poet" (pp. 301–11) describes her first visit to St. Elizabeths in 1952 when she was Miss Chih-ying Jung, a foreign student from China, and how, over a period of four months, she met Olga Rudge, Dorothy Pound, and T. S. Eliot during her visits and worked with Pound on *Cathay*, the Confucian Odes, and the difficulties of translation. Marcella Spann Booth (who collaborated with Pound in editing the anthology *Confucius to Cummings* [1964]) speaks intimately about the last year at St. Elizabeths ("Through the Smoke Hole," pp. 329–34), especially his advice to visitors, the housekeeping problems, other inmates, and his prolific production: letters and cantos.

Charles Olson describes in "First Canto" (*Paideuma* 3:295–300) his first meeting with Pound in 1945 at his arraignment before Bolitha Laws, chief justice of the district court for the District of Columbia. "He was grey and alone," Olson remembers; and he later talked about his incarceration in a tent in Pisa and at Gallinger Hospital, Washington, about Mary and Omar, the English people, the American government, and his work in progress. Carlos Baker recalls in close detail a one-day visit with Pound on the poet's 80th birthday ("Pound in Venice, 1965" [*VQR* 50:597–605]). His single remark at Gianfranco Ivancich's luncheon party was a criticism of the *malfatta*; he pushed away his plate and said to Mrs. Baker, "Too heavy." Peter Russell's lengthy reminiscence was written in Venice in December 1972 after Pound's funeral. "Ezra Pound: The Last Years: A Personal Memoir" (*MHRev* 29:11–44) deserves reprinting for many reasons, chief among them the warmth of this old friendship and the aura of daily conversations and meaningful silences that both author and subject obviously cherished. Russell moved to Venice in 1964, and he records Pound's appraisal of old friends (Ford, Williams, Eliot, Lewis) and new enthusiasms (Ginsberg, Burroughs, Lowell), his joy in making tapes of his poems, his continuing love of music. "For all the disagreement about him," Russell concludes, "[he] had radiated energy and inspired others with that energy."

To these essays must be added two interviews which offer a potpourri of biographical detail. Carroll Terrell spliced a series of dialogues with David Gordon, whose first meeting with Pound was in 1952: "Meeting E. P. and then..." (*Paideuma* 3:343–60). The conversations are confined to the St. Elizabeths' years but range widely in subject matter. The second half of "Allen Verbatim" (*Paideuma* 3:253–73) records Allen Ginsberg's reactions to the news of Pound's death, his recollection of a visit in 1967 ("Pound told me he felt that the Cantos were 'stupidity and ignorance all the way through' and that his 'greatest stupidity was stupid suburban anti-Semitic prejudice' "), and his introducing Pound and Olga Rudge to music by Bob Dylan and the Beatles. Interviews, unfortunately, are almost impossible to condense, even to excerpt. These are worth reading whole.

c. Criticism: Books. No major books appeared in 1974, but these are useful. James J. Wilhelm's *Dante and Pound: The Epic of Judgement* (Orono: Univ. of Maine Press) is not, as the author says at once, for the "seasoned Dantista" but for the reader who wants to watch "the dramatic shift in Pound's uses of the Italian master." Chapter 1 rehearses Dante's life in considerable detail and then sees Pound's in the same general pattern: youthful exile, attempts at reconciliation, and final separation. Wilhelm next treats the two poets as lyrists, both greatly influenced by Guido Cavalcanti (the Dante-Guido relationship was every bit as intricate as the Pound-Eliot), and then devotes a whole chapter to monarchy and money (Dante's *De Monarchia*, Pound's *ABC of Economics*). The last third of the book tries (not wholly successfully) to place the *Inferno-Purgatorio-Paradiso* next to the Early-Middle-Late *Cantos* through close inspection of Pound's use of Dante's imagery. There is no doubt, however, that Wilhelm writes with contagious enthusiasm about what he calls "the most intellectually alive poem of the [20th] century." Grace Schulman's *Ezra Pound: A Collection of Criticism* (New York: Mc-Graw-Hill) is divided into three parts. "The Poet's Own Testimony: 1913–1962" reprints "A Retrospect" (1918, on Imagism), "How I Began" (1913), and Donald Hall's interview for the *Paris Review* (1963)—a strangely unrepresentative choice. "General Criticism" is limited to essays by Marianne Moore ("Our debt to Ezra Pound is prodigious for the effort he has made to share what he knows about writing"), Hugh Kenner (the explicit use of Sappho in his work, from *The Pound Era*), Sister Bernetta Quinn (a chapter from her 1972 study, emphasizing Pound's prose, both the literary criticism and the economic treatises), and T. S. Eliot (the introduction to *Selected Poems of Ezra Pound*, 1928). Six essays (five are excerpted from books) make up the last section, "Specific Works and Stages." They make familiar reading (Thomas Jackson on the London years, Hugh Kenner on *Mauberley,* Donald Davie on *The Pisan Cantos,* M. L. Rosenthal on the architecture of the first 109 Cantos, Daniel Pearlman on Canto I as microcosm) except for Richard Pevear's arguments in "Notes on the Cantos of Ezra Pound": Cantos 110–17 are "the ordained end" towards which Pound "has been working from the start," but "the later cantos are not a *Paradiso.* Dante's poem is a comedy, but the *Cantos* are tragic . . . the vision of paradise has vanished or has been lost." Suzanne Juhasz, in *Metaphor and the Poetry of Williams, Pound, and Stevens* (Lewisburg, Pa.: Bucknell Univ. Press) travels over wholly familiar ground in her introductory chapter, and in 56 pages devoted to the *Cantos* (concentrating on the first 30) she also rehearses what Kenner, Dekker, and Davie have already told us. Juhasz is at her best when she discusses Pound's compound-word metaphors, but even here her commentary is disappointingly listless. Williams's poetry is much more her métier.

d. **Criticism: Articles.**   The *Italian Quarterly* (16[1973]:1–120) is a special issue on Ezra Pound and Italy which deserves belated notice, however brief, before turning to the 1974 publications. The 10 contributions are of various importance. James Wilhelm's contribution is better read in the context of his book, *Dante and Pound,* described above. Massimo Bacigalupo's essay on Canto 106 is also an extract from a book, *L'ultimo Pound* (Rome, 1973). Eugenio Montale's "Uncle Ez" was originally published in *Corriere della sera* (Milan, 1953) and is here translated for the first time. Angela Palandri's "Italian Images of Ezra Pound" is a condensed version of the introduction to a forthcoming volume with that title. The rest were newly written for this issue: Carlo Izzo discusses "Three Unpublished Letters by Ezra Pound" (two dated 1956, one from 1958); Hugh Kenner reflects on Pound's love for Italy, especially Lago di Garda, in "The Magic of Place"; Riccardo M. degli Uberti offers a "history of a friendship" between Pound and his father, Ubaldo degli Uberti (see Cantos 77, 78, 89, and 95); Aldo Tagliaferri revaluates *Jefferson and/or Mussolini;* Gian Piero Barricelli comments on Pound's translation of Leopardi's "Sopra il ritratto di una bella donna"; and Georg M. Gugelberger offers an unusually lucid analysis of *The Spirit of Romance* and the Cantos as "an endless conversation with the works of

Dante" in a beautifully written essay, " 'By No Means an Orderly Dantescan Rising.' "

Three essays on Pound and politics are the most illuminating work of the year, certainly for the general reader. Timothy Materer, in "The English Vortex: Modern Literature and the 'Pattern of Hope' " (*JML* 3:1123–39), tries to understand "the depth of Pound's disappointment [with himself as well as Eliot and Wyndham Lewis], the sense that the failure of the Vortex implied the crash of an entire culture." (Pound concludes bitterly in Canto 102: "But the lot of 'em, Yeats, Possum, Old Wyndham/ had no ground to stand on.") Materer shows in a commendably concise essay how the Vortex, the association Pound began with Lewis and Eliot in 1914, moved from the excitement of publishing *Blast* through the devastations of World War I to the dissolution of the triumvirate when Eliot began editing the conservative *Criterion,* Lewis foolishly supported German National Socialism in "a book he almost immediately regretted, *Hitler,*" and Pound had moved to Italy and was supporting Major Douglas's Social Credit and Mussolini's authoritarian rule. It is a mark of Materer's skill in condensation that he also manages to show us Lewis and Pound at the end of their careers "painfully disillusioned" as they contemplated the shards of their "pattern of hope." In "The Dragon and the Duel: A Defense of Pound's Canto 88" (*TCL* 20:114–25), James Wilhelm searches for historical fact as background to the duel between John Randolph of Roanoke and Henry Clay, notably Thomas Hart Benton's autobiography *Thirty Years' View* (1854–56). Pound aligns Randolph with the Chinese emperor T'ang, Emperor Antoninus, St. Ambrose, Delacroix, "Master" John Adams, and Major C. H. Douglas. Wilhelm concludes: "The true guide to history lies in the heart, the emotional recreation of it. . . . This is the *poetic* use of historical material. . . . The poet acknowledges emotion, slanting, and error." Thomas H. Jackson's "The Poetic Politics of Ezra Pound (*JML* 3:987–1011) offers the most closely reasoned arguments of all, difficult to excerpt or condense, but undoubtedly a major contribution to this phase of Pound scholarship. Jackson sees Pound as neither eccentric nor crank in his political writings but "a perfectly bourgeois political thinker" who "does not understand the notion of class struggle." The central figures in the *Cantos,* he argues, are "persons of ever increasing social relevance": Sigismundo Malatesta, Jefferson, John Adams—examples of the *artifex,* the man who can adduce appropriate order from the flux, whose key values are concreteness, a sense of gradations (discernment), and agility of mind. Jackson then demonstrates how Jefferson and Malatesta were, for Pound, "one type of importantly *polumetis* statesmen, the many-counseled Odyssean man"; but his brave attempt to mythologize Adams "sinks beneath a barrage of historical details" and quotation of "arid political prose" en masse. He concludes that Pound's major concern was "to bring valid poetic language back into contact with the culture which for long now has scorned it." His method—"to create a poetry that could contain politics."

In "Olson's Relation to Pound and Williams" (*ConL* 15:15–48), Robert von Hallberg sees all three poets as antisymbolists in absolute opposition to Eliot. He admires Pound's "mythological vision [which] apprehends the familiar directly" and sees Canto 17 as one of the best means of illustrating Pound's attempt to blend the actual Venice at dawn with his vision of Dionysus. But Olson, he argues, thought Pound's vision "too much his own" (he calls it Pound's EGO-POSITION) and "his idiosyncratic interpretations of history are finally not shareable." Charles Doria, in "Pound, Olson, and the Classical Tradition" (*Boundary* 2:127–43), sees Pound using the classical tradition (5th-century Athens to 1st-century Rome) "both as canon and methodology for what it teaches about the rise of Europe and for its cultural conservatism" but sees Olson viewing it "as an outsider." He believes that the major persona of the *Cantos* is Odysseus and that *Cantos* was not chosen as a title "for its descriptive value but as a metaphor to direct our attention to various aspects of the Classical Tradition." The bulk of the article, admittedly, concerns Olson.

Whatever is said here about *Paideuma* 3 in this brief survey will be wholly inadequate. It continues to be a handsomely printed, intelligently edited repository of biographical and bibliographical information (see above), notes, queries, reviews, work in progress, and reprints of reference material as well as (in the 1974 volume) six longish exegetical articles which are most assuredly not for the beginner. Five of them treat Pound's study of Chinese language and literature. David Hsin-Fu Wand examines Pound's use of Chinese mythology in "To the Summit of Taishan" (pp. 3–12). He concentrates on Pound's interest in Confucianism and his impatience with Shamanism, Taoism, Buddhism; his invoking the name of Kuanon (Kuan-yin), the goddess of mercy in Chinese legends; and his use of Taishan ("exalted mountain"), located in the province of Shantung, as symbol of freedom from worldly strife. Through a Chinese goddess Pound reaches the top of a Chinese paradise. Carroll F. Terrell pursues Pound's search for paradise on earth in a fascinating illustrated article, "The Na-Khi Documents I" (pp. 91–122), which traces the poet's interest in Oriental art and landscape from his friendship in 1911 with Laurence Binyon, author of *The Flight of the Dragon*, to his discovery in the summer of 1956 of a book by Peter Goullart, *Forgotten Kingdom* (1955), as well as Joseph F. Rock's impressive work, *The Ancient Na-khi Kingdom of Southwest China* (1947). Terrell concludes by saying that Pound's "hieratic landscapes (whether in the land of the Na-khi, Provence, the roads of France, or the scenes from Pisa . . .) all evoke a spiritual dimension as suggested by *The Flight of the Dragon*. And with the nicest of art these spiritual dimensions are intensified as we journey into 'Thrones' and the paradisal cantos." Eugene Eoyang studies Pound's translations of the *Shih Ching* (or *Book of Songs*) in "The Confucian Odes" (pp. 34–47). He sees these translations of 305 poems as interpretations of Confucianism, as "modern American poems inspired by ancient Chinese originals," and as problems in the art of translation itself. He prints the Karlgren and the Waley translations as well as the Chinese text for four complete odes. A knowledge of Chinese would assist every reader of David Gordon's comparison of the Legge, the Mathews, and the Karlgren translations with Pound's versions in " 'Root/Br./By Product' in Pound's Confucian Ode 166" (pp. 13–32). Equally demanding is his study of Pound's use of the *Sacred Edict*, "Thought Built on Sagetrieb" (pp. 169–90), concentrating on Canto 99, lines 694–712. He shows us by a few main examples how "Pound has not merely 'digested' the *Edict*, but allowed the *Edict* itself to shape a new structure of The Cantos' spiralling form." But the very title of Gordon's article needs explanation. He reads Sagetrieb to mean, literally, tradition-instinct, and adds: "Sagetrieb can only have any value in passing down a tradition when the tradition is *made new* each time, just as Kang, Yong and Wang made the *Sacred Edict* new each time they passed it down to Pound who again made it new." Kenner translates it differently but confirms Gordon's point (*The Pound Era*, 534n): "A lexicographic puzzle, not in the German dictionaries. 'Saying-force'? In Canto 90 it is paired with 'tradition,' but its etymology suggests paideumic energies, not passive inheritance."

The sixth notable essay is Leon Surette's "'A Light from Eleusis': Some Thoughts on Pound's *Nekuia*" (pp. 191–216). He begins with two books Pound reviewed in 1906: *Origine et esthétique de la tragédie* (1905) and *Le Secret des troubadours* (1906), both by a minor author, Josephin Péladan, and demonstrates in detail how strong in time their influence was in stimulating Pound's interest in the Eleusinian Mysteries ("a fertility cult at whose centre lies the mystery of human sexuality") and their connection with the Odyssean *nekuia* (descent) in Canto 1. "I believe," Pound wrote in reply to Eliot's query as to what he believed, "that a light from Eleusis persisted throughout the middle ages and set beauty in the song of Provence and of Italy." Surette argues that "since Pound's descent leads to a kind of *visio beatifica* as in the Eleusinian rites, the Eleusinian allusion provides a bridge between the *Commedia* and the *Odyssey* so far as their relevance to the *Cantos* is concerned." We are now a far distance from Péladan, but close to the relevance of both Homer and Dante, two disparate poets, to the architecture, even to the literal meaning, of Pound's epic.

ii. Eliot

a. **Bibliography.** The first appearance in spring 1974 of the *T. S. Eliot Newsletter*[1] (ed. D. E. S. Maxwell and Shyamal Bagchee, York University, Toronto) provides a much-needed clearing house for bibliographical updating as well as notes on work in progress, dissertations, recent publications, and the usual brief research papers. It will appear twice a year. The first two issues contain commentary on current critical articles and the announcement that *TSEN* is in process of preparing a bibliography of articles in English, 1916–55, to supplement Mildred Martin's *Half-Century of Eliot Criticism*. Every college library will need this journal.

b. **Biography.** One way to cope with T. S. Matthews's biography, *Great Tom: Notes Toward the Definition of T. S. Eliot* (New York: Harper & Row) is to repeat James Breslin's just conclusion (*VQR* 15:632–37): "More than a disappointment, it is an embarrassment.

---

1. *Editor's Note*: This newsletter changed its name to the *T. S. Eliot Review* in 1975.

Great Tom is careless in its scholarship, shallow in its observations on Eliot's character." One must also add gauche in its critical judgments and maddening in its reliance on rhetorical questions that lurch into soap-opera language: "Was there resentment as well as guilt on Eliot's side? . . . Was it partly that he did not fully return [Vivienne's] love? . . . Did he feel that he had sacrificed another human being?" In his preface Matthews warns us that "all biographies, whether they are official, definitive or, like this one, intermediate, must be to some extent guesswork," but a biographer need not impose *all* his guesses on the reader with interrogation points: "What sort of person was Eliot? Can we trust his friends to tell us? Can we trust his friends? . . . . When you start peeling the onion, where do you end?" We certainly end with less respect for Matthews than for his subject. Denied access by Valerie Eliot to any unpublished papers, he might have concentrated on known facts, published work, documented letters, and personal interviews. Instead he quotes Eliot's supposed remarks without documentation and borrows from Mrs. Eliot's introduction to the facsimile edition of *The Waste Land* without acknowledgment. His commentary on Eliot's conversion ("just as Boston had been a better address than St. Louis, and London a better address than Boston, so the Church of England was a cut above the Unitarian Church") is as insensitive as his reflections on the critic's role are gross ("The scholars continue to peck away at Eliot's poems like sparrows picking at horse shit that still smokes with life and still gives off fresh ammoniac fumes"). We agree with one judgment in Matthew's preface: "An authoritative biography of Eliot is needed." *TSEN* has announced that Frank S. Jewett, M.D. (psychiatry, Columbia University) is assembling material for a biographical study.

William Empson pokes around Eliot's puzzling relationship with his father and "the monstrosity of the [Unitarian] religion" in his review/article on Valerie Eliot's facsimile edition of *The Waste Land* (*EIC* 22[1972]:417–29). He believes "Eliot wanted to grouse about a father and lambasted some imaginary Jews instead," and argues, in fact, that "the central theme of *The Waste Land*, or symbol as one might say, is about a father." Perhaps Mrs. Eliot's forthcoming edition of her husband's letters will be followed by a life of the poet written by a scholar like Richard Ellmann and based on the whole Eliot archive. We need it now.

c. **Criticism: Books.** Before approaching the books published in 1974, two European volumes from earlier years need to be mentioned. Kristian Smidt's *The Importance of Recognition: Six Chapters on T. S. Eliot* (Tromsø: Peder Norbye, 1973) concentrates in part on the major poems (*The Waste Land*; "Journey of the Magi" and *Ash-Wednesday*; *Four Quartets*) in terms of the recognition of pattern, of allusion, and of experience, respectively. Two chapters on Eliot's drama discuss the theories behind his dramatic output and the influence of Ibsen. The final chapter is on Eliot, Yeats, and their mutual influence. Smidt on Ibsen is convincing, especially the indebtedness of *Murder in the Cathedral* to *The Pretenders* and *The Family Reunion* to *Rosmersholm* and *John Gabriel Borkman*. In *Mythos-Neuplatonismus-Mystik: Studien zur Gestaltung des Alkestisstoffes* (Munich: Wilhelm Goldmann, 1972), Ortwin Kuhn devotes a very long chapter to *The Cocktail Party* and its relation to Euripides' *Alcestis*, Robert Browning's *Balaustion's Adventure*, A. W. Verdall's *Euripides the Rationalist* (1885), the psychological theories of C. G. Jung, and the idealism of F. H. Bradley. The last section ("Weltanschauung und Literaturkritik") is especially acute on Eliot's conversion and his "tragisches Lebensgefühl."

Seven more recent volumes made a variety of contributions to the scholarship on Eliot, few of them indispensable. The general criticism first. The subject of Mowbray Allan's *T. S. Eliot's Impersonal Theory of Poetry* (Lewisburg, Pa.: Bucknell Univ. Press) is Eliot's critical thought, not his taste or his "judgments on specific writers." In six chapters he analyzes the fundamental terms in Eliot's critical vocabulary: point of view, thought and sensation, self-consciousness, object, personality, and form, as well as the concepts "objective correlative" and "dissociation of sensibility." He leans heavily on F. H. Bradley because he tries to prove that Eliot's critical thought derived from an idealist theory of knowledge, but Allan also pays close attention to the influence of Arnold, Babbitt, and de Gourmount with a glance at Hume and Hegel. He succeeds in focusing attention on the definition of these terms rather than the multiple examples he could have excerpted from the body of Eliot's prose, but he does so, of course, at the risk of not supplying the supporting evidence some readers will demand. The book is not nearly so acute as recent work by Allen Austin, John D. Margolis, Marion Montgomery, and Bernard Bergonzi; but for the general reader he clarifies what Eliot meant by certain terms he used and reused in the light of traditional philosophic usage, the poet's own beliefs, and especially his changes of emphasis throughout his critical career.

Thomas R. Rees hopes to "prove that the technical methods used in Eliot's poetry, however dissimilar from traditional English poetic style, particularly in regard to prosody, conform rigorously to a system of aesthetic principles common to all arts." *The Technique of T. S. Eliot: A Study of the Orchestration of Meaning in Eliot's Poetry* (The Hague: Mouton) moves from Eliot's Harvard "apprenticeship" poems through *The Waste Land* (the longest chapter) to *Four Quartets*, all of it methodical and predictable, not to say tautological ("When Prufrock says 'There will be time,' he is postponing the need to make a great decision"). Mr. Rees has a good ear and is intent on showing us how Eliot's music builds desired effects, but this book's concern with the objective/subjective stance and the eclecticism arguments comes late in the growing volume of critical studies of Eliot's poetry.

Two volumes from Europe are more limited in scope but far more perceptive in their critical judgments. Heinz Wetzel's *Banale Vitalität und lähmendes Erkennen: Drei vergleichende Studien zu T. S. Eliots "The Waste Land"* (Bern und Frankfurt: Herbert Lang) does not offer a systematic interpretation of *The Waste Land* but investigates instead a theme at the heart of the poem: "the casual connection between triviality and life on the one hand and sterility and knowledge on the other." The first essay ("The Prophet and the Spring") uses as a point of departure Tonio Kröger's conversation with the artist Lisabeta Ivanovna over Adalbert, the novelist, and his argument that "[spring] is and always has been the most ghastly time of the year." A knowledge of Tonio's dilemmas is vital to an understanding of this essay. The second ("The Art of Allusion") confines itself to lines 196–206 in "The Fire Sermon" with an emphasis, naturally, on John Day, Andrew Marvell, Ovid, Verlaine, and Wagner. The third and longest piece, devoted to tracing the influence of Joyce's *Ulysses* on the poem, relies heavily on the original manuscript edited by Mrs. Eliot for publication in 1971. Alessandro Serpieri's *T. S. Eliot: Le Strutture Profonde* (Bologna: Il Mulino), is also a collection of essays, moving from *Prufrock and Other Observations* through *Four Quartets*. Serpieri borrows his subtitle, "deep structures," from Noam Chomsky's writings on transformational grammar; opens his book with a "study

of the functionalism of the images: Eliot's metaphysical arabesque";
and then approaches the poetry directly, devoting about a third of
his pages to *The Waste Land*, trying to demonstrate by close reading
Eliot's shift from the mythic method to the allegorical. The reader
needs some knowledge of structuralism and phenomenology to follow
Serpieri's arguments, but he is repaid several fold by the cogency of
the prose, the author's wide reading, and his poetic imagination, especially in the section on *Four Quartets* called "the flight of time."

Two books from England will be helpful to teachers of Eliot especially. A new edition of B. C. Southam, *A Student's Guide to the
Selected Poems of T. S. Eliot* (London: Faber) is "designed to eluci-
date one particular kind of difficulty—the special problems of meaning which face the reader immediately, on the very surface of the
poems." The book, admittedly indebted to Grover Smith's *T. S. Eliot's
Poetry and Plays*, treats *Prufrock and Other Observations* (1917)
through the Ariel Poems and Choruses from *The Rock* (1934). Nevill
Coghill's edition of *The Cocktail Party* (London: Faber) adds to a
reprint of the text some comments on the play taken from the author's
private correspondence, a set of notes (factual, referential, interpretive), and a lively essay on the structure and meaning of the play.
"Although in some monumental yet admirable way," Coghill argues,
"*Murder in the Cathedral* must be rated as Eliot's greatest dramatic
masterpiece, I prefer the spanking allegro of *The Cocktail Party*
which takes his problems in holiness out of the Church in order to
show them to us in our comparatively godless daily lives, where we
need not keep straight faces for more than a brief moment." Coghill
is especially good on the language of the play, admitting early on
"that [although] the lines are written in verses [it] does not mean
that they are staking a claim to be considered as 'poetry.' "

Linda W. Wagner's *T. S. Eliot: A Collection of Criticism* (New
York: McGraw-Hill) reprints nine essays, six of which were origi-
nally published since 1969. The earliest is Pound's note on the 1917
Prufrock volume, first published in *Poetry* (1917), then Arthur Miz-
ener's essay from *Sewanee Review*, "To Meet Mr. Eliot" (1957), and
Leonard Unger's discussion of *Ash-Wednesday* and "The Hollow
Men" (1966). More recent work is Bernard Bergonzi on the early
poems, M. L. Rosenthal on "*The Waste Land* as an Open Structure,"
Daniel R. Schwarz on the unity of "Gerontion," and William T.
Moynihan in a lengthy discussion, "Character and Action in *Four*

Quartets," in which he argues that "there are few, if any, ideas in the *Quartets* which are not in the *Choruses* [from *The Rock*]" but "the *Quartets* presents both the speaker in the act of recalling his experience of life and the emotional effect of that recalling." The volume concludes with Katharine Worth's essay on Eliot and the "living theater" and Dame Helen Gardner's brief overview of the poet's career in which she feels that "the literary historians of the future, however they rank Eliot among the English poets, will have to speak of the years between the two wars as 'The Age of Eliot.' . . . I cannot believe that future ages . . . will not respect in Eliot's poetry the voice of the conscience of civilized man speaking out of an age of anxiety and despair, and that even those who reject the formulations of his faith will not respond to the accent of faith, and honor him as a man and a poet who chose not to despair."

d. **Criticism: Contributions to Books.** In a 46-page chapter in *A Common Sky: Philosophy and the Literary Imagination* (Berkeley: Univ. of Calif. Press), A. D. Nuttall concentrates on Eliot's doctoral dissertation on F. H. Bradley (he is chiefly concerned with Eliot's conversion from Bradleian idealism to Christianity) but also branches out to perceptive commentary on Arnold, Browning, William James, Graham Greene, and Sartre without ever forgetting the major residue of Eliot's reading: the poetry. Several of Nuttall's obiter dicta are delightfully startling, coming as they do from an English philosopher: "[Eliot] is no more an Englishman than Milton was a Greek"; "Both [Eliot and Henry James] are suckers for refinement"; "I suspect that the anti-semitism which notoriously recurs in the poetry of Eliot (than whom few men were less anti-semitic) is in substance almost rhetorical"; "But the tradition to which Eliot belongs is precisely that of romanticism"; "Almost from the first his poetry was marked by a hunger for God." This is a stimulating chapter in a book about "solipsistic fear" and "the story of [its] rise, obvious in philosophy, less obvious perhaps in literature." George A. Panichas writes with equal verve on Eliot and D. H. Lawrence in a chapter of *The Reverent Discipline: Essays in Literary Criticism and Culture* (Knoxville: Univ. of Tenn. Press). A self-styled "generalist critic and a Christian Humanist," he takes his title from Lawrence's belief that "the critic, like a good beadle, should rap the public on the knuckles and make it attend during divine service. And any good book is divine service."

He recalls that Eliot found Lawrence culturally rootless, without a sense of history, trapped by a "romanticism of despair," able to attain "only a religion of autotherapy," in short, a "heretic." Lawrence thought Eliot's "classiosity" all "bunkum, but still more cowardice," and thought the man was "like a beautifully carved skeleton—no blood, no guts, no marrow, no flesh." Yet Panichas argues that "an underlying sympathy of religious vision ultimately unites the two." They were our two major apocalyptists, and he points to *Women in Love* (1920) and *The Waste Land* (1922) "as 'dramatic poems' containing a presentation of 20th-century European civilization." In contrast, the chapter called "Poetry and Thought" in Joachim Ritter's *Subjektivität* (Frankfurt: Suhrkamp) is modest in its assertions and philosophic in its approach. Ritter sees the theme of Eliot's poetry in its "infusing an Otherness into the ordinary aspects of human experience. The sense of the 'other' is dissolved in the images and symbols which are not to be identified or grasped directly but inform common elements of life with this special sense of their otherness . . . [for example] winter sun on the ice, rose and yew tree, the time between midnight and dawn, the burnt city, ash on the sleeve of an old man's coat." Ritter does not argue for reading Eliot as a romantic, however, but as a poet of "stern sobriety" who "preserves the eternal meanings and associations which a rational reality has dispossessed."

e. **Criticism: Articles.**   Since *The Arizona Quarterly* (30:5–94) is an entire issue devoted to Eliot, it is as good a place as any to begin. Of the four short pieces, two stand out. Nancy D. Hargrove's "Landscape as Symbol in T. S. Eliot's *Ash-Wednesday*" (pp. 53–62) argues that in all six sections—the fertile garden, the desert garden, the stair or pathway, the serene garden, the coast of New England, and the rocky solitary landscape—the landscape symbolizes "the arduousness of the spiritual ascent as well as the final joy which awaits the determined soul." Marion Montgomery's "The Awful Daring: The Self-Surrendered in *The Waste Land*" (pp. 43–52) reads the poem as "an elegy for the self, for the old man that must be put off on the authority of Paul . . . St. Paul describes a condition of surrender, requiring no less than everything." He also reads "Gerontion" as "a summary of the burden of self-knowledge the journey of *The Waste Land* expands upon." The two longer essays are Audrey T. Rodgers's "The Mythic Perspective of Eliot's 'The Dry Salvages'" (pp. 74–94), which sees the poem as "a record of man's alienation from a life-giving source, here in the symbol of the water" (what most men have to learn is that "sacrifice is the route to spiritual salvation," not divination, depth psychology or palliative drugs) and F. Peter Dzwonkoski's "'The Hollow Men' and *Ash-Wednesday*: Two Dark Nights" (pp. 16–42) in which he expands Montgomery's concern with time in *The Waste Land* to the earlier *Ash-Wednesday* where the persona moves toward "the attainment of a health of spirit which enables him to desire time-lessness while still existing in time."

Three articles on *The Waste Land* investigate quite diverse sub-jects. In "*The Waste Land* Manuscript" (*AL* 45:557–70), Lyndall Gordon traces the growth of the poem through all the stages of its composition by grouping the fragments according to the different batches of paper Eliot used and then establishing a chronological order by a variety of other clues. These clues are ingeniously de-scribed (especially "The Death of Saint Narcissus" and "London") and lend credence to Gordon's argument that when Eliot wove a first draft out of a "hoard of fragments" he intended his poem to be "a dirge for aspects of [his own] identity that he had lost [during the previous decade]." At Lausanne he "shifted the emphasis from per-sonal case history to cultural disease" and as a consequence he had to "rewrite his saint's life in more explicit terms in *Ash-Wednesday* and *Four Quartets*." An important article. Marjorie Donker's "*The Waste Land* and the *Aeneid*" (*PMLA* 89:164–73) assembles quantities of shared themes in the two poems: mythic configuration, initiation pat-tern, war and loss, memories of a sea voyage, the desert, a "lost girl," fire as a symbol for both purgation and lust. Marion Perret's "Eliot, the Naked Lady, and the Missing Link" (*AL* 46:289–303) concen-trates on John Day's *The Parliament of Bees* and lines 187–206 of "The Fire Sermon."

Two charming articles, both brief, could well be prologomena for longer treatments of their subjects. Audrey T. Rodgers's "Dance Imagery in the Poetry of T. S. Eliot" (*Criticism* 16:23–38) sees an insistent pattern of opposites in the poems: "the dance as a ritual of transcendence, a symbol of unity, a celebration of human and cosmic harmony on the one hand; and, on the other, a symbolic *danse maca-bre*—the rhythmic gestures of futility that constitute activity in the modern world." She leads us to a little-known Eliot poem, "The Death of Saint Narcissus," as well as "Portrait of a Lady," *Ash-Wednesday,* and "East Coker." James Rother's "Modernism and the Nonsense Style" (*ConL* 15:187–202) talks of Eliot's debt to Lewis Carroll, notably in *The Waste Land*, and the poet's attempt to "counterfeit" reality, that is, to use linguistic formulae as something more familiar to us than "either the world we know from within or the world we guess at from without." Rother is fascinating on what he calls Eliot's "moog" eclecticism, the mixing of sounds (inflectional idiosyncrasies of personal speech) in order to create a synthesis, "a generalized dialect of Anglo-American civilization."

Two long articles on the poetry, both by Barbara Everett, appeared in *Critical Quarterly* 16. Both could stand cutting, but they are rich with insight and take their subjects very seriously indeed. "In Search of Prufrock" (pp. 101–21) insists that the poem began as exploration though it may have ended as "love song." "The primary impression is not at all one of unifying mood and theme . . . but of a variegated collection of passing thoughts and feelings, all stamped with one style; and that style is not the style of tragic satire. Prufrock wants . . . to go for a walk around the evening city." Ms. Everett then searches for new sources, and uncovers Turgenev's "The Diary of a Superfluous Man," the cheerful comedy of a *Punch* serial called *The Diary of a Nobody*, Whitman's "Song of the Open Road," Dante's 26th Canto, and the "peculiar mimetic rhythmical skills of W. S. Gilbert." "A Visit to Burnt Norton" (pp. 199–224) is less ingenious but equally iconoclastic. Her reading of the poem insists that we look closely at the opening movement as "an experience of terror," and she explicates the lines in terms of ghost story, a genre which leads her to the obvious Henry James, the less likely Charles Dickens (Dr. Manette's house in *A Tale of Two Cities*), and then back to Eliot's own poems, notably "The Death of Saint Narcissus," "East Coker," and "Little Gidding."

Three essays on Eliot as dramatist cover familiar ground but still deserve mentioning. In "Eliot's *The Cocktail Party*: Comic Perspective as Salvation" (*MD* 17:301–06), Gary T. Davenport sees Eliot reconciling "two seemingly incompatible elements: high moral seriousness and 'light' comedy in the Noel Coward idiom." The salvation of such a character as Edward depends directly on "sustaining a comic overview of life and a sense of [his] own potential absurdity." In a far more ambitious article, "T. S. Eliot's Plays and the Tradition of 'High Comedy'" (*CritQ* 16:127–40), P. G. Mudford traces the last four plays not only to the obvious Greek sources but also to the large tradition of "high comedy" we know in such work as *A Midsummer Night's Dream, The Marriage of Figaro, L'Avare, The Dunciad, Don Juan,* and *Pickwick Papers.* Yet he sees Eliot's extension of the tradition of high comedy as a qualified success, particularly in *The Elder Statesman.* John Cutts's study of the Becket play, "Evidence for Ambivalence of Motives in *Murder in the Cathedral*" (*CompD* 8:199–210) concentrates wholly on the main character. Becket's sermon "marks his conscious manipulation of orthodoxy to suit his own purposes and betrays his 'delight' in the paradox of his situation." In opening the doors of the church, he admits "men who are slightly tipsy with drink" and thus "*commands* his own martyrdom." In the midst of this martyrdom, Cutts argues, "Christ's forgiveness of his enemies is totally lacking."

The last group of critical articles is devoted, for the most part, to Eliot's reading, his prose, and his relationship to other writers. Ronald Schuchard's careful reproduction of the syllabi of Eliot's lectures in Yorkshire, Southall, and Sydenham under the auspices of Oxford University and the University of London shows "how thorough was Eliot's grounding in French and English literature, literary criticism, social and intellectual currents, moral and philosophical attitudes, political and economic theories" ("T. S. Eliot as an Extension Lecturer, 1916–1919" [*RES* 25:164–73, 292–304]). Two pieces by Marion Montgomery need enlarging to make a wholly convincing argument, but they are nevertheless important. In "Eliot and the Particle Physicist: The Merging of Two Cultures" (*SoR* 10: 583–89), he notes that the year before Eliot published *For Lancelot Andrewes,* Werner Heisenberg propounded his "Principle of Uncertainty" which holds it "impossible to determine both the position and the velocity of an electron at the same time." In six pages Montgomery tries to discuss the ramifications of particle physics in philosophy and religion. Unfortunately he seems more concerned with Wyndham Lewis, *Science News,* and Ezra Pound than with Eliot's poetry as a source of a future merger. In "Eliot's Autobiography" (*IllQ* 37:57–64), Montgomery is also easily sidetracked. He tries to demonstrate that Eliot's strictures against a future biography are unimportant because he has already written it in his essays, beginning with "Tradition and the Individual Talent" (1919) and ending with "To Criticize the Critic" (1961). But Montgomery then be-

comes embroiled in such problems as the rise of criticism in the 19th
century, the dislocation of the poet from society, Edmund Burke's
theory of aesthetics, and Eliot's reaction to Poe, Baudelaire, and the
English Romantics. James Torrens, S.J., concentrates on the influence
of one Frenchman on Eliot's intellectual growth ("Charles Maurras
and Eliot's 'New Life'" [*PMLA* 89:312–21]) and reminds us that
Maurras's daily newspaper, *L'Action Française*, declared early in the
20th century that its program would be *classique, catholique,* and
monarchique. Eliot dedicated his study of Dante to Maurras (1929),
defended him in the pages of *The Criterion* (1928), and, Torrens
believes, was eventually "at the point of thinking of Maurras as his
Virgil leading [him] into the world of Dante." The "new life" was
"the recovery of that ancient harmony that existed before the Fall."
After *Ash-Wednesday* and his move toward the plays and *Four
Quartets,* the tutelage of Dante grew and that of Maurras receded.
Graham Hough's article ("Dante and Eliot" *CritQ* 16:293–305) is
the right complement to Torrens's last sentences. Hough believes that
Eliot's long Dante essay of 1929 is likely to remain "the clearest path
to Dante for an English reader" and that as we come to understand
how he employed Dante's words in his own poetry, "we see them as
briefly opened doorways into a whole imaginative world." Hough
calls this "cultural blood-transfusion—the importing of a whole order
of feeling from a different civilisation," an operation which Eliot
"repeatedly performs, with great richness and subtlety." Explication
is not Hough's intent here; he discusses assimilation, slow conversion,
inconsistencies, Eliot's fears that poetry might become a substitute
religion, his great reliance on Santayana, and much more. One hopes
this delightful essay will be reprinted.

   Two others in this final group are worthy of reprinting, but for
quite different reasons. James Smith, professor emeritus at the University of Fribourg, died before the appearance of his "Notes on the
Criticism of T. S. Eliot" (*EIC* 22[1972]:333–61). Editor F. W. Bate-
son calls it "perhaps the very best article this journal has published
in its twenty-two years' life." Smith's attack is among the most vehement Eliot's criticism has suffered. He compares Eliot to Hobbes,
marking their power over words but also "an integrity or pig-
headedness—choose which word you will—which drives them to
apply theories to facts which cannot do other than shatter the theories." Smith decries the validity of Eliot's concept of "the objective

correlative" and "dissociation of sensibility," his "nefarious theory of organic wholes" (particularly in relation to Shakespeare), his "minimal acquaintance with what Englishmen wrote in medieval times," and concludes by calling his prose "a huge gallimaufry," the work of a man Smith felt was inept, impercipient, sarcastic, arrogant, and preposterous. The charges are substantiated at length. At equal length George A. Panichas's "T. S. Eliot and the Critique of Liberalism" (*ModA* 18:145–62) defends the social criticism as the work of "one of the great modern prophets." He thinks Eliot's contribution to the critique of modern liberalism has been "misunderstood and misrepresented as an example of 'right-wing millenialism'" because "he refused to accept indiscriminatingly the view that cultural change is the law of life." For Eliot overcentralization and uprootedness embody "the two most rife conditions of this century's cultural malady," and his rejection of liberalism as "the wave of the future" was incontrovertible. With telling results, Panichas places John Dewey's *Liberalism and Social Action* (1935) next to Eliot's *After Strange Gods* (1934), then moves on to contrast Dewey's *Freedom and Culture* (1939) with Eliot's *The Idea of a Christian Society* (1939), repositories of even less reconcilable viewpoints. In disparaging liberalism, Panichas argues, Eliot did not necessarily embrace the new Humanism, chiefly because he felt Irving Babbitt like Matthew Arnold risked usurping the place of revealed religion. Only in what Jacques Maritain called *humanisme intégral*, humanism with a "metaphysics of transcendence," could man hope to find a genuine spiritual ally in the war against liberalism. "There is a sense," Eliot wrote in 1941, "in which wisdom that is not Christian turns to folly." Religious sensibility is the "cement" our culture so desperately needs, not the anodynes of scientific liberalism. Panichas has opened old wounds here, but he is clearly the man to debride, not bandage, them.

Princeton University

9. Faulkner

Karl F. Zender

i. Bibliography, Editions, and Manuscripts

The disappointment over the editing of *Flags in the Dust* (New York: Random House [1973]) continued in 1974 with the appearance of the paperback edition (New York: Random House, Vintage Books). This edition contains a completely reset text, and a brief comparison with the hardbound text indicates that a number of typographical errors have been corrected. So much to the good. But the paperbound edition is not newly edited, and it reprints without alteration Douglas Day's inadequate and misleading introduction. In a rather acrimonious reply to Thomas McHaney's strictures on the introduction and text of the hardbound edition (*FCN* 2[1973]:7–8; discussed in *ALS 1973*, p. 135), Albert Erskine, Vice-President and Editorial Director at Random House, argues that "Random House is not, should not be and does not intend to be a competitor of the EETS [Early English Text Society]" (*FCN* 3:2–3). This is a position with which one may have considerable sympathy. Faulkner is a major figure in our cultural heritage, and his work should be made available, even if imperfectly, to the widest possible audience in moderately priced editions. But it is difficult to understand why the implication that only "nonsubstantive alterations in spelling and punctuation have been made" is allowed to stand unaltered in the

Editor's note: I am very much indebted to my colleague Karl Zender, who stepped in at the last moment to write this chapter when the expected version failed to materialize. I also wish to thank Louise Schleiner for writing a notice of Dieter Meindl's *Bewusstsein als Schicksal*, which is included in Section *iii*. Finally, I must correct an error that appeared in Professor Meriwether's Faulkner chapter last year. In a quotation from an article by Nancy Norris (*Mosaic* 7,i: 213–35), *ALS 1973* on p. 147 reads as follows: ". . . 'the combination of letters' in the last name of Labove 'suggests the separation of "love" by "Ab," a man characterized earlier in *The Hamlet* as [angered at] having been beaten at horse trading.'" The words in square brackets were omitted from *ALS*.

introduction to the paperback edition, when Erskine himself admits
that much larger editorial changes were required by the condition of
the typescript of *Flags*. As matters now stand, we have an inexpensive
text of *Flags in the Dust* for classroom use. This is a cause for joy, but
also for caution.

A *Faulkner Miscellany*, edited by James Meriwether (Jackson:
Univ. Press of Miss.), reprints a number of items by Faulkner that
were first published in *MissQ* (26[1973]; see *ALS 1973* for a description and discussion of these items). This book also prints for the first
time three other items of some textual interest. In "New Material for
Faulkner's *Intruder in the Dust*" (pp. 107–12), Patrick Samway, S.J.,
reproduces and discusses a letter from Faulkner to Robert Haas containing a revision of Gavin Stevens's "Sambo" speech that Faulkner
wished to include in any subsequent printings of the novel. The other
two items, of lesser interest, are Meriwether's presentation and discussion of the text Faulkner wrote for the World War II monument in
Oxford (pp. 105–106), and his reproduction of the Spanish text (together with Muna Lee's translation) of Faulkner's speech of acceptance for the Andres Bello award, given him in Caracas in 1961 (pp.
164–66). In the annual Faulkner issue of *MissQ* (27), Meriwether
reprints two further items. "Faulkner's 'Ode to the Louver'" (pp.
333–35) is of some interest. It reproduces a comic poem, together
with a cover letter signed by "Ernest V. Simms," sent by Faulkner to
Phil Stone from Paris in the fall of 1925. The second item, of less significance, is "Faulkner's Speech at the Teatro Municipal, Caracas, in
1961" (p. 337).

Meriwether is also responsible for the only recent work of bibliographic interest other than the standard ones published by the MLA
and *American Literature*. The "Supplement" section of his essay on
Faulkner in *Sixteen Modern American Authors*, ed. Jackson R. Bryer
(Durham: Duke Univ. Press [1973], pp. 258–75), carries his extremely useful survey of scholarship and criticism forward through
1972, with occasional reference to reviews appearing in 1973. Both
the original essay, which first appeared in *Fifteen Modern American Authors* (Durham: Duke Univ. Press [1969]), and the supplement are well informed, judicious, and wide-ranging. They deserve
greater use than the quality of much recent scholarship on Faulkner
indicates the original essay to have received.

ii. Biography

The most important event of the year—indeed, of the history of Faulkner studies—was the appearance of Joseph Blotner's long-awaited *William Faulkner: A Biography*, 2 vols. (New York: Random House). The book was worth the wait. Massive in intention and in accomplishment, it chronicles with an incredible wealth of detail the course of Faulkner's life and career. It rectifies errors and illuminates what was formerly obscure. On matters as widely divergent as Faulkner's marriage, his Hollywood career, his relations with his literary contemporaries, his reading, his travels, and the genesis, revision, and publication of his fiction, Blotner shows us whole and clear what we have too often known only in fragment or in error.

This is not to say that the work is without either its drawbacks or its detractors. A book as large as this one, taking a dozen years to complete, and relying to an unprecedented degree on oral interviews with acquaintances and colleagues of its subject, will inevitably contain errors of fact and of judgment. Blotner's book contains a high number of them, in the transcription of quotations from Faulkner's work, in the footnoting of sources, and in the arrangement and presentation of its data. The nature and something of the extent of these errors are detailed in James Meriwether's review-essay, "Blotner's *Faulkner*" (*MissQ* 28[1975]:353–69). Anyone interested in the biography would be well advised to consult this detailed essay. (I should note in passing an error in one of Meriwether's corrections of Blotner. Surely it is Flem Snopes—not, as Meriwether says, Lump Snopes—whom Ratliff imagines having sex in exchange for sardines in *The Hamlet*.)

More than errors of fact, a central problem in judgment distressed the early reviewers of Blotner's biography. It is not fair to say that it is a book without an idea, but it is true that Blotner mainly eschews any attempt to interpret the shape and significance of Faulkner's career, and the interrelationship of his life and art, in favor of a chronicle rendering the events of that life. Unfortunately the disavowal of interpretation is incomplete: it slips in the side door, in embarrassingly unsophisticated forms. This is the substance of David Littlejohn's criticism in "How Not to Write a Biography" (*NewRep* 23 March:25–27), and I think that it is in the main an accurate one.

It is hardly instructive to see Blotner repeatedly discuss Faulkner's alcoholism merely as an escape from social obligation or as an anodyne for physical pain. Nor is it instructive to see him rely on "shyness" as a categorical explanation for many of the mysterious, and frequently cruel, aspects of Faulkner's behavior. The present state of knowledge concerning the human personality is more advanced than Blotner's gestures toward analysis and interpretation would seem to imply.

Perhaps I am only saying that ideally one might prefer a biography of Faulkner on the order of Edel on Henry James. But given the present state of the Faulkner scholarship, the time perhaps has not yet come for such a study. What we most need now are accurate dates, accurate records of events, accurate renderings of Faulkner's personal and professional relationships. To a great extent, this is what Blotner has given us. But even when the book is viewed as a chronicle biography, there are occasional grounds for disquietude. Something—either his personal adulation for his subject, or the fact that many of Faulkner's relatives and acquaintances are still living—has led Blotner into curious discretions and evasions, especially in the area of Faulkner's sexual life. As David Minter points out in "Faulkner and the Uses of Biography" (*GaR* 28:455–63), "There is no way . . . to justify devoting several pages to the history of New Orleans and but a few lines to Estelle Faulkner's highly theatrical attempt to drown herself in the Gulf of Mexico on a honeymoon following a long-delayed marriage." Some questions are simply not asked, some answers not given.

Still though, much is asked and much is given, and for what Blotner provides we should be grateful. Whatever its defects of interpretation and presentation, Blotner's biography will do what few works of scholarship can be said to do: it will change the course of the study of its subject for the foreseeable future. It is quite a remarkable achievement.

Beside Blotner's book, the year's other biographical items are only of ephemeral interest. James Dahl's "A Faulkner Reminiscence: Conversations with Mrs. Maud Falkner" (*JML* 3:1026–30) provides some slight insight into the character of Faulkner's mother in her later years. Malcolm Franklin, Faulkner's stepson, has published an excerpt from a projected book of reminiscences of his stepfather. The excerpt, entitled "A Christmas in Columbus" (*MissQ* 27:319–

22), recounts a visit in 1930 or 1931 with the Franklin family, but contains nothing of interest on Faulkner. Also of little interest is Murry C. Falkner's "The Coming of the Motor Car" (*SoR* 10:170–80), a highly romanticized account of the first automobiles in Oxford. Falkner tells us little that we did not already know from John B. Cullen's *Old Times in the Faulkner Country*. Thomas Inge's "The Virginia Face of Faulkner" (*Virginia Cavalcade* 24,i:32–39) is a popularized account of Faulkner's visit to the Southern Writers' Conference in 1931 and of his tenure as writer-in-residence at the University of Virginia.

iii. Criticism: General

a. **Books.** Panthea Broughton in *William Faulkner: The Abstract and the Actual* (Baton Rouge: La. State Univ. Press) has written the one important book-length study of the year. She brings a fresh and engaging intelligence to bear on Faulkner's fiction. Although her title would seem to promise another in the series of studies praising Faulkner's discovery of his own "little postage stamp" of concrete subject matter and condemning (or excusing) his use of abstraction in his later fiction, her emphasis is actually rather different. Broughton sees, as some Faulkner critics do not, the necessity as well as the danger of the human impulse toward abstraction. She thus examines the use of abstraction by Faulkner's characters and by Faulkner himself *in propria persona* not only as a way of evading reality but as a way of ordering and comprehending it. This is to the good, for it provides a basis for a sympathetic understanding of characters and works too often devalued or ignored. But when Broughton turns from theory to practical criticism, some problems arise that limit the usefulness of her study. She demands "authenticity" of response both to experience and to abstraction from Faulkner's characters before she will view them sympathetically, but her standards of measure for this quality are so rigorous as to seem almost puritanical. (Given the prominence of the term "authenticity" in Broughton's critical vocabulary, it is odd that she does not mention Lionel Trilling's *Sincerity and Authenticity*, a major work on the subject.) The leading heroes (and heroine) of her aesthetic are Lucius Priest in *The Reivers*, the runner in *A Fable*, Harry Wilbourne in *The Wild Palms*, and Judith Sutpen in *Absalom, Absalom!*—a pale cast in comparison with the "inauthentic" others. A less rigorous application of her theory, one that would view sympathetically such characters as Lucas Beauchamp in *Go Down, Moses,* Labove and Jack Houston in *The Hamlet,* and Mink Snopes in *The Mansion,* would be welcome. Nevertheless Broughton's book exhibits a needed break with the old clichés about Faulkner's use of abstraction, and points toward (even if it does not fully achieve) a new aesthetic for his fiction.

Dieter Meindl's *Bewusstsein als Schicksal: Zu Struktur und Entwicklung von William Faulkners Generationenromanen* (Stuttgart: Metzler), though not as valuable as Broughton's book, is still a worthwhile study. Defining a *generationenroman* as a novel depicting a central figure in relation to the dead founder of his family, Meindl inspects *Sartoris, Absalom, Absalom!* and *Go Down, Moses.* He detects a movement toward increasing awareness on the part of the central character of the significance of his ancestral past, but his study as a whole suffers from excessive schematization, and draws some odd conclusions about the nature of Ike McCaslin's relationship with the wilderness.

Faulkner's Indians have long been a neglected aspect of his fiction. Lewis Dabney, in *The Indians of Yoknapatawpha* (Baton Rouge: La. State Univ. Press), does little to overcome this neglect. Dabney has a good, even if underdeveloped, idea in his suggestion that Faulkner presents master-slave relationships between Indians and blacks with a clarity of judgment not to be found when these relationships involve whites and blacks. But this idea alone cannot compensate for the book's other deficiencies. It exhibits only rudimentary command of scholarly and critical method, and it is frequently incoherent. At one point, in an altered version of Allen Tate's analogy, Dabney describes the whites in "Lo!" as "upstart Greeks" and the Indians as "older, more civilized Trojans." But in the next paragraph he says that "these Trojans" are "people who would drown you in a swimming race, who leave bones on your rug," a statement which seems to make nonsense out of the analogy. At another point, Dabney speaks of "a scene which both reasserts and parodies the traditions of chivalry and valor," but does not say how this is possible. At yet another point he says that *Death in the Afternoon* "appeared two years before 'Red Leaves' " when he must mean that it appeared two years after. Examples of such failures in exposition and in critical and scholarly method are distressingly frequent in this book.

Even more bothersome are the difficulties Dabney has in dealing with the order of composition of the Indian stories. Following Cowley, he asserts that the Indian materials form a sub-chronicle within the Yoknapatawpha saga. He acknowledges that the stories were not written in the order of the events they depict. He acknowledges as well that when Faulkner came to republish them in the *Collected Stories* he did not arrange them in their chronicle order. Yet he treats the stories and *Go Down, Moses* in the order of their depicted events, with the result that he frequently loses sight of the order of composition. Thus, when Dabney says of "Red Leaves" that "this is Faulkner's last vision of the Indian within a basically Indian society," we must puzzle over the ambiguity of the phrase "Faulkner's last vision." "Red Leaves" is the "last vision" only in the order of depicted events; it is the first Indian story that Faulkner wrote. Three of Faulkner's later "visions"—the other three Indian stories—deal with earlier and hence more "basically Indian" societies. Faced with such confusion, I can only conclude that Faulkner's Indians still await serious study.

Two studies of varying merit consider Faulkner's work in relation to the doubtful future of the novel as a form. Alvin Seltzer, in *Chaos in the Novel—The Novel in Chaos* (New York: Schocken Books), insists with apocalyptical shrillness on the imminent demise of the novel. Concentrating mainly on the fiction of the 1930s, he sees Faulkner as a writer who is only barely able to contain chaos within aesthetic form. This view has a venerable history, but few recent adherents. Seltzer does not document his critical indebtednesses, but he seems to have been influenced by nothing more recent than Walter Slatoff's *Quest for Failure*. In *Vision and Response in Modern Fiction* (Ithaca: Cornell Univ. Press), Arnold Weinstein takes a similarly pessimistic view of the future of the novel, but he informs it with intelligence and a refined and subtle sensibility. Because he discusses only *The Sound and the Fury*, and *Absalom, Absalom!* among Faulkner's novels, his treatment of these works will be discussed in sections *v* and *vi* below.

b. **Articles.** Little of general significance appeared in article form during the year. Joseph Trimmer, in "V. K. Ratliff: A Portrait of the Artist in Motion" (*MFS* 20:451–67), provides a welcome reminder of the importance to Ratliff of aesthetic considerations in his "Snopes watching." His assertion that Ratliff is "symbolic of Faulkner's conception of the role of the artist" is most convincing when it is applied to *The Town*, least convincing when it is applied to *The Hamlet*. Richard Reed's "The Role of Chronology in Faulkner's Yoknapatawpha Fiction" (*SLJ* 7,i:24–48) labors the obvious. It adds nothing new to our understanding of the chronology or of its inconsistencies, which seem to bother Reed overly much. He exhibits uncertain command of another important chronology—the order of Faulkner's novels—when he says that "*Sartoris* was written after *The Sound and the Fury* but was published before."

Despite its ambitious title, Morse Peckham's "The Place of Sex in the Work of William Faulkner" (*Studies in the 20th Century* 14:1–20) is a casual, error-filled performance by a critic from whom we have come to expect better. Concentrating mainly on *A Fable*, Peckham argues that Faulkner depicts an irreconcilable but humanly necessary tension between illusory idealism and unbearable reality. His inattention to detail extends even to a repeated confusion over the relative valuation Faulkner places on the terms "endure" and "prevail" in the Nobel Prize speech. Glenn O. Carey's "William Faulkner on the Automobile as Socio-Sexual Symbol" (*CEA* 36:15–17) gives brief consideration to scattered passages in which Faulkner views the automobile negatively. Carey ignores the nostalgic image of the automobile in *The Town* and *The Reivers*.

iv. Criticism: Ideas, Influences, Intellectual Background

In "Faulkner's 'The Hill'" (*SLJ* 6,ii:3–18), Michel Gresset subjects an early prose sketch to a careful, patient, and thoroughly convincing examination, and reveals it to contain in embryo a number of long-lived Faulknerian themes and symbolic clusters. This essay is a model of subtlety and sophistication in the study of literary genetics. If Gresset had been aware of "Nympholepsy," a revision and expansion of "The Hill" recently published in *A Faulkner Miscellany* (see section *i*), he would have found additional evidence in support of his already strong argument.

Joan Korenman's "Faulkner's Grecian Urn" (*SLJ* 7,i:3–23) is valuable for its display of the longevity of Faulkner's association of images of still water with refuge from time. But the main thesis—

that Faulkner was attracted to Keats's "Ode" because of its attitude toward time and change—is shopworn. Surely we already know this. The remaining items in this section may be quickly covered. John Ditsky, in " 'Dark, Darker than Fire': Thematic Parallels in Lawrence and Faulkner" (*SHR* 8:497–505), argues for parallels between scenes in *The Rainbow* and scenes in Faulkner's fiction, most notably in *Soldier's Pay* and *As I Lay Dying*. In "*Don Quixote* and Selected Progeny: Or, the Journey-man as Outsider" (*SoR* 10:31–58), Louis D. Rubin, Jr., gives brief consideration to Faulkner's use of "the mock-epic possibilities of the Quixotean journey." Matthew O'Brien's brief note, "Faulkner, General Chalmers, and the Burning of Oxford" (*AN&Q* 12:87–88), argues that Faulkner mistakenly spoke of a "Yankee Brigadier Chalmers" in a letter to the editor of the Oxford *Eagle* because a Confederate brigadier of the same name had demoted his great-grandfather.

v. Individual Works to 1929

Faulkner's first two novels received no independent attention, but I wish to mention again Panthea Broughton's *William Faulkner: The Abstract and the Actual* (section *iii. a*). Broughton's treatment of the discussion of aesthetic theories in *Mosquitoes* affords valuable insight into this neglected work. Michel Gresset's "Faulkner's 'The Hill' " (section *iv*) also deserves mention here, as does William Boozer's *William Faulkner's First Book: "The Marble Faun" Fifty Years Later* (section *x*).

In the absence of an authoritative text of *Flags in the Dust* (section *i*), we need to learn what we can from what we have. This Richard P. Adams begins to do in his review-essay, "At Long Last, *Flags in the Dust*" (*SoR* 10:878–88). He concludes that *Flags* is, as Liveright said, diffuse and disorganized, but he attributes this failure to Faulkner's discovery during the composition of the novel of "the incredible wealth of his . . . material." We do not need to use the appearance of *Flags* as an excuse to rush into print with ill-conceived comparisons between it and *Sartoris*, which is what Patricia Kane does in "The Narcissa Benbow of Faulkner's *Flags in the Dust*" (*NConL* 4,iv:2–3).

Sartoris will undoubtedly continue to receive attention as a part of the Faulkner canon, but it received none of merit in the year under review. In "Faulkner's *Sartoris*: The Tailor Re-Tailored" (*SCR* 6,ii:56–59), Carter Martin makes the unremarkable—and unproven—suggestion that the name "Sartoris" derives from Carlyle's *Sartor Resartus*. (The same suggestion is made independently by Peckham [discussed in section *iii. b*].)

The work on *The Sound and the Fury* is more extensive than that on the earlier novels, but not much more noteworthy. In *Vision and Response in Modern Fiction* (see section *iii. a*), Arnold Weinstein makes a welcome resolution to attend to the sequence of events in the novel, rather than to an abstracted and rearranged chronological sequence. But other than a good explanation of Quentin's "development" toward suicide in the second section of the novel, his reading provides us with little we did not already have; it does not compare in value with his excellent interpretation of *Absalom, Absalom!* (see section *vi*). Donald Messerli's "The Problem of Time in *The Sound and the Fury*: A Critical Reassessment and Reinterpretation" (*SLJ* 6,ii:19–41) is ambitious but thesis-ridden. Messerli provides a good review of previous discussions of the problem of time in the novel, but he objects to these past readings not because of their inaccuracy but because of the unacceptability of their moral and philosophical implications and proposes an alternative based on the phenomenology of Eugene Minkowski.

J. C. Cowan's "Dream-Work in the Quentin Section of *The Sound and the Fury*" (*L&P* 24:91–98) offers nothing new in the way of a Freudian analysis. Cowan makes the odd assumption, surely incorrect, that Caddy owned the first automobile in Jefferson. Denis Murphy's "*The Sound and the Fury* and Dante's *Inferno*: Fire and Ice" (*MarkhamR* 4:71–78) would seem more promising, since one might expect some Dantesque influence on at least the Quentin section of the novel. But despite Murphy's efforts to make a case he exhibits no likely evidence of this influence. Finally, because of a strained effort to discover a parallel between the myth of Agenor and the Compson family in her inappropriately titled "Eliot's 'Tradition' and *The Sound and the Fury*" (*MFS* 20:214–17), Diane Naples provides an inaccurate reading of some of the details, as when she says that "Caddy exhibits herself naked" in the scene at the stream on the night of Damuddy's death.

vi. Individual Works, 1930–1939

As I Lay Dying received no individual attention during the year, and *Sanctuary* received almost none. André Malraux's previously translated preface to *Sanctuary* has been retranslated by Violet Horvath (*SoR* 10:889–91). This preface is important evidence of the nature of the French response to the novel. In "Faulkner's *Sanctuary*: The Last Laugh of Innocence" (*NMW* 6:73–80), Robert Schmuhl ignores the ambiguity and complexity of Faulkner's renderings of idiot figures in order to give undue prominence to Tommy, and to claim that "he represents both goodness and knowledge." The number of typographical errors in this essay (and in many others in *NMW*) is difficult to excuse.

Sally Padgett Wheeler's "Chronology in *Light in August*" (*SLJ* 6,i[1973]:20–42) provides a convenient and, as far as I have checked, accurate chronology for the novel. Wheeler does not cite the previous valuable work done on this subject. Don Graham and Barbara Shaw make a convincing case for Faulkner's indebtedness to "Wesley Everest," an earlier version of the "Paul Bunyan" section of *1919*, in "Faulkner's Small Debt to Dos Passos: A Source for the Percy Grimm Episode" (*MissQ* 27:327–31). The only essay devoted to *Pylon*, Joseph McElrath, Jr.'s "*Pylon*: The Portrait of a Lady" (*MissQ* 27: 277–90), argues persuasively for a more sympathetic view of Laverne Shumann than any found in earlier criticism. She is hardly, however, the center of the novel, as McElrath claims.

Absalom, Absalom! received more attention than any of Faulkner's other novels, some of it of very good quality. Arnold Weinstein's discussion of the novel in *Vision and Response in Modern Fiction* (see section *iii. a*) is especially noteworthy. Weinstein displays convincingly the ways in which both the form and the theme of the novel are designed to engender in the reader an act of passionate identification something like the one that Shreve and Quentin undergo. It is this act, he argues, and not the accuracy or inaccuracy of the discoveries made about the past as a result of it, which is the central concern of the novel. In Weinstein's view—and now in my own—*Absalom, Absalom!* is concerned with how we know and how we love, not with what we know and what we love. A similar study, though more limited in scope and less successful in accomplishment, is John Middleton's "Shreve McCannon and Sutpen's Legacy" (*SoR* 10:115–24). Middleton argues that "as a bystander drawn into what he observes, [Shreve] illustrates the possibility of a reader being vitally affected by a work of fiction." It is unfortunate that Middleton makes this worthwhile suggestion while denying the other functions rightly ascribed to Shreve by Hyatt Waggoner and Cleanth Brooks.

Ralph Behrens's "Collapse of Dynasty: The Thematic Center of *Absalom, Absalom!*" (*PMLA* 89:24–33) is a competent study, but it seems old-fashioned in comparison with Weinstein's book and Middleton's essay. Behrens seems to want one right interpretation, not of the novel, but of Sutpen's "design." To this end he provides a worthwhile review of the major interpretations of the significance of Sutpen's downfall, and then proposes that its meaning can be most completely determined through an inspection of the analogy (implied by the novel's title) with the rise and fall of Biblical dynasties. But Behrens rides the analogy with the house of David quite hard; his interpretation should be read in conjunction with the cautions about the use of this analogy that are voiced by John Hagopian in "The Biblical Background of Faulkner's *Absalom, Absalom!*" (*CEA* 36:22–24).

Harry B. Henderson III provides another useful reading of *Absalom, Absalom!* in *Versions of the Past*. As his title implies, Henderson examines the ways in which American novelists have imagined the past. His chapter on *Absalom, Absalom!* existed only in draft form at the time of his death in an automobile accident, which may account for the presence of occasional obscurities in expression and argument. The chapter nevertheless provides a useful view of Quentin as a figure caught between mutually unacceptable "holistic" and "progressivistic" views of history.

The remaining studies of *Absalom, Absalom!* are of less use. Virginia Hlavsa, in "The Vision of the Advocate in *Absalom, Absalom!*" (*Novel* 8:51–70), argues strenuously but unconvincingly that the novel has the structure of a nine-part trial—the first four of which turn out to be parodies of courtroom uses of evidence, and all nine of which are in composition and order based on no courtroom procedure with which I am familiar. It is depressing that an essay concerned with the rules of law should be so eccentric in its treatment of literary evidence. (By punning on "sutler" and "penitentiary" and taking "hundred" in the sense of "an old English jurisdictional area," Hlavsa interprets "Sutpen's Hundred" to mean "a prison of low commerce"!) In "What Quentin Saw 'Out There'" (*MissQ* 27:323–26), Hershel Parker expends considerable ingenuity in an effort to convince us that Quentin learns the secret of Charles Bon's birth by seeing Jim Bond's physiognomic resemblance to other members of the Sutpen family. Finally, R. S. Kellner's oddly titled "A Reconsideration of Character: Relationships in *Absalom, Absalom!* (*NMW* 7:39–43) may safely be ignored.

vii. Individual Works, 1940–1949

Joseph Trimmer's essay (see section *iii. b*) deserves mention here for its discussion of *The Hamlet*. Almost all of the other significant work for this period deals with *Go Down, Moses*. Walter Taylor, in "Horror and Nostalgia: The Double Perspective of Faulkner's 'Was'" (*SHR* 8:74–84), engages in a welcome attempt to read this story apart from its function in the whole of the novel. But he loads the story with a weight of significance it could hardly bear even if its foreshadowings of later parts of the novel were being taken into account. In "A Hand of Poker: Game and Ritual in Faulkner's 'Was'" (*SSF* 11:53–60), Karl F. Zender examines the conclusion of this same story in terms of the formal requirements of games and of rituals.

Any lingering belief in Marvin Klotz's argument (*AL* 37[1965]: 1–16) that economic considerations motivated Faulkner's revisions of the short story originals of *Go Down, Moses* should be dispelled by Joanne V. Creighton's workmanlike "Revision and Craftsmanship in Faulkner's 'The Fire and the Hearth'" (*SSF* 11:161–72). It is unfortunate that Creighton was unable to round out her competent study by examining the manuscript versions of the unpublished original of the third section of "The Fire and the Hearth." Ike McCaslin, that favorite figure for analysis, surprisingly received only one independent treatment. R. D. Ackerman, in "The Immolation of Isaac McCaslin" (*TSLL* 16:557–65), attempts to revive the conception of Ike as a saint (in his terms, a Tiresias) who dies to the world of civilized corruption and is reborn to a kind of beatific inaction and indifference. The attempt is unsuccessful, partly because of the eagerness with which Ackerman lays seemingly contradictory kinds of "corruption" at the door of civilization. We are told at one point that "Ike's imagination merges with the life-death continuum of nature, ultimate unity instead of division; the *mine-thine*, subject-object basis of civilization will not be the root of his own consciousness." But when Ackerman addresses the famous passage in "Delta Autumn" in which Ike contemplates with horror a world in which *"Chinese and African and Aryan and Jew, all breed and spawn together,"* he sees it as a picture, not of a state of nature, but of a civilized world made up of "distinctionless chaos." Another item to be noted in this section is *Le Blanc et le Noir chez Melville et Faulkner* (see section *x*). Evidently nine of the 11 essays on Faulkner in this volume deal with *Go Down, Moses.* Patrick Samway's essay on *Intruder in the Dust* (see section *i*) also deserves mention here.

viii. Individual Works, 1950–1962

With the exception of Joseph Trimmer's essay (see section *iii. b*), nothing of much significance was done on the work of Faulkner's last phase. Morse Peckham's consideration of *A Fable* has been discussed in section *iii. b.* In " 'Endure' and 'Prevail': Faulkner's Modification of Conrad" (*N&Q* 219:375–76), Christof Wegelin reexamines Faulkner's indebtedness to Conrad in the Nobel Prize speech and concludes, not unremarkably, that Faulkner is more optimistic than Conrad. Two essays on *The Reivers* complete the output for this period: Edwin Moses, "Faulkner's *The Reivers*: The Art of Acceptance" (*MissQ* 27:307–18), and M. E. Bradford, "What Grandfather Said: The Social Testimony of Faulkner's *The Reivers*" (*Occasional Review* 1:5–15). Of the two, only the former is of value. Moses provides a welcome inspection of the retrospective quality of the novel, but one may demur when he claims for it the status of a major work. It may be, as Moses says, that in *The Reivers* "Faulkner is laughing, not only at passionate people, but at his own previous passionate description of them." But is such an attitude all gain? Incidentally, anyone interested in inspecting Bradford's essay should be advised that the editors of *Occasional Review* evidently only found one occasion to publish their journal before it folded. I found it in the library of the Institute for Governmental Studies at the University of California at Berkeley.

ix. The Stories

Faulkner's short stories received considerable attention, but as has been the case in the past, much of it is characterized by inattention to (or ignorance of) both the rest of the canon and previous scholarship and criticism. In addition to Dabney's book (see section *iii. a*), three essays give attention to one or another of the Indian stories. M. E. Bradford's "That Other Patriarchy: Observations on Faulkner's 'A Justice'" (*Modern Age* 18:266–71) is vitiated by his assumption that Sam Fathers is here, as in *Go Down, Moses,* the son of Ikkemotubbe. Without doubt, in "A Justice" Sam Fathers is the son of Craw-ford. Gilbert H. Muller's "The Descent of the Gods: Faulkner's 'Red Leaves' and the Garden of the South" (*SSF* 11:243–49) is a competent but rather heavily religious reading of this story. Muller overburdens this spare and classical tragedy when he finds in it a call for human redemption, but his treatment of the theme of slavery in the story may be profitably compared with Dabney's (section *iii. a*). In "Ikkemotubbe and the Spanish Conspiracy" (*AL* 46:389–91), Richard A. Milum explains the significance of Faulkner's mention of Carondelet and General Wilkinson in "Red Leaves." His explanation will not surprise anyone conversant with American history.

The three items dealing with "A Rose for Emily" make one wish that a moratorium could be declared on the study of this overanalyzed and overrated story. Neither W. V. Davis, "Another Flower for Faulkner's Bouquet: Theme and Structure in 'A Rose for Emily'" (*NMW* 7:34–38), nor C. H. Edwards, Jr., "Three Literary Parallels to Faulkner's 'A Rose for Emily'" (*NMW* 7:21–25), nor J. F. Kibler, "Faulkner's 'A Rose for Emily'" (*Expl* 32:item 65), deserves attention. It is a relief to turn to Sharon Smith Hult's "William Faulkner's 'The Brooch': The Journey to the Riolama" (*MissQ* 27:291–305), a competent study of the significance of the reference in this story to W. H. Hudson's *Green Mansions.* Though more concerned with displaying a method of teaching than with literary analysis, Joseph M. Garrison, Jr.'s "Faulkner's 'The Brooch': A Story for Teaching" (*CE* 36:51–57) offers occasional comments of value.

The two remaining items are both by Kenneth G. Johnston. In "The Year of Jubilee: Faulkner's 'That Evening Sun'" (*AL* 46:93–100), Johnston attempts to establish a tenuous connection between

the story and the 50th anniversary (the "jubilee year") of the Emancipation Proclamation. The argument hangs on the doubtful assertion that Quentin Compson was born in 1889, rather than in the
more widely accepted 1890. Nor does Johnston explain why Faulkner, if he wished to make this connection, should have chosen to set
Quentin's retelling of the story, rather than its events, in the jubilee
year. In "Time of Decline: Pickett's Charge and the Broken Clock in
Faulkner's 'Barn Burning'" (*SSF* 11:434–36), Johnston says that the
time indicated by the broken clock in Ab Snopes's wagon in "Barn
Burning" is approximately the same as the time of Pickett's charge at
Gettysburg, given the hour difference between the Eastern and
Central time zones. There is no doubt that this is true.

x. Unexamined Items

I have seen notices of but have not examined the following books:
William Boozer, *William Faulkner's First Book: "The Marble Faun"
Fifty Years Later* (Memphis: The Pigeon Roost Press); Edgar Loh-
ner, ed., *Der Amerikanische Roman im 19. und 20. Jahrhundert: Inter-
pretationen* (Berlin: Erich Schmidt Verlag) [see Chap. *21, ii*]; Robert
Rougé, *L'Inquiétude Religieuse dans le Roman Américain Moderne*
(Paris: Librairie C. Klincksieck) [see *ALS 1973*, p. 439]; Viola Sachs,
ed., *Le Blanc et le Noir chez Melville et Faulkner* (The Hague:
Mouton); and Jean Weisgerber, *Faulkner and Dostoevsky: Influence
and Confluence*, trans. Dean McWilliams (Athens: Ohio Univ.
Press). This last is a translation of a familiar work, first published in
Brussels in 1968. The *U.S. Military Academy Library Occasional
Papers* (no. 2) is devoted to Faulkner. It contains the following:
Jack Capps, "Introduction: William Faulkner and West Point" (pp.
1–5); Albert Erskine, "Authors and Editors: William Faulkner at
Random House" (pp. 14–19); W. W. S. McIntosh, "A Selective Listing of the William Faulkner Collection at the United States Military
Academy" (pp. 20–28); and Robert Moore, "The Faulkner Concordance and Some Implications for Textual and Linguistic Studies"
(pp. 6–13). I should also note here Will Fridy's " 'Ichthus': An Exercise in Synthetic Suggestion" (*SAB* 39:95–101).

University of California, Davis

10. Fitzgerald and Hemingway

Jackson R. Bryer

All the excitement generated in 1974 by publicity for the lavish movie version of *The Great Gatsby* and for a prime time television program on Fitzgerald's life did not, unfortunately, produce a meaningful increase in worthwhile scholarly activity on either Fitzgerald or Hemingway. This year's survey reflects a general decrease, in fact, in the volume of material. There was, for example, no full-length critical study of either writer. But, as always, there were some pleasant surprises. They include a valuable and attractive pictorial autobiography of the Fitzgeralds and a collection of original essays on Hemingway which contains a remarkably large number of fresh and important pieces. And the trend, noted at the beginning of last year's survey, toward an increasingly higher percentage of the work being worthy of comment has also continued. Regrettably, the 1974 edition of the *FHA*, perennially a source of some of the year's best work, was not available in time to be included.

i. Bibliographical Work and Texts

The first volume in the South Carolina Apparatus for Definitive Editions (SCADE) Series is Matthew J. Bruccoli's *Apparatus for F. Scott Fitzgerald's "The Great Gatsby"* [*Under the Red, White, and Blue*] (Columbia: Univ. of S.C. Press). The SCADE Series, as Bruccoli has explained in an earlier note (*PBSA* 67[1973]:431–35), is designed to present the "apparatus only, without the text, for a definitive edition of a work in copyright—or of a work that is not feasible to republish." As Bruccoli makes clear in this note, as well as in his several other pieces on this subject, the publication history of *Gatsby* involves continual corruptions of the text by editors and publishers; so the *Apparatus* is a welcome beginning towards correcting this situation.

After a brief "Historical Introduction" (which Bruccoli acknowledges is drawn from the much fuller discussion in his introduction to
the 1973 *Gatsby Facsimile*), there are 10 parts to the main body of
the volume: textual notes on the emendations to the copy-text; editorial emendations in the copy-text; revisions in Fitzgerald's marked
copy of the novel; collation of the revised galleys against the first
printing; historical collation; plate alterations in the second printing;
collation of the printings of the Scribner Library edition; end-of-the-
line hyphenation in the copy-text; pedigree of editions and printings
of *The Great Gatsby*; and explanatory notes. The book is thus designed so that anyone who wants to prepare an established text of
Gatsby can do so by marking up his copy (presumably he will be
using the Scribner Library edition, not the rare and expensive first
printing) based on the various collations and emendations Bruccoli
presents. The *Apparatus* is undeniably useful; that it is, occasionally,
misleading and confusing is suggested in a very recent review (*TLS*,
5 Sept. 1975) by Denzell S. Smith. While some of Smith's criticisms
themselves are cryptic, he does note several errors in the book which
ought to be corrected.

Whatever the value of Bruccoli's *Apparatus*, it is certainly the
most significant bibliographical contribution of the year. The others
are hardly more than footnotes to previous scholarship. Thus, John
M. Meador, Jr., in "Addendum to Hanneman: Hemingway's *The Old
Man and the Sea* (*PBSA* 67[1973]:454–57), corrects some errors in
Hanneman's descriptions of first editions of the novel, and then
points out the numerous textual variants which exist in the American
resettings and reprintings. In "The Corrections Lists for F. Scott
Fitzgerald's *This Side of Paradise*" (*SB* 26[1973]:254–64), James
L. W. West, III, traces the fates of the several lists of corrections in
the first printing of the novel, which were offered to the publisher
by Fitzgerald, F. P. Adams, Maxwell Perkins, and Robert Bridges.
West shows how, in general, Scribner's did not heed them and notes
that the 1960 edition (the one now generally used) contains 187
variants from the 1920 text, of which only 40 "enter the 1960 text
legitimately from plate alterations in the first edition." Some of the
corrections in those lists remain unchanged in the latest printing.
This piece, as well as Meador's and Bruccoli's *Apparatus*, adds further evidence to the case for textually pure editions of Fitzgerald's
and Hemingway's books. West, in a review-essay on Bruccoli's Fitz-

gerald descriptive bibliography (*Costerus* n.s. 1:165–76), also suggests the need for further bibliographical research on Fitzgerald's short stories, asserting that the texts in such collected volumes as *Afternoon of an Author, The Crack-Up,* and *The Pat Hobby Stories* are "generally unreliable" when compared to the original magazine versions. In this review West, who praises Bruccoli's book as "the most thorough and comprehensive full-dress bibliography of a major American writer ever published," also includes a brief list of addenda and corrigenda for entries in Section A, admitting that it took him many hours to find even these.

In "Hemingway's Manuscripts: The Vault Reconsidered" (*SAF* 2:3–11), Philip Young reluctantly rehashes the familiar story of his experiences going through the over 19,000 pages Hemingway left behind at his death. He does, however, draw three new conclusions. None are very surprising, but all suggest areas for future research. Young asserts that Hemingway "was not a particularly good judge of how well or badly he was writing, from day to day, over some *very* extended periods of time"; that he "never really had either an agent or an editor"; and that he "did not revise very much." In an intriguing postscript to this essay—which was originally delivered as a talk at the 1973 Pennsylvania State University Conference on Bibliography —Young tells of some additional Hemingway materials which he found in Key West. These included revised galleys of *Winner Take Nothing,* in which the author had personally excised the four-letter words he'd originally used; galleys of *Death in the Afternoon,* which contained an ending that was later removed; and a notebook "where he had listed the various ways he liked to think of dying—most suicidal, contradicting everything else he wrote about that—and not including by shotgun."

Two notes add to the enumerative listings on Fitzgerald and Hemingway. James L. W. West, III, in "Mencken's Review of *Tales of the Jazz Age*" (*Menckeniana* 50:2–4), reprints a hitherto unlisted review from *The Smart Set* for July 1923. Kenneth Rosen's "Ten Eulogies: Hemingway's Spanish Death" (*BNYPL* 77:276–77) offers an unannotated compilation of 1961 pieces, observing in his brief prefatory remarks that "the notion that Hemingway's final act is existential and completely understandable and in full accord with the philosophy expressed in his writings is a pervasive one in these Spanish responses." This summary accurately describes the tone of

José Luis Castillo-Puche's book-length memoir (see below); and it would be of value to compare his impressions with those of some of the others on Rosen's list.

No new Fitzgerald or Hemingway material appeared in 1974, aside from the first publication of Fitzgerald's brief 1924 essay "The Pampered Men" in Bruccoli, Smith, and Kerr's *The Romantic Egoists* (see below). Scribner's did issue the first American edition of *Bits of Paradise*, previously available only in England (see *ALS 1973*, pp. 155–56), as well as *The Enduring Hemingway: An Anthology of a Lifetime in Literature*, ed. Charles Scribner, Jr. Usefully arranged around six motifs in Hemingway's work—his apprentice fiction, World War I, bullfighting, big-game hunting in Africa, the Spanish Civil War, and the sea—this ample (864 pages) selection includes three complete books, *In Our Time*, *A Farewell to Arms*, and *The Old Man and the Sea*, as well as substantial portions of *The Green Hills of Africa*, *The Sun Also Rises*, *For Whom the Bell Tolls*, and *Islands in the Stream*. Each section is helpfully introduced by an appropriate piece of Hemingway's nonfiction, and there is also the first book appearance of "Miss Mary's Lion" from "The African Journal." The entire book has been designed to be readable and it succeeds admirably. Scribner's brief introduction is a graceful and informative survey of Hemingway's life and career.

ii. Letters and Biography

The most significant publication on either Fitzgerald or Hemingway in 1974 was *The Romantic Egoists: A Pictorial Autobiography from the Scrapbooks and Albums of Scott and Zelda Fitzgerald*, ed. Matthew J. Bruccoli, Scottie Fitzgerald Smith, and Joan P. Kerr (New York: Scribner's). This book has received neither the amount nor the kind of attention it deserves, undoubtedly because of its $25 price-tag and its "coffee-table book" appearance. Not only is it a beautifully designed volume, it is also a gold mine for scholars, students, and just plain "fans" of the Fitzgeralds. Drawn entirely from the scrapbooks, the photo albums, Fitzgerald's *Ledger*, letters, manuscripts, and published writings, it is divided into six chronologically arranged sections. Basic reliance is on clippings and photographs from the scrapbooks; but the true genius of the editing job lies in the interpolated passages from letters and published works which are inserted at exactly the right place in the narrative. Thus a brief but significant excerpt from a 1933 letter to John O'Hara in which Fitzgerald comments on his Irish heritage appears among his baby pictures and portraits of his parents and of his boyhood home.

Among the numerous riches to be found are letters to Fitzgerald, praising his work (usually on the occasion of the publication of a novel), from, among others, O'Hara, Thomas Wolfe, Edith Wharton, T. S. Eliot, John Dos Passos, and Robert Benchley; a portfolio, mostly in color, of Zelda's paintings; clipped reviews of *Save Me the Waltz*; clippings of reviews, interviews, and articles which are not listed in Bryer's *Critical Reputation* because they are not identified in the scrapbook and could not be located; pages from the original magazine publication of stories and articles, worth having if only for the often marvelous illustrations which add a flavor of the time; the previously mentioned first publication of "The Pampered Men"; reproductions of some of Zelda's letters; and a brief last section which includes clippings of obituaries and posthumous editorials, as well as snippets from Zelda's letters to her daughter. The body of the book is bracketed by a short but typically charming and modest introduction by Mrs. Smith, and Bruccoli's final survey of Fitzgerald's "Posthumous Vindication" which manages to be both thorough and succinct. My only quibble with this remarkable volume is that it is not always clear what in it comes from the scrapbooks and albums (and thus represents something Zelda or Scott chose to include) and what has been assembled by the editors. Mrs. Smith asserts that only 10 percent of the material falls into this latter category but it would be useful to know more specifically what this includes.

The two major biographical books of the year on Fitzgerald and Hemingway, coincidentally, both focus on the last years of their respective writer's life. Both were written as personal reminiscences by persons who only met their subject late in his life; and, finally, both picture their subjects as ill and depressed. Tony Buttitta's *After the Good Gay Times: Asheville—Summer of '35: A Season With F. Scott Fitzgerald* (New York: Viking) presents a remarkably vivid and full re-creation of conversations with Fitzgerald. Buttitta was the proprietor of the Intimate Bookshop in Asheville's George Vanderbilt Hotel and Fitzgerald often stopped by to talk and reminisce. Buttitta kept careful notes on these conversations, he tells us, on the flyleaves of some 60 books which were then as now in his personal

library. From these he has reconstructed the events and dialogues of
that summer. Fitzgerald emerges as frequently drunk and consistently pessimistic, mourning the loss of his talent and his youth.
There is a good deal of attention paid to his affair with a married
woman and his more casual flirtations with a local prostitute. Buttitta
also describes a marvelous scene when a slightly inebriated Fitzgerald
tried to rent a room in Thomas Wolfe's mother's boarding house, only
to be turned away when Julia Wolfe noticed his "shaky movements"
and remarked proudly, "I never take drunks—not if I know it."
Throughout, Buttitta stretches our faith in his credibility with his
pages of supposedly quoted conversations. Some of it sounds patently
unlikely, as, for example, Fitzgerald's "I've lost the knack and the gay
parade's passed me by"; but the overall picture is undoubtedly an
accurate one and Buttitta's method does give it a sharpness which it
otherwise would not have.

Buttitta's focus is almost entirely on Fitzgerald, with only occasional digressions into autobiography or literary criticism. In contrast, José Luis Castillo-Puche, in *Hemingway in Spain: A Personal
Reminiscence of Hemingway's Years in Spain By His Friend* (Garden
City, N.Y.: Doubleday), mars what otherwise would have been a
valuable and evocative portrait by his dual obsessions with trying to
understand and explain Hemingway's suicide and with demonstrating
the factual inaccuracy of parts of *For Whom the Bell Tolls*. Originally
published in Spanish in 1968, the book is best when it recalls Hemingway's last visit, in 1959, to the San Fermín fiesta in Pamplona, or his
pilgrimage to the bedside of a dying Pío Baroja. There should be
more of this sort of first-hand account. As Buttitta does, Castillo-
Puche repeats long conversations verbatim, and the resulting effect
is, again, a successful evocation. And again the picture is not a pretty
one. Hemingway is seen as ill, as an old man trying to recapture his
youth by surrounding himself with pretty young women while an
ever-tolerant and patient Mary Hemingway ministers to his every
need. But this should have been a much shorter book than it is (388
pages). Castillo-Puche as literary critic is far less successful than he
is as biographer. His tendency to read Hemingway's fiction as literal
autobiography is irritating; and his persistent nit-picking about *For
Whom the Bell Tolls* belies his own contention that fiction should not
be evaluated as fact.

Alice Hunt Sokoloff's *Hadley: The First Mrs. Hemingway* (New

York: Dodd, Mead [1973]), overlooked in last year's survey, is also too long. Its 111 pages could easily have been condensed into a long article. As it is, this account of the life of Hemingway's first wife is based entirely on four interviews Mrs. Sokoloff had with Hadley Richardson Mowrer in 1970–72, and on her letters, mostly to Ernest, which she apparently put at Mrs. Sokoloff's disposal. There is no attempt to go beyond these by interviewing others who knew the Hemingways or even by reading other published accounts of this period. When one adds to this the fact that *Hadley* is full of proof-reading errors, the inescapable conclusion is that this book should never have been published.

All of the three shorter biographical pieces are on Hemingway; and one of them, Leah Rice Koontz's "My Favorite Subject Is Hadley" (*ConnR* 8,i:36–41), is an acknowledged footnote to the Sokoloff biography. Koontz interviewed Hadley after the book appeared; but her comments add little to the earlier work, except perhaps for her confirmation of Hemingway's anti-Semitism as manifested in his portrait of Harold Loeb as Robert Cohn. Herbert Ruhm, in "Hemingway in Schruns" (*Commonweal* 99[1973]:344–45), recounts a sentimental pilgrimage he took to the Hotel Taube in Schruhns, Austria, where Hemingway spent the winters of 1925 and 1926. Ruhm finds unchanged the hotel which Hemingway describes in *A Moveable Feast* and mentions in "The Snows of Kilimanjaro"; and he reminisces about the important events in Hemingway's life which occurred there—his rewriting of the first draft of *The Sun Also Rises*, his meeting with Pauline Pfeiffer (later to become the second Mrs. Hemingway), and his succumbing to the easy life of the rich. This is an unpretentious and well-written piece. David L. Inglis's "Morley Callaghan and the Hemingway Boxing Legend" (*NConL* 4,iv:4–7) relies almost entirely on Callaghan's *That Summer in Paris* (1963) to dispel the myth of Hemingway's boxing prowess.

iii. Criticism

a. **Collections.** Both new collections are on Hemingway. Linda Welshimer Wagner's *Ernest Hemingway: Five Decades of Criticism* (East Lansing: Mich. State Univ. Press) is, in all but one instance, entirely drawn from previously published reviews and articles. The focus, Wagner indicates in her introduction, is on "Hemingway as writer, as craftsman, seeking to shape his statement of beliefs about life with all the love and finesse of any gifted artisan." The volume is divided into four sections. The first deals with his early writing, his views of other writers, and Hemingway as literary critic; the second contains essays which survey his total work from different thematic perspectives; the third includes studies of his style; the fourth presents eight essays, each a treatment of one work. Because only 6 of the 22 essays selected have previously been collected, and most have been written within the last decade, this collection is relatively unique and fresh. The one original piece, Richard Hasbany's on *In Our Time*, will be discussed below.

Unlike Wagner's collection, *Hemingway in Our Time*, ed. Richard Astro and Jackson J. Benson (Corvallis: Ore. State Univ. Press), is composed entirely of new essays, all of which were originally delivered as papers at a Hemingway Conference held at Oregon State University in April 1973. The focus of the collection is on "the novelist's literary reputation, on his late and posthumous works, and on his influence on contemporary fiction," with the aim of stimulating further discussion. Benson's introduction is a chatty and entertaining attempt to show the extent of Hemingway's importance and influence and to account for his popularity. Reasons for the latter, Benson feels, lie "in the nature of the work itself. Simply stated, his position is in a closer alignment with our felt positions than that of any other modern writer." (The individual essays are discussed below and referred to as Astro and Benson.) The total impression of the volume is of a rarity among recent collections on Hemingway or Fitzgerald, a useful and worthwhile venture. As has been continually noted in these surveys, despite the annual flow of material, there are new areas left untouched. Perhaps the best way to draw attention to this fact is to assemble a group familiar with the previous scholarship and have them deal with some of these. *Hemingway in Our Time* certainly reflects the success and value of one such project.

b. **Full-Length Studies.**   As noted earlier, no full-length study of either Fitzgerald or Hemingway appeared in 1974. This is, obviously, a mixed blessing. On the one hand, we were spared the unpleasant task of plowing through a redundant or inflated manuscript. On the other, however, it means that none of the myriad of scholars and critics concerned with these two popular figures was able to produce

a full examination of an area needing further research, such as Fitzgerald's style, either writer's short stories, or either writer's critical
reputation.

The one full-length study to be discussed here, inadvertently
omitted from last year's survey, is itself decidedly a mixed blessing.
Robert B. Pearsall's *The Life and Writings of Ernest Hemingway*
(Amsterdam: Rodopi [1973]) does include, particularly in his sections on *A Farewell to Arms* and the short stories, flashes of critical
insight. But Pearsall's biographical details are rehashes of Baker, and
he is glib to the point of critical irresponsibility. Any reader should be
wary of a book which, on its first page, dismisses Sherwood Anderson
and Ring Lardner as "pygmy writers" and rejects Faulkner's fiction
as too narrowly regional in its concerns. Pearsall's fascination with
the sound of his own prose and his desire constantly to render judgments extend also to his treatment of Hemingway. Thus, he calls
"The Killers" "the best-known of all American short stories," says of
"Mr. and Mrs. Elliot" (which he misspells "Eliot") only that it is an
"ugly little story," simplistically remarks of Lady Brett that "Hemingway hated her, and meant to make her hateful," and sees *Torrents of
Spring* as having been written deliberately to alienate Hemingway
from Boni and Liveright "so that he could move on to the richer firm
of Charles Scribner's Sons." Despite Pearsall's repeated insistence
that he is a Hemingway enthusiast, his subject emerges from this
study as a very unattractive person, whose life is too often used to
cast light on his work. Hopefully, there will be better full-length
works than this one in the future.

c. General Essays.   Principally because of the large number of them
included in the Astro and Benson collection, there is an abundance of
good general essays this year. One, Peter L. Hays's "Hemingway and
Fitzgerald" (Astro and Benson, pp. 87–97), links the two subjects of
this survey through a comparison of *Gatsby* and *The Sun Also Rises*.
Previous critics have noticed minor similarities; but Hays contends
that Hemingway may well have been influenced by Fitzgerald's
novel. In support of this, he points to such plausible connections as
the influence on both of *The Waste Land*, how sports is used as a
metaphor for the lives of the characters in both novels, and the fact
that both involve "frustrated patterns of initiation." But Hays is most
illuminating when he acknowledges an important difference: "Fitz-

gerald's novel is a criticism of society couched in lush prose that conveys his own romantic hope; while Hemingway's book transmutes Eliot's and Fitzgerald's material into a philosophical statement about a harsh universe, a statement expressed in a flatter, less lyric prose more attuned to the author's view of life's very limited possibilities."

One of the most interesting and original points Hays makes in his essay is the suggestion that, in the end, Nick is a part of the corruption of the East that repels him, and that "most readers who accept Nick as their moral norm throughout the novel [should] realize the significance of their own tacit approval of his silence, of his refusal to judge or condemn, and of his pandering." In "Fitzgerald in the Fifties" (*SNNTS* 5[1973]324–35), Barry Gross takes a tack which seems diametrically opposed to Hays's by seeing Nick at the end of the novel as an heroic figure through his commitment to Gatsby. Further, Gross attributes the Fitzgerald Revival in the 1950s largely to young people's identifying with Nick, whom he sees as cautious, avoiding entanglements, and unwilling to pass judgments, yet a bit restless too—for excitement and romance. Gross, like Hays, presents his thesis well; and the pieces represent two convincing opposing views.

The other good general essay on Fitzgerald is Scott Donaldson's "Scott Fitzgerald's Romance With the South" (*SLJ* 5,ii[1973]:3–17). Donaldson explores what he sees as Fitzgerald's two-part attitude toward the South. The first, reflecting his relationship with Zelda, began as a highly romanticized view, reflected in short stories like "The Ice Palace" (1920), where Sally Carrol Harper is seen as a warm and charming southern belle. But by 1929 when he wrote "The Last of the Belles," this figure has been transformed into the cruelly vicious and selfish Allie Calhoun. The second part of Fitzgerald's attitude was molded by his view of his father and remained quite constant: though he was permanently disillusioned by Edward Fitzgerald's business failure, Scott always venerated his father as a southern gentleman; and he never abandoned, in his own life and work, the pride in manners and breeding his father symbolized to him. This is an original and lucidly argued essay.

The two other general pieces on Fitzgerald are more nearly notes. Both take their points of departure from recent books. H. Alan Wycherley, in "The Fitzgerald Fad" (*CEA* 36,ii:29–30), continues his attack on the Fitzgerald Revival articulated in earlier essays by

here bemoaning sentimental appraisers who try "to blurb into immortality a writer of limited talent and scope." The latest culprits he
indicts are Callahan (see *ALS 1972*, p. 138) and Mayfield. That these
two books are deficient is certainly an arguable contention; but that
their subject is unworthy of better treatment is also debatable. Dan
Isaac seizes upon Tony Buttitta's quotation of Fitzgerald's remarks
on radical politics, and, in "The Other Scott Fitzgerald" (*Nation*
219:282–84), asserts that "it is about time that we begin to recognize
the other F. Scott Fitzgerald—the Fitzgerald who was desperately
striving to become a serious historical and political writer, and took
a final shot at writing a proto-Marxist novel with *The Last Tycoon.*"
The few examples that Isaac assembles to support his contention and
the fact that he never really says very much at all about *The Last
Tycoon* make this a weak essay. His conclusion—that Fitzgerald was
not a "joiner" but was a "sentimental Marxist"—seems highly equivo-
cal in comparison with his earlier statements.

Four very good general essays in the Astro and Benson collection
study the body of Hemingway's fiction from four valid perspectives.
Robert W. Lewis's concern (pp. 113–43) is with "Hemingway's Sense
of Place." While Lewis's style is occasionally too self-conscious and
his survey too often rambles, he has a very perceptive section on the
short stories; and his basic thesis—that place is basic to Hemingway's
work and that it has a significance that is more than geographical—
is undeniable, given the evidence he assembles. John Clark Pratt's "A
Sometimes Great Notion: Ernest Hemingway's Roman Catholicism"
(pp. 145–57) suggests a paradox in Hemingway's attitude toward
the Church: "If he did not want to be known as a Catholic writer,
neither for obvious reasons did he want to be seen as an overtly anti-
Catholic writer." Pratt sees Hemingway as consistently "attracted to"
and "even obsessed with Roman Catholicism" because "above all
other Christian beliefs, Roman Catholicism is a 'code' religion, ritualistic in precisely the manner Hemingway found so appealing in aspects of war, sport, and life itself." Tracing Catholicism through
characters and themes in the fiction, Pratt notes a shift after *A Farewell to Arms*: "Few of the stories in his first two collections carry
religious overtones, but almost all of his later works show a careful
consideration of Catholic elements, presented allusively as well as thematically." Castillo-Puche, in his biographical memoir (see above),
implies a good deal about Hemingway's ambivalence regarding

Catholicism; and Pratt's essay serves as a valuable expansion and exploration of this worthwhile subject.

John Griffith's "Rectitude in Hemingway's Fiction: How Rite Makes Right" (pp. 159–73) also deals with a key aspect of Hemingway's art and makes an important new distinction. His contention is that "while ritual correctness and moral right are related concepts, they are distinguishable, and . . . the special Hemingway sense of doing things right consistently has more in common, philosophically and psychologically, with correct observance of ritual than it has with systematic morality." Griffith feels that Hemingway often confused ritual with morality because he didn't see that "where morality attempts to adapt itself to every human circumstance, ritual refuses to alter its form; it rigidly repeats itself, for its meaning is in the action itself, not in its effect on the world." Thus, Robert Jordan's death is "almost wholly a ritual action" because it is an admitted waste, unmitigated by any heroism that will contribute to the Cause. This is an excellent essay, one of the two or three best this year on either writer.

Michael Friedberg, in "Hemingway and the Modern Metaphysical Tradition" (pp. 175–89), also manages to deal freshly with a seemingly hackneyed subject, in this case the Hemingway style. Friedberg's point is that "Hemingway's style is basically the language of the new metaphysical ideology of twentieth-century fiction" in that it mirrors the irony inherent in a universe which is describable on a superficial objective level but unknowable and uncontrollable on a level beyond that. This is an uneven and sometimes opaque essay; but it rewards careful reading.

Coincidentally, two essays this year deal with Hemingway and Henry Adams. One, George Monteiro's "The Education of Ernest Hemingway" (*JAmS* 8:91–99), deals exclusively with this subject; while the other, Richard Lehan's "Hemingway Among the Moderns" (Astro and Benson, pp. 191–212), uses the Adams connection merely as a starting point for a more ambitious and far-ranging study. Monteiro begins with such superficial parallels as "identity in names, the shared metaphor of 'education,' similar interests in cathedrals, and the similarity of attitudes and narrative methods." Beyond these, however, he sees Hemingway as finding in *The Education of Henry Adams* "an exact and exacting definition of the world his generation had inherited, along with a set description of the historical milieu in which he himself must live and work." That definition was Adams's awareness "that the human mind was helpless before the multiplication of forces which inevitably defeated its most disciplined efforts." Monteiro then traces this theme through Hemingway's first two novels briefly and, at greater length, through *Winner Take Nothing*, with emphasis on "A Clean, Well-Lighted Place," which he considers the clearest expression of Adams's influence. This is a well-presented thesis and a very suggestive essay.

Lehan's study touches on the Hemingway-Adams connection in passing at the outset when he notes how Adams provided in *The Education* a challenge for modern writers to find a substitute in modern civilization for the Virgin which had held together the 12th century by giving "the individual a frame of ordering reference outside himself." Three who accepted Adams's challenge were Pound, who found the substitute "in the meaning of the fifteenth century"; Eliot, who found it "in a classical tradition"; and Williams, who found it in "a return to American roots." But Hemingway, Lehan feels, rejected these solutions, "demythologized modern literature," and turned to "an idea of pre-history—to a belief in residual, primitive values that are inextricable from the rhythms of life and death and the land." Lehan's thesis is that Hemingway, as a primitivist, "rejected the modern world and reduced all values to those that could be reconciled with the elemental" and he traces this through several of the novels and a selection of short stories. He notes also the theme of "seeing and mis-seeing" in Hemingway's fiction, observing how those in touch with the elemental see literally and figuratively, while those who are not do not achieve either. Along with John Griffith's essay, Lehan's is the best in a very good collection.

Two of the other general essays on Hemingway are less scholarly—by design—and more informally presented. In "Ernest Hemingway: The Popular Writer as Popular Culture" (*JPC* 8:91–97), John Raeburn examines Hemingway's role as a "public writer" and celebrity, a man who first established his position through his writings but later was known to and honored by far more people than the readers of his books. Raeburn feels that Hemingway sought this role and encouraged it through publication of self-revealing nonfiction and by playing upon the public's desire for an idol who was warrior, sportsman, and "bon vivant." In the shadow of this created figure, Raeburn contends plausibly, "the master of modern prose lingered

palely in the background, esteemed but only of secondary interest."
This persuasive essay implies the need for a full-length investigation
of the way Hemingway's reputation as a writer changed through his
lifetime and after his death. Surely the removal of the living legend-
ary figure made it easier to examine the work by itself.

Philip Young's "Posthumous Hemingway, and Nicholas Adams"
(Astro and Benson, pp. 13–23) is an extremely useful survey and
evaluation of just what has happened since the living legend was
removed. Young begins with his assessments of the four posthumous
volumes: *A Moveable Feast* is "a minor masterpiece, a small jewel,
flawed ever so slightly here by sentimentality, and just a little there
by malice, but glittering none the less, and cut to last"; *By-Line:
Ernest Hemingway* is "journalism, which is not the same thing as
literature, and there is an ominous drift to it in which the reporter
begins by interviewing certain notables and ends interviewing himself, by then among the foremost of them"; *Islands in the Stream* is a
disappointment, primarily because "in relating all the experience the
book deals with [Hemingway] had never . . . discovered its meaning"; and *The Nick Adams Stories* (for which Young was largely responsible) "might have been better, but if I didn't think it was
worth having I wouldn't have proposed it, or would subsequently
have bowed out of it." In connection with the last-named project,
Young has some interesting observations to make on the reviews it
received and on the disputes he had with Scribner's over what ought
to be included. Young's conclusions—about whether posthumous
publication has hurt or helped Hemingway's stature—are that, on
balance, it has been a good thing: "we've now got a larger territory
to operate in, and some new material."

Two much briefer pieces also deal generally with Hemingway.
Nicholas Canaday, Jr., is concerned with "The Motif of the Inner
Ring in Hemingway's Fiction" (*CEA* 36,ii:18–21). Canaday defines
the "Inner Ring" as "a name for varying degrees of intimacy within a
closed circle" and sees this motif dominating Hemingway's works.
Though brief, Canaday's exploration is intriguing. More ephemeral
is Robert O. Johnson's "Hemingway's 'How Do You Like It Now,
Gentlemen?': A Possible Source" (*AL* 45[1973]:114–17), in which
Hemingway's question, as reported in Lillian Ross's *New Yorker*
profile, is traced to Act III of George Villiers's 1671 play, *The
Rehearsal.*

d. **Essays on Specific Works: Fitzgerald.** All but four of the 17 essays discussed in this section are devoted at least partially to *Gatsby*. When one adds to this the quasi-literary attention received by the movie—represented, most prominently, by *Newsweek* (Feb. 4) and *Time* (Mar. 18) cover stories, and Bruce Bahrenburg's paper- back account, *Filming "The Great Gatsby"* (New York: Berkley)— the dimensions of this imbalance are even more apparent. These sta- tistics are somewhat misleading, however, in that three of the *Gatsby* articles are about the movie principally and four others are brief notes.

The two best essays are both, ironically, 1973 pieces, Giles Gunn's "F. Scott Fitzgerald's *Gatsby* and the Imagination of Wonder" (*JAAR* 41[1973]:171–83), and David Parker's *"The Great Gatsby*: Two Versions of the Hero" (*ES* 54[1973]:37–51). Gunn perceives the novel as "a story about Gatsby's poetry of desire, his imagination of wonder" that Americans have lost because "we can no longer be so vulnerable." This wonder, which requires "an openness to the unan- ticipated, a certain susceptibility to surprise," is not without vulgari- ty; but in the end of the novel Fitzgerald redeems even "the crude and sordid materials in terms of which it [wonder] is expressed." This is an unpretentious study which makes its claims clearly and succinctly.

Parker's aim is to examine *Gatsby* against the background of English literature in order to understand its Americanism more com- pletely. He finds that Fitzgerald, in his portrayals of Gatsby and Nick, incorporates two versions of the hero in English literature: the hero of the romance, an idealist searching for some transcendent object; and the hero of the novel of "sentimental education" whose journey is an inward quest. Thus he compares Gatsby to Browning's Roland with respect to attitudes ("neither is destroyed by delay or the prospect of failure"), landscape (a wasteland), and the atmo- sphere in which pursuit of the ideal takes place (lies, suspicion, ambiguity). Nick is more briefly compared with the narrator of *Wuthering Heights*; but the bulk of Parker's article, happily, is a close consideration of the two figures in Fitzgerald's novel, in which he notes differences between the two kinds of hero, especially in their attitudes toward time and reality. To the hero of romance time is insignificant and reality is in dreams; to the hero of the novel of sentimental education time represents the possibility of change, and reality is elusive and discovered only when the education is completed. If Parker's distinctions occasionally seem too pat, his thesis enables him to make some extremely illuminating comments on *Gatsby*.

Kenneth Eble's "*The Great Gatsby*" (*ColL* 1:34–47) is worthwhile less for its startling new insights than for its judicious review of previous approaches to the novel and its separation out of what Eble, one of the most sensible Fitzgerald critics, considers to be the important aspects of *Gatsby*. Trying to answer the question of "what there is that argues for the novel's greatness," Eble finds evidence in three areas: "a greatness of theme," the design of the novel, and its style. Eble is best in discussing the second of these as he stresses Fitzgerald's craftsmanship as evidenced in his revisions and rewriting. Unfortunately, his section on the style, while suggestive, is far too brief and too dependent on quotations without analysis. But he correctly puts the emphases where they ought to be and this article could serve very well as a primer for future studies.

Tom Buchanan, perhaps the least-studied of the novel's major characters, is the subject of two essays this year. In "Tom Buchanan and the Demise of the Ivy League Athletic Hero" (*JPC* 8:402–10) Christian Messenger demonstrates convincingly how Fitzgerald's portrait embodies all the disagreeable aspects of a former Ivy League athlete. Messenger then notes that this is a radical shift from the beginning of this century when the Ivy League athlete was the embodiment of the American hero, praised by everyone from Teddy Roosevelt and George Santayana to Jack London and Stephen Crane. This piece suggests how Tom fits the novel's pattern of shattered ideals just as the others do. John B. Humma's "Edward Russell Thomas: The Prototype for *Gatsby*'s Tom Buchanan?" (*MarkhamR* 4:38–39) is less ambitious in its speculations regarding similarities between Tom and Daisy and socialites Edward Russell and Linda Lee Thomas (she later became Mrs. Cole Porter). The parallels are striking and persuasively presented.

Two of the essays on *Gatsby* deal with parallels between Fitzgerald's novel and Raymond Chandler's *The Long Goodbye*. Leon Howard's "Raymond Chandler's Not-So-Great Gatsby" (*MDAC* 2 [1973]:1–15) begins with the many superficial comparisons that he sees—principally between major characters and in plot details. But the emphasis soon shifts to a more thorough examination of the differences between the two novels. These focus on Chandler's narrator, Philip Marlowe, as compared to Nick, and on Fitzgerald's respect for wealth and the rich contrasted with Chandler's antipathy. Howard also sees Chandler as able to draw the line between crooks and honest men far more easily than Fitzgerald; but this, of course, is a result of the requirements of a detective novel as opposed to a traditional novel. Howard's conclusion, that Chandler was influenced by *Gatsby*, seems inescapable; his further speculation, that Chandler "was genuinely serious about moral values and apparently so offended by those he found implicit in Fitzgerald's novel that he sacrificed his own craftsmanship to an attack on respect for wealth and tolerance for crooks," is intriguing but obviously more debatable. But it is surely one of the greatest merits of this article that it does more than make a comparison and claim of influence; it explains the significance of the connections. In a footnote to Howard's essay, Lawrence D. Stewart notes the similarities in design between "The Dust Jackets of *The Great Gatsby* and *The Long Goodbye*" (*MDAC* 2[1973]:331–34); but his emphasis is also on stressing differences: "Fitzgerald's wrapper seems to have been designed to help him, fortuitously, in the creation of his book; Chandler's, to help the reader in his reading."

Three essays in the Summer 1974 issue of *Literature/Film Quarterly* study the film of *Gatsby*, with varying degrees of attention paid to the novel. But even Irene Kahn Atkins's "In Search of the Greatest Gatsby" (*LFQ* 2:216–28), which is entirely concerned with a comparison of the 1949 and 1974 versions, makes fascinating reading. Atkins emphasizes the fidelity to Fitzgerald's novel in all aspects of the later production (her section on the care Nelson Riddle took in making sure that his musical score was faithful to the period is particularly interesting) and the anachronisms and distortions present in the earlier version.

Edward T. Jones also praises the 1974 movie for its close adherence to the novel in "Green Thoughts in a Technicolor Shade: A Revaluation of *The Great Gatsby*" (*LFQ* 2:229–36); but, unlike Atkins's, his essay has a good deal to say about literature. Jones is extremely good at stressing both where the film and novel are close together (in "characterization by gesture," in "scenic narration," and in care and detail given to minor characters) but also where film cannot capture novel due to differences in media. Thus, he sees the movie as rendering the Buchanans more sympathetically only because we cannot have the benefit of Fitzgerald's "often satirical portraiture" of them. Jones's essay is a balanced appraisal and is a useful corrective to reviews of the film which totally disregarded many of the careful distinctions he makes. In "A Linking of Legends: *The Great Gatsby* and *Citizen Kane*" (*LFQ* 2:207–15), Roslyn Mass presents evidence of correspondences between the novel and Welles's movie, in characters, in the use of the automobile, in the circular narrative form of both, and in the common ancestor both have in Conrad. This is a slight but otherwise worthwhile study.

Two studies link *Gatsby* with other works by Fitzgerald. The more substantial of these, Robert A. Martin's "The Hot Madness of Four O'Clock in Fitzgerald's 'Absolution' and *Gatsby*" (*SAF* 2:230–38), seems almost to be an answer to Lawrence D. Stewart's essay (see *ALS 1973*, p. 169), which called the two works "basically irreconcilable." Martin contends that they are "linked by numerous parallels that reflect Fitzgerald's original conception of the novel as an extended treatment of Jimmy Gatz's metamorphosis and career as Jay Gatsby." The parallels he cites—the prevalence of four o'clock and the number four in both, emphasis on clock time and calendar time, and other details—hardly seem startling; but they do support his claim that "some of the original links that would have tied 'Absolution' to *Gatsby* as prologue to novel are still visible beneath the surfaces." Less significant but worth noting are the links Roderick S. Speer finds between *Gatsby* and Fitzgerald's 1924 essay, "The Cruise of the Rolling Junk," in "*The Great Gatsby's* 'Romance of Motoring' and 'The Cruise of the Rolling Junk'" (*MFS* 20:540–43). Speer sees a similar sense of disappointment lurking beneath the idealism in the two and also observes serious themes of *Gatsby* fermenting in the essay.

Finally, in "'Gatsby and the Dutch Sailors'" (*AN&Q* 12[1973]: 61–63), Robert A. Martin notes that the paragraph about the Dutch sailors which appears on the last page of the novel was originally positioned at the end of chapter 1. This, he feels, accounts "for a number of subsequent references scattered throughout the novel in which Gatsby is closely associated with water and nautical objects connected with water." Although highly speculative, this note, along with Martin's other piece on "Absolution," both serve to show how carefully structured *Gatsby* is and what a meticulous craftsman its author was. Studies which emphasize this are never too numerous.

There are only two studies of Fitzgerald's other novels, continuing that regrettable trend in criticism of this author. In "Technical Potential and Achievement in *Tender Is the Night*" (*DQR* 3[1973]: 49–55), F. G. F. Schulte deals rather woodenly with what he sees as the two seemingly irreconcilable views on the novel's rhetoric: one, that "Fitzgerald had lost his power of clarity and control"; and, two, that "he had mastered his medium in a perfect way." Schulte's answer, that the rhetoric ultimately fails because Fitzgerald suppresses knowledge of the flaws in Dick's character and does not clearly define the forces working against him, seems too simplistic.

Kermit W. Moyer's "Fitzgerald's Two Unfinished Novels: The Count and the Tycoon in Spenglerian Perspective" (*ConL* 15:238–56) is valuable in two ways. Not only does it provide a unique reading of *The Last Tycoon* by viewing it from a Spenglerian perspective, but it also presents studies of the four published sections of Fitzgerald's abortive and critically ignored novel, "The Count of Darkness." Moyer traces the Spenglerian elements through the stories and then shows how *The Last Tycoon* expresses them as well, concluding that, "in *Tender Is the Night*, Fitzgerald had focused upon historical decline; in *The Last Tycoon*, his focus shifted, or widened, to include the element of rebirth and historical repetition." Moyer's approach is certainly a narrow one; but his insights are such that we accept his viewpoint as central to an understanding of the novel and the stories.

In one of the only two studies of Fitzgerald's short stories (another deplorable trend which continues), Edwin Moses looks briefly at "The Ice Palace," providing in "F. Scott Fitzgerald and the Quest to the Ice Palace" (*CEA* 36,ii:11–14) a very useful explication of a popular story. Moses feels that the ice palace, "which in symbolic terms is the object of Sally Carrol's quest, represents the essence of Harry's society"—cold, with a "dimness made brilliant by artificial lights." But, when Sally rejects the ice palace of the North and returns to the South, the latter—static and backward-looking—is not ideal either. "What is really needed," Moses asserts, "is a synthesis of the feminine qualities of the South and the masculine ones of the North." Sally, of course, is incapable of achieving this; but, as Moses points out, neither were "better Fitzgerald characters than she."

The other study of the stories is Ruth Prigozy's workmanlike "The Unpublished Stories: Fitzgerald in His Final Stage" (*TCL* 20: 69–90). It is good to have such full discussions of the seven unpublished pieces which she covers, only three of which are also included in Jennifer M. Atkinson's earlier survey (see *ALS 1971*, p. 121), but only infrequently do they seem to warrant either all this attention or the significance Prigozy attributes to them. To claim, as she does, that "they tell us more" than Fitzgerald's commercial successes is excessive; and with some of them—notably "Thank You for the Light"—she seems to be straining to find any redeeming features.

e. **Essays on Specific Works: Hemingway.** The essays on Hemingway's full-length works are more evenly distributed this year than in the recent past. While *A Farewell to Arms* and *The Sun Also Rises* lead in numerical terms, as usual, with five and three, respectively, we have at least two pieces on each of four other books.

Taken as a group, the essays on *A Farewell to Arms* are very strong. The best is Robert O. Stephens's "Hemingway and Stendhal: The Matrix of *A Farewell to Arms*" (*PMLA* 88[1973]:271–80). A model for influence studies, this carefully documented piece demonstrates through a convincing marshalling of internal and external evidence the extent of Hemingway's debt to *The Charterhouse of Parma*. Stephens focuses first on the retreat from Caporetto and on Frederic's response to it: and then moves on to a comparison of Frederic's development and education with that of Stendhal's protagonist, Fabrizio. This last comparison leads Stephens to the conclusion that *A Farewell to Arms* "is a novel about the conditions of love in the modern world more than it is about war" and it therefore belongs "within the ethical rather than the naturalistic tradition."

Bernard Oldsey's "Of Hemingway's *Arms* and the Man" (*ColL* 1:174–89) is the first two parts of a planned six-part monograph which deals with various questions about *Arms* that "have remained fuzzy, fugitive, or relatively unattended." Here he 'deals with two, the significance of the title and the light shed on the novel by biographical information and a knowledge of Hemingway's other works. Oldsey sees the title as an ironic parody on its source, George Peele's poem "A Farewell to Arms." Where Peele speaks positively of the ideals of duty, faith, and love, Hemingway depicts these qualities negatively. Oldsey is particularly balanced in his remarks on Hemingway as autobiographical novelist, noting that "His form of art demanded that he take substance from actuality, provide it with mimetic reflection, and produce his own form of combining fiction."

Thus, *Arms* emerges ultimately as a "culminating and rounded variation on themes stemming in part from experience and . . . in fine short works written before the novel."

In "Tragic Form in *A Farewell to Arms*" (*AL* 45:571–79) Robert Merrill deals sensitively and sensibly with the structure of the novel in an attempt to show it is tragic but not in the Aristotelian sense. Its tragedy derives not from any tragic flaw in its hero but from the tragic effect it produces. While Merrill may seem at times to be manipulating his definition of tragedy to suit his purposes, his framework enables him to make some cogent observations about *Arms*. Similarly, J. F. Kobler's thesis—that *A Farewell to Arms* is "a strongly anti-romantic novel"—is an intriguing though debatable point of view. In "Let's Run Catherine Barkley Up the Flag Pole and See Who Salutes" (*CEA* 36,ii:4–10), Kobler finds evidence for his assertion in three aspects of the novel: Frederic's "stylistic flatness" (beneath his spoken words lies his real meaning); Catherine's avoidance of his real name, indicating that he is serving as a substitute for her first love; and Frederic's need for other amusement, an indication that he is not, unlike Catherine, completely immersed in their relationship. As Merrill does with "tragedy," Kobler seems to be using the term "anti-romantic" rather loosely here; but he provides some useful readings.

Of the three pieces on *The Sun Also Rises*, two are little more than notes. The one substantial essay, Terrence Doody's "Hemingway's Style and Jake's Narration" (*JNT* 4:212–25), is a careful close reading which takes the position that Jake's style is not his own but Hemingway's. He cites sections where this discrepancy is apparent; but concludes that, while it is a weakness of the novel, it is also a strength. Throughout, Doody is sensitive to the effectiveness of Jake's narration as well as to the points where it falters.

In "Jacob Barnes' Name: The Other Side of the Ledger" (*EngR* 24,i[1973]:14–15), Joseph M. Flora notes that, in addition to the Biblical connotations of Jake's name, there are the meanings excrement, filth, and privy (from the plural *jakes*—in modern British, "a dirty mess"). This term, Flora contends, would have been familiar to Hemingway because Twain uses it in *Huckleberry Finn*. This meaning, along with the Biblical one, suggests the complexity of Hemingway's attitude toward his character. Charles C. Walcutt's "Hemingway's *The Sun Also Rises*" (*Expl* 32:Item 57) very briefly rebuts

James Twitchell's criticism of the novel's characters as adolescents. They are damaged people trying to survive in a damaged world.

There are two essays this year on *To Have and Have Not*: the better of these is Gerry Brenner's "*To Have and Have Not* as Classical Tragedy: Reconsidering Hemingway's Neglected Novel" (Astro and Benson, pp. 67–86). Brenner's title is misleading, for he shows how Hemingway's novel has features of Renaissance Revenge Tragedy and the "common man" tragedy of Arthur Miller, as well as Aristotelian tragedy. This approach tends to make the essay rambling and overlong; but, throughout, the focus is on the text and on close reading. William Kenney is more limited in his approach, in "Hunger and the American Dream in *To Have and Have Not*" (*CEA* 36,ii: 26–28). He traces two motifs through the novel–hunger and personal relationships–and their relationship to the American Dream, the myth of unlimited plenty and the belief that "an individual, through self-reliance and hard work, can succeed at anything he undertakes." Kenney sees the falsity of this Dream asserted throughout the novel —nature has become predatory and personal relationships have turned to perversions.

There are only two notes on *The Old Man and the Sea* this year. Both are helpful; neither is very significant. Stephen D. Warner, in "Hemingway's *The Old Man and the Sea*" (*Expl* 33:Item 9) focuses on "the repeated references to Africa and the lions on the beach" in the novel; but his analysis hardly seems worth the effort. George Monteiro's squib on "The Reds, the White Sox, and *The Old Man and the Sea*" (*NConL* 4,iii:7–9) claims plausibly that Santiago, by incorrectly placing the Reds in the American League, is not showing his ignorance of baseball but rather is joking with Manolin, who is senselessly worried about the ability of the Yankees to defeat all opponents.

The one essay on *For Whom the Bell Tolls*, Robert D. Crozier, S.J.'s "For Thine Is the Power and the Glory: Love in *For Whom the Bell Tolls*" (*PLL* 10:76–97), rests rather securely on a comparison of Jordan's journey to death with the "ladder of love" of St. John of the Cross. While Crozier may seem to go too far in his analogies here, his essay provides a good reading of the novel and also gives us additional evidence of Hemingway's complex religious attitudes.

We have an excellent essay this year on *The Green Hills of Africa*,

James Schroeter's "Hemingway Via Joyce" (*SoR* 10:95–114). Uniquely among studies of this book, Schroeter approaches it as a literary work, rather than as travel literature or autobiography, and contends that we must find a key to it, as we do with *Finnegan's Wake*. The key which he supplies is the word "pursuit," meaning both "chase" and "vocation," and his discussion is happily centered on the literary craftsmanship Hemingway displays. This is an important study and a useful corrective to previous scholarship.

Similarly, Joseph M. DeFalco's "Hemingway's Islands and Streams: Minor Tactics For Heavy Pressure" (Astro and Benson, pp. 39–51) tries to correct attempts to read "Hemingway's fiction as autobiography and to judge his work by standards alien to fiction." Relating *Islands in the Stream* to *Across the River and Into the Trees* and *The Old Man and the Sea*, DeFalco sees all three reflecting "a major shift to the affirmative mode in the realism of Hemingway's later fiction." This is a closely argued and convincing essay.

The Astro and Benson collection also contains two good essays on *A Moveable Feast*. In "Sketches of the Author's Life in Paris in the Twenties" (pp. 25–38), George Wickes deals with "what Hemingway put into his last book and what he left out," examines "how he selected certain episodes and sketched certain individuals," and tries to explain why. His conclusion—that the book is "just about as slightly fictionalized as *The Sun Also Rises*, but with one all-important difference: that it is presented in the guise of memoirs written with scrupulous precision"—is demonstrated convincingly through his careful review of Hemingway's portraits of Fitzgerald, Pound, Eliot, Stein, and Ford.

Starting where Wickes ends his article—with the assumption that *A Moveable Feast* is more fiction than fact—Faith G. Norris's "*A Moveable Feast* and *Remembrance of Things Past*: Two Quests for Lost Time" (pp. 99–111) cites the "illuminating parallels" she finds between the two works. These include similarities in theme (both proclaim that "time is an ever-flowing substance which, once gone, will never return"), in approach (both authors omit "certain experiences discreditable to them" but "give us a God's plenty when dealing with the weaknesses of others"), and technique (both describe episodes and persons without much regard for chronological time). These correspondences are convincing; what is considerably less plausible is Norris's labeling of both works as novels of manners.

Two recent articles on the short stories deal with the *In Our Time* collection, and both present attempts to find a unity in the volume. Carl Wood's "*In Our Time*: Hemingway's Fragmentary Novel" (*NM* 74[1973]:716–26) sees unity in its plot involving a single composite personality represented in several characters. Wood is best in showing the thematic interrelationships between the stories. Richard Hasbany, in "The Shock of Vision: An Imagist Reading of *In Our Time*" (Wagner, *Five Decades*, pp. 224–40), also is strongest in his explications of the individual pieces. His discussion of Imagism is a familiar one and his delineation of the imagistic techniques and devices in the stories is often hazy.

In "The Family in Hemingway's Nick Adams Stories" (*SSF* 11: 303–05), Frank W. Shelton sees Nick's changing attitudes toward family relationships as an organizing principle. Thus, his apparent rejection of fatherhood and marriage before the war alters as he realizes progressively that family relationships, though often painful, can prevent isolation and cushion one from the world's brutality. Shelton's approach is a useful one. In another overview of Hemingway's stories, George Monteiro, in "Hemingway, O. Henry, and the Surprise Ending" (*PrS* 47[1973]:296–302), compares and contrasts the endings of "The Last Leaf" and "A Day's Wait" to show the different views of human experience implied in their respective surprise endings. Hemingway uses his to emphasize his belief that life is inescapably ironic. Finally, Delbert E. Wylder's "Internal Treachery in the Last Published Short Stories of Ernest Hemingway" (Astro and Benson, pp. 53–65) deals with "Two Tales of Darkness" (1957). He provides good close readings of these little-studied works; but his claim that they are "the most complex of all his short stories" seems extravagant and in need of further explanation.

There are far fewer studies of individual Hemingway stories than usual, and most are very brief. One of the two pieces on "A Clean, Well-Lighted Place" (the only story which is the subject of more than one article this year) is, predictably, yet another rehashing of the textual problems in the story, Warren Bennett's "The New Text of 'A Clean, Well-Lighted Place'" (*LHY* 14,i[1973]:115–25). Decidedly more worthwhile is Annette Benert's "Survival Through Irony: Hemingway's 'A Clean, Well-Lighted Place'" (*SSF* 11:181–87), which takes the position that the story presents as many "anti-'nada'" images of light, cleanness, and quiet as "nada" images.

The year's best study of a Hemingway short story is Kenneth G. Johnston's "Hemingway's 'Wine of Wyoming': Disappointment in America" (*WAL* 9:159–67). This is an extremely perceptive and clearly argued explication of a story which is often dismissed lightly. Johnston sees it as concerning "the American 'melting pot' and the discrepancy between the dream and the reality of American life." He points out how the recurrent mention of Al Smith's presidential candidacy and the repeated descriptions of the snow-capped mountains which form the backdrop for the action are related to this theme. Throughout, Johnston's attention is totally on the text; and his claims for it are modestly and logically presented.

Three of Hemingway's most critically studied stories are each the subject of one essay. In "The Structure of 'The Killers'" (*LHY* 15,i: 114–19), M. S. Nagarajan writes awkwardly of "the near-perfect fusion" between "the outward form and the inner life" of the story. H. H. Bell, Jr., in "Hemingway's 'The Short Happy Life of Francis Macomber'" (*Expl* 32:item 78), sees Wilson's treatment of Margot as that of a true hunter who must kill a wounded animal for the protection of others. Thus, Margot, "wounded" by her husband's achieving of manhood, is dangerous; and Wilson "kills" her by breaking her pride. This view probably deserves a fuller treatment. The title of Scott MacDonald's "Hemingway's 'The Snows of Kilimanjaro': Three Critical Problems" (*SSF* 11:67–74) suggests its scope. The three problems are: the significance of Harry's imagined flight to Kilimanjaro; the reasons for Hemingway's use of italics; and the implications of the epigraph. MacDonald's examination of these areas is useful; but his attempt to tie them together at the end of the essay seems strained.

Finally, in "Hemingway's 'Miracle' Play: 'Today Is Friday' and the York Play of the Crucifixion" (*MarkhamR* 4[1973]:8–11) Robert D. Arner investigates "the possibility that the York Play of the Crucifixion (*Christi Crucifixio*) could have served as a source for Hemingway's play" and demonstrates how the York Play adds perspective and meaning to "Today Is Friday." The similarities cited— in characters, language, and the representation of Christ—do support Arner's contention that Hemingway's play is "richer and more inter-

esting" than previously acknowledged. And his essay is a fitting conclusion to this survey in that its concern with Hemingway's religious
views and themes is an echo of several of the other pieces noted above.

f. Dissertations.   The steady stream of doctoral research on Fitzgerald and Hemingway slowed to a trickle in 1974. There were not
any dissertations dealing exclusively with either writer, although one
concerned a comparison of the role of women in their works. Aside
from this, both are among the writers considered in two or three
general dissertations.[1]

University of Maryland

1. This essay could not have been completed without the research assistance
of Nancy Prothro.

Part II

11. Literature to 1800

Robert D. Arner

One of the dismal disappointments of this past year in early American studies was to find the early South almost totally neglected, but with the assurance of better things to come I have preserved my predecessor's separate category. On the positive side of the ledger, this was a good year for historical studies and biographies, with Paul Boyer's and Stephen Nissenbaum's account of the Salem witch trials, David F. Hawke's masterful biography of Paine, and Edmund and Dorothy Smith Berkeley's life of Dr. John Mitchell heading the list. Among bibliographical studies, C. William Miller's handsome book on Franklin's Philadelphia printing stands out, while of book-length critical treatments, the section on Phillis Wheatley in Merle A. Richmond's book on Wheatley and George Moses Horton merits special attention here, as does also William J. Scheick's discussion of Edward Taylor. An important diary kept by Ebenezer Parkman was issued in book form, and two first-rate anthologies of essays appeared, one edited by Sacvan Bercovitch and the other, a collection of articles and notes by Douglass Adair, edited by Trevor Colbourn. An interesting sidelight, spurred by Fawn M. Brodie's biography of Jefferson, was the renewal of the controversy over Jefferson's relations or nonrelations with the slave girl Sally Hemings.

Among shorter pieces those by Norman Pettit and Sargent Bush, Jr., on Thomas Hooker seem especially well done, while William J. Scheick's analysis of Nathaniel Ward's *Simple Cobler* is also sound. Karen Rowe has written a nice essay on Edward Taylor's meditations on Canticles, and Leo M. Kaiser has edited a number of John Leverett's Latin writings. Sacvan Bercovitch's essay on Cotton Mather clarifies Mather's relationship to some of his American successors, while in a more modest way Carl Dolmetsch attempts the same feat for William Byrd. Good essays on Franklin were hard to come by, but Paul Ilie's at least deserves attention; Franklin's sometime alter

ego, Edwards, was sensitively studied by David Weddle, and J. A.
Leo Lemay took a look at another writer of the Great Awakening in
his examination of one of Joseph Green's previously unpublished
satires. Not surprisingly, worthwhile essays on Revolutionary and
early National writers were relatively plentiful in this year of Bicentennial celebration, with Edwin Gittleman and Julian Boyd contribut-
ing significant essays on Jefferson, Gordon S. Wood on Richard Henry
Lee and the *Federal Farmer*, and Robert D. Arner on Freneau. Early
novelists were also favored; Charles Brockden Brown alone was the
subject of four solid essays, one each by William L. Hedges, Michael
D. Bell, Paul C. Rodgers, Jr., and Paul Witherington, and the sea
motif in early fiction was ably discussed by Roger B. Stein.

i. Edward Taylor

Of major significance to Taylor scholarship is William J. Scheick's
The Will and The Word: The Poetry of Edward Taylor (Athens:
Univ. of Ga. Press), which carries on the critical tradition of examining Taylor's intellectual and theological backgrounds while also reflecting the recent interest in close exegesis of given poems and image
patterns. Particularly impressive is Scheick's ability to bring together into meaningful patterns clusters of images scattered throughout 40 years of Taylor's work. At the same time, the philosophical
foundations of the study seem occasionally too shaky to support
the total weight of Scheick's argument about Augustinian faculty
psychology and the renewed will as motive force and theological
and psychological center of Taylor's meditations; also, the tightly
structured prose of the book seems ill-suited to convey Taylor's controlling theme of Love, but Scheick's overall command of the poet's
work and his understanding of the Puritan mind in general, marred
only by Perry Miller's familiar monolithic flaw, makes his argument
a formidable one that will have to be reckoned with by any future
Taylor scholars wishing to set aside or significantly modify his
conclusions.

   Another good contribution is Karen E. Rowe's "Sacred or Profane? Edward Taylor's Meditations on Canticles," *MP* 72:123–38.
Rowe spends a bit too much time on the old problem of Taylor's sensuous imagery, but she correctly points out that most of those questionable images derive from Canticles, a book on which Taylor wrote

49 meditations all told. Tracing Taylor's marked preference for "spiritual expositions" rather than "prophetical and political analyses" of Canticles to Arthur Jackson's and James Durham's commentaries, Rowe then suggests an organizational pattern for the Second Series of *Preparatory Meditations*: "From the historical and typological poems (II. 1–30) that prefigure Christ and those that despair over the degeneracy of the human condition and his personal state, Taylor moves in later life toward meditations on Christ's immediate presence and reconciliation with the redeemed."

For most of us Michael D. Reed's news that Taylor was strongly influenced by "Puritan meditative tradition and religious doctrine" ("Edward Taylor's Poetry: Puritan Structure and Form," *AL* 46: 304–12) will seem a bit stale, but Reed freshens it up somewhat with the observation that Taylor's conceits "insist on and maintain the gap between the human and the divine" to a degree that English metaphysical poetry does not and that individual meditations tend to end either as petitions or in the "hypothetical mode" as a way of maintaining tonally the balance between the sin of wanhope and the sin of spiritual self-assurance within a Puritan context. The only other note on Taylor this past year, Jesse C. Jones's "A Note on the Number of Edward Taylor's *Preparatory Meditations*," *EAL* 9:81–82, is an exercise in elementary arithmetic and surely need not have been published.

ii. Puritanism

Two first-generation Puritan historians come in for careful scrutiny in William J. Scheick's "The Theme of Necessity in Bradford's *Of Plymouth Plantation*," *SCN* 32:88–90, and Edward J. Gallagher's "The Case for the *Wonder-Working Providence*," *BNYPL* 77(1973): 10–27. Scheick argues that Bradford and the Pilgrims originally ascribed to divine providence "actions which actually derived from the corrupt necessity of the innately depraved heart," and as the progress of historical events gradually made this enlarged meaning of necessity clear to them, they lost their lofty faith and confidence; this descent and its consequences, says Scheick, exactly parallel the patterns described in different terms by David Levin, Alan Howard, and Jesper Rosenmeier. In contrast, Edward J. Gallagher asserts that Edward Johnson's *Wonder-Working Providence*, motivated by the

"doctrine of the Second Coming of Christ," transcends historical circumstances to become "myth, history illuminated and governed by an
imaginative conception aimed at satisfying an existential need"; it
represents "the first sustained mythicizing of the American experience
written by an inhabitant." Yet another early historian, one who has
never been believed, is the subject of Robert D. Arner's "Pastoral
Celebration and Satire in Thomas Morton's *New English Canaan*,"
Criticism 16:217–31. Arner's concern is not with Morton's historical
method, however, but with his literary technique; Morton, Arner
argues, borrows from English folk tradition two complementary and
yet antithetical voices, those of the May Lord and the Lord of Misrule. As his fortunes take a decided and final downward swing, Morton abandons both of those for the Biblical Jeremiah, implicitly ac-
knowledging that the spirit of festivity has been defeated in New
England.

The only other 17th-century New Englander known to possess a
sense of humor, Nathaniel Ward, is discussed by William J. Scheick
in "The Widower Narrator in Nathaniel Ward's *The Simple Cobler
of Aggawam in America*," *NEQ* 47:87–96. The essay advances our
appreciation of Ward's command of rhetorical resources by isolating
a pattern of cross-referenced images and metaphors relating to marriage and, according to Scheick, the symbolical marriage of man to
Truth. The impact of another minister, Thomas Hooker, on New
England thought was assessed by Norman Pettit ("Hooker's Doctrine
of Assurance: A Critical Phase in New England Spiritual Thought,"
NEQ 47:518–34). Focusing on Hooker's controversy with John Cotton over the issue of immediate assurance and Cotton's dangerous
verging on Antinomianism, Pettit concludes importantly: "Hooker
was the first of the Jacobean Puritan divines fully to discuss the
doctrine of assurance as it related to man's resistance to the Spirit"
and "the first to be concerned with certain habits of mind the dangers
of which later became apparent in New England; and among these
were overintrospection and excessive reliance on 'feeling' and 'sense.'"

Hooker's writings are also the topic of Sargent Bush, Jr.'s "Four
New Works by Thomas Hooker: Identity and Significance," *RALS*
4:3–26, which recovers from a well-known entry in the *Stationers
Register* (November 13, 1637) four new titles: *The Sinners Salvation,
The Properties of An Honest Heart, Spirituall Thirst*, and *The Stay of
the Faithfull*. In addition to the initials "T. H.," already established

as referring to Hooker for two of the seven works lumped together in this single entry, the evidence for attribution is both internal—style, structure, and theme—and external: Hooker's demonstrated associations with the printer Robert Dawlman, for example. Bush not only argues these attributions very convincingly but also discusses the evidence for definitely attributing to Hooker yet another of the seven works, *Spirituall Munition*, long thought to be Hooker's but not previously examined closely. This last work and *The Stay of the Faithfull* are among only four known to have been "preached directly on England's troubles during the reign of Charles I," while *Properties* is one of the relatively few works by Hooker "prepared specifically to be read." The other two new titles extend our knowledge of Hooker's concern with "the long series of stages through which the elect soul passes on his way to grace and beyond."

As the bibliography of one Puritan divine increases, another's shrinks. The loss this time is John Norton's, who, according to Wayne Franklin ("John Norton the Printer: An Attribution," *SB* 27:185–87) is pretty definitely not the author of *An Answer to a Late Scurrilous and Scandalous Pamphlet* (1642) long credited to him; the rebus of "NOR" over a keg or "tun" which seemed to hint at his authorship is really an identifying mark of John Norton, a London printer. To counterbalance this small diminution, however, Thomas M. Davis reprints from Edward Taylor's "Extracts" Solomon Stoddard's sermon on Galatians 3.1 ("Solomon Stoddard's Sermon on the Lord's Supper as a Converting Ordinance," *RALS* 4:205–24). The sermon is dated 1679, a full decade before Stoddard returned to the same subject with more success (Winter 1690), and Davis credibly conjectures that on this first occasion even so persuasive a minister as Stoddard failed to convince his congregation of his point of view.

Some minor Puritan poets emerged momentarily from obscurity this past year, among them John Fiske, whom James Bray studied in "John Fiske: Puritan Precursor of Edward Taylor," *EAL* 9:27–38. Bray discusses Fiske's use of puns and paradoxes but does not probe much beyond the surface of Fiske's language in arguing the poet's similarities to Taylor. Leo M. Kaiser carefully edits and annotates "Thirteen Early American Latin Elegies: A Critical Edition," *Humanistica Lovaniensia* 23:346–81, ranging from Elijah Corlet's elegy on Thomas Hooker (1647) to the first known Southern elegy in Latin, William Dawson's (?) verses on John Randolph's death in 1737.

Meanwhile Anne Bradstreet, hardly an obscure poet, was highlighted in three studies, none of them exceptional. Kenneth R. Ball rather unconvincingly relates the structure of Bradstreet's verses to "the Puritan morphology of conversion," ignoring distinctions of kind and intention which, in the epitaphs at least, easily account for the theme of humility and the concluding contemplation of paradise ("Puritan Humility in Anne Bradstreet's Poetry," *Cithara* 13[1973]:29–41). Kenneth A. Requa, "Anne Bradstreet's *Poetic Voices*," *EAL* 9:1–18, discusses once again the public and private qualities of Anne's work but does not add anything significant to what has already and long ago been said. The best of the Bradstreet essays is Jane Donahue Eberwein's "The 'Unrefined Ore' of Anne Bradstreet's Quaternions," *EAL* 9:19–26, which is also keyed to traditional tensions but deals with poems that do not often receive attention.

Single-handedly, Leo M. Kaiser almost elevates John Leverett, tutor and later president of Harvard, to the stature of a major writer, at least in terms of critical attention. Kaiser introduces and reprints three of Leverett's Latin writings in "Seventeenth-Century American Latin Prose: John Leverett's Welcome to Governor Sir Edmund Andros," *Manuscripta* 18:30–37; "A President Accepts," *The Classical Outlook* 52:40–41; and "John Leverett and the Quebec Expedition of 1711: An Unpublished Latin Oration," *HLB* 22:309–16. In all of these Kaiser notes Leverett's command of the language, his "capacity for vivid expression," and his ability to express dangerous sentiments tactfully (as in the welcome to Andros). Another minor figure of the period, though not a Latinist, is Robert Roule, whose account of the massacre of Indian captives by enraged women is reprinted by James L. Axtell in "The Vengeful Women of Marblehead: Robert Roule's Deposition of 1677," *WMQ* 31:647–52.

Increase Mather and his famous offspring seem also to be making a collective bid for major stature. In *Increase Mather* (TUSAS 246), Mason I. Lowance, Jr., struggles with the straitjacket of Twayne format and the extra complication of diverse audiences but manages to accomplish what he modestly hopes for the book, an extension of Kenneth Murdock's fine *Increase Mather: The Foremost Puritan* (1925). Increase's son Cotton is treated in the company of Jonathan Edwards in Stephen J. Stein's "Cotton Mather and Jonathan Edwards on the Number of the Beast: Eighteenth Century Speculation about the Antichrist," *PAAS* 84:293–316, which points out that the two Puritan divines, though separated in time, both subscribed to Francis Potter's *An Interpretation of the Number 666* (1642). Not only does this shared borrowing demonstrate the "continuities in the English tradition" of apocalyptic interpretation, but it also underscores an American tendency to invest diverse local issues with ultimate significance "and to transform power struggles into crusades against the forces of the beast." In " 'Nehemias Americanus': Cotton Mather and the Concept of the Representative American," *EAL* 8:220–38, Sacvan Bercovitch extends Stein's speculations about Mather's relevance to later American culture by brilliantly tracing the inherited impulse which led "the major figures of the American Renaissance" to find "the way out of private despair" in "the affirmation of a national self-hood which allows the individual to create himself in the image of America even as he spiritualizes America into a metaphor for the journey of the soul." This conflation of country, saint, and church, Bercovitch shows, is precisely what Mather accomplishes in dealing with Winthrop, whose identity Mather comes to share as he declares "*himself* the meaning of America." The life of Winthrop "merits our attention . . . for the biographical method it sets forth, and the heroic concept it establishes, a concept larger than the disparate 17th-century elements it contains, because it defines the representative American." To pass from such erudition to Sigrid Moe's "Cotton Mather's Literary Output: A Reassessment," *AN&Q* 12:102–06, and hear that Mather did not really write as many original pages or books as stunned critics give him credit for, since he often plagiarized himself, is to make the proverbial journey from sublimity to ridiculousness. Put Mather into a collected edition, urges Moe, and you will have only 20 or so modern volumes of around 400 pages each—"not a staggering accomplishment for 44 years of incessant writing." *Sic transit gloria mundi.*

Those archantagonists of the Puritan establishment, the Quakers, also came in for some attention this year. John Ditsky's "Hard Hearts and Gentle People: A Quaker Reply to Persecution," *CRevAS* 5:47–51, examines Francis Howgill's *The Heart of New England Hardened through Wickedness* (1659) as a reply to John Norton's *The Heart of New England Rent . . .* (London edition, 1660). Except for his failure to forestall some confusion by telling us that Norton's book had a 1659 printing in New England, Ditsky's summary of Howgill's refutation and then counterattack is competently done, though he should be less surprised about the anger that Quakers could work up. J. William Frost recounts another Quaker struggle, this time in Rhode Island, in "Quaker Versus Baptist: A Religious and Political Squabble in Rhode Island Three Hundred Years Ago," *QH* 63:39–52, which discusses the furor over George Fox's visit to the colony in May 1672, when the Quaker Nicholas Easton was governor; Frost also reprints Fox's sermon notes of May 25 and Thomas Olney's rejoinder, "Ambition Anatomized." Finally, Michael P. Graves offers "A Checklist of Extant Quaker Sermons, 1650–1700," QH 63:53–59, in order to disprove the stereotype that the Quaker form of worship allowed for little emphasis upon the spoken word.

We have yet to deal with two fine books, one an anthology of critical essays, the other an historical-sociological study. The first is Sacvan Bercovitch's *The American Puritan Imagination: Essays in Revaluation* (Cambridge: The Cambridge Univ. Press), which is divided into three sections—Approaches, Themes, and Genres; Four Major Writers (Bradford, Bradstreet, Taylor, and Mather); and Continuities—and which brings together some of the finest essays written during the last decade and a half. Bercovitch has laid under contribution the talents of Norman Grabo, Larzer Ziff, David Minter, Cecilia Tichi, Jesper Rosenmeier, Robert D. Richardson, Jr., Karl Keller, David Levin, Daniel B. Shea, Jr., John F. Lynen, and Ursula Brumm. There is no point remarking on the essays in detail; most have long since proved their value to the study of Colonial letters. The best, to my mind, is Grabo's "The Veiled Vision: The Role of Aesthetics in Early American Intellectual History" (orig. in *WMQ* 19:493–510), but also fine is Bercovitch's introduction, the only previously unpublished piece in the collection; it not only shapes and directs the book but also summarizes some of the key challenges and possibilities of early American studies.

As for the historical inquiry, Paul Boyer's and Stephen Nissenbaum's *Salem Possessed: The Social Origins of Witchcraft* (Cambridge, Mass.: Harvard Univ. Press) I believe to be the best treatment yet in print of that much-discussed episode. It is not only thorough but full of original insights, plausible theories that grow out of the authors' close examination of the Putnam and Porter families and the interfamily quarrels often inspired by the drive toward autonomy for Salem Village, which the Putnams championed and the Porters opposed. Economics, geography, and the pressures of a changing society, Boyer and Nissenbaum argue cogently, separately and together played a part in shaping the Putnams' attitudes toward their own ill luck, but there were psychological factors as well which the authors speculatively explore. Especially illuminating is their treatment of Samuel Parris's sermons in the months before and during the outbreak, his fascination with betrayals and money, and by focusing on the psychological dimensions of the ritual of public confession, the authors also offer a convincing explanation of why no confessing "witches" were executed.

iii. The South

Once again the faraway and forgotten country, the colonial South, attracted the interest of only two critics this past year, both identified with Southern Colonial studies for some time. In a review essay focused on Pierre Marambaud's *William Byrd of Westover, 1674–1744* (Charlottesville: Univ. Press of Va. [1972]), Carl R. Dolmetsch argues that Byrd must be approached not only from a sociohistorical perspective, as Marambaud does, but also from an aesthetic one ("William Byrd of Westover," *EA* 27:320–23). Byrd, Dolmetsch contends, is indeed a writer of note and not simply a colonial whose best work does not compare with that of his London contemporaries; London, in fact, offers no basis for comparison, both because its population was so much greater than that of early Virginia and because fashionable English literary models proved unserviceable to Byrd, who practically had to invent his own form for the "Histories." Quite correctly, Dolmetsch also points out that Byrd was only one of several talented early Southern writers, and in coincidental support of that thesis Robert D. Arner offers an analysis of " 'Clio's *Rhimes*': History and Satire in Ebenezer Cooke's 'History of Bacon's Rebellion,' " *SLJ* 6:91–106. Cooke's "History," says Arner, has in the past been judged by democratic standards, when what is obviously required is an assessment of contemporary 18th-century political attitudes. Viewed in this light, Cooke's conservatism is easily understood; his political faith helps the satirist to elevate a local rebellion and rebel leader into symbols of universal folly as well. Both dimensions of the rebellion are kept before us by a satirist-historian who in both capacities shared with his age the ideas of David Hume and others that human nature and human folly remain unchanged from century to century and culture to culture.

iv. Franklin and the Enlightenment

It took C. William Miller 20 years to compile his *Benjamin Franklin's Philadelphia Printing: A Descriptive Bibliography* (Philadelphia: Amer. Philosophical Soc., MAPS 102), but the effort paid off. Here is a book which is truly indispensable for colonial scholars, an impressive labor of love which opens with short surveys of the problems of colonial printers, of type fonts and foundries, of Franklin's instrumental role in the establishment of a thriving paper mill industry in the Middle Colonies, and of early American bookbinding, among other things. An outstanding feature of the main text is the photographic reproductions, some of them necessarily diminished, of all of Franklin's available title pages—a photographic essay, if you will, on Franklin's skill at typographic design. Examples of Franklin's early type are provided in an appendix, and, to make the book still more useful, a final concordance cross-references titles to Evans, Shipton and Mooney, Bristol, and the *Franklin Bibliography*. With convincing evidence as his argument, Miller removes some 86 items from the list of Franklin or Franklin and Hall imprints. An extraordinarily handsome volume as well, Miller's book is not likely ever to be superseded.

Another facet of Franklin's literary career is explored by Betty Kushen in "Three Earliest Published Lives of Benjamin Franklin, 1790–93: The *Autobiography* and Its Continuations," *EAL* 9:39–52. Despite its title, the essay is less bibliographical than analytical, detailing the shifts in Franklin's reputation in the years immediately following his death. Kushen discusses the mixture of praise and censure in James Jones Wilmer's *Memoirs* (London, 1790), in which the Loyalist Wilmer predictably blackens Franklin's character, in Buisson's *Mémoires* (Paris, 1791), and in the anonymous but clearly republican *Private Life* (London, 1793); the alternating pattern of defamation and defense, Kushen notes, has remained as the rhythm of Franklin biographies ever since. And in another essay on the *Auto-biography*, Paul Ilie ventures a comparative analysis of "Franklin and Villarroel: Social Consciousness in Two Autobiographies," *ECS* 7:321–42, concluding, not surprisingly, that the American and the Spaniard present contrasting attitudes towards religion, the value of work, and the ideal of social mobility; Franklin's life stands as an exemplum for the upward bound middle class, while Villarroel's both reflects and promotes "the mentality of social dependence."

Two of Franklin's friends and correspondents, John Bartram and Dr. John Mitchell, kept him company on this year's critical roster. In "Humor in John Bartram's Journals," *AN&Q* 12:90–93, John J. Gill notes that many of the passages inexplicably omitted from Helen Cruickshank's reprint of *Travels in Pennsylvania and Canada* (New York: Devin-Adair, 1957) are humorous and that they establish at once Bartram's indebtedness and contributions to the "tradition of American humor." Bartram's humor, Gill maintains, depends less upon "verbal wit than on incongruity or comic elements of the incidents," but, frankly, I did not find anything funny in Gill's examples, and in any case the "tradition of American humor" requires further defini-tion. On the other hand, Edmund and Dorothy Smith Berkeley's *Dr. John Mitchell: The Man Who Made the Map of North America* (Chapel Hill: Univ. of N. C. Press) is not only the first biography of this intriguing man but also a first-rate one. The book takes off from Theodore Hornberger's assessment of Mitchell as "for a time perhaps the ablest scientific investigator in North America" and "a key to the problem of intellectual life in the colonies" (*HLQ* 10[1947]:277). What emerges is the life of an American scientist, Virginia born, who, like his countrymen in the arts, founded his career on the close obser-vation of nature and practical experimentation but who, also like them (Benjamin West, J. S. Copley, *et al.*), constantly lamented the lack of trained companions and his great distance from the "*books and learning*" of Europe. Forced by ill health to move to England, Mitch-ell continued a career that had already produced tracts on an epi-demic of Weil's Disease, which he mistakenly diagnosed as yellow fever, and a detailed anatomy of the opossum; in England, he met or was introduced in correspondence to John Bartram, Franklin, Cadwallader Colden, John Custis, and William Byrd, among other notables, and it was here, too, that his carefully prepared map brought

him cartographic fame. Strictly speaking, the Berkeleys' treatment of
Mitchell's English career falls beyond the specific scope of my remarks, though not of my strong commendation.

v. Edwards and the Great Awakening

The best essay of the year on Jonathan Edwards is David Weddle's
"Jonathan Edwards on Men and Trees, and the Problem of Solidarity," *HTR* 67:155–75, which discusses Edwards's use of tree and
branch imagery to present his concept of the solidarity of man both
as saint and sinner. The grafting image, says Weddle, speaks of
growth and history as well as of divine establishment, and it is precisely here, in his theory of inherited depravity through historical
identity, that Edwards's break from an Augustinian concept of the
"natural" unity of the race as "physical" is most apparent. By maintaining the balance between "disposition as a generic characteristic
and action as an individual responsibility," Edwards was able to
arrive at a theory of "racial unity in Adam . . . without the unfashion-
able assumptions of Platonic realism on the one hand or the ethically
precarious implications of federalism [i.e., the claim that man sinned
through his representative, Adam, a notion that 18th-century political
developments were even then rendering unsavory and untenable] on
the other." In "Family, Conversion, and the Self in Jonathan Edwards's *A Faithful Narrative of the Surprising Work of God*," *TSL*
19:79–89, William J. Scheick ranges through many of Edwards's other
works as well to support his contention that the motif of the family is
at the heart of *Faithful Narrative* and to argue that contemplation of
the family led Edwards to a new understanding of the experience of
grace. In the saint, Edwards came to realize, the stages of conversion
"generally thought to be preparatory could in actuality be responses
to the presence of grace in the soul." Finally, Stephen J. Stein contributes an interesting note on "Jonathan Edwards and the Rainbow:
Biblical Exegesis and the Poetic Imagination," *NEQ* 47:440–56, in
which Stein examines Edwards's early musings, scientific and spiritual, on the rainbow; this background frames Stein's analysis of the
"meteorological and theological" dimensions of an extended entry in
Edwards's "Biblical Notebooks," which Stein finds unconventional
in that it deemphasizes the literal and contextual implications of the

Biblical rainbow. Such exercises in the explication of natural symbols, says Stein, served Edwards as a release from the more rigorously intellectual pursuits of sermonizing and philosophizing, though the probing revealed in *Images and Shadows* does not tend to support Stein's conclusion about release and relaxation.

Francis G. Walett's edition of *The Diary of Ebenezer Parkman* (Worcester, Mass.: American Antiquarian Society), originally published serially in *PAAS* (vols. 71 to 76, 1961–66), provides a conservative view of the Great Awakening which Edwards was instrumental in inspiring. Parkman was acquainted with Edwards and George Whitefield, among other leaders of the revival, but his responses to revivalism and the intellectual ferment of the Awakening were nonetheless cautious. The Diary tells the story of Parkman's life from 1719 to 1755, first as a student at Harvard and then as the minister of the church at Westborough, Massachusetts; like the more famous diary of Samuel Sewall, which it both complements chronologically and contrasts in its rural setting, Parkman's is also something of a self-portrait—see, for example, the entries dated April 30 and May 1, 1750—and an invaluable resource work, covering topics from folkways to psalm singing and literary tastes. Walett's attempt to identify in footnotes most of those whose paths crossed Parkman's own greatly enhances the value of this diary.

One instance of the religious controversy touched off by the spread of revivalistic fervor is the subject of J. A. Leo Lemay's "Joseph Green's Satirical Poem on the Great Awakening," *RALS* 4:173–83. An indefatigable reseacher who has already turned up many colonial treasures, Lemay here presents another small gem, Green's 1742 (?) attack on the Rev. William Cooper. Delightfully scurrilous, the poem is its own justification of Lemay's call for more thorough explorations of colonial commonplace books in manuscript collections. Another discovery along the same lines, though beyond the immediate scope of the Great Awakening, is William G. McLoughlin's find of "Ebenezer Smith's Ballad of the Ashfield Baptists, 1772," *NEQ* 47:97–108. McLoughlin calls the work an example of "primitive protest poetry," though it is not really a ballad; moreover, the claim for its importance as an ancestor of Woody Guthrie's and Bob Dylan's songs seems a bit far-fetched, if only because many earlier, better (and more ballad-like) poems deserve that distinction. Smith was not a good poet, to say the least, but his crude verses at least apprise us of the intense passion he threw into the struggle to free Baptists from compulsory taxation to support the Congregational Church.

vi. Revolutionary and Early National Periods

In contrast to the year just passed, patriots far outnumber Tories in 1974, which is, I suppose, as it should be. Only James E. Mooney's "Loyalist Imprints Printed in America, 1774–1785," *PAAS* 84:105–218, breaks the silence on the Tory side, while the struggles of a patriot printer, David Hall, are taken up by Robert D. Harlan in "David Hall and the Townshend Acts," *PBSA* 68:19–38, an essay that points out the contrast between Hall's reluctant resistance to the Stamp Act and his patriotic response to the Townshend Acts; self-interest, says Harlan, played some part, especially since William Franklin and Joseph Galloway's *Pennsylvania Chronicle* was substantially undercutting Hall's profits, but there can be no doubt from the record of his printing that he had indeed become a patriot in the few years intervening.

Still on the purlieus of the struggle, Sheldon B. Cohen goes searching for "Student Unrest in the Decade Before the American Revolution," *ConnR* 7,ii:51–58, and though he finds familiar causes for complaint—bad food, authoritarian faculty and administration— he also finds students at Yale, Harvard, and the Colleges of Rhode Island and New Jersey wearing clothes of American manufacture, helping to burn storehouses of tea, and delivering nationalistic commencement orations; still, in Cohen's eyes, the chief service of American colleges in those years was to prepare an impressive number of young men for leadership during and after the Revolution: hardly a striking conclusion. And as the conflict grows still nearer, Fred R. McFadden, Jr., calls attention to the oedipal aspects of the Revolution as manifested in polemical writings and popular iconography ("Popular Arts and the Revolt Against Patriarchism in Colonial America," *JPC* 8:286–94).

In his biography of the penman of the Revolution, *Paine* (New York: Harper & Row), David F. Hawke has managed to write a lucid book about a difficult subject, a man whose life has been clouded by lies and legends. One of the things that makes this the best life of Paine available is the thoroughness of Hawke's scholarship; another is the clarity with which he handles complex issues, as in the case of the political manueverings that trapped Paine in the Reign of Terror; and yet another is the soundness of his literary judgments. He places *Agrarian Justice* high on the list of Paine's achievements, for instance, locates *The Age of Reason* in a tradition of deism that is neither Anglo-American nor French, and observes that Paine's great accomplishment in that work and in *The Rights of Man* is that both reinforce their messages by means of a style calculated to undermine "traditional deference of plain people." If Hawke's study errs at all, it is slightly on the side of idealizing its subject, somewhat after the fashion of John Wesley Jarvis's portrait of Paine that adorns the book jacket. In contradistinction to Hawke's study, Joseph V. Metzgar's "The Cosmology of Thomas Paine," *IllQ* 37:47–63, errs by saying nothing new about Paine's acceptance of a Newtonian universe and the notion of a Great Chain of Being; only when Metzgar points out the contradiction between Paine's concept of God as an impersonal Prime Mover and the vengeful Jehovah who will interfere on behalf of the cause of freedom does his essay show some strength, and the remission is only temporary. Finally, Jerome D. Wilson sets out to provide in bibliographical overview an account of the vicissitudes of Paine's modern reputation in the country he helped to bring to birth ("Thomas Paine in America: An Annotated Bibliography, 1900–1973," *BB* 31:133–57, 180).

Many of the pieces in Douglass Adair's *Fame and the Founding Fathers: Essays by Douglass Adair*, ed. Trevor Colbourn (New York: W. W. Norton) have appeared previously, most in *WMQ* which Adair edited from 1946 to 1955. All are of great interest to historians and students of literature, but the most important are "The Authorship of the Disputed Federalist Papers" (pp. 27–74), which challenges the Benson list and restores Madison to 40 percent authorship; "The Tenth Federalist Revisited" (pp. 75–106), which examines the growth of Madison's faith that the pluralism of American society would prevent anarchy; "The Mystery of the Horn Papers" (pp. 203–32); and "A Note on Certain of Hamilton's Pseudonyms" (pp. 272–85). This last points out that not only do most of Hamilton's pseudonyms fit the contemporary situation, but all also refer to classical heroes who despised the mob, were eventually deposed by the rabble, and then vindicated by the later course of historical events.

It is too bad that Adair did not live to review Fawn M. Brodie's *Thomas Jefferson: An Intimate History* (New York: W. W. Norton), because in "The Jefferson Scandals" (pp. 160–91), one of the few previously unpublished pieces in the book, he states categorically that "it is possible to *prove* that Jefferson was innocent of [James T.] Callender's charges" that Jefferson kept a slave mistress, Sally Hemings, and fathered children by her. Adair accuses Jefferson's nephew Peter Carr instead, and if he does not quite prove Jefferson's innocence to anyone's full satisfaction except, perhaps, his own, still in accidental prophecy of 1974 his article constitutes the best argument against Brodie's book that I have yet seen. By and large Adair's scholarly method is superior to Brodie's, for whom suppositions on one page become established premises on the next. Brodie also accepts Sally Hemings's word (as reported by a son, Madison Hemings, in 1873) that she was pregnant by Jefferson in Paris in 1790 and that only the promise of freedom for her sons at age 21 brought her back to Virginia from a country where the status of slave was not recognized; yet Jefferson's *Farm Book*, upon which Brodie relies for many other details (and even reads omissions from the record as Jefferson's conscious or unconscious suppressions of his passion for Sally), dates the birth of Sally's first child in 1795, a significant discrepancy between legend and fact which Adair points out. Adair receives support from Dumas Malone ("Mr. Jefferson's Private Life," *PAAS* 84: 65–72), who reproduces a letter from Ellen Randolph Coolidge to her husband, Joseph Coolidge, Jr., addressed precisely to Callender's charges; but even with this piece of family testimony (which Brodie also uses to other ends) Malone concedes that "it is difficult to prove a negative," though he is willing to dismiss the accusation on the basis of Jefferson's known character.

Unwilling to disturb the balance of power in this stand-off, Max Beloff, in his review article on "A 'Founding Father': The Sally Hemings Affair," *Encounter* 43 (Sept.):52–56, circumspectly contents himself with distinguishing between Brodie's attitude toward miscegenation—she believes it humanizes Jefferson—and those of Merrill Peterson, Malone, and Winthrop Jordan. A final word: if neither Adair nor Malone proves a negative, Brodie also fails to prove a positive, and so the story remains alive and well and will undoubtedly be dredged up again at any time by any one wishing to make capital of it.

Not everyone who wrote on Jefferson was schooled in scandal. Julian P. Boyd's excellent "Jefferson's Expression of the American

Mind," *VQR* 50:538–62, traces the development of Jefferson's political thought from his immersion in legal studies (1762–67), when "he . . . made himself the best informed student in America on the rights, duties, and accountability of those elected to positions of public trust," to his "Declaration of rights and League for their support by the inhabitants of Virginia," which Patrick Henry refused to sponsor in the Virginia Assembly; the difference between this document and the *Summary View of the Rights of British America* lies in the greater emotional charge of the *Rights* and in Jefferson's "pragmatic insistence that political freedom is the indispensable prerequisite to all other forms of liberty." The next step, of course, is the *Declaration of Independence,* and Edwin Gittleman has closely examined that in a fine essay, "Jefferson's 'Slave Narrative': The Declaration of Independence as a Literary Text," *EAL* 8:239–56. Gittleman compares Jefferson's document with the one Congress finally adopted and finds that congressional substitution of "domestic Insurrections" for the original grievance against slavery not only destroys the logic of Jefferson's composition but also and more seriously exposes an "unforgivable [American] hypocrisy and . . . tyranny" far worse than the crimes charged against George III. Obviously less important than Gittleman's article is Harry R. Skallerup's "'For His Excellency Thomas Jefferson, Esq.': The Tale of a Wandering Book," *QJLC* 31:116–21, which reports that Jefferson's authorially inscribed copy of Jose de Mendoza y Rios's book on navigation, long lost from the Library of Congress, has been located at the U.S. Naval Academy.

Political writings attributed to another southerner, Richard Henry Lee, are the subject of Gordon S. Wood's "The Authorship of the *Letters from the Federal Farmer,*" *WMQ* 31:299–308. Wood suggests no other writer, but he builds a strong case for Lee's not being the author; his argument is based in part on the contemporary political environment, in part on the differences in style between this work and others known to be by Lee, and in part on Lee's failure to claim them for his own.

Among poets active during and immediately after the Revolution, none was more important than Freneau, whose struggles to survive in the society which the war brought into being are the subject of Thomas D. Cowan's "Philip Freneau: The Artist in the Early Republic," *PNJHS* 92:225–39, a superficial treatment of Freneau's alienation as an artist in a nation of artisans. More substantial are two articles that argue the case for Freneau's poetic competence, Carol A. Kyle's "That Poet Freneau: A Study of the Imagistic Success of *The Pictures of Columbus*," *EAL* 9:62–70, and Robert D. Arner's "Neoclassicism and Romanticism: A Reading of Freneau's 'The Wild Honey Suckle,'" *EAL* 9:53–61. Kyle discusses the discovery theme of *Pictures* "as an act realized through a reenactment in the form of the poem"; Columbus as artist first imagines the New World, then translates the fiction into geographical reality through direct action, just as Freneau imagines and then "discovers" the historical and mythically poetic presence of Columbus. Arner examines the persona, tone, and imagery of Freneau's best-known poem and cautions against reading the poet anachronistically, from a romantic rather than a neoclassic perspective.

Victor E. Gimmestad's book on another Revolutionary poet, *John Trumbull* (TUSAS 240), will hardly stand as the definitive critical study of this accomplished satirist, but it is competently done and, as an added feature, offers discussions of a good many poems not often mentioned by other critics. Gimmestad also, in "John Trumbull's 'Epithalamion,'" *YULG* 48:178–82, corrects errors in Irving N. Rothman's earlier "John Trumbull's Parody of Spenser's 'Epithalamion,'" *YULG* 47 (1973):193–215 by pointing out that the poem originally appeared in editions earlier than Rothman had cited and by extending the list of Trumbull's sources well beyond Spenser; according to Gimmestad, the poem confirms Trumbull's claim that his "satirical turn was not native," for in this early performance the poet was writing innocent burlesque rather than barbed satire.

Thanks largely to a special issue of *JSR* (6,i) and Merle A. Richmond's *Bid the Vassal Soar: Interpretive Essays on the Life and Poetry of Phillis Wheatley and George Moses Horton* (Washington, D.C.: Howard Univ. Press), America's first published black poet came in for more than her usual share of attention. Essays in the special number of *JSR* include Dorothy B. Porter's "Historical and Bibliographical Data of Phillis Wheatley's Publications" (pp. 54–60) and some interesting speculations about the poet's connections with the abolitionist cause and the Earl of Dartmouth by Margaret G. Burroughs, "Do Birds of a Feather Flock Together?" (pp. 61–73). In the same issue, Paula Giddings's "Critical Evaluation of Phillis Wheatley" (pp. 74–81) examines once more the charge that the poet lacked black consciousness; much of Giddings's article is taken from

Richmond's book, which is by far the best biographical and critical treatment of Wheatley to date, even though the repeated assertions that Wheatley was as accomplished as any other American poet then writing are, to say the least, annoying. Richmond places the poet in "a strange, ambiguous twilight zone" between black and white societies and suggests that Wheatley's blackness may paradoxically be seen in her failure to strike many notes of protest; slavery is responsible for this deprivation of personal and cultural identity, the disappearance of Wheatley as an individual behind the conventions of white society and literature. Finally, Kenneth Silverman ("Four New Letters by Phillis Wheatley," *EAL* 8:257–71) adds to the Wheatley bibliography correspondence with the English philanthropist John Thornton, letters that, among other things, date her manumission some three months before the death of her mistress Susanna Wheatley; they also underscore a tension between the poet and her missionary friends, who "had led her to Homer, Milton, and Newton, but wished her to settle in Annamaboe" and preach to her own race.

vii. Brown and Contemporaries

Immensely aided by a special issue of *EAL*, the Charles Brockden Brown revival proceeds apace, and we shall shortly have an authoritative CEAA edition of *Wieland* as one result of it. Meanwhile that novel is the subject of Joseph A. Soldati's "The Americanization of Faust: A Study of Charles Brockden Brown's *Wieland*," *ESQ* 20:1–14, which presents Theodore Wieland as a Faustian hero who combines Icarian impulses (the flight outward and above mortal limitations) with extreme narcissism (the inward pull toward self-love, self-contemplation, and self-destruction). His murder of Catherine and the children and his attempt on Clara's life are simultaneously efforts to regain the feeling of soaring in the company of the gods and acts designed to destroy external projections of his inner self. But James D. Wilson, "Incest and American Romantic Fiction," *SLitI* 7:31–50, sees both *Wieland* and William Hill Brown's *Power of Sympathy* in other terms, works in which incest as symbol registers the self-destructive element implicit in America's experiment in democracy, the "tension between solipsism and the need for community."

Both William L. Hedges, "Charles Brockden Brown and the Culture of Contradictions," *EAL* 9:107–42, and Michael D. Bell, " 'The Double-Tongued Deceiver': Sincerity and Duplicity in the Novels of Charles Brockden Brown," *EAL* 9:143–63, undertake to comment at least briefly on all of Brown's works, both repeat a good deal of what has already been said about many of these, but both go on to make sound and original contributions. Hedges reserves his best for *Arthur Mervyn*, whose protagonist "has to act in a new world which dogma and tradition have insufficient power to shape, a world of infinite complexity which only slow tentative observation can chart." Franklin and Woolman provide contemporary but contradictory models, the first insisting that self-realization is to be found in the external trappings of success, the second quietly asserting that it is an internal quality attained only "through total identification with suffering humanity"; Arthur's actions reveal his lack of a secure sense of identity (something Hedges feels modern Americans have also inherited from the Woolman-Franklin tradition) in a world where city and country are equally innocent, equally corrupt; he responds by borrowing identities from other characters in the novel and even, as he takes over his own narrative from Dr. Stevens, the literary personalities of Sterne and Shakespeare.

Bell, too, is best on *Mervyn*, in which he finds a persistent and deliberately ironic counterpointing of assertion and action both in the title character and in the form of the book: "Against the novel's apparent vindication of narrative sincerity stands the welter of suppressed motives revealed briefly in the final dream [of Achsa Fielding's returning first husband]." Bell links Brown to Poe, Hawthorne, and Melville as an author who exploited the power of fancy even while distrusting it, and sees in nearly all Brown's novels that "the artistic conflict between sincerity and duplicity emerges as only one aspect of a more general opposition—literary, psychological, and political—between energy and order."

Although a few of his arguments seem to confuse the probabilities of the real world with the possibilities of a fictional one, Paul C. Rodgers, Jr., has nonetheless argued plausibly and well for the "haphazard process" of composition which brought Brown's least highly regarded romance into being ("Brown's *Ormond*: The Fruits of Improvisation," *AQ* 26:4–22). He accounts for the widely diverse critical interpretations of the book by suggesting that Brown was pressured to meet his printer's deadline, tried to keep his story moving by using a variety of items of contemporary interest, and "had no controlling thematic or symbolic end in view." Two late Brown novels interest Paul Witherington in "Brockden Brown's Other Novels: *Clara Howard* and *Jane Talbot*," NCF 29:257–72, who offers some reasons why these books have been neglected and then relates them to Brown's major romances on the basis of shared concerns with "the rebellious individual chastened and reunited with society" and "the theme of moderation" between the extremes of rationality and emotion. Although the discussion of Brown's attitude toward art and the artist might have profited from a consideration of Stephen Dudley (*Ormond*) and although the conclusion that these last novels are "technically superior" to their predecessors is highly debatable, the essay is a sound and solid one.

Two bibliographical essays on Brown's work, one of them authored by Witherington, take different tacks. In "Charles Brockden Brown: A Bibliographical Essay," *EAL* 9:164–87, Witherington surveys the peaks and troughs of Brown's American reputation, identifying three high water marks of interest: 1815–30; 1875–1920; 1940 to the present. An important omission is any coverage of contemporary responses and reviews, but S. W. Reid's "Brockden Brown in England: Notes on Henry Colburn's 1822 Edition of His Novels," *EAL* 9:188–95, touches on that subject slightly in calling attention to the continuing English publication of Brown's books even at a time when they were out of print in America. Reid also notes that someone, most likely Colburn himself, made considerable editorial changes in an effort to tidy up Brown's prose for English audiences, presumably more discerning than American readers in matters of style and diction.

Brown's biographer William Dunlap is the subject of Jack Zipes's "Dunlap, Kotzebue, and the Shaping of American Theatre: A Revaluation from a Marxist Perspective," *EAL* 8:272–84, a strange piece filled with sweeping generalizations; far from a thoroughgoing Marxist analysis and much too brief to call itself a revaluation, Zipes's essay nevertheless seems to have the best of it against Oral Sumner Coad's (*William Dunlap*, 1917; repr. 1962) and Robert Canary's (*William Dunlap*, 1970) views of Kotzebue's political makeup. Dunlap and Kotzebue, Zipes argues, are "partially responsible for promoting what are essentially negative features in the history of American theatre," the "flashy commercial dramatic production which works upon our consciousness so that we shall excuse our 'ruling fathers.'"

Perhaps no one else knows the business of editing quite as well as G. Thomas Tanselle, and in his review of Marius B. Péladeau's edition of *The Prose of Royall Tyler* ("The Editing of Royall Tyler," *EAL* 9:83–95) he demonstrates once again that good intentions do not necessarily guarantee a sound text. His conclusion, that Péladeau's edition is both confusedly conceived and inaccurately executed, is a word of warning to Tyler critics who might otherwise be tempted to take editorial competency as a matter of faith. Another article on Tyler is Larry R. Dennis's "Legitimizing the Novel: Royall Tyler's *The Algerine Captive*," *EAL* 9:71–80, which skillfully treats Tyler's novel as an "exploration of the various forms of captivity" familiar to Americans, including literary captivity by English sentimental and romantic traditions, but which also takes too hard a slap at Susanna Rowson, who could be (and often was) equally critical of these traditions in *Sarah, Mentoria,* and *Charlotte Temple,* among others. Rowson herself is featured in Wendy Martin's "Profile: Susanna Rowson, Early American Novelist," *WS* 2:1–8, which amounts to little more than a hasty overview of Rowson's extraordinary career by way of underlining a final irony: that a woman so active and economically self-sufficient should have contributed to American literature only stereotypes of "passive, martyred heroines." But Rowson's women are more complex than this suggests, and some of them even manage to be self-assertive; nor is it ironic, considering Rowson's goals as an educator, that so many of her women should fit a pattern not much different from what male novelists were able to imagine.

A fine essay on the sea motif in early American fiction is Roger B. Stein's "Pulled Out of the Bay: American Fiction in the Eighteenth Century," *SAF* 2:13–36, which sensitively examines the sources, literary and otherwise, of early sea fiction. Stein argues that Franklin's account of his passage from New York to Philadelphia may be regarded as the definitive statement of the shape and purposes of the early American novel, a literary tradition that appropriates providential biography for the purposes of the adventure narrative and that attempts through manipulation of narrative voice to balance the conflicting claims of inner and external dimensions of the same experience. Stein offers sound readings of the sea symbolism in Royall Tyler's *The Algerine Captive* and William Williams's *Mr. Penrose,* and he also demonstrates how in *Charlotte* the experience of seduction at sea is transmuted into "an effective (and affective) language for inner states of feeling." To Stein's assertion that definitions of the American novel derived retrospectively from 19th-century performances only obscure the importance of early formative efforts at a native fiction, I can only add a fervent amen and the postscript that this is also true of colonial poetry, humor of the 17th and 18th centuries, and, perhaps, the entire notion of what the word *American* meant in those early years.

Although he is not really an American, as Jayne K. Kribbs points out in "Setting the Record Straight on the Real John Davis," *PBSA* 68:329–30, any author so closely connected with the Pocahontas legend deserves mention in American literary history; Kribbs's note simply distinguishes the novelist from several other contemporaries of the same name and adds that none of the 15 libraries listed as holding Davis papers in *American Literary Manuscripts* actually possesses any belonging to the writer. Like Davis, Drake and Halleck also may not fall immediately within the scope of this chapter, but Joseph Slater's "The Case of Drake and Halleck," *EAL* 8:285–97, is devoted to two writers so neglected that it deserves mention here in the event that it might be overlooked elsewhere. Slater's essay is a calm, level-headed one which concludes sanely: "What 'The Culprit Fay,' the *Croaker* poems, and *Fanny* chiefly need" is not explication but "a publisher who will put them and a handful of other Drake-Halleck poems into a pamphlet that can help to supplement and vary our portly, taste-shaping, canon-forming anthologies." And in a brief note on another poet roughly Drake and Halleck's contemporary, J. M. Bonnet ("John Blair Linn and Alexander Gerard: Taste, Imitation and Genius," *ES* 55:361–63) shows that Linn's preface to *The Powers of Genius*, in which he argues that genius must be counterbalanced by taste, is heavily indebted to Gerard's *An Essay on Genius* and, beyond Gerard, to the whole Scottish school of common sense philosophy.

viii. General and Miscellaneous Studies

In some ways Donald Stauffer's *A Short History of American Poetry* (New York: E. P. Dutton) is a welcome change from historical surveys which barely find space for Taylor and Bradstreet; Stauffer's first chapter mentions these two along with Urian Oakes, John Fiske, Richard Steere, and other Puritans, as well as the New Amsterdamers Henricus Selijns and Nicasius De Sille. His treatments are standard rather than striking, though he does a good job on Steere's "On a Sea-Storm nigh the Coast"; but there are still no Southern poets mentioned, and once Stauffer gets to his second chapter, the last that is of interest to early Americanists, the line-up of 18th-century poets is tired and familiar: Freneau and the Connecticut Wits.

A fine volume to complement Roger Stein's study of sea fiction (see section *vii*, above) is Keith Huntress's edition of *Narratives of Shipwrecks and Disasters* (Ames: Iowa State Univ. Press). Many but not all of these narratives are American and belong to the 17th and 18th centuries, but all may be read as once they were, for the sake of adventure alone; Huntress also provides introductory discussions identifying appropriate narratives as sources for Poe, Melville, and Wordsworth, among others.

One facet of early American book publishing is illuminated by Madeline B. Stern in "Saint-Pierre in America: Joseph Nancrede and Isaiah Thomas," *PBSA* 68:312–25. Stern reprints an exchange of six letters between the young Frenchman and Harvard tutor Nancrede, publisher of the first American edition of Bernardin de Saint-Pierre's *Paul et Virginie*, and the prominent printer Isaiah Thomas. Thomas was commissioned to print Saint-Pierre's *Studies of Nature* for Nancrede, and Nancrede's anxious letters to him reveal his deep concern with "paper and type, engraving and binding, the rate of production and the number of copies in an edition, the preparation of preface and dedication" which went into this expensive and exceedingly handsome book.

Chief among checklists, bibliographies, and additions to bibliographies which will prove useful to students of early American culture is Jackson C. Boswell's "A Check List of Americana in A Short-Title Catalogue of Books Printed in England, Scotland & Ireland and of English Books Printed Abroad 1475–1640," *EAL* 9 (sup.):1–124. By narrowing his focus to Pollard and Redgrave, Boswell has managed a degree of thoroughness rarely met with in other checklists of books relating to America. Other bibliographical listings include Marcus McCorison's "Additions and Corrections to *Vermont Imprints*," *PAAS* 84:402–04, and William Matthews's *American Diaries in Manuscript, 1580–1954: A Descriptive Bibliography*

(Athens: Univ. of Ga. Press), which is admittedly neither exhaustive—Edward Taylor's diary is not listed, for instance—or fully descriptive. These sins are, however, easily forgivable in so extensive an undertaking; subsequent scholars will be greatly in Matthews's debt.

University of Cincinnati

12. 19th-Century Literature

Warren French

Evaporation of critical interest in 19th-century American poets except Poe, Whitman, and Emily Dickinson and spotty attention to fictionists except Cooper, Hawthorne, Melville, Twain, James, and Crane, countered by increasing attention to those whom David Levin has called "Romantic Historians," requires a reorganization of the survey of scholarship about those 19th-century writers not granted separate chapters in this volume. The present essay replaces "19th-Century Fiction" with a more inclusive chapter in the hope of doing justice to the minor poets and to intriguing figures like Henry Adams who have not been consistently treated in previous volumes. It also provides a matrix into which the separate analyses of the Transcendentalists and other much-discussed authors may be set.

i. General Studies

At once a difficulty arises concerning this new procedure. While books like Richard H. Fogle's *The Permanent Pleasure: Essays on Classics of Romanticism* (Athens: Univ. of Ga. Press) lend themselves admirably to the new plan, since their concerns are limited to such major writers as Hawthorne, Poe, and Melville, consideration of really general studies of the century would seem to have to be fragmented among chapters of this book in a manner that would fail to suggest the studies' continuity. At least this year, however, the problem failed to materialize, because scholar-critics produced no such overviews. Even Harry B. Henderson, III's *Versions of the Past,* which announces the broadest aims of any book considered here, splits up upon examination into a series of insightful reports about individual writers and books that are only tenuously related to each other.

The most truly general study of the century's literature to appear recently—Joan R. Sherman's *Invisible Poets: Afro-Americans of the Nineteenth Century* (Urbana: Univ. of Ill. Press)—will be treated next year in the chapter on black writers, though it should be noted here—since these poets must be considered in a period as well as a racial context—that the 26 studied out of 130 who have been identified as filling what was previously considered a gap between Phillis Wheatley and Paul Laurence Dunbar fail on the basis of the evidence presented to support Sherman's assertion that their work is "impressive both in quantity and quality."

If little was published in 1974 about 19th-century American literature generally, the number of dissertations completed may have alarming implications for the future. Omitting those on major figures, I count at least two dozen on general topics and more than 30 on in-individual writers among those reported. Only a handful, however, appear to enhance our knowledge of the period. While not many conclude (though one does) that the writer's appraisal of his subject's work brought him "to the general conclusion reached by most earlier critics," the group as a whole distressingly recapitulates familiar points.

ii. The Age of Elegance—Irving, Cooper, and Their Contemporaries

The promotion of the bicentennial of our national independence and related anniversaries seems to assure the reverent restoration not only of historic houses and monuments but also of our classic literature.

A model for the attractive presentation of such ventures, one that even may win these honored works the reading they deserve, is provided by the publications of Sleepy Hollow Restorations at Tarrytown, New York, especially an illustrated edition of the two keystones of our national storytelling tradition, "Rip Van Winkle" and "The Legend of Sleepy Hollow." Another of the press's delightful works, ideally suited as a gift book yet useful to the scholar, is *The Worlds of Washington Irving, 1783–1859: An Anthology Exhibition from the Collections of the New York Public Library*, ed. Andrew B. Myers, a meticulously annotated assemblage of reproductions of prints, drawings, letters, and manuscripts. Myers has also edited another tasteful, illustrated volume that further indicates the scope of the Restoration's publishing program, *The Knickerbocker Tradition: Washington Irving's New York*, a scholarly symposium of six essays, of which the editor's "Sunnyside: From Saltbox to Snuggery to Shrine" (pp. 88–115) and Michael L. Black's "Political Satire in Knickerbocker's *History*" (pp. 65–87) are of most literary interest, though all the essays provide valuable background material for understanding social and political contexts of Irving's work. Black, treating Irving's early work as a late flourishing of 18th-century wit, describes him as "one of the best writers of American political satire, a genre that has not flourished in this country," who focused his real attack on Thomas Jefferson and the dangers to the national interest from those of his economies that resulted from his theory that the government that governs least governs best. Myers in his essay describes how in the development of his rural retreat, Sunnyside, Irving created a virtual self-portrait of himself in his later years as a Romantic artist.

Per Seyersted, pace-setter of the Kate Chopin revival, in "The Indian in Knickerbocker's New Amsterdam" (*Indian Historian* 7: 14–28) takes us back also to Irving's early satire to try to work out his attitude toward native Americans. Although Seyersted broods at length over chapter 4 of book 1 of the Knickerbocker *History* to show that Irving established there "the sympathetic view of the Indians which we find in some of his later writings," the critic is compelled to admit that in the *History*, "Knickerbocker tells us surprisingly little about the undoubtedly very important Dutch relations with the natives" and that Irving's "later treatments of the original Americans mark a sad anticlimax for a writer who started out as one of America's strongest critics of his countrymen's merciless robbing and killing of the Indians."

Considering later Romantic writings, Donald A. Ringe in "Irving's Use of the Gothic Mode" (*SLitI* 7:51–65) studies the relevant tales to illustrate Irving's ultimate dedication to the Scottish "Common Sense" school of philosophy by showing that "the world of common sense and prosaic daylight, though less attractive perhaps than the world of fantasy," is the one in which Irving always finally anchored his tales. Tom Scanlan takes a look at what happened on the stage to one of the most famous of these tales in "The Domestication of Rip Van Winkle: Joe Jefferson's Play as Prologue to Modern American

Drama" (*VQR* 50:51–62). He demonstrates how the famous adaptation affirmed the importance of family structure in a way the original tale did not, although the play also avoided facing the implications of the contradiction it depicts between the fear of responsibility for family and "the worth of family structure with its mutuality and the secure embrace of obedient love." This is the very dilemma, Scanlan argues, that is central to the drama of Eugene O'Neill, Tennessee Williams, and Arthur Miller.

Taking from the shelf one of Irving's often overlooked works about Spain, Earl N. Harbert theorizes in "Washington Irving's *Conquest of Granada*: A Spanish Experiment that Failed" (*ClioW* 3:305–13) that the book marked "a departure from any earlier approach to history or simple story-telling" by "employing the weight of documentation to counterbalance the romantic tendencies" of the imagination. Readers' negative reactions to this new mixture of history and fiction helped Irving decide that the experiment "should be reworked to become a more conservative exposition of verifiable history."

Finally, Richard H. Cracraft writes *Washington Irving: The Western Works* (WWS 14) to introduce readers who are more familiar with modern Western stories than with Irving's writings to *A Tour of the Prairies* and other works by "the first American writer to discover a literary bonanza in the trans-Mississippi West." Cracraft describes Irving as "wavering between hymning the ideal, the primitive, and the romantic, and hymning the economic exploits of hardheaded realistic businessmen and their often uncouth and uncivilized employees" and presenting "too much foreground and too little background" to uncover the West as the setting for a national tradition (p. 39). In another contribution to the same series, *George Frederick Ruxton* (WWS 15), Neal Lambert presents his subject's blend of history and fiction in *Life in the Far West* as a more important prototype than anything that Irving produced of the literature of the mountain man.

Regardless of specialized interests, all scholar-critics can benefit from pondering the powerful caution to source-and-influence hunting in Barton W. Browning's "Cooper's Influence on Stifter: Fact or Scholarly Myth?" (*MLN* 89:821–28), which questions August Sauer's long-accepted attribution of the influence of Cooper's *The Deerslayer* on Adalbert Stifter's poem *Hochwald*—an attribution based on remarkably strong, detailed parallels between the works—on the grounds that the German poem had been set in type before the novel was published. Also indispensable to Cooper scholarship is Lance Schachterle's classification in "The Three 1823 Editions of James Fenimore Cooper's *The Pioneers*" (*PAAS* 84:219–32) of the complicated relationship between the two different American editions and between both and the first British edition. William L. Vance's " 'Man and Beast': The Meaning of Cooper's *The Prairie*" (*PMLA* 89:323–31) does more than Nicolaus Mills in *American and English Fiction in the Nineteenth Century* (see *ALS 1973*, pp. 210, 434) to bring out "novelistic" qualities in Cooper's book by showing how it explores the question of man's ambiguous identity as "an animal with a difference," especially through Natty Bumppo's conversations with the naturalist, Dr. Battius. "At every moment of decision in the book," Vance argues, "a more or less prolonged debate on what constitutes human behavior occurs." Cooper resolves the debate in his last image of the Bush family by emphasizing "the conception of man as first and last a social animal who finds that human nature in its passions and necessities fundamentally requires the sustenance of tradition and the restraint of law."

What is surprising recently is to find *The Headsman*, Cooper's hitherto usually overlooked novel about Switzerland, an object of perceptive attention. In one of the year's most sensitive and artful essays, "Cooper's Artistry in *The Headsman*" (*NCF* 29:77–92), Constance A. Denne argues that, although the novel is usually read as a sociopolitical work, it really describes a visionary journey from a lower world into a rarefied atmosphere—the physical journey paralleled by a metaphysical one, in which "true values are made visible." The partially happy ending that sociopolitical critics have objected to, Denne finds, is neither imposed nor inconsistent if the characters are seen as transcending mundane concerns and behaving generously toward one another in an effort "to create the only kind of future possible in a fallen world." This reading should inspire a general reconsideration of Cooper's works, which are still being given the limited readings Denne protests. A case in point is Harold T. McCarthy's *The Expatriate Perspective: American Novelists and The Idea of America* (Rutherford, N.J.: Fairleigh-Dickinson Univ. Press.) In the only chapter considering books discussed in this essay, McCarthy presents Cooper's "European novels," *The Bravo* and *The Heidenmauer* as well as *The Headsman*, against the background

of Cooper's political preoccupations during his travels in Europe.
He maintains that in *The Headsman*, "the man [Cooper] conditioned
by American ideals of what constituted a republic and a democracy
chose some episode from European history that afforded the trappings of romance in order to demonstrate not only how false were
that period's concepts of republic and democracy, but how false
were the present age's pretensions" (p. 26).

Harry B. Henderson, III, in *Versions of the Past* concentrates on
this European trilogy in describing the "holist imagination" that he
believes Cooper shared with historian Francis Parkman. Henderson,
like Vance, succeeds more nearly in aligning Cooper's aims with Sir
Walter Scott's than Mills does, because Henderson argues that this
"holist imagination" is "most palpable in that feature of Cooper's
novels which critics have held in least esteem, namely the conventional lovers [who] assure the continuity of the race and unbroken
possession of the wealth to which Cooper's heroes are inevitably
heir" (p. 50). As Cooper's "miniature panorama of progress approaches the modern situation," Henderson discerns "an effort to
restore stability and cultural complexity to the center of the social
spectrum" (p. 68). He also observes that Harvey Birch, the peddler
in *The Spy*, "redeems the anarchy of revolution by symbolizing the
principle of nationalism" (p. 57), a point made also in Robert Fink's
"Harvey Birch: The Yankee Peddler as an American Hero" (*NYFQ*
30:137–52), which examines the way in which Birch's true character
is revealed "through his patriotic and humanitarian actions."

Turning to Cooper's controversial works about his return to the
United States after his extended European junket, Jack Kligerman
advances in "Style and Form in James Fenimore Cooper's *Homeward
Bound* and *Home as Found*" (*JNT* 4:45–61) the complex but well-
contrived argument that in these books "Cooper faces back to the
eighteenth century, back to a use of language according to a theory
which keeps ideas and images separate" by effectively divorcing
"theme from action" in *Homeward Bound* and reducing "action to
the mere illustration of theme" in *Home as Found* instead of turning
forward to the metaphorical fusion of idea and image as did writers
of the American Renaissance. Cooper's backward look would have
met with the approval of an earlier editor, Joseph Dennie, whose
"ability to excite a love of elegance" is cited in Randolph C. Randall's
"Joseph Dennie's Literary Attitudes in the *Port Folio*, 1801–1812"

(*Gohdes Festschrift*, pp. 57–91). This was the reason for the success of this magazine that anti-Rousseauist Dennie, who "deplored the American Revolution as a disaster," edited in Philadelphia as a voice for "authoritarianism in literature as in politics," devoted to campaigning to curb "political and linguistic change."

Several major efforts have been made recently to improve our acquaintance with such less familiar contemporaries of Irving and Cooper as Dennie. Two additions to the Twayne series illustrate its virtues and vulnerabilities. Edward Halsey Foster's *Catharine Maria Sedgwick* (TUSAS 233) reminds us that, although this western Massachusetts novelist/moralist is almost unknown today, she was once as highly regarded as an example of America literary maturity as Cooper. Halsey provides not only the necessary summaries of her obscure works to demonstrate the formal shortcomings of her efforts to devise plots to embody her aristocratic sentiments, but he also does his most valuable work in recreating the social, political, and geographic context in which she worked. He gives us a sense of the life of a well-to-do family of the Federalist period moving between Stockbridge and New York City in what was probably the nearest equivalent we have achieved in this country to the town-and-country life-style depicted in 18th-century British novels. Awareness of this context enables us to understand why Miss Sedgwick's artlessly constructed museum pieces were once highly regarded, especially by European reviewers hopeful about the future of American culture. Foster deftly traces how the author through the satires of the upper-class life that she knew intimately became "the *only* woman who was widely considered a major American writer" before Harriet Beecher Stowe (p. 21) and then how she declined in critical esteem when she turned to didactic tales that sought to upgrade society.

Allen F. Stein in *Cornelius Matthews* (TUSAS 221) fails, on the other hand, to provide an adequate context for understanding his subject's forgotten works. Tediously hammering away at Matthews's life-long demands for "literary nationalism" and the protection of an adequate copyright act, Stein gives no sense of the reasons for Matthews's obsessions during his erratic career (extremely prolific between 1838 and 1856, he lived until 1889 without producing any further major work). Preoccupied with Matthews's banal ideals, Stein presents this querulous figure in a virtual social vacuum. He fails to realize that if he is just in writing of one of Matthews's poems, "It is important to remember that a major reason for its sloppiness is that Matthews was wrestling with conceptions which were too large for his abilities" (p. 49), we are dealing with a writer whose motives are much more interesting than his limited accomplishments.

One wonders after examining the fifth volume of *The Writings of William Gilmore Simms, Stories and Tales* (Columbia: Univ. of S. C. Press)—a gargantuan 860-page collection of 15 previously "unpublished" or "uncollected" works—to what extent the last comment about Matthews may apply to Cooper's Southern counterpart. Editor John Caldwell Guilds, however, blames the previous neglect of these works largely on their inaccessibility and maintains that three of the tales included "alone put Simms front-and-center in the tradition of American humor," with which he has not heretofore been adequately linked.

iii. Popular Writers of the American Renaissance

A recognized classic of the tradition with which Guilds seeks to link Simms, *A Narrative of the Life of David Crockett,* is available in two new editions: a large-format facsimile of the original edition, edited by James A. Shackford and Stanley J. Folmsbee (Knoxville: Univ. of Tenn. Press, 1973) and an edited version with an introduction by Joseph J. Arpad (New Haven, Conn.: College and Univ. Press). Nancy B. Sederberg has also made a painstaking addition to our knowledge of the genre by cataloguing in "Antebellum Southern Humor in the *Camden Journal*: 1826–1840" (*MissQ* 27:41–74) the many examples appearing in that South Carolina paper and concluding that the editors treated both reprinted and original material generally quite casually as fillers.

The most comprehensive survey published recently of the writings under consideration here is "History and Literature in a Romantic Age," third chapter of Russel B. Nye's *Society and Culture in America, 1830–1860* (New York: Harper & Row). After providing valuable information about developments that facilitated the production and distribution of all kinds of publications during these decades, Nye capably discusses for readers with little specialized knowledge of the period the concern of American Romantic writers for subjective impressions and organic form. His remarks reflect the increasing con-

cern recently with the "romantic historians" considered in the next
section of this essay.

Presuming, on the other hand, that his readers have considerable
specialized knowledge of the writings of the period, John T. Irwin
discusses in "The Symbol of the Hieroglyphics in the American
Renaissance" (*AQ* 26:103–26) the importance of François Champol-
lion's decipherment of Egyptian hieroglyphics through the Rosetta
stone in focusing the attention of American writers on the linguistic
aspects of the symbolic process. Although Irwin discusses only Emerson, Thoreau, and Hawthorne, many less memorable writers were
intrigued by these findings and Irwin's account sheds more light on
the cryptic intentions of popular authors than the discussion of one
of the most notorious of them in J. V. Ridgely's "George Lippard's
The Quaker City: The World of the American Porno-Gothic" (*SIL*
7:77–94), which proves a strained discussion that reaches only the
dismally inadequate conclusion that this incipient demagogue with
delusions of grandeur wrote "in dread."

Illuminating about the movement which led from grotesque excesses like Lippard's towards the fiction that would mark America's
literary maturity is Robert F. Marler's "From Tale to Short Story:
The Emergence of a New Genre in the 1850's" (*AL* 46:163–69). Marler shows how the figures of the once immensely popular tale decayed
into "romance figures or stereotypes illustrating popular values and
ideals" (such as those in Catharine Maria Sedgwick's late didactic
works) with "no interior life beyond what the invariably omniscient
narrator asserts they have" and were then replaced in a new genre
by characters possessing distinctive personalities and inner con-
sciousnesses, foreshadowed in the critical commentary and practice
of Poe, Hawthorne, and Melville, and exemplified before the Civil
War in the work of Harriet Prescott Spofford, Rose Terry Cooke, and
Rebecca Harding Davis. (Marler explores an important early contribution to this new genre in "'A Dream': Howells's Early Contribution to the American Short Story," which is discussed below.)
Even earlier, Benjamin Lease argues in "John Neal and Edgar Allan
Poe" (*PoeS* 7:38–41), Neal had contributed to this change by trans-
forming "what he considered Cooper's excessively bland vision of the
American landscape into his own wild, darkly ironic, and peculiarly
American Gothicism" in his best tale, "David Whicher." (Lease

previously amassed the evidence to argue "The Authorship of 'David Whicher': The Case for John Neal" [*JA* 12(1967):124–36].)

The battle for realism was not, however, won so quickly as Marler implies; authors like Hawthorne and Melville and literate publishers were far in advance of a growing public. As Henry Nash Smith points out in "The Scribbling Women and the Cosmic Success Story" (*CritI* 1:47–70), an examination of three of the most popular novels of the period between the early 1850s and 1870s, Susan B. Warner's *The Wide, Wide World* (1851) was rejected by the leading publishers as "fudge"; but the public still demanded works in which "the surrender of inner freedom, the discipline of deviant impulses into rapturous conformity, and the consequent achievement of both worldly success and divine grace merge into a single mythical process, a cosmic success story" (p. 51). While the American and British literary establishments disdained the pious heroines of popular fiction, they did admire the "nongenteel characters" whom popular novelists depicted with a "surprising flair." The dilemma, as Smith puts it, was that "the characters in popular fiction representing ideal values were inert puppets whom no one really believed in; yet the characters who possessed color and interest seemed to be permanently condemned to inferior status." As Marler suggests happened earlier in the magazine story, however, a revolution got underway in the popular novel as writers began to deal with the problem of "how to confer full humanity on the commonplace characters without 'idealizing' them" (p. 68).

At the center of this struggle stood that "scribbling woman" who more memorably than any other bridged the gap from didactic idealism to "quaint" local color writing, Harriet Beecher Stowe. Evan Brandstadter in "Uncle Tom and Archy Moore: The Antislavery Novel as Ideological Symbol" (*AQ* 26:160–75) presents the first antislavery novel, Richard Hildreth's *The Slave, or Memoirs of Archy Moore* (1836) as much inferior to *Uncle Tom's Cabin* because of Hildreth's failure to create characters the reader can empathize with or to use the vernacular effectively. As even Hildreth recognized also, Mrs. Stowe owed her greater success to the religious character of her novel that presented Uncle Tom as not primarily slave, but Christian hero. Randall Miller in "Mrs. Stowe's Negro: George Harris' Negritude in *Uncle Tom's Cabin*" (*CLQ* 10:521–26) objects to this very quality of her work, noting that in *A Key to "Uncle Tom's*

Cabin" she attributes Harris's aggressiveness, unique among the black characters, to "white qualities of intelligence and energy," thus reducing all totally black characters to passive stereotypes. Pursuing this line of argument to the extreme point of outrage, Alfred R. Ferguson in "The Abolition of Blacks in Abolitionist Fiction: 1830–1860" (*JBlS* 5:134–56) maintains that "unconscious racism" shows through the sentimental mask of abolitionist Christian virtue, which actually called for the abolition not of slavery, but of blacks as a separate race. A reason for what is now considered this failing of not just abolitionist fiction, but early Afro-American fiction, is suggested by Bernard W. Bell's "Literary Sources of the Early Afro-American Novel" (*CLAJ* 18:29–43), which acknowledges the influence upon early black writers of the Bible and abolitionist tracts, but stresses their even greater dependence upon early white popular fiction in which the unifying metaphor is an archetypal quest, usually cast in a Christian framework, for identity as a free man.

Mrs. Stowe's relationship to this concern about racial integrity is examined in Theodore R. Hovet's "Christian Revolution: Harriet Beecher Stowe's Response to Slavery and the Civil War" (*NEQ* 47:535–49). Hovet traces "the failure of radical reform in America in the 1850s and 1860s" to many antiinstitutional radicals' entering into "an alliance with a society they supposedly mistrusted and feared," because they supposed that this effort would make a better world, an individual and social reality, rather than a Christian evangelical dream. In so doing, Hovet feels, "they strengthened the political and social structure" to a degree that made their perfectionist hopes a hopeless dream. Exploring a specific example of Mrs. Stowe's concerns in "Harriet Beecher Stowe's Interest in Sojourner Truth, Black Feminist" (*AL* 46:359–63), Jean Lebedun argues that the novelist found "the best elements of the Woman movement" epitomized in this powerful former slave who became a vigorous campaigner for feminism.

Other articles show how interesting Mrs. Stowe has become, not just as a writer, but as a person. Frederick Trautman's "Harriet Beecher Stowe's Public Readings in New England" (*NEQ* 47:279–89) describes the mixed success of the one tour that she made to raise money between September and December 1872; and Barbara Rotundo's "Harriet Beecher Stowe and the Mythmakers" (*AN&Q* 12:131–33) traces amusingly the way in which various friendly

biographers have added appealing but misleading details to the
Stowe legend. Finally Walter J. and Ruth I. Meserve's *"Uncle Tom's
Cabin* and Modern Chinese Drama" (*MD* 17:57–66) demonstrates
the surprisingly far-reaching consequences of the play based upon
her novel. After being the first modern play performed by Chinese
students in Tokyo in 1907, it retained its popularity as revolutionary
drama in China until the 1964 Cultural Revolution demanded examples of what Mao calls "the drama of utopia."

Obliquely but importantly related to Mrs. Stowe and the problems of literary racism is Chadwick Hansen's "The Metamorphosis
of Tituba, or Why American Intellectuals Can't Tell an Indian Witch
from a Negro" (*NEQ* 47:3–12), which shows that the concept of the
race and role of the servant Tituba as black witch in the Salem hysteria derives not from primary sources but from Longfellow's play
Giles Corey of the Salem Farms, in which this character, previously
identified as an Indian, is described as the half-Indian, half-black
daughter of an African Obi magician. The other major Longfellow
piece this year does not put the once-revered poet in a much more
favorable light. Steven Allaback's "Longfellow's 'Galgano'" (*AL*
46:210–19) reprints a verse translation of Giovanni Fiorentino's *Il
Pecorone*, which was intended as the student's contribution to *Tales
of a Wayside Inn*. Allaback theorizes that it was replaced at the last
moment by the famed "The Falcon of Sir Federigo" because the
"consistently, if faintly, erotic" tone of "Galgano" might have proved
offensive to Longfellow's audience. Richard Harwell and Roger
Michener reprint in "As Public as the Town Pump" (*LJ* 99:959–63) a
letter that Longfellow wrote to his father from Germany in 1829,
arguing for support of public libraries as the real basis for higher
education; and Ernesto Ardura's attractively illustrated "Poet of
Two Cultures" (*Americas* 25[March 1973]:25–29) praises the poet's
translations from Spanish.

That exciting discoveries may still be made through close scrutiny
of Brahmin literature is illustrated by Stanton Garner's *"Elsie Ven-
ner*: Holmes's Deadly 'Book of Life'" (*HLQ* 37:283–98). Garner
proposes that in "the most provocative novel of the decade," Holmes
tried to counter the pessimism of Hawthorne and Melville, but found
reality less malleable than he had anticipated, since the price of the
passionless gentility of the Brahmins proved the sacrifice of the
passionate Elsie. While the novel accomplished what Holmes had

hoped in redirecting American fiction away from philosophical principles that he thought erroneous, Garner argues, it also accomplished
what he did not foresee in redirecting this fiction "toward a realism
which he did not like and a pessimistic determinism that he did not
want."

Such cheerless speculation may in part account for the uncus-
tomary attention recently granted one melancholy branch of our
popular literature. Thomas Bender's "The 'Rural' Cemetery Movement" (*NEQ* 47:196–212) examines tracts used to promote the development of suburban burying grounds; and Stanley French's "The
Cemetery as Cultural Institution: The Establishment of Mount Au-
burn and the 'Rural Cemetery' Movement" (*AQ* 26:37–59) elaborates
upon this phenomenon by focusing upon its most famous early example in Cambridge, Massachusetts. Closely related to this movement
that led to today's "memorial parks" are the writings examined in
Ann Douglas's "Heaven Our Home: Consolation Literature in the
Northern United States, 1830–1880" (*AQ* 26:496–515), a contribution to a special issue devoted to "Death in America."

iv. Henry Adams and the "Romantic Historians"

One star that is looming constantly larger among American literary
constellations is Henry Adams. Future studies of his most discussed
work will be greatly benefited by Ernest and Jayne M. Samuels's new
edition of *The Education of Henry Adams* (Boston: Houghton Mif-
flin), incorporating and discussing changes from several copies of the
original private (1907) edition that Adams annotated during his lifetime. That *The Education* is still being rediscovered is indicated by
the journalistic approach of some recent articles that emphasize Adams's concept of himself as a failure. Judith N. Sklar, a professor of
government at Harvard, writing of the book in an issue devoted to
"Twentieth Century Classics Revisited" (*Daedalus* 103:59–66) explains that in this "public autobiography," Adams was not interested
in accurate recollection, but the remembrance of the past "as a free
activity of the present imagination." She finds that this "last Puritan"
did genuinely fail as a result of "his disastrous decision to fashion a
science of history," but that his confession redeems his failure and
teaches his readers much. Ross Lincoln Miller's "Henry Adams: Making It Over Again" (*CentR* 18:288–305) puts forward the view that

Adams's sense of failure may obscure his real achievement, which Miller sees as a description of the three major intellectual stages of life. These we now can identify as stages of consciousness, so that if Adams and others had pursued the lead his studies provided, they might have given "profitable impulse to the nascent psychological studies of his day." Denis Donoghue in "The American Style of Failure" (*SR* 82:407–32) presents the Philistine view that one suspects Adams "of taking pleasure in failure, cultivating it for all the moral superiority to be got from it," since one finds his third-person protagonist "implying that whatever happens to the protagonist is bound to be in the nature of things rather than in the nature of his personal choice."

Earl N. Harbert's more sophisticated approach in "*The Education of Henry Adams*: The Confessional Mode as Heuristic Experiment" (*JNT* 4:3–18) questions Adams's "contrived case of personal failure" and argues that his book is "less a disguising of self-revelation as impersonal art than a disguising of impersonal and experimental art as self-revelation," aimed ultimately at the education of readers. Harbert's view is that the "total experience" of *The Education* depends upon what the reader can do with it "to create for himself a unified interpretation of experience quite unlike the insistent polarity of Adams's view," so that considered as "an experiment with words, *The Education* would fail only when readers failed it." In reaching these conclusions, Harbert disappointingly overlooks reinforcing arguments in John Conder's *A Formula of His Own: Henry Adams' Literary Experiments* (Chicago: Univ. of Chicago Press, 1970), which presents both *The Education* and *Mont-Saint-Michel and Chartres* as unique literary structures devised to deal with the issue that underlies all Adams's work of whether man has free will or is determined.

Two further essays argue that *The Education* is paralleled by important later works that it probably did not directly influence. George Monteiro's "The Education of Ernest Hemingway" (*JAmS* 8:91–99) discusses the appearance of Adams's characteristic ideas in Hemingway's writings, but judiciously observes that they are so much a part of the characteristic disillusionment of the first decades of this century that they are most thought-provoking as parallels rather than as specific echoes. Gordon O. Taylor probes in "Of Adams and Aquarius" (*AL* 46:68–82) a much more complex "evolutionary link" between *The Education* and Norman Mailer's *Of a Fire on the Moon*. He sees both "author-protagonists" as intent on absorbing and reacting to a set of facts in a "spent, deluded attitude" and then similarly structuring their responses to the situations with emphasis "on the moment of imaginative crisis, the instant of time enfolding some shift in the nature of reality as perceived or experienced." As a result, both sequences reveal something of the discontinuity "between what was unknowable . . . and what we can no longer avoid knowing."

Of unusual interest in connection with these speculations is the analysis of an earlier American third-person account of the writer's "education" in Howard Feinstein's "The Double in *The Autobiography* of the Elder Henry James" (*AI* 31:293–315). Feinstein argues that Stephen Dewhurst, the double of the novelist's minister-father in a sketch entitled *Inner Life*, had all of the ideal qualities which the elder Henry aspired toward, after a lifetime of spiritual development, although, curiously, the double was depicted as having ultimately been driven to his death by the kind of useful social work that James himself avoided.

Henry Adams's closest friend, John Hay, is also receiving new attention as an artist. Charles Vandersee edits a reprinting of Hay's novel *The Bread-Winners* (New Haven, Conn.: College and Univ. Press) and also in "The Great Literary Mystery of the Gilded Age" (*ALR* 7:245–72) tells the story of the efforts to discover the identity of the author of this notorious anonymously published novel about the labor question. Vandersee feels that if Hay had been identified as the author, he subsequently might not have been confirmed as secretary of state.

Henry Adams's historical writings are beginning to receive almost as much attention as *The Education*. Cruce Stark focuses in "The Historical Irrelevance of Heroes: Henry Adams's Andrew Jackson" (*AL* 46:170–81) upon a single aspect of *History of the United States during the Administrations of Thomas Jefferson and James Madison*, arguing that the treatment of Jackson presents frontier violence as a lower-class blight on democratic virtue and suggests that Jackson's actions "if not always beneath reproach, seldom rose above suspicion." Two books present much more sweeping analyses and continue the exploration begun in David Levin's *History as Romantic Art* of the work not only of Adams, but of Bancroft, Prescott, Motley, and Parkman. Harry B. Henderson, III's *Versions of the Past* is concerned with "two distinct and fully developed techniques and traditions, represented by Bancroft and Motley on the one hand, and Prescott and Parkman on the other" (p. 17). Henderson resolves "the vexing problem" of labeling them by choosing "progressive" from a list that includes "Whig," "Idealist," "liberal" and "Germanic" for the Bancroft-Motley approach and "holistic" for the Prescott-Parkman approach ("functionalist" and "Gestalt" carry "too many distracting overtones)." Henderson then presents the works of Henry Adams and his brother Brooks as "as much an attempt to resolve the tension between the holist and progressive traditions in a synthesis as it is to make a new departure in the name of 'scientific' history" (p. 42). Henderson's effort has been succinctly appraised in a review by David Levin (*AL* 47[1975]:292–94): "the polarizing lenses that his categories place between us and the literature . . . shut out more light than they transmit, and they commit him to a narrative which begs questions and excludes important evidence." As Levin generously acknowledges, however, Henderson's "practical criticism" of the historical imagination evinced in major fiction gives his book lasting value. An example is Henderson's judgment that in Henry Adams's novel *Democracy*, he "seems to be saying that the generation that survived the Civil War has converted an idealized view of progress and its agents into a progressive philosophy of dirty hands" (p. 217), which Adams himself rejects.

Beside the complex if uneven analysis that Henderson did not live to see through the press, Richard C. Vitzthum's study of some of these same historians' relationship to their sources in *The American Compromise: Theme and Method in the Histories of Bancroft, Parkman, and Adams* (Norman: Univ. of Okla. Press) appears relatively superficial. Vitzthum finds his subjects' work constituting a tradition characterized by what he labels an "*e pluribus unum* approach" that tends "to measure American history in terms of moral character," praising those who "eschew private ambition, political disloyalty, or social anarchy." Although Vitzthum feels that Adams's work could not have been done without the example of his predecessors, his "greater awareness of the relationship between his own and the sources' voices" and his more penetrating thought makes his work the most successful example of a now vanished tradition.

Robert H. Canary's *George Bancroft* (TUSAS 266), an entire book in a "literary" series devoted to one historian, presents a view much like Vitzthum's that the reading public preferred Bancroft's democratic predispositions in *The History of the United States from the Discovery of the Continent* (his life's work) to efforts to demythologize the figures that he dealt with. Though today we may dissent from Bancroft's predispositions, Canary feels that we still respond to a vision that imposes a meaningful structure on the facts of history and makes his work "an impressive literary achievement as well" (p. 115).

Providing further evidence that the "romantic historians'" qualities are primarily literary, Gordon Brotherston shows in "An Indian Farewell in Prescott's *The Conquest of Mexico*" (*AL* 45[1973]:348–56) that in the treatment of Nezahualcoyotl, ruler of Tezcoa in the 15th century, whom Prescott regarded as a moral balance to the barbaric Aztecs, the historian ignores what may have been authentically Indian about the leader in the poems he draws upon in order to fashion a portrait of the kind of "spiritual pagan" that many Romantic artists dream of fondly.

v. The Local Color Movement

Turning to a question closely related to these "historical" endeavors, E. Stanly Godbold, Jr., investigates the historical qualities of regional literature in "A Battleground Revisited: Reconstruction in Southern Fiction, 1895–1905" (*SAQ* 73:99–116). He suggests in this most general of a cluster of works about Southern local color writers this year a diversity that precludes generalization of the views of six novelists (Cable, Thomas Nelson Page, Thomas Dixon, John S. Wise, Joel Chandler Harris, Ellen Glasgow). He uses differences among the group, however, to highlight Harris's neglected *Gabriel Tolliver*, "an almost pathetic call for national and racial good will," as "the most extraordinary, and unread" treatment of the controversial subject. Turning to Harris's more familiar work, Louis D. Rubin, Jr., in "Uncle Remus and the Ubiquitous Rabbit" (*SoR* 10:787–804) also argues that the Georgia writer importantly advanced the literary representation of the black man's humanity, but that his works besides the animal fables did not survive because in them "he became too much the sentimentalist . . . unable to look at life without making everything come out right."

Rubin in "The Other Side of Slavery: Thomas Nelson Page's 'No Haid Pawn'" (*SLitI* 7:95–99) presents in a much different light an exceptional story by another writer noted for his sentimentality, provocatively suggesting that there are dark implications in "this terrible tale of horror, guilt, fear and depravity" in the middle of *In Ole Virginia*, which otherwise glorifies "the joys and delights of plantation life before the war." The same story is cited in Kimball King's "Local Color and the Rise of the American Magazines" (*Gohdes Festschrift*, pp. 122–33) as one of those that *Scribner's* editors insisted must be toned down. King goes on to list as the "fundamental values" of the local colorists in the sentimental era after the Civil War, "respect for authority, a rather static vision of social order, and affirmation of charity, self-sacrifice, and a stoical and emotional acceptance of life's vicissitudes" (p. 131).

The major work of one writer uncomfortable about these requirements, upon whom *Scribner's* editor R. W. Gilder thought he exercised "a refining influence," is studied in Michael L. Campbell's "The Negro in Cable's *The Grandissimes*" (*MissQ* 27:165–78). Campbell reports that George Washington Cable despaired of the blacks' improving their own situation, because he recognized that economic power must be the basis for the reform of any society, but also ironically recognized that those who reached a position to carry out such reforms had often become in the process "soulless, emasculated, and completely ineffectual." In *Versions of the Past*, Harry B. Henderson, III, elucidates even broader reasons for believing that Cable foresaw "no successful overthrow of cultural barriers," so that in his work "the essentially tragic view of the holist imagination prevails despite [his] search for grounds for progressive hope" (p. 209).

Southerners besides Cable had difficulty with Northern editors. Rayburn S. Moore's "Paul Hamilton Hayne and Northern Magazines, 1866–1886" (*Gohdes Festschrift*, pp. 134–47) traces the poet's annoyance with the difficulties that he had after the Civil War placing poems in leading Northern journals, whose busy editors could not always give his writing the attention it deserved. Reese M. Carleton in his introduction to "Mary Noailles Murfree (1850–1922): An Annotated Bibliography" (*ALR* 7:293–378) also attributes the failure of this Tennessee local colorist who often wrote under the name "Charles Egbert Craddock" to realize her early promise to her refusal to listen to unfavorable criticism and to her yielding instead to the demands of the readers of the popular magazines of the period. Another useful reference tool besides Carleton's extensive listing of writings by and about Murfree is C. H. Edwards, Jr.'s "Bibliography of

Sidney Lanier: 1942–1973" (*BB* 31:29–31), which updates volume 6 of the Centennial Edition of Lanier's works.

Cable's Louisiana looms large in recent local color studies as another once-neglected writer continues to attract attention. Per Seyersted has followed up his *The Complete Works of Kate Chopin* (1969) with a selection, *"The Storm" and Other Stories, with "The Awakening"* (Old Westbury, N.Y.: Feminist Press), for which he provides an introduction stressing again the shocked reaction to Chopin's work at the turn of the century. Bert Bender in "Kate Chopin's Lyrical Short Stories" (*SSF* 11:257–66) meanwhile praises "the lyrical voice embodied" in the kind of works Seyersted collects as "the antithesis of both the formal rigidity and the genteel, comic tone of the 'short story.'" Finally, Bernard J. Koloski forcefully argues in "The Swinburne Lines in *The Awakening*" (*AL* 45:608–10) that two lines quoted from a sonnet in the novel reinforce the atmosphere of impending death that should prepare the reader for Edna's suicide. Turning to contemporaries of Chopin's, Robert Bush in "Charles Gayarré and Grace King: Letters of a Louisiana Friendship" (*SLJ* 7,i:100–131) gracefully recounts the melodramatic story of the touchy relationship between two proud Creoles. The older Gayarré sees his possessions and the life he knew disappearing while he inspires in the younger King the love of her native state that will lead to her historical work.

Charles Chesnutt's works transcend the limited framework of Southern local color and will be treated next year in the chapter on black fiction. William Andrews's "The Significance of Charles W. Chesnutt's 'Conjure Stories'" (*SLJ* 7,i:78–99) deserves notice here, however, because of its argument that when *The Conjure Woman* appeared in 1889, the author's race was not known and his work was judged by the same standards as his white contemporaries' and that the book maintains its distinction today because it expanded and occasionally transcended the tradition of Joel Chandler Harris and Thomas Nelson Page. Chesnutt is, unfortunately, not being well served by major efforts to enhance his reputation. Robert M. Farnsworth points out in a review (*ALR* 8[1975]:85–86) that J. Noel Heermance's repeated references in *Charles W. Chesnutt: America's First Great Black Novelist* (Hamden, Conn.: Archon) to Chesnutt's "greatness" are "critically embarrassing," and Richard E. Baldwin in another review (*AL* 47[1975]:280–81) points out editorial shortcomings in *The Short Fiction of Charles W. Chesnutt* (Washington, D.C.: Howard Univ. Press) that minimize the value of the collection.

Other local color writers outside the South struggle along without the advantage of bevies of regional enthusiasts. Katharine T. Jobes' "From Stowe's Eagle Island to Jewett's 'A White Heron'" (*CLQ* 10:515–21) takes a perceptive look at the two Maine writers and observes that Jewett sees the artist not in Stowe's "ministerial conception" as a passive spiritual medium through whom God's truth flows to enlighten others, but rather as "an active individual seeking to discover her own nature and its relationship to the world around her."

The major contribution in 1974 to the study of New England local color writing was Dorothea Walker's *Alice Brown* (TUSAS 239). The Twayne series has often been scolded for a too-rigid format, but authors seem to depart from it to their detriment. Alice Brown is a curious and important figure; and it is the merit of Walker's study that it calls attention to her again. It fails, however, to satisfy the interest it rouses because of the critic's structuring of the discussion. A New Hampshire farm girl, Alice Brown published no significant fiction until she was nearly 40; yet she went on to become president of the Boston Authors' Club. Instead of carrying us stage by stage through Alice Brown's life, however, Dorothea Walker chooses to study Brown's work by genres, devoting much of the book to strained comparisons between obscure novels published at widely separated times. Even from this fragmented analysis, one perceives that Brown's work underwent a marked change and became increasingly "mystical" after the death of her closest friend, Louise Imogen Guiney, in 1920; but this first book-length study of an influential, but extremely secretive woman provides us with no guide for understanding the progress in the changes of her views manifested through her writings. Only two early chapters on the short stories that won Brown her reputation and on her plays are as useful as they might be in drawing comparisons between Brown's career and those of other regionalists.

A generalization useful for such purposes is drawn by Patrick Morrow in "Bret Harte, Popular Fiction, and the Local Color Movement" (*WAL* 7[1973]:123–31), one contribution to an entire issue devoted to Harte. Morrow argues that Harte's brand of local color was popular for a generation because of Americans' "pastoral desire" after the Civil War "to get back to our agrarian roots and rediscover the good and true American nature." More important, Morrow shrewdly speculates that a similar urge is being strongly felt today with the result that the local color movement is again particularly relevant to readers' interests.

Other contributors to the issue deal with narrower subjects. Roscoe L. Buckland speculates in "Jack Hamlin: Bret Harte's Romantic Rogue" (*WAL* 7[1973]:111–22) that, though this character who appears in 20 stories between 1869 and 1901 has no biography one can reconstruct, Harte used him to develop "a dashing hero for sentimental romance, a rogue for comedy of manners, and possibly a projection of unfulfilled desire." Donald E. Glover's "A Reconsideration of Bret Harte's Later Work" (*WAL* 7[1973]:143–51) rejects the American interpretation of Harte's working in England after 1860 as "the tragic descent" of a literary artist into "despair, penury, and hackwork" for the British view of him as a *raconteur* with an inclination "to bend realistic local color for the purpose of excellent story telling." Jeffrey T. Thomas's lengthy "Bret Harte and the Power of Sex" (*WAL* 7[1973]:91–109) ponders Henry Adams's unelaborated remark in *The Education* that he could think of only Whitman and Harte as American artists who had insisted upon the power of sex and concludes that although Harte speaks of sex "as the strongest and most magic of all human passions" in only one story, "The Judgment of Bolinas Plain," Adams knew what he was talking about. Jack Scherting looks at a little-considered body of Harte's work in "Bret Harte's Civil War Poems: Voice of the Majority" (*WAL* 7[1973]: 133–42) and finds that it provides "an inside approach" to Californians' "active interest in the Union cause," in which "the moral issue of slavery was apparently subordinated to the practical cause of union."

None of these essays probe as deeply as Fred E. H. Schroeder's reading, with the aid of Freud, in "The Development of the Super-Ego on the American Frontier" (*Soundings* 57:189–205), of Harte's "The Luck of Roaring Camp." Schroeder sees the story as an allegory that should receive the attention one gives Hawthorne's stories, since "compressed into an isolated society of one hundred men and four seasons' passage of time, the primitive and barbaric has passed and true civilization has replaced it" as a new kind of distinctively American culture born out of the frontier experience.

vi. William Dean Howells and Genteel Realism

That this development Harte reputedly summarized led to "true civilization" is questioned in two intriguing essays about one of Howells's most acclaimed novels. George Perkins in "*A Modern Instance*: Howells' Transition to Artistic Maturity" (*NEQ* 47:427–39) argues that earlier critics have overemphasized the treatment of divorce in the novel and have failed to recognize the importance of the background conflict "between country and city values." "If Howells inserted a social message into the novel," Perkins insists, "it was not about the evils of divorce, but about the laxness of a society that encourages rather than retards the development" of such an opportunist as Bartley Hubbard. Fred G. See in "The Demystification of Style: Metaphoric and Metonymic Language in *A Modern Instance*" (*NCF* 28:379–403) sees divorce as still the chief theme and the novel as setting itself against the conventions of domestic sentiment prevailing in Howells's time. "Bartley's deconstruction and manipulation of language," See argues in currently fashionable jargon, "which robs Marcia of a self, and at the same time permits him to invent his own, is thus only one of a number of symptoms of cultural disintegration with which the novel provides us."

Both essays suggest that Howells may not be so easily dismissed as "old-fashioned" as he has sometimes been in recent years. Kermit Vanderbilt reviews the novelist's critical status in "Howells Studies: Past, or Passing, or to Come" (*ALR* 7:143–53), and Clayton L. Eichelberger provides further material for the study of Howells's period in *A Guide to Critical Reviews of United States Fiction, 1870–1910*, volume 2 (Metuchen, N.J.: Scarecrow) by concentrating on listing reviews of works by obscure authors in inconveniently indexed or unindexed periodicals. Joseph Katz calls in "Bibliography and the Rise of American Literary Realism" (*SAF* 2:75–88) for further work toward the same end by stressing the importance of acquiring new information about the activities of early newspaper syndicates in fostering realistic fiction.

Other articles about Howells suggest relationships with other writers ranging across centuries. Earl Hilton's "Howells's *The Shadow of a Dream* and Shakespeare" (*AL* 46:220–22) finds similarities between a main character and the opening situation in the novel and *A Winter's Tale*, and Lloyd N. Dendinger's "Emerson's Influence on

Frost through Howells" (*Frost Centennial Essays*, pp. 265–74) discusses Howells's and Frost's respect for each other, based on the
common concern that they shared with Emerson for the common and
the low, modified by Howells's dropping of Emerson's "transcendental rationale for his aesthetic theories." Alfred Kazin's chatty
"Howells the Bostonian" (*ClioW* 3:219–34) compares Howells to J. D.
Salinger as "a charming writer" of the type that pleases us by becoming the best articulator of what we already know. Kazin finds that the
pleasure in reading Howells comes from the novelist's revealing the
existence of social distinctions in a society that does not like to admit
them, although Kazin thinks that this appeal fails to endure because
Howells felt too many obligations to the conventional goodness of
his period. John W. Crowley provides reinforcement for this view in
"The Sacerdotal Cult and the Sealskin Coat: W. D. Howells in *My
Mark Twain*" (*ELN* 11:287–92). He chooses passages from the book
to show that since Howells felt a profound conflict between the values
of his native West and his adopted East, Twain may have made him
feel that he had sold out his birthright.

A tougher view is taken in Robert F. Marler, Jr.'s "'A Dream':
Howells's Early Contribution to the American Short Story" (*JNT*
4:75–85), which shows Howells writing as early as 1861 a story built
around the theme familiar in his later work that "romantic dreams are
dangerous and misleading." Paul A. Eschholz also questions Howells's
capitulation to the East by pointing out in "*The Landlord at Lion's
Head*: William Dean Howells' Use of the Vermont Scene" (*Vermont
History* 42:44–47) the way in which Howells exposes the effete Bostonian artist Westover's "inability to appreciate human nature fully."

Although concerned only glancingly with Howells's Altrurian
novels, Kenneth M. Roemer continues to add to the wealth of speculations on late 19th-century American utopian fiction. In "The Heavenly City of the Late 19th-Century Utopians" (*JASAT* 4[1973]:5–17)
—which includes four fascinating illustrations from works cited—
Roemer describes the ways in which visionaries would have turned
the American city into "an idealized medieval or baroque city complete with people who knew their places." While Roemer acknowledges that it would be easy to explain away this ambivalence toward
progress "by labeling the utopian authors as elitist reformers with
rural backgrounds who advocated radical means to achieve conservative or backward-looking ends," he feels that the phenomenon

must be viewed as an indication of the extent of the "cultural shock" produced by rapid urbanization. He advances much the same argument in " 'Utopia Made Practical': Compulsive Realism" (*ALR* 7: 273–76), which suggests that this "compulsive realism" betrays an ambivalence that suggests that the authors did not fully believe in the reasonable paths to utopia that they outlined and used them as covers "for acute frustrations and longings growing out of the rapid changes of the late nineteenth century."

An explanation of an even more profound inner need to create utopias is convincingly provided by J. Wayne Baker's "Populist Themes in the Fiction of Ignatius Donnelly" (*AmerS* 14,ii[1973]: 65–83). Baker reviews the failure of all the "entrepreneurial schemes" of the author of *Caesar's Column* and analyzes him as one frustrated both in business and politics "who identified with others in society who had experienced similar economic and social disappointments" and who used his fiction as "one way among many in which he expressed his case against this apparently hostile society," in the hope that he would hit upon one device that would "launch him at last into national political prominence."

The continuing fascination of this utopian fiction is shown by the completion within the year of three more dissertations about it, including Robert E. Hogan's " 'Decorous Fancies, Sober Imaginations, Goodish Sentiments': The Literary Career of Edward Bellamy" (*DAI* 35:1625A). Hogan's work is of particular interest for choosing as Bellamy's best fiction not *Looking Backward*, but *The Duke of Stockbridge*, a tale of Shays's rebellion of 1786–87 in the section of western Massachusetts also portrayed in Catharine Maria Sedgwick's aristocratic fictions. The same choice also was made by Harry B. Henderson III in *Versions of the Past*, which describes Bellamy's "proletarian romance" as indicating—like Mark Twain's *A Connecticut Yankee*—where "distrust of man's ability to create the new society through a revolt of the oppressed" was to lead for the American writer—to "the impulse for change resulting in catastrophe," once the progressive dream is aborted (p. 203). (Henderson finds Donnelly's *Caesar's Column* and Jack London's *The Iron Heel* perfectly illustrating this development.)

Essays about two other prominent exponents of realism raise problems about agrarian or frontier nostalgia. Lonnie E. Underhill and Daniel F. Littlefield, Jr.'s "Hamlin Garland at Isleta Pueblo"

(*SwHQ* 78:45–68) reprints Garland's account of his first experience with the Pueblo Indians, which the editors feel manifests a feeling for the Indian previously lacking in his work. Probing much more deeply into the work of a more tortured author, George Spangler in "Theron Ware and the Perils of Relativism" (*CRevAS* 5:36–46) reexamines especially the roles of Celia Madden and Sister Soulsby in Harold Frederic's *The Damnation of Theron Ware*. He reaches the conclusion that the novel is not "an affirmation or even a resigned acceptance of moral relativism," but a cautionary tale dramatizing the frightening meaning of Americans' devotion to the "practical," "with all the unprincipled and hence unpredictable behavior it implies."

vii. The Ironic Vision of Stephen Crane

The perception of this very unpredictable behavior that upset Harold Frederic fueled the "ironic vision" that makes Stephen Crane a principal forerunner of the 20th-century "modernist" writers. The late Marston LaFrance, who analyzed Crane's vision in *A Reading of Stephen Crane* (see *ALS 1971*, pp. 183–84) in one of his last writings, surveys "Stephen Crane Scholarship Today and Tomorrow" (*ALR* 7:125–35) to find that critics are just settling down to serious work after having "outgrown the innocence of naturalistic and Freudian speculation" and "the bumptiousness of symbolic absurdity." His judgment that "the critical hammering needed even for classification renders most naturalistic readings of Crane faintly comic" should eventually bring to a halt such florid tributes as Arno Karlen's "The Craft of Stephen Crane" (*GaR* 28:470–84), which treats his works as naturalistic and concludes with a comment that, ironically, better fits the critic than his subject: "He often seems an innocent whose powers sporadically triumphed over his simplistic ideas and slovenly craftsmanship."

LaFrance's further observation that even Crane's early writings about the slums cannot be "wedged into the naturalistic pigeonhole" is brilliantly supported by Alan Trachtenberg's "Experiments in Another Country: Stephen Crane's City Sketches" (*SoR* 10:265–85), which relates the 19th-century concept of the city as a mystery to the problem of "a fragmented urban landscape, the mystery of which is located in the alarming incommunicability" of what Robert Paul has called the "moral regions" that make the city "a mosaic of little

worlds which touch but do not interpenetrate." Trachtenberg relates this perception to Crane's efforts in the best of his city sketches
(like the companion pieces "Experiment in Misery" and "Experiment
in Luxury") to discard a traditional moral posture and try "to convey
physical landscapes equivalent to his perception of the subjective
lives of the characters." A difference between Crane's and James
Agee's vision that is related to this perception of urban experience is
discussed in Warren French's "*Face to Face*: Film Confronts Story"
(*ESP* 4:43–74), which argues that the alterations that Agee made in
the story line of "The Bride Comes to Yellow Sky" for a 1953 film
version "represent not necessary adjustments of the material to a new
medium, but the alteration of one socially-minded artist's material by
another with his own particular axe to grind." French thinks that
Agee's work might be most suitably titled "The Church Comes to
Yellow Sky," since it substitutes "churchification for Crane's feminiza-
tion . . . as the enemy of irresponsible male playfulness in the Old
West."

George Monteiro discusses this same short story in his contribution to a special issue of *Arizona Quarterly* devoted to articles on
Crane, "Stephen Crane's 'Yellow Sky' Sequel" (30:119–26) pointing
out that in "Moonlight on the Snow," Crane shows a western town,
Warpost, Texas, "drifting toward the rudimentary dictates of a more
conventional order," but losing in the process "its bravado and independence, along with something that we could call its total innocence"—as happens also in the more familiar story. Dealing with
another little-known work, Charles W. Mayer in "Stephen Crane and
the Realistic Tradition: 'Three Miraculous Soldiers' " (*ArQ* 30:127–
34) provides evidence to support the thesis proposed in Marston La-
France's book that "the chief motif of Crane's fiction may [be] his
exploration of the discrepancies between illusion and reality" operat-
ing as "a thematic and structural basis" through a discussion of a character's discovery that "war is a singularly unromantic affair in which
grand ideas and purposes evaporate in the face of the meaningless
death of ordinary men." Turning to a familiar story, May L. Autrey
offers in "The Word Out of the Sea: A View of Crane's 'The Open
Boat' " (*ArQ* 30:101–10) a questionable moralistic reading that the
death of the oiler, the only man in the boat to rely on his own physical
prowess, completes the lesson that "the word out of the sea" need not
have been "Death," but only "Submit." Rita K. Gollin's " 'Little Souls

Who Thirst for Fight' in *The Red Badge of Courage*" (*ArQ* 30:111–18) indulges in similar superficial moralizing by describing Henry Fleming as remaining "a young Everyman, vulnerable to injury, quick to anger, and ignorant about the future," typical of those ignorant men whose inverterate quarrelsomeness as individuals leads to "the large quarrel which is war." Reid Maynard's "Red as Leitmotiv in *The Red Badge of Courage*" (*ArQ* 30:135–41) is yet another "color" study that finds red symbolic of Crane's cosmic views of both universal struggle and transformation. (Katharine G. Simoneaux's "Color Imagery in Crane's *Maggie: A Girl of the Streets*" [*CLAJ* 18:91–100] is another piece in the same vein that lists *all* the color words in the novel to show how Crane uses them to convey emotional impressions.)

In the most ambitious article in the Arizona gathering, "Twin Lights on Henry Fleming: Structural Parallels in *The Red Badge of Courage*" (*ArQ* 30:149–59), Clinton S. Burhans, Jr., studies the division of the novel into 12-chapter halves to reach another dubious, moralistic conclusion—this one that the novel is a cautionary tale expressing Crane's conviction that society needs reshaping, because Henry Fleming is depicted as so totally committed to his society's martial ideas and values that he is unable "like too many others then and since, to recognize their complete irrelevancy to the new realities of modern war and human psychology." Burhans pursues this reading in "Judging Henry Judging: Point of View in *The Red Badge of Courage*" (*BSUF* 15,ii:38–48) by arguing that readers share Henry's life as he experiences it, "but only in the language by which Crane orders and articulates that experience." Thus we are led to the "compassionate but finally negative" verdict that Henry may think he has become a man, but that he still has a long way to go, because his "final self-evaluation bears the shape of his society." In both pieces Burhans skillfully describes Crane's techniques only to arrive at conventional conclusions that articulate the analyst's quarrel with the world.

Robert M. Rechnitz's "Depersonalization and the Dream in *The Red Badge of Courage*" (*SNNTS* 6:76–87) also pictures Henry as self-deluded in the final paragraphs of the novel. He argues that in the course of his experience, Henry "exchanges his subjective delusions for a socially devised and sanctioned vision . . . as far removed from reality as was his abandoned private vision," so that he has found a home in the army, but at an exorbitant price. In *Versions of the Past,* Harry B. Henderson, III, treats *The Red Badge of Courage* as marking "the predicament in which the American historical imagination found itself at the end of the nineteenth century as the result of the rising influence of naturalism" (p. 198). Henderson, too, apparently considers Henry self-deluded at the end of the novel, arguing that the character "never *defines* himself at all," because in a naturalistic world of power without a master, "the History revered in Everyman's consciousness . . . offers neither roles nor ideals but rather the primitive enshrined as civilization" (p. 231).

Against the literal interpretations of war as *war* in these articles may be placed Jan Van Meter's metaphorical reading (that we should have anticipated as inevitable) of war as *sex:* "Sex and War in *The Red Badge of Courage*" (*Genre* 7:71–90). Following a stream of sexual imagery Van Meter is led to the conclusion that the novel parallels an initiation ritual in which Henry Fleming defeats "his impotence in the face of masculine challenge," so that "now he can see the world and its struggles with the confidence of a sexually mature adult." Even more reductivist than Van Meter's reading are D. B. Graham's "Dreiser's Maggie" (*ALR* 7:169–70), which humorlessly reads into a passing jocularity in *Sister Carrie* "further evidence of Crane's stimulating presence in Dreiser's imagination," and Jon M. Kinnamon's "Henry James, the Bartender in Stephen Crane's 'The Blue Hotel'" (*ArQ* 30:160–63), which airs the vulgar notion that Henry the bartender in the story is a spoof on Henry James, whom Crane loved to harass because of James's detestation of violence.

Tim A. Pilgrim contributes something helpful in dealing with the same story in "Repetition as a Nihilistic Device in Stephen Crane's 'The Blue Hotel'" (*SSF* 11:125–29). He accounts for the heavy use of repetitive dialogue as an indication of the failure in communication that results from all of the characters' being so wrapped up in themselves that they are lacking in truthful introspection, and he also accounts for the repetition of episodes as indicative of Crane's nihilistic conviction that men who are thus both socially and self-alienated are trapped within recurring cycles of time.

viii. Frank Norris and the 1890s: Naturalism and Decadence

Despite the unevenness of Crane criticism, the completion of the University of Virginia edition of his collected works assures at least a reliable starting point for dealing with the often unsuspected complexities of his writings. What are needed now are comparable editions of the works of his contemporaries, so that the two recent dissertations related to this period that we should most welcome in print are Jesse S. Crisler's "A Critical and Textual Study of Frank Norris's *McTeague*" (*DAI* 35:396A) and Joseph R. McElrath, Jr.'s "A Critical Edition of Frank Norris's *Moran of the Lady Letty*" (*DAI* 34:5981A). Crisler tells with justified outrage the story of the dispersion of the *McTeague* manuscript as a money-making scheme, and McElrath at last compares all the newspaper versions of Norris's sensational sea-story to demonstrate that the book versions "have been thoroughly revised, bowdlerized, and house-styled."

Charles L. Crow's "The Real Vanamee and His Influence on Frank Norris's *The Octopus*" (*WAL* 9:131–39) also provides valuable information by identifying the original for this key character as "a San Francisco painter, stained-glass craftsman, writer and art patron named Bruce Porter," who served Norris, as Vanamee served the poet Presley in the novel, as "an intelligent and encouraging critic, a tutor of Western history and a source of persuasive and consoling doctrine." Less striking is D. B. Graham's doubtful perception in "Frank Norris's Afternoon of a Faun" (*PLL* 10:307–12) of a parallel to Stéphane Mallarmé's poem "L'Après-midi d'un faune" in the conventional pastoralism of Presley's meditation in the opening chapter of *The Octopus*. A sounder argument in Keith S. Sheppard's "A New Note for McTeague's Canary" (*WAL* 9:217–18) is that the bird may have come up from the mine with McTeague, since songbirds are used in deep mines to detect lethal gases.

One of the most complex interpretations so far given Norris's *McTeague* is Joseph H. Gardner's "Dickens, Romance, and *McTeague*: A Study in Mutual Interpretation" (*EIL* 1:69–82). Gardner advances two arguments to demonstrate that "as the nineteenth century became the twentieth, Dickens had lost none of his value as a presence in American fiction." The first argument is that Dickens influenced Norris's shifting in treating lower-class characters "from explaining human phenomena in terms of the simple to an honest attempt to grapple with the complex." The second is that although in *McTeague*, Norris may have set out to write a simple "naturalistic" study, he produced "a Dickensian exploration of the relationship between attitudes toward sex and attitudes toward money."

Much more impressionistic than Gardner's thoroughly reasoned piece is Russell Roth's "Ambrose Bierce's 'Detestable Creature'" (*WAL* 9:169–76), which reveals that Bierce thought so poorly of his mother that we should not be surprised that he "would have imagined a snake staring at [a character in 'The Man and the Snake'] with his dead mother's eyes." A more significant clue to Bierce's craftsmanship is provided by Cathy N. Davidson's "Literary Semantics and the Fiction of Ambrose Bierce" (*ETC.*, 31:262–71)—an argument that the storyteller "does not compose fictions which evolve in some preordained fashion with the prolonged passage from ignorance to innocence" but stories that proceed by associations related to the psychology of the protagonists. Davidson reads "An Occurrence at Owl Creek Bridge" in the light of the doomed Farquhar's "semantic aptitude," as depicting how, ironically, when he is about to die, "he finally begins to appreciate the values inherent in much of his previous life [that] his former rhetoric led him to contemn." Davidson's advice did not appear in time to deter Robert C. McLean's effort to use traditional logical methods in reading "The Deaths in Ambrose Bierce's 'Halpin Frayser'" (*PLL* 10:394–402) to find the evidence that this tale, although usually viewed as a piece of traditional supernatural gothicism, is actually an ambiguous narrative in which Bierce "unobtrusively presents an intelligible pattern of clues" to suggest the rational explanation that the title characer is cold-bloodedly murdered by his father.

McLean makes Bierce's tale sound like the popular fantasies described in Daryl E. Jones's "Clenched Teeth and Curses: Revenge and the Dime Novel Outlaw Hero" (*JPC* 7[1973]:652–65). Jones traces the way in which Edward L. Wheeler, who described himself as a "sensational novelist," created in 1877 for the Beadle and Adams dime novels, the character of Deadwood Dick, prototypical virtuous outlaw, whose "justification for taking the law into his own hands rests on society's refusal to take a stand against the social evil which [his foes] represent," a technique that provided the public with "heroes who possessed a capacity for resolving in fantasy the otherwise insoluble cultural conflicts of the age." Robert E. and Katharine M. Morsberger's "Christ and a Horse-Race: *Ben-Hur* on Stage" (*JPC* 8:489–502) doesn't tell us how General Lew Wallace's even more popular hero appealed to public fantasies, but it does explain that although the play version of his novel became one of the most phe-

nomenal hits in the history of the American theatre, it did not open
until November 29, 1899, nearly two decades after the publication
of the novel in 1880, because of Wallace's fears that a theatrical production would lack the proper reverence that he tried to maintain in
an earlier tableau version that proved too static to suit theatre-goers'
tastes.

The revelation that Herbert Mayes's 1928 biography of another
popular writer, Horatio Alger, Jr., is a hoax, for which Mayes himself
provided the entries from a nonexistent diary that was announced
as its principal source, should be pretty well circulated by now, for
it is discussed in both Gary F. Scharnhorst's "The Alger Problem:
The Hoax about Horatio Revealed" (*BSUF* 15,ii:61–65) and Jack
Bales's "Herbert R. Mayes and Horatio Alger, Jr.; or The Story of a
Unique Literary Hoax" (*JPC* 8:317–19), as well as a number of newspaper features. Since Edwin P. Hoyt learned the truth before writing
Horatio's Boys: The Life and Works of Horatio Alger (Radnor, Pa.:
Chilton), he was able to avoid the trap into which many recent cele-
brators of Alger have fallen by trusting in Mayes's account. Yet although Hoyt's book is avowedly based upon material at Harvard, its
tone and value as scholarship are adequately suggested by a sentence
which ends the opening chapter's juicy revelations of pederasty by
informing us that after Alger's exposure he "would sink or swim in the
ink of his pen." Also of strictly entertainment value is Robert Con-
row's *Field Days: The Life, Times and Reputation of Eugene Field*
(New York: Scribner's), a cute, well-illustrated tribute to the Chicago newspaperman-versifier.

Another long-neglected Chicagoan fares much better. As John
Pilkington's generous review (*AL* 47[1975]:127–28) points out, Bernard R. Bowron, Jr.'s waiting to publish his *Henry B. Fuller of
Chicago: The Ordeal of a Genteel Realist in Ungenteel America*
(Westport, Conn.: Greenwood Press) "until experience and scholarly
maturity have given him the discerning judgment necessary for the
handling of such a complex personality as Fuller" serves "as an excellent example to young scholars of the value of not rushing one's doctoral dissertation into print." Although Bowron's bibliography lists
only a few works like Edmund Wilson's on Fuller published since
the completion of his dissertation in 1948, the writer has obviously
spent the quarter century meditating on his perplexing subject and
polishing his own genteelly understated style until his work reflects

in the appropriate manner of a period miniaturist the identification
with its subject that Leon Edel's massive biography of Henry James
does in the boldly appropriate style of a Boldoni portrait. It is hard
to believe that Fuller can be judged more fairly and fully than he is in
this conclusion to Bowron's book:

> One can disdain a way of life and still respond intensely, as an
> artist, to life itself. Lacking that passion for experience, Fuller
> substituted for it an unusually strict concern for the literary
> mold in which experience may be cast. But in spite of his in-
> sistence on the primacy of form, Fuller realized that there was
> something lacking in all his fiction; he could not achieve a mov-
> ing sense of life. . . . Time and again he recognized the limita-
> tion imposed by his diffidence and reserve: his unwillingness
> to pry into the private lives of his characters, the uneasy ret-
> icence that compelled him to veer away both from emotional
> crises and from the improprieties that the "better element"
> did not discuss. He thought such reserve a virtue in the gentle-
> man, but he came to realize that it was a virtue the American
> novelist could scarcely afford (p. 234).

My only reservation about Bowron's accomplishment rises from
the hope he expresses in his introduction that his book may end the
neglect of Fuller, who "was not just a good novelist but, in his fictional
themes and experimental techniques, an important one" (p. xv).
Bowron's book seems most likely to end not the neglect of Fuller, but
the consideration of him, for it seems so clearly to say the last word
about him. There seems scant likelihood of reviving widespread interest in a fiction characterized by the genteel reserve that has often
disabled our "better element" while the vulgar flourished.

In a rare example of bad timing in the program of comprehensive
bibliographical surveys that have so much facilitated the study of
turn-of-the-century realists, *American Literary Realism* published
its piece on Fuller, Jeffrey Swanson's " 'Flesh, Fish, or Fowl': Henry
Blake Fuller's Attitudes toward Realism and Romanticism" (7:195–
210), followed by "A Checklist of the Writings of Henry Blake Fuller
(1857–1929)" (pp. 211–43), just too early to include the mention of
Bowron's book. A delay might have made the bibliography for all
practical purposes definitive and might also have prompted Swanson,
on the basis of Bowron's soundly documented analyses of Fuller's

motivations, to recast his now already outdated reflections on Fuller's once seemingly erratic swings between realism and romanticism. Swanson provides only the lame explanation that perhaps Fuller was "a real eclectic who neither rejected idealistic romanticism nor blushed at the harsh realities of Chicago life." And despite the seeming finality of Bowron's book, two more dissertations about Fuller were completed in 1974.

Indiana University–Purdue University at Indianapolis

13. Fiction: 1900 to the 1930s

David Stouck

With its coverage of a shorter time span, this essay will now focus primarily on eight novelists whose work receives serious critical attention each year. The eight include Anderson, Cather, Dos Passos, Dreiser, Lewis, London, Stein, and Wharton. These writers will be treated in separate sections of the essay, and the sections will be arranged in an order that reflects the amount of significant scholarship published on an individual author during the year. Other writers such as Glasgow, Cabell, Tarkington, Toomer, Sinclair, who receive less critical scrutiny, will be grouped together according to kindred interests or regions. Generally speaking, my approach in this essay will be to give considerable space to important material and to omit or just mention briefly items which I consider to be of marginal value.

If there was a marked trend in criticism during 1974, it was toward the reexamination of the fiction in this period from a feminist point of view. The world reflected in the novels of Lewis, Anderson, and Wharton is still a palpable presence for most of us, and critics are drawn to examining the attitudes and ideas in those books that helped shape the lives of our mothers and grandmothers. The danger of feminist literary criticism is a too narrow sociological bias, but a thoughtful consideration of a novel from a feminist vantage point can greatly increase our understanding and appreciation of an author's imaginative world. Feminism is especially prominent in the titles of dissertations.

There were no general book-length studies of fiction from 1900 to 1930, and only one essay of note which touched generally on the writers of this period. The latter is Jeremiah J. Sullivan's "Conflict in the Modern American Novel" (*BSUF* 15:28–36). Using Irving Babbitt's criticism of Dreiser as a point of departure, Sullivan begins by stating that Babbitt's conscience versus impulse formula has never been an adequate description of conflict in the American novel. He

contends that in James and Twain the real conflict is between conscience and convention (a code of social behavior) and that the conflict is replaced in Dreiser and Anderson by impulse versus social
convention, society's inhuman codes and conventions remaining the
real enemy. Sullivan says Dreiser and Anderson believed the only
genuine order possible would be fashioned out of human desires and
impulses. Sullivan sees Hemingway's hero reversing the process and
constructing a code or set of social conventions to protect himself
from the destructive nature of his impulses, while the modern existential novelist, recognizing all values as artificial and absurd, must
choose between "grades of disorder, rather than order and disorder."

Although there were few general criticisms of the literature in this
period, a valuable research tool appeared in James Woodress's *American Fiction, 1900–1950: A Guide to Information Sources* (Detroit:
Gale Research Co.). Woodress has taken all the American novelists
of any worth in this period and listed their works, bibliographies,
manuscripts, editions and reprints, biographies and criticisms. In
listing biographies and criticisms, Woodress evaluates as well as describes the different entries. This is an indispensable aid for the
serious researcher in American fiction.

i. Willa Cather

Of the authors covered in this essay, by far the greatest amount of
critical attention in 1974 was given to Willa Cather—26 articles and
4 dissertations. This rivals the work done annually on Fitzgerald and
Hemingway. The marked increase in Cather criticism represents the
first fruits of scholarship prompted by the observances of Cather's
centenary in 1973. There were at least four seminars organized to
mark this event: a "precentennial" symposium at Merrimack College
in October 1972; the illustrious International Seminar held in Lincoln, Nebraska, in October 1973; the first Willa Cather seminar at
MLA in Chicago in 1973 (which continues to meet annually), and a
special seminar on Cather sponsored by the Renascence Society in
April 1974. The papers given at these various meetings are now beginning to appear in print; what is encouraging is that so many of
them are of a very high quality.

The most prestigious group of essays is that edited by Bernice
Slote and Virginia Faulkner and published as *The Art of Willa*

Cather (Lincoln: Univ. of Nebr. Press). Along with interviews, excerpts from panel discussions, and notes submitted by the participants, these essays represent the proceedings of the International Seminar. The essays are divided into "Reassessments" and "Recollections." The latter group consists of Leon Edel's opening address to the seminar entitled "Homage to Willa Cather" (pp. 185–204), in which he describes some of the special problems that confronted him when asked to complete the Cather biography begun by the late E. K. Brown, and a reminiscence, "Miss Cather" (pp. 205–24), by Alfred A. Knopf, who was Willa Cather's friend and publisher for 27 years.

"Reassessments" begins with Eudora Welty's "The House of Willa Cather" (pp. 3–20), which draws attention to the remarkable physical quality of Cather's work. Miss Welty says that Cather's "own living world is around us as we read, present to us through our eyes and ears and touch," and emphasizes that Cather's physical landscape comes alive to us exactly because the descriptions always contain the subjective element—it is always a thing perceived. Miss Welty also suggests that Cather's work embodies, above all else, passion; and whether it is the struggle for survival in a harsh landscape or the desire for greatness in art, it takes the form of strenuous physical life in every novel. Two prominent American critics who have written on Cather before give their reassessments of this author. In his essay "Willa Cather: American Experience and European Tradition" (pp. 43–62), James Woodress suggests that Willa Cather's success as a writer owes much to her fusion of native American experience (the life of her emotions) with European culture derived from books and travel (the life of the mind). Woodress points out that among major American novelists of the first half of the century Willa Cather is unique for her erudition and that her learning always gives her American material universal reference. Less satisfying is James E. Miller, Jr.'s "Willa Cather and the Art of Fiction" (pp. 121–48). Miller assesses Cather's achievement in the light of James's theory of fiction and sees her most successful novels as those from *My Ántonia* (1918) through *My Mortal Enemy* (1926) in which Cather, like James, either used an observer to tell a story or created a drama of consciousness in one character. The narrowness of this critical approach is evident when we find *One of Ours* (1922) designated one of Cather's major achievements, while *Death Comes for the Arch-*

bishop (1927) is seen as initiating a downward trend in her art. Objections to Miller's approach are recorded in the discussion of the seminar participants.

Four of the papers are by scholars from other countries. Michel Gervaud's "Willa Cather and France: Elective Affinities" (pp. 65–81) considers the idealization of French culture in Cather's novels and the French influences, both literary and personal, on her writing. Hiroko Sato's "Willa Cather in Japan" (pp. 84–97) describes the reception of Willa Cather's work in her country and singles out certain facets of Cather's art, such as love for nature, the importance of the family and the importance of tradition, which have a particular appeal for the Japanese. In "Italian Perspectives" (pp. 103–118) Aldo Celli first rehearses the reception of Cather in Italy (also the author's oblique references to Italy in her fiction), then goes on to show how various aspects of structuralist criticism popular in Europe (considerations of horizontal and vertical lines of narrative, lexical and syntactical structures in language, patterns of folk tale and melodramatic gesture) can enrich our appreciation of Cather's artistry. In "The Two or More Worlds of Willa Cather" (pp. 21–42) the British historian Marcus Cunliffe examines Cather as "a product and an exponent of a whole set of tensions between West and East." He points out that in her art she transcends the rhetorical question of her day over whether East (civilization, culture) or West (frontier, strength, hardihood) was superior, and that in her novels the real dramatic opposition is between the creative individual at home in his environment and the false human being who is a hater and spoiler of both persons and places. He also points out that, unlike Frederick Jackson Turner, Cather did not celebrate the uniqueness of the American frontier, but saw it in relation to historical recurrence stretching back to the poetry of Virgil and Horace.

The outstanding piece in the collection is Donald Sutherland's essay, "Willa Cather: The Classic Voice" (pp. 156–79). Willa Cather is frequently referred to as a classical artist and Sutherland explores some of the actual influences of Greek and Latin literature on her fiction. He finds that the greatest influence on Cather is in the expressive quality of voice, that Willa Cather's novels, like the classics, are written primarily in a vocal mode, that even classical allusions are more important for their sonority than for ideas associated with them. Sutherland compares Cather's voice to that of Virgil who similarly wrote of farming and of life's brevity, and whose middle style (neither inflated nor thin) could command great passions. Part III, "Afterviews," includes a note by John J. Murphy who, with Bernice Slote, urges future Cather critics to look at "the specifics of the text"; an overview of Cather's work in the light of the pictorial arts by Warren French; and miscellaneous observations of interest such as Leon Edel's "hunch" that some day Cather will rank above Hemingway in the pantheon of American authors.

Another first-rate collection is *Five Essays on Willa Cather: The Merrimack Symposium*, ed. with a preface by John J. Murphy (North Andover, Mass.: Merrimack Coll.). Richard Giannone's "Willa Cather and the Human Voice" (pp. 21–49) is in a vein similar to Sutherland's, arguing that Cather brought back an oral and auditory dimension to the modern novel. In this sophisticated essay Giannone points out that Cather, who was raised in what was in some respects a preliterate society, transferred the effects of oral storytelling to much of her ficion both thematically and formally. The sound of voice, he says, is frequently the only access to the inner soul of Cather's characters: for example, Ántonia's physical appearance has changed, "but the 'husky, breathy voice' Jim 'remembered so well' authenticates her enduring identity." Similarly, according to Giannone, form in Cather's novels (epic in *O Pioneers!*, the georgic in *My Ántonia*) often refers us to preliterate, oral narration where storytelling is not product but process. The approach through voice taken by Giannone and Sutherland is, I feel, a particularly fruitful one for future Cather criticism.

Bernice Slote's "Willa Cather: The Secret Web" (pp. 1–19) demonstrates the richness and complexity of allusions in Willa Cather's writing. Slote shows how apparently casual references in the novels, when investigated, often reveal a subtle network of associations and hidden inferences which open up the pattern and the meaning of a story. Among the examples cited is the epigraph to *O Pioneers!* from Mickiewicz's epic poem *Pan Tadeusz* which, when scrutinized, points to a number of parallels between Cather's writings and the work of the Polish poet, an influence never considered previously. In a comprehensive overview titled "Willa Cather: The Widening Gyre" (pp. 51–74) John J. Murphy argues that in the Nebraska novels Willa Cather's male characters fail to establish fruitful relationships with women because they insist on idealizing them as pure maternal figures or else on rejecting them as fallen women. In *The Professor's House*, Murphy continues, the hero recognizes this false division in his life between the ideal and the real, while in the subsequent Catholic novels the two are joined together in the figure of the Virgin Mary, who inspires her missionary priests to make the religious ideals of civilization a concrete reality. In "Willa Cather and the Pastoral Tradition" (pp. 75–96) John H. Randall, III, sets forth the familiar thesis that Cather's prairie novels acquire universality from being written in the classical pastoral tradition. But he goes on to illustrate the proximity beween scenes in these novels and the idyls of Theocritus and the eclogues and georgics of Virgil. He argues, debatably I think, that Cather's writing is weakest when she deviates from the norm of classical pastoral, as in the conclusion to *My Ántonia* which nostalgically returns the narrator to his childhood instead of directing him back to the real world of the present, and in *A Lost Lady* where the angry denunciations of materialism disrupt the contemplative spirit of pastoral. In "The Poetics of Willa Cather" (pp. 97–119) Lillian D. Bloom argues that Cather's critical principles were determined by her organic view of art. She says that as a novelist Cather rejected invention and manipulation of subject matter, for she felt that a novel had its own inevitable design and that it was the artist's task to render that design as faithfully and sympathetically as possible.

Two more journals have followed the example of *Western American Literature* (see *ALS 1972*, pp. 237–38) and *Colby Library Quarterly* (see *ALS 1973*, pp. 228–29) in devoting an issue to Willa Cather. *Arizona Quarterly* (Winter 1973) published three articles on Cather's major novels. Mary E. Rucker's "Prospective Focus in *My Ántonia*" (29:303–316) sees Jim Burden as moving from a childhood desire to merge with nature to a social desire for love and community and then back again, as an adult, to desiring union with the impersonal forces of nature on the prairie. This critic wants to put the emphasis not on Jim's memory shaping the novel, but on the conflicts of his growing up, particularly his desire to reconcile agrarian values and letters. The essay, however, makes what are already familiar points: that Jim Burden is the novel's center of focus, that Jim tries to escape reality by his idealized vision of the land. David C. Stineback's "Willa Cather's Ironic Masterpiece" (29:317–30) argues that *The Professor's House* is Cather's renunciation of nostalgia, that in the novel the professor, in order to survive, must give up his ideal vision of the past embodied in Tom Outland for the "bloomless" realities of the present symbolized by Augusta. Mary-Ann and David Stouck's "Art and Religion in *Death Comes for the Archbishop*" (29:293–302) suggests that the vision informing this novel is "the renunciation of earthly power and ambition," and that in the latter part of her career Cather saw religion and religious art, because of their communal, impersonal character, as the only possible sources of an enduring happiness.

Prairie Schooner (Summer 1974) also published three pieces under the heading "Willa Cather: A Portfolio." In "*My Ántonia* and the American Dream" (48:112–23) James E. Miller, Jr., argues that Jim Burden's failure to find happiness and fulfillment as an adult is another instance in American literature of the failure of the American dream. He compares Jim Burden to Fitzgerald's Jay Gatsby and the protagonist of Williams's *Paterson*, because their common pursuit of a golden ideal can only lead them into the past. In "Cather's *My Mortal Enemy*" (48:124–33) Elizabeth Gates Whaley states her belief that Cather's purpose in this novel was "to show the tragedy of the misspent life where love did not last." She suggests that Cather must have seen something of herself in Myra, and where Myra turned to religion to see herself clearly, Cather had her art to illuminate her life. Particularly interesting for Cather specialists is L. Brent Bohlke's "Beginnings: Willa Cather and 'The Clemency of the Court'" (48:134–44), which shows that even in as early a story as "The Clemency of the Court" Cather was drawing on a combination of literary and factual sources for her fiction. The story of the ill-fated Russian boy, Bohlke argues, likely owes something to a couple of similar stories by Turgenev, but was probably prompted and shaped in its details by a scandalous incident at the Nebraska State Penitentiary in Lincoln in 1893 in which a young convict was found dead in the solitary cell.

Amidst these riches there appeared inevitably articles of less substance and value. In a lengthy and diffuse piece entitled "Nature and Character in the Novels of Willa Cather" (*CLQ* 10:391–412), John Ditsky examines Cather's 12 novels three different times according to her use of the land: first, the land seen as the "embodiment of history or witness to the past, secondly as a "source of hope and reflection of human dreams," and thirdly as the "shaper of individual character, especially in terms of orientation to art." The novels are treated too briefly and the approach is too thesis-ridden to be very valuable, although this article as a whole does underscore rightly enough the importance of the land as an abiding metaphor in Cather's art. A philosophy of the land has been Sister Lucy Schneider's special interest, but her "Permanance [sic] and Promise: Cather's *Shadows on the Rock*" (*Renascence* 26:83–94) is little more than a series of personal impressions, positive and negative, on Cather's Quebec novel. More interesting is novelist Margaret Howe Freydberg's "Willa Cather: the Light Behind Her Books" (*ASch* 43:282–87). Freydberg feels the essence of Cather's artistry derives from the fusion of her detailed observation of life with her profound moral integrity (the intensely personal dimension of art). And in "Symbolic Representation in Willa Cather's *O Pioneers!*" (*WAL* 9:187–96) Maynard Fox argues the density of Cather's apparently simple prose by showing how many of the scenes in *O Pioneers!* anticipate through their seemingly casual details the future relationships of the characters.

Finally, an invaluable addition to Cather scholarship must be noted in Margaret Anne O'Connor's "A Guide to the Letters of Willa Cather" (*RALS* 4:145–72). According to Cather's will, her letters cannot be collected for publication, nor quoted directly in print. Cather scholars are faced accordingly with the monumental task of consulting libraries all over the country if they want to avail themselves of the biographical and literary information the letters contain. O'Connor's guide gives the location of some 900 letters (there are 43 collections altogether) and helps direct the scholar to the area of his particular interest. In brief notes about the collections O'Connor gives particular emphasis to describing important letters in small holdings that have not been used extensively by Cather's biographers.

ii. Jack London

The other novelist to receive a great deal of critical attention in 1974 was Jack London. The London revival in fact reached a significant milestone with the publication of Earle Labor's *Jack London* (TUSAS, 230). This is the first full-scale critical study of London and his writings to appear in English, and it is a worthy if belated tribute to

London as his centenary approaches in 1976. This book is probably the very best that its kind (the Twayne series) can offer—a critical introduction that is at once comprehensive and insightful. Labor's immense enthusiasm for his subject gives his study a special zest; but the book is always a balanced account of London, ready to recognize the author's limitations as quickly as to single out his virtues. Labor's approach to both the man and his work is primarily mythic. He opens his study by considering the phenomenon of London's success as a personality, accounting for it in terms of the American myth of rugged individualism and the Rags-to-Riches Dream. He argues that the best of London's writings have a mythic dimension that cannot be fully described or accounted for in literary critical terms.

Labor sees *The Call of the Wild* and *White Fang* as London's two most successful books, neither of which he says can be classified as conventional novels. He defines *The Call of the Wild* as a mythic romance, and in some detail shows how the book is a parable about the darkest impulses in man. *White Fang* he classes a sociological fable written according to a moral vision. Both he says are beast fables which comment not on the plight of animals but on the human situation. He feels *The Call of the Wild* is the more engaging book because it holds the reader "for no other purpose than the unique experience of art" and directs us toward "the everlasting mystery of life itself." It is on such sound literary judgments as these that Labor's study is built. Labor also discusses at length some of London's more uneven productions. He comments, for example, on the sentimentality of the love story in *The Sea-Wolf* and the credibility of the protagonist's suicide in *Martin Eden*. But these are novels, he reminds us, which have tremendous popular appeal, and he accounts for this in terms of their archetypal dimensions. Wolf Larsen, he says, is the "psychopathic overreacher," whose literary archetype includes Milton's Satan and Melville's Captain Ahab. He places *Martin Eden* in the tradition of the *Bildungsroman* and relates its hero to both the American archetype of the dangerous innocent and to the potent myth of Rags-to-Riches. Labor also considers London's socialism and his political allegories, but sees these books betrayed by the pamphleteer and reformer in London. In his conclusion Labor states that "London's ultimate greatness derives from his 'primordial vision' and the mythopoeic force which animates his finest creations." Let me say

again that this is a first-rate book: admirable for its comprehensive-
ness and density within the scope of the Twayne format and always
well written.

Another important addition to London scholarship is the reprinting of Hensley Woodbridge's *Jack London: A Bibliography* (Mill-
wood, N.Y.: Kraus Repr. [1973]) in an enlarged edition which increases the number of entries by almost 50 percent over the 1966
edition. Further supplements to this new edition have appeared in
Vols. 6 and 7 of the *Jack London Newsletter*. Less significant is Dale J.
Walker's *Jack London, Sherlock Holmes and Sir Arthur Conan Doyle*
(Amsterdam, N.Y.: Alvin S. Fick). This brief study relates London
as a detective-story writer to Doyle only in the broadest sense. Walker
fails to establish London as a reader of Sherlock Holmes and does not
explore the possibilities of a literary relationship between the two
writers. There were also four dissertations wholly or partly concerned
with London.

The vitality of the London revival is reflected in the variety and
frequently high quality of articles printed by the *Jack London Newsletter*. Grappling, like Labor, with the problem of Martin Eden's
suicide, Roy Weitzel in "Towards a 'Bright White Light': London's
Use of Swinburne in *Martin Eden*" (*JLN* 7:1–8) argues for London's
artistry by showing how the allusions to Swinburne and his poetry
foreshadow the course of the action and the fate of the artist in the
novel. Similarly concerned with London's artistry, Lynn De Vore in
"The Descent of White Fang" (*JLN* 7:122–26) shows how in Biblical
images that change from Old to New Testament London portrays
the socializing of the wolf dog.

Most of the articles are concerned with more strictly philosophical
issues. Frances W. Kaye's "Jack London's Modifications of Herbert
Spencer" (*JLN* 7:67–72) shows how London's individualism, supported by Herbert Spencer's doctrine of survival of the fittest, was
always being altered in some way by his socialism. Kaye argues that
London could not really formulate a coherent socialist solution to the
problems of capitalism, and that his definition of the good life in
Burning Daylight and *The Valley of the Moon* is a reversion to the
pastoral idyll which is neither Spencerian nor Marxist. In her article
Kaye refers to *The Sea Wolf* as Nietzschean in philosophy, but in the
following number of the newsletter (*JLN* 7:109–10) Anthony Bukoski
quotes London's claim that *The Sea Wolf* was an attack on Nietzsche

and on the idea of the superman. He also points to Charmian London's recollection that her husband said he was trying to prove the failure of the antisocial superman in modern life. Edwin Erbentraut's "The Key to Complexity: Jack London and the Theory of Complementarity" (*JLN* 6[1973]:119–22) attempts to explain such contradictions in London's philosophy and character by reference to a theory in physics which holds that two seemingly opposing ideas can be simultaneously valid. Meanwhile in "The Wolf in London's Mirror" (*JLN* 6[1973]:111–18) Ann Upton suggests that London's favorite animal, the culturally ambivalent wolf (both destroyer and preserver), reflects the dichotomy in London and his philosophy between the lone wolf, or Nietzschean superman, and the wolf of the pack, the man who turned to socialism seeking friendship, justice, and love.

The Call of the Wild continues to receive the most individual attention. Jonathan H. Spinner in "A Syllabus for the 20th Century: Jack London's *The Call of the Wild*" (*JLN* 7:73–78) argues that in Buck's joining the wolf pack, London is saying the dilemmas of modern man are going to be resolved through violence, that allegorically Buck in the North is learning to cope "with his loss of identity, his feeling of alienation, and his loss of faith in a world he neither created nor knew existed." In "*The Call of the Wild*: Parental Metaphor" (*JLN* 7:58–61) Andrew Flink sees another kind of allegory, one about fatherly love and desertion that London was projecting on to the protagonists of his famous novel.

One of the policies of *JLN* is to provide evidence of how other countries view London and his work. Do Duc Duc's "Jack London's Dream at the Turn of the Century" (*JLN* 6[1973]:133–45) is a 1966 article by a Vietnamese Communist critic who sees London exclusively as a socialist writer. He argues that London was not a racist, but had sympathy for the native people in his stories, that his descriptions of brute strength and survival of the fittest were descriptions of contemporary American society, and that *The Iron Heel* is London's most important work which, in view of continuing social struggle, has not lost its timely character.

Other articles of interest include Lou Burton's "Some Monstrous Worm" (*JLN* 7:117–21), a reading of the short story "Love of Life" which shows how London reduces his protagonist to a primitive worm form seeking the sea in its struggle for survival. And Kathleen

B. Hindman in "Jack London's *The Sea Wolf*: Naturalism with a
Spiritual Bent" (*JLN* 6[1973]:99–110) shows how Humphrey Van
Weyden appropriates much of Wolf Larsen's natural philosophy to
his own life, but how in the end he remains a man in whom the
spiritual side still has priority of place.

iii. Gertrude Stein

Gertrude Stein's centenary was marked appropriately by a book about
her life—James R. Mellow's *Charmed Circle: Gertrude Stein and
Company* (New York: Praeger). Mellow has immersed himself in
countless collections of letters and memoirs (particularly the Stein
collection at Yale) and has produced an affectionate but unbiased
account of Gertrude Stein's life. Mellow's book, however, is not a
definitive biography, nor is it meant to be; as the title suggests, it is
as much about the circle of artists, friends, and acquaintances that
surrounded Gertrude Stein as about the author herself. In the "Afterword" Mellow admits a nostalgic desire to recapture something of a
brilliant episode in American literary history, to hear the voices of
Picasso, Matisse, Hemingway, to recreate the texture of a writer's
daily life, and to catch something of that special relationship between
Gertrude Stein and Alice Toklas that lasted nearly 40 years. These
things Mellow has done beautifully. *Charmed Circle* is the biography
of a milieu, full of anecdotes and leisurely elaborations on the
various persons who, over the years, formed part of that extraordinary company.

While *Charmed Circle* affords the reader immense pleasure, it is
not a book which significantly extends our understanding of a difficult writer's works. Mellow is fascinated with Gertrude Stein as a
celebrity (he impresses on us her inordinate desire for fame), but he
seems curiously disinterested in her writings as literature. Mellow
does not really attempt, as Richard Bridgman did in *Gertrude Stein
in Pieces*, to unravel the complexities and ambiguities of her works.
More frequently one finds Mellow complaining of a deliberately
perverse and tedious quality to her writing. For example, he refers
to *Two: Gertrude Stein and Her Brother* as another of the author's
"lengthy and frequently boring word portraits." And when Mellow
discusses the novels his particular interest is in relating them to the
events of Stein's life rather than exploring their stylistic experiments.

Mellow takes as epigraph for the first half of his book a sentence from the memoirs of D. H. Kantweiler, the Paris art dealer: "You must understand that we lived in an atmosphere of euphoria, youth and enthusiasm that can hardly be imagined today." The achievement of Mellow's book is in recreating something of that atmosphere.

The serious treatment of Stein's fiction wanting in Mellow's book can be found in David D. Cooper's article, "Gertrude Stein's 'Magnificent Asparagus': Horizontal Vision and Unmeaning in *Tender Buttons*" (*MFS* 20:337–49). Cooper first distinguishes between the psychological mode, whose transparent style always directs us to subject matter, and the visionary mode, whose opaque style bodies forth universal, unconscious impulses at the expense of meaning. He continues further to distinguish between the vertical visionary like Blake or Whitman who ascends or descends the entire range of universal human experiences, and a writer like Gertrude Stein whom he describes as a "horizontal visionary" because she focuses on the exterior world of sense experiences. Where the vertical visionary sees into the essence of experience, the horizontal visionary sees into its substance. He suggests that *Tender Buttons* deals solely with objects and how we perceive them; the message of such a book is that real perception is to recognize chaos and unmeaningfulness, and the richness of the exterior world free from the time continuum.

Another significant publication related to Gertrude Stein is *Staying on Alone: Letters of Alice B. Toklas*, ed. Edward Burns, introd. Gilbert A. Harrison (New York: Liveright, 1973). The seriousness of Stein's life and her dedication to writing is enhanced by Alice's letters. In the more than 20 years after Gertrude died Alice dedicated all her energies to getting the manuscripts published; the letters record much of these efforts. They also give a feeling for the relationship between Gertrude and Alice and for the style of life of 27 Rue de Fleurus.

iv. Theodore Dreiser

The most significant event in Dreiser scholarship in 1974 was the long-awaited publication of Dreiser's *Notes on Life*, ed. Marguerite Tjader and John J. McAleer; introd. John Cowper Powys (University: Univ. of Ala. Press). We are told that Dreiser started to gather material for this book of philosophical reflections as far back as 1915, though he did not begin a systematic classification of his materials until the 1930s. Dreiser died before the book was ready for publication, so it lacks the author's coherent and ordered presentation of his philosophical writings. The editors accordingly have had a difficult task: how best to arrange the large amount of material that had not been catalogued? They chose first to print only materials not previously published, which means some of Dreiser's major philosophical essays are omitted here in favor of short notes and jottings. In this respect the book is partial. Secondly, since many of the essays and notes could be included under several topic headings, the editors had to devise their own system of classification. This was obviously necessary, but more obvious should have been the necessity of an index to provide a comprehensive guide (through cross-reference) to any given topic. Amazingly, and regrettably, an index was not included. This is potentially an important and useful book because Dreiser's philosophy, like London's, was always rambling and inconsistent, but without the index its usefulness is severely limited.

There were no major articles on Dreiser in 1974. The *Dreiser Newsletter*, however, continues to bring together interviews, biographical information, and brief notes. In "'Along the Wabash': A 'Comedy Drama' by Theodore Dreiser" (*DN* 5,ii:1–4) Donald Pizer tells us that while critics know little of what Dreiser was doing for most of 1895, a group of letters in the copyright office of the Library of Congress reveals he was attracted to the idea of becoming a playwright. Dreiser filed copyright for a comedy drama to be titled "Along the Wabash." A deposit copy of the play was never received by the Library of Congress, but the title phrase does appear in the first line of the popular song "On the Banks of the Wabash" written by Dreiser's brother, Paul Dresser. D. G. Kehl in "Dreiser and the Winebrennarians" (*DN* 5,ii:5–9) suggests that Dreiser's reference in *An American Tragedy* to the presence of Winebrennarians on the lake at the point when Clyde is going to drown Roberta may be an artful allusion to underscore Clyde's false idea of free will. Kehl points out that Winebrennarians (Church of God) put strong emphasis on free will in their faith, a concept which becomes wholly ironic by the conclusion of *An American Tragedy*. More far-fetched is Beverlee Calvert's "A Structural Analysis of *Jennie Gerhardt*" (*DN* 5,ii:9–11), which tries to account for the arrangement of *Jennie*

Gerhardt's 62 untitled chapters through a juggling of numbers related to ages, dates, weeks in a year, days in a week, etc.

A couple of notes in *American Literary Realism* prove to be of some interest. The title of John C. Hirsh's article, "The Printed Ephemera of *Sister Carrie*" (*ALR* 7:171–72) refers to tickets, menus, business cards, newspapers, etc. mentioned in the novel, which, Hirsh points out, have "all the impermanence of a cut flower, but none of the beauty, and thus [are] an appropriate symbol for the urban and material world of sentimental values and failed idealism which Carrie finds in Chicago and New York." In "*Sister Carrie*: A Possible Source for the Title" (*ALR* 7:173–74) Allen F. Stein speculates that a Civil War song titled "Sister Carrie," which appeals to South Carolina not to secede from the Union (not to leave home) might be the source of Dreiser's title. Finally, Philip L. Gerber's "Frank Cowperwood: Boy Financier" (*SAF* 2:165–74) shows how Dreiser built up his account of Cowperwood's childhood for *The Financier* when so little factual documentation on the early life of Charles Tyson Yerkes, Jr., the prototype of Cowperwood, was available. Gerber gives evidence that Dreiser used details from the life of Jay Cooke, historical information from public records as well as his own boyhood memories.

v. Edith Wharton

Edith Wharton has become a subject of special interest for feminist critics. Elizabeth Ammons in "The Business of Marriage in Edith Wharton's *The Custom of the Country*" (*Criticism* 16:326–38) maintains that critics have not recognized that "Wharton's real subject matter is woman and that she directs her social criticism . . . primarily against cultural attitudes which demean or inhibit women." Ammons argues that Wharton's main target in *The Custom of the Country* is not the nouveaux riches, but the institution of marriage in the leisure class, and defends the ruthless, unsympathetic heroine of the novel by demonstrating that "Undine Spragg is no more exploitive than the culture which produced her. She just accepts marriage for the speculative, economic institution it obviously is." In a more thoughtful essay entitled "Viewing the Custom of her Country: Edith Wharton's Feminism" (*ConL* 15:521–38) Margaret B. McDowell suggests that Wharton's sympathy for her women characters and her insights into their lives reveal an implicit feminism in her writing. McDowell points out that while Wharton's women at first appear humble and acquiescent, they prove firm and courageous in the end while the male characters are revealed as passive and ineffectual. Moreover, she writes, Wharton's women ask questions about themselves and their roles in society and if they settle for conformity and compromise, they do so knowing why. Further, McDowell points out that Wharton's novels provide a document on the changing role of women in society, particularly in relation to divorce and the extramarital affair.

More literary in its assumptions and purpose is Cynthia Griffin Wolff's "Lily Bart and the Beautiful Death" (*AL* 46:16–40). In this nicely argued essay Wolff traces the tragic death of Lily Bart in *The House of Mirth* to a confusion between the ideal and the real reflected in current attitudes in the representation of women in art. She demonstrates that Lily was raised to be a decorative object, a symbol of her family's affluence and respectability, and that her models were the figures of female elegance in Art Nouveau and the female figures of moral righteousness in neoclassical murals then in vogue in public buildings. She then argues that Selden only responds to Lily as an "aesthetic-moral object" and that their relationship and Lily's image of self-worth disintegrate because she cannot become the flawless embodiment of virtue that her outward appearance symbolically represents.

Of some biographical interest is Adeline R. Tintner's " 'The Hermit and The Wild Woman': Edith Wharton's 'Fictioning' of Henry James" (*JML* 4:32–42), which shows how the details of Wharton's pseudo-life of a saint, "The Hermit and The Wild Woman" (1906), and her imitation medieval poem, "Ogrin the Hermit" (1909), can be identified with the personal relationship between Wharton and Henry James (the latter had advised Wharton on her marital affairs around the time the pieces were written). Tintner's thesis is a rebuttal of R. W. B. Lewis's statement that Walter Berry rather than James was the prototype of the hermit.

vi. John Dos Passos

The major discussion of this author in 1974 is to be found in John P. Diggins's "Visions of Chaos and Visions of Order: Dos Passos as

Historian" (*AL* 46:329–46). Diggins argues that in *U.S.A.* Dos Passos was not a historian, for a historian relives in his mind the experiences of the past and reveals their determinant content, but rather that he was a chronicler recording with his camera-eye technique the dead, inert events, empty of potential, that have chaotically swept over man in a capitalist society. He states that in *U.S.A.* Dos Passos's historical vision as such is "the totality of chaos." He points out, however, that in later novels Dos Passos changed and viewed history as the study of great men, thus reversing from his naturalistic position to seeing men, not as passive creatures, but as characters shaping the course of human events. Diggins argues that this final conservative view of history is confused, for Dos Passos believed American democracy sprang naturalistically from the freedom inherent in the environment of America rather than from the possibilities of the political mind. The other Dos Passos article of special interest and value is David L. Vanderwerken's "Dos Passos' *Streets of Night*: A Reconsideration" (*MarkhamR* 4:61–65). Vanderwerken examines the structure of Dos Passos's third novel and finds an intricate series of triangular relationships formed around the three central characters, Fanshawe, Nan, and Wenny. According to this critic these three characters form the central triangle, but within each character's consciousness exists another triangle, responsible for inner conflict, that is similar to Freud's tripartite division of the psyche (ego, superego, id). Vanderwerken also sees the wheel or circle as another controlling structural image, used to dramatize the characters' belief that they are "doomed to recapitulate the destiny of their ancestors." Finally Vanderwerken points out that this somewhat anomalous, self-consciously literary novel is similar to other Dos Passos novels in that the pattern of futility in the characters' lives reflects the sterility and stagnation of the whole country.

Two notes on Dos Passos are also of interest. David E. E. Sloane's "The Black Experience in Dos Passos' *U.S.A.*" (*CEA* 36,iii:22–23) suggests that the almost complete absence of black people in Dos Passos's major work objectively reflects the peripheral nature of black life in upward–mobility–oriented America. He points out that the few oblique references to blacks are wholly racist in import. Meanwhile in "Faulkner's Small Debt to Dos Passos: A Source for the Percy Grimm Episode" (*MissQ* 27:327–31) Don Graham and Barbara Shaw credit Dos Passos as a significant influence on Faulkner, arguing that Faulkner's Percy Grimm sequence in *Light in August* likely had its origin in Dos Passos's *1919* where a Warren Grimm leads the mob that lynches a leader of the Wobblies. *Dos Passos: A Collection of Critical Essays*, ed., introd. Andrew Hook (Englewood Cliffs, N.J.: Prentice-Hall) makes more readily available a substantial number of previously published essays on the author.

vii. Sherwood Anderson

Anderson is also represented now in the Prentice-Hall series. *Sherwood Anderson: A Collection of Critical Essays*, ed., introd. Walter B. Rideout (Englewood Cliffs, N.J.: Prentice-Hall) is a judicious selection of the best pieces available on the author. There were no major new additions to criticism of Anderson in 1974, but William J. Scheick's "Compulsion Toward Repetition: Sherwood Anderson's 'Death in the Woods'" (*SSF* 11:141–46) proves one of the most interesting treatments of a short piece of fiction. In a psychological reading of the story Scheick argues that the narrator as a boy was afraid of growing up and that he subconsciously identifies with the old woman who has died, as a way of evading the painful realities (specifically sexual) of becoming a man.

Two other pieces focus on Anderson's short stories. William V. Miller's "In Defense of Mountaineers: Sherwood Anderson's Hill Stories" (*BSUF* 15,ii:51–58) describes the 13 stories Anderson set in Virginia and points out that the author was concerned to debunk the romantic myths about these people. Miller says Anderson wanted to reveal the harsh economic and social realities of their lives, while at the same time suggesting something of the pride and courage with which they fronted life. Luther S. Leudtke in "Sherwood Anderson, Thomas Hardy and 'Tandy'" (*MFS* 20:531–40) draws an analogy between Anderson's story, "Tandy," and the central situation in Hardy's *Jude the Obscure*, suggesting that an influence on Anderson was likely. He points out that the struggle to find love and fulfillment in rural communities that have been left behind by modern technology dominates the fiction of both Anderson and Hardy. Anderson is compared unfavorably to James Purdy, another Ohio author, in Frank Baldanza's "Northern Gothic" (*SoR* 10:566–82). Baldanza points out that both Anderson and Purdy are centrally concerned with the lonely, questing adolescent and that both are preoccupied with what Anderson termed the "grotesque." But this article is marred by the author's quarrelsome determination to reveal Anderson as an inferior artist.

viii. Glasgow, Cabell

The only substantial discussion of Ellen Glasgow's work was C. Hugh Holman's "April in Queenborough: Ellen Glasgow's Comedies of Manners" (*SR* 82:263–83), first presented at the gathering at Mary Baldwin College, Staunton, Virginia, in the fall of 1973 to mark the author's centenary. This masterly essay relates the critical success of the Queenborough novels (*The Romantic Comedians, They Stooped to Folly, The Sheltered Life*) to Ellen Glasgow's ability in late middle age to view her characters disinterestedly rather than as surrogates of her anguished self. Holman describes the protagonists in all three novels as aging characters, like James's Lambert Strether, who recognize they have missed life's delight. But Holman says they never become tragic figures because the narrator always views their world from a "detached, amused, gently satiric" perspective. In "Ellen Glasgow's *Virginia*: Preliminary Notes" (*SB* 27:265–89) Oliver Steele reproduces the notebooks Glasgow made as she was planning her novel, *Virginia*. In a discussion of the notebooks Steele singles out a number of features of composition that are reflected in the changes Glasgow made between the notes and the novel. Reflecting the current trend in literary criticism are two dissertations on feminism in Glasgow's novels.

Two articles in an issue of *Mississippi Quarterly* describe the city of Richmond in which Ellen Glasgow and James Branch Cabell lived. In "Cabell's and Glasgow's Richmond: The Intellectual Background of the City" (27:375–91) Maurice Duke gives a brief historical sketch of the city describing the theatre and the kinds of books that were available in Richmond, while Edgar E. MacDonald in "Glasgow, Cabell and Richmond" (27:393–413) describes the kind of society that these writers grew up and lived in, pointing out that both wrote "novels of manners." A third article in the same issue, "Glasgow and the Southern Renaissance: The Conference at Charlottesville" (27:415–34) by Dorothy Scura, describes Glasgow's failure to organize a Southern writers conference that would continue to meet annually. Scura attributes this failure in part to Glasgow's conservatism.

The articles in the 1974 *Kalki* do not further our appreciation of Cabell significantly. The only comprehensive treatment of Cabell's fiction is Maurice Duke's "The Ornate Wasteland of James Branch Cabell" (*Kalki* 6:79–89), which asks "What is the statement made by Cabell's ambitious Biography of the Life of Dom Manuel?" Duke's answer is that beneath the dazzling surface of urbanity and ironical wit in Cabell's mythical Poictesme "lies a spiritual wasteland, not unlike Eliot's, in that in Poictesme nothing is really worth the effort because nothing can really ever be accomplished." The only other substantial piece is Geoffrey Morley-Mower's "James Branch Cabell's Flirtation with Clio: The Story of a Collaboration" (*Kalki* 6:39–53), which gives an account of how Cabell worked with the historian, A. J. Hanna, to write a book, *The St. Johns* (1943), for Farrar and Rinehart's The Rivers of America Series. Morley-Mower shows how Cabell was always searching out the scandalous and ridiculous in the historical facts provided by Hanna.

ix. Sinclair Lewis

Lewis too is the subject of feminist criticism. Nan Bauer Maglin's "Women in Three Sinclair Lewis Novels" (*MR* 14[1973]:783–801) considers *The Job, Main Street*, and *Ann Vickers* in a feminist light and concludes from these books that "Lewis was consciously exploring through fiction the choices and pressures that women felt personally and socially during the first third of the twentieth century." She shows that the central dilemma for Lewis's women, as for any woman today, was the choice of work or marriage.

The *Sinclair Lewis Newsletter* continues to publish brief articles, some of high quality. In a rather unique piece entitled "*Babbitt:* The Sound Track of a Satire" (*SLN* 5–6[1973–74]:1–4) Robert L. Coard draws attention to all the repetitive, discordant sounds in the novel (e.g., the grinding *g*, the booming *b*) which Lewis uses to underscore the noisy, irritating, and mechanical nature of middle-class American life in the 1920s. In another interesting piece, "Sinclair Lewis's Plot Paradigms" (*SLN* 5–6[1973–74]:4–6), Stephen S. Conroy points out that Lewis, who has been faulted for lack of plot construction in his novels, used two plot designs based on the journey motif. In one design the journey is linear, with the protagonist moving toward some never-quite-reached goal; the other design, found in *Main Street* and *Babbitt* and *Dodsworth* among others, is the journey as a temporary escape, with the protagonist circling back home by the end. In "The Unfortunate Failure of *Kingsblood Royal*" (*SLN* 5–6[1973–74]:13–15) T. J. Matheson argues that the novel is damaged by Lewis's own confusion regarding racism. He points out that on the one hand Lewis denies there are differences in race, but "on the other he seems convinced that Negroes are in fact superior to whites and thus 'different.'" In another short piece, "H. L. Mencken's Reviews of Sinclair Lewis's Major Novels" (*Menckeniana* 51:2–7), Matheson suggests that Mencken's bias for satire made him blind to Lewis's other virtues as a novelist and made him comment in a review of *Dodsworth* that Lewis's work is "irritatingly uneven." The *Newsletter* is less valuable when it publishes articles like Grace S. Wurster's "The Hollow Note in Lewis's Satire" (*SLN* 5–6[1973–74]: 15–18), a quarrelsome little piece that strikes its own hollow note. For example, Wurster attacks Lewis for creating simple stereotypes as the targets of his satire, but later in the article she says Lewis confuses his readers by looking at Gopher Prairie from several points of view.

x. The Harlem Renaissance

Interest in the beginnings of black studies in the 20th century has abated somewhat during the last year. Most of the articles pertinent to this critical survey are to be found in a special number of *Studies in the Literary Imagination*. Leon Coleman's "Carl Van Vechten Presents the New Negro" (7:85–104) describes three forms of aid and encouragement that Van Vechten gave the artists of the Harlem Renaissance: his writing about Negro arts and artists; his assistance in getting works by Negroes published; and his promotion of social contacts between Negro and white artists at his famous parties during the 1920s.

In "Jean Toomer and the South: Region and Race as Elements within a Literary Imagination" (7:23–37) Charles T. Davis relates Toomer's awakening to the question of race and home to his awakening as an artist and distinguishes between the South-North-South movement in geography in *Cane* and the North-South-North movement of the artist's consciousness in the book. Letters between Sherwood Anderson and Toomer around the time *Cane* was published in 1922 are described and reproduced in part by Darwin T. Turner in "An Intersection of Paths: Correspondence Between Jean Toomer and Sherwood Anderson" (*CLAJ* 17:455–67). In these letters Anderson is moving towards the artist's dedication to his craft, while Toomer is moving away from art towards a concern for society and psychology.

xi. Popular Fiction (Tarkington, Dixon, O. Henry, and Others)

Of the writers in a more popular vein considered in this chapter, Booth Tarkington has received the largest amount of significant critical attention. Keith J. Fennimore's *Booth Tarkington* (TUSAS, 238) is a very readable introduction to one of this century's most prolific writers. Fennimore has chosen to discuss Tarkington as a novelist and probably the major strength of his book lies in his attempt to relate Tarkington's special brand of realism to the critical theories and practice of other realists, especially Howells. Fennimore is also greatly interested in how Tarkington conducted his career (what the author did when, etc.), but here his book is always overshadowed by James Woodress's biography. More substantial and original are his discussions of Tarkington's remarkable talent for creating women characters (will he next be "discovered" by feminist critics?) and the effects he achieved in the Penrod stories. Fennimore, of course, looks at the *Growth* trilogy and other major novels like *Alice Adams*, but in this area his book is more a review of Tarkington's career and novels than a critical study, a flaw inherent perhaps in the Twayne series format. One does wish Fennimore had attempted to evaluate Tarkington's novels as works of art. This is the strength of Adam J. Sorkin's " 'She Doesn't Last, Apparently': A Reconsideration of Booth Tarkington's *Alice Adams*" (*AL* 46:182–99), which takes a careful look at one of the author's more successful books. Sorkin concedes at the outset that Tarkington is not a great writer, that his ambitious *Growth* trilogy does not earn him a prominent place in the American literary tradition. He argues, however, that *Alice Adams* is an exception and worth reconsidering, for in that novel Tarkington's realism triumphs over his own attitudes of conformity and pious acceptance of the status quo. Sorkin points out that Tarkington thought the book insignificant and argues that the author's relative detachment from his characters and their fate (he viewed them comically and unsentimentally) allowed him to present them realistically. Accordingly, he says, the social and personal defeat of the heroine is clearly seen as the direct result of her social and economic situation. He concludes by pointing out that *Alice Adams* is a vivid picture of life in the middle-class society of a growing midwestern town in the early 1920s and that it is ironically a sign of Tarkington's limitations that he portrays its limited, unrewarding nature without fully recognizing it himself.

Another Twayne series study of a popular writer is Raymond A. Cook's *Thomas Dixon* (TUSAS, 235). Cook follows up his biography of Dixon, *Fire From the Flint*, with a closer look at Dixon's novels. He gives in his new book a concise biographical sketch of Dixon and an account of his other careers, including lawyer, minister, actor, movie-maker, politician, but the largest part of the book deals with Dixon as a novelist. *The Clansman*, made into the film *Birth of a Nation*, is Dixon's best-known work and receives the greatest amount of critical attention. Cook discusses in detail the racial views that made Dixon and his novel the subject of so much heated controversy in the earlier part of the century, particularly Dixon's belief that the Negro was inherently inferior to the white man and that the Negro should submit to the superiority of white civilization or live separately in a country of his own. Cook examines in an unbiased way some of Dixon's other reactionary social theories such as his repudiation of socialism, his fear of communism, and his stand against the emancipation of women. Only on the last topic does Cook himself suggest a sympathy with his subject, for he writes: "If Dixon were living today, he would doubtless be writing effective satire about some of the ludicrous aspects of the so-called women's liberation movement." Cook asserts several times over that Dixon, because of his immense popularity and influence, is an important figure in American social and cultural history, but he admits at the same time that as a writer he ranks as "a popular sub-literary novelist." In describing the novels he says there is too much that is sensational and repetitious to hold the reader's continued interest, and one can't help wonder at the end of such a book whether a literary-focused study of the man is really necessary.

Two substantial articles on other popular writers leave the same impression. Geoffrey Blodgett's "Winston Churchill: The Novelist as Reformer" (*NEQ* 47:495–517) focuses on this author's progressivist political activities with very little reference to the novels he wrote. Edward Ifkovic's "Harold Bell Wright and the Minister of Man: The Domestic Romancer at the End of the Genteel Age" (*MarkhamR* 4:21–26) looks carefully at the novels but finds them only of sociological interest. Ifkovic sees Wright's sentimental novels as crystallizing the values of middle-class America: "God and the home, America and provincialism, articulated morality and hard work." He singles out Wright's raising of the minister figure from a supporting to a leading character in the domestic novel as the unique feature of his work.

O. Henry is seen in a more literary context and compared with other writers. In "Hemingway, O. Henry, and the Surprise Ending" (*PrS* 47[1973]:296–302) George Monteiro points out that what interested O. Henry was not character or setting, but action that would lead to the surprise ending. Hemingway dismissed O. Henry as something of a hack writer, but Monteiro argues that Hemingway too practiced a brand of surprise ending—the ending that comes unexpectedly, in the middle of things as it were, and is highly ironic. In "O. Henry and Dickens: Elsie in The Bleak House of Moral Decay" (*ELN* 12:35–37) Patricia Marks notes the parallelism between Dickens's commentary upon Jo's death in *Bleak House* and O. Henry's epilogue following Elsie's moral downfall in "Elsie in New York" and demonstrates that O. Henry found his theme of the innocent destroyed by righteous social mores in Dickens.

Finally, mention must be given to two writers, Robert Herrick and Mary Austin, who are not exactly popular novelists, but who do not draw enough critical attention to warrant a separate section in this chapter. Phyllis Franklin's "The Influence of William James on Robert Herrick's Early Fiction" (*ALR* 7:395–402) considers the preoccupation with apathy in Herrick's early stories and relates this interest to James's psychology of failure. Franklin says generally of Herrick's characters: "Their wills are deficient; their acts automatic, reflexive; and they drift apathetically, responding to chance external stimuli." In "Western Literary Realism: The California Tales of Norris and Austin" (*ALR* 7:278–80) Lee Ann Johnson distinguishes the realism of these two writers by suggesting that Norris presents heredity while Austin presents environment as the greatest influence on man. But this brief article is little more than a plea that the early stories of Norris and Austin be collected. Much more valuable is J. Wilkes Berry's "Characterization in Mary Austin's Southwest Works" (*SwAL* 2[1972]:119–24) which suggests that Austin's characters are seldom stereotypes and that their complexity derives from the relationship to the desert which destroys them or makes them disciples of its harsh code of existence. In addition Berry takes note of the narrator herself who often is "officious, meddlesome, humorless," but who emerges as an imposing presence in her works.

Simon Fraser University

14. Fiction: The 1930s to the 1950s

Margaret Anne O'Connor

The expedient of splitting the burgeoning field of 20th-century fiction into three periods rather than the two of previous editions of *ALS* might have resulted in what seems an oddly truncated middle chapter to some readers. Indeed, limiting this chapter to writers who grew to prominence in the years from 1930 to the early 1950s has produced an odd mixture. Such writers as Welty, Nabokov, and Warren who continue their rich careers even today appear with writers of proletarian fiction whose careers are more easily encompassed by the chapter's chronological boundaries. Still, setting figures writing today with those who began their careers at the same time succeeds in displaying the dimensions of their achievements. A major trend in this year's criticism of authors of this period is the desire to expand the boundaries of prose literature. Thus arguments are put forth for the creative genius of Katherine Anne Porter's personal correspondence, screenplays by Agee, Chandler, and Steinbeck, Woody Guthrie's autobiography, and Anaïs Nin's five-volume *Diary*. Critics, too, claim reevaluation of popular writers of the 1930s and 1940s is now in order and suggest that many of these writers are due a more prominent place in American literary history. The lion's share of critical attention, however, has gone to recognized figures—Steinbeck, Warren, Welty, Nabokov, and West.

James Woodress's *American Fiction, 1900–1950: A Guide to Information Sources* (Detroit: Gale Research Co.) is certain to prove an invaluable tool in working with many writers covered in this chapter. Woodress's volume contains concise bibliographical essays on 44 writers "who seem in 1973 to be the most significant producers of fiction during the first half of the twentieth century." The format for author entries consists of a single paragraph biography and general assessment of current importance; a list of works of fiction; comments on editions and reprints; an assessment of biographical ma-

terials and interviews; and a survey of most valuable criticism with
sources measured one against another in terms of present interest to
scholars. A major emphasis is on foreign criticism, a dimension lacking in other bibliographic surveys of this type. The conciseness of
entries on major figures such as Faulkner, Hemingway, and Fitzgerald is of great value now that materials have proliferated to such
an extent, and the essays on figures such as J. P. Marquand, Vardis
Fisher, Walter Van Tilburg Clark, and others covered in the body
of this chapter provide the most up-to-date and thorough bibliographic surveys available on these less prominent authors.The critical sense displayed in the essays is even and dependable. Readers
are warned of unreliable sources and directed toward studies of
greatest worth. Woodress's volume is the first in a projected series
on American, English, and world literature from Gale and its sets a
high mark of excellence for the subsequent volumes to equal.

i. Dissenting Voices—"Art for Humanity's Sake"

The manifesto of *The Rebel Poet*, a precursor of *The Anvil*, pro-
claimed its artistic creed as "art for humanity's sake" and the statement remained a guiding precept in *The Anvil* as well. In *Writers in
Revolt: The Anvil Anthology, 1933–1940* (New York: Lawrence Hill
Co., 1973), Jack Conroy and Curt Johnson edit a selection of short
stories and poetry which originally appeared in *The Anvil* and *New
Anvil* under Conroy's editorship. Conroy's introduction to the volume
gives an informative and occasionally amusing account of the magazine's history, and selections include works of fiction by Nelson Algren, Erskine Caldwell, James T. Farrell, Langston Hughes, Jesse
Stuart, William Carlos Williams, and Frank Yerby. Many of these
and other selections in the anthology are unavailable in other sources
and the notes on contributors identifies many of the shadowy figures
who played a role in proletarian fiction of the period. Jack Conroy
himself is the subject of Jack Salzman's "Conroy, Mencken, and *The
American Mercury*" (*JPC* 7[1973]:524–28). Salzman terms Conroy's
The Disinherited "one of the few essential testaments of the 1930's"
and recognizes the importance of Mencken's contribution to its success through publishing five short stories which ultimately became
part of the novel. Salzman's article is followed by a chapter of Con-

roy's autobiography which he is in the process of writing ("Charlie was our Darlin,'" *JPC* 7[1973]:529–36).

John M. Reilly considers six novels dealing with the National Textile Worker's strike in Gastonia, North Carolina, of April 1929 in "Images of Gastonia: A Revolutionary Chapter in American Social Fiction" (*GaR* 28:498–517). Sherwood Anderson's *Beyond Desire* (1932) is the best known of the group, which also includes Mary Heaton Vorse's *Strike* (1930), Dorothy Myra Page's *Gathering Storm* (1932), Grace Lumpkin's *To Make My Bread* (1932), Fielding Burke's *Call Home the Heart* (1932), and William Rollins, Jr.'s *The Shadow Before* (1934). Reilly uses these novels to make general points about the purposes and characteristics of radical fiction. The essay displays admirable attention to the literary implications of ideologically inspired fiction. While no new points are raised, older issues growing from Walter Rideout's *The Radical Novel* (1956) are settled in terms of these six novels.

Kenneth McCollum's *Nelson Algren: A Checklist* (Detroit: Gale Research Co. [1973]) lists all editions and printings of Algren's book-length works in English, as well as the first magazine appearance of stories, poems, articles, essays, interviews, reviews, and published letters. Studs Terkel introduces the *Checklist* in "Nelson Algren: An Appreciation" (pp. 1–4) by assessing Algren's achievement: "My hunch is his writings will be read long after acclaimed works of the Academe's darlings, yellowed on coffee tables, will be replaced by acclaimed works of other Academe's darlings. For in the spirit of a Zola and a Dreiser, he has captured a piece of that life 'behind the billboards.'" A facsimile of an essay fragment titled "Salomon and Morris: Two Patriots of the Revolution," which Algren wrote on assignment for the WPA "for the B'nai B'rith or some similar organization," is appended to the *Checklist* (pp. 87–107). The wide margins, full-page division markers, and 22 full-page photos of dustjackets and memorabilia suggest that this checklist could well have appeared as a medium-length journal article instead of the $15.00 thin volume at hand.

Woodress's review essay on John Steinbeck (*American Fiction*, pp. 183–93) is a good place to begin the job of sifting through the mountain of material which is rapidly accumulating on this author. Tetsumaro Hayashi has the same evaluative purposes in mind in the collection of reviews he edits titled *Steinbeck Criticism: A Review of Book-Length Studies* (*1939–1973*), Steinbeck Monograph Series 4. Many of the reviews originally appeared in *StQ* while others have been prepared specifically for this monograph. The study would be more helpful if it included an essay synthesizing the findings of the 17 separate reviews. Hayashi also edits *A Study Guide to Steinbeck: A Handbook to his Major Works* (Metuchen, N.J.: Scarecrow), an extremely handy tool for teaching Steinbeck. Each of the twelve contributors to the volume's treatment of individual works has prepared an essay following a useful format which presents background information on the work, a plot synopsis and explication, suggestions for research projects, and an annotated bibliography of relevant secondary sources. Introductory essays by Warren French and Peter Lisca aim at the general problems of teaching Steinbeck while a concluding essay by Robert E. Morseberger considers Steinbeck and his work in films.

In his introduction to Howard Levant's *The Novels of John Steinbeck: A Critical Study* (Columbia: Univ. of Mo. Press), Warren French writes the essay which might well have been the synthesizing element in Hayashi's *Steinbeck Criticism* mentioned above. French briefly reviews the major works of criticism on Steinbeck, both book-length studies and articles, and ranks them in terms of their value to present scholars. He proclaims Levant's work "a turning point in Steinbeck studies" because "it provides an objective framework for analyzing the causes of a decline [in the quality of Steinbeck's work] that has hitherto been attributed almost entirely to events in the author's private life" (p. xi). Levant's study, a revision of his 1962 Cornell dissertation, treats Steinbeck's major works chronologically in order to show the balance of "structure" and "materials" (terms drawn from Wellek's and Warren's *Theory of Fiction* [1949]) in his best work as opposed to the imbalance between them in works written after 1945. For a study covering so much ground, the absence of an index is vexing, as is the heavy reliance on early scholarship, despite the existence of pertinent, more recent material. Still, Levant presents a valuable overview of Steinbeck's entire career.

The majority of periodical articles on Steinbeck in 1974 appeared, appropriately enough, in *StQ*, edited by Tetsumaro Hayashi. Most articles in *StQ* shied away from the well-ploughed fields of Steinbeck's major novels and dealt instead with recurring images and themes in several works seen as a group or with works of less recognized merit. In the first category is "Steinbeck and the Automobile" (7:18–24) in which George Spies, III, pulls together references to the automobile in Steinbeck's fiction and essays to confirm his reputation as "Poet Laureate of the Jalopy." Robert M. Benton makes a plea for more attention to Steinbeck's scientific interests in future criticism in "A Scientific Point of View in Steinbeck's Fiction" (7:67–73). As if in response to Benton, Betty L. Perez discusses Steinbeck's knowledge of marine biology in "Steinbeck, Ricketts, and *Sea of Cortez*: Partnership or Exploitation?" (7:73–79). Citing unpublished letters and journals, Perez shows that the work was a true collaboration, not, as many critics have assumed, the artistic work of Steinbeck and the scientific work of Ricketts. In "The Expository Prose of John Steinbeck" (parts 1 and 2, 7:41–52, 88–102), Sanford E. Marovitz finds *Sea of Cortez* "one of the most strikingly beautiful and significant volumes in the entire Steinbeck canon" and, despite the problems of coauthorship, an example of Steinbeck at his journalistic best.

In "Steinbeck's *Burning Bright*: Homage to Astarte" (7:79–84), John M. Ditsky finds that the attempt to combine "allegorical and naturalistic" elements results in a work which Ditsky himself admits is somewhat "unsettling and even ludicrous." Tracing both patterns in relation to the Blake poem which gives rise to the novel's title, however, Ditsky argues that "it would be naive to believe that John Steinbeck did not fully intend the paradoxical elementing to which some of us object, and malicious to fault him for trying." Lawrence William Jones plays on an epithet Malcolm Cowley coined in "Poison in the Cream Puff: The Human Condition in *Cannery Row*" (ed. Marston LaFrance, 7:35–40). Jones reads the work as a parable on the human condition and not primarily a comic work as some critics view it. The breadth of the topic is too much for such a brief article, but the grounds for Jones's view are clear.

Two articles in *StQ* focus on *The Pearl* and see the work as a record of a man triumphing over the temptations of materialism. In "*The Pearl* as the Novel of Disengagement" (7:84–88), Tetsumaro Hayashi uses concepts from Zen philosophy to explain the emotional dilemma the pearl presents to the novel's protagonist, Kino. By casting away the valuable pearl, Kino achieves the state of *Gedatsu*:

"He restores himself by means of his total self-negation." Sydney J. Krause finds a similar pattern in his "*The Pearl* and 'Hadleyburg': From Desire to Renunciation" (7:3–17). In these pieces both Mark Twain and Steinbeck picture characters succumbing to greed. The endings of the two pieces demonstrate their authors' differing views of mankind. In "The Man That Corrupted Hadleyburg," casting off the object of greed occurs too late to save the Richardses; Kino and his wife, however, are given the chance to triumph over human frailty.

The final article on Steinbeck's work in *StQ* presents a unique reading of a well-known story. In "The Original Manuscripts of Steinbeck's 'The Chrysanthemums'" (7:102–11), Roy S. Simmonds suggests that Elisa is more the villain than the victim in her passion-less marriage, based on the original intent of the story to be gleaned from the early drafts and Steinbeck's marginal comments on the MS. Simmonds feels Elisa has "deprived" and "emasculated" her husband, not been driven to a denial of her own femininity by his neglect as is a more common view. Charles A. Sweet, Jr., takes an alternate view, though one with its own "twist" of the standard interpretation of the story in "Ms. Elisa Allen and Steinbeck's 'The Chrysanthemums'" (*MFS* 20:210–14). Developing a hint given by Peter Lisca (in *The Wide World of John Steinbeck*, 1958) when he refers to Elisa's "silent rebellion against the passive role required of her as a woman," Sweet suggests readers regard Elisa Allen "as an embryonic feminist" in order to understand Steinbeck's purposes in the story. Through Elisa's degradation at the end of the story, Sweet feels Steinbeck is pointing out "that the sexuality inherent in woman prevents her from attaining equality." Sweet concludes: "Though not to the degree of Hemingway, Steinbeck's world is a man's world, a world that frustrates even minor league women's liberationists."

Mark Spilka discusses the Miltonic overtones of the novel and play versions of *Of Mice and Men* in "Of George and Lennie and Curley's Wife: Sweet Violence in Steinbeck's Eden" (*MFS* 20:169–79). Spilka draws the term "sweet violence" from *Tortilla Flat* and finds the evocation of paradoxical emotions suggested in the oxy-moron to be a dimension Steinbeck achieves in his best work. In "The Turtle or the Gopher: Another Look at the Ending of *The Grapes of Wrath*" (*WAL* 9:53–57), Stuart L. Burns argues unconvincingly that the parable of the tenacious turtle is inappropriate to the themes of the novel, particularly in light of the "logical and inexorable movement toward tragedy or pathos" Burns sees at the novel's end. He would substitute the parable of the gopher which appears in *Cannery Row*, illustrating a more bitter lesson that "peace and prosperity are attainable only if one is willing to sacrifice love and companionship." As the novel stands, however, the turtle only illustrates what Burns sees as "Steinbeck's inability to see where his novel came out thematically."

Henry Roth's lone novel *Call It Sleep* prompted five articles and a dissertation this year. Three of the articles and the dissertation ("the first full-length critical study of Roth," *DAI* 34:4271A) are by Bonnie K. Lyons. In "Roth's *Call It Sleep*" (*Expl* 33:item 10), Lyons illustrates Roth's control of language through the single example of his use of the Yiddish word "zwank" throughout the novel. He plays on the sound of the word as well as its English meaning, "tongs," in the climactic scene of the novel. Lyons gives a history of Roth's attempts to follow the success of his first work with a second, never-completed novel in "After *Call It Sleep*" (*AL* 45:610–12). In this article she draws from her interview with Roth in 1972, which was published in its entirety as "Interview with Henry Roth" (*Shenandoah* 25,i[1973]:48–71). The interview itself presents a wealth of information on Roth's life at the time he wrote *Call It Sleep*, his knowledge of the works of Eliot and Frazer, his method of composition (he says, for instance, that he did not allude to Eliot's or Frazer's works consciously), and his attitude toward Judaism. On this point, Roth mentions that he does not consider *Call It Sleep* "a Jewish Novel." This interview is preceded by an excerpt from Roth's journal, "Prolog in Himmel" (*Shenandoah* 25,i[1973]:44–47), suggesting that his Jewish heritage is still of great concern to him, however. In "The Ethnic Experience and Aesthetics in Literature: Malamud's *The Assistant* and Roth's *Call It Sleep*" (*Journal of Ethnic Studies* 1,iv:45–50), M. Thomas Inge finds Roth's work concerned primarily with "the loss of the Jewish identity in the modern civilized waste land" as opposed to Malamud's novel in which Jewishness is basically a metaphor for the tragic dimensions of everyman's life. Inge does not find Roth's ethnic orientation limiting, however. He sees its value in its "portrait of minority experience" as well as in the skill of its execution. Recognizing the many strains of influence in *Call It Sleep*, including Roth's Jewish heritage and proletarian political leanings, Mary Elrich Redding chooses to investigate the "basic Jungian Oedipal structure," which also underlies the novel, in "Call It Myth: Henry Roth and *The Golden Bough*" (*CentR* 18:180–95). Redding notes the many symbols in the novel obviously drawn from Roth's reading of Frazer. Her biographical support for asserting Roth knew Frazer's work well is strengthened by the Lyons interview, which apparently was unknown to Redding at the time she wrote this study.

James T. Farrell and Edward Dahlberg have received scant attention recently. Charles E. Robinson's "James T. Farrell's Critical Estimate of Hemingway" (*FHA* [1973]:209–14) traces Farrell's changing attitude toward Hemingway's work, which culminated in his 1960s assessment that Hemingway "did not grow." Discussing Farrell's 1936 letters concerning conversations with Hemingway, Robinson notes Hemingway's stated views on such writers as Malcolm Cowley, Dos Passos, Faulkner ("the best"), and Wolfe ("a phoney"). Robinson has done an excellent job of editing the unfinished article titled "Ernest Hemingway" that Farrell began in 1964. Robinson's carefully annotated version following this article was approved by Farrell himself in 1971 (*FHA* [1973]:215–25). Edward L. Shaughnessy compares the protagonist of George Santayana's only novel, *The Last Puritan*, to Farrell's Studs Lonigan in "Oliver Alden and Studs Lonigan: Heirs to Spiritual Poverty" (*MarkhamR* 4:48–52), finding that "each novel tells the story of a young man who suffers a moral atrophy brought on by cultural desolation." In a note to an excerpt from Edward Dahlberg's new satiric novel, "From 'The Olive of Minerva'" (*Prose* 8:45–72), the editors report that Dahlberg is at work on a third volume of his autobiography. In addition, John O. Cech makes use of unpublished correspondence and biographical data on Dahlberg in his University of Connecticut dissertation, "Edward Dahlberg and Charles Olson: A Biography of a Friendship" (*DAI* 35:2260A).

Three other "dissenting voices," James Thurber, Nathanael West, and J. D. Salinger—whose dissatisfaction with American life is less political than cultural—were also the subjects of critical attention in 1974. Thurber's voice is more subversive than dissenting according to Carl M. Lindner's "Thurber's Walter Mitty—The Underground American Hero" (*GaR* 28:283–89). Lindner finds Mitty one of a long line of heroes in American literature who are in conflict with a female-dominated society and seek escape. Rip Van Winkle and Huck Finn achieved physical escape, but "today, Thurber seems to say, the combat is so unequal that the path to heroic action lies through the inner mind." F. V. Bernard's "A Thurber Letter" (*ELN* 8[1971]:300–301) presents a brief letter from Thurber to a Korean War pilot recuperating from wounds. Thurber displays a bit of Walter-Mitty-like envy for the proverbial "red badge."

In an overview of Nathanael West's fiction, S. Betsky-Zweig's "The Cannonballed of Popular Culture: Nathanael West's *Miss Lonelyhearts* and *The Day of the Locust*" (*DQR* 4:145–56) compares West to Hieronymus Bosch as both are "incapable . . . of making sinners palatable or sin enticing." Joan Zlotnick, too, finds parallels between West and painters, in this case on the grounds of technique in "Nathanael West and the Pictorial Imagination" (*WAL* 9:177–85). Like a painter, West "communicates primarily through images" in his fiction. She finds specific ties in techniques to the Cubists and Surrealists and the more popular art form of the comic strip. Basing his textual evidence primarily on *Miss Lonelyhearts*, Charles Baxter argues in "Nathanael West: Dead Letters and the Martyred Novelist" (*WCR* 9,ii:3–11) that a major subject of all of West's fiction is the response of the artist to the outrageous demands of the mass audience. In "The War Within Nathanael West: Naturalism and Existentialism" (*MFS* 20:181–202), Daniel R. Brown oversimplifies and distorts the philosophic tenets of the two schools when he speaks of a "clash" in West "between naturalistic proletarian sympathies and existentialist elitist disdain for the ignorant majority." Brown categorizes West as a naturalist but finds "a true point of difference between West's style and [that of the] naturalists is his use of comedy." According to Brown, "strict naturalists are rarely amusing—intentionally. They do not see the plight of their characters as anything but serious and pathetic." Such unsupported—and unsupportable—generalizations make Brown's overlong article less than useless.

Despite its ominous purpose in providing "a full-fledged psychoanalytical reading," James Bryan's "The Psychological Structure of *The Catcher in the Rye*" (*PMLA* 89:1065–74) avoids the jargon prevalent in such studies and presents a clear, persuasive discussion of the structure of the novel dependent on Holden Caulfield's mental state. Bryan's views on the incestuous overtones of Holden's interest in his sister Phoebe creep up on the reader and before he can balk at

the absurdity of the suggestion, Bryan succeeds in convincing him of
his position. Paul Kirschner completes his "Salinger and His Society:
The Pattern of *Nine Stories*" (*LHY* 14,ii[1973]:63–78), which was
begun in the same journal in 1971. In the current article he gives
excellent readings of "Teddy" and the other stories in the latter half
of the collection but, failing to fit these readings into the findings of
his 1971 article, he declares the pattern "flawed."

ii. Expatriates and Emigrés

Charles Baxter finds that Djuna Barnes has compared the situation
of the contemporary novelist to that of "a defrocked priest" in "A
Self-Consuming Light: *Nightwood* and the Crisis of Modernism"
(*JML* 3:1175–87). Using the techniques of structuralist Roland
Barthes, Baxter analyzes the ineffectual "alchemist" Matthew O'Connor in the novel: "Behind the outline of Matthew O'Connor looms the
shadow of the 20th century novelist in theoretical trouble; intoxicated
with his own power, endlessly talking to no audience . . . trying to
change the course of history and totally failing to do so, growing
more and more artful, and secretly becoming a thief."

Another notable American expatriate, Henry Miller, was the subject of three dissertations recorded in 1974. In one intriguing study,
Douglas Stone argues the importance to "the history of American
and internationalist literature of the '30s" of "Henry Miller and the
Villa Seurat Circle, 1930–1940" (*DAI* 34:6664A [Calif., Irvine]).
These studies suggest that the lull in published comment on Miller
this year is only to be a temporary one.

Anaïs Nin, also a member of the Villa Seurat circle, was the subject of three recent dissertations, primarily dealing with her *Diary*,
the fifth volume of which also appeared in 1974. In his introduction to
A Casebook on Anaïs Nin (New York: New American Library), editor Robert Zaller puns on his title in stating the volume's "thesis":
"The case is for Anaïs Nin as one of the most significant artists and
figures of our time." Zaller garners support for his case by reprinting
early critical comments on Nin's work from Stuart Gilbert, Lawrence
Durrell, Edmund Wilson, and Henry Miller. Seven of the remaining
sixteen articles in the collection are printed for the first time. Paul
Grimley Kuntz's "Art as Public Dream: The Practice and Theory of
Anaïs Nin" (pp. 77–99) is particularly noteworthy. Kuntz traces

Nin's interest in Jungian psychology and the work of Otto Rank, noting that she was herself a lay analyst for a short time. While he confines his close reading of texts principally to *Winter of Artifice* and the first volume of the *Diary*, Kuntz speaks of her whole corpus of works when he says, "We stand to learn much from her about the artist's use of dreams and the important transformation of dreams in the creative process." Benjamin Franklin's "Anaïs Nin: A Bibliographical Essay" (pp. 25–33) presents the publication history of Nin's work as well as a brief discussion of secondary sources. He also announces the imminent publication of his *Anaïs Nin: A Bibliography* (Kent, Ohio: Kent State University Press), which should solve many of the tangled bibliographic problems he outlines in this short article. Zaller's range of articles in the collection is very wide and the book is useful.

Anaïs Nin explains the function of her *Diary* in freeing her from the demands society placed on her as a woman and an artist in "On Feminism and Creation" (*MQR* 13,i:4–13). Her concept of "creation" is not simply artistic; she feels the supreme "creation" is the shaping of one's own life and sees her *Diary* as the record of such creation.

If further evidence were needed to establish Vladimir Nabokov's importance to contemporary literature, the appearance of four book-length studies, a collection of critical essays, six articles, and six dissertations on Nabokov in the last year would certainly present a persuasive argument. Donald E. Morton's admirable *Vladimir Nabokov* (New York: Frederick Ungar) surveys all of Nabokov's novels with the chapter on *Pale Fire* of particular merit. Morton includes a useful chronology of Nabokov's career, a concise biographical introductory chapter, a chronological consideration of each of his novels, a bibliography of primary and secondary sources, and an index. While he briefly reviews Nabokov's early Russian novels, he wisely refrains from presenting these works as more than background material to the English language novels which are the major focus of his study. A second general introduction to Nabokov is Douglas Fowler's *Reading Nabokov* (Ithaca, N. Y.: Cornell Univ. Press), which grows from Fowler's 1972 Cornell dissertation of the same title. Fowler confines his study primarily to five novels and three short stories. He begins with an examination of *Bend Sinister*, finding there "a set of thematic, moral, and narrative constants" which function in later works as well. Fowler's major point concerns the existence of Nabokov's "equivalent" as the protagonist of his best fiction. Fowler asserts that "in protecting his favorites from our condemnation or dislike," Nabokov "is hardly the icy puppeteer both he and his critics keep giving us as the Nabokov persona" (p. 153).

In *The Literature of Exhaustion: Borges, Nabokov, Barth* (Durham, N.C.: Duke Univ. Press), John O. Stark confirms the thesis of John Barth's "The Literature of Exhaustion" (*Atlantic* 220[1967]: 29–34), which groups these three writers together because they "use as a theme for new works of literature the agonizing hypothesis that literature is finished." Stark finds Borges "the archetypal writer of the Literature of Exhaustion" and sees the concept as central to Barth's work as well. Of Nabokov, however, Stark notes: "Many of his distinguishing characteristics . . . fall outside my concerns here. This largeness indicates that he, a truly major writer, has done more important work than have the other two. In other words, this study deals with Borges, Barth, and a part of Nabokov" (p. 2). The extended Nabokov chapter dealing with *Lolita*, *Pale Fire*, and *Ada* shows similarities in structure between these works and those of Borges. It is, however, the weakest chapter in support of his general thesis and suggests that Stark might have profited by deemphasizing Nabokov.

Amazingly, the vague title of Carl R. Proffer's collection of criticism on Nabokov aptly fits its contents—*A Book of Things About Vladimir Nabokov* (Ann Arbor, Mich.: Ardis). Selections range from D. Bartson Johnson's highly technical "Contrastive Phonoaesthetics, or, Why Nabokov Gave Up Translating Poetry as Poetry" and "Synesthesia, Polychromatism, and Nabokov" through Francis Bulhof's arcane "Dutch Footnotes to Nabokov's *Ada*," to end whimsically with "A *Lolita* Crossword Puzzle" by Kerry Ahearn. Most of the material included appears for the first time and the collection as a whole suggests the same eclectic spirit as the author it concerns.

Bobbie Ann Mason's *Nabokov's Garden: A Guide to "Ada"* (Ann Arbor, Mich.: Ardis) is based on her 1972 University of Connecticut dissertation. While it is the first full-length study of *Ada* to be published, its focus on nature imagery excludes many other important aspects of the novel and reduces its value as a general "guide" to the work. *Ada* is also the major subject of Paul K. Alkon's "Historical Development of the Concept of Time," which appears in a collection of essays otherwise concerned with genetics (*Biorhythms and Human Reproduction*, ed. Michel Ferin et al. [New York: Wiley], pp. 3–22).

Alkon finds Nabokov the contemporary heir to St. Augustine's concern for restructuring time.

Two brief notes solve some of the riddles Nabokov is so fond of posing for his readers. Thomas A. Reisner finds Hamlet's words "To be or not to be" the answer to the tantalizing word puzzle in "Nabokov's *Speak, Memory*, Chapter III, Section 4" (*Expl* 33: item 18). Edward Profitt identifies the pedant who introduces *Lolita* in "A Clue to John Ray, Jr." (*MFS* 20:551–52). He is, according to Profitt, "a spokesman for fictional modes" or "the voice of gen-re."

In "*Lolita* and Pure Art" (*EIC* 24:169–84), Michael Bell notes Nabokov's "dependence on formal funning" and discusses the Flaubertian aesthetic at its base. James Joyce's carefully wrought "*Lolita* and Humberland" (*SNNTS* 6:339–48) links the novel with the figure of Lewis Carroll. Joyce notes that the wordplay of both authors has much in common and reminds the reader that Nabokov translated *Alice in Wonderland* into Russian while still in college. On another level, Joyce sees Lewis Carroll/Charles Dodson as a model for Humbert Humbert since both men share "a perverse interest in little girls."

iii. The Southerners

W. U. McDonald, Jr., contributes a very useful bibliographic article in his "Eudora Welty Manuscripts: A Supplementary Annotated Finding List" (*BB* 31:95–98, 126, 132). Here he updates his original list (*BB* 24[Sept.-Dec. 1963]:44–46) of Welty holdings in the Mississippi Department of Archives and History in Jackson and the Humanities Research Center at the University of Texas, Austin. The collections now include typescripts of *Losing Battles, The Wide Net and Other Stories*, and several early versions of *The Optimist's Daughter*. Carefully annotated entries are divided into four categories—published fiction, published nonfiction, unpublished writings, and personal letters. The information in this article should prove particularly useful now that the success of Welty's most recent novels has sparked interest in her entire career.

Two articles appearing in 1974 were presented as part of the Eudora Welty Celebration held at Hollins College, near Roanoke, Virginia, in the spring. In "Speech and Silence in *Losing Battles*" (*Shenandoah* 25,iii:3–14), James Boatwright discusses the meaning of silence in the thematic structure of the novel: "The weapons in that battle as it is fought out in this novel, are speech and silence. By speaking we honor the whole world of duty, of love, of our community with others . . . . In silence we assert our separateness, our joy in the soul's integrity." J. A. Bryant, Jr., delineates a differing set of polarities in "Seeing Double in *The Golden Apples*" (*SR* 82:300–315). He agrees with earlier critics who argue that the work has the integrity of a novel, despite shifts in time, place, and characters among the "chapters." It is the character of King MacLain who searches for "The silver apples of the moon,/The golden apples of the sun" who provides this unity. It is MacLain, a character of "double vision," who inhabits the real world as well as one of mythic proportions. Through him and the novel as a whole, Welty shows that "the commonplace and even the repulsive must be respected, for nothing we see is merely what it seems to be, and the familiar may, and often does, conceal a miracle."

Two brief explications of early Welty short stories also demonstrate the vitality she achieves through the creation of essentially unresolved and unresolvable conflicts of antithetical forces. William B. Stone's "Eudora Welty's Hydrodynamic 'Powerhouse' " (*SSF* 11:93–96) suggests Welty is presenting a concept of race relations through her imagery in the story. The black characters are described in terms of the power of rushing water and the white characters are associated with structures which harness that power such as windmills. In "Ruby Fisher and Her Demon-Lover" (*NMW* 7:63–68), Carol Hollenbaugh identifies the psychological conflict in "A Piece of News" as a product of the sexual fantasies of a young housewife and her unresponsive husband, Clyde, who returns home wanting supper, not her.

Jeffrey Helterman sees Perseus's confrontation with the "stupifying sisters" as a key to understanding the conscious and subconscious motivations of three sterile women in "Gorgons in Mississippi: Eudora Welty's 'Petrified Man'" (*NMW* 7:12–20). Margaret Bolsterli is less successful in "Mythic Elements in 'Ladies in Spring'" (*NMW* 6:69–72) in delineating the mythic strains underlying this story. She alludes to Frazer, the wasteland setting at the beginning of the story, and the theme of the fisher-king, but somehow a synthesis of these elements eludes her in this undocumented treatment of the story.

In "Windsor in Spencer and Welty: A Real and an Imaginary Landscape" (*NMW* 7:2–11), Hunter M. Cole traces the appearance of a colonial mansion on the Old Natchez Trace in Welty's essays and the short story "Asphodel," as well as in Elizabeth Spencer's story "A Southern Landscape." Since Cole fails to posit a reason for this recurring image, the value of the information is not clear.

Eudora Welty, too, added to this year's critical comment on her work in "Artists on Criticism of Their Art: 'Is Phoenix Jackson's Grandson Really Dead?'" (*Critl* 1:219–21, followed by "A Worn Path," pp. 222–28). Welty leaves the reader to decide for himself if Phoenix's journey to get medicine for her grandson is a hopeless one but suggests that such a reading adds artificially to the poignancy of the mission. She discusses the genesis of the story and her intent to focus only on the journey itself. In a concluding paragraph, she associates Phoenix's mission with the role of the writer: "Like Phoenix, you work all your life to find your way . . . to reach a meaning— using inventions of your imagination, perhaps helped out by our dreams and bits of good luck. And finally, too, like Phoenix, you have to assume that what you are working in aid of is life, not death."

Joan Givner reviews the letters of Katherine Anne Porter recently donated to the University of Maryland's McKeldin Library in "Porter's Subsidiary Art" (*SwR* 59:265–76). Givner records several anecdotes to be gleaned from the letters but finds the collection's major value to literary historians in the account the letters give of the progress of *Ship of Fools*. Givner finds first mention of the work in a letter of December 3, 1937, three years before critics have dated the beginning of composition. Givner's major thesis, however, is that Porter's letters are more than mere aids in gathering biographical information: "The personal letter is an ideal vehicle for her. In her hands it assumes a special form, poised somewhere between fact and fiction, and perhaps ranking with or complementary to her fiction."

In "Looking-glass Reflections: Satirical Elements in *Ship of Fools*" (*SR* 82:316–30), Jon Spence defends Porter's only full-length novel against the criticism of several reviewers who think the novel shows that "the author's philosophic view of man [is] pessimistic and misanthropic." Spence points out the Swiftian techniques of satire in the novel, most notably the animal imagery and the depiction of physical deficiencies as manifestations of spiritual failure. The essay is well argued, though the charge of misanthropy is not the most damaging criticism leveled against the novel. As Woodress briefly notes in his review article on Porter in *American Fiction, 1900–1950* (pp. 157–60), critics have charged the novel with being "boring, repetitive, and a technical failure," and a defense of the novel on any grounds should take these criticisms to task.

The work of James Agee prompted four dissertations listed in the 1974 volumes of *DAI*, most pertaining to his film criticism and work in documentaries. Critical articles, however, still approach Agee through his written fiction and poetry. Victor A. Kramer continues his work on the difficult MSS of posthumously published *A Death in the Family* in "Premonition of Disaster: An Unpublished Section for Agee's *A Death in the Family*" (*Costerus*, N.S. 1:83–93). The excerpt of the MS is transcribed with author's emendations noted and a head-note discusses the problems presented by the group of MSS and this section in particular.

William J. Rewak, S.J., discusses the religious symbolism in "James Agee's *The Morning Watch*: Through Darkness to Light" (*TQ* 16,iii[1973]:21–37). Rewak notes the obvious flaws of the work, primarily its overly symbolic action, but sees it as a necessary stage in the evolution toward the more balanced *A Death in the Family*. Donald E. Stanford turns his attention toward Agee's verse in "The Poetry of James Agee: The Art of Recovery" (*SoR* 10,ii:xvi–xix). He praises in particular the religious verse and love sonnets appearing in Robert Fitzgerald's 1968 collected edition of his poetry and gives an account of his own meeting with Agee in 1940, before the success of his prose writings made him turn away from his early interest in poetry. Stanford laments that "toward the end of his life he was re-ported to have said that poetry was his 'true vocation.' I wish he had stuck to it. He might have become a major poet."

Nancy Joyner analyzes "that complex and paradoxical myth of the southern lady" in "The Myth of the Matriarch in Andrew Lytle's Fiction" (*SLJ* 7,i:67–77), referring most frequently to Lytle's novel *The Velvet Horn* and two well-known short stories, "Jericho, Jericho, Jericho" and "Mr. Macgregor." According to Lytle, "man's attitude to woman is the foundation of society, under God. In the South, be-cause of the prevailing sense of family, the matriarch became the defining image." The women in Lytle's fiction, confirming Anne Firor Scott's 1970 study *The Southern Lady*, are capable and often ruthless business women, not the pampered dependents of the myth of the Southern Belle. Joyner finds, however, that "women do not fare well" in Lytle's fiction. They are cold and unsuccessful as "exceptions" to the myth of the southern lady "and are decidedly not admirable characters."

In "Carson McCullers and the South" (*GaR* 28:19–32), Delma E. Presley finds that McCullers basically disliked the South, had little respect for its provincialism, and "poked fun at back-woodsmen-come-to-town" as in "The Ballad of the Sad Cafe." For the most part, Presley explains McCullers's antipathy for the South biographically, rather than through a close reading of her works. With the notable exception of "The Ballad of the Sad Cafe," Presley thinks that all of McCullers's work after *The Heart is a Lonely Hunter* lacks vitality. To Presley, the reason for this decline is McCullers's later reliance on the imaginative use of language and the neglect of the solid foundation of place which had been an early strength of her work: "She left it [the South] before she really understood it" in Presley's view.

Temira Pachmuss finds McCullers and Lawrence heirs to the spirit of Dostoevsky in "Dostoevsky, D. H. Lawrence, and Carson McCullers: Influences and Confluences" (*GSlav* 4:59–68). All three authors "depict contemporary man as being hopelessly alone in a diseased city of modern culture, civilization, philosophy, and industrialization." Tracing similarities in prose style to support this influence, Pachmuss also recognizes a common "tension between the comic and tragic" in the work of each. The essay suffers from a common problem of "influence studies," however, in that similarities in world-view are not shown to be a direct product of reading the work of the earlier author. Pachmuss presents no biographical evidence that either Lawrence or McCullers knew Dostoevsky, though such evidence exists. Pachmuss could extend her list of contemporary writers influenced by Dostoevsky endlessly and still not go beyond the thesis stated in the passage quoted from Nina Garfinkel's *Dostoevsky: Our Contemporary* (1960), which opens Pachmuss's essay: "Who has not borrowed from Dostoevsky . . . We live in a Dostoevskian universe and the issue of the struggle, which arises here, is vital to all of us."

In "Rejection of the Feminine in Carson McCullers's *The Ballad of the Sad Cafe*" (*TCL* 20:34–43), Panthea Reid Broughton also recognizes a common plea for breaking through the isolation of the individual in the works of Lawrence and McCullers. Broughton's study goes beyond the issue of "influence," however, to delineate

the causes of isolation in McCullers's work. Broughton takes issue
with critics who view the characters as comic in their inability to love;
instead, Broughton finds this flaw a key to the human tragedy in the
story. In the small town of the story which serves as a microcosm of
the contemporary world, the inability to love grows from the denial
of the qualities of warmth and tenderness identified as "feminine."
The townspeople have denied a part of themselves and refuse to
honor it in others: "The human psyche has then been split . . . into
qualities which are feminine and contemptible on the one hand and
masculine and admirable on the other." Broughton quotes from *The
Heart is a Lonely Hunter* to support this view of the psyche: "By nature all people are both sexes." Broughton presents a convincing reading of the novella and her thesis could well be extended to explain the
key issue in much of McCullers's work. Irving H. Buchen also uses the
terms *masculine* and *feminine*, though in a differing sense, in his
treatment of the role of art and the artist in "Divine Collusion: The
Art of Carson McCullers" (*DR* 54:529–41). The recurring figure of
the artist in McCullers's fiction must exercise two kinds of discipline
in Buchen's view: "The first is the discipline of surrender which is re-
ceptive, self-effacing, almost feminine. The second is the discipline of
control which is exacting, aggressive, almost masculine." Dealing
primarily with McCullers's extended essay "The Flowering Dream:
Notes on Writing" (from which the title of this essay is drawn),
Buchen finds that "in McCullers' world, wholeness is defined by all
the characters who never achieve it."

Laurence Perrine gives a sensitive reading of a McCullers story
in "Restoring 'A Domestic Dilemma'" (*SSF* 11:101–04) in response
to an explication of the story in *SSF* in 1972 which saw the protagonist
as wooden and lifeless. Perrine supports his differing view well with
specific references to the text.

Several biographical and textual studies offer some new perspectives this year on the life and works of Thomas Wolfe. In "Seeds of
Destruction: The Death of Thomas Wolfe" (*SAQ* 73:173–83), James
Meehan reviews the medical records at Johns Hopkins and posits an
alternate diagnosis for the cause of Wolfe's death. His death certifi-
cate states tuberculosis of the brain as the immediate cause of death,
a diagnosis which, according to Meehan, appeals to the romantic instincts of his public who see Ben's terminal illness in *Look Homeward, Angel* finally catching up with brother Eugene. Meehan sees a

more likely cause to be a case of desert fever, or coccidioidomycosis, contracted on the trip Wolfe took through the Southwest in the weeks before his death. Admitting that such a diagnosis is impossible to prove conclusively, Meehan, with the support of Dr. Michael L. Furcolow, "a recognized authority on fungus diseases," asserts that desert fever is the most probable cause of death.

Fred W. Wolfe, the model for Luke in *Look Homeward, Angel* and the sole surviving member of Wolfe's immediate family, was interviewed twice in 1974. The relaxed atmosphere created by interviewers Richard J. Calhoun and Robert W. Hill make " 'Tom, Are You Listening?' An Interview with Fred Wolfe" (*SCR* 6,ii:35–47) the more revealing discussion. Fred Wolfe shares several anecdotes and explains the relationship between real-life models and their fictional representations in many early works. Wolfe also discusses his brother's relationship with F. Scott Fitzgerald, calling it one of "friendly enemies." John Daniel Walther's " 'Luke' Looks Homeward: An Interview with Fred W. Wolfe" (*MissQ* 27:141–63) covers much of the same ground as the *SCR* interview, but it is marred by the interviewer's tendency to pose long questions and to lead Wolfe into expected responses. Fred Wolfe's reactions to biographers and negative critics of his brother's work are interesting aspects of this interview, however.

In "Thomas Wolfe's 'No Door': Some Textual Questions" (*PBSA* 68:45–52), Sharon Doten makes a detailed examination of the remaining drafts of Wolfe's 1933 "No Door." The difficulties of detecting who was responsible for the editorial changes before publication make Doten question the value of this short story, and by extension all of Wolfe's short fiction extracted from longer works for periodical publication: "Recent studies have begun to adopt the position, first advanced by [C. Hugh] Holman, that in the short novels Wolfe displays a sense of form that is absent from his huge, rambling novels, and thus that the short novels show his true artistic potential . . . . Before so important a claim is made, much more attention must be directed to such textual matters as are noted here."

"That Harriette Arnow will go down in the American literary chronicle as a major figure is, at this point at least, highly improbable," asserts Wilton Eckley in *Harriette Arnow* (TUSAS 245). He justifies the worth of this first critical volume to appear on Arnow on the grounds of the excellence of two of her four novels, *Hunter's Horn*

(1949) and *The Dollmaker* (1954). The chronology and introductory biographical chapter, both prepared through interviews with Arnow, are virtually the only biographical sources available on this neglected figure. The chapter treating Arnow's short fiction of the 1930s gives excellent readings of the stories, though readers familiar with *The Dollmaker* will be surprised at Eckley's reading of the ending of the work, which he sees as affirmative. Despite Eckley's unequivocal single sentence under the heading of "Secondary Sources" in his bibliography—"To date there have been no significant studies dealing with the works of Harriette Arnow"—Joyce Carol Oates's careful reading of *The Dollmaker* (in *Rediscoveries: Informal Essays in Which Well-Known Novelists Rediscover Neglected Works of Fiction by One of Their Favorite Authors*, ed. David Madden [New York: Crown, 1971], pp. 57–66) certainly deserves mention. In this essay she states: "There are certainly greater novels than *The Dollmaker*, but I can think of none that have moved me more, personally, terrifyingly, involving me in the solid fact of life's criminal exploitation of those who live it—not hard, not sentimental, not at all intellectually ambitious, *The Dollmaker* is one of those excellent American works that have yet to be properly assessed" (p. 66). Eckley's study still leaves this task unfinished.

Five dissertations on the themes of Robert Penn Warren's fiction are listed in the 1974 volumes of *DAI*, making him the most popular subject among the Southern writers for doctoral theses. Marshall Walker makes a contribution to American scholarship with "Robert Penn Warren: An Interview (*JamS* 8:229–45). In it Warren briefly traces the history of the Fugitive and Agrarian groups and his involvement. He parallels these movements with similar forces in Ireland, suggesting affinities in attitudes "though it was not specified often—the notion of a somewhat backward society in an outlying place with a different tradition and a rich folk-life, facing the big modern machine." Warren also stresses the importance of Yeats's aesthetic to the formation of common poetic standards of the Fugitive group. Walker knows Warren's work well and asks perceptive questions about Warren's entire career, his position on the Negro, and in particular, the genesis of *All the King's Men*.

In "On the Politics of the Self-Created: *At Heaven's Gate*" (*SR* 82:284–99), James H. Justus notes that while this novel is not arguably better than *All the King's Men*, it is deserving of attention in its own right, not simply for what it adds to an understanding of the later work. Justus finds *At Heaven's Gate* "the closest Warren ever came to writing an agrarian novel." The New South appears as "a homegrown waste land" with all the virtues of agrarian life "conspicuously missing in the lives of the major characters, but their very absence is a measure of their importance." Flo Witte relies heavily on Leonard Casper's "Trial by Wilderness" (*WSCL* 3[1962]) in her reading of the theme of self-definition in "Adam's Rebirth in Robert Penn Warren's *Wilderness*" (*SoQ* 12:365–77), so much so that the argument presented is simply repetitive.

In "Search for an Eternal Present: *Absalom, Absalom!* and *All the King's Men*" (*ConnR* 8,i:95–100), Mary Ann Wilson finds that Faulkner and Warren share Bergson's belief in the fluidity of time as shown in the form and content of these two novels. Both authors also create main characters who, with Bergson, recognize that "the ultimate responsibility for understanding the past devolves on the individual."

In "The Case of the Vanishing Narratee: An Inquiry Into *All the King's Men*" (*SLJ* 6,ii:42–69), Simone Vauthier employs the techniques of the structuralist to account for the abrupt change in prose style at the end of the novel, which has been seen as a flaw by many of the novel's critics. Using a vocabulary drawn from the works of French structuralists writing as recently as 1972, Vauthier analyzes the appearance of the "you" of direct address and finds the prevalence of the form in the major portion of the novel a symptom of the diffuseness of the narrator, Jack Burden: "Unable to see himself clearly, he posits in the disjunctive 'you' the double that embodies *him*, that makes him visible because *he* can address it." It is only after he comes to know himself that the "you" disappears. A complex essay, which uses mathematical symbols to objectify difficult concepts, the value of the conclusions more than justifies the vocabulary-building process the reader must go through to follow the argument.

iv. The Popular Novelists—Surviving Success

The favorite novelists of the mass audiences of the 1930s to the 1950s are being reassessed from today's perspective with some surprising results. In "*Gone with the Wind* as Bildungsroman or Why did Rhett Butler Really Leave Scarlett O'Hara?" (*GaR* 28:9–18), Dawson Gaillard finds an allegorical level of the novel, which adds dimensions to the work for the literary scholar, though the popular audience seems to need no further "aids" to find value in the work. Gaillard sees Mitchell contrasting the image of the antebellum southern lady with postwar Scarlett, who is "the New Woman," and suggests that Mitchell was ambivalent concerning whether this change was good or bad. She finds, however, that Mitchell was, perhaps unconsciously, trying "to write a success story . . . about a woman who was successful in breaking away from the life of self-effacement" of earlier southern women. When Rhett Butler turns away from Scarlett at the novel's end, he shows he could love her only as a child, not as "a twenty-eight-year-old serious-minded woman."

Samuel I. Bellman suggests that the acclaim of winning a Pulitzer Prize does not always serve a writer's subsequent career well. In his *Marjorie Kinnan Rawlings* (TUSAS 241), he credits the author with fine work in *The Yearling* as well as in her autobiography *Cross Creek* (a Book-of-the-Month-Club selection in 1942), but sees that public acclaim often led Rawlings to publish inferior work. Discussing her short story "Black Secret" of 1945, which he sees as "a carelessly handled travesty," Bellman notes: "The writing, particularly of the dialogue, is unbelievably bad; and one of the most incredible features of this story is its having been published at all (even in *The New Yorker*), its winning an O. Henry prize, and its being reprinted in two anthologies." Bellman's critical eye is excellent and he has avoided jumping on any bandwagons in his measured assessment of Rawlings's work.

Two other Pulitzer Prize winners have apparently survived recognition of their contemporaries and achieved the acclaim of a new generation of readers and critics. Pierre Michel's *James Gould Cozzens* (TUSAS 237) finds *Guard of Honor* (1948) to be Cozzens's finest novel though he terms *By Love Possessed* (1957) his most "ambitious" work. A brief chronology tracing Cozzens's career is virtually the only biographical information in the volume and Michel notes Cozzens's reluctance to share such information with his reading public and, for that matter, to become the kind of public man interest in his work might well tempt him to be. Michel treats all of Cozzens's fiction and attempts a definition of the label "conservative," which many critics have placed on the writer. This is a valuable study which concludes with an annotated bibliography of primary and secondary sources.

Political scientist Michael Dillon finds an analysis of the roots of tyranny to be Thornton Wilder's purpose in his "most political novel," *The Ides of March*. In "Poet and Statesman: Thornton Wilder's Political Vision in *The Ides of March*" (*InR* 9:149–58), Dillon uses his treatment of this novel to support his larger thesis that political scientists have much to learn from literature. Dillon agrees with Goethe that "a great dramatic poet . . . may succeed in making the souls of his plays the souls of the people." Edward Ericson, Jr., analyzes the bonds between literature and philosophy in "Kierkegaard in Wilder's *The Eighth Day*" (*Renascence* 26:123–38). Ericson supports his assertion that Kierkegaard's Knight of Faith is the model for Wilder's man of faith in the novel, both through textual evidence and Wilder's confirmation of his findings in personal correspondence with Ericson.

John Leggett's *Ross and Tom: Two American Tragedies* (New York: Simon and Schuster) is biography written for the popular market, which argues that Ross Lockridge and Tom Heggen were victims of "The American Bitch-Goddess Success." The two writers, however, had complex emotional problems which complicate Leggett's attempt to support his general thesis. Lockridge and Heggen both committed suicide at the moment their first novels brought them money and critical acclaim and, in the spirit of A. Alvarez's *The Savage God*, it is these suicides that are Leggett's major interest in the book. Not much is said about the two novels that propelled these two authors into the limelight, though Leggett suggests that both *Raintree County* and *Mister Roberts* are deserving of critical attention. The informal, "novelistic" style of the biography follows the pattern of Budd Schulberg's *The Four Seasons of Success* (New York: Doubleday, 1972), which dealt with six authors' reactions to success—Sinclair Lewis, William Saroyan, Scott Fitzgerald, Nathanael West, John Steinbeck, and Tom Heggen. Leggett corrects several inaccuracies in Schulberg's chapter on Heggen ("Taps at Reveille," pp. 169–86), but the earlier work is more successful in its investigation of the effect of critical acclaim on the work of American writers.

"The literary reputation of James M. Cain is evidence of justice denied" according to Tom S. Reck in "J. M. Cain's Los Angeles Novels" (*ColQ* 22:375–87). Reck finds Cain's three novels set in Los

Angeles to be "a kind of proletarian fiction" which is "more direct and accurate" than works by Steinbeck or Upton Sinclair and which attest to Cain's "serious intent" as a novelist. In *The Postman Always Rings Twice*, *Double Indemnity*, and *Mildred Pierce*, Cain adds his own innovations to the format of the crime novel while writing of the American Dream turned nightmare. In "Morris' *Cannibals*, Cain's *Serenade*" (*JPC* 8:59–70), David Madden explains how the pairing of "popular" and "serious" novels can be a useful teaching aid in introductory literature courses. As an example, he discusses his teaching of Wright Morris's *Love Among the Cannibals* with Cain's bestseller *Serenade*. He finds value in both works and leaves college teachers to ponder their role as arbiters of taste.

Leon Howard's provocative thesis in "Raymond Chandler's Not-So-Great Gatsby" (*MDAC*[1973]:1–15) is that Chandler's purpose in writing *The Long Goodbye* was to debunk the myth of the romantic crook presented in Fitzgerald's *Gatsby*. Not accepting Fitzgerald's adoration of the rich and tolerance for corruption, Chandler turned the plot of *Gatsby* into a detective story with Philip Marlowe replacing Nick Carroway as the first-person narrator. The similarities Howard finds between the two works are striking and help to outline Chandler's moralist stance. As a companion piece to Howard's article, Lawrence D. Stewart discusses "The Dust Jackets of *The Great Gatsby* and *The Long Goodbye*" in the same issue of *MDAC* (pp. 331–34). He sees the jackets as reflecting similarities in the novels, not necessarily as evidence that the *Gatsby* jacket was the model for that of *The Long Goodbye*. Photos of the jackets are included.

Although more than a third of Steven Marcus's "Dashiell Hammett and the Continental Op" (*PR* 41:363–77) simply reviews familiar biographical information, in the remainder of the essay he does a fine job of delineating the "sense of sustained contradiction" at the base of Hammett's best fiction. The Continental Op, who metamorphosed into Sam Spade in later works, lives by a rigid moral and ethical code, though one which differs from prevailing social standards. Marcus argues in conclusion that "Hammett was able to raise the crime story into literature" through the complexity of this character. George J. Thompson continues the serial publication of his 1972 University of Connecticut dissertation, "The Problem of Moral Vision in Dashiell Hammett's Detective Novels," in *ArmD* (part 4:

The Maltese Falcon, 7:178–92; part 5: *The Glass Key,* 7:270–80; part 6: *The Thin Man* 8:27–35).

The author of best-seller *The Bad Seed* is the subject of Roy S. Simmonds's "William March's *Company K*: A Short Textual Study" (*SAF* 2:105–13). Simmonds presents a comparison of the magazine and book version of many of the 113 vignettes that make up March's first "novel," in order to show March's method of revision.

Another genre of popular fiction, the Western, continues to attract the attention of critics. Gary Topping finds in "Zane Grey's West" (*JPC* 7[1973]:681–89) that Grey presents "a barometer to the popular thought of his time." The discussion of Social Darwinism in Grey's work is the most valuable aspect of Topping's essay. The notes are extensive and give a fine review of criticism on Grey's work and the traditions from which it grew.

Looking at a later generation of authors who wrote about the West, Richard Astro discusses "*The Big Sky* and the Limits of Wilderness Fiction" (*WAL* 9:105–14). Astro identifies Vardis Fisher, Frederick Manfred, and A. B. Guthrie, the author of *The Big Sky*, as "the best wilderness novelists." He finds, however, even Guthrie's excellent example of a work in the literary subgenre a "testament to the bankruptcy of primitivism." By definition wilderness novels do not show a character moving to the fullness of maturity which grows from "meaningful social contact." His assessment of the wilderness novelists is that they "can create exciting plots which are true to history, and interesting, one-dimensional characters to live in unbounded space. And by doing so, they present a valuable record of what once was . . . . To ask more from Guthrie or any wilderness novelist is to demand more than they can legitimately provide."

Two Western writers who go beyond the limitations of the wilderness novelist as Astro defines them are the subjects of excellent monographs in the Boise State University Western Writers Series. Robert Bain discusses the poetry and fiction of Pulitzer Prize winner *H. L. Davis* (WWS 11), noting his Faulknerian preoccupation with "the need for human community" and his search for a usable past in such novels as *Honey in the Horn* (1937) and *Winds of Morning* (1952). Bain quotes from Davis's collection of essays *Kettle of Fire* (1959) in ranking his priorities in writing: "Landscape counts in the character of a place, but people count more." In *Frederick Manfred*

(WWS 13) Joseph M. Flora sees Manfred's best novels as those treating man in society, particularly within the family, and the responsibilities placed on him by these human relationships. In his most popular works, the five novels set in 19th-century Siouxland called the Buckskin Man Tales, Manfred makes a judgment on the American past and present through his picture of "the wholeness and health" of Indian community life. Flora argues for the continuing value of these works as well as *This is the Year* (1947), "Manfred's major novel of the soil," on the basis of its fully developed characterizations and realistic picture of an emigrant Frisian family in the American Midlands of the 1920s and 1930s.

In "Man and Nature in Clark's *Track of the Cat*" (*SDR* 12,iv: 49–55), Douglas G. Rogers argues for the relevance of this novel to today's world. Rogers gives a reading of the novel emphasizing the symbolic structures which suggest the threat of materialism to nature. Rogers's thesis seems almost revisionist in relation to Max Westbrook's emphasis on the psychological struggles within the individual, which he saw as overshadowing the environmental concerns of Clark's novels (see *ALS 1970*, pp. 229–30).

In "The Art of Autobiography in *Bound for Glory*" (*SwAL* 2 [1972]:135–43), Terrell F. Dixon sees Woody Guthrie's autobiography as part of that body of literature which documents "the unresponsiveness of his country's institutions" during the depression years. Dixon approaches the work through its language, imagery, and symbolism and finds the kind of control demonstrated in the work to be evidence of Guthrie's skill as a writer. He notes that *Bound for Glory* is "an excellent addition to the art of autobiography and an important part of the literature of the American Southwest."

University of North Carolina, Chapel Hill

15. Fiction: The 1950s to the Present

James H. Justus

For the first time in several years there is no new book on Flannery O'Connor to report—but essays on and explications of her work continue unabated. Mailer and Bellow remain popular, but on the basis of sheer quantity alone 1974 is the year of Updike. Interest in theory, particularly as it relates to the post-Modernist, antirealist fiction, is high. The number of dissertations reported (45) shows a decrease of more than 20 percent from last year, which may reflect our parlous marketplace more than it does a slackening of interest in contemporary American fiction, but there is also a noticeable shift in the pattern of authors chosen. While nine dissertations on O'Connor were completed last year, only three were reported for 1974; Barth, the subject of three last year, holds the record for 1974 with six (and he is included in four additional multiple-author studies). Also in 1974 Hawkes was the subject of four dissertations, followed by Mailer, Updike, and Kosinski, with two each. John Cheever and Shirley Jackson, whose work has so seldom been studied, were the subjects of two dissertations each. Studies of several authors grouped according to shared techniques or themes continued to be popular, along with special topics (Jewish "character," the war novel, southern historical consciousness, and that old standby favorite, alienation).

Much of the criticism unfortunately also continues along the lines so evident in the past: repetitiveness, superficiality, sloppy form, pedestrian writing. Editors of university presses must take partial responsibility for the growing habit among younger scholars of relying on ephemeral paperback editions of their authors' works for reference and citation; and editors of journals hospitable to criticism of contemporary American fiction must take major responsibility for printing the work of young critics who announce their enthusiasms as if their fellow critics had not covered much the same ground two, three, five, or seven years ago. Much of the work confirms the pervasive suspicion in many English departments that contemporary fiction is the "field" for the lazy, the incompetent, and the opportunistic. Without some regard for the same canons of accuracy, reasoned argument, and substance our colleagues in the earlier periods are expected to honor, the work recorded in this chapter of *ALS* may well be as short-lived as the classroom paperbacks from which Barth, Malamud, and O'Connor are taught.

i. General Studies

a. **Overviews and Special Topics.**   David H. Richter's *Fable's End: Completeness and Closure in Rhetorical Fiction* (Chicago: Univ. of Chicago Press) is both an historical account and theory of fictions whose structures are generated "not by plot but by doctrines, themes, attitudes, or theses." Exploring the principles of construction and the sources of our sense of completeness in *Rasselas, Candide*, Pynchon's *V.*, Heller's *Catch-22*, and Bellow's *Herzog*, Richter contends that the formal end of such fiction rests not in a protagonist's change of fortune or a sense of a shift in consciousness, but in authorial "inculcation of some doctrine or sentiment concerning the world external to the fiction." Impressive in both its scholarship and criticism, *Fable's End* is weakest when Richter attempts to relate formal properties to affective response. He speaks bluntly about "intentions"—of both authors and works—and suggests the importance of paying attention to readers' intuitive feelings about the success of a piece of fiction or its elements which make us feel "comfortable." How such matters can be aesthetically measured or evaluated is a thorny problem which Richter all but ignores.

Morris Dickstein sings his "Cold War Blues: Notes on the Culture
Modern Occasions 2 (Port Washington, N.Y.: Kennikat Press), edited by the late Philip Rahv, is an interesting, if slightly old-fashioned collection of new fiction, criticism, and poetry. Mark Rudman's "On Sontag" (pp. 228–41) may still be of interest to some; in "Is the Novel Dead?" (pp. 73–87), Francis X. J. Coleman tries out a "new" theory of "the dialectic of literature" to convince himself that it is not, but his essay is too meandering to be very helpful in this annual quiz.

Morris Dickstein sings his "Cold War Blues: Notes on the Culture of the Fifties" (*PR* 41:30–53) with energy and smugness. Translating the public and political trademarks of the Eisenhower era into its literary equivalents, he finds them at once dreary and heartbreaking. He sounds petulant in noting that Saul Bellow, unlike Delmore Schwartz, not only survived but prospered; he recoils alike from the political intellectuals who praised American "pluralism and pragmatism" and the literary intellectuals who eschewed politics to pursue "private myths and fantasies." Dickstein commends the hardy few who still maintain "an adversary stance."

Dickstein summarizes the Jewish novel of the 1950s as "*an atonement for Jewish radicalism*," perfectly reflective of the time: ruminative, private, morally austere, self-conscious, and apolitical. Unfortunately, Sanford Pinsker's account of "The Rise-and-Fall of the American-Jewish Novel" (*ConnR* 7,i[1973]:16–23) is neither provocative nor substantial. And if Dickstein is still the angry partisan, Jack Behar is merely jaded in "Notes on Literature and Culture" (*CentR* 18:197–220), which are jottings about, among others, F. R. Leavis, Lionel Trilling, and their "elevated quarrel" with society, and Richard Gilman, "an unrepentant old modernist" whose ideas about the avant-garde are a "poor thing."

What Jeremiah J. Sullivan means by "Conflict in the Modern American Novel" (*BSUF*, 15,ii:28–36)—which is both ambitious and confused—is the clash between demands of conscience and the need to follow the "order-giving codes of the day." In recent years what he detects as a Dreiserian strain (natural impulse vs. social norms) can be seen in such diverse books as *The Confessions of Nat Turner* and *Mr. Sammler's Planet.*

In a firmer essay, " 'Noble Shit': The Uncivil Response of American Writers to Civil Religion in America" (*MR* 14[1973]:709–39), Leo Marx muses on the connections between language and conscience in certain 19th-century predecessors and contemporary ones, especially the effort to "invest the highest political authority with religious legitimacy." Norman Mailer shares with Emerson, Whitman, and Mark Twain the belief in linguistic freshness for generating a genuine patriotism.

The nonfiction novel is the chief beneficiary of "A Typology of Prose Narrative" (*JLS* 3:67–80) by Mas'ud Zavarzadeh, a fiercely theoretical, complex, but clearly reasoned essay. The premise behind "metamodernist" aesthetics—that changes in contemporary reality have created new literary realities which cannot be dealt with by traditional taxonomy—is applicable to authors both early (Defoe) and Modernist (Agee, Mailer) as well as to such contemporary texts as Andy Warhol's *a*. Despite the dazzling barrage of schema and coinages (*fictual*: the "puzzling blend of the fictional and the factual"), this is an important essay, even for those whom it may not convince.

"A Final Word for Black Humor" (*ConL* 15:271–76) is Jerome Klinkowitz's epitaph for a movement which was alive and well only a decade ago. Its only writers to develop into major talents—Vonnegut, Barth, Pynchon—are those, says Klinkowitz, who violated the traditions of Black Humor, "which included an accommodation by laughter to the world's insanity and a deliberate refusal to find any new forms in fiction appropriate to the strange new worlds they described." John Boni's subject in "Analogous Form: Black Comedy and Some Jacobean Plays" (*WHR* 28:210–15) is really the contemporaneity of Jacobean drama, but along the way there are some pertinent insights into *Slaughterhouse-Five*, *Catch-22*, and *The Ginger Man*. Both forms share goals—survival in a corrupt world—and both decline to rely on available value systems.

William H. Gass's fascinating essay on what he calls "the measurement of nature," "Groping for Trouts: On Metaphor" (*Salmagundi* 24[1973]:19–33), also suggests ways of reading his own fiction. Every metaphor, he says, "establishes between its terms a quite specific *angle of interaction*, and the movement of the mind which reaches, exploits, and dwells on this, so swiftly as to seem quite effortless, is nevertheless a momentous factor." Philip Stevick collects and comments on a full page of "Metaphors for the Novel" (*TriQ* 30:127–38), pointing out the reductionist nature of critical metaphors. Although some are no longer useful in contemporary fictional practice, one that survives healthily is "the novel is a game." Robert M. Adams discusses "Transparency and Opaqueness" (*Novel* 7:197–209), mostly in terms of Modernist fiction; his key term, *transparency*, is that quality in which one pattern is "felt through another without either being granted unequivocal primacy," a mode of "multiple speech" and the opposite of allegory.

"Old Genre, New Breed: The Postwar American Picaro" (*Genre* 7:205–11) may be simplistic and reductive, but Patrick W. Shaw at least grapples with the shared "voluntary alienation" of such varied protagonists as Augie March, Holden Caulfield, Malcolm, and Sebastian Dangerfield. Behind them all is "the artist at war with the mass mediocrity of his society." Using Erich Segal's *Fairy Tale* and the popularity of Tolkien as symptomatic of the contemporary American's "longing for the home to which nobody has ever been," Frank Bergmann speculates a little too casually on the resurgent fairy tale as an operative form in the 1960s in "Under the Sign of the Unicorn's Head: Adult Fantasy and Contemporary America" (*Amerikastudien* 19:50–57). In "The College Novel in America: 1962–1974" (*Crit* 16,ii:121–28), John O. Lyons updates the bibliography of his 1962 study with 90 new items and an interesting observation—that the feminist movement has not touched the form at all.

b. The New Fiction: Theories and Modes. A useful introduction to the biases and practices of post-Modernist fiction is "Understanding New Fiction" (*MFS* 20:307–16) by Myron Greenman. Like traditional art, the new fiction is *"a vital attempt at self-preservation,"* though "to apprehend the world" its creators shift the mimetic reference from externals (the aesthetic object) to their own activity (authorial beliefs). Greenman, who insists that mimesis is still the only valid "literary reality," acknowledges that for some fictionists "reality" does not precede mimesis: "the impulse to, and the act of, mimesis can be viewed as the reality itself."

In his "Notes on the Rhetoric of Anti-Realist Fiction" (*TriQ* 30:3–50), Albert J. Guerard prefers the term *antirealist* to *fabulist* or *surrealist* because it is ethically neutral and because it describes those writers dedicated to the reimagining of a world bankrupted by inherited forms and manners (i.e., "the 1850–1950 longueurs of social realism"). Guerard stresses the sense of delight in the new fiction, studies the rhetoric of Hawkes and Kosinski in detail, and cites Jerome Charyn's as a "representative career."

Stanley Fogel and Charles Russell write separate essays on the importance of language in the new fiction. In " 'And All the Little Typtopies': Notes on Language Theory in the Contemporary Experimental Novel" (*MFS* 20:328–36), Fogel says that language is not a "transparent medium" but is itself "the essential property out of which the novelist makes his construct." He illustrates the changing concepts by analyzing a passage from D. H. Lawrence and contrasting its linguistic assumptions with those of William Gass, Robert

Coover, and others. In "The Vault of Language: Self-Reflective Artifice in Contemporary American Fiction" (*MFS* 20:349–59), a description of how the self-reflective fictionists are questioning the
nature of language, especially metaphor, Russell sees two related
schools—those writers who explore the world of apparent chaos by
means of the creating consciousness (Pynchon, Kosinski, Brautigan,
Barthelme, Sukenick) and those who focus on the "prescriptive
structure" of language in which the writers' own structural devices
are their subject (Nabokov, Borges, Barth, Coover, Gass). Common
to both groups is the feeling that if "we see, or create, meaning, it is
recognized as one more artifice."

Richard Pearce analyzes one important component of "surfiction"
in "Enter the Frame" (*TriQ* 30:71–82): as the narrator of contemporary fiction enters the frame, "the medium asserts itself as an independent source of interest and control," and the narrative voice loses its
once dominant status. In "surfiction" at its best, the reader confronts
images in which narrator, subject, and medium merge. Robert S. Ryf
discusses "Character and Imagination in the Experimental Novel"
(*MFS* 20:317–27), concluding rather desultorily that the author-
character relationship serves as an analogy to, and even embodies,
"the epistemological function of the imagination."

Theodore Solotaroff, who has been instrumental in the great pro-
liferation of talent in the last decade, contributes "Some Random
Thoughts on Contemporary Writing" (*TCL* 20:270–76). The dif-
fusion is so marked, he says, because of the transformation from "an
essentially elite literary culture" to a democratic one—"more fluid
and disorderly than even Congress." William H. Pritchard is considerably more conservative in his estimate of "Novels and Novelists
in the 1960s" (*Modern Occasions 2*, pp. 188–209). He is most convincing in his remarks about the "traditional ironists" (Evan S. Con-
nell, Frederick Buechner); he is too hostile to those who scorn plot
and the traditional mimetic approach to add very much to our understanding of Barth or Pynchon, but he praises Updike as still the "most
daring, resourceful, and necessary" novelist after Bellow and Mailer.

David Caute's "Commitment Without Empathy: A Writer's Notes
on Politics, Theatre, and the Novel" (*TriQ* 30:51–70) is a plea for a
"truly dialectical and critical literature" based on the principle of
alienation. The cultural style loosely associated with the New Left

"generates a lot of Fun," says Caute, but its attempts to marry socio-political commitment with an adventurous approach to literary forms have resulted not only in illiteracy but also antiliteracy: "the cult of spontaneity and improvisation" really capitulates to "the commercial inebriation it affects to fight." He scores those who derisively dismiss all knowledge as "mere subjectivity" and history as chaotic and arbitrary and who write novels as if they were "merely an extended slogan."

Though he gets some historical perspective by beginning with the "iconoclastic pioneers" (Kafka, Joyce, Proust, Woolf) and in-cluding the practitioners of the New Novel, Charles I. Glicksberg concentrates on those young Americans who "have gone the whole hog" in "Experimental Fiction: Innovation Versus Form" (*CentR* 18:127–50). While he gives high marks to Pynchon and Barthelme, he condemns the purveyors of anarchy and chastises Steve Katz and Ronald Sukenick for their stagy crusading efforts and their persis-tently intrusive narrating voice. Though Glicksberg's sympathies are clear, his arguments are those which the innovative fictionists have heard before and, for better or worse, rejected as irrelevant to their aims.

Sukenick is one of the 12 writers represented in *The New Fiction: Interviews with Innovative American Writers* (Urbana: Univ. of Ill. Press), edited by Joe David Bellamy, who is also responsible for about half of the interviews. For "Susan Sontag" (pp. 113–29), Bel-lamy dutifully passes on that woman's self-congratulatory placing of herself in history (she takes the credit for getting 1950s fiction out of the doldrums: "after I wrote that essay ["Against Interpretation"], people got more international again"). This important primary volume has an admirable and brief introduction in which Bellamy cites the nonmonolithic nature of the new fiction and pays tribute to Louis D. Rubin, Jr., who in his 1966 *Kenyon Review* essay, "The Curious Death of the Novel," astutely anticipated the premises and practices of the newer fictionists who have flourished in the past decade.

ii. Norman Mailer

Though written so leisurely and copiously as to suggest the self-indulgence of its subject, Robert Solotaroff's *Down Mailer's Way*

(Urbana: Univ. of Ill. Press) may well be the finest work yet on this important writer. Especially admirable is the way Solotaroff, while obviously engaged by Mailer's life and work (like Richard Poirier), is able to distance himself from his subject (which Poirier is not always able to do). In his links with Emerson and Whitman (the role of "moralist-prophet") and in his commitment "to trace the spoor of possibility wherever he finds it" Solotaroff finds the strain which encompasses Mailer's various assays into anarchism, revolutionary socialism, hipsterism, and his own brands of conservatism and existentialism. Mailer attempts throughout his career, argues Solotaroff, "to ground the intuitive in the factual, the mystical in the phenomenal, the psychic in the biological, and the apocalyptic in the historical." Although in the 1960s the trendy Mailer resembled an "intellectual answering service," he has always written "the best that he had in him at the moment"; being impatient to wait for a time when better writing might come is the price he has paid in order to "dramatize possibility."

Stressing the continuities between the first novel and the work of more than two decades later, Solotaroff correctly assesses the centrality of *The Naked and the Dead* in the most exhaustive exposition of that novel now available. Croft (the "secret hero") he finds the most compelling of Mailer's characters, with the possible exception of Mailer himself in *The Armies of the Night*. The tentativeness of both *Barbary Shore* and *The Deer Park* derives from a confused author who did not clarify his purposes until about 1958, when he became committed to a belief in the ongoing duel between an existentialist God of goodness and courage and an equally powerful Devil of evil and cowardice, a view which colors the fiction and nonfiction equally. Solotaroff is perceptive in tracing connections between *The Presidential Papers* and *An American Dream* and between *Cannibals and Christians* and *Why Are We in Vietnam?* Richly strewn along the way are casually offered *aperçus*: though Mailer dislikes Marshall McLuhan, his D.J. is an avid McLuhanite; the energizing vernacular of *Vietnam* results partly from Mailer's reading of *Naked Lunch;* the spirit of Henry Adams's *Education* hovers over *Armies.*

Paul N. Siegel's "The Malign Deity of *The Naked and the Dead*" (*TCL* 20:291–97) could have benefited from Solotaroff's complex coverage; what Siegel finds in the first novel is a fairly simplified naturalism presided over by a God who is no more than a "cruel practical joker." In "Myth and Animism in *Why Are We in Vietnam?*" (*TCL* 20:298–305), Rubin Rabinovitz treats Mailer's use of opposites and parallels: electromagnetic radiation suggests psychic radiation, and supernatural events underscore the physical action. The technological metaphors (notably anode and cathode) reinforce the initiation, which measures the hero's ability to confront his own psychic irrationalities.

"Norman Mailer's Early Nonfiction: The Art of Self-Revelation" (*WHR* 28:1–12) is Robert Merrill's survey of the nonfiction prior to 1967. To nobody's surprise, "The White Negro" is named the significant essay of this early period because it transcends its own cultural and political analysis to become a sociological "fiction." But only with *Advertisements for Myself*, with its strong personal voice, is there a breakthrough in the creation of vital personae. Merrill is especially fresh in his discussion of "Ten Thousand Words a Minute," in which the subject is not the Patterson-Liston fight but Mailer himself.

Despite the "dazzling footwork" of a writer who "seems to require the invention of new genres before critical discussion of his works is possible," Mailer works in traditional modes: this is Kenneth A. Seib's well-argued "Mailer's March: The Epic Structure of *The Armies of the Night*" (*EIL* 1:89–95). The triumph of this work is its form, for just as its theme echoes the *Iliad*, so does the epic determine its narrative structure and content. At once epic hero and epic author, Mailer attempts to "justify the ways of America to whatever gods that be."

If Solotaroff detects the figure of Henry Adams behind *Armies*, Gordon O. Taylor in a superb essay, "Of Adams and Aquarius" (*AL* 46:68–82), sees him as a "spectral presider" over several of Mailer's recent efforts. Mailer's mood in 1969, like Adams's in 1905, is "spent, detached." Common to both the *Education* and *Of a Fire on the Moon* are the third-person authorial device, the concept of history recast as personal experience, and the author-protagonist's adjusting his imagination to a set of facts.

Robert F. Lucid, combining biography, gossip, psychological theory, and cultural criticism, contributes a fascinating essay on Mailer's power as a public figure in "Norman Mailer: The Artist as Fantasy Figure" (*MR* 15:581–95). Like Stephen Crane, Mark Twain, and Hemingway before him, Mailer proves that the human imagination possesses "the art and the metaphor which will allow it to transcend those literal circumstances, internal and external, which seem bent on its destruction." Though his context is quite different, Richard Poirier ("The Aesthetics of Radicalism," *PR* 41:176–96) similarly observes that Mailer tends to transfer villainy from the self to science and technology "and then to set himself up as the creator of the salvaging literary metaphor."

Despite his title, "The Novel of Nightmare: Norman Mailer's 'An American Dream'" (*Americana-Austriaca*, pp. 10–23), Robert H. Fossum imaginatively surveys most of the work as it relates to the notion of the American Dream, not as a "dream gone wrong" but simply as one which arises out of "the subterranean chambers of the Id." Because he equates the source of "corruption" with that of "purification," Mailer stresses the need to distinguish between the destructive and creative uses of violence.

The variety and versatility of Mailer as both public and private figure are emphasized in the 15 previously published articles of varying quality now collected in *Will the Real Norman Mailer Please Stand Up*, ed. Laura Adams (Port Washington, N.Y.: Kennikat Press). They deal with the fiction, poetry, journalism, and drama and with the author as entertainer and metaphysical politician. Like many others, Adams points out in her introduction that Mailer's most prodigious and interesting period is from *Advertisements for Myself* (1959) through *The Armies of the Night* (1968). Her own version of Mailer's esthetic is succinct, accurate, and happily free of the pretentiousness of a few of her contributors. Though some of his attempts to revolutionize the consciousness of his time have been ill-conceived, she believes "it is the process itself and the governing esthetic" which make Mailer important. Adams is also the compiler of *Norman Mailer: A Comprehensive Bibliography* (Metuchen, N.J.: Scarecrow), with an introduction by Robert F. Lucid.

iii. John Updike

Two books and a special number of *Modern Fiction Studies* confirm William T. Stafford's remark (*MFS* 20:115–20) that the critical literature on Updike is fast approaching the bulk of the primary work. There is still some repetitiveness in both the books and the essays, a tendency to wonder aloud whether Updike has anything to "say." In the religious readings, the explicit, exegetical, and simplistic approach has been succeeded by a syncretistic, mythic, and far fuzzier methodology.

The rubrics in Edward P. Vargo's *Rainstorms and Fire: Ritual in the Novels of John Updike* (Port Washington, N.Y.: Kennikat Press, 1973) are *sacralized* and *transcendent*. Updike is fascinated with material details, says Vargo, because the physical and spiritual are fused in "sacramental understanding" of the universe. The need for transcendence takes several forms in *Rabbit, Run*—basketball, golf, sex—but the ultimate trap is the disintegrating matter of this world; the characters in *The Centaur* are able to develop a "sacralized universe through the paradigmatic use of myth, and consequently are able to go on living in a desacralized milieu."

The etherealized generalizations in *Rainstorms and Fire* have a certain rhetorical panache, but their solidity is shaky and their pertinence sometimes dubious. Vargo asserts but does not demonstrate how Updike resembles the "novelist-entropologists" (i.e., Pynchon, Heller, Purdy, and Burroughs). The word on *Rabbit Redux* illustrates the pervasive critical softness of this book: "The price [Rabbit] pays is the price that we all must pay: the necessity of living for the rest of our lives with what cannot be undone." This is no doubt true, but it is a tattered critical banner to follow.

If in its approach and demonstration Vargo's study tends to be more elusive than palpable, Joyce B. Markle's book has a well-defined thesis which is reiterated, sometimes in interesting variations, in each chapter. The ambitious aim of *Fighters and Lovers: Theme in the Novels of John Updike* (New York: N.Y. Univ. Press, 1973) is to provide "a broad and extended schematic of the central issues and values" in Updike's longer work. Of the several major thematic lines —"the flight from death," the need for "lovers," man as creator, man's ability to relate to others in society—clearly the most crucial for Markle is Updike's concept of "specialness": the drive for stature, its function, and the human consequences when it is missing. The first five novels "chart the lives and problems of protagonists with the vision that makes special, the love that gives life," and *Of the Farm* is thematically the most complex because the emphasis is on the mother, who both gives and restricts love. Because the hero, with a vivid sense of his ordinariness, occupies a "landscape of in-action,"*Bech: A Book* is unambiguously comedic. Most of Markle's analyses are precise and detailed, and though she disclaims any major interest in stylistic study, her readings are filled with useful insights into Updike's techniques. Authorial values she sees in the use of antagonists (Conner, Eccles, Thorne) and children (who represent the world of external concerns which must be meshed into any scheme of personal fulfillment); and she relates the imagery of ascents and descents in *Rabbit, Run* to a larger pattern in which basketball, sex, and religion operate in a geometry of "ups and downs, circles and straight lines, nets and spaces."

Some impressive essays appear in the Updike number of *MFS* 20. Robert A. Regan's "Updike's Symbol of the Center" (pp. 77–96), stuffed with too many "little congruencies and arabesques" (as Up-dike once termed his own style), may not be quite the radical departure which its author claims—it is too long, and its tone is au-thoritative to a fault—but it is a valuable piece which draws upon aes-thetics, art history, and epistemology to make its seemingly simple subject a basic component of Updike's art. Based on the rigid struc-ture and inherent limitation of the eye, Updike's "center" organically annexes "the inner and outer realms in a sameness of conceptual order." It is this novelist's belief, says Regan, that to live is "neces-sarily to be furrowed within visual perspective"; and despite the "disquieting bias of each man's perspective—of each man's eye and I—there is unity and agreement to be found . . . in the 'freedom' and 'form' of visual apprehension." Emerson, Kant, and Bergson may be too heavy for their relevance to Updike, but Regan is convincing in his invoking of these diverse "sources."

Robert S. Gingher asks the familiar question, Has John Updike Anything to Say? (pp. 97–105), and answers yes. The reasons seem to be that Updike treats large Faulknerian issues in the "subsurface architectonics of his fiction"; he concludes that Updike deals less with individual psyches than with "an aggregate portrayal of the human condition." More persuasive answers come in two other articles, Joseph Waldmeir's "It's the Going That's Important, Not the Getting There: Rabbit's Questing Non-Quest" (pp. 13–27) and Wayne Falke's "*Rabbit Redux*: Time/Order/God" (pp. 59–75). Waldmeir's is a modified no. Against those who argue that Updike

sees mystery revealed through perception and contemplation, Waldmeir asserts that the main thing consists of "scene, situation, character, even argument—as perceived, with no revelation beyond the
perception. Because he honestly has no revelation to make." Falke,
however, believes Updike "has too much to say" in *Rabbit Redux,*
which, though it is old-fashioned in its concern for social issues, is
Updike's most mature work because of its tough-minded refusal to
accept either "corrupt Christianity" or "corrupt humanism."

In "Updike's *Couples*: Squeak in the Night" (pp. 45–52), Paula
and Nick Backscheider find Piet's search for happiness as the main
movement in *Couples*, especially his progression from one false god
to another; though Foxy is a "false redemption," some residue of
Piet's Calvinism remains. Alan T. McKenzie conjures up memories
of Jane Austen in " 'A Craftsman's Intimate Satisfactions': The Parlor
Games in *Couples*" (pp. 53–58). The first game ("Impressions") is
a centrifugal and the second ("Wonderful") a centripetal method
for revealing character both among the characters within the novel
and to the reader.

Taking hints from Updike's 1968 *Paris Review* interview and the
epigraph from Karl Barth, John B. Vickery explores the significance
of the story-teller and his art lying within the ethical meaning in
"*The Centaur*: Myth, History, and Narrative" (pp. 29–43). "What
Chiron and Caldwell achieve, the existential narrator achieves"—
i.e., by sacrificing his own "verbal identity" he gains the "total freedom of the story-teller to whom narrative aware of its mythic origins
is the conceivability of the inconceivable."

In his study of "John Updike's Literary Apprenticeship on *The
Harvard Lampoon*" (pp. 3–12), Robert McCoy finds that the aspir-
ing artist who wished to emulate Jan Vermeer and excelled in caricature and cartoon also produced 60 poems and 25 articles and
stories during the 1950–54 undergraduate years. Notes on two stories
are lesser pieces—Alfred F. Rosa's "The Psycholinguistics of Updike's
'Museums and Women' " (pp. 107–11) and Albert J. Griffith's "Updike's Artist's Dilemma: 'Should Wizard Hit Mommy?' " (pp. 111–
15). Arlin G. Meyer and Michael A. Olivas, the compilers of "Criticism of John Updike: A Selected Checklist" (pp. 121–33), bring
this satisfying number to an end.

Of the remaining items from other sources, two should be noted.

Roger Sharrock's thin little comparison of "Singles and Couples:
Hemingway's *A Farewell to Arms* and Updike's *Couples*" (*Ariel*
4,iv[1973]:21–43) turns on the fact that both novels are about sexual
love and that the participants resent the intrusion of time, generation,
or biology into their enclosed worlds. Lewis A. Lawson, in "Rabbit
Angstrom as a Religious Sufferer" (*JAAR* 42:232–46), argues for an
ontological interpretation of Rabbit's moral failure. Though much
more deeply concerned with the "transempirical plane of existence
than most of his fellow Americans," Rabbit shuns a religion which
requires acknowledgment of sin and "the necessity of a redeemer":
he wants a religion in which "all his decisions will be made for him
by a Benevolent Dictator."

iv. Flannery O'Connor

Despite the lack of new book-length studies of O'Connor, the tenth
anniversary of her death finds no marked diminution of scholarly
interest in her fiction. In his general survey of the phenomenon,
Stuart L. Burns assesses the significance of the criticism in "O'Connor and the Critics: An Overview" (*MissQ* 27:483–95) and finds that
it suffers from the fallacy of imitative form: "the criticism, like its
subject, is both rich and redundant." Though more commemorative
than critical, a two-day session at Georgia College drew an imposing
number of O'Connor specialists, who also occasionally grappled with
the nature of the criticism of her work. Marion Montgomery suggests, in a panel discussion transcribed at that meeting, that those
who write about O'Connor are not interested in what "needs to be
done" in O'Connor criticism; they are attempting to discover why
they are fascinated by the work, and the criticism, even by hostile
critics, is "an act of piety."

Among the essays emerging from the Georgia College meeting
which comprise the *Flannery O'Connor Bulletin* (*FOB* 3) is Montgomery's "Flannery O'Connor: Prophetic Poet" (pp. 79–94), which
moves the southerner into "high cotton": Aeschylus, Sophocles,
Dante, Eliot. Her symbols, says Montgomery, are meant "to open
upon larger spiritual concerns, not simply to satisfy the subjective
impulse toward meaning" so common in many symbol-hunting
critics. In an unsatisfying "Rebels and Revolutionaries: The New

American Scene" (pp. 40–56), Caroline Gordon writes of O'Connor's great affinity with Henry James. We are asked to believe that O'Connor's angle of vision (Catholic orthodoxy) is as revolutionary in the history of fiction as James's discovery of the central intelligence. She is right in praising both writers' grasp of "architectonics," but her own essay is notably infirm in architectonics.

The two most persuasive essays are Robert Drake's "Flannery O'Connor and American Literature" (pp. 1–22) and Frederick Asals's "Flannery O'Connor as Novelist: A Defense" (pp. 23–39). Drake still believes that O'Connor is sui generis (as he argues in his milestone pamphlet of 1966), but he is now more willing to trace a few of her links to a tradition which he terms the "Loyal Opposition": O'Connor follows Hawthorne, Melville, Poe, Dickinson, Faulkner, and Eliot in suggesting that "the universe is an inscrutable mystery, too tangled for man's unaided mind to sort out alone." In a healthy minority report, Asals disputes the critical commonplace that O'Connor is a better short-story writer than novelist. *Wise Blood* and *The Violent Bear It Away* are "brief, intense, poetically conceived, highly condensed works" in the tradition of *The Scarlet Letter*, *The Great Gatsby*, and *Miss Lonelyhearts*—what Nathanael West called the "lyric novel." Important in this subgenre is the scene, which is "refracted into symbolic forms of expression" rather than delineated by analysis of its constituent parts.

In a view similar to that of Martha Stephens (*ALS 1973*, pp. 267–68), Claire Katz takes issue with the theological critics in "Flannery O'Connor's Rage of Vision" (*AL* 46:54–67). The fiction suggests a "psychological demand which overshadows her religious intent," shaping plot, image, character—and especially a narrative voice which preserves a primitive, sadistic quality associated with the parent. O'Connor pillories those characters who partially represent herself: an intellectual woman who because of her illness is also a child dependent upon her mother. The result is a universe "fixed by infantile conflict" and closed to adult interrelations. Katz's essay is a compelling example of intelligent psychological criticism: sensible, tactful, demonstrable—and liberated from the jargon which debilitates the work of most critics who write with her orientation.

James F. Farnham, who also quarrels with those critics who see only illustrated religious beliefs in the works, argues in "Disintegration of Myth in the Writings of Flannery O'Connor" (*ConnR* 8,i:11–19) that attention to myth "in its wider secular sense" is an important key to O'Connor. Without myth, man becomes a Displaced Person, a pervasive O'Connor type representing the "distortion of whatever traditional models we might have of a human being." Curiously, it turns out that the myths which Farnham has in mind are all of the religious variety.

Concentrating on "Violence and Belief in Mauriac and O'Connor" (*Renascence* 26:158–68), James M. Mellard discusses the two writers' shared preoccupation with violence in connection with a vision of sin and redemption; the physical violence in their works is paralleled by "stylistic violence." Though some of these similarities have been noted before, Mellard traces them economically and forcefully.

Anneliese H. Smith ("O'Connor's 'Good Country People,'" *Expl* 33:item 30) sees Joy-Hulga's self-identification with Vulcan as appropriate, since in mythology Vulcan was never successful "as an autonomous figure." David R. Mayer argues in "Apologia for the Imagination: Flannery O'Connor's 'A Temple of the Holy Ghost'" (*SSF* 11:147–52) that the Incarnation serves as a paradigm for the writer's vision and art; just as the fictive child merges images from Catholic ritual, saints' lives, and sayings of the nuns with her own experience in order to understand herself, so O'Connor in her career was similarly affected by images from the Bible, church history, and ritual. In "The Pauline 'Old Man' in Flannery O'Connor's 'The Comforts of Home'" (*SSF* 11:96–99), Joseph R. Millichap says that although the protagonist is a cynical "doubting Thomas" who can recognize the devil in others but not in himself, O'Connor suggests that the catastrophe may be a "fortunate fall."

Thomas F. Gossett draws upon 135 pieces of correspondence for two source studies: "Flannery O'Connor on Her Fiction" (*SWR* 59:34–42) and "Flannery O'Connor's Opinions of Other Writers: Some Unpublished Comments" (*SLJ* 6,ii:70–82). Because of Regina O'Connor's strictures against an edition of O'Connor's letters, Gossett must paraphrase rather than quote (and he enriches that information with his memory of conversations with the writer from the mid-1950s to her death in 1964). Even in paraphrase, the O'Connor voice comes through, showing both her remarkable wit and her occasional exasperation. The letters, says Gossett, show a writer "extraordinarily sure of the effects she strove to achieve."

v. Saul Bellow, Bernard Malamud, and Philip Roth

M. Gilbert Porter describes himself as an unapologetic though non-militant New Critic, and his *Whence the Power? The Artistry and Humanity of Saul Bellow* (Columbia: Univ. of Mo. Press) is more a series of critical analyses, which rigidly follow the plot of each novel, than it is a well-focused, comprehensive unity. Some chapters are excellent for all that in their insights into Bellow's important imagery (*Seize the Day*), narrative levels (*The Victim*), and the functional use of opposites (*The Adventures of Augie March*). Porter perceptively traces not only the musical imagery but also the narrative movements in *Henderson the Rain King* ("horizontal" and fast-paced before Henderson begins his "lion therapy," after which it is "vertical").

If his discussion of *Herzog* ("a secular theodicy for our time") seems unduly thin, it is partly because Porter refuses to drag out the central issue—ideas vs. experience—to the tiresome extent of many previous critics; and his treatment of *Mr. Sammler's Planet* is as uncompromisingly cerebral as the novel itself, which Porter terms "a staged performance . . . heavy on ideas, light on fictional concretions, thematic embodiments." A final chapter is a comparative review of Bellow's heroes, out of which comes Porter's placement of Bellow in what he calls "neo-transcendentalism," a tradition which includes Ralph Ellison, Ken Kesey, and Bernard Malamud, who reaffirm "human possibilities of the dream despite the power of the dread."

With her treatment of Bellow's comedy, Sarah Blacher Cohen is frankly more restricted, but she skillfully transforms this seemingly narrow topic into an extrapolated method for understanding the most crucial aspects of an author who is so powerfully central in contemporary letters. *Saul Bellow's Enigmatic Laughter* (Urbana: Univ. of Ill. Press) is, like Porter's book, a chronological analysis of the novels through *Mr. Sammler's Planet*. Cohen argues that the novels avoid both strict naturalism and the tragic mode, since somewhere in between these forms Bellow finds the most congenial arena for probing man's complexities and subtleties. This in-between area is comedy, though at times the term enjoys a wider latitude than some readers will be willing to grant: the comedy of the first two novels turns out to be "mordant lacerations" (*Dangling Man*) and "fiendish ironies" (*The Victim*); and for all the fine arguments I am not convinced that *Seize the Day* is Bellow's "most hopefully resolved" comedy.

Overall, however, Cohen's is a strong book, tactfully reasoned and well-written, whose major thesis is convincing—that Bellow's strengths do not lie in comic situations (though there are some superbly staged ones) but in the comedy of ideas; and Cohen rightly concentrates on allusions, catalogs, juxtapositions of the sacred and the profane, and sheer verbosity as signs of the writer's belief in the cognitive power of language to rout the banal. The treatment of *Augie March* demonstrates happily that language is the key not only to Augie's irrepressible rhetoric but also to an entire vision of man (Cohen calls her chapter "The *Animal Ridens*"), and her best segment is on *Henderson*, whose "fabulous voyager" hero employs the "humor of verbal retrieval." Bellow's fictions, even the jeremiadical *Mr. Sammler's Planet*, are secular comedies of man "vacillating between recidivism and reform of his detestable practices." Cohen also contributes "Sex: Saul Bellow's Hedonistic Joke" (*SAF* 2:223–29), in which she shows that the novelist's use of this "comic leveler" is an important clue to his humor in the social relationship of men and women.

In his elegant polemic, "Saul Bellow and the Modern Tradition" (*ConL* 15:67–89), Daniel Fuchs argues that the explicit thrust of Bellow's fiction is "to deny nihilism, immoralism, and the aesthetic view" (i.e., the Modernist aesthetic with its "bloodless intellectuality, its coldness of heart, its reactionary ideology"). Certain aspects of Modernism—alienation, the break with tradition, the magnification of subjectivity—appear, however, as part of Bellow's stylistic tensions, between affirmation and skepticism, the manic and depressive, action and revery, common sense and mystical feeling, the colloquial and the learned, "Yiddish inflection and latinate elongation."

A fit companion to Fuchs's essay is "Saul Bellow: The Theatre of the Soul" (*Ariel* 4,iv[1973]:44–59) by E. R. Zietlow, who tackles the Modernist and anti-Modernist impulses from a slightly different angle. Through *Seize the Day*, Bellow is the Modernist writing of the Age of Anxiety, creating characters who define the self through action; beginning with *Henderson*, the concern is to achieve being, a state represented as "an agreeable harmony of the ego with the self's deeper reality."

In "*Dangling Man*: Saul Bellow's Lyrical Experiment" (*BSUF*

15,ii:67–74), James M. Mellard explores Bellow's first novel in light of Ralph Freedman's 1963 work on lyric fiction. The structures of *Dangling Man* are to be discovered in the interactions of image patterns, and the novel is the objective form for the mind's "engagement with the varied craters of the spirit." "Koheleth in Chicago: The Quest for the Real in 'Looking for Mr. Green'" (*SSF* 11:387–93) may be overargued (Grebe as the modern Preacher looking for the meaning of existence), but Eusebio L. Rodrigues's suggestion that this story issues from a creative mood poised precariously between the belief that man is a victim of the human condition and the awareness that he can somehow transcend this condition explains the peculiar transcendentalized Dreiserian elements in this transitional work.

Bellow's most controversial novel is based on contrast and opposition rather than on the "dialectical tension leading to a synthesizing conclusion," says Douglass Bolling in "Intellectual and Aesthetic Dimensions of *Mr. Sammler's Planet*" (*JNT* 4:188–203). The juxtaposition of farcical effects and philosophical concerns shows man as "*both* lover of wisdom and fool," as a creature "not only worthy but morally compromised." Although Bolling draws some useful analogies from painting and relevant parallels from the ethical intuitionists, the coherence is dissipated in an article much too long.

In an entertaining and informative biographical sketch, "Bellow Observed: A Serial Portrait" (*Mosaic* 8,i:247–57), Rosette C. Lamont recalls a friendship with the author during the pre-*Herzog* days when Bellow lived in Dutchess County in New York; for the post-*Sammler* years, we get revealing glimpses of the author's attitudes toward some of his younger critics ("He has no friends among the New Left, nor does he wish to have any").

The most skillful explorer of family relationships is Bellow, says Andrew Jefchak, who in "Family Struggles in 'Seize the Day'" (*SSF* 11:297–302) sees the distance between father and son as a poignant measure of the distance between the world at large and the individual self. Rita K. Gollin, in a general article on "Understanding Fathers in American Jewish Fiction" (*CentR* 18:273–87), counters the popular misapprehension about the hegemony of the Jewish mother in modern Jewish life and letters; the father is important, she says, as a "transmitter of a moral tradition." In the most important works of Bellow—as well as those of Malamud, Roth, and Singer—the father is responsible for posing serious and moral problems for his child; though he may be ineffectual or tyrannical, the child "learns to accept, to pity, and sometimes to love."

In *Bernard Malamud and the Trial by Love* (Amsterdam: Rodopi) Sandy Cohen glosses the novels and related short stories according to the dominant theme of self-transcendence. The motif of every work is the painful progress from egocentric frustration and lust to the disinterested love of others, and to be successful the Malamud protagonist must learn to live outside the myth that controls him. A number of critics would quarrel with Cohen's assertion that "Malamud has from the first wanted to present man as he strives toward perfection through self-transcendence," since it leaves little room for Malamud's exquisite sense of the phenomenal world and its imperfect denizens; but even in Cohen's own terms, many of Malamud's protagonists are failures. The hero's turn toward transcendence in *The Natural* is only implied; in *The Fixer* the issue seems to be absorbed into the whole Hasidic universe in which the "physical world of man and the metaphysical world of God are one"; for the painter of *Pictures of Fidelman*, self-transcendence is "a parody"; and *The Tenants*, though it is called a "departure," ends with "little hope for self-transcendence." This arbitrary and schematic book seems never to have passed through an editor's hands.

In talking about the "seamless perfection" of Malamud's tales in "Serial Form and Malamud's Schlemihls" (*Costerus* 9[1973]:109–16), Stanley Poss relies on rhetorical overkill to supply some minor illuminations. We should keep in mind, he says, "that the integritas and consonantia of a work add up to an ultimately unanalyzable claritas." That advice has little to do with the modest discovery that Malamud's notion of a story owes more to the older traditions of the "tale" ("rambling and episodic") and the Yiddish tale-teller than it does to the Joycean epiphanic story.

M. Thomas Inge's purpose in "The Ethnic Experience and Aesthetics in Literature: Malamud's *The Assistant* and Roth's *Call It Sleep*" (*JEthS* 1,iv:45–50) is to redefine our traditional standards by which we teach literature. Although Henry Roth's novel is a "private and ethically oriented piece of fiction" compared to Malamud's more universally applicable work, both are successful fictions in their own terms; the specialized novel should not be relegated to the second-rate category.

John N. McDaniel stresses the "hard core of social realism" in *The Fiction of Philip Roth* (Haddonfield, N.J.: Haddonfield House), in which he finds a perspective more secular and skeptical than Jewish. Even in the satire and fantasy, the Rothian hero "must go out into the world—even if it is only to discover that he is a man without a country, invisible, homeless, a stranger to himself and his deepest beliefs—before he can go underground to wait for a new spring and the promise of home." If his description sounds more like Ellison's Invisible Man than Portnoy, it is because McDaniel sees in Roth's protagonists a summary of the "strongest hopes and deepest fears of contemporary American authors." The activist heroes (Ozzie Freedman, Eli Peck, Neil Klugman) examine possibilities for self-assertion within the community, and the victim-heroes (Lon Epstein, Paul and Libby Herz, Lucy Nelson) succumb to the forces of social absurdity and psychological compulsion. Both fictional types of this "most 'marginal' of Jews" are defined in their several-fronted assault upon the American experience. McDaniel's thesis is crisp and its demonstration clear and convincing; but the frequent typos, the overreliance upon previous critics, and the use of paperback editions for his texts tend to erode confidence we might have in the critical insights.

Charles M. Israel would agree with McDaniel's thesis insofar as it applies to "The Fractured Hero of Roth's *Goodbye, Columbus*" (*Crit* 16,ii:5–11); Klugman's failure of insight and untrustworthiness as a storyteller come primarily from "a collapse of authority around and inside him"—a crisis which is American and Western, not exclusively Jewish. "The secret of the terror behind Roth's fiction is the realization that the father is impotent," says Mark Shechner in "Philip Roth" (*PR* 41:410–27); the son's chief concern is to escape the father's wrath and to "short-circuit his sentimentality." Just as his books read like case histories, "so does the profile of his entire career." After *Portnoy's Complaint*—called the breakthrough novel—Roth dispenses with symptoms in favor of style. Shechner thinks *My Life as a Man* has the most sustained writing of any of the novels because Roth's talent is engaged fully "at its most frantic, its most ironic, and its most subtle." Pierre Michel contributes "*Portnoy's Complaint* and Philip Roth's Complexities" (*DQR* 4:1–10). Despite the restrictions of his title, "*The Great American Novel* and 'The Great American Joke'" (*Crit* 16,ii:12–29), Bernard F. Rodgers, Jr., demonstrates that sources in traditional American humor, both Down East and South-western, can be found in *Our Gang* and *Portnoy's Complaint* as well as in the more recent work. Rodgers's fine work here may well indicate future lines of investigation.

Both Rodgers and McDaniel contribute bibliographies. In "Philip Roth: A Checklist 1954–1973" (*BB* 31:51–53), McDaniel covers the novelist's work through March 1973, including paperback editions and excerpts from novels, and the major book reviews, critical articles, and book chapters. Rodgers's *Philip Roth: A Bibliography* (Metuchen, N.J.: Scarecrow) covers the same period, but is annotated and a bit fuller than McDaniel's; it also includes review essays, interviews, dissertations, and previous bibliographies.

vi. John Barth, John Hawkes, and Thomas Pynchon

Barth's well-known essay is the basis for John O. Stark's *The Literature of Exhaustion: Borges, Nabokov, and Barth* (Durham, N.C.: Duke Univ. Press), the defining characteristic of which, however, is most succinctly expressed by Susan Sontag: "discovering that one has nothing to say, one seeks a way to say *that*." Buttressing his analysis with the recent work of George Steiner, Ihab Hassan, and Richard Poirier, Stark decides that the ultimate argument in this kind of literature is that "the domain of language and literature paradoxically contains all reality and that the 'real' world contains none."

Unlike Borges and Nabokov, Barth shows the complex relation between reality and imagination by mixing the two domains rather than setting boundaries around each. Barth's created world "continually moves," says Stark, because of its creator's interest in process rather than product. *The Sot-Weed Factor* typifies the first stage of the literature of exhaustion "because it creates and exhausts an infinite set of possibilities." The later works are more dubious about such possibilities, although to suggest that realism had to be invented too, Barth makes his bard in "Anonymiad" invent a new kind of literature.[1]

Stark is perceptive in showing how Barth's use of opposites is not only an ethical and aesthetic principle but also one which accounts

1. D. Allan Jones, in "John Barth's 'Anonymiad'" (*SSF* 11:361–66), also sees the Mycenaen minstrel, who espouses his creator's aesthetic, fusing out of tragedy and satire a new kind of literature—a "single, comprehensive genre."

for a style richly compounded of contradictory elements. He relates this kind of literature to allied movements (the so-called Literature of Silence, the *nouveau roman*, Camp and Black Humor, fabulation); but Stark's chapter on Barth is oddly, haphazardly organized, and the observations rarely go beyond what has already been noted about Barth's specific works. References "when possible" are to notoriously undependable paperback editions. But the most astonishing lapse is Stark's comment that Barth "has too few readers perhaps because he has too few critics." To prove that existing critical work consists "mainly" of "ephemeral" book reviews, Stark compiles a highly selective bibliography which ignores most of the reputable work on Barth of the last five or six years. Had he consulted Joseph N. Weixlmann's 1972 checklist, as he did Jackson Bryer's of 1963, he would have found some more of these "too few critics."

In *John Barth: The Comic Sublimity of Paradox* (Carbondale: So. Ill. Univ. Press), Jac Tharpe reaffirms most readers' general feeling that as a group, all of Barth's novels "comprise a history of philosophy," the emphasis of which is on ethics in the early work and on ontology and cosmology in the later. Tharpe's real contribution, however, is in showing the relationship between these metaphysical investigations and Barth's notion of man as *homo faber*: the central question finally is what Barth thinks of "the value of human activity." If ultimate answers are elusive, man can at least be engaged in a "craft" and learn to be a "better performer." Life style, then, becomes a matter of pride in technical craftsmanship. Barth himself is the hero-artist "at some ontogenic level removed from merely personal biography"—the "heroic craftsman, who orders a chaotic funhouse." Even if craftsmanship and creativity in perfect union "are insufficient to produce the final holy utterance," it also means that something is always left to be said (*Lost in the Funhouse*); if the universe is chaotic, "perhaps a chaotic new tongue will describe it" (*Chimera*). Although the unlikely shade of Hemingway hovers over this interpretation of Barth, it may help to make the later works seem less masturbatory.

Harold Farwell finds that Barth's writing reaffirms the persistent, if tenuous, belief in the possibility of love, though love is seen as "the very essence of the absurd," not an absolute value but one "more precious for its very fragility." "John Barth's Tenuous Affirmation: 'The Absurd, Unending Possibility of Love'" (*GaR* 28:290–306) includes an interesting look at Barth's 1952 M.A. thesis, in which Farwell finds the familiar unresolved triangle, and a consideration of the recent "Dunyazadiad."

In "*Giles Goat-Boy*: Satyr, Satire, and Tragedy Twined" (*Genre* 7:148–63), James T. Gresham cites Barth's use of intellectual systems and catalogs to suggest that the fourth work is Menippean satire. The doubling device illustrates that the romantic and burlesque heroes are "undifferentiable." John W. Conlee finds that "John Barth's Version of *The Reeve's Tale*" (*AN&Q* 12:137–38) can be found in chapters 12–14 of *The Sot-Weed Factor*.

In *Comic Terror: The Novels of John Hawkes* (Memphis: Memphis State Univ. Press), Donald J. Greiner places his author squarely in the Black Humor camp while suggesting some of the continuities with the 18th-century satirists. Even without benefit of a "benevolent social norm," we can still appreciate the good offices of comedy, since we are horrified and amused simultaneously at some of the responses of Hawkes's characters; and, like traditional comedy, Hawkes's maintains faith in the "invulnerability of basic values: love, communication, sympathy." Hawkes has always insisted on freedom from constraint in matters of point of view, motivation, and sequential logic, but Greiner sees a detectable shift from the earlier parodying of genre (detective thriller, the Western) to the parodying of the fictional process itself. Paradoxically, the later fiction, though more lyrical (thus suggesting "life's power to balance death"), gradually assumes the shape of "conventional fiction": if the earlier work abounds in highly controlled set pieces full of self-conscious inventions and amusing twists, the later shows a tighter rein on language and imaginative vision.

Greiner finds *The Owl* the most successful of the early works because of its controlled blend of violence and humor; *The Beetle Leg*, an "irreverent comedy" which "reverses the myth of love and fertility," is the most horrifying; and he finds a kind of trilogy on the varieties of love in *The Lime Twig, Second Skin*, and *The Blood Oranges*. In his finest chapter—on *The Lime Twig*—Greiner argues persuasively that the Bankses may be banal, but they are not the kind to be hopeless, innocent victims, and gives fresh observations on Sidney Slyter and on Hencher's poignant first-person chapter. Throughout, Greiner is skillful in showing how Hawkes achieves coherence not through plot, theme, or character development, but through verbal patterns and recurring motifs. What is occasionally unconvincing is Greiner's insistence upon seeing comedy *in* the terror (Tremlow's beating of Skipper is termed "hilarious"). Despite some inevitable disagreements in Greiner's evaluation of tonal effects, most readers will benefit from *Comic Terror*.

In discussing the genesis of *Second Skin* ("Notes on Writing a Novel," *TriQ* 30:109–26), Hawkes himself says that this was the first novel in which he was "explicitly attempting to write comic fiction," and he remarks that he is no longer interested in such a "safe" mode: "from now on I want to come still closer to terror." In another essay, dating from a 1966 lecture, Hawkes discusses some of the similarities of "*The Floating Opera* and *Second Skin*" (*Mosaic* 8,i:17–28). He cites a catalog of "alarming parallels" between his own work and that of our "comic Melville" (first person, comic treatment of death, derangement, pain of sexual experience); both novels are "tenuous or hard-won affirmations of life."

Despite his deceptively simple title, Ron Imhoff succeeds in writing the year's most pretentious essay. In "On *Second Skin*" (*Mosaic* 8,i:51–63), he argues that structure is "the primary substance" of the novel; with some help from the Prague structuralists, he provides some elaborate charts which supposedly help us in "decoding the text," but which merely suggest that abstract patterns are perceptible. The parts of *Second Skin* "form a vibrant, deanatomized whole that is identifiable and connected but not interpretable in any fixed and unchanging way." In a more helpful essay, "Hawkes' *Second Skin*" (*Mosaic* 8,i:65–75), Richard Yarborough writes that Skipper is a "creative artist, ordering and manipulating his materials" in a way reminiscent of Henry in Berryman's *Dream Songs*. Both are "two tragic artists manipulating their memories in a passionate attempt to face death and truth, to find an order, a good in the evil and fear" of their lives.

The sterile universe of Hawkes's novels is marked by paralysis, disorder, and repressive forms and codes, says André Le Vot in "Kafka Reconstructed, ou le fantastique de John Hawkes" (*RANAM* 6[1973]:127–41). The tradition of American romance as well as Kafka accounts for the fantasy, poetic metonomy and metaphor, ambiguous narrative voices, the "pénétration—ou ce surgissement—du surnaturel" in the works from *The Goose on the Grave* to *The Blood Oranges*.

In "What Stencil Knew: Structure and Certitude in Pynchon's *V.*" (*Crit* 16,ii:30–44), Richard Patteson observes that this first novel consistently undermines the belief that knowledge can be increased. Facing the "horrors of randomness" in the universe, Stencil accepts discovered or created form, elevated finally to conspiracy as invented form. In the second novel the protagonist becomes suspicious that she only imagines connections and unity—a reflection, says Manfred Puetz, of the general Modernist urge to uncover patterns in the structure of things. "Thomas Pynchon's *The Crying of Lot 49*: The World Is a Tristero System" (*Mosaic* 7,iv:125–37) contains a succinct comparison with *V.*

John P. Leland believes that Pynchon explores "the possibilities of language and fiction" so substantively that the second novel is "not only about entropy but is itself entropic." "Pynchon's Linguistic Demon: *The Crying of Lot 49*" (*Crit* 16,ii:45–53) is a conjectural demonstration that language for Pynchon is a meaningless accident, a medium incapable of establishing contacts beyond its own closed system. Linda W. Wagner, in "A Note on Oedipa the Roadrunner" (*JNT* 4:155–61), sees the novel as an attempt to recreate physically the quality that dominates our culture—"the demonic speed that obscures any truth and confuses the strongest character." Except for an unfruitful comparison of Oedipa and Nick Carraway, Wagner's article is persuasive.

In an early review, Earl Rovit called *Gravity's Rainbow* "a 760-page Rube Goldberg machine which depresses the soul." But in a well-researched and plainly written essay, "Science as Metaphor: Thomas Pynchon and *Gravity's Rainbow*" (*ConL* 15:345–59), Alan J. Friedman and Manfred Puetz make great sense out of that "machine" by showing the relationship between the compost-garden image and the V-2 rocket. Advancing beyond the earlier novels through what he calls "Entropy Management," Pynchon sees that death and decay are the larger disorder that makes possible "the endless variety and renewal of life." Friedman and Puetz commend the scientific accuracy of the novel and in a valuable footnote cite the few slips.

Although Friedman and Puetz discuss briefly the tension between the Pavlovian determinist and the statistician who sees life as a freak deviation from the probable, Lance W. Ozier concentrates entirely on the successful characterizations and thematic significance of Roger Mexico and Ned Pointsman in "Antipointsman/Antimexico:

Some Mathematical Imagery in *Gravity's Rainbow*" (*Crit* 16, ii:73–90). The novel dramatizes an archetypal confrontation of spiritual and intellectual freedom with mechanical determinism, although the opponents are only vaguely comprehending. In "*Gravity's Rainbow* Described" (*Crit* 16,ii:54–67), Scott Simmon calls the novel an "historical and cultural synthesis of Western actions and fantasies." With its dual vision, tending simultaneously toward the "cataclysmic and the comic," *Gravity's Rainbow* resembles *The Confidence Man* and *The Day of the Locust* more than it does the Black Humor fiction of the 1960s. Simmon also contributes "A Character Index: *Gravity's Rainbow*" (*Crit* 16,ii:68–72) keyed to the Viking-Compass edition.

vii. Joseph Heller, Ken Kesey, and Jerzy Kosinski

The number of fresh approaches and worthwhile insights of the Heller critics has not been commensurate to the almost obsessive interest in *Catch-22*. In *Critical Essays on "Catch-22"* (Encino, Cal.: Dickenson Pub. Co.), James Nagel has reprinted five "representative" reviews and nine essays along with five new pieces, the best of which is his own contribution, "Yossarian, the Old Man, and the Ending of *Catch-22*" (pp. 164–74). The old man in the Roman bordello functions as Yossarian's alter ego, whose actions and philosophical stance duplicate the protagonist's psychological movement.

Nagel's comment on the hero's flight to Sweden—that it is a "positive affirmation" which links Yossarian to Huck Finn, Natty Bumppo, Henry Fleming, and Frederic Henry—is echoed or disputed in three other essays. Daniel Walden (" 'Therefore Choose Life': A Jewish Interpretation of Heller's *Catch-22*," pp. 57–63) says that Yossarian chooses to exchange adaptation to an irrational world for the "older heritage-oriented world" represented by Hasidim. Suffused with moral content, the novel is "loyal to civilization, to the law, to the heart, and to humanity." James J. Martine agrees, in "The Courage to Defy" (pp. 142–49), that Yossarian's final act, though it seems to be existential and solipsistic, is an act of hope. Like Nagel, Howard J. Stark ("*Catch-22*: The Ultimate Irony," pp. 130–41) sees the old man—together with Orr and Colonel Korn—as philosophic models for Yossarian. As "symbols of man's moral disinterestedness," all three adapt to and acquiesce in "dissemblance," and Yossarian is an "existential dupe who . . . succumbs to a false message." The ultimate irony, however, is that those who stay to adjust or flee to forget are equally " 'disappeared' by Catch-22"; the novel thus shows the absurdity and irrationality of a disordered universe.

The title, "What Manner of Men Are These?" (pp. 45–56), by Jess Ritter seems to refer to the announcement that *Catch-22* is a Menippean satire, and although he points out some pertinent details about the Jonsonian names and functions of characters, the argument gets lost in a discussion of the clash of a morality of love and the capitalistic system.

Elsewhere, in "*Catch-22* and Angry Humor: A Study of the Normative Values of Satire" (*SAH* 1:99–106), James Nagel tackles the generic issue more substantially. Analyzing the framework, characters, "selective targets," and internal patterns of tone and structure, Nagel sees the novel essentially as a Juvenalian satire. Since traditional conservative norms have been abandoned in our society, a dominant "uneasy humor" must depend upon the "singularity of the narrative base" in this satire, a humor which questions the prevailing ethical norm rather than depending upon it. In an interesting note Nagel also reprints and comments upon "Two Brief Manuscript Sketches: Heller's *Catch-22*" (*MFS* 20:221–24). The leaves reveal that Heller originally conceived of his novel in Hemingwayesque terms and with strong emphasis on ethnic stereotypes.

Walter R. McDonald sees Yossarian as an ascetic embracing a radical individualism in "He Took Off: Yossarian and the Different Drummer" (*CEA* 36,i[1973]:14–16); in "Look Back in Horror: The Functional Comedy of *Catch-22*" (*CEA* 35,ii[1973]:18–21), McDonald focuses on the savage humor, the purpose of which he says is to turn "the world on end in order to arouse a jaded audience." W. K. Thomas is another who comments on Yossarian's flight in "The Mythic Dimension of *Catch-22*" (*TSLL* 15[1973]:189–98); he believes the upswing, upbeat conclusion is justified by the mythic aspect of narrative, which itself becomes "a hope for regeneration." Louis Hasley, in "Dramatic Tension in *Catch-22*" (*MQ* 15:190–97), says the final impression of the novel is pessimistic, an effect rendered largely through Heller's knack for interweaving and juxtaposing the comedy and the horror.

Les Standiford's "Novels Into Film: *Catch-22* as Watershed" (*SHR* 8:19–25) will be more enlightening for cinema buffs than for readers of Heller's novel, which Standiford terms a "rambling, predominantly humorous narrative." Finally, Joseph Weixlmann contributes "A Bibliography of Joseph Heller's *Catch-22*" (*BB* 31:32–37), a chronological listing of editions, interviews, and previously published bibliographies.

The most imaginative essay on Kesey this year is John Wilson Foster's "Hustling to Some Purpose: Kesey's *One Flew Over the Cuckoo's Nest*" (*WAL* 9:115–29). Kesey's problem, argues Foster, was to forge some kind of synthesis out of the collision of two attitudes (associated with hierophany and politics) that would harmonize with current realities of American society without permitting the apocalyptically inclined "to imagine that either total victory or total defeat is imminent." Although the games with which McMurphy hustles men (Monopoly, blackjack, poker, the World Series) are little models of the free enterprise system, the thrust of the novel is revolutionary: "The entrepreneur who is converted to the cause of the disfranchised is a firm part of revolutionary mythology," and McMurphy's shift is merely an "extension of his transformation from hustler to victim."

In "The Cowboy Saint and the Indian Poet: The Comic Poet in Kesey's *One Flew Over the Cuckoo's Nest*" (*SAH* 1:91–98), Carol Pearson contends that this novel is based on the "romantic myth of the king, the hero, and the fool": Big Nurse (the old king) is foiled by the fool (McMurphy) in order to nourish and train the "mythic hero (and future king)" (Bromden). The Indian poet then acts under this tutelage by writing his book about McMurphy. Barry H. Leeds's "Theme and Technique in *One Flew Over the Cuckoo's Nest*" (*ConnR* 7,ii:35–50) is a little late, in view of previous work on Kesey. It is frankly an admiring introduction to the novel, an investigation of symbol patterns and narrative devices.

In the most compelling parts of "The Gifts of Strangeness: Alienation and Creation in Jerzy Kosinski's Fiction" (*PolR* 19,iii–iv:171–89), Ivan Sanders concentrates on the "alienating and creative potentials of language" in all four novels, each of which is about outsiders whose aim is "to master a situation, to understand, to control, to *possess* experience—visually, verbally, if not always physically." While Kosinski distrusts language as a block to communication, he also strives for the precise word, as if he has been liberated by his adopted language. Samuel Coale argues in "The Cinematic Self of Jerzy Kosinski" (*MFS* 20:359–70) that Kosinski's anti-heroes follow the Robbe-Grillet formula that characters, existing as "one more visual surface," can be defined solely in terms of their actions. Though he thinks the last two novels inferior to *The Painted Bird* and *Steps*, they are the novels which best illustrate Coale's thesis.

"The Three Denouements of Jerzy Kosinski's *The Painted Bird*" (*ConL* 15:370–85) is David H. Richter's textual analysis of the variant endings of Kosinski's first novel, the popularity of which allowed the novelist to alter and refine his work in three separate editions (1965, 1966, 1970). Frederic E. Rusch's "Jerzy Kosinski: A Checklist" (*BB* 31:6–9) is "limited to works by and about Kosinski in English through March, 1973."

viii. Kurt Vonnegut and Richard Brautigan

Edward Grossman's "Vonnegut and His Audience" (*Commentary* 58,i:40–46) is a dispirited analysis of plot patterns, characters, and style as well as audience. If his apolitical politics earned Vonnegut his wide readership, even more important in sustaining it is his style —brief sentences, repetitive phrases, and a mock-naïve rhetoric; but if Grossman's description of Vonnegut's heroes is accurate, one wonders why readers even bother ("mechanized contrivances bathed in a stroboscopic glare—fleshless robots . . . moving jerkily toward the next joke, moral, or plot-advancing surprise").

In "*Breakfast of Champions*: The Direction of Kurt Vonnegut's Fiction" (*JAmS* 8:101–14), Peter B. Messent argues that Vonnegut's recent novel is a fictional cul-de-sac: like the new surfictionists, Vonnegut examines the basis of fictional form, discovers that words are less important than their sounds, and experiments with tired aural-visual responses. Readers looking for something new about Vonnegut's most popular novel will not find it in Arnold Edelstein's "*Slaughterhouse-Five*: Time Out of Joint" (*ColL* 2:128–39).

The most important scholarly tool yet to appear for the study of Vonnegut is Asa B. Pieratt, Jr., and Jerome Klinkowitz's comprehensive *Kurt Vonnegut, Jr.: A Descriptive Bibliography and Annotated Secondary Checklist* (Hamden, Conn.: Archon), which cites all the material by and about the author from 1950 through 1973, including dissertations and previous checklists.

Two of Brautigan's most popular works are the subject of a clutch of essays in a special number of *Critique* (16,i). Both Thomas Hearron ("Escape Through Imagination in *Trout Fishing in America*," pp. 25–31) and David L. Vanderwerken (*"Trout Fishing in America* and the American Tradition," pp. 32–40) praise Brautigan for his attempt to bridge the gap between the nation's mythical past and a dispossessed present through the sheer power "of imagining America otherwise." Hearron makes considerably more of the novelist's metaphorizing technique than is necessary to show "the city's incursion into the wilderness," but his point that the manner in which one thinks and describes reality can alter reality itself is a useful guide to Brautigan generally. Vanderwerken insists that Brautigan is the legatee not only of the uncompromising strain of idealism in American writing but also, because his work is "symbolic, parabolic, and fantastic," the grand tradition of American romance.

In "Author's Intent: *In Watermelon Sugar*" (pp. 5–17), Patricia Hernlund argues that the novel consciously projects a traumatized, closed society of joyless humans—a stultified utopia. Even more depressing is Harvey Leavitt's reading in "The Regained Paradise of Brautigan's *In Watermelon Sugar*" (pp. 18–24): because of the Biblical analogues, the commune is "man's second great attempt to obtain an earthly paradise." In this revised Eden, the passive narrator is "Adam II," the archetype of the prophet of the future; and, like the Old Testament, *In Watermelon Sugar* is a work of teaching and guidance which deserves its function as the Bible of the contemporary college generation.

"Richard Brautigan: A Working Checklist" (pp. 41–52), compiled by James Wanless and Christine Kolodziej, is complete through 1973, annotated, and useful despite its sometimes dubious authority (the phrase "said to have appeared in" recurs much too often).

ix. William Styron, Walker Percy, Reynolds Price, and James Dickey

Although most of his *William Styron* (Bowling Green, Ohio: Bowling Green Univ. Popular Press) has previously appeared as articles, Melvin J. Friedman provides a succinct (72 pp.) account of most of the important aspects of Styron's art. An earlier chapter relates his subject to the "new fiction" of the 1950s (Styron was among those who tried to rid fiction of both "too much experimentation" and a "too-rigid" reliance on traditional form), and in a new final chapter,

Friedman compares Styron to his contemporary John Hawkes and to such post-Modernists as Barthelme and Barth.

Whereas Friedman suggests that *The Confessions of Nat Turner* might appropriately have been termed a "nonfiction novel," David Eggenschwiler, in "Tragedy and Melodrama in *The Confessions of Nat Turner*" (*TCL* 20:19–33), calls the book "historical melodrama" whose facile aspects are qualified by the ironic structure of the first-person technique. While the narrator is making "consoling melo-dramatic fictions out of his intolerable understanding of his condi-tion," Styron constructs his melodrama from the stereotypes, popular myths, and obsessive images that "our culture has used to avoid painful understanding." In "An Interview with William Styron" (*SoR* 10:923–34) conducted by Ben Forkner and Gilbert Schricke during the writer's week-long tour of French universities, the author himself stresses the liberties he took with the historical Nat (a deranged man of "unredeemed fanaticism") for the purposes of humanizing him.

Although *Love in the Ruins* gets most of the attention of the Percy critics, in "The Catholic Novel and the 'Insider God'" (*Com-monweal* 101:78–81), Robert E. Lauder examines more generally the contrasting visions of Graham Greene and Walker Percy. The British novelist focuses on God's special action, through special rites, in special places, and with a select group of people; Percy, writing under the influence of Vatican II, stresses God as "the loving outsider" who makes his sinners realize that they are really saints.

W. L. Godshalk's "Walker Percy's Christian Vision" (*LaS* 13: 130–41) and Thomas LeClair's "The Eschatological Vision of Walker Percy" (*Renascence* 26:115–22) are complementary despite the use of different terminology. Godshalk believes that the existentialist approach has been overstressed, and that the last novel particularly is about man's Faustian pride, "his fall from grace, his call for spiritual aid, and his final return to the common life of Christendom." LeClair argues that because of its apocalyptic frame, *Love in the Ruins* is the clearest example of Percy's primary concern—eschatology both "immanent" and "transcendent" (i.e., death as condition and death as part of the "economy of salvation").

LeClair's passing observation about Percy's belief in "linguistic freshness" becomes Jared W. Bradley's topic in a disappointingly conventional article, "Walker Percy and the Search for Wisdom" (*LaS* 12[1973]:579–90): language for Percy is described as "a symbol of our comprehension of life around us," a metaphysical link between empiricism and existentialism. In "Walker Percy and the Self" (*Commonweal* 100:233–36), Lewis J. Taylor, Jr. discusses the novelist's concern with forfeited "sovereignty"—a dilemma resulting from the application of abstract theories of science and technology to human relationships.

In "Recent Southern Fiction: Percy, Price and Dickey" (*Handelingen XXIXe Vlaams Filologencongres*, pp. 188–98), T. A. Westendorp surveys the second generation of fictionists, those writing under the shadow of Faulkner, and finds that Reynolds Price's *A Generous Man* is a deliberate attempt towards limitation of the Faulkner tradition; that Dickey has not "fully grasped the tradition of the Southern novel" in *Deliverance* (because of its lack of insight, its inaccurate descriptions, and its interchangeable characters); and that in *Love in the Ruins* Percy has created the "most promising opening on to the future without having closed the door to the past." A more favorable estimate of Price can be seen in Simone Vauthier's "Nom et visage dans *A Long and Happy Life*" (*RANAM* 5[1972]: 243–63), a graceful but attenuated piece on Price's concern with relationships between fathers and children, the recurring intimations of mortality, and the importance of courage and love. Vauthier sees "The Names and Faces of Heroes" and its rich metaphors as pertinent to the novel.

In a densely packed essay, "James Dickey's *Deliverance*: The Ritual of Art" (*SLJ* 6,ii:83–90), Henry J. Lindborg argues that through its references to harmony, relation, and perspective, this novel is not merely about the art of killing but that it is "an exploration of the process of creation." Initiation is the ritual "commonly shared only through the medium of the novel itself," in a "secret ceremony which takes place in a dream state" or through sleep, during which what is imagined is made real.

William Stephenson stresses the role of Drew in "*Deliverance* from What?" (*GaR* 28:114–20)—the musician who is both the innocent bystander drawn into a tragic conflict and the orphic poet. Ed is saved not through reckless freedom and violence (Lewis's aegis) but through music and law (Drew's aegis).

x. Gore Vidal, Joyce Carol Oates, and James Purdy

Bernard F. Dick's major discovery about Vidal—that his interest in movies dates back to his juvenilia from the Phillips Exeter *Review*—is applied ruthlessly throughout *The Apostate Angel: A Critical Study of Gore Vidal* (New York: Random House). *Williwaw* becomes a "sort of elegiac *Story of G.I. Joe*, somewhere between a hymn to the survivor and a threnody for the misbegotten"; the hero of *In a Yellow Wood* is a "human photon" inspired by Karloff films; in fact, most of the novels "resemble film scripts" (though in another mood Dick says they show Vidal as a "classicist"). A talk-show cuteness invariably intrudes just when some critical point should be made (the discussion of *The City and the Pillar* is queered from the beginning by Dick's title, "Huck Honey on the Potomac"; the video-adaptation of a Faulkner story is praised because Vidal was able "to cut through the dense prose to the core of the story").

Dick writes with a breezy 1950s colloquialism punctuated alternately by such learned borrowings as *Wanderjahr, l'homme engagé, porte-parole,* and *roman policier*; simple-minded *sententiae* ("Seduction can be physical or verbal," "the swinging pendulum never rests," "Most tragedies are poetic constructs"); and vulgarisms ("the bitch who suckles neither wisely nor well," "the *donna* who philosophizes between her legs," "the female executive breaking her incipient balls to rise to the top of a man's profession"). Though the style is a compound of divergent impulses, it is hammered out with heavy predictability. Instead of taking a good if not great writer seriously, Dick rapturously quotes Vidal's witticisms and summarizes plots in the manner of a bright undergraduate; he describes Vidal's writing as "cut to the contour of the author's pumpkin grin," an inaccurate if not meaningless image which suggests nothing short of Alfred E. Newman. *The Apostate Angel* is the most wretched critical book of 1974.

In his discussion of "The Short Stories of Joyce Carol Oates" (*GaR* 28:218–26), Samuel F. Pickering, Jr., contends that what began as a fictive world depicting a comparatively objective reality (and stressing the "positive aspects of community") has turned into a more subjective enterprise reflecting Oates's fascination with the dreary psychology of suburbanites and academics. G. F. Waller, however, in "Joyce Carol Oates' *Wonderland*: An Introduction" (*DR* 54:480–

90), finds throughout the fiction a consistent concern for "the fragility of the human personality in contemporary America"; but in *Wonderland,* her most completely realized novel, Oates shows the phenomenological influence of Sartre and Heidegger. Waller fails to demonstrate how such an influence makes the fiction better.

Frank Baldanza continues his solid work on Purdy with four new essays. In "James Purdy on the Corruption of Innocents" (*ConL* 15: 315–30), he describes the most prominent feature of the fiction as "the relationship between a young innocent and the corrupt adult world in which he must make his way." Baldanza makes clear, however, that Purdy's innocents are also resilient, more existential than earlier examples of the type in Spanish picaresque and English sea fiction. This relationship Baldanza examines from another angle in "The Paradoxes of Patronage in Purdy" (*AL* 46:347–56). Although the patron-protégé situation, a pervasive one in the author's microcosm, is "acidulous, bickering, and recriminative," Purdy assumes it to be basic to society at large.

"James Purdy's Half-Orphans" (*CentR* 18:255–72), a companion piece to Baldanza's earlier essay on orphans (*ALS 1970*, p. 277), are those recurring characters who live with one parent or grandparent but whose dilemmas are as excruciating as those of full orphans: both point to Purdy's central theme, "the failures of love." In "Northern Gothic" (*SoR* 10:566–82) Baldanza places this author in the tradition of Sherwood Anderson. The fictive zones of both Ohio writers are the dispossessed, desperate, and eccentric; both are gothic in their "predilection for the abnormal, the irregular, the alienated, the soul *in extremis.*"

Douglass Bolling, in "The World Upstaged in James Purdy's *I Am Elijah Thrush*" (*UDR* 10,iii:75–83), concentrates on the false mythologizing and self-dramatizing ploys of those unwilling or unable to relate themselves authentically to "reality." Their stratagems to put boundaries around reality with myths and ego-requiring images reduce the world at large to the status of a minor actor.

xi. Others

a. **Edward Lewis Wallant and Elie Wiesel.** In his brief but suggestive "Edward Lewis Wallant as Urban Novelist" (*TCL* 20:252–61), Leo Gurko finds that though his New York and New Haven are

"anti-Periclean," Wallant manages to turn their ugliness into a celebration of "swarming vitality." Believing so much in the regenerative
powers of the city, he revives and dramatizes in contemporary form
"nothing less than the Periclean ideal."

Elie Wiesel's attitude toward the Holocaust is the subject of two
essays. In "Link and Promise: The Works of Elie Wiesel" (*SHR*
8:163–70), Samuel H. Joseloff asserts that the writer rejects nihilism,
cynicism, or anger in order to fulfill his duties as a storyteller, "writing
legends and tales, singing through words" about a vanished world.
Josephine Knopp's more substantial "Wiesel and the Absurd" (*ConL*
15:212–20) interprets Wiesel's protests against the destruction of
European Jewry as a protest against God's failure to intercede; the
underlying purpose of the first five novels is "to reconcile Auschwitz
with Judaism, to confront and perhaps wring meaning from the
absurd," which emerges as the novelist's true antagonist. Molly
Abramowitz contributes *Elie Wiesel: A Bibliography* (Metuchen,
N.J.: Scarecrow Press). In addition to a biographical sketch, she gives
a "fairly complete" listing of the work in English; only representative
items in Hebrew, Yiddish, and French are given.

b. Donald Barthelme and Robert Coover.   Jerome Klinkowitz con-
tributes "Donald Barthelme," one of the interviews in *The New
Fiction* (pp. 45–54).[2] Barthelme tends to shun generalizations about
premises or aesthetics of fiction writing, warns several times about
mistaking his characters' views for his, and praises the Germans for
their innovative directions in fiction. Charles Moran makes an odd
pedagogical case with his "Barthelme the Trash-Man: The Uses of
Junk in the Classroom" (*CEA* 36,iv:32–33): since its language is
"sublimely poor," Barthelme's work encourages students to collect
"bad language."

Larry McCaffery has compiled "Donald Barthelme, Robert Coover, William H. Gass: Three Checklists" (*BB* 31:101–06), which is
especially useful for noting the uncollected work of all three writers.
Neil Schmitz concentrates on *Pricksongs & Descants* in "Robert

---

2. Joe David Bellamy, ed., *The New Fiction: Interviews with Innovative
American Writers* (Urbana: Univ. of Ill. Press). This important collection repre-
sents a dozen writers, including William Gass, John Hawkes, Tom Wolfe, Ronald
Sukenick, John Gardner, and others.

Coover and the Hazards of Metafiction" (*Novel* 7:210–19), with emphasis on the demystified narrator's own contrivances. Coover's metafiction ("the discipline of the elect") is directed toward the technique of writing, not toward writing "as metaphysical risk-taking"; in the absence of "furniture and *ficelles*," the metafictionist has only himself working in the "cannibalistic forms of parody and farce."

c. **Edwin O'Connor and J. F. Powers.** In "Priests and Politicians: The Fiction of Edwin O'Connor" (*Crit* 16,ii:108–20), David Dillon traces "the death of Irishness" in America—O'Connor's dominant theme. From Skeffington of *The Last Hurrah* to Kinsella of *All in the Family*, the turn is from the tribal and paternalistic to that of the political and patrician. Gerald Haslam, drawing parallels between James M. Curley of Boston and the fictional Skeffington, says in "*The Last Hurrah* and American Bossism" (*Rendezvous* 8,i[1973]: 33–44) that O'Connor's novel adheres to its own internal logic, but that it is a "weak generalization when applied to bosses as a group."

In "Christian Folly in the Fiction of J. F. Powers" (*Crit* 16,ii:91–107), Thomas R. Preston argues that the great subject of both the stories and *Morte d'Urban* is not so much clerical life as it is the nature of the Christian life: Powers uses the *contempus mundi* tradition of Christian folly as a means for making characters realize that they must die to the world in order to live truly for the faith.

d. **Popular Fiction.** The appreciation of popular fiction is represented this year by vastly differing strategies and with varying success. At one extreme are "The Illusion of Fiction in Frank Conroy's *Stop-Time*" (*MFS* 20:391–99), in which Roger Ramsey modestly observes that Conroy realizes the importance of "suggestive memory"; and for those who are curious about such things, the overstuffed *Irving Wallace: A Writer's Profile* by John Leverence (Bowling Green, Ohio: Bowling Green Univ. Popular Press), which also includes the transcript of an interminable interview with the bland but egoistic author. At the other extreme are Craig Challenger's "Peter De Vries: The Case for Comic Seriousness" (*JAH* 1:40–50), a respectable argument for the "integrated view of tragedy and comedy" in *The Blood of the Lamb* and *The Vale of Laughter*; Ian Kennedy's

"Dual Perspective Narrative and the Character of Phineas in 'A Separate Peace'" (*SSF* 11:353–59), which suggests that the combined points of view of Gene the boy and Gene the man succeed "in dissolving the limitations of conventional first-person narration"; and Louis Auchincloss's stylish autobiography, *A Writer's Capital* (Minneapolis: Univ. of Minn. Press), which reveals selective glimpses of the novelist's early life at Groton, Yale, and Virginia, his wartime experiences aboard an LST, and his friendship with Vance Bourjaily and other writers of the early 1950s.

James Jones, now one of the exiles returned, may or may not turn out to be an important figure, but he is well served by John R. Hopkins's *James Jones: A Checklist* (Detroit: Gale Research Co.), which lists books, stories, articles, interviews, and published letters from 1951 to present work in progress. Included is "The Writer Speaks: A Conversation Between James Jones and Leslie Hanscom," a transcription of a previously unpublished 1962 radio program.

In an intelligent gloss on " 'The Lottery': Symbolic Tour de Force" (*AL* 46:100–07), Helen E. Nebeker shows that the horror of Shirley Jackson's tale is that man is not a fated victim of his darkest urges but of "unexamined and unchanging traditions." Robert Lima gives a historical synopsis of Satanism, an account of the modern continuity of its beliefs, and a reading of Ira Levin's popular shocker in "The Satanic Rape of Catholicism in *Rosemary's Baby*" (*SAF* 2:211–22).

Robert H. Moore's "The Last Months at *Harper's*: Willie Morris in Conversation" (*MissR* 3:121–30) is somewhat mistitled, since this interview, recorded in 1971 but withheld, is more about opinions of Faulkner, Dickey, and his own *North Toward Home* than it is about Morris's departure from the editor's chair at the magazine. L. Moody Simms, Jr., surveys the career of "Alice Walworth Graham: Popular Novelist" (*NMW* 6:63–68), who was well known in the 1950s for her historical romances of the Natchez country; and George M. Kelly conducts "An Interview with Thomas Hal Phillips" (*NMW* 6:3–13), a former student of Hudson Strode and author of five novels in the 1950s.

Jack L. and June H. Davis discuss a Southwestern writer in "Frank Waters and the Native American Consciousness" (*WAL* 9:33–44), especially his search for a philosophical principle by which Indian consciousness can be described and related to its Anglo-American counterpart. Gerald Haslam pays tribute to Jack Schaefer's "slate-hard style," narrative skill, and historical truth in "*Shane*: Twenty-five Years Later" (*WAL* 9:215–16).

e. Detective and Science Fiction. Ross Macdonald buffs are represented by several items, the most solid of which is "Ross Macdonald's Violent California: Imagery Patterns in *The Underground Man*" (*WAL* 9:197–203) by Elmer R. Pry, who in examining "the best" of the Lew Archer novels concludes that Macdonald's historical analyses are attempts to explain the violence of his milieu. The novelist himself speaks of California as "the central place in the world," a "bellwether," in Jerry Tetunjian's "A Conversation with Ross Macdonald" (*TamR* 62:66–85), in which he also discusses his influences (Dashiell Hammett more than Raymond Chandler, Marshall McLuhan, Morley Callaghan) and his reading favorites (Hemingway, Vonnegut). Ralph B. Slipper also contributes "An Interview with Ross Macdonald" (*MDAC* [1973]:53–58). Readers may also be interested in Steven R. Carter's "Ross Macdonald: The Complexity of the Modern Quest for Justice" (*MDAC* [1973]:59–82) and a more general survey by Max Byrd, "The Detective Detected: From Sophocles to Ross Macdonald" (*YR* 64:72–83).

The most notable of recent work on science fiction are Brian Aldiss's *Billion Year Spree: The True History of Science Fiction* (Garden City, N.Y.: Doubleday [1973]), Donald A. Wollheim's *The Universe Makers: Science Fiction Today* (New York: Harper [1971]), and Thomas Clareson's edition of *Science Fiction Criticism: An Annotated Checklist* (Kent, Ohio: Kent State Univ. Press [1972]). Marjorie Miller's *Isaac Asimov: A Checklist* (Kent, Ohio: Kent State Univ. Press [1972]) is now followed by Joseph F. Patrouch, Jr.'s *The Science Fiction of Isaac Asimov* (Garden City, N.Y.: Doubleday), the last section of which covers Asimov items since 1969; an admirable introduction, in which Patrouch describes the techniques of science fiction, is a model of its kind. See also Lemuel Reilly's "An Interview with Isaac Asimov" (*DLR* 3:28–34).

In "The Startled Muse: Emerson and Science Fiction" (*Extrapolation* 16:64–66), Michael N. Stanton shows that the epigraph from *Nature* in Asimov's "Nightfall" dramatizes the gulf between transcendental and existential attitudes. Jo Allen Bradham traces both biblical analogies and allusions to *Finnegans Wake* in "The Case in James Blish's *A Case of Conscience*" (*Extrapolation* 16: 67–80).

f. **Miscellaneous.** Richard Goodman, Jr., spends "An Evening with William Burroughs" (*MQR* 13:18–24), whose views of Norman Mailer and complaints about the difficulties of filming *Naked Lunch* may interest some. In a raffish tribute to "Kerouac" (*CarolinaQ* 26, iii:92–99), Allen Ginsberg describes his friend's prose style as "long, symphonic-sentenced, heavy-voweled periods" with some occasional cadences from Milton and Thomas Wolfe. In "The Delicate Dynamics of Friendship: A Reconsideration of Kerouac's *On the Road*" (*AL* 46:200–206), George Dardess defends the structure of the novel (a love story, not a travelogue), whose "outfanning geographical movement" represents the turn from "the limitations of possibilities to their expansion."

In "Secret and Symbol: Entrances to Goyen's *House of Breath*" (*SWR* 59:248–53), Robert Philips emphasizes two important aspects of the novel which launched William Goyen's career; the symbols are large, archetypal, mythical (air, earth, water), while the secrets, the private revelations of characters, are structural, "refractions of the teller's memory."

In "Myth and Ritual in the Short Fiction of Bruce Jay Friedman" (*SSF* 10:515–16), Stuart Lewis argues that while in the novels Friedman dramatizes man's alienation from society, in the stories he suggests that man is also alienated from nature. In likening J. P. Donleavy's most celebrated novel to *The Satyricon* in "'The Skull Beneath the Skin': J. P. Donleavy's *The Ginger Man*" (*MichA* 6: 273–80), Donald E. Morse notes that the omnipresence of death lends a "fierce pleasure" to Dangerfield's grim humor, revealing Donleavy's view that the value of the few brief moments of joy "lies only in their immediacy or in recollecting them in suffering." *Searches and Seizures* is the occasion for "On Stanley Elkin" (*FI* 2,iii:140–44), a frank appreciation by Raymond M. Olderman of a novelist whose books have grown progressively more involved with wonder and mystery in their protagonists' continual grapple with death.

Except for his concentration on the last three novels in "On Wright Morris" (*FI* 2,iii:144–47), Joseph Schwartz adds little to what others have observed—that Morris has an agrarian bias in his critical examination of American manners. In "Nothingness and Beyond: Joan Didion's *Play It as It Lays*" (*Crit* 16,i:64–78), David J. Geherin asserts that this work is neither a Hollywood novel nor a psychological novel; Maria's Camusian sickness is ontological. Marjorie Ryan surveys "The Novels of Diane Johnson" (*Crit* 16,i:53–63) and places the three works in the "satiric-comic-realistic" tradition. Robert Scholes's "The Good Witch of the West" (*HC* 11,ii:1–12) is about Ursula Kroeber Le Guin, who since 1966 has published eight novels of "speculative fabulation." "On Dan Wakefield's Superfiction" (*FI* 2,iii:126–32) is an informal appreciation by Jerome Klinkowitz, who rightly praises one of the most solid of the "new journalists" for his novel, *Going All the Way*.

Pat Ensworth and Joe David Bellamy provide one of the most entertaining interviews in years with "John Gardner: An Interview" (*FI* 2,iii:33–49). Gardner cites some of his influences (Melville, William Gass, Walt Disney) and stresses the importance of storytelling in the new fiction. Manfred Puetz supplies a fine introduction to the author of *Flats* ("On Rudolph Wurlitzer," *FI* 2,iii:134–39), and Harris Dienstfrey writes about the comic inventiveness of *Double or Nothing* in "On Raymond Federman" (*FI* 2,iii:147–50).

Indiana University

16. Poetry: 1900 to the 1930s

Richard Crowder

i. General

The profile of this chapter has been somewhat altered recently. We entertained Eliot for one time only: he has now departed to share a chapter with Pound. Since most of the foreign contributions are noted elsewhere, this chapter is considering only two essays from abroad. Black poets are omitted this year. And, finally, we have definitely adopted all the Fugitives, who have been in and out for several years; Tate and Warren are joining Ransom and Davidson.

We appear to be in a period of taking stock, finding out what we have to work with. There are seven books on Frost, varying greatly in quality. One book catalogues Frost materials at the University of Virginia; two more are devoted (with differing purposes) to Frost's critics; one article provides a checklist of Frost's critical comments. One book anthologizes critical and review articles on Robinson up to 1916; an article provides a checklist of early Robinson criticism; another informs us of recently acquired materials on Robinson at Colby College. Two essays detail Jeffers research materials. Another book is a summary of critics' opinions on Masters for 60 years. Two books and three articles present correspondence of our poets.

Now—what are we going to do with this material? Useful as this kind of work and publication is, we need, armed with such enriching background, to return to the poems themselves, to the original matter which made checklists and critical anthologies possible. Bless Reginald Cook and M. D. Uroff for their books on Frost and Crane.

Unfortunately missing here are serious extended studies of the poetry of Tate, Warren, Aiken (the single article notes his poetry only incidentally), Millay, H. D., and MacLeish. They should not be relegated to the shelves of nominal memory, for they all wrote good verse which deserves to be explored in greater depth. Furthermore, as Alvin Rosenfeld pointed out in this chapter in *ALS 1972*, we ought by this time to be focusing not so much on the individual poets as on the period as a whole. The time of the richest flowering of these poets is almost a half century into history. That surely is far enough away for gainful perspective.

Granted, Donald Barlow Stauffer's *A Short History of American Poetry* (New York: E. P. Dutton) gives the period some attention, but it deserves more. Of necessity Stauffer has to be fairly brief in his treatment of individuals, but he manages nevertheless to make incisive comments about most of the poets of concern to this chapter, some statements naturally being more extended than others. He expresses views on Stickney, Lodge, and Moody in chapter 7; on Robinson, Frost, Millay, Teasdale, Sandburg, Lindsay, and Masters in chapter 8; on H. D., Fletcher, and Wylie in chapter 9; and on Cummings, Aiken, Jeffers, Ransom, Warren, Tate, and Hart Crane in chapter 10. Though summary in nature, these brief essays are brightly written and suggest some fresh approaches. The book is worth examining.

The *Explicator* (vols. 32–33) gives little space to our poets. Frost is the subject of four items, Cummings of two, and Robinson of one. *DAI* (vol. 35) records 17 dissertations (mostly from 1973). Robinson and Frost, along with two composers, are the subject of one; Jeffers and Masters with three other poets are treated in another; Crane and two other poets are the point of focus in a third. The rest are devoted to single poets: Frost, Jeffers, H. D., Robinson, Crane, and Cummings—two each (though one of the Cummings studies is on the plays); Millay and John G. Neihardt—one each.

ii. Frost

Robert Frost: A Descriptive Catalogue of Books and Manuscripts in the Clifton Waller Barrett Library, University of Virginia, comp. Joan St. C. Crane (Charlottesville: Univ. of Va. Press), is a well organized and accessible listing. The front matter contains an essay by Barrett on his personal experiences. A preface by Lesley Frost Ballantine based on warm family recollections follows. Fredson Bowers contributes a "Bibliographical Introduction." Then the cataloguer herself explains her procedures and makes the usual acknowledgments.

The main section of the book is divided into two parts, "Printed Works" and "Manuscripts and Letters." In addition to lists of American and English editions of "Books and Pamphlets" and an 11-page catalogue of "First Appearances," the interesting phenomenon of Frost's "Christmas Cards" is given 37 pages (pp. 108–44). The "Manuscripts" division includes illustrations of some of the holographs. "Letters" (pp. 197–257) is generous with not only third-person descriptions of the contents but many direct quotations also. The bibliography details most of the principal background books, from W. B. Shubrick Clymer and Charles R. Green's 1937 bibliography through Arnold Grade's *Family Letters* (see *ALS 1972*, p. 319). Reference is facilitated by a thorough index.

The introduction to Peter Van Egmond's *The Critical Reception of Robert Frost* (Boston: G. K. Hall) is marred by graceless writing. On the first page the author inexcusably misspells the first name of Lawrance Thompson (which he spells correctly on the following page). He misuses the adverb *hopefully* in the current egregious manner and has taken up the popular *overview* for *survey*. In one sentence he uses the blanket word *things* twice: "those things associated with Robert Frost's work" and "other similar things." Clichés appear at every turn: "eminently quotable," "to lay the groundwork." It is regrettable that too many literary scholars are losing sight of fresh style as they go about the business of compilation and criticism.

The main body of Van Egmond's book (305 pp.) is an elaborate descriptive catalog of items relevant to Frost's reception, both critical and popular. Twelve divisions cover the ground. All available reviews (262 items) of all the books from *A Boy's Will* to *In the Clearing* lead the lists. There follow 159 "Interviews and Talks," beginning with Frost's high school valedictory and concluding with the *Cornell Library Journal* publication (1970) of a 1950 address, "A Tribute to Wordsworth." Van Egmond says that these items show that "the poems are what count ultimately." In introducing the section on "Published Letters," the editor compares Frost to Twain as letter writer, thinking constantly of the recipient, but always aware of his obligation as an American artist.

Under "News Items" the editor attempts to separate out the "non-evaluative" news stories concerning Frost and his family. This can obviously be only a representative listing. There are 16 "Bibliographies and Checklists." "Books and Pamphlets," from Gorham B. Munson's pioneer *Robert Frost* (1927) to Elaine Barry's *Robert Frost on Writing* (*ALS 1973*, pp. 316–17), are followed by "Parts of Books":

Amy Lowell's *Tendencies in Modern American Poetry* (1921) to William H. Pritchard's essay in Reuben A. Brower's *Forms of Lyric* (1970). Descriptive notes on 706 articles from periodicals arranged chronologically from 1915 to 1973 provide a developing survey of the tides of Frost's reputation, his variants and his constants. A selective list of anthologies (129) names many of the poems included by the editors, the most frequent of which appear to be "Stopping by Woods...," "Fire and Ice," and "Design." Tributes by other poets (72) "range from the fatuous to the sublime." Thirty-one dissertations (through 1970) are listed. Van Egmond's claim that "several" have become books is somewhat overextended. George W. Nitchie published *Human Values in the Poetry of Robert Frost*, and Elizabeth Isaacs wrote a sound introductory book, but these hardly add up to "several" outgrowths of dissertations. "Foreign Criticism" (95 items) has come from over the world, Iran to South America. (Van Egmond groups all Latin American countries together.) The book closes with an "Index to Critics" (*critics* used loosely). Van Egmond's industry is commendable. Now what's to be done with the poems, given all these lists?

Donald J. Greiner goes beyond the annotated bibliography. *Robert Frost: The Poet and His Critics* (Chicago: American Library Association) treats the entire body of writing related to Frost over a period of more than 60 years. For this reason, as he himself points out, Greiner has to be selective, even at the cost of omitting mention of someone's "favorite article." His six chapters, however, evaluate in some depth critical comment through the years. The first discusses quite frankly the collections of letters, the biographies, and various memoirs. When there are differences concerning facts, the author defers to Thompson as generally most reliable. The second chapter, addressing itself to "The Early Criticism" from 1913 to 1925, looks at the reviews of the four books of verse of this period and the few longer commentaries (before the onslaught of Frost criticism as a major industry). A division on "The English Criticism" and a much longer division on "The American Criticism" demonstrate that most early opinions were favorable.

Greiner now turns to critical comment considerably less than adulatory. For example, he shows how Frederic I. Carpenter, in viewing the 1930 *Collected Poems*, tries to sound approving, but in reality is finding fault with the poet for lack of "fertility," by which he seems to mean "quantity," in spite of the admitted perfection of certain poems. Newton Arvin, furthermore, thinks Frost a highly biased writer, and others make negative judgments, including Rolfe Humphries, R. P. Blackmur, and Yvor Winters, who "implies that Frost's themes are minor because they deal with stone walls rather than with contemplation of death and eternity." In contrast to the detractors Greiner sees Frost as a serious commentator on the ills of our century.

Chapter 4, "The Literary Heritage of Robert Frost," shows how the critics connect the poet with Wordsworth, Emerson, Thoreau, and New England in general. Greiner finds more to say here than in chapter 3 as he analyzes books of criticism by such writers as John Lynen, Reuben Brower (for whom he has high praise), and Lawrance Thompson as well as articles by thoughtful writers like Hyatt Waggoner and Reginald Cook. In pointing out that Hayden Carruth and Malcolm Cowley are at opposite ends with regard to Frost's place in the New England tradition, Greiner appears to favor Carruth's affirmative view. In a chapter on nature, the author finds that Frost is not to be considered logically consistent in his view of the natural world, for he interacted all his life in varying ways with "nonhuman otherness."

The last chapter looks at Frost as craftsman—not only his own views but the opinions of careful readers. (Greiner considers the "Introduction" to Robinson's posthumous *King Jasper* one of the best sources of Frost's ideas about poetry.) There is now a need, says the author, for critical weighing of Frost's ideas about the craft as they developed through the years. In fact, Greiner calls for comprehensive studies of his entire achievement. Each of the six chapters is followed by a good listing of materials relevant to the subject under consideration, and at the end of the book three pages are devoted to "Additional Study Guides." A searching index adds value to this broadranging and indispensable survey.

Greiner agrees with Elaine Barry that Frost was not a practical critic in spite of his lectures, written remarks, and memoirs—most of them still to be evaluated. In "Robert Frost, the Poet as Critic: An Analysis and a Checklist" (*SCR* 7:48–60), he says that Frost's theories were nonetheless innovative, sophisticated, and creative and were backed by wide reading. The poet was most concerned with "drama, sound, organic development, form, and metaphor." "Education by Poetry" (1931) was probably the poet's highest critical attainment. A "Selected Checklist of Sources for Robert Frost's Critical Theory" (pp. 57–60) is divided into five sections: Letters, Interviews, Essays, Lectures, and Memoirs. Greiner has done us a service in directing us to these widely scattered materials.

Three other items in the same issue of SCR 7 are about Frost. "Frost in the Carolinas," recorded and edited by Richard J. Calhoun (pp. 3–12), presents hitherto unpublished remarks by Frost, a speech, in his informal manner, made at the University of North Carolina in the spring of 1957. This is primary material beyond the province of this chapter, rambling reminiscences and meditations introducing the poems he reads. Kathryn Gibbs Harris spells out "Robert Frost's Early Education in Science" (pp. 13–33) in the first part of a promised book-length study. A biographical account up through his first sojourn in England, the article examines Frost's mother's Swedenborgianism and the influence of a school friend, Carl Burrell, with whom he "shared intellectual freedom." Absorbed by physics and astronomy, Frost found William James's books stimulating. Bergson's *Creative Evolution* excited him (led to "Design," says Harris). Interested all his life in scientific discoveries and their implications (he frequently enjoyed the *Scentific American*), Frost followed his mother's Swedenborgian belief that knowledge of the world leads to knowledge of God. "In fact, much of the effect of the mystical in the poems arrived through the poet's knowledge of science." In "Words in the Rush of Everything to Waste: A Poetic Theme in Frost" (pp. 34–47), David Alan Sanders pursues the poet's obsession with the power of language to give permanent form to the world which the imagination perceives, that imagination which is paradoxically compelled to witness the destruction involved in all change. Sanders explores the nuances of this idea of control through words in various poems, e.g., "Nothing Gold Can Stay," "In Hardwood Groves," and "The Wood-Pile."

Reginald L. Cook presents background material, then admirably goes on to make critical use of that material. *Robert Frost: A Living Voice* (Amherst: Univ. of Mass. Press) serves three purposes: (1) Cook describes his encounters with the poet; (2) he transcribes several of Frost's talks and conversations; and (3) he makes critical comment on the voice in the poetry. Cook knew Frost through the Bread Loaf experience, though he talked with him countless other times.

Chapter 2 develops at length four of these meetings. The next chapter stresses Frost's mighty sense of place and time. The long center section of the book records Frost's own words, with unobtrusive introductions by Cook explaining the situation and Frost's manner during each session. This part is a distinct contribution to Frost studies, offering as it does not only the voice cadences but variations on Frost's intellectual and emotional concerns.

The third section of the book (110 pp.) is comprised of the author's own critical estimates. Cook is of the opinion that Frost never consciously assumed a disguising mask and that for Frost poetry was in its own way as rigorous and precise as science. (See Harris, above.) He has found that Frost's best poems are more about art than about society or politics, though the poet does not ignore these matters. Frost, he points out, was unsympathetic with over-readers who worry symbols to death. In his discussions Cook takes a close look at a number of poems as, for example, he reinforces his belief in Frost's capacity for "containment" of vision. "The climactic point in reading Frost originates in the simultaneity of the vision, of separability and inseparability, of part and whole . . . of star and constellation. This is the Grand Design." Cook's faith is that Frost will survive not for his picturing of rural New England but for "the old intuitive knowledge and the simple truths of the human heart." The book contains an index to Frost quotations as well as a thorough general index. Cook's essay "Robert Frost: An Equilibrist's Field of Vision" (*MR* 15:385–401) has been incorporated in revised form in this book.

A different sort of project is Kathleen Morrison's *Robert Frost: A Pictorial Chronicle* (New York: Holt, Rinehart, & Winston). The author was Frost's secretary-manager for nearly a quarter of a century. Her book, recording much of the poet's activity after his wife's death in 1938 (with occasional backward glances), takes up the life story from the point at which Lawrance Thompson's *The Years of Triumph* closes.

The style is unhappily monotonous; the sing-song details are tiresome: "After a night of partying, Robert talked next day to the Rhodes Scholars, and, following lunch with Lord and Lady Beveridge, returned to Wadham to pack for his journey into the Cotswolds" (p. 89). "In Israel Robert faced a demanding program, which included two lectures, two so-called talking sessions, a reception, a large luncheon, and many informal meetings with members of the university faculty" (p. 106). Why does Mrs. Morrison insist on calling her subject "Robert" on every page? It's just too, too Harvard-wifely.

The book further substantiates what we already know of the complexities of the poet's personality: his jealousies, demands, fears, vindictiveness, chauvinism, racism, and so on. It will be of some use to the person who assumes the formidable task of finishing the biography Thompson so admirably built through two volumes. Mrs. Morrison has arranged the material in roughly chronological order, but she should have gone to the trouble of an exhaustive index, partly because activities and people get lost in those undigested lists. We have here a kind of log of raw materials that Frost might have called a "matrix," details that should be sorted, evaluated, and shaped into a portrait characterized by sharp intuition, by compassion without sentimentality, and by sensitive nuance. The numerous photographs are of greater interest than the text.

Another book of undigested data is Nancy Vogel's *Robert Frost, Teacher* (Bloomington, Ind.: Phi Delta Kappa). Principally through quotation of Frost's comments on teaching and through memories of people who knew him or interviewed him, the author gives us a chronological portrait of the poet as mentor. Her comments, as introductions and as a means of coherence, are generally flat, e.g., "Robert Frost did not like pretentiousness and snobbishness." As a handbook this job of work is made up of stuff that could be the core of a study full of insights and creative interpretation.

Monumental (xii + 610 pp.) is the word for *Frost: Centennial Essays*, compiled by the Committee on the Frost Centennial of the University of Southern Mississippi. Marice C. Brown, chairman of the committee, introduces the collection with "The Quest for 'All Creatures Great and Small.'" The head editor, Jac L. Tharpe, contributes the "Afterword: Frost as Representative of the Eidolons." Between these two articles are presented 40 other essays by as many hands, some more familiar than others—Reginald Cook, Philip Gerber, Lawrence Perrine, George Monteiro, James M. Cox, and John Lynen, for example.

The editors have attempted rough groupings of the collection by subject matter. Under "Achievement," in addition to Cook's and Gerber's essays (the one a review of critics' opinions and the other a speculation on the poet's reputation a hundred years hence) are a study of Frost as guru, a long look (27 pp.) at Frost's sense of reality,

and a dialogue with James Dickey. Other sections present essays on
"Nature," "Themes," and "Contexts" (Frost and Eliot, and Howells,
and Hawthorne). Eight pieces concern "Method and Theory" (e.g.,
Lewis H. Miller, Jr.'s "Design and Drama in *A Boy's Will*" and Donald J. Greiner's "Robert Frost's Dark Woods and the Function of
Metaphor"). Sections on "Religion" and "Biography and Reminiscence" (including an interview with John Ciardi) are followed by
two important papers under the plain heading of "Robert Frost."
James M. Cox, in "Robert Frost and the End of the New England
Line" demonstrates Frost's descent from Emerson and Thoreau. "Relations with God may be more tentative, but relations with people, if
not more happy, are certainly more necessary." John F. Lynen ("Du
Côté de Chez Frost") places Frost in modern literature by an un-
hurried analysis (33 pp.) of "Directive."

A rather informal index, with the help of the table of contents,
should direct readers to passages useful for the interest of the hour.
For example, Emerson and Whitman are the "influence" poets referred to most frequently, and "After Apple Picking" is the choice as
"one of the finest poems" of Gerber and Dickey among others. This is
a gold mine of a book. Any library without it would be depriving
readers of all levels of a source of richness and variety of insight into
the work and personality of a great poet.

Lesley Frost (Ballantine), in "Certain Intensities" (*BSUF* 15,iii:
3–8), says that her father taught her from the beginning to write
stories with strict awareness of "intensities of dialogue, scene, character, and situation." She traces, with examples from her writing, her
education from preschool days to college. She details her father's
ingenious ways of interesting his children in learning, quoting some
of Frost's letters to herself.

The contemporary poet William Stafford writes of "The Terror
in Robert Frost" (*NYTM*, 18 Aug.:24–26, 31, 33, 35–36, 38). The long
opening is largely biographical. Then Stafford explains how "Frost
walks through the valley of the shadow and fears evil." He exposes
Frost's well-known lack of orthodoxy in the classroom, his jealousies
and prejudices, his life-long pursuit of the relation of sound to meaning, and the importance to him of "individuality in language"—nothing new, but clarifying for *New York Times* readers the stance of the
"real" Frost.

"Robert Frost: The Contrarieties of Talent and Tradition" (*NEQ*

47:351–67) is the title of James R. Vitelli's study of how our acknowl-edgment of the myth of Frost increases our capacity for getting into the poems. Frost wanted to be a popular poet and succeeded through accommodating his talent to the American tradition, as, for example, in his use of common speech idioms. At the same time he was deeply conscious of the power of design. Vitelli calls attention to Frost as rôle-player, as much an original creation as any figure in his poems (contrast Cook, above). He meets head on the traditional hostility of Americans to poetry (this being the base of his design). Reality he handles paradoxically because of his innate desire to make of himself a public myth and at the same time come to an understanding of his own identity as poet. Vitelli examines "The Axe-Helve" to prove his point, that contrarieties are at work in the poet. Public bard and private poet are also in counterpoint in "Provide, Provide." Con-sciously designing, Frost is inevitably modern, while making rich use of American tradition.

V. Y. Kantak's contention in "Poetic Ambiguity in Frost" (*WHR* 28:31–46) is that the poet infuses flat language and literal tone with Emersonian noumenism. Far from the received pastoral tradition, Frost's nature poems are sophisticated and profoundly wise. If he enters with a fact, he emerges with a verity, though perhaps only suggested. Kantak sees this device as the result of Frost's love of a practical joke. Emersonian transcendentalism informs "Directive" as he reads it. For support, he reminds us that *A Masque of Reason* calls "Uriel" "the greatest Western poem yet."

In "Barriers and Boundaries: Wall Imagery in Frost" (*BP* 16 [1971]:19–30), Ramesh Srivastava takes the stand that Frost is not an isolationist. Rather, he employs walls to defend himself from out-side perils; to show how reason and passion are related; to express his ideas on poetic theory, on politics, and on society; and to illuminate his attitude toward institutions, man, and nature. Frost is a citizen of the world who works at transcending natural barriers. Throughout all these metaphorical functions, the wall imagery maintains a pas-toral charm all its own.

Floyd C. Watkins claims to differ with Sidney Cox and Lawrance Thompson in that he cannot find that Frost took a firm stand either as a believer or as a skeptic. "Going and Coming Back: Robert Frost's Religious Poetry" (*SAQ* 73:445–59) develops the idea that what may at first appear to be orthodox in Frost raises doubts on examination, though Watkins grants that the poems are not as vacillating in religious views as are the poet's prose comments. The poems of relative belief come early and late and tend toward abstraction and emotional flabbiness. For Watkins the best poems (that is, of the middle period) express doubt and are characterized by vivid imagery and the high tension of genius, though he concedes that even in his last period Frost wrote six or seven marvelous poems, such as "Design" and "Neither Out Far Nor In Deep."

Richard Poirier sees the vision and the actual composing of a poem as a frequent theme in *A Boy's Will*. This can be translated into the form and irony with which Frost seeks to control terror, confusion, and darkness. In "Robert Frost: The Sound of Love and the Love of Sound" (*AtM* 233,Apr.:50–55) Poirier holds that one of the poet's recurring themes is the peril of silence produced "by failure in love." The fact of sound is important to Frost. "Never Again Would Birds' Songs Be the Same" Poirier considers "one of the most beautiful poems in our language . . . a marvelous illustration of the creative power of love upon sound and upon form."

William H. Shurr's interpretation of "Stopping by Woods . . ." springs from an analysis of the poet's "specific diction and its provenances." In "Once More to the 'Woods': A New Point of Entry into Frost's Most Famous Poem" (*NEQ* 47:584–94) Shurr indicates that Frost here is recording an encounter of the mind with Emersonian transcendentalism of the first chapter of *Nature*. The "lovely, dark and deep" woods are the true subject, which Frost has been resisting in the irrelevant details of the first 12 lines. The promised "new point of entry" comes from "A deep and dazzling darkness" (a name for God) in Henry Vaughan's "The Night," with which Shurr says Frost had acquaintance. Line 13 of the Frost poem is in the language of the mysticism which interested Grierson, Eliot, and Evelyn Underhill. William James used similar diction. Shurr refutes the reading of the poem as a Freudian death-wish and finds it based in transcendent experience, which, says Shurr, Frost fought against all his life. "Design" supports Shurr's argument that Frost, far from longing for darkness, wanted to stave it off.

Lewis H. Miller, Jr., has contributed "The Poet as Swinger: Fact and Fancy in Robert Frost" to *Criticism* 16:58–72. Frost, the author proposes, does justice to the chaos of reality as we know it by constantly swinging between fact and fancy. Miller close-reads "Birches,"

"Mowing," and "The Wood-Pile," the ending of which sums up his
theme: the coziness of a distant fireplace is small comfort when we
are confronted with the slow burning of decay; in spite of momentary
halts in our sense of chaos, destruction wins in the end. Such recognition, Miller says, puts Frost in line with the modern view of man in
an alien universe.

Presenting evidence that Frost combined events and details from
both *The Conquest of Peru* and *The Conquest of Mexico* by William
Prescott and added material of his own invention, J. M. Linebarger,
in "Sources of Frost's 'The Vindictives,' " (*AN&Q* 12:150–54) says
that the result is "a poem that is historically inaccurate and ethically
unpleasant, but revelatory of how the poet's mind worked." He suggests that possibly this poem was written in jealous reaction to Mac-
Leish's *Conquistador*, published a few years earlier. At any rate, it
fails because of its "acceptance of revenge as a value."

Roy P. Basler's "Robert Frost: Lobbyist for the Arts" (*QJLC*
31:108–15) reviews the poet's career in Washington beginning with
his appointment as Consultant in Poetry at the Library of Congress in
1958–59 to the time of his death. He worked indefatigably to make
the government aware of the need to support the arts. Reproductions
of several Frost manuscripts, if irrelevant, are of independent interest.

NConL 4 published three brief explications of Frost poems: Dennis Vail's "Frost's 'Mowing': Work and Poetry" (Jan., pp. 4–8), his
"Point of View in Frost's 'The Peaceful Shepherd' " (Nov., pp. 2–4),
and Fred Schutz's "Frost's 'The Literate Farmer and the Planet
Venus': Why 1926?" (Nov., pp. 8–11).

This was a very heavy year for Frost studies. Unfortunately, there
was some duplication of effort that added to the mass of material.
Much of what was said has already been said in former years. In an
era of consciousness of waste maybe scholars should be more aware
of what's been said already, more sensitive to the paper shortage and
rising costs of printing, and, just as important, more sympathetic toward a reader's impatience.

iii. Robinson

Richard Cary is a dedicated Robinson scholar. Before his recent re-
tirement not only did he publish books and articles, but he was the
assiduous editor of *Colby Library Quarterly,* the principal journal

regularly accepting work on Robinson. This year Cary's *Early Reception of Edwin Arlington Robinson: The First Twenty Years* (Wa-
terville, Me.: Colby College Press) gives us the full text of all known
reviews, interviews, and essays on Robinson's work, arranged chronologically under the title of each book (from December 16, 1896, to
August 27, 1915). Cary has headed each entry with a telling phrase
extracted from the article: "Can this man do it?" (from the first
known review); "at last coming into his own" (from the last review
of the 1915 revision of *Captain Craig*). In addition, the editor has
written an interesting introduction discussing the main trends of the
reviewers' comments, e.g., "Literary Analogues," "Originality," "Obscurity," "Pessimism," and "Humor." Of this latter, Cary generously
points out that Robinson's humor is an investigative subject "still in-
vitingly open."

The reviews of each volume are introduced by essays chiefly
biographical, picturing the milieu out of which the book came. Careful documentation of these essays is at the back of the book. On the
other hand, notes on each review follow that review immediately.
Cary identifies the reviewer, follows up the relations between poet
and reviewer, and juxtaposes the poet's reactions with the critics'
comments. There are two indexes: "General" and "Robinson's Writings." Not for Robinson scholars alone, Cary's book is a fascinating
investigation of the problem of the poet's minimal reputation up to
the appearance of *The Man Against the Sky* (1916). Though over
160 items of appraisal have been unearthed, the fact remains that
Robinson was rebuffed, disdained, and ignored for the first 20 years
of his career, the period during which, many critics maintain, he
wrote his best poems.

A related contribution of Cary's is "The First Twenty Years of
Edwin Arlington Robinson Criticism: A Supplementary Annotated
Checklist" (*RALS* 4:184–204). This list adds over 90 items to those
catalogued in the bibliographies of Charles Beecher Hogan and
William White—reviews published between 1896 and 1915. Editorial
notes describe the nature of the comments in each review. An index
not only lists the reviewers but locates their articles and indicates
their references to other writers (e.g., Poe, Whitman, Frost, and
Masters).

We are not through with Cary yet. *CLQ* 10 contains three contributions by its editor. "Additions to the Robinson Collection: II"

(pp. 385–88) brings the Colby bibliography up to date. " 'The Clam-Digger: Capitol Island': A Robinson Sonnet Recovered" (pp. 505–11) presents evidence that this poem, in *The Reporter Monthly* for April 1890, is indisputably Robinson's. "Robinson's Friend Arthur Davis Variell" (pp. 372–85) recounts events of boyhood friendship renewed for seven years beginning in 1922. The foundering of the contacts in 1929 was no doubt due to "expanding introversion, infirmity, distance." Cary labels Robinson's habit of keeping his acquaintances apart his "self-shielding *modus vivendi* of archipelago friendships."

CLQ 10 carries seven other articles on Robinson. Carlos Baker, in " 'The Jug Makes the Paradise': New Light on Eben Flood" (pp. 327–36) suggests a parallel between "Mr. Flood's Party" and James Kirk Paulding's "The Old Man's Carousal," which was in Robinson's copy of Stedman's *An American Anthology*. Both protagonists drink to the past and experience regret. Ronald E. McFarland reconsiders "Robinson's 'Luke Havergal' " (pp. 365–72), relating it to the "Inferno," with which Robinson was familiar as early as 1890. In his poem Dante as sinner is lost in the world without his Beatrice. McFarland points out several analogous passages. "Juxtaposition as Structure in 'The Man Against the Sky' " (pp. 486–94) engages the interest of John Newell Sanborn, who proposes that the poet does not follow Aristotle's formula of beginning, middle, and end with one theme but here places counter themes side by side to bring about a new comprehension. Sanborn cites similar structure in Chaucer, Ovid, Milton, and elsewhere. Immortality and pessimistic existentialism are interwoven throughout the poem.

John H. Miller has discovered that Robinson arranged his poems by theme in his earliest book ("The Structure of E. A. Robinson's *The Torrent and The Night Before*," pp. 347–64). Between an introductory group of poems on money-making and death and the concluding narrative, Robinson deals with four main themes: art, death, light in a dark world, and love and idealism as a means of survival. "The Night Before" (the final poem), however, is a warning that living only in the spirit is to alienate oneself from reality.

Don Richard Cox points out, in "The Vision of Robinson's Merlin" (pp. 495–504), that Merlin is free to leave Broceliande whenever he chooses (an innovation of Robinson's). As visionary prophet inferior only to God and Fate, Merlin transcends Time until at last he must succumb, as he understands, to Change and Time as well. It is true, however, that he has been able to see beyond the view of ordinary mortals. His vision is the central theme of the poem. Vivian shows him the parallel between his own search for order and "the reflected visions of Camelot and Arthur." When Merlin discovers, though, that she is not after all that ideal he has been seeking, he leaves her and returns to Camelot, where he sees in the visions of the fool Dagonet ironic similarities with his own.

Laurence Perrine catalogues Arthurian works that may have influenced Robinson and records the poet's reaction to the stories as told by others. In "The Sources of Robinson's Arthurian Poems and His Opinions of Other Treatments" (pp. 336–46) Perrine discusses Malory, the Vulgate *Merlin*, William Morris, Joseph Bédier, Wagner, Swinburne, Arnold, Masefield, Lowell, Hermann Hagedorn, and G. L. Kittredge, whose translation of *Sir Gawain and the Green Knight* fascinated Robinson. He thoroughly disliked Richard Hovey's four Arthurian poetic dramas just as he opposed Tennyson "in spirit, characterization, and moral outlook."

George Monteiro writes an introduction to a newly discovered article in the short-lived *Touchstone* (1906). In " 'The President and the Poet': Robinson, Roosevelt, and *The Touchstone*" (pp. 512–14), Monteiro points out that "An Idyll of Little Old New York" (reproduced in facsimile) is a satire on the relationship of the two men. It is amusingly illustrated and concludes with a parody of "Richard Cory" entitled "John Rockefeller."

iv. Crane

After several preliminary articles on Crane (see *ALS 1970*, p. 301, and *ALS 1971*, pp. 284–85), M. D. Uroff has published her completed study, *Hart Crane: The Patterns of His Poetry* (Urbana: Univ. of Ill. Press), in which she brings the shorter poems into equal focus with *The Bridge* through a study of the way "recurrence of patterns" demonstrates the operation of the poet's imagination. The author delineates in detail the poet's acts of violation and possession (creating tension), the world's flight and stasis (tension again), and the poet's "Impulse to Mastery" (chapter 6). Uroff discovers in the whole body of Crane's poetry (not just *The Bridge*) a unifying weaving of "words, images, and metaphors" which belies the frequent disjointedness that a study of genre (epic vs. lyric) seems to generate. She concludes that, in addition to the transcendent longings of *The Bridge*, Crane possessed a desire to express very human "sensations, sufferings, and ecstasies." In contrast with the "fastidiousness and preciosity" of his contemporaries, his poetry is inclusive, consistently yea-saying, emotionally vital and powerful. Furthermore, he escapes mere oracular outbursts and produces varied and intricately worked patterns through wide-open responsiveness to the interplay of the forces of the language he uses. After the Unterecker life, the Weber and the Lewis letters, the Schwartz and Schweik bibliography, and the ponderous, virtually unreadable *Hart's Bridge* of Sherman Paul, there is need for a book like Uroff's, which returns us to the poems themselves studied in a definable framework of ideas.

Thomas S. W. Lewis has edited the *Letters of Hart Crane and His Family* (New York: Columbia Univ. Press). The preface sets forth the foreseeable uses of the book: information for "anyone concerned with biography," parallels with passages in the poems, documentation of the unusual family relationships, and Crane's rise from an unlikely middle-class environment to a position of poet of extraordinary genius. Lewis's chronology, drawn from the contents and dates of the letters, helps to set times and places straight. The letters, from the hands of Crane, his parents (Clarence and Grace), and his grandmother (Elizabeth Belden Hart), deal mostly with quotidian routines, with travels, jobs, and encounters. Grace Crane's emotional stranglehold on her son and Clarence Crane's businessman's view of success are prominent. The parents' divorce, remarriage, and subsequent divorce and Clarence's other marriage are exhausting to follow, but not so tiring as Hart's constant restlessness—from one job to another, from one friend's abode to another, from one city to another. He had to be a highly disciplined artist to accomplish what he did in the unceasing whirl of this mobility. The text (letters and commentaries) runs to 657 pages—ample for getting the feel of the personalities and interrelationships of the family. The index is composed chiefly of a list of persons named in the letters as well as a few key topics like "Christian Science" and "Rhythmical Physical Culture" (both being interests of Grace Crane). Writing to one's father, mother, and grandmother about the cost of living, rooming houses, even parties and dinners with the high achievers in the arts is probably not going to inspire one to subtle comments on the nature of poetry, problems of structure, man's place in the universe, and other topics suitable to intellectual analysis. One reviewer suggests that these letters are worth reading if only to show that a great poet has as many daily concerns and family problems as the rest of us. Well, maybe.

Other Crane letters are brought to light by Thomas Parkinson in "The Hart Crane–Yvor Winters Correspondence" (*OhR* 16,i:5–24). Since the Winters letters are not available, this essay is based on Crane's contribution. Winters did not keep letters generally, but, according to Allen Tate, must have kept these to prove that he was not trying to destroy Crane's reputation. Of the 43 communications from Crane to Winters, this essay uses 9 letters to show how warm and fruitful the relationship between the two poets was from 1926 to 1928. Parkinson supplies biographical information (in part from interviews with Mrs. Winters) and quotations from Winters's publications to demonstrate how, despite their opposing points of view and life-styles, the two men were engaged in a productive friendship for over two years.

Philip Yanella claims that "For the Marriage of Faustus and Helen" is the first Blakean (as opposed to Eliotic) poem of consequence in America, preceding the work of Patchen, Rexroth, and Ginsberg in this tradition. In " 'Inventive Dust': The Metamorphoses of 'For the Marriage of Faustus and Helen' " (*ConL* 15:102–22) Yanella sees it as expressing faith in the American city. He concludes that "Metamorphosis is at its center; the transforming, synthesizing imagination is its kingpin; the idea of absolute freedom of the will to create anew is its basis." "Wilbur Underwood: Hart Crane's Confidant" (*MarkhamR* 4:66–68) by Philip K. Jason is a biographical sketch of a poet of minor achievement mentioned by Crane's biographers. The author (generally unacknowledged) of the widely known "The Kitchen Prayer," Underwood took the credit for bringing Crane to the works of Melville, though he had to admit, for the most part, that Crane's work puzzled him.

v. Ransom and the Fugitives

After the death of Ransom, *SR* 82 devoted over 90 pages to encomium, recollection, and reexamination. Allen Tate's "Reflections on the Death of John Crowe Ransom" (pp. 545–51) records Tate's student dislike of his teacher Ransom, partly because he saw in him what he

now knows were his own traits of calculation and competition. He
envied the older man's self-control and traces through the years the
course of his own "dislike," commenting along the way on his inso-
lence in replying to a Ransom essay. He now admits that fear was the
soil from which aversion sprang. Tate thinks Ransom's late urgency to
revise his poems was "the last infirmity of a truly noble mind," but he
still admires the logic and insight of Ransom's critical essays, couched
in "perspicuous . . . engaging . . . elegant prose."

Tate's confession is followed by another of Thomas Daniel Young's
biographical essays (see ALS 1973, p. 325), which follows Ransom's
three years as a Rhodes Scholar at Oxford, citing his correspondence
with his family in Tennessee, recounting his experiences with his
tutors, tracing his travels around England and to the continent, describing his daily routines, and detailing his reading. His "indoctrina-
tion into a foreign culture accentuated his natural inclination toward
a formality of manner." In the ensuing 20 years his creed took definite
form: "In manners, aristocratic; in religion, ritualistic; in art, traditional." *Poems About God* (1919) is "a hungry book," in the opinion
of Louis D. Rubin, Jr. ("The Wary Fugitive: John Crowe Ransom,"
pp. 583–618), who feels that Ransom was seeking a richer, more
meaningful place to stand but was not yet finding it. *Chills and Fever*
(1924) is a stronger book, in which wit and extravagant language
shield "domestic imagery." One finds violence and satire as the poet
decries the theology of Methodism and the tendency to water down
religious faith. Several later poems show him characteristically impatient with the modern: "Antique Harvesters" was a 1925 statement
of his point of view in *I'll Take My Stand*, a defense of rural life. He
justifies the urge to religion in poetry through "the logic of ontology
and aesthetics," in spite of which, or in addition to which, however,
he was profoundly passionate. "He held strong convictions, felt emotions powerfully, and when he took his stand, he meant it." George
Core, in "Mr. Ransom and the House of Poetry" (pp. 619–38), examines Ransom's prose, especially *The World's Body*, in some detail
and decides that the man had, with grace and wit, reconciled the
world and himself. What he contributed by way of "ontological
criticism" has had a tremendous influence in the rebirth of Southern
literature as well as overall criticism of our day. Though the New
Criticism banned biography in interpretation, Core urges analysis

of the facts of Ransom's career in order to reach an understanding of the complexities of his writing.

Thomas Daniel Young supplies further biographical detail in "Without Rank or Primacy" (*MissQ* 27:435–45). After two years at Vanderbilt, Ransom took two years off to teach. He was "a strict disciplinarian and a demanding teacher." Back at Vanderbilt, he was initiated as a junior into Phi Beta Kappa. The author lists the courses Ransom took in his last two years in college. These are some of the details that Core says one must study to appreciate the poetry and prose of this Fugitive leader.

Michael O'Brien has edited "A Correspondence, 1923–1958: Edwin Mims and Donald Davidson" (*SoR* 10:904–22). Mims, chairman of the Department of English at Vanderbilt for 30 years, in contrast with the Agrarians was a liberal who leaned toward an understanding with the industrial North. Tate, Warren, and Andrew Lytle despised him; Ransom was polite, but disdainful in private. Most unregenerate of the Agrarians, Davidson was, on the other hand, grateful to Mims for tolerating him; hence, their personal differences were submerged beneath their common love of the South, to the point where Davidson could even forgive Mims for letting Ransom leave Vanderbilt in 1937. By 1958 both men felt left behind. Mims thought men of Davidson's view were the cause of his being forgotten; Davidson thought the progressiveness that Mims supported had contributed to his own oblivion. Ironically, it was these opposing frustrations that brought them together. This article is based on three letters from Mims, five from Davidson.

John Tyree Fain and Thomas Daniel Young have brought together 248 letters from the files of Davidson's correspondence in Nashville and of Tate's at Princeton in *The Literary Correspondence of Donald Davidson and Allen Tate* (Athens: Univ. of Ga. Press). The editors have limited their selection to literary discussions, avoiding personal matters where possible. The foreword by Lewis P. Simpson places Davidson and Tate historically in the line "of Carlyle's grand vision of men of letters as the priests of a restoration of an age of faith in the face of an age of science." Their differences are in Tate's reaffirmation of "the humane tradition" as against Davidson's "mystical secularism." The introduction by the two editors traces the growth of the two men's interest in and judgment of T. S. Eliot as an example of "the fascination of discovery" in store for the reader of these letters. There follows a Register of virtually all the Davidson-Tate letters in the two files (short notes, fragments, etc., omitted) with brief descriptions of those not included in the book.

The letters themselves (403 pp.) are divided into four sections: the years of *The Fugitive*, the years between *The Fugitive* and *I'll Take My Stand*, the period from *I'll Take My Stand* to the end of the Agrarian movement, and later years—in all, from 1922 to 1966. They are frank, exciting, analytical, cool, candidly complimentary, dissenting, responsible, adult, critical—a splendid adventure for the informed reader. Knowledgeable headnotes introduce each section; footnotes, as consistent with clarity, are kept to a minimum. One comes from this book with a full sense of the unshaken belief of these writers that art, to be true, must be deeply rooted in its "cultural soil." These letters are of vastly greater interest to readers of poetry than are most of those in the Crane family collection.

vi. Cummings, Jeffers, Masters, and Others

Bethany K. Dumas has produced a turkey called *E. E. Cummings: A Remembrance of Miracles* (New York: Barnes & Noble). This very dull book opens with two sentences that set the pace: "From Cambridge, Massachusetts, to New York City is no great distance, geographically speaking. The trip is five hours by train, one hour by plane." The concluding paragraph of a chapter on the plays begins: "And the message is couched in that very traditional form, blank verse, which has long and generally been accepted as that best adapted to dramatic verse in English." This same paragraph is glued together by these phrases: "as being essentially one which," "that in which," "the agent who," "is one which."

Granted a deadening style, what about the contents? Six chapters discuss the poet's life, the poems (one chapter on juvenilia), the prose, and the plays and attempt a concluding appraisal. In the preface the author labels the book "a brief look at the man and writer E. E. Cummings as he was and grew and became." It is certainly no more than that. The content follows the style—hackneyed and actually destructive of interest. How many times have we heard that Cummings "revived the lyric" and "created a poetic language?" How pompous and condescending can a professor get? Witness, "At his best, he forced the reader into a kind of re-reading that results in the finest kind of education available to most of us, that in which [!] we continue to educate ourselves." After saying nothing really stimulating for 148 pages, the author ends with this lullaby: "he was the most traditional of innovators and the most innovative of traditionalists." Warning: do not—repeat: do not—read this book.

The second chapter of Tomaž Ložar's master's thesis at the University of Toronto appeared in *AN* 4 (1971):61–72. Entitled "E. E. Cummings: The Poem as Improvisation," it draws on McLuhan's insight that relates Cummings's poetry to jazz. Aware of the evanescence of beauty, the poet tries to capture it as it passes. Hence performance, "the saying of the right things at the right moment," is central. To Cummings and jazzmen alike surprise, discovery, and joy are essential. This is not to say that Cummings is a *naïf*: he is a skilled craftsman, a literate sophisticate. The usual critical comments, however, are not sufficient, for his constant experiments, "necessitated by the making impulse," require a special approach in getting at his technique, which is at once fragile and certain (that is, says Ložar, defiant).

Two explications focus on the element of love in Cumming's nature. William V. Davis argues that "E. E. Cummings's 'Except in Your'" (*ELN* 11:294–96) turns admiration for a lady into a comment on the poet and his muse. G. J. Weinberger's "E. E. Cummings's Benevolent God: A Reading of "when you are silent, shining host by guest" (*PLL* 10:70–75) shows Cummings's capacity for going beyond self in the discovery of joy.

E. N. Lockard reports a 45-minute conversation with Jeffers in "A Visit to Robinson Jeffers in 1945" (*ELN* 12:120–23), during which he found the poet to be shy and unexpansive but courteous and kind as he showed his visitors the well-known tower. The conversation was disconnected, jumping quickly from Frost to Steinbeck to Edmund Wilson to Frank Lloyd Wright. Jeffers admitted that his isolation here helped him "to sift out the irrelevant" from his poetry.

The *Robinson Jeffers Newsletter* continues to be the chief repository of Jeffers material. *RJN* 39 typically contains news, notes, and reports of research in progress as well as abstracts of articles and dissertations. James Martin Kirwan, artist, testifies to the influence of Jeffers on his posters (pp. 6–8). Robert J. Brophy, the doughty editor of the newsletter, points out "Biblical Resonances in Jeffers' 'Signpost'" (pp. 10–12), and Edward Nickerson thinks it "curious" that Jeffers was briefly interested in rhyme about 1942 ("The Return to Rhyme," pp. 12–21). *RJN* 39 concludes (pp. 21–26) with a description of Jeffers materials at California State University, Long Beach. *RJN* 40 follows the same layout. The two principal essays are by Brophy—"Jeffers' 'Second-Best': A Vocational Crisis" (pp. 7–9)— and by Denis Van Dam—"Greek Shadows on the Monterey Coast: Environment in Robinson Jeffers' Poetry" (pp. 9–11). Brophy clarifies Jeffers's view that, unless the writing of poetry is "a vocation from God," it can be only anemic and second-hand; he contends that the work of Jeffers is "God-linked" and therefore "not second-best." Van Dam's essay (documented with 34 footnotes) sees the Monterey coast and ancient Greece as both having "their primitive myths, people, and places." Nickerson, in describing in some detail "Jeffers Scholarly Materials: Library of Congress" (pp. 17–20), studies particularly an incomplete draft of "Cawdor." Persistent, searching, and informative for Jeffers scholars and others interested in the poet's work, which Brophy leads in keeping alive, *RJN* deserves wider circulation.

In *Edgar Lee Masters: The Spoon River Poet and His Critics* (Metuchen, N.J.: Scarecrow), John T. Flanagan says that a solid, updated biography of the writer is needed. His book summarizes and evaluates what critics said of some 50 of Masters's books written between 1898 and 1942, when his health failed. Divided into ten chapters, beginning with a biographical essay, the book follows Masters's writing career through the eyes of the reviewers and critics. By far the longest chapter is devoted to the reception of *Spoon River Anthology*—in spite of its detractors the most widely praised of any work of Masters. The critics were almost unanimous in finding a few, if very few, admirable poems in the five books that followed. Chapters on *Domesday Book*, the dramatic verse narratives, and the novels note that commentators eventually thought Masters would do well to turn to fiction exclusively, for in spite of sharp detail his later verse could not stand up to *Spoon River Anthology*. As biographer he was said to be biased, hurried, erroneous, and superficial. Flanagan's last chapter is quantitative, showing how little space (if any at all) has been allotted the poet in literary histories and anthologies for the classroom and the public. The author concludes from this analysis that

Masters still has an audience, however limited. At least the Spoon River poems "are unlikely to die from complete neglect."

Charles E. Burgess, in "Masters and Some Mentors" (*PLL* 10: 175–201), traces the poet's intellectual debt to several Illinois figures: William H. Herndon, author of the *Life of Lincoln*; the Rev. Robert Don Leavy Miller, local historian and superintendent of schools; John Hill, newspaper editor; Mary Fisher, high school teacher; and Dr. William Strode, physician and naturalist. Burgess gives almost ten pages to the writing and personal relationships of Margaret Gilman George Davidson, a poet of modest ability whose success in publication (*The Century, Youth's Companion, Harper's Weekly,* etc.) served as incentive to Masters, who felt himself in intellectual and aesthetic competition with many people, in varying degrees his guides and teachers.

Though not mainly about poetry, Stephen E. Tabachnick's "The Great Circle Voyage of Conrad Aiken's *Mr. Arcularis*" (*AL* 45:590–607) makes note of Aiken's disappointment at not being noticed by critics nor included in anthologies as often as his contemporaries, a trend, Tabachnick speculates, triggered by Aiken's inclination toward "philosophic inquiry" rather than the language devices that so magnetized the New Critics. The author sees the Aiken canon as characterized by "a real coherence, a staggering thematic and symbolic unity, a philosophic argument" as Aiken tried to solve metaphysical problems. The article traces Aiken's "great circle" voyage (with images of "ships, stars, seagulls, and freezing temperatures") through *Preludes*, the fiction, *Ushant*, and finally the drama *Mr. Arcularis* and comments that Aiken led a reflective life of complex concerns which he wrote about "with an astonishing simplicity." The author is guardedly optimistic about the future of Aiken criticism.

Robert T. Self, in editing "The Correspondence of Amy Lowell and Barrett Wendell, 1915–1919" (*NEQ* 47:65–86), directs attention to the warm epistolary relationship between Wendell, representative of the old guard, and Lowell, proponent of the new radicalism. Lowell's letters reveal a good deal about her attitude toward her work as poet and about the innovations of the current verse writers, but they also show that she profoundly appreciated Wendell's help, encouragement, and influence. On the other hand, Wendell's letters show him as suspicious of anything novel or adventurous. This collection testifies to the constant interaction in literature between past (Wendell) and present (Lowell).

Codline's Child: The Autobiography of Wilbert Snow (Middletown, Conn.: Wesleyan Univ. Press) takes its title from Codline Foster, the Maine midwife who assisted at the birth of Snow, a child of poverty who became governor of Connecticut (for two weeks). A minor poetic figure, Snow was acquainted with many of his contemporary poets. Of particular interest is the chapter on "The Robert Frost I Knew" (originally, in slightly longer form, an article in *TQ*), which reveals, among other details, that Frost in reality admired and respected Robinson more than any other living poet. The book discloses several autobiographical events as the provenience of Snow's verse. In covering 90 years of the man's life, it is entertaining, conversational, unpretentious.

Three articles relevant here appeared in *Midamerica 1974*: Blair Whitney's "Vachel Lindsay: The Midwest as Utopia" (pp. 46–51); Paul J. Ferlazzo's "The Urban-Rural Vision of Carl Sandburg" (pp. 52–57); and Frances Ewart's "Edgar A. Guest: Twentieth Century Paradox" (pp. 98–119).

Purdue University

17. Poetry: The 1930s to the Present

Linda Welshimer Wagner

i. General

In 1974 scholarship of contemporary poetry continued its track upward, with new interest in comparative studies. Forty-six dissertations were completed on the poets included in this chapter: eight on Wallace Stevens; five on William Carlos Williams; four on Theodore Roethke; three on James Dickey; two each on H. D., Marianne Moore, Sylvia Plath, Charles Olson, Robert Creeley, James Wright, Robert Lowell, the Black Mountain group of poets, and feminist poetics. Several more broadly comparative dissertations also appeared.

Two essays this year attempted to define the modern poem. James Guimond's "After Imagism" (*OhR* 15,i[1973]:5–28) is a complete discussion of what Sir Herbert Read once termed "one clear line of progress." Guimond views Imagism in painting and photography as well as poetry, commenting—with illustrations—on the "highly materialistic" art of Charles Sheeler, Walker Evans, William Carlos Williams, and Robert Bly. He finds that Bly's poems differ from Williams's because his images are less likely to be external. Howard Nemerov asks "What Was Modern Poetry?" (*Salmagundi* 25:30–46) and answers "that written between 1910 and 1925," having as its most apparent characteristics freedom from conventional forms, a dominant metaphor or image, some cognizance of formal criticism, and myth used rather than religion. Nemerov uses some early poems by Williams to illustrate these modern tendencies. Of them he chooses "The Semblables" as most effective because its "meaning" rises from "the collocation of things all by itself" (p. 46).

Octavio Paz gives a broader definition of the term *modern* in his *Children of the Mire: Modern Poetry from Romanticism to the*

Avant-Garde (Cambridge, Mass.: Harvard Univ. Press), trans. Rachel Phillips. Paz traces modern Western poetry to "its birth in English and German Romanticism," and follows its "metamorphosis into French Symbolism and Spanish American *modernismo*," and finally into 20th-century avant-garde. He finds its basic mode to be analogy, but analogy changed variously by irony. Its primary theme, according to Paz, is "a contradictory dialogue with and against modern revolutions and the Christian faiths." As a body of work, modern literature has been enriched and modified by an awareness of criticism that previously did not exist.

Basic to his definition is Paz's premise that "Modernity is an exclusively Western concept which does not appear in any other civilization" (p. 23) It rises from the Western concern that with time comes change and social self-consciousness, and that art is, at least sometimes, a criticism of that society. Paz considers Romanticism in this context, finding that much of its impact occurred because it was not only a literary movement but also "a new morality, a new eroticism, and a new politics" (p. 58). So too was the 20th-century avant-garde, with the difference that "The *idea* of change was the cornerstone of modern poetry," a premise that led to the modern "fusion of prose and poetry. The results were marvelous monsters, from Rimbaud's prose poem to Joyce's verbal epic" (pp. 158–59). From this position, Paz believes art will begin a new cycle once again, but that modernism per se has ended.

One ramification of the end of modernism as Paz defines it is described by James F. Mersmann in *Out of the Vietnam Vortex: A Study of Poets and Poetry Against the War* (Lawrence: The Univ. Press of Kans.). Set against a brief survey of the poetry of World Wars I and II, Mersmann's study of poems of the sixties provides more than close readings of the work of Allen Ginsberg, Denise Levertov, Robert Bly, Robert Duncan, and others (discussed in separate sections of this chapter). Mersmann's thesis is that so-called "war" poetry by these people is not in any way inferior to their less political writing, and that the growth of protest poetry reveals a new humane consciousness developing in Western civilization. Whereas "resignation" was the mood of World War II poetry, the Vietnam poets were, in comparison, violently outspoken. Mersmann sees the shift in voice as a result of free poetic forms: "'Open poetry' and 'open forms,' we may infer, are somehow importantly tied to an 'open universe'" (p. 27). As a result of these new freedoms, he finds that "poets now have a new attitude toward human possibility, and a faith that men can or could create a peaceful, anarchic, orderly, spiritual, and ecstatic community."

Robert B. Shaw, in "The Poetry of Protest," pp. 45–54 of his essay collection *American Poetry since 1960: Some Critical Perspectives* (Cheadle, England: Carcanet Press [1973], essays elsewhere referred to in appropriate sections) is less enthusiastic about this view of poetry. He remarks that protest poems "lend themselves so easily to classification" (diatribe, documentary, autobiography, or satire) that separating individual poems is difficult. Shaw criticizes Levertov's poetry as maudlin, Bly's as limited satire, and Duncan's as exaggerated: "the American nightmare seems as inhibiting to serious poetry as the American Dream at its rosiest ever was" (p. 53).

M. L. Rosenthal sees poetry, both of today and of the past, as the highest expression of man's humanity to and for man, and has written his refreshing *Poetry and the Common Reader* (New York: Oxford Univ. Press) as testimony to that belief. The short book is a set of statements about the importance of poetry in every person's life. That poetry is rooted in "everything we know and feel and are" Rosenthal proves by finding its uses in capturing past or forgotten memories, emotions, and political feelings. He incorporates discussions of poems by Frost, Stevens, Yeats, Williams, Whitman, Paul Blackburn, Wordsworth, Lowell, Auden, and others (thematic readings, for the most part), and provides a readable text for anyone interested in the poems. He concludes that the best poetry, that closest to each of us as common reader, "brings out the latent music of our awareness in such a way that we recognize ourselves as never before."

Rosenthal's affirmative view of poetry in general and modern poetry in particular is shared by Vernon Young ("Poetry Chronicle: Sappho to Smith," *HudR* 27:597–614) and Richard Lattimore ("Poetry Chronicle," ibid., pp. 460–74) but spoken against by Paul Ramsey ("American Poetry in 1973," *SR* 82:393–406). Ramsey considers more than 100 books of poetry, and concludes that they form a single genre—"personal, self-expressive, fragmented," with most poems short and relatively obscure. "It is not a good genre: poems in it lack completeness, clarity, maximum eloquence, and achieved understanding."

Whatever the critical impression, several paperback books were published to take advantage of the present interest in contemporary poetry. *Contemporary Poetry in America*, ed. Robert Boyer (New York: Schoken Books) is a reprint of the poetry issue of *Salmagundi*, 1973; *The Craft of Poetry: Interviews from the New York Quarterly*, ed. William Packard (Garden City, N.Y.: Doubleday) reprints interviews with Auden, Blackburn, Sexton, Ginsberg, Levertov, Wilbur, Creeley, and others. *The Poetics of the New American Poetry*, ed. Donald M. Allen and Warren Tallman (New York: Grove Press [1973]) contains statements on poetics from those written by Walt Whitman and Ernest Fenollosa to comments by Louis Zukofsky, Gary Snyder, and Frank O'Hara. A companion volume, at least in intention, to the poetry anthology which appeared 15 years ago (*The New American Poetry: 1945–1960*, ed. Donald M. Allen [New York: Grove Press, 1960]), this book is of importance chiefly for the practitioners of the Pound–Williams–Black Mountain group of poets. Also of interest in this grouping is the overlooked Samuel Charters's *Some Poems/Poets: Studies in American Underground Poetry Since 1945* (Berkeley: Oyez [1971]). Charters has included essays on the work of Olson, Duncan, Snyder, Ginsberg, Creeley, and other San Francisco poets.

Donald Barlow Stauffer's *A Short History of American Poetry* (New York: E. P. Dutton) concentrates mostly on poetry before 1900. The modern writers are grouped into only three chapters, one on "Pound, Eliot and the Imagists"; another titled "The New Poets: Regionalism and the Renewal of Language," in which Frost, Sandburg, Millay, Masters, Teasdale, Robinson, and others all collide; and a third—"New Thresholds, New Anatomies"—grouping Aiken, Cummings, Warren, Tate, Ransom, Williams, and Stevens together. The composition of the latter two chapters might just as easily be reversed—might not the Southern poets be placed as accurately in the "regionalism" chapter as in affinity with plain-speaking Williams? Similarly, Stauffer places poets from Lowell and Roethke to Berryman in "The Middle Generation" and—most concentrated chapter of all—poets ranging from Theodore Weiss and Isabella Gardner to Anne Sexton in the final chapter, "Some Contemporaries." One would wish for a more contemporary listing; as Vernon Young notes in his *HudR* essay on the Robert O'Clair–Richard Ellmann *Anthology of Modern Poetry* (New York, 1973), the real directions of contemporary poetry are simply not indicated by this kind of sampling of current work.

Stauffer's approach is historical and descriptive. He does not assume to be a critic primarily; he may note that Williams's *Paterson* is somewhat like Pound's *Cantos*, but he does not explain or elaborate the observation; and he seldom moves beyond the barest of generalizations. Space limitations can probably be blamed for much of this telescoping—both of poets and of comments about their work.

ii. Wallace Stevens

Two books, part of a third, and numerous essays treat the writing of Wallace Stevens. Adalaide Kirby Morris's *Wallace Stevens: Imagination and Faith* (Princeton, N.J.: Princeton Univ. Press) is in many ways a summary book. Morris gives ample credit to previous work as she builds from it to create a convincing study of Stevens's identification of poetry and religion; poetry *as* religion. For Stevens, the ancestral heritage of formal orthodoxy was a force to counter; skeptical of the old faiths, however, he was actively engaged in creating a new, personal, and more expansive religion, what Morris calls a "transvaluation" of the Christian trinity.

Man as poet and creator becomes Godlike, and Stevens's insistence on nature, on the concrete and the commonplace becomes an integral part of his symbology. Yet his sacramental system also includes such images from Biblical and Christian tradition as rocks, grass, glass, doves, rainbows, stars, and the burning bush. Underlying these images which connect even his most disparate poems is Stevens's belief in "the morality of the right sensation." Like Arnold (and also Williams and Pound), Stevens believed that poetry was the means of helping people "live their lives": "we have to turn to poetry to interpret life for us, to console us, to sustain us."

While much of this study has been anticipated, Morris does justice to Stevens's use of such major Biblical structures as parable and anecdote, proverb, prayer, hymn, and psalm; and to his language as reminiscence of "Biblical quotation, rhythm, words, and phrasing," at least in part.

Diane Wood Middlebrook's *Walt Whitman and Wallace Stevens* (Ithaca, N.Y.: Cornell Univ. Press) is in many ways similar to the

Morris book, in that her attention too falls on the way Stevens created his fictive world, but it is also much more original in its pairing of the two poets. Stressing that Whitman and Stevens "made analogous contributions to American literature and to modern poetry," Middlebrook examines Whitman's *Song of Myself* and Stevens's *Notes toward a Supreme Fiction*. She finds the chief resemblance between the two poets to be their concept of the poet as "supreme" imaginator, capable of creating myths viable for other human imaginations. Important in the work of each is the fictive "I," though never in a confessional sense: "the momentary confrontation between mind and object becomes the central drama" (p. 18).

Concerning Stevens, Middlebrook emphasizes the gradual evolution of his image of man as hero of even the fictive world. The year 1942 she labels *Annus Mirabilis*, for Stevens then wrote both the essay "The Noble Rider and the Sound of Words" (which laments the loss of heroes in modern art) and *Notes toward a Supreme Fiction*. Coming 20 years after *Harmonium*, Stevens's concept of heroic man "differs substantially in character from Whitman's." The end result, however, is quite similar. The latter part of the study traces Stevens's growing concept and his use of it in later poems, his transformation of "difficult self-acceptance" to a Whitman-like belief in person as icon, as "mythic form."

In *Metaphor and the Poetry of Williams, Pound, and Stevens* (Lewisburg, Pa.: Bucknell Univ. Press), Suzanne Juhasz also recognizes the primacy of the imagination to Stevens, but she is more interested in his method of arranging his constructs than in his philosophy of writing and living. Working from *Notes toward a Supreme Fiction*, "Thirteen Ways of Looking at a Blackbird," "Someone Puts a Pineapple Together," and other poems, she sees Stevens working with parts, images, which relate to each other in patterns more spatial than linear. She correlates his method in the poems with that of the prose of "Adagia," only to conclude that—because Stevens uses such a random structure—there is no resolution. "Stevens concludes by admitting, not a solution, but the perpetual existence of a war." Juhasz seems to feel that Stevens's poems emit only contradictions, both in their consistent mixture of language, which is both abstract and concrete, and in what she terms "the inconsistencies of his theoretical position."

Stevens's work holds a comparatively pejorative position in this study; Juhasz's preference for Williams is evident in both the structure of the book (she discusses Williams's short poems early, and then concludes with a long chapter on *Paterson* as representative of the most expert use of metaphor) and in her readings of his poems. She finds that his use of metaphor was consistent. It appeared in both early poems and late, but by the time of *Paterson* V or "Asphodel," Williams had built up such patterns of accumulated meaning that even simple metaphors had wide impact (so too did Pound throughout the *Cantos*). While this book is an interesting view of three central modern poets, and while Juhasz's focus on the use of metaphor is practical, her limited selection may be less than fair. To choose only one of Stevens's major poems seems self-defeating (how can we see the patterns of metaphor accumulate with so small a sample of his writing given?), and her definition of metaphor never comes clear, at least to this reader.

Several essays provide interesting insight into Stevens's work. James Rother's "Modernism and the Nonsense Style" (*ConL* 15:187–202) discusses Stevens (and Eliot and Hemingway) as not above using "nonsense" words, phrases, poems—much to the bewilderment of the serious modernist critics), sometimes for "serious" satiric purposes. Rother sees this approach as connected with Lear and Carroll, and reads "Last Look at the Lilacs," "Snow and Stars," and "The Comedian as the Letter C" in this context.

"Wallace Stevens and the Scientific Imagination" by Judith McDaniel (*ConL* 15:221–37) describes the poet's use of the new concepts of modern science, as formulated by T. H. Huxley, Alfred North Whitehead, Max Planck, and other theoretical physicists, with particular reference to Stevens's poems in *The Rock*.

Allison Ensor's " 'Tennessee' in Wallace Stevens' 'Anecdote of the Jar' " (*SHR* 7 [1973]:315–21) relates the poet's visits to Tennessee in the year before the poem was written, and his ambivalence about the state, to the ambivalence within the poem.

John Killinger, in his *The Fragile Presence* (Philadelphia: Fortress Press [1973]), uses Stevens's attitude of achieving "wonder" through an accumulation of the finite and detailed as an example of the modern artist's approach to religion. Like Roethke, whom Killinger also discusses, Stevens treated this "apprehension of the whole" as "a transcendent act of mind, a moment of vision in which the act of reality behind or beyond the existences of discrete or individual objects is grasped and exalted." Stevens's term for this was "major reality" (p. 105). More pagan than Tillich's "ultimate reality," Killinger yet finds affinities between modern artistic concepts like this of Stevens's and more doctrinaire statements of religious belief.

Louis Zukofsky's remarks on Stevens ("Addenda to *Prepositions: The Collected Critical Essays*," *JML* 4:91–104) stress his enduring quality, not for his philosophical wisdom or importance so much as for his inherently poetic quality ("an instant certainty of the words of a poem bringing . . . peoples together").

Isabel G. MacCaffrey provides valuable readings of some of the 25 poems included in *The Rock*, the last section of *Collected Poems*, which never saw separate book publication ("A Point of Central Arrival: Stevens' *The Rock*," *ELH* 40:606–33). She considers this group Stevens's "final soliloquy," "the concluding movement in the dialogue of a mind with itself," "an old poet's dream." Discussing the group structurally, she finds that its organization and themes are integral to the "whole of *Harmonium*."

William Bevis suggests one means of reading several of Stevens's troublesome poems in "Stevens' Toneless Poetry" (*ELH* 41:257–86). What Bevis means by *toneless* is poems that "convey no feeling" but rather "they articulate a non-feeling state of consciousness. The poet is neither affirming, denying, nor caring." He includes in his discussion "A Snow Man," "A Clear Day and No Memories," "The Course of a Particular," "Of Mere Being," "Not Ideas About the Thing but the Thing Itself," and "The Plain Sense of Things."

In a broad discussion of modern poetry, Eugene P. Nassar uses Stevens's belief in art as the product of an ordering imagination, yet undercut by the sense that such a belief is "pretend" as the basis for his reading of poems by Williams, Frost, Pound, Hart Crane, and Stevens ("Illusion as Value: An Essay on a Modern Poetic Idea," *Mosaic* 7, iv:109–23). Because such a dichotomy is somewhat discomforting, Nassar finds a dark tone even "beneath the gaiety and bravura of surface in much of his early poetry."

Leonora Woodman, in "'A Giant on the Horizon': Wallace Stevens and the 'Idea of Man'" (*TSLL* 15:759–86), finds Stevens's later poems failures because they only "dimly apprehend" a "realm of order." Stevens seems content to find this order in his art, at times; again—in the later poems—that "supreme fiction" does not appear to satisfy him. Woodman comments on his use of rhetorical questions, traces his definition of "pure poetry" through his writings (with emphasis on "Ananke," Stevens's symbol for the essential imagination), and concludes by finding the poet's ambivalence toward the "supreme fiction" disquieting.

Important information appears in J. M. Edelstein's "The Poet as Reader: Wallace Stevens and His Books," *BC* 23:53–68. Other essays dealing with the interpretation of single poems are *"The Man with the Blue Guitar* by Wallace Stevens" (*LHY* 14[1973]:49–60) in which Akhtar Oamber discusses the poem's connection with Picasso's *The Guitarist*, exhibited in 1934 in Hartford, Connecticut; Carol Flake's "Wallace Stevens' 'Peter Quince at the Clavier': Sources and Structure," *ELN* 12:116–20; Robert F. Fleissner's "Stevens' 'Of the Surface of Things': An Echo of Faust," *AN&Q* 12:115–16; Philip Furia's "Nuances of a Theme by Milton: Wallace Stevens' 'Sunday Morning,'" *AL* 46:83–87; and Peter L. McNamara's "Wallace Stevens' Autumnal Doctrine," *Renascence* 26:72–82, which discusses "The Auroras of Autumn."

iii. William Carlos Williams

In addition to the Juhasz book reviewed in the previous section, Ron Loewinsohn edited and introduced Williams's 1928–30 manuscript, *The Embodiment of Knowledge* (Norfolk, Conn.: New Directions), and two other critical books appeared. *William Carlos Williams*, ed. Charles Angoff (Rutherford, N.J.: Fairleigh Dickinson Univ. Press) consists of four papers presented as the Levertov lectures. With the exception of Emily Wallace's essay on Williams's use of tree imagery in his poems, the papers are thin. Kenneth Burke discusses Williams's fragmentation, contrasting his dissociative process with Conrad Aiken's *Ideenflucht*, and comparing it to modern traffic. Norman Holmes Pearson comments briefly on the people using the Williams Collection at Yale; A. M. Sullivan speaks of Williams as humanist.

Joseph Riddel's *The Inverted Bell: Modernism and the Counter-poetics of William Carlos Williams* (Baton Rouge: La. State Univ. Press) attempts a purely critical approach to Williams's work. Even though Riddell states that he is interested in Williams's poetics rather than his poems, beginning with a long discussion of Claude Lévi-Strauss and Jacques Derrida provides a cumbersome introduction at best. The relationship between these critics and Williams is never explained; the composite seems little more than arbitrary.

My chief objection to the book is that Riddel discusses very little of Williams's poetry and poetics (toward the end of the book, he does include some segments of *Paterson,* "Asphodel," and other of the late poems). As far as Williams's poetics is concerned, whenever Riddel needs a buttressing quote, he turns to Stevens or—in what is surely a first for literary criticism—to Charles Olson. Most often, in the critical first half of his book, Riddel gives us Heidegger's criticisms of Hölderlin's poems.

Riddel's chief objection to Williams's expressions of his own poetics is his "naivete and lack of rigor that repels systematic thinkers." The inherent contradiction between Riddel's opinion and the very poetics he is yet somehow drawn to explicate may prevent this study from being satisfying.

A valuable bibliographic addition to work in Williams studies is Neil E. Baldwin's and Steven L. Myers's "The Manuscripts and Letters of William Carlos Williams in the Poetry Collection of the Lockwood Memorial Library, SUNY at Buffalo: A Descriptive Catalogue," available from the Lockwood Library. Craig A. Lahm also lists "Additions to *A Bibliography of William Carlos Williams* by Wallace" in *Serif* 11,ii:40–43.

Bernard I. Duffey's important essay, "The Experimental Lyric in Modern Poetry: Eliot, Pound, Williams" (*JML* 3:1085–1103) stresses the similarities between Williams and the other poets. *Paterson* is also a discontinuous lyric, like *Cantos* and *The Waste Land,* having as its subject "uncertainty of feeling." "The three poets are all equally in the business of filling out the basic poetic questions of the times: how to feel, how to say?"

By using four manuscript versions of the opening of *Paterson* I, Douglass F. Fiero concludes that the concept of the poet-persona was the transforming element that helped Williams make *Paterson* into more than a patchwork of physical details ("Williams Creates the First Book of *Paterson, JML,* 3:965–86). A short appendix lists the four versions, from the Yale and Buffalo collections.

D. B. Graham comments on Howells's *Their Wedding Journey* (1871), which also uses the Sam Patch legend as an image of American daring in "A Note on Howells, Williams, and the Matter of Sam Patch," *NConL* 4:10–13.

Two essays point to specific themes within Williams's poetics: "Flowers and the Unicorn in *Paterson*" by Robert Davis (*Graduate English Papers* 6:28–33) and Charles Doyle's "Kora and Venus: Process and Object in William Carlos Williams" (*Person* 17:189–97). Hugh Fox summarizes much of the poet's poetic in "The Genuine Avant-Garde: William Carlos Williams' Credo," *SwR* 59:285–99. Emphasizing the "Prologue" to *Kora in Hell*, Fox finds its importance in "dismissing Eliotesque and Poundian posturing," and seeing "the real function of the imagination as breaking through the alienation of the near at hand and reviving its wonder." Fox has reservations about Williams's ultimate work, however, finding some of it marred by cloddish realism (the novels), but considers the writing of the 1920s important to any concept of avant-garde writing.

iv. Theodore Roethke

Richard A. Blessing's *Theodore Roethke's Dynamic Vision* (Bloomington: Ind. Univ. Press) is a good account of the poet's theory and practice, with special attention to Roethke's ability to convey the effect of motion or dynamism while writing in traditional metric forms. Blessing sees the real sense of a Roethke poem to lie beyond " 'thinky-think' " or content, to be connected inextricably with the movement of the whole: as Roethke liked to say, "Motion is equal to emotion.' "

Blessing divides his study into three sections: the earliest Roethke (undergraduate poems and essays); the greenhouse-childhood poems; and the later sequences, in which he is particularly interested. He makes much good use of unpublished materials from the University of Washington collection and furnishes important and accurate insights into Roethke's poetic process.

Among the essays dealing with Roethke's work, Dennis E. Brown's "Theodore Roethke's 'Self-World' and the Modernist Position" (*JML* 3:1239–54) is an important step toward defining the nature of identity within the poetry. In contrast to Eliot and Pound, who wrestled with the concepts of selfhood posed by Henri Bergson and William James, Roethke developed "his exploration of the self-world from within," offering by this process "a way back to a sane relationship between self and world," a relationship ultimately based on love.

Brian Swann agrees with Brown's view of Roethke's "process," at least an early stage of it, as described in his "Theodore Roethke and 'The Shift of Things,'" *LitR* 17:269–86. Using poems from the earlier periods, Swann demonstrates the poet's concept "'that to go forward as a spiritual man it is necessary first to go back. . . . Are not some experiences so powerful and so profound . . . that they repeat themselves . . . each time bringing us closer to our own most particular (and thus more universal) reality?'"

The Roethke chapter in John Vernon's *The Garden and the Map: Schizophrenia in Twentieth Century Literature and Culture* (Urbana: Univ. of Ill. [1973]) presents Roethke's personal and poetic vision of world as garden. Vernon sees the poems in *Praise to the End!* as illustrating sane schizophrenia. Unfortunately, the world created in the poems "is a total alternative to the dualistic structures of classical Western thought."

A structuralist approach is taken in Bernard Heringman's "Roethke's Poetry: The Forms of Meaning," *TSLL* 16:567–83; and several other essays treat the poems from thematic and mythic perspectives: Anthony Libby's incisive "Roethke, Water Father," *AL* 46:267–88, and William V. Davis's "Fishing an Old Wound: Theodore Roethke's Search for Sonship," *AntigR* 20:29–41.

v. Olson, Ginsberg, Duncan, Zukofsky, Blackburn, Dorn

George Butterick's *Olson: The Journal of the Charles Olson Archives* includes several critical essays as well as primary items. No. 1 (Spring) contains the moving "Robert Duncan, Letter to Jess after his last visit to Olson in New York Hospital, 1970," pp. 4–6; an August 1969 interview with Olson by Herbert A. Kenny ("'I know a man for whom everything matters,'" pp. 7–44), rich in comments about Cape Ann and Gloucester; and the first part of Butterick's annotated list of books important to the poet: "Olson's Reading: A Preliminary Report (A–C)," pp. 54–82. Items D–G are included in No. 2 (Fall), pp. 70–96, along with items from Black Mountain College. Butterick has also edited *Charles Olson, Additional Prose: A Bibliography on America, Proprioception & Other Notes & Essays* (Bolinas, Calif.: Four Seasons Foundation). Among the miscellaneous writing is Olson's review of Creeley's *For Love*.

Among essays on Olson (in addition to the special Olson issue of

Boundary 2, reviewed in *ALS 1973*) are several excellent pieces. Robert von Hallberg's "Olson's Relation to Pound and Williams" (*ConL* 15:15–48) carefully documents the relationships among the three poets, considering them as "post or anti-symbolists." Drawing from unpublished material, von Hallberg presents Olson's objections to the older writers (*Paterson*, for example, did not reach far enough back into time, and Williams's view of New Jersey was too pastoral). Steve Ballew emphasizes that Olson's use of history as both character and place is the connecting strain that unifies the *Maximus* poems. Olson's epic he finds "open" and "unfinished" but possessed of "exciting range" ("History as Animated Metaphor in *The Maximus Poems*," *NEQ* 47:51–64).

Gordon Ball has edited *Allen Verbatim: Lectures on Poetry, Politics, Consciousness by Allen Ginsberg* (New York: McGraw-Hill). As the subtitle indicates, Ginsberg's interviews and lectures include comments on politics, war, consciousness, survival, and recent poetry. He speaks of his reverence for Pound ("the greatest poet of the age"), Williams, Blake, Kerouac, Stein, and makes helpful remarks about John Ashbery (his poems are marked by "the gaiety of improvisation") and Kerouac (his work is distinguished by "the musical sequence" of American speech).

For James F. Mersmann (*Vietnam Vortex*, pp. 31–75) Ginsberg remains a central figure for the 1960s and 1970s (not "the best" and "not typical," however). In "Allen Ginsberg: Breaking Out," Mersmann describes the crash through the palings of convention that Ginsberg finally achieved, but only after years of restraint and terror. A close reading of *Empty Mirror* provides explanation for the poet's analysis of life's evils as "lacklove." For Ginsberg, war was just another of those evils, and he censured it in the same terms he did other social problems. Mersmann sees "Howl," for example, as "a vehement anti-war poem" because it attacks the myriad of "controls." He finds Ginsberg's best protest poem—emphatic in its seeming casualness—to be "Wichita Vortex Sutra."

Diane Middlebrook ("Bound Each to Each," *Parnassus* 2:128–35) agrees with Mersmann's interpretation of the early Ginsberg as she reviews two collections of his early poems. For her the poet's process of development was maturation, although she admires some of the poems in *The Gates of Wrath*.

Mersmann's chapter on Robert Duncan (*Vietnam Vortex*, pp.

159–204) is a clear, cogent introduction to this still largely ignored poet. In "Robert Duncan: Irregular Fire—Eros Against Ahriman," Mersmann locates the difficulty of Duncan's poems not so much in their many allusions as in "the aura of the mythic that invades the language at all levels." Duncan's themes are cyclic, most of them oriented around love; and his vision, syncretic. As part of his thematic concentration, his protest poems are affirmative rather than satiric. Mersmann discusses three other central concepts in the poems: green flowering, the dance, and "the unthinking ready thing."

The *JML* "Gathering" for Louis Zukofsky (4:74–108) includes three essays by Zukofsky (one mentioned in the Stevens section of this chapter) and two essays on the poet's work. Philip R. Yannella sees Zukofsky's work as "wonderfully balanced . . . a poetry insistently possessed of a voice like no other even while it is very much a part of a tradition." He emphasizes the 700-page poem "A," then nearing completion ("On Louis Zukofsky"). Hayden Carruth affirms Yannella's excitement by allowing that Zukofsky may have some problems with verbosity and attenuation, but beyond that "*all* his words inhere" ("The Only Way to Get There from Here").

Guy Davenport's essay "Zukofsky's 'A'–24" (*Parnassus* 2:15–24) stresses the poet's acceptance everywhere but in his own country and claims that he is a "poet's poet's poet," perhaps "the last man of the great generation of . . . 1914, the inventors of the art of the century." See also the special Zukofsky issue of *Maps*, 5 (1973).

Clayton Eshleman reviews Paul Blackburn's poetry in "A Mint Quality," *Boundary* 2, 2:640–48, describing it as "modest," "unassertive, almost passive, yet sturdy." He finds Blackburn's handling of the line adept and is interested in the way Blackburn's visionary poems are likely to "forecast experience-chains" for his own life. M. L. Rosenthal comments that Blackburn was "probably our finest poet of city life since Kenneth Fearing," but he is most impressed by Blackburn's range, his "lyric scope and many-sided sensibility" ("Paul Blackburn, Poet," *NYTBR* 11 Aug.:27).

Ross Feld laments the kind of inattention Blackburn's work has received in "It May Even All Be Alright," *Parnassus* 2:73–86, pointing to his similarities with Pound, Williams, and Zukofsky and describing the greater range of his work.

The first issue of an interesting literary-critical journal was devoted to the work of Ed Dorn. *Vort* (Fall 1972) included essays by

Donald Davie, Robert Kelly, Tom Raworth, and the editor, Barry Alpert. Subsequent issues of the journal have treated the writing of Ted Berrigan, Anselm Hollo, David Bromige, Ken Irby, Fielding Dawson, Jonathan Williams, Robert Kelly, Gilbert Sorrentino, and Donald Phelps.

vi. Schwartz, Kunitz, Jarrell, Nemerov, Merton

Richard McDougall's *Delmore Schwartz* (TUSAS 243) is a complete, generally well-documented book. Sympathetic though McDougall is to Schwartz's life and problems, he admits early that the writer eventually passed into manic-depressive and paranoid madness, although his poetry remained sound: "At their best, Schwartz's creative work and his criticism show a wholeness of vision and a soundness of judgment that put both on the side of sanity and light. By formal means, by means of art, he was able to transcend his bias and to present a vision of modern life that has a wide relevance" (p. 16).

William Barrett reminisces at length in "Delmore, a '30s Friendship and Beyond" (*Commentary* 58,iii:41–54), capturing Schwartz's seemingly boundless promise, his growing anxieties, and tense relationships from the 1930s on. (Barrett also gives some attention to Paul Goodman.) Lila Lee Valenti discusses unpublished material discovered after Schwartz's death in 1966 in "The Apprenticeship of Delmore Schwartz" (*TCL* 20:201–16). She too notes his amazing ability in all genres, and gives special attention to the early "Sonnets" and "Songs," some reprinted here.

Three interviews with the influential Stanley Kunitz were published in 1974: one with Michael Ryan (*IR* 5:76–85); one with Cynthia Davis (*ConL* 15:1–14); and one in Selden Rodman's *Tongues of Fallen Angels* (Norfolk, Conn.: New Directions), pp. 93–111.

In addition to dissertations, several essays focused on Randall Jarrell's poetry. Russell Fowler, writing in "Randall Jarrell's 'Eland': A Key to Motive and Technique in His poetry," *IR* 5:113–26, notes that, while Jarrell's criticism is highly esteemed, critics appear divided on judgment of his poems, at least partly because they fit no "school." Fowler sees his pervasive mode to be "an insistence on unfettered improvisation, an absolute refusal to be systematic or to provide a theoretical or symbolic paradigm for his own work." Jarrell's poetry is "emotional and quasi-mystical." Frances C. Ferguson comments on the wide range of his poems and attitudes in "Randall Jarrell and the Flotations of Voice" in *GaR* 28:423–39.

Raymond Smith's essay "Nemerov and Nature: 'The Stillness in Moving Things'" (*SoR* 10:153–69) sees Nemerov as one of our most distinctive voices, especially in his meditative mode, with nature his concern. Close attention is given to "Runes" and "Blue Swallows." In Nemerov's view, however, man always remains outside nature.

Marquita Breit's *Thomas Merton: A Bibliography* (Metuchen, N.J.: The Scarecrow Press and American Theological Library Association) includes both primary and secondary materials, with a biographical introduction by Brother Patrick Hart, O.C.S.O. A relatively general essay is Dennis Q. McInerny, "Thomas Merton and the Awakening of Social Consciousness" (*AmerS* 15:37–53), while Michael W. Higgins follows Merton's interest in Blake (his M.A. thesis was on Blake's poetry) in "A Study of the Influence of William Blake on Thomas Merton" (*ABR* 25:377–88).

vii. Robert Lowell and John Berryman

A large amount of critical activity was in evidence this year. Lowell's publication of three books, several controversial, and Berryman's relatively recent death triggered a veritable landslide of criticism, some of it excellent. Alan Williamson's book *Pity the Monsters, The Political Vision of Robert Lowell* (New Haven, Conn.: Yale Univ. Press) has as thesis the premise that Lowell's private poems served as a means of his social understanding, that the self-analytical and the public poems are interdependent. Williamson considers "politics" in the large sense of life-view, and proceeds by close readings of many poems from early collections as well as *Near the Ocean* and *Notebook*. He points out examples of "excessive adolescent hatred" in the otherwise controlled, innovative early poems, and reiterates the importance of *Life Studies* to American poetry per se. After that collection, Williamson contends that Lowell had to forge a new public conscience, one he sees as fairly unpredictable yet authoritative, based on both experience and psychoanalytic thought. The progression is described in this segment (p. 111): "In *Near the Ocean*, Lowell's stance becomes more dynamic and ambivalent, partly because his direct juxtaposition of political and confessional material brings more personal feelings into play, and partly because the issues are timely and pressing ones: the war in Vietnam, racism, police brutality. *Near the Ocean* both extends the psycho-political themes of *For the Union Dead* . . . and partly transcends its bad conscience about political belief and anger." Williamson finds *Notebook*, as well, to be a way of Lowell's achieving his own poetic language, and therefore a highly satisfying achievement.

John F. Crick's *Robert Lowell* (New York: Barnes & Noble) is meant to be an introductory book. Crick covers much of Lowell's published writing, using as approach biography (and seeing that Lowell in 1973 has experienced a career that "suggests an agonised Prometheus tied to a rock of tragic contemporary experience"). In addition to this kind of chronological method, Crick relates Lowell's poetics to those of Williams, and also sees the later work created by an imagination perhaps dangerously out of control but still viable. Crick sees the "liberated sonnets" of the last books as previewing an important direction for contemporary poetics.

Among the essays of interest this year are Arthur Oberg's "I Am To Myself, and My Troubled Self Sings" (*OhR* 15:108–11), a review of Lowell's three 1973 books as presenting "serious aesthetic and moral problems." The "best poems are powerfully executed," but Oberg feels that the "long work is uneven and shaky." He concludes that the man and the life behind the poems are "too unsettled for him to make good poetry." On the other hand, Oberg finds Berryman's *Dream Songs* superior, even though the earlier Lowell poems are in some ways better than Berryman's entire canon.

Frances Ferguson's chapter in Shaw's *American Poetry Since 1960* ("Appointments with Time: Robert Lowell's Poetry through the Notebooks," pp. 15–28) sees that Lowell's poetry embodies the essence of modernity, "the thrust towards ever-more-direct confrontations with time." In his work imitation becomes one means of recapturing earlier confrontations, as does revision. In the later books Ferguson finds that the concern with time becomes an obsession, adding to an obscurity which had been present before but never so Hegelian. Other discussions of Lowell as both modern and political include Rosemary Sullivan's "Notebook: Robert Lowell as a Political Poet," *EA* 27:291–301 and Max Richards's "The Citizenship of Robert Lowell," *Meanjin* 33:201–06.

Readings of other Lowell work are also helpful. George Lensing studies Lowell's attitudes toward morality, toward man as fallible, and toward New England as historical continuity, finding them similar to Edwards's in "Robert Lowell and Jonathan Edwards: Poetry in the Hands of an Angry God," *SCR* 6:7–17. Lensing believes that Lowell's use of Edwards as subject in his poetry reveals a consistency in point of view that spans the three decades of his writing. Steven G. Axelrod ("Robert Lowell and the New York Intellectuals," *ELN* 11:206–09) discusses the poem of that title as it appears in the last three collections. An atypical poem (in its bitter and satirical tone), it has gained from various revisions. Axelrod sees the poem as Lowell's farewell to New York.

"*Lowell* Had Been Misspelled *Lovel*," *IR* 5:98–121, is a major assessment of the poet through his 1973 collections. Arthur Oberg sees Lowell caught squarely amid the "difficulties of the public and private art and life" and sees his poetics as a revelation of his need to take "extensive stock of who he is, where he is, and what he takes poetry to be." Despite his feeling that the quasi-sonnet form of the last poems is less effective than other of Lowell's experiments, Oberg finds the poet's importance to lie in his virtuosity, and not merely technical virtuosity. As Oberg describes Lowell: "He can be medieval in his obsession with last things, Renaissance in his admiration for the infinitely gifted man, classical or Augustan in his judgment and taste, Romantic and Victorian and Modern by turn. And it may be in his position as Modern that he tried to hold together what in any other age either never would have had to be reconciled, or would have been so overwhelming as to lead to madness or death" (p. 100).

J. M. Linebarger's *John Berryman* (TUSAS 244) is a careful study, hampered somewhat by the publishers' limitations on the amount of poetry to be quoted. Linebarger sees the sonnets and *Homage* as transitional, and *Dream Songs* as the culmination of Berryman's art, where certain qualities of both Beat and Academic poetry are evident. Occasional forced interpretations and a tendency toward overgeneralization are the book's weaknesses.

Edward Mendelson's essay in Shaw's *American Poetry Since 1960* ("How to Read Berryman's *Dream Songs*," pp. 29–44) warns against "explicating" the poems, an irony since one of the themes in them is Berryman's satire of critics. Mendelson points out the formal numerology and structure of the *Songs*, considering Berryman's theme—the idiosyncratic reveries of the old poet—his greatest risk. Boring as many of the poems are, Mendelson still considers this poem sequence "the most courageous and interesting poetic experiment of their decade."

Peter Stitt defines Berryman as more than a confessional poet because he maintains an important distance between his persona Henry and his own view of the poet—humor and candor are significant elements. This chronological survey in "John Berryman: The Dispossessed Poet" (*OhR* 15,ii:66–74) points to a continuing religious strain. Ultimately Stitt feels that even religion fails the poet, as do all the traditional answers.

Much insight into Berryman the person is gained through William Heyen's "John Berryman: A Memoir and an Interview," ibid., pp. 46–65. The memoir depicts Berryman during a 1970 visit; Jerome Mazzaro participated in the interview.

Michael Browne's "Henry Fermenting: Debts to the Dream Songs" (*OhR* 15,ii:75–87) considers Berryman's major poem a great achievement for its uses of language.

Ernest C. Stefanik, Jr., has compiled "A John Berryman Checklist" (*BB* 31:1–4, 28) and the full *John Berryman: A Descriptive Bibliography* (Pittsburgh: Univ. of Pittsburgh Press). Stefanik also edits the new *John Berryman Studies*, a quarterly devoted to essays on Berryman and other middle-generation poets (805 W. First Ave., Derry, Pa.). The first numbers will be reviewed in *ALS 1975*.

viii. Dickey, Stafford, Berry, Ignatow

Three dissertations on James Dickey's poetry and several essays about his novel *Deliverance* indicate the continuing interest in this relatively controversial poet. Michael Mesic's "A Note on James Dickey" (*American Poetry Since 1960*, pp. 145–53) describes the poet as creating a poetry of "the common man," a male unfortunately much too indoctrinated with the harsh American ethic of masculinity. Mesic suggests that perhaps the prose and subject of *Deliverance* is more suitable for Dickey than poetic forms.

In contrast, Joyce Carol Oates sees Dickey as our age's Whitman. Damned with the heritage of one generation, admittedly masculine, he survives into another, recording the process with brutal honesty. She describes Dickey's poetry as rarely confessional but "always personal—at times contemplative, at times dramatic." Oates discusses the continuum of his work, finding most interesting his exploration into an "otherness"; most pervasive, his view of "life-as-battle" and "man-as-combatant" ("Out of Stone into Flesh: The Imagination of James Dickey," *MPS* 5:97–144).

David C. Berry's view of Dickey is in an orphic configuration, connecting the world of the living and the dead, particularly the dead of his family, for the purpose of finding continuity ("Harmony with the Dead: James Dickey's Descent into the Underworld," *SoQ* 12:233–44.

Many of the most interesting essays on Dickey written from 1965 to 1971, and several unpublished ones, have been collected by Richard J. Calhoun in *James Dickey: The Expansive Imagination* (Deland, Fla.: Everett/Edwards [1973]). Opening with "A Conversation with James Dickey" by Carolyn Kizer and James Boatwright, the book contains essays by Peter Davidson, H. L. Weatherby, Laurence Lieberman, Thomas O. Sloan, Daniel B. Marin, Richard Kostelanetz, and two essays by Calhoun. The new material includes essays by Arthur Gregor (on Dickey as romantic), William J. Martz (on "Cherrylog Road"), Robert W. Hill (on Dickey as comic poet), George Lensing (on Dickey's imagination), and Paul Ramsey (on meter and structure in the poetry). The book conludes with a checklist by Robert W. Hill.

John Lauber treats the poems of William Stafford with perception in "World's Guest—William Stafford," *IR* 5:88–99. He sees that the poems reveal various "pieties," toward earth, region, home, parents, a man's "total past." As Stafford himself wrote in 1970, "poetry, the stance that accepts, may be salvational."

Richard Howard discusses *Someday, Maybe* ("Ecstasies and Decorum," *Parnassus* 2:217–20) as the work of a minor poet. Disappointed because "the poems accumulate but they do not *grow*; they drift like snowflakes into a great and beautiful body of canceling work," Howard sees Stafford as positioned where he was a decade ago. Bernard F. Engel, writing in "On Nailing the Octopus; or, On Midwestern Popular Poetry" (*Midwestern Miscellany* 1:21–27), explains this sameness in Stafford's poems because the poet's view remains the same—"semi-religious," firmly grounded in the beliefs and attitudes of the postmodern, Midwestern generation. Engel sees the Stafford persona as "not alienated" but "typically alone."

Edwin Fussell assesses the writing of Wendell Berry in his essay "Farm Poets and Garage Critics" (*Parnassus* 2:25–32). Locating him as a "Farm Poet," claiming that rewards go to the genre writers who can be so distinguished, Fussell seems to object to Berry's subjects, the brevity of his poems, and his way of life. Morgan Speer also places Berry's prose and poetry in the farmer-agrarian tradition of Thoreau, finding his growth chronological and thematic: "a steady clarification" leading to a growing concern with death. His interest in death is, however, positive because he is a moralist: "he constructs an ideal according to the life he is trying to lead" ("Wendell Berry: A Fatal Singing," *SoR* 10:865–77). John Ditsky too admires Berry's theme—"the continuity of life in Nature"—and his work in "Love as a Farm and a Forest," *MPS* 5:92–93.

A major essay on David Ignatow, "Earth-Hard: The Poetry of David Ignatow" by Ralph J. Mills, Jr., appeared in *Boundary 2*, 2:373–429. Mills stresses that Ignatow is both a lyric poet interested in the self and a social one fascinated by New York. The quality of "personal meditation," however, characterizes both. A more than usually informative interview with Ignatow was published in *Boundary 2*, 2:442–81. Beginning and closing with Ignatow's poetics, this "dialogue" between the poet and William Spanos covers the range of modern poetry and its great figures. Also of interest is "David Ignatow Talks to Galen Williams" (the director of Poets & Writers, Inc.) in *APR* 3, iv:43–47.

ix. Bly, Wright, Kinnell, Snyder

Alan Williamson's grouping of these four poets in his essay "Language Against Itself: the Middle Generation of Contemporary Poets" (*American Poetry Since 1960*, pp. 55–68) provides a new location for the "middle generation" label (previously used for Lowell, Berryman, Schwartz, etc.) Williamson finds parallels among these poets in these areas: (1) language as "at least as much the enemy as the facilitator of essential creativity"; (2) a concern with the literally primitive as a means of new information; (3) a search for simplicity in language and structure, both sentence and poem; (4) presentation of a vision that is both philosophically and aesthetically whole, pure. Williamson finds these writers in a group by themselves, not influencing the younger writers to any great extent—for various reasons.

In Robert Bly's essays, his concern with the second and third points are particularly clear. "The Network and the Community," one of his columns for *APR* (3,i:19–21), discusses the ways people relate to each other, and some of Bly's interpretations of Freud and Jung. *Field* (no. 10:31–35) includes his notes, "Reflections on the Origins of Organic Form," his reply to an essay by Donald Hall. Hall reviewed a recent collection ("Notes on Robert Bly and *Sleepers Joining Hands*," *OhR* 15, i[1973]:89–93) and termed Bly "the most systematic poet in the U.S." (with Gary Snyder a close second), describing them both as "learned, eclectic priests . . . born teachers." He also describes Bly (and Kinnell) as poets "of the soul's journey."

James F. Mersmann's chapter on Bly ("Robert Bly: Watering the Rocks," *Vietnam Vortex*, pp. 113–57) stresses his effective political poems that benefit from his sometimes irritating single-mindedness. He finds Bly outside the groups of most contemporary poets because "Bly's interest has always been with content rather than form, and life rather than 'art' " (p. 116). Perhaps the increasing interest in Bly signals the end of the craft-oriented poetics of the 1960s (although the deluge of work being done on the Black Mountain poets would tend to indicate not a death of interest, perhaps more a modification). Mersmann does object to Bly's "easy" stone-throwing, his tendency to find simple reasons for complex economic and political situations; but he finds the image patterns in Bly's poems—related nearly always to his pervasive life-view—important new avenues for subsequent writers.

Among the essays on James Wright, Cor van den Heuvel's "The Poetry of James Wright" (*Mosaic* 7:163–70) is most affirmative. Seeing Wright as a very strong poet, able to explore both inner and outer worlds, van den Heuvel considers him a "classicist," a craftsman who can put the traditional devices of his art to new uses. Edward Butscher's opinion differs, however ("The Rise and Fall of James Wright," *GaR* 28:257–68). He finds the late poems to be "almost embarrassing in their lack of sensitivity and basic poetic skill." He objects primarily to Wright's attitudes which are conducive to "sentimentality" and "self-indulgence," and sees his returning to Ohio themes as lacking in "good taste." Belle M. McMaster's "James Arlington Wright: A Checklist" appeared in *BB* 31:71–82, 88.

Interest in Galway Kinnell remains high since the 1971 publication of *The Book of Nightmares*. Arthur Oberg's "The One Flea

Which Is Laughing" (*Shenandoah*, 25[Fall 1973]:85–91) calls the long poem "major poetry," inspired by some terrible "inner generosity." "If it is a violent, dark dreams book, it is also a gentle book." John Hobbs discusses "Galway Kinnell's 'The Bear': Dream and Technique" in *MPS* 5:237–50 as an allegory of the poet, and perhaps man, feeling that coming to grips with Kinnell's longer poems is important in realizing his whole vision. William Thompson attempts to discuss the complete Kinnell in his essay "Synergy in the Poetry of Galway Kinnell" (*Gypsy Scholar* 1,ii:52–70). Thompson is concerned with the imagery, diverse yet compatible, and the effect of transcendence that Kinnell's poems produce. He reads the major recent poems, and concludes that *Body Rags* is primarily a quest; 'The Bear' is the culmination of that quest; *The Book of Nightmares* is a song for the poet's daughter: a story of mistakes made, searches undertaken . . . and a message from the present to the future . . . a meditation." A dissenting view, in part, comes from *Parnassus* as Donald Davie questions the overemphasis in Kinnell's poetry on the spiritual confusion of modern man ("Slogging for the Absolute," 2:9–22). Davie prefers *Flower Herding on Mount Monadnock* of all the collections.

Ben Pleasants's "Ontology of Language in the Poems of Eliot & Snyder" (*Tuatara* 12:53–63) relates Snyder's pilgrimage to Eliot's, finding that Snyder moved from "phenomenologist induction into silence," while Eliot moved from meaning to ritual. He connects Snyder's vision with Zen, Fenollosa, and American Indian beliefs, concluding that his final poetry will be word pictures that end in silence. Nathan Mao adds depth to this suggestion with his "The Influence of Zen Buddhism on Gary Snyder," *TkR* 5:125–33; and Rudolph L. Nelson's essay " 'Riprap on the Slick Rock of Metaphysics': Religious Dimensions in the Poetry of Gary Snyder," *Soundings* 57:206–21, places Snyder as prophet, writing as a "voice from our wilderness," and by his emphasis on Zen and Indian beliefs adding this aspect to other kinds of contemporary statement. Snyder's recent collection of poems, *Turtle Island* (Norfolk, Conn.: New Directions), includes prose sections on the need for change in population, pollution, and the general physical condition of this earth. Another essay is titled "Energy Is Eternal Delight," and others are on teaching and poetry.

x. Levertov, Plath, Sexton, Rich, Wakoski, Bogan, and Others

James F. Mersmann's chapter on Denise Levertov ("Denise Levertov: Piercing In," *Vietnam Vortex*, pp. 77–112) suggests that whereas *"balanced* and *whole"* were adjectives that characterized her earlier poetry, the protest work has been important because it has intensified her view of life's mystery, *claritas*. Mersmann posits that intellect has outweighed feeling and mystery in Levertov's poetics, yet those other elements are also present, and intellect in her case is pitched at its highest manifestation: the "clean, precise perception that arises from attending closely while the will is quieted and the intellect is warmed by the emotions" (p. 78). Because she saw war as "ultimate unreason and disorder," her poems against it were angry, unforgiving, and perhaps no longer balanced. Mersmann feels that she is being true to her original vision, although perhaps the poetry has suffered because of her alienation during the war period.

Hayden Carruth (in "Levertov," *HudR* 27:475–80) defends even the later poems and finds them revelations of Levertov's "good sense and practical wisdom," based always in a neoplatonism. He thinks the title essay of the *Poet in the World* should be every modern writer's credo. New insights into the Levertov background appear in Ronald Younkins's "Denise Levertov and the Hasidic Tradition," *Descant* 19,i:40–48.

Peggy Rizza points out in her essay, "Another Side of Life: Women as Poets," *American Poetry Since 1960*, pp. 167–79, that women have concerns as poets that may differ appreciably from their lives as women. Since the trend in contemporary poetics, however, has been to the personal, the obvious differences in women's lives and preoccupations should have been more noticeable in current poetry. Rizza considers Elizabeth Bishop, Anne Sexton, Maxine Kumin, and Mona Van Duyn, and pleads for evaluation as poets, on the basis of work, instead of on autobiography or genre.

Sylvia Plath is the obvious example of the woman poet judged exclusively as female, with the connotations of hysteria and submission that Rizza mentions. One of the best essays on Plath was Anthony Libby's dual treatment, "God's Lioness and the Priest of Sycorax: Plath and Hughes," *ConL* 15:386–405. Drawing on all the poetry of both Plath and Ted Hughes, Libby points to similarities (and possible influences) and differences. Plath's immersion, and transcendence, in nature, and Hughes's greater tendency toward violence and animal imagery are seen as central; Libby feels that myth and earth-mother imagery provide the key to both poets' work. D. F. McKay's "Aspects of Energy in the Poetry of Dylan Thomas and Sylvia Plath" (*CritQ* 16:53–68) explains part of the semantic difficulty of both poets as corollary of their terriffic vitality, evident in speed, sudden shifts of images, and suprasyntax. A thematic reading is Andrew Taylor's "Sylvia Plath's Mirror and Beehive," *Meanjin* 33:256–65; a descriptive approach is taken by M. D. Uroff in "Sylvia Plath's Women," *CP* 7,i:45–56; and the underlying tensions in her work are the basis for Deborah Ashford's "Sylvia Plath's Poetry: A Complex of Irreconcilable Antagonisms," *CP* 7,i:62–69. James E. Miller, Jr., in "The Creation of Women: Confessions of a Shaken Liberal" (*CR* 8:231–45) uses Plath's life and literary reception as "the best example we have . . . of what it means to grow up female and talented in this country, perhaps in the modern world."

Sylvia Plath and Anne Sexton: A Reference Guide by Cameron Northouse and Thomas P. Walsh (Boston: G. K. Hall) includes both primary and secondary materials. In addition to the many laments for Sexton in the aftermath of her suicide (one of interest being "Remembering Anne Sexton" by Erica Jong, *NYTBR* 27 Oct.:63), several essays that attempted to assess her writing positively also appeared: Robert R. Armstrong's "Sexton's *Transformations*: Beyond Confessionalism," *IEY* 24,iii:57–66 and Rise B. Axelrod's "The Transforming Art of Anne Sexton," *CP* 7,i:6–13.

Albert Gelpi assesses the poetry of Adrienne Rich in "The Poetics of Change," *American Poetry Since 1960*, pp. 123–43, finding in the changes in her poetry a paradigm for the changes in the 20 years of American poetry since World War II. Beyond the obvious move from the formalist, ironic structure to a free shape consonant with the poet's attitudes and themes, Gelpi finds that Rich's subjects have widened. Part of the change he attributes to her willingness to recognize "the animus as a power within herself through which psychic experience . . . can emerge into articulation." Her resulting "deepening subjectivity," however, has led not to withdrawal but to an increased involvement with other human beings.

Along with several dissertations, the work of Marianne Moore has been recognized in Gary Lane's *A Concordance to the Poems of Marianne Moore* (New York: Haskell House) and Maurice J. O'Sullivan's essay "Native Genius for Disunion: Marianne Moore's 'Spenser's Ireland,'" (*CP* 7, i:42–47. Louise Bogan is represented by *What the Woman Lived, Selected Letters of Louise Bogan, 1920–1970*, ed. Ruth Limmer (New York: Harcourt, Brace [1973]), a collection rich in literary history drawn from more than a thousand letters available.

Daniel J. Cahill's 1973 study, *Harriet Monroe* (TUSAS 222), provides a clear, accurate survey of the interesting history of *Poetry*, but his discussion of Monroe's own writing is so brief as to be inadequate. Cahill does reprint some of Monroe's poems and several of these, "At the Prado" and "A Power-Plant," suggest that her work is worth republishing.

Muriel Rukeyser's 1949 essay collection, *The Life of Poetry*, has been reissued in paperback by William Morrow & Co. Important as a poetics and a defense of poesy combined, the book bears interesting resemblances to Levertov's *Poet in the World*—and important differences as well. A good overview of Rukeyser's career is Virginia R. Terris's "Muriel Rukeyser: A Retrospective" (*APR* 3, iii:10–14). Rukeyser also considers Kafka's letters in the same issue of *APR* (pp. 8–9). Her continuing work suggests (and Terris finds this true also) that Rukeyser may endure like Whitman, whom she called "the poet of possibility," giving "the meanings of possibility, produced by his own age, their further meaning and image in poetry."

xi. O'Hara, Ammons, and Ashbery

Marjorie Perloff discusses O'Hara's work in "New Thresholds, Old Anatomies: Contemporary Poetry and the Limits of Exegesis," *IR* 5:83–99. She places his poetry in relation to his work as curator of the Museum of Modern Art rather than as symbolist, using his 1961 poem "Essay on Style" as illustration. Susan Holahan (in *American Poetry Since 1960*, pp. 109–22) considers O'Hara a New York poet increasingly concerned with time and its "separate moments"—hence, his poetics.

Arthur Oberg's comment on Ammons ("Frazzling Reality," *OhR* 15,iii:107–10) describes him as "one of our most important poets." Oberg sees that he uses Williams's "particularity" and Stevens's "relentless circling meditations" to create his own sense of world, "less edgy and more engaging" than it is for some poets.

Harold Bloom discusses "John Ashbery: The Charity of the Hard Moments" (*American Poetry Since 1960*, pp. 83–108), seeing the poet as a direct descendant of Stevens, his work characterized since 1956 by "a skeptical honesty, self-reflexive, and an odd faith in a near-inscrutable order." Dismissing the poems in *The Tennis-Court Oath*, Bloom reads the body of Ashbery's work as steady progress toward "Fragment," "the crown of *The Double Dream of Spring* and, for me, Ashbery's finest work" (p. 98).

Again faced with the problem of which poets to include in this increasingly overwhelming essay, I turn for conclusion to Harvey Gross's retrospective essay on the poetry of the 1960s ("The Problem of Style and the Poetry of the Sixties, *IR* 5:69–74). Gross finds most important during the decade of the 1960s the reemergence of Ezra Pound at the center of the American poetic tradition (reasserting the native line in American poetry, and emphasizing its antiintellec-tual qualities), rather than T. S. Eliot; and the new freedoms in form, voice (the abandonment, in many cases, of the persona), and metaphor ("very personal combinations," "a deepening of the Imag-ist method"). The poems of the 1970s might still be characterized by such a description, and in that kind of stasis, perhaps criticism will have a chance to catch up.

Michigan State University

18. Drama

Jordan Y. Miller

i. From the Beginning to the Early 20th Century

The early period, particularly the 19th century, received a rather high proportion of scholarly emphasis during 1974. The *Emerson Society Quarterly*'s third quarter issue is devoted entirely to a symposium on the subject and includes several excellent illustrations of leading theatrical personalities of the day such as the Hodgkinsons, Edwin Forrest, and others. The issue is introduced by Kent C. Gallagher (20:143–47) who justifies the symposium on the basis of learning how the early nation met some of its cultural needs in a theatre that was both entertainment and a straight business enterprise. Gallagher sees William Dunlap as attempting to move away from the still strong British influences and notes that the early Republic was probably prevented from developing a significant drama because of three factors: the economics of the theatre, the requirements of the Romantic school of acting, and the nature of the entertainment for which the public clamored.

The appeal of the first article, "Hodgkinson and His Rivals at the Park: The Business of Early Romantic Theatre in America" (20:148–69), by Billy J. Harbin, is mainly to theatre buffs who are historically and statistically minded with interests in the problems of moving into the new Park Row Theatre in 1797 and the various salaries received by the company ($100 a week for Hodgkinson) and such. The notorious Thomas Abthorpe Cooper receives considerable discussion, but so do several others. Critical reception of the performances is also discussed, with special emphasis on the comments of William Coleman of the New York *Evening Post*.

The second article, "The American Drama and Theatre in the Nineteenth Century: A Retreat from Meaning" (20:170–86), by William R. Reardon, advances some very practical reasons for the lack of dramatic achievement in the 19th century: lack of talented dramatists, an assumption that the age required farce, economic problems within the theatre business due to rapid changes and growth in the nation at the time, and the less felicitous nature of national topics for the drama. The third article, Kent Gallagher's "The Tragedies of George Henry Boker: The Measure of American Romantic Drama" (20:187–215) presents a good analysis of Boker as a Romantic decidedly different from the tradition of Bird's *The Gladiator* and Stone's *Metamora*. Boker's *Francesca da Rimini* receives the main emphasis as one play which brought American drama some early if not lasting distinction in diction, characterization, and action. The final item, "A Congress of Wonders: The Rise and Fall of the Dime Museum" by Brooks Mc-Namara (20:216–32), asserts the legitimacy of the freak shows as being in the tradition of popular entertainment and not merely a "quaint corruption" of the legitimate stage. Peale's, Barnum's, and Hanlon's museums were strictly American in origin, unique to the time and place. The article is certainly relevant these days in view of contemporary scholarly interest in popular culture.

In the same "popular" line is David L. Rinear's "Burlesque Comes to New York: William Mitchell's First Season at the Olympic" (*NCTR* 2:23–34), which is a fairly detailed account of what went on during the 1839–40 season, although one wonders if knowing all this about the subject is worth the effort. A bit more significant is the analysis in "The Minstrel Show as Theater of Misrule" (*QJS* 60:33–38) by Jules Zanger, who finds that there was a plainly evident two-way display of class and social prejudice in these theatre pieces. The elaborate costumes and pomposities of the interlocutor represented an attack on the educated classes, and the parodies of grand opera in particular represented a gross caricature of upper-class culture. Equally prejudicial was the stock parody of blacks through the end men of Tambo and Bones.

William Dunlap comes in for some interesting comments in two articles. One is a brief item by Gerald Argetsinger, "Dunlap's André: Beginning of American Tragedy" (*Players* 49:62–64), which reviews works that had impressed Dunlap such as *The Prince of Parthia*, *Ponteach*, and *The Contrast*. Argetsinger makes a strong attempt to justify André as a tragic hero who is destroyed as a result of a single fall from virtue which André himself understands and accepts. The obvious Romantic tragic tradition of the play, in a direct line with *Camille*, as Argetsinger admits, together with the patriotic "Hail

Columbia" aspects make it difficult to accept in full Argetsinger's view. More fascinating and certainly more controversial is "Dunlap, Kotzebue, and the Shaping of American Theater: A Reevaluation from a Marxist Perspective" by Jack Zipes (*EAL* 3:272–84). Here an admitted "party line" is taken which blames a great deal of our present commercial sentimentality and "kitsch" in contemporary stage, TV, and cinema on Dunlap's admiration for and production of his own translations of Kotzebue's Gothic "mellers." While Zipes asks that Dunlap be taken seriously for what he attempts in trying to be moral and beneficial in the entertainment he produced, Zipes notes the ultimate failure, and one seriously questions whether or not Zipes really proves that all of the flaws of our present mass entertainment are such direct linear descendants of the Dunlap-Kotzebue influence and tradition. The author himself admits that hardly anybody today knows anything about the two men anyway.

In a discussion of 19th-century American Romanticism Marlin J. Bennison and Barry B. Witham in "Sentimental Love and the Nineteenth Century American Drama" (*Players* 49:127–29) find that American plays presented an inversion of the traditional myth of Romance with the seducer becoming the seduced and the traditional female temptress becoming the pursued virgin. Despite the advances of the likes of *Margaret Fleming* and *Hazel Kirke* the author contends that most dramatists of the century maintained the underlying assumption of a moral view of world order, with values still placed on the Puritan work ethic. In his doctoral dissertation "Percy MacKaye's Vision of the National Drama as an Expression of the American Identity" (*DAI* 35:3764A, Kent State) Duncan J. Rollo finds MacKaye a "philosophic idealist," one who seeks to define the uniqueness of the American people through an indigenous drama, in contrast to the escapist-oriented commercial theatre of the day.

J. F. S. Smeal in "The Idea of Our Early National Drama" (*NDQ* 42,i:5–22) uses George Berkeley's "Westward the Course of Empire" as his thesis that somehow America is in the final act of empire in terms of Berkeley's four acts completed and one to go. The article is obviously based on considerable scholarly background, but it is not always clear. In view of the Continental Congress's Discontinuance Acts of 1774 and 1778, Smeal arrives at the speculation that perhaps early American plays were not meant to be staged at all but only to be read, but the reasoning does not seem convincing.

Tom Scanlan offers an interesting perspective on the Rip Van Winkle story in his "The Domestication of Rip Van Winkle: Joe Jefferson's Play as Prologue to Modern American Drama" (*VQR* 50:51–62). Rip is seen to prefigure the family plays of O'Neill, Miller, and Williams. This may be a bit hard to swallow, but Scanlan makes clear that the Jefferson adaptation softened and sentimentalized the Irving story and put considerable emphasis on the importance of family structure. Walter J. Meserve and R. I. Meserve provide some unique historical information in "Uncle Tom's Cabin and Modern Chinese Drama" (*MD* 17:57–66), noting that the beginning of modern drama in China was a 1907 production under the title "The Negro Slave Sighs to Heaven," the first full-length modern play ever produced by the Chinese.

Two items on James A. Herne contribute to the limited scholarship on this "first" American realist. Gene A. Saraceni in "Herne and the Single Tax: An Early Plea for an Actor's Union" (*ETJ* 26:315–25) provides considerable information about Herne's political activities and his active involvement with the idea of abolishing land ownership to provide more equal distribution of wealth. Corollary to this was Herne's interest in getting actors unionized, and Saraceni speculates that the Klaw and Erlanger syndicate might never have achieved its powers had the actors listened to Herne and organized earlier. John Perry in "Selected Bibliography on James A. Herne" (*BB* 31:50) does precisely as indicated and provides a useful bibliography of books and plays in which Herne was involved as well as criticism of his works appearing in the 1880s.

A variety of items of historical interest close out studies in the early era. Peter J. Ventimiglia's Fordham dissertation "The William Winter/Augustin Daly Shakespeare Productions, 1885–1898" (*DAI* 34:5127A) examines the direction that Shakespearean production was taking in the American theatre of the 19th century, particularly under Daly and under certain pressures from Winter as critic of the New York *Tribune*. Loren K. Ruff provides a history of the "moral lectures" and other stratagems in Boston in "Joseph Harper and Boston's Board Alley Theatre, 1792–1793" (*ETJ* 26:45–52). Robert Montilla in "The Building of the Lafayette Theatre" (*ThS* 14:105–29) goes into considerable detail with area maps, diagrams, and complete structural statistics in a thorough documentation of the story of this important structure. J. Dennis Rich and Kevin L. Seligman provide a complete history of the ill-fated but noble attempt to bring a truly national theatre into being in "The New Theatre of Chicago, 1906" (*ETJ* 26:53–68). Edward C. Powers in "Tommaso Salvini: An American Devotee's View" (*ThS* 15:130–42) reports on the detailed diaries kept by one Thomas R. Sullivan, a worshipper of the Italian performer who acted Othello during the time of Booth and Irving. In two highly specialized reports of interest mostly to regional readers we learn of many of the struggles of the frontier theatre. First, Douglas McDermott in "Touring Patterns on California's Frontier, 1849–1859" (*ThS* 15:18–28) involves the theatre outside San Francisco, including Sacramento, Nevada City, Sonora, and the like. The second, by Frederick W. Gilliard, "Theatre in Early Idaho: A Brief Review and Appraisal" (*Rendezvous* 8,i:25–31) makes some interesting observations on the insights into frontier attitudes which touring companies provided in the generally crude impersonations of blacks and Chinese, but, oddly enough, not the Indians. Finally, Faye E. Head discusses the very specialized situation of "The Theatrical Syndicate *vs.* the Child Labor Law of Louisiana" (*LaS* 13:365–74).

ii. The Modern Period

The entire issue of *Yale Theatre* for spring 1974 was devoted to improvisational theatre under the collective title "Tonight We Improvise," with an introduction by Rocco Landesman and Robert Marx (5:6–9). Two articles are worthy of special note. Lee Gallup Feldman writes "A Brief History of Improvisational Theatre in the United States" (5:128–51) which is actually a fairly comprehensive account crammed into 23 informative pages. He includes everything from the first steps in the Compass and then the Second City in Chicago in the 1950s and 1960s on down to Nichols and May, the Premise in New York and the Committee in San Francisco in the 1970s. A valuable piece of research. Janet Coleman's article "Improvisational Theatre in America: Variations on a Theme" (5:10–25) relates experiences with David Shepherd and Paul Sills and the development of the Compass. Coleman makes a telling comment in her observation that too many improvisational performers are interested in being entertainers and are not taking their artistic responsibilities seriously. Other items are mostly interviews and conversations with improvisational theatre personalities. In order: Paul Sills and R. G. Davis, "A Dialogue" (5:26–

55); Landesman, "A Conversation with David Shepherd" (5:56–65) and also Landesman, "Interview: Theodore J. Flicker" (5:66–81). Allan Albert contributes "Notes on the Proposition" (5:90–117). There is also a Compass scenario entitled "The Real You" (5:84–89) which helps to convey the *commedia dell'arte* nature of the improvisational techniques.

Modern dramatic themes and techniques are the subjects of three items. Roger Gross, "The Play as Dramatic Action" (*Players* 49:32–35), looks into the whole concept of dramatic action as the "Formal Cause" of a play. That is, if one can follow the reasoning in the fairly limited space given to it, the action of the play, according to Gross, is the "Master Psychic Event" with the play perceived as *being* an action, rather than *having* action. Perhaps it is clearer to quote Gross specifically. The action, he says, is "the structured meaning-response seen from a particular point of view as a virtual event." The story can be repeated, but the action cannot. Alan H. Casty delves into a popular depression-age subject in his UCLA dissertation "The Gangster and the American Social Drama of the Thirties: A Study of the Interaction of an Icon of Popular Culture and the Conventions of Drama" (*DAI* 34:7224A). Noting that the drama of the 1930s has a "persistent subtext" of "double crisis of self and society," Casty finds that because there were serious questions about basic processes of the economy and society, certain aberrant forms of will and action developed through various individual psychological blocks and distortions, with the gangster an example. Patrick J. Nolan, Bryn Mawr, writes "The Drama of Illusion: Memory Plays in American Drama, 1920–1940" (*DAI* 6651A), in which he finds that the playwrights wrote their works using remembrance as a perspective critical of contemporary reality. Rice, Odets, Howard, Sherwood, and Hellman, much the same group treated by Casty, reflect the processes that produced a "failed society," while O'Neill, Barry, and Anderson deal with whether or not the "separated" individuals can create meaningful lives apart from society.

Four books close out the significant contributions in this area. Of signal importance is John F. Wharton's *Life Among the Playwrights: Being Mostly the Story of the Playwrights Producing Company, Inc.* (New York: Quadrangle/New York Times). This is a very readable informal account of how the Playwrights Company came into being as a rebellion against the controlling interests. The volume is interspersed with a great number of illustrations, mainly portraits of those involved, with considerable reprinting of correspondence among the participants. Of greatest value is the second appendix, a full chronological record of all productions from 1938 to 1960. Malcolm Goldstein adds to the increasing literature of the between-wars activist theatre with *The Political Stage: American Drama and Theater of the Great Depression* (New York: Oxford). A number of somewhat superfluous play summaries takes up a lot of space, but there is a detailed review of everything in the genre from the 1920s to 1940s with discussion of political views of both writers and various organizations such as the Group Theatre and the Guild. This is a fine companion volume to Clurman's *Fervent Years*, Flanagan's *Arena*, and Himelstein's *Drama Was a Weapon*.

Of more contemporary interest is Joseph Wesley Zeigler's *Regional Theatre: The Revolutionary Stage* (Minneapolis: Univ. of Minn., 1973). This "personal look" at the Margo Jones, Tyrone Guthrie, Joseph Papp theatres and others (Arena in Washington, Actors Workshop in California, and others) over the past couple of decades, provides some valuable accounts of the important regional theatres, with a lot of good illustrations included. Zeigler notes that there are growing excellent alternatives to New York in such strong groups as New Haven's Wharf and Providence's Trinity Square, with a total of some 40 such theatres today as against less than a dozen 20 years ago. Finally, there is the excellent revelation of a lot of the cultural views of this country in John Hohenberg's *The Pulitzer Prizes: A History of the Awards in Books, Drama, Music, and Journalism Based on the Private Files over Six Decades* (New York: Columbia Univ. Press). Drama is, of course, but a small portion of the 434-page volume, but there are full and straightforward accounts of many of the problems involved with controversies between the Advisory Board for Drama and the jurors who made the final decisions. The book covers the history of all awards from the initiation of Pulitzer's "grand scheme" in 1902 and the first awards of 1917 into 1974. One can find here all the information about why such obviously insignificant plays as Zoë Akins's *The Old Maid* (1935) and Owen Davis's *Icebound* (1923) won over *The Children's Hour* and *The Adding Machine*.

a. **Eugene O'Neill.** Two major bibliographic volumes are of invaluable assistance to the O'Neill scholar. Jordan Y. Miller's second edition of his critical bibliography, *Eugene O'Neill and the American Critic* (Hamden, Conn.: Shoestring, 1973) came out early in 1974 and represents a complete revision and updating of all the material that first appeared in 1962. This edition has dropped the outdated introductory essay and concentrates on all the facts and figures of O'Neill's life, productions, first publications, and critical material about all of the plays into 1973. The life chronology has been corrected with the assistance of Louis Sheaffer. Of perhaps even greater significance to the O'Neill scholar is the appearance of Jennifer McCabe Atkinson's *Eugene O'Neill: A Descriptive Bibliography* (Pittsburgh, Pa.: Univ. of Pittsburgh). This is a long-needed scholarly effort which carries on where the original Sanborn and Clark bibliography of 1931 leaves off. Sanborn and Clark appeared while O'Neill was still an actively producing playwright, and now that we have virtually everything, barring new discoveries among the Yale papers, the Atkinson bibliography is for now a final and definitive effort. It is a beautifully produced work including a complete listing of everything from *Thirst* of 1914 through *Children of the Sea* in 1972. The extremely valuable appendices include a list of all published acting scripts; O'Neill's contributions to newspapers and periodicals, including items from the New London papers; promotion blurbs, auction material, and book dealer catalogues; a listing of plays in anthologies; and film, radio, and musical adaptations.

The most extensive critical work on O'Neill in 1974 is Winifred Frazer's monograph, *E.G. and E.G.O.: Emma Goldman and The Iceman Cometh* (Gainesville: Univ. of Fla.). Mrs. Frazer is one of the most active contemporary O'Neill scholars, and she has done a truly remarkable work in these slightly more than 100 pages in discussing how the career of Emma Goldman, the radical leader of the turn of the century, touched and directly affected O'Neill's life and plays. Frazer spends considerable time in analyzing the various characters of *Iceman* with respect to their reflection of real-life acquaintances, including the apparent equating of Emma Goldman herself to the off-stage mother of Don Parritt. A brief review of O'Neill's works as *stageplays*, heavily dependent on theatrical techniques, as opposed to most routine criticism of the *playscripts* appears in *Americana-Austriaca* (3:24–32), in "Eugene O'Neill: Man of the Theatre" by Bruce Granger. The article represents a fine start on a subject which ought to be even more fully explored.

The tiny international review *Adam* (Arts, Drama, Architecture, Music) has an article by Willard Booth, "Haunting Fragments from Eugene O'Neill" (39[1973]:37–40) in which there is discussion of and speculation about what happened to the last plays, mainly those of the *Possessors* cycle. Most of it is assumptions taken from the various titles and other evidence, since nothing much else exists outside of *Touch of the Poet* and *More Stately Mansions.* James Corey's "O'Neill's *The Emperor Jones*" (*AN&Q* 12:156–57) is a line-for-line comparison of how O'Neill patterned his witch doctor scene after Conrad's *Heart of Darkness.* John Krimsky's "*The Emperor Jones*: Robeson and O'Neill on Film" (*ConnR* 7:94–99) provides some hitherto unavailable information about the troubles in censorship and race prejudices encountered in filming the 1933 production.

Issue no. 50 of *Yale French Studies* is devoted entirely to "Intoxication and Literature," and one of the important items is by Stephen B. Brecco, "High Hopes: Eugene O'Neill and Alcohol" (pp. 142–49). Brecco holds that O'Neill was unable to rise very far above his contemporary dramatists in most of his works up to 1933, despite the continual critical comparison with the Greeks and other great names, because of his alcoholism. The best plays of the later period, beginning with *Iceman*, all came after O'Neill had become a virtual teetotaler. *Iceman* itself reflects the hellish deathlike quality of heavy drinking and the "poison" that drinking itself represents. O'Neill, says Brecco, uses the trauma of alcohol thematically in the later plays, rather than reportorially as in the early ones.

The very early O'Neill is discussed in James Milton Highsmith's "'The Personal Equation': Eugene O'Neill's Abandoned Play" (*SHR* 8:195–212), noting that only Louis Sheaffer's biography gives more than passing notice to this play begun at Harvard. In this excellent bit of research Highsmith, working from an undated typescript at the Houghton Library, Harvard, thoroughly discusses the play scene by scene and shows how certain thematic and structural elements of the play appear later in *Beyond the Horizon* and the one-act sea plays.

Four doctoral dissertations indicate the continuing scholarly interest in O'Neill. Joseph J. Brennan, NYU, writes about the lighter side of O'Neill in "The Comic in the Plays of Eugene O'Neill: The Use of Characterization, Situation, and Language in Relation to Henri Bergson's Theory of Comedy" (*DAI* 35:1088A). The later plays are seen to treat the human condition as more comic than tragic.

Ralph L. Corrigan, Jr., Fordham, in "The Function of the Green World in Selected Plays of Eugene O'Neill" (*DAI* 34:5162A) explores O'Neill's themes of disharmony with and alienation from the natural world. Joan P. Fleckenstein, Wisconsin, and Regina Poulard, Loyola of Chicago, write very similar studies of some of the fairly familiar aspects of Nietzsche in "Eugene O'Neill's Theatre of Dionysus: The Nietzschean Influence upon Selected Plays" (DAI 34:2805A) and "O'Neill and Nietzsche: The Making of a Playwright and Thinker" (*DAI* 35:2271A).

Two final items are John R. Cooley's "The Emperor Jones and the Harlem Renaissance" (*SLitI* 7,i:73–83) and Edwin J. Blesch, Jr., "O'Neill's Hugie: A Misconceived Experiment?" (*Nassau Review* 2,v:1–8).

b. **Albee, Miller, Williams.**   The three major dramatists other than O'Neill each received two or three items worthy of note during the year. E. G. Bierhaus, Jr., in "Strangers in a Room: *A Delicate Balance* Revisited" (*MD* 17:199–206) writes a very close study of the play in terms not of its focus on friendship, which seems apparent at first encounter, but in terms of its political focus and its moral and intellectual content. The character names are extensively analyzed, found to be essentially biblical with "surprising permutations" of character. All characters seem to be "in it together," aware of functioning in a kind of play or contest with everything coming back at the end to the original starting point. This is an analysis well worth attention, although there could be a question or two about excessive "reading into" the play. Ruth M. Schneider, SUNY Albany, discusses *The Zoo Story* in "The Interpolated Narrative in Modern Drama" (*DAI* 34: 6605A), but the main body of the dissertation is concerned with Pinter and others. The aspect of Albee's "absurd" qualities in Esslin's terms is discussed at some length in "Myth and Romance in Albee's *Who's Afraid of Virginia Woolf?*" by James P. Quinn (*ArQ* 30:197–204). Existential vision and ironic parody of romance are held to balance each other. Martha's unseen father is the sterile king, Martha the princess, and George the dragon killer. The monster is Western culture's perverted values. This is a provocative study, among the best of the serious treatments of this play in recent years.

One dissertation on Miller, Irving F. Jacobson's "The Fallen

Family: A Study in the Work of Arthur Miller" (*DAI* 35:2271A, UCLA), attempts to show how Miller's characters have lost a primal past which they continually seek through "regression and progression." Irving Jacobson's "The Child as Guilty Witness" (*L&P* 24:12–23) is mainly a discussion of Miller's story "I Don't Need You Any More," but it does touch upon many of the same family relationships seen in the plays with the child who becomes the outcast, the guilty witness to family strife.

Williams is found to be more religiously oriented than commonly acknowledged in a dissertation by Henry R. Beasley, Louisiana State, in "An Interpretative Study of the Religious Element in the Work of Tennessee Williams" (*DAI* 34:5954A). Instead of the Freudian emphasis, with the misleading sexual aspect, Beasley holds that Williams's plays are about the struggle of the outsider to fulfill the Will to Meaning in Colin Wilson's terms, and he finds Christian symbolism and the figure of Christ in passion to be central. Charles W. Cole and Carol I. Franco look at some of the lesser Williams work in such plays as *The Gnadiges Fraulein* and *Slapstick Tragedy* in "Critical Reaction to Tennessee Williams in the Mid-1960s" (*Players* 49:18–23). Alan S. Chesler offers a summary of a quarter century of criticism in "A Streetcar Named Desire: Twenty-five Years of Criticism" (*NMW* 7:44–53), which includes many of the standard daily and periodical press reviewers.

c. Others. E. E. Cummings (or e. e. cummings, if you prefer) receives the nod in two articles relative to *Him* (or *him*). "Damn Everything but the Circus: Popular Art in the Twenties and *him*" (*MD* 17:43–55) by Marjorie Smelstor, S.C., is mainly about the emerging interest in the lively arts as opposed to the Great Arts of the 1920s. Cummings is found to have created his work in the atmosphere of the lively arts, with *him* being explored as "a product of and response to the contemporary artistic scene." The artist, says Smelstor, "must damn everything but the circus—*everything* is the circus." Cummings was doing this in *him*, but the critics failed to recognize it. A fine companion piece to Smelstor's analysis is William I. Oliver's detailed explanation of how a production of Cummings's play was staged in "Him—A Director's Note" (*ETJ* 26:327–341), which the writer regards as "this most ambitious of our American plays," with its "intensely personal" expression. There are several photographs and sketches of how the play was staged in a kind of Brechtian "epic" style with slides and various projections. Of particular note is the fact that the play was staged before full houses in the midst of the Berkeley campus unrest in the 1969 riots, with performances often delayed by roadblocks and tear gassing.

John Leggett's *Ross and Tom: Two American Tragedies* (New York: Simon and Schuster) tells of the sad life of Thomas Heggen with a complete account, including the palm-tree episodes, of the real-life events that went into the short stories and *Mister Roberts*. Arthur Dorlag and John Irvine have edited *The Stage Works of Charles MacArthur* (Tallahassee: Fla. State Univ.), which contains all of the plays MacArthur wrote or collaborated on. The general introduction is a review of MacArthur's life and plays, and there are special brief prefaces by his wife, Helen Hayes, by Nunnaly Johnson, Richard Fallon, and John D. MacArthur. This is a fine addition to collections of fairly hard-to-come-by plays.

A dissertation on Clifford Odets, "The Early Plays of Clifford Odets" (*DAI* 35:399A) by Richard J. Dozier, North Carolina, discusses the difficulties in resolving differences between the early and later plays. The early plays, he feels, were more Biblical than Marxist. America's greatest expressionistic play is treated in Richard A. Weaver's *"The Adding Machine*: Exemplar of the Ludicrous" (*Players* 49:130–133), which sees the play as being a fine example of the comedic principle of the ludicrous as well as our best expressionistic work. Rice is also the subject of a doctoral study in Anthony F. R. Palmieri's "Elmer Rice: A Playwright's Vision of America" (*DAI* 35:3760A, Maryland), which regards Rice as a serious, though secondary, American dramatist whose 30 produced plays of some 50 written demonstrate an artist of integrity. From the evidence here this dissertation should be a valuable addition to the very limited material on Rice and could form the basis for an eminently publishable book.

In "The Augustus Thomas Collection at the University of North Carolina" (*RALS* 4:72–89) Jim G. Lewis publishes information concerning the location of over 75 plays by Thomas written between 1890 and 1925, plus other materials including hundreds of manuscripts and typescripts. In a dissertation at NYU Robin Taylor investigates German influences in "Elements of German Expressionism in American Drama, 1920–1940" (*DAI* 34:7921A).

iii. Black Theatre and Drama

Norma R. Jones's dissertation at Bowling Green, "The Image of the 'White Liberal' in Black American Fiction and Drama" (*DAI* 34: 5178A) is a study of the picture of the white liberal as seen by black writers as different from the white oppressor. Fiction is emphasized more than drama, but the topic is pertinent. Some of the prejudices of the black writer toward certain social aberrations, particularly homosexuality, are attacked by Jon L. Clayborne in "Modern Black Drama and the Gay Image" (*CE* 36:381–84). Clayborne notes that many of the already proven fallacies and stereotypes of the male homosexual are perpetuated as fact by many black writers including Bullins, Baraka, and Gordone. Clayborne pleads well for the abandonment of these stereotypes if black drama is to realize its development potential. Robert L. Tener in "The Corrupted Warrior Heroes: Baraka's *The Toilet*" (*MD* 17:207–15) takes the play as a demonstration of movement from boyhood to manhood. Baraka sees society as something like a cowboy and Indian movie "with the reel running out."

The historical position of blacks in the American theatre during the Great Depression is treated by Ronald Ross in "The Role of Blacks in the Federal Theatre, 1935–1939" (*JNH* 59:38–40). Included are the Federal Negro Theatre, Negro Youth Theatre, and Lafayette Theatre. A good history of a subject that needs further exploration. Lloyd W. Brown's "The Cultural Revolution in Black Theatre" (*NALF* 8:159–64, 166–72) and Robert J. Willis's "Anger and the Contemporary Black Theatre" (*NALF* 8:213–15) are further contributions.

iv. Miscellaneous

Yvonne B. Shafer's "The Liberated Woman in American Plays of the Past" (*Players* 49:95–100) begins with Rachel Crothers's 1909 *A Man's World* and carries through Sophie Treadwell, Rose Franken, S. N. Behrman, and John Van Druten. Tice L. Miller's review of the career of New York critic Alan Dale in "Alan Dale: The Hearst Critic" (*ETJ* 26:69–80) contrasts Dale as one setting a new tone of criticism as against William Winter of the *Tribune* and J. Rankin Towse of the *Post*, who were the respected genteel critics of the turn of the century. Dale, noted for the "smartness" of his style in attacking the "images and idols" of Victorian culture is held to be one who significantly helped shape modern critical styles.

A handful of general items closes out the year's collection. Wayland D. Hand in "Folk Beliefs and Customs of the American Theatre: A Survey" (*SFQ* 38:23–48) compiles a list of the superstitions and taboos from backstage and onstage that have developed within the American theatre. Charles A. Carpenter's "Modern Drama Studies: An Annual Bibliography" appears in *MD* 27:67–120, covering 1972–73. F. L. Warner provides some useful information in "Recorded Original Performances from the American Theatre Prior to 1943" (*ETJ* 26:101–07) with a list of available recordings up to the time the first "original cast albums" began to appear when Decca issued *Oklahoma!* in 1943. Arnold Moss with "Will You See the Players Well Bestowed? The Guest Artist Program at American Colleges and Universities" (*ETJ* 26:231–41) discusses the scope and problems that are faced by institutions hosting guest artist performances in the face of some "antiquated" Equity rules. And finally, Albert E. Johnson lists some 66 dissertations in the United States currently under way in everything from early theatre through Edward Albee in his "Doctoral Projects in Progress in Theatre Arts 1974" (*ETJ* 26:242–48).

University of Rhode Island

19. Folklore

John T. Flanagan

Folklore research continues to attract a wide diversity of scholars whose traditional concern with ballads and tales remains unabated but who reveal a growing interest in theory and methodology. Collecting data is still important, but there seems to be general agreement about the need to compile current bibliographies, to arrange folklore materials in readily available archives, and to study the bearers of folklore as well as the texts themselves. This chapter like its predecessor for 1973 will deal only with verbal materials. Data on folk life must perforce be handled elsewhere.

i. Bibliography and Archives

In an essay entitled "The Gordon Wilson Collection" (*TFSB* 40:82–94) Diana Zacharias describes the extensive holdings of Mammoth Cave folklore at Western Kentucky University. The collection is especially rich in folk speech, proverbial lore, and folk belief. Such omnium gatherums prompted Robert A. Georges, Beth Blumenreich, and Kathie O'Reilly to offer "Two Mechanical Indexing Systems for Folklore Archives: A Preliminary Report" (*JAF* 87:39–52). The authors outline their plans and explain how punch cards which are easily sorted can facilitate filing and using. A similar suggestion was made by Bruce A. Rosenberg and John B. Smith in "The Computer and the Finnish-Geographical Method" (*JAF* 87:149–54). With the aid of a computer scholars could encode each narrative, keypunch it accurately, and presumably analyze it more easily. But there is no way to avoid the initial step of reading each tale. Rosenberg and Smith suggest that Stith Thompson's study of "The Star Husband Tale," based on 86 versions, could have been done more quickly if a computer had been available at the time.

Bibliographical work in 1974 took many forms. Richard E. Bueh-

ler and his corps of assistants summarized 1,057 items in *AFS* and
revealed the usual wide range of coverage. But the annotation is
uneven, many listed items are very old, and the journals abstracted
often seem eccentrically chosen. Topographic names are the subject
of a survey by Richard B. Sealock and Margaret S. Powell, "Place-
Name Literature, United States and Canada 1971–1974" (*Names*
22:150–64). There is more history than folklore in "Humor of the
Old Southwest: a Checklist of Criticism," by Charles E. Davis and
Martha B. Hudson (*MQ* 27:179–99), but folklore material is scattered throughout. More limited compilations are William K. Mc-
Neil's "An Annotated Bibliography of Indiana Folklore" (*IndF*
6[1973]:100–137); and John F. Szwed's "Black Folk Culture in
Pennsylvania" (*KF* 19:113–21).

Frank Hoffman provides a good deal of data about a generally
unexplored field in his 1973 volume, *Analytical Survey of Anglo-
American Traditional Erotica* (Bowling Green: Bowling Green Univ.
Popular Press). Because of his wide survey and the attention given
not only to books but also to magazines and ephemeral literature,
Hoffman's book should have special utility. His review of the roadblocks set up even by libraries for the collector of erotic material is
enlightening.

Two bulky volumes issued by the MLA provide much folklore
data, but of course are neither exhaustive nor up to date. The 1972
International Bibliography lists some 2,400 items, a large part of
which have no American relevance, and includes the obvious folklore categories. The citations are accurate but there is no annotation
and much trivia seems to have been included. The general geographical plan of listing items aids users considerably. The 1972 *Abstracts
of Articles* compiled by Walter S. Achtert and Eileen M. Mackesy,
presenting summaries of articles usually done by the original authors, is so sketchy as to be virtually useless. Only 16 items deal with
folk tales and scattered abstracts concern proverbs, riddles, songs,
and material folklore.

An unusually complete bibliography by Joseph Hickerson occupies pp. 775–816 of Duncan Emrich's *American Folk Poetry, an
Anthology* (Boston and Toronto: Little, Brown). Hickerson's "Bibliography of American Folksong" is limited to material in English
but shows an astonishing catholicity: lullabies, fiddle pieces, Child

ballads, hymns, spirituals, carols, occupational ballads, shanties, chants, protest songs, and blues. Hickerson has geared his bibliography to the divisions of Emrich's anthology but adds general collections of folk songs, regional material, and volumes of Negro folk song. Despite the lack of annotation this list is both convenient and helpful.

At the time of writing this essay the annual bibliography of folklore provided by Merle E. Simmons for 10 years was unavailable. This compilation has appeared in *SFQ* since 1964 but was shifted in 1974 to *JFI*. It has not yet been published.

ii. History and Theory

In his 1974 presidential address to the English Folklore Society, "Folklore and History," H. R. Ellis Davidson proposes the thesis that history and folklore are intertwined and can be mutually helpful (*Folklore* 85:73–92). He concludes that oral traditions are important, patterns can shape memories of the past, and folklore itself may alter the course of events but not necessarily for the best. He cites historical figures to whom folklore has become attached but pays scant attention to American examples.

Theory and methodology also stimulated other discussions. In a long and overly detailed article entitled "The Memorate and the Proto-Memorate" (*JAF* 87:225–39) Linda Dégh and Andrew Vázsonyi reconsider two terms first proposed by Carl Von Sydow. The concept of *fabulat* has been generally accepted but the two authors find the *memorat* invalid since it cannot be easily distinguished and the criteria seem undependable. Their own suggestion of *proto-memorate* to serve as a postulative memorat seems only additional jargon. A whole issue of *Folklore Forum* edited by Gerald Cashion (Special Series 12) is given over to 14 papers on "Conceptual Problems in Contemporary Folklore Study." Among the subjects discussed are an oral history project, the history of folklore scholarship, ethical problems, communication among folklorists, new terms, and a triadic approach to folklore (oral, kinesiological, and material). A more practical approach to the subject is described in Kay Hardman's "An Experiential Approach to Folklore Studies for Teachers" (*FForum*, 7:192–97), which is the results of her experience in teaching methods to potential instructors in a California classroom. She relied heavily on personal experience, variant interpretations, and class analysis.

The rapidly developing interest in the performer as well as the performance is demonstrated again in an article by Thomas A. Burns (*KF* 19:61–94). In "Aesthetic Judgment: the Interpretive Side of the Structure of Performance" he pleads for more attention to the style of the folk performance and more consideration of such variables as place, season, time, and environment. He chooses a professional football game to exemplify external and internal variables. Some of these points are also made by Diane Wolkstein in "An Interview with Harold Courlander" (*LJ* 99:1437–40). Courlander, a prolific compiler of folktales from Africa, Haiti, and the Indian Southwest, speaks freely of his methods of obtaining materials and making the necessary contacts with informants. He does not try for verbatim translation but frequently polishes the narration and often excludes violent or erotic material.

David J. Hufford in "Psychology, Psychoanalysis, and Folklore" (*SFQ* 38:187–97) pleads for greater interaction between folklore and psychology. It is not enough to employ psychoanalysis and personality theory; the folklorist would do well to use the psychological laboratory and to enter freely into interdisciplinary research. Hufford does not always make clear just how his goal is to be achieved.

In "On Folklore and Women Folklorists" (*Folklore Feminists Communication* no. 3:4, 29–37) Richard Reuss gives an historical account of the contribution made by women to folklore scholarship and of their inadequate recognition. He cites the well-known work of Ruth Benedict, Elsie Clews Parsons, and Louise Pound but suggests that several other female scholars were quickly forgotten. Moreover, women have held less than their share of offices in professional organizations, even in the American Folklore Society in recent years. Correction of this obvious imbalance seems slow in coming.

Another article by Reuss, with a long and rather stupid title, " 'That Can't Be Alan Dundes! Alan Dundes is Taller Than That!' The Folklore of Folklorists" (*JAF* 87:303–17), gives an amusing picture of professional folklorists supported by anecdotes about Kittredge, Thompson, Taylor, and other notables as well as by personal recollections of younger scholars. Reuss outlines the route by which graduate students in folklore eventually reach professional eminence and pays due attention to fieldwork, publishing, and attendance at conventions. His thesis seems to be that folklorists themselves generate folklore and are therefore worth scholarly attention.

Freddye Belle Stansberry in "Folklore and Its Effects Upon Black History" (*MissFR* 7[1973]:115–22 discusses Negroes in the United States, pointing out that although the first slaves arrived without a common language or culture, they did bring with them a legacy of tales, dramatic speech, and musical forms. As a result Negroes have contributed animal tales, tales about the generic slave John, a kind of oratory, blues, ragtime, and "signs" or superstitions. But she feels that blacks should strive today to make their unique heritage part of the American experience.

The January issue of *WF*, under the guest editorship of Don Yoder, is given over to essays on folk religion with examples taken from Italian-Americans in Philadelphia, folk art in the Southwest, Greek-Americans in Philadelphia, and the life of a Methodist exhorter in Tennessee in the early 1800s. Yoder himself contributes an excellent definition of folk religion in which he assays some of the important elements: superstition, magic, witchcraft, dreams, prophecies; he also provides a valuable bibliography (23:16–34).

In "The Rhetoric of the Radio Ministry" (*JAF* 87:318–27) William M. Clements reports on his study of folk preachers who use the radio extensively in two counties of northeastern Arkansas. Broadcasts of sermons and exhortations to the Pentecostal sects in this area reveal many of the qualities that characterize the discourses of folk preachers facing actual congregations. The radio preacher, to be sure, is strictly limited in time, cannot depend on gestures or facial changes, and is deprived of immediate audience response. But like his counterpart in church he can paint scenes vividly, make emotion-charged appeals, and even indulge in semichants. Clements contends that radio preaching in Craighead and Poinsett counties is highly effective in its appeal to the folk.

iii. Ballads and Songs

Research in folk ballads and songs continues to exemplify a wide spectrum, including history and theory, examinations of individual ballads, discussions of particular genres like lullabies and spirituals, and useful collections, notably Duncan Emrich's *American Folk Poetry.*

Thomas Adler in "The Ballad in Blugrass Music" (*FForum* 7:3–47) prints the texts of 32 ballads from phonograph records, some very familiar, and concludes that bluegrass music utilizes a repertoire with deep traditional roots. Howard Wright Marshall in " 'Keep On the Sunny Side of Life': Patterns and Religious Expression in Bluegrass Gospel Music" (*NYFQ* 30:3–43) discusses at some length American evangelistic and fundamentalist religion as expressed in music. He is also concerned with the cultural and musical nature of bluegrass, which he conceives to be one manifestation of the revival of nativism. In an article entitled "A Century of Song: Popular Music in Minnesota," James Taylor Dunn is more concerned with popular than with folk music but points out the link between ragtime and the folk. His article is embellished with reproductions of the title pages of songs (*MinnH* 44:122–41).

In "American Balladry: the Term and the Canon" (*KF* 19:3–10) Tristram Potter Coffin argues that relatively few ballads have national recognition in the United States although there is much local balladry. He lists some 50 ballads which he believes can properly be called pan-American. Some, incidentally, are Child ballads. Ivan M. Tribe focuses on a narrower theme in "The Continuing Tradition of Tragedy and Disaster Ballads: A Case Study of Silver Bridge Songs" (*JEMFQ* 9[1973]:147–58). Tribe surveys ballads about caves and wrecks, then concentrates on the songs written about the collapse of an Ohio River bridge in 1967. He insists that no single event in American history has inspired so many ballads.

Bess Lomax Hawes is the author of an interesting article on lullabies (*JAF* 87:140–48). In "Folksongs and Function: Some Thoughts on the American Lullaby" she discusses the bizarre words used by American mothers to lull their babies to sleep and comments that the child remains in close proximity to the mother but must be trained shortly for self-reliance. Thus the mother often sings to it about isolation, about going away. She feels that American lullabies are often a mother's conversation with herself about eventual separation.

In another general article Ivan M. Tribe discusses "The Hillbilly Versus the City: Urban Images in Country Music" (*JEMFQ* 10:41–

51). In Tribe's view much country music was antiurban, picturing the city as evil and immoral and using the honky-tonk or the bar as the milieu. But some cities, nevertheless, notably Memphis, Dallas, Louisville, and Kansas City, were accorded more favorable treatment.

John Lovell, Jr., published his *Black Song: the Forge and the Flame* in 1972 (New York: Macmillan), an excellent investigation of the genesis and development of the Negro spiritual. He considers the impact of camp meetings and revival services, and the interrelationship of spirituals with blues, jazz, and ragtime. Chapter 15 is a stimulating discussion of the American spiritual as a folk song.

Individual ballads were treated briefly in several articles. Brenda Joyce Quillin's "Nell Cropsey Died—But How?" (*NCarF* 22:43–54) deals with the death of a young North Carolina woman in 1901 and a local ballad commemorating the event. It has been compared to "Pearl Bryan." Michael B. Dongan in "Two Manuscript Folksongs from Civil War Arkansas and Their Background" (*MidSF* 2:83–88) prints one Confederate and one Union song. A Spanish language ballad about the bursting of a dam in California in 1928 is the subject of Bess Lomax Hawes's discussion, "El Corrido de la Inundacion de la Presa de San Francisquito: The Story of a Local Ballad" (*WF* 33: 219–30). The *corrido* in eleven stanzas without a refrain is given in full, and the author supplies a translation and comments on *corrido* style.

The most thorough study of a ballad published in 1974 is Norm Cohen's "Robert W. Gordon and the Second Wreck of 'Old 97'" (*JAF* 87:12–38). Cohen deals with two themes here: the importance of Gordon's collecting activities, and his contributions both to the Library of Congress folk-song archive and to the history of the ballad itself. The Southern Railroad train which was wrecked near Danville, Virginia, in 1903 produced one of the best known American occupational ballads and one which has confused students ever since. Even today the authorship is not clearly established although the ballad has been sung and recorded frequently. Cohen suggests that a later ballad about another train wreck may have clouded the whole issue.

Individual singers also attracted some attention. David Evans in "Bubba Brown: Folk Poet" (*MissFR* 7[1973]:15–31 sketches the life and work of John Henry "Bubba" Brown, a black musician from Mississippi who wrote a number of blues and was self-trained as violinist and guitarist. John D. Robb in "H. V. Gonzales: Folk Poet of New

Mexico" (*NMexFR* 13:1–6) gives data about Higinio V. Gonzales (c. 1830s–1922), a schoolteacher who wrote poems in "decimas" about personal or family matters. Barbara Kempf in "Meet Doc Williams: Country Music Star, Country Music Legend" (*JEMFQ* 10: 1–13) describes an Ohio-born coal-miner who with his wife became important in the country music field. Steven A. Schulman in "Howess Dewey Winfrey: the Rejected Songmaker" (*JAF* 8:72–84) claims that although Winfrey's songs were not accepted by his community they are of the type that would be accepted elsewhere. The argument hardly seems valid.

Several collections of folk songs demand mention. In *Sang Branch Settlers: Folksongs and Tales of a Kentucky Mountain Family* (Austin and London: Univ. of Tex. Press), Leonard Roberts brings together some previously published material about the Couch family of eastern Kentucky. The volume contains tales, songs, and riddles; many of the ballads are well known. David Seneff McIntosh in *Folk Songs and Singing Games of the Illinois Ozarks*, ed. Dale Whiteside (Carbondale: So. Ill. Univ. Press) presents material collected in 32 southern Illinois counties and includes local songs and ballads as well as play-party games, singing square dances, and ropeskipping rhymes. The local songs reflect politics, disasters, immigration, and crime. Some variants of Child ballads appear among the traditional folk songs. The book is attractively produced and contains a bibliography as well as notes.

Roger D. Abrahams in *Deep the Water, Shallow the Shore: Three Essays on Shantying in the West Indies* (Austin: Univ. of Tex. Press) once more draws on his collecting experiences in the Caribbean islands. Two chapters deal with fishing and seining activities on Tobago and Nevis; another is concerned with whaling off the island of St. Vincent. Abrahams contends that the shanty is by no means obsolete, but he says little about individual performances or the relationships between singers and audience.

The most ambitious collection of American folk song to appear during the year is the anthology edited by Duncan Emrich, *American Folk Poetry*, a volume of 831 pages with an excellent bibliography by Joseph Hickerson (already alluded to in section i). Emrich in his introduction observes that folk poetry is anonymous, has no established texts, is constantly varied, and since it is written in the language of the folk generally lacks other aesthetic merits. He excludes minstrel songs, vaudeville songs, and college songs, as well as crusading ditties. Most of his material comes from Library of Congress recordings, with their origins scrupulously indicated. The book is divided into many sections, such as children's songs, play-party songs, Child ballads (some 56), hymns, occupational songs, disaster ballads, and songs loosely called the "expression of a growing nation" (cowboys and outlaws to Mormons and railroaders). Emrich provides no annotation besides his identification of singers, dates, and places of recording. But he has produced a highly attractive volume.

iv. Tales and Legends

Folklorists continue to speculate on the origins of tales, study their development, collect from informants in the field, or publish compilations of narratives. The material assembled encompasses a wide geographical range.

In "A Morphology of the Modern Fable" (*JPC* 8:15–27) Bruce A. Lohof contends that the brief short stories in *Good Housekeeping*, 1965–69, have all the attributes of the traditional fable. His 52 examples seem to suggest a clear structural pattern.

David A. Walton writes in *Ohio Folklore* on "Folklore as Compensation: A Content Analysis of the Negro Animal Tale" (no vol. [1974?]:1–11). Challenging the old idea that Negroes viewed the animal tales as entertainment, he finds a major conflict between the weak and the strong therein, with cleverness generally overcoming force. More examples would have aided his familiar argument. Margaret Gillis Figh and Margaret B. Kirkpatrick in "The Development of an Alabama Folktale" (*SFQ* 38:109–20) deal with an old Alabama legend about a man lynched for desertion during Civil War days. Some 15 variant fragments confirm the strength of the traditional story and are consistent in the main elements.

A number of brief tales were collected in various journals. Lee and Joy Pennington in "Two Tales from Bloody Harlan" (*AppalachianJ* 1[1973]:139–42) and Ralph C. Worthington, Jr., in "Five Tar-Pitt Tales" (*NCarF* 22:15–29) simply print their stories without substantial comment. Ovid S. Vickers in "Five from Gum Swamp" (*MissFR* 7:33–38) presents tales from South Georgia. William R. Ferris in "Black Folktales from Rose Hill" (*MissFR* 7:70–85) collects 13 short tales from Vicksburg, most of which are animal stories, Wade

Wellman's "Folk Yarns and Other Matters" and F. Roy Johnson's "Yarns Old and New" in the same issue of *NCarF* (22:102–08, 114–18) include North Carolina ghost stories. Judy Trejo in "Coyote Tales: A Paiute Commentary" (*JAF* 87:66–71) prints four tales about such speaking animals as coyote, bear, and bobcat, and observes that although they have chiefly entertainment value they can also teach proper behavior. Here the coyote has his usual traits of greed, curiosity, malice, and lechery.

C. E. Schorer presents in *SFQ* two more tales of Indian life from the collection made by C. C. Trowbridge in the Detroit area in the 1820s; the manuscripts are owned by the State Historical Society of Wisconsin. "The Fisherman" (38:63–71) deals with murder and transformation; the last of the 11 narratives simply entitled "A Story" (38:233–41) includes courtship, vengeance, and the sudden change of men into animals. As in previously edited tales Schorer analyzes the action, cites parallels, and compares themes and events with those in other Indian stories.

The Southwest is the scene of tales recorded in two articles. Rubén Cobos in "Five New Mexican Spanish Folktales" (*NMexFR* 13:11–18) presents stories collected in Albuquerque, two of local origin and three suggesting a European provenience. There is little annotation. Mary Lee Nolan's "Stories Told by Refugees from the Mexican Revolution (1910–1920)" (*MidSF* 2:63–76) uses Texas A. and M. University archives to piece together the tales of fugitives who escaped across the border from Nuevo Laredo. The interviews contain much summarized history.

In "Folklore in the Library, Old Schuylkill Tales" (*PF* 23,iii:44–48) Mac E. Barrick discusses a collection of Indian tales, legends, ghost stories, and local anecdotes which was published originally by Ella Zerbey Elliott in 1906. The book attracted little attention then, but it obviously derives from oral tradition and sheds light on public opinion of the time.

Barrick also discusses " 'The Barber's Ghost': A Legend Become a Folktale" (*PF* 23,iv:36–42), a well-known Pennsylvania story which once had wide credence and is preserved today as an entertaining narrative. Another legend is treated by William E. Holloman in "The Ice-Cold Hand" (*NCarF* 22:3–8), an old tale of a man who jilted a girl. She died shortly afterward as did the man, whereupon the girl's face supposedly appeared on his headstone. Even though the evidence is contradictory, the tale, like other Carolina legends, survives.

Collections of folk tales published in 1974 represent a wide range of interest. Iona Opie and Peter Opie in *The Classic Fairy Tales* (New York: Oxford) print 24 famous tales using the earliest English text for each. Nineteenth-century illustrations add to the book's appeal. There are of course no American stories included.

Hector Lee's *Tales of California* (Logan: Utah State Univ. Press) includes 20 stories about California history and celebrities, most of which originally served the author as television or radio talks. They are by no means folk tales although they occasionally deal with the folk and present outlaws and local heroes. Reduced to print, they seem rather bland.

A very different kind of collection is Stephen Dow Beckham's *Tall Tales from Rogue River, the Yarns of Hathaway Jones* (Bloomington and London: Indiana Univ. Press). Jones (1878–1936) was an Oregon pioneer, a hunter and woodsman and mail carrier who happened also to be a creative liar. He was both tough and voluble with a talent for self-dramatization. Beckham collected the stories by and about him from various sources and makes of them a kind of tall tale cycle dealing with monstrous animals and the Münchhausen-like adventures of the narrator. Jones thought nothing of taming a skunk or a raven, riding down a flume on a bear's carcass, swimming a river by holding on to the tail of a salmon, or carrying a deer and a bear simultaneously. By adding certain realistic touches Jones makes his yarns almost believable.

A well-balanced anthology of aboriginal material is *The Portable North American Indian Reader*, ed. Frederick W. Turner, III (New York: Viking). Turner presents the literature by and about the American Indian, which ranges from authentic myths and tales to poetry, fiction, and history by recognized writers (Freneau, Melville, Parkman). The first half of the book is the most useful since it includes legends and stories from 11 tribes as well as a sampling of chants and oratory from the whole continent. Turner also finds room for samples of captivity narratives and for Paul Radin's *Autobiography of a Winnebago Indian*. Much of the earlier material comes from reports of the Bureau of American Ethnology and from *JAF*.

The final pages even when they are the work of authors of Indian extraction like N. Scott Momaday or Vine Deloria seem less important, at least to the folklorist.

v. Superstitions and Cures

Collections of superstitions and cures continue to appear, generally regional in nature but occasionally focused on occupations. Jane C. Beck in "A Traditional Witch of the Twentieth Century" (*NYFQ* 30:101–16) presents data about Dolorez Amelia Gomez, a Philadelphia Negress who learned folk medicine from her grandmother. She utilizes roots and herbs but depends also on mental powers and as a practicing Catholic finds no incompatibility between religion and witchcraft.

Ruth Ann Musick in "Witchcraft and the Devil in West Virginia" (*Appalachian J* 1:271–76) gives details about the evil eye and witchcraft, which she supports by brief tales derived chiefly from European immigrants. Two articles by Addie Suggs Hilliard in *TFSB* list beliefs and therapy about illness. "On Swallowing Punkin Seed" (40: 119–21) deals with pregnancy and forecasts about children. The euphemisms for pregnancy are rather amusing: "got caught," "out of whack," "carrying precious cargo," "damned the red river," and the title of the article. In "What'll We Give to the Baby-O?" (40:41–46) cures for infant sicknesses traditionally accepted by the author's Scotch-Irish ancestors are listed. It is claimed that swallowing a live minnow will cure whooping cough and that wine made from flowers of the lily-of-the-valley will make a useful brain tonic.

Three articles in the *NCarF* deal with agricultural superstitions and folk medicine. Suzanne Maley in "North Carolina Animal and Weather Superstitions" (22:21–25) gives 82 rural beliefs derived mostly from college students. Bruce W. Whitehurst in "Plant and Animal Husbandry Beliefs from Daughtry's Crossroads" (22:9–14) lists folk beliefs from a single family in Northampton County. Initial comments on animal care, planting, and home remedies are followed by 54 specific beliefs. Leonidas Betts in "Folk Medicine in Harnett County" (22:84–94) collects cures and medical traditions from two white informants and one Negro female. Ringworm, warts, croup, burns, and "risings" are some of the ailments prescribed for.

An article of a very different kind is Wayland D. Hand's "Folk

Beliefs and Customs of the American Theater: A Survey" (*SFQ* 38:23–48). Deriving his evidence from the folklore archives at UCLA and from an experienced Los Angeles actor and play director, Hand lists a number of bad luck and good luck tokens to which actors pay more than lip service. Thus broken mirrors, the number 13, whistling on the stage, open umbrellas, borrowed makeup, and the color yellow in stage props or costumes invariably connote misfortune to theater people; while knocking on wood, wearing medals, rubbing a horseshoe, placing a rabbit's foot in the makeup box, or putting a left shoe or stocking on first (at least in California) either bring good luck or ward off evil. Hand's essay indicates that actors are an abnormally suggestible group.

vi. Folk Heroes

The folk hero remains a perennial theme and continues to attract both theorists and biographers. William M. Clements in "Savage, Pastoral, Civilized: An Ecology Typology of American Frontier Heroes" (*JPC* 8:254–66) attempts to classify his examples in relation to the environment. Savage heroes such as Crockett and Fink identify with their surroundings and often imitate the Indian in savagery and ruthlessness. Pastoral heroes like Boone, Carson, and Johnny Appleseed feel a rapport with the landscape and reveal bravery and independence without sacrificing the influences of civilization. Civilized heroes, generally synthetic and best represented by Paul Bunyan and Pecos Bill, are technically oriented and lack a real basis in either history or folklore. Clements admits that his theory is limited to frontier figures and necessarily excludes other types of heroes.

Robert A. Fink in "Harvey Birch: the Yankee Peddler as an American Hero" (*NYFQ* 30:137–52) goes back to Cooper's *The Spy* to find a folk hero and covers familiar ground in his discussion. In contrast William A. Sullivan selects an Arkansas river rat as his candidate for a folk hero. In "Perry Martin: Hero of the River Rat Folk" (*MidSF* 2:3–6) he gives data about a timber worker, moonshiner, and ex-convict who was widely known in the area around Rosedale, Mississippi. In his later life Martin was respected for his honesty and generosity.

One of the most interesting recent evaluations of an American

hero is Bruce A. Rosenberg's *Custer and the Epic of Defeat* (Univ.
Park and London: Penn. State Univ. Press), a careful attempt to explain what happened before and after the Custer massacre. Rosenberg sifts the limited historical evidence thoroughly, examines biographies and memoirs, and then compares Custer's last stand with
mythical and factual accounts of other famous defeats. His parallels
at times seem rather remote: Saul, Leonidas, Roland, for example;
and sometimes needlessly erudite, e.g., the Anglo-Saxon poem "Battle of Malden." But Custer remains a symbol of reckless daring to
the American public, in Rosenberg's words "far and away the most
celebrated military hero of the American people." The almost instant
mythologizing of the martyr of the Little Big Horn remains a fascinating story.

vii. Folk Speech

In the amorphous category of folk speech one can include names,
jokes, riddles, proverbs, and professional cant, all of which have
stimulated scholarly investigation. Indeed the language of the people not only shows amazing variation but also preserves linguistic
aberrations and traditions in fascinating ways.

Donald Kay, in "British Influence on Kentucky Municipal Place
Names" (*KFR* 20:9–13), provides a slight discussion of the subject
and then prints in parallel columns the original English name and
its Kentucky equivalent. Raven I. McDavid, Jr., and Sarah Ann
Witham in "Poor Whites and Rustics" (*Names* 22:93–103) summarize
their inquiry into the names used to define rural inhabitants on the
Atlantic seaboard. It is no surprise to find "backwoodsman" commonly used, followed by "countryman," "hayseed," "poor white
trash," "backwoodser," and "hick."

In 1973 Alvin Schwartz compiled his *Witcracks: Jokes and Jests
from American Folklore* (Philadelphia: Lippincott), a collection of
puns, shaggy dog stories, Wellerisms, and moron jokes intended for
a younger audience. There are brief notes on the subgenres of humor.

A thoughtful article by Nathan Hurvitz, "Blacks and Jews in
American Folklore," (*WF* 33:301–25) examines white Christian
folklore about two minority groups. Hurvitz examines some of the
stereotypes commonly held, prints familiar graffiti as well as political
doggerel, and terms the Negroes outsiders on the basis of color, the

Jews on the basis of religion. Much of the folk jesting about the two groups is bland and amusing, but it can also be hostile and vicious. Hurvitz suggests that the folklorist who collects data can help to eliminate group cleavages.

The December issue of *SFQ* is given over to six papers on the practical joke (38:253–323). Three essays deal with Canadian material, practical jokes in the Newfoundland seal fishery, wedding night pranks in New Brunswick, and juvenile tricks in children's camps mostly in Newfoundland and Ontario. In a theoretical paper entitled "A Generic Approach to the Practical Joke" Richard Tallman attempts to classify jokes into a kind of index which might prove useful to future investigators (pp. 259–74). Since at the moment "jokelore" is unorganized and seldom studied, some kind of classification system is probably desirable; but to at least one reader the attempt to impose scientific terminology on practical jokes seems a joke in itself. Roger Welsch contributes two essays to the symposium, a note on personal experience (pp. 253–57) and "Bigger'n Life: the Tall-tale Postcard" (pp. 311–23). In the latter Welsch gives a brief history of the picture postcard and observes that the period 1905–15 was the heyday of this particular phenomenon. By careful trickery photographers could show gigantic corncobs, hogs, cicadas, the visual exaggerations corresponding in many ways to the oral tall tales which were equally familiar. Freak postcards of this type were known throughout the country but were most common in the plains states where weather excesses were common.

Riddles are no longer a common pastime, as Charles S. Guthrie asserts in the foreword to his *Riddles from the Cumberland Valley* (Bowling Green, Ky.: Kentucky Folklore Society [1973]), but they are fun in themselves and well worth serious attention. Guthrie prints 124 riddles from Cumberland county, most of which reflect a rural background and farm life. Some 66 are termed true riddles while the rest are tricks or puzzles. William Hugh Jansen provides an introduction to the booklet.

Three other brief collections of riddles have also been published recently. Donald M. Hines, in "Rare Blooms from a Rude Land: Frontier Riddles from the Inland Pacific Northwest" (*IndF* 6:205–40 [1973]), presents 230 riddles and conundrums found in the weekly press of Oregon and Washington, some of which seem to reflect the midwestern origins of the speakers. Douglas McReynolds in " 'Mys-

terious Names': Riddles in the Ozarks" (*BMHS* 30:205–07) prints
several riddles from Missouri which deal with a predatory animal
whose name is disguised. Danny W. Moore in 'The Deductive Riddle:
An Adaptation to Modern Society" (*NCarF* 22:119–25) collects
16 riddles from North Carolina college students which are longer than
the traditional riddle and thus stimulate orderly reasoning and skill
in puzzle solving. He argues that they include modern elements and
thus may be a subgenre of the classic riddle.

Proverbs too command attention. Addie Suggs Hilliard's article,
"Shakespeare Proverbs in Chester County, Tennessee" (*NCarF*
22:63–74), comments on the English and Scotch-Irish settlers who
came to Tennessee in the early 19th century and lists the proverbs
which are still current among their descendants and which resemble
proverbs in Shakespeare's plays.

Wolfgang Mieder published three articles on proverbs in 1974.
"The Essence of Literary Proverb Studies" (*NYFQ* 30:66–76) makes
a strong plea for a more systematic study of proverbs, including editions, indexes, and textual quotations to confirm usage. American
proverb studies, he contends, seem to deal mostly with regional
writers like Jesse Stuart and Harry Harrison Kroll. Mieder's article
also appeared in *Proverbium* (23:888–94). In "The Proverb and
Anglo-American Literature" (*SFQ* 37:49–62) he expands his argument slightly. Proverbs have been inadequately dealt with, he believes, despite the yeoman work of Archer Taylor and B. J. Whiting.
The methodology of collecting needs improvement, and much attention should be given to American writers of the 19th century and to
20th-century poets. Mieder provides a helpful bibliography.

Two articles deal with the diction of special occupations. Thus
Mac E. Barrick in "The Folklore Repertory of a Pennsylvania Auctioneer" (*KF* 19:27–42) analyzes the role of the auctioneer and provides examples of his spiel. Barrick's chief informant remains anonymous but uses proverbs, folk comparisons, rhymes or jingles, and
various jokes. In "The View from the Water Table: Folklore of the
Offshore Oilfield Workers" (*MidSF* 2:63–76) Mary C. Fields describes the work and the speech of men stationed on the drilling rigs
in the Gulf of Mexico. They have their rituals, superstitions, and
customs, and they use a peculiar terminology which only the initiated can understand.

Somewhat different in focus is Charles K. Wolfe's "Southwestern

Humor and Old-Time Music: Lunsford's 'Speaking the Truth,' "
(*JEMFQ* 10:31–34). The article deals with a burlesque sermon recorded by Columbia in 1930 but probably in oral circulation before
and after the recording. It ridicules both the backwoods preacher
who addresses "Brethering and Sistering" and the preacher turned
recording artist as well.

Another kind of folk speech, coarse and obscene but sometimes
very funny, appears in an article by Anthony M. Reynolds, "Urban
Negro Toasts: A Hustler's View from L.A." (*WF* 33:267–300).
Toasts are defined here as rhymed couplets assembled from a variety
of sources and performed before an appreciative Negro audience.
The speakers are identified as gamblers and street people who will
often recite lengthy toasts incorporating details of their own lives or
repeating narratives learned from other speakers or even from print.
Reynolds gives the toasts he recorded as well as the sources if they
were available. In a similar article Dennis Wepman, Ronald B. Newman, and Murray B. Binderman deal with "Toasts: the Black Urban
Folk Poetry" (*JAF* 87:208–24). To these authors the toast is oral
literature, generally narrative but occasionally merely boasts or modern flytings. In particular the toast depicts "the spirit of a black sub-
culture—the Life—in our cities."

Earl F. Robacker's "Victorian Wall Mottoes" (*PF* 23,iii:2–10)
combines folk speech and folk art. He describes the samplers, once
common in Pennsylvania homes, which framed common aphorisms or
admonitions ("United We Stand," "Knowledge is Power," "Abide
With Me") in elaborate needle work. Generally the sampler included
the name of the domestic artist and the date of completion.

A curious article by Alan Dundes entitled "The Henny-Penny
Phenomenon: A Study of Folk Phonological Esthetics in American
Speech" (*SFQ* 38:1–9) deals with common American practices and
provides a multitude of examples. Traditional pairs of words, which
he terms binomials, are represented by *kith and kin* and *hit or miss*.
Reduplicatives can be identical (*tom-tom* or *ding-dong*), can change
vowels (*hee-haw* or *zig zag*), or can rhyme (*hocus-pocus* or *mumbo
jumbo*). Dundes notes that one of the Aarne-Thompson tale types is
called "Animals with Queer Names" (whence the title of this article),
and then theorizes that the English language seems to prefer "h-p"
locutions: *hen party, house party, horse power, half price, half pint,*
and many more. His examples are persuasive.

A special kind of folk speech is defined by Kay L. Cothran in "Talking Trash in the Okefenokee Swamp Rim, Georgia" (*JAF* 87: 340–56). Based on her University of Pennsylvania dissertation, this article collects some of the whoppers, tall tales, personal experience tales, and accounts of practical jokes which are an essential part of male conversation in southeastern Georgia. Like other oral narratives they are told for amusement and continue to delight a willfully credulous audience. Ms. Cothran admits that collecting such material from Okefenoke fishermen and woodsmen is sometimes stultifying for a woman but contends that she could often infer from female behavior in the back country what the males did not always articulate. At any rate her hoard of verbal "trash" is amusing and revealing.

viii. Folklore in Literature

Articles dealing with the use of folklore themes by American writers continue to appear. Witchcraft, superstition, and conjuration are some of the themes identified and discussed, while the writers generally selected are novelists. Only one major poet apparently attracted folkloristic attention in 1974. In "Emily Dickinson's Valentines" (*AQ* 26:60–78) Vivian R. Pollack points out that there were three valentines among the poet's early work and argues that they utilize some of the conventions of the English Valentine's Day. The evidence is thin and the article needlessly long but the verse does demonstrate Emily Dickinson's command of wit and parody.

Chadwick Hansen in "The Metamorphoses of Tituba, or Why American Intellectuals Can't Tell An Indian Witch from a Negro" (*NEQ* 47:3–12) gives an interesting account of the half-breed woman who figured in the Salem witchcraft trials and became a character in a dramatic poem by Longfellow and in plays by William Carlos Williams and Arthur Miller. In *The Crucible* Miller makes Tituba into a Negress practicing voodoo, although historically she was probably Indian. In her article entitled "Power Unequal to Man: the Significance of Conjure in Works by Five Afro-American Authors" (*SFQ* 38:91–108), Helen Jaskoski analyzes *conjure* (by which she means hoodoo, voodoo, gopher, root work) in works as varied as the different versions of Frederick Douglass's autobiography, short stories by Charles W. Chesnutt, and novels by Ernest J. Gaines and Ann Petry. She concludes that conjure can serve as a source of power within and for the community but if misused it can be destructive. Chesnutt's tales, incidentally, have been collected by Sylvia Lyons Render. *The Short Fiction of Charles W. Chesnutt* (Washington, D.C.: Howard Univ. Press) includes 55 items and an introduction which claims that the author faithfully reproduced popular folkways, dialects, superstitions, and even parts of folk sermons. Chesnutt obviously knew the work of Joel Chandler Harris and modeled his own Julius McAdoo after Uncle Remus.

Another Negro writer, Zora Neale Hurston, is the subject of an essay by Ann L. Rayson. In "The Novels of Zora Neale Hurston" (*SBL* 5:1–10) she stresses the fact that Hurston collected black folklore in Florida and Georgia so that as a consequence she could fill her fiction with folk idioms and folkways. Indeed, "Her novels are extended ballads composed through incremental repetition and traditional characters and situations."

Two writers who used early 19th-century backwoods material also stimulated revaluation. Leonard Williams in "An Early Arkansas 'Frolic': A Contemporary Account" (*MidSF* 2:39–42) provides data about Charles Noland who contributed sketches to periodicals under the pseudonym of Pete Whetstone. The particular "frolic" mentioned here involved a quilting party, a dance, fiddle tunes, and a marching game. In the *Appalachian Journal* (1:82–93) Ormonde Plater deals with five stories by George Washington Harris about the Sut Lovingood family. Plater points out in "The Lovingood Patriarchy" the use of trickster stories, practical jokes, drunken wakes, and rather unusual erotic humor.

A perceptive article by Joseph J. Arpad, "The Fight Story: Quotation and Originality in Native American Humor" (*JFI* 10[1973]: 141–72) deals with the basic episode of much early frontier narrative, the conflict between river boatman and wagoner. It is usually presented as the account of an eyewitness on the Mississippi or other western rivers. Arpad remarks that actually most of these confrontations depend on earlier printed versions rather than on personal experience. Perhaps the seminal text comes from James K. Paulding in 1817. Later versions appear in works by Bird, Crockett, Longstreet, and Mark Twain.

Robert C. Wess in "The Use of Hudson Valley Traditions in Washington Irving's *Knickerbocker History of New York*" (*NYFQ* 30: 212–25), focusing on the 1848 revision of the book, reviews Irving's handling of tall tales and the derisive pictures of the early Dutch preserved in folklore. A more original discussion of fictional practice is S. M. Bennett's "Ornament and Environment: Uses of Folklore in Willa Cather's Fiction" (*TFSB* 40:95–102). In the Nebraska novels the author used folklore somewhat ornamentally, to embellish or illustrate character and to add color to incidents. In the novels about New Mexico and Quebec the folklore, basically religious, became important to the author in her attempt to define the clash or mixture of cultures. Church art in the Southwest and folk medicine in Quebec were freely introduced into the pages of the novels and became functioning elements therein.

Folklore has also entered the work of more recent writers. Richard Gray argues in "Signs of Kinship: Thomas Wolfe and His Appalachian Background" (*AppalachianJ* 1:309–19) that Wolfe in his last unfinished work, *The Hills Beyond*, deliberately and consciously employed North Carolina mountain traditions and legends for greater authenticity. In similar fashion John Steinbeck turned to an old whaling village on Long Island and used references to weather and fishing lore in a late novel. Kevin McCarthy's "Witchcraft and Superstition in *The Winter of Our Discontent*" (*NYFQ* 30:198–211) points out that the folklore is introduced not only for genuine local color but also to provide irony and parody. Steinbeck even includes a banker who will not step on the sidewalk cracks although his mother has been dead for some years.

In an article entitled "Traditional Themes in Faulkner's 'The Bear'" (*TFSB* 40:57–64) Judith W. Hess asserts that critics have not precisely documented Faulkner's dependence on folk materials. But her citation of Thorpe's "Big Bear of Arkansas" story and some of Davy Crockett's hunting exploits is hardly news in 1974.

ix. Miscellaneous

The articles discussed here reveal the extraordinary diversity of folklore research. Advertising, computers, country weeklies, the Teddy Bear fad, high school yearbooks, and a manual for collectors illustrate the limitless directions in which folklorists can project their inquiries profitably.

Nancy B. Sederberg in "Antebellum Southern Humor in the *Camden Journal*: 1826–1840" (*MissQ* 27:41–74) examines a South Carolina periodical and finds a number of courting, political, and religious anecdotes. Each item is summarized. Two country newspapers interested other writers. Hugh Don Johnson in "Ora Jane Bawcum's Fox Ridge News" (*MidSF* 2:89–94) gives an account of a column of local news appearing in the Parsons, Tennessee, *News Leader*. It is gossipy, incoherent, and semiliterate but fascinating in its account of personal and domestic life. Andrew Badger's "Rural Salesmanship: Some Gleanings from *Thigpen's Store News*" (*MidSF* 2:19–26) concentrates on the announcements and advertisements in a four-page paper distributed gratis by the proprietor of a store in Picayune, Mississippi. Some of the howlers printed therein seem inspired ("Wanted —an old time dining table by an old lady with square legs").

Another article based on newspaper evidence is Ormond Loomis's "The Ford-McCoy Killing" (*FForum* 7:244–59), a discussion of a family feud in Monroe County, Indiana, in 1907 which is still remembered but differently interpreted.

Several essays confirm the claim that modern folklore is not necessarily rural. Bruce E. Nickerson in "Is There a Folk in the Factory?" (*JAF* 87:133–39) answers his question positively. He uses his own plant experience to prove that although factory workers do not engage in storytelling or use particular folklore genres, they definitely observe traditional customs, permit horseplay, and perform "government jobs" (work done for themselves on company time). Michael J. Preston in "Xerox-Lore" (*KF* 19:11–26) argues that technical inventions spawn new lore. A xerox print thus can be visual, can produce mock directions, and can circulate parodies. Similarly Richard S. Thill in " 'A Rose by Any Other Name': Computers, Traditions, and the Folklorist" (*TFSB* 40:1–8) comments on computer jokes but suggests more seriously that computers can aid researchers in other ways than storing data. He seems rather vague about specifics.

Tom E. Sullenberger in an adroit article entitled "Ajax Meets Jolly Green Giant: Some Observations on the Use of Folklore and Myth in American Mass Marketing" (*JAF* 87:53–65) ties folklore to advertising. Sullenberger claims that both manufacturers and salesmen have used folklore concepts to good advantage and chooses examples from advertising symbols in the canning, baking, detergent, and automobile industries. Automobiles named Jaguar, Cougar, Barracuda, and Mustang benefit from their obvious connotations, although Demon seems possibly unwise and Gremlin suggests a mischievously evil figure. To the author such labels are clever and successful "folklure."

Norine Dresser in " 'The Boys in the Band is Not Another Musical': Male Homosexuals and Their Folklore" (*WF* 33:205–18) uses material gleaned from visiting gay bars in Los Angeles to reach certain conclusions about homosexuals. Isolated from family, society, and religion, the homosexual readily admits his deviation but defensively shifts pronouns, adopts feminine names, exchanges in-jokes, and imitates female manners. The article gives definitions for some 20 commonly used terms in the homosexual environment.

In two articles William R. Ferris deals with southern railroad and religious lore. He claims in "Railroad Folklore: An Overview" (*NCarF* 22:169–76) that the railroad has been probably the greatest single catalyst for folklore in American life. It was not a great social leveler since most railroad folklore came from ethnic groups, but it did stimulate work chants, folk tales, and slangy diction. Ferris points out the wide usage of railroad nicknames and occupational terms. In "Black Delta Religion" (*MidSF* 2:27–33) he comments on Negro church practices ranging from evangelical preaching and the mourners' bench to hymn-singing choirs and total immersion. Ferris also includes anecdotes about baptism and parody sermons. Photographs enhance his text.

Consideration of three widely different essays, a workers' manual, and a state ethnic collection will conclude this roundup of miscellaneous items. Jeremiah J. Sullivan and James F. McCloy in "The Jersey Devil's Finest Hour" (*NYFQ* 30:233–39) revive interest in a diabolic manifestation once visible in 18th-century New Jersey. It supposedly reappeared briefly in 1909. Steven J. Zeitlin's "As Sweet as You Are: the Structural Element in the Signed High School Yearbook" (*NYFQ* 30:83–100) turns to autographed class books from the 1965–72 period to discover folk forms. The results are trivial. Peter Tamony, on the other hand, in "The Teddy Bear: Continuum in a Security Blanket" (*WF* 33:231–38) traces the appeal of the Teddy Bear fad and connects it with Theodore Roosevelt, the Steiff toys of Würtemberg, Russian folklore, the bear flag of California, and a warm and comfortable chemise. Teddy Bear's progeny, Tamony observes, include Smokey the Bear, Yogi Bear, and the cuddly toy carried by Dennis the Menace.

The entire 1974 issue of *Northeast Folklore* (15:1–76) is given over to "A Manual for Field Workers," a project which had its inception in the folklore archives and courses of Edward D. Ives at the University of Maine. Although specifically keyed to local conditions the manual has a wider utility, and people who heard Ives talk on the subject begged him to make it more easily available.

A pleasant little book entitled *The Harvest and the Reapers* is the work of Kenneth and Mary Clarke (Lexington: Univ. Press of Ky.). Part of the Kentucky Bicentennial Bookshelf, the volume surveys the oral history of the Bluegrass State and includes succinct accounts of Kentucky folk speech, yarns, ballads, and legends. Representative examples are a classic of horse racing, "Ten Broek and Mollie," and a summary of the Beauchamp-Sharp tragedy which inspired both William G. Simms and Robert Penn Warren. Probably the most useful part of the volume is the biographical material about prominent Kentucky folklorists like Josiah H. Combs, E. C. Perrow, Marie Campbell, Leonard Roberts, and Gordon Wilson. The book unfortunately lacks an index.

As its contribution to the American Bicentennial the Texas Folklore Society issued in 1974 *The Folklore of Texan Cultures*, ed. Francis Edward Abernethy (Austin, Tex.: Encino Press). The 366–page book includes short essays by 43 different writers on the ethnic groups native to or immigrating to Texas; the typographical format is attractive and excellent photographs enhance the text. The folklorist will find a good deal of interest here: Mexican *corridos*, Cajun cookery, Spanish religious miracles, Negro "Juneteenth" tales, the ritual and traditions of Italian gulf coast fishermen. Folklore is also scattered through the accounts of some of the less known ethnic groups in what used to be the largest American state: Greeks, Irish, Poles, Chinese, Jews. But on the whole the book is stronger in regional and local history than in folklore. Most of the authors have academic connections although there are a few journalists and businessmen included. The volume is a pleasure to dip into and to sample; probably only a genuine Texas aficionado would wish to read it carefully from cover to cover.

x. Obituaries

Obituaries of folk performers and folklore scholars appeared in various places in 1974. W. Amos Abrams contributed a reminiscent account of Horton Barker to *NCarF* (22:141–53) in which he paid tribute to the surprising repertoire of a blind singer. William Hugh Jansen wrote a notice of Bascom Lamar Lunsford (1882–1973) for *JAF* (87:155). Lee Knight published an obituary of Marjorie Lansing Porter (1891–1973) in *NYFQ* (30:77–80). And in 1973 Anne Warner and Frank Warner contributed to the *Appalachian Journal* (1:163–93) a long account of Frank Profitt (1913–65), replete with pictures, anecdotes, and excerpts from letters.

D. K. Wilgus's tribute to Francis Lee Utley (1907–74) in *WF* (33:202–04) emphasized Utley's interests in Chaucer, medieval literature, and onomastics as well as folklore.

The death of Archer Taylor in 1973 produced memorials in various periodicals. Alan Dundes in *American Folklore Newsletter* (3:3) and Donald J. Ward in *Fabula* (15:124–27) wrote tributes. The longest account came from Wayland D. Hand in *JAF* (87:3–9), a fervent eulogy to Taylor's versatility, scholarship, and erudition. Hand especially emphasized Taylor's mastery of bibliography, German literary history, and proverbs.

University of Illinois, Urbana

20. Themes, Topics, Criticism

Michael J. Hoffman

I shall continue this year the practice I adopted in the last edition of *ALS*, of dealing only with full-length books that seem to me to make a significant contribution to literary criticism in English and to overviews of American literature. There were to my knowledge no major anthologies published during the past year and, literary cycles being what they are, there were many fewer attempts at an overview of American literature published than there were in 1973. Although the list of books I have examined does not pretend to be complete, it does, I am confident, represent the critical works of 1974 that are worth remembering.

i. Overviews of American Literature

One of the few comprehensive overviews was Dan Vogel's *The Three Masks of American Tragedy* (Baton Rouge: La. State Univ. Press). It is less about the theater than about the tragic possibilities and characteristics of American literature. In his opening chapter Vogel uses Aristotle to establish his critical metaphor. While the basic outline has promise, Vogel's treatment of *The Poetics* is too skeletal. As a result, his thesis is underdeveloped.

Vogel asserts that tragedy always "flourishes at a time of prosperity for the respective societies in which it was written. . . . In America, tragedy was first written in the middle of the nineteenth century, coincident with the supreme confidence of a republic flexing its manifest destiny" (p. 13). This is hardly a new suggestion, and Vogel's presentation of the "tragic" sides of Hawthorne, Melville, and company has had more than one precedent. Still, his development of Oedipus, Job, Christ, and Satan as tragic models is well done and does provide us with some fresh insights into such individual works as *Moby-Dick*, *The Scarlet Letter*, and *Death of a Salesman*. Vogel's narrative presentation is thematic rather than chronological, and I wonder if his purposes wouldn't have been better served by a more historical approach. I also missed any reference to Charles Williams's *Modern Tragedy*, a book whose major insights Vogel seems in large measure to share.

A better-done book is David Ketterer's *New Worlds for Old: The Apocalyptic Imagination, Science Fiction, and American Literature* (New York: Doubleday, paper; Bloomington: Indiana Univ. Press, hardbound). This is one of the best books ever written on science fiction; however, the reader uninterested in that subject should not pass it by because it is about much more than the title suggests. For Ketterer the apocalyptic impulse is basic not only to science fiction but to much of what is most vital in this country's literature. His major influences are William Blake, Frank Kermode's *Sense of an Ending*, Bruce Franklin's *Future Perfect*, and Northrop Frye's *Anatomy of Criticism*.

Not surprisingly, Ketterer's archetypal sci-fi author is Poe, whose "Fall of the House of Usher" he uses as a historical model for apocalyptic fiction. He divides the various kinds of science fictional writing into the following categories: the visionary tradition, utopian fantasy, millenialism, differing perceptions of reality, differing concepts of man, new concepts of space-time, outside controlling forces in the universe (God or otherwise). There are long chapters on Poe, Brown's *Wieland*, Twain's *Connecticut Yankee*, Melville's *Confidence Man*, and Vonnegut's *The Sirens of Titan*. Ketterer presents Kurt Vonnegut as a culmination of American science fiction and *The Sirens of Titan* as perhaps the finest literary work in the genre. One does not have to agree with that judgment, however, to find *New Worlds for Old* an erudite, well-written book.

An equally interesting book by Lawrence Chenoweth, *The American Dream of Success* (North Scituate, Mass.: Duxbury Press), uses documents of popular culture to study "The Search for the Self in the Twentieth Century." Chenoweth has read "1140 articles published in *Reader's Digest* sample issues from 1926 through 1969 and 707 articles and stories published in *The Saturday Evening Post* sample issues from 1917 through 1967" (p. ix). In addition, the author claims to "have studied the 47 best-selling self-help books published between 1917 and 1969" (p. ix). In addition, Chenoweth discusses "Superman," "Little Orphan Annie," and "Peanuts" as well as relevant sociological and historical works concerned with the same period. His thesis is that "to retain American values and ignore the conflicts among our basic beliefs, self-help writers increasingly have resorted to rationalizations which have made our philosophies of life outdated and contradictory to the point of absurdity" (p. 1). The book is an extended exemplification of the theory that there is in American culture a paradoxical conflict between its stated ideals and our lived ideologies, as classically presented by Reinhold Niebhur in *The Irony of American History*. The author's attitudes are what I would call "academic radical," but they are well stated and not merely rhetorical. He makes his case well, although I am not sure that we finally learn much more than we already knew. And the choice of *The Reader's Digest* and *The Saturday Evening Post* certainly stacks the deck. There were, after all, other mass cultural attitudes than those of the rednecks so often pandered to by those two magazines. What I should like to see is a more extensive coverage of the same ground through examination of radio and television programs, films, advertising, and other forms of mass media. Chenoweth mentions these in passing, but we need more evidence. Still, the book is a good beginning and bodes well for the interest in popular culture currently burgeoning in academia.

A thoughtful, promising work by Harry B. Henderson, III is *Versions of the Past*. It contains an excellent discussion of American attitudes toward history, with primarily 19th-century American novelists and historians as subjects and models. Henderson's intention is to establish a theoretical base for discussing, *à la* Georg Lukacs, the historical novel in American Literature.

To establish his thesis, the author divides his figures according to two structures or "frames of acceptance" which he claims underlie all American historical writing, fictional and otherwise. The first is the "progressive" frame, which asserts the "eternally constant nature of man and the idea of history as consisting of measurable change on an absolute scale" (p. 14). This structure derives from the Puritans, with Bancroft and Motley its key 19th-century figures among historians. The second, "holist," frame derives from Vico. "It is characterized by a relativistic view of time-bound man and by a belief that historical change is not measurable except *in terms of the period un-*

der consideration" (p. 14—author's italics). Here the exemplars are Prescott and Parkman. This interesting thesis demands, I am afraid, too much manipulation of evidence to stand without qualification. However, Henderson's readings of individual works—among them *The Last of the Mohicans, Billy Budd, The Scarlet Letter, Democracy, A Connecticut Yankee in King Arthur's Court,* and *Absalom, Absalom!*—are sensitive and intelligent enough that they need not rigidly adhere to a thesis to be valid.

The 30-year-old Henderson was killed in a traffic accident shortly after this book—his first—was accepted for publication. It is a pity that so promising a career will not have a chance to develop further.

Mary Helen Dohan's story of the American language, *Our Own Words* (New York: Knopf), is not going to replace H. L. Mencken's book on the same subject but then it hardly intends to. This is a high-level popular history, written from a broadly philological point of view. The author is not only a good scholar, she is also skilled at making linguistic and philological concepts accessible to the non-specialist. Each chapter is a short history of some particular language category traced often from Indo-European origins through the various influences on British English to the various stages of the growth and development of American English. Dohan traces the influence on our language of such sources as Indians, immigration, industrialism, urbanization, and television. Her book is the best one-volume history of American English I know of for anyone other than the professional linguist. While it does not match Mencken for virtuosity and wit, it is still a very well-written piece of cultural history.

The final book in this section is not literary, but it is one that professors of American literature ought to know about. It is *The Flowering of American Folk Art* (New York: Viking Press), by Jean Lipman and Alice Winchester, originally the sumptuously illustrated catalogue for a major exhibition of folk art at the Whitney Museum. The historical area covered is the first century of the Republic, 1776–1876, and the text consists primarily of descriptive passages about the various areas of American folk art that the authors have used to divide the field—areas such as paintings, sculpture (ship carvings and cigar-store figures, for instance), home and highway decorations, and home furnishings. The authors make a good case for the beauty of American folk and "primitive" art and their excellent selections are beautifully reproduced. The book gives the reader a better insight into the American folk consciousness than most books that are more elaborately theoretical, and I would recommend it as an excellent way to understand the settings of many literary works of that period.

ii. Thematic and Historical Studies

The renewed interest in literary history has recently been served and symbolized by the distinguished journal, *New Literary History*, edited by Ralph Cohen. A set of essays from that journal now appears as a book under the editorship of Professor Cohen, *New Directions in Literary History* (Baltimore: Johns Hopkins Univ. Press). It is a distinguished collection with a variety of focuses and excellent pieces from some people not always thought of as literary historians, such as Geoffrey Hartman, Michael Riffaterre, and Barbara Herrnstein Smith. The latter has contributed, I think, the book's most distinguished essay, "Poetry as Fiction," which I hope will find its way into a new book by the author.

Almost everything in this volume is concerned in some way with the reader's response to works of literature, which indicates how far we have gone beyond the "intentional fallacy." As one might expect, the orientation of many of the writers is phenomenological, particularly the European contributors. But the book's point of view is eclectic rather than ideological. This is a collection that anyone interested in literary theory ought to take a look at, for it marks off a number of directions that literary study will be taking in the next decade.

A literary and cultural historian whose career has covered almost five decades, Howard Mumford Jones, has published yet another book, *Revolution & Romanticism* (Cambridge, Mass.: Harvard Univ. Press), the third in a series after *O Brave New World* and *The Age of Energy*. This is a summatory work, not one of original scholarship, but as readers of Jones might expect, it is well written. The book is better as narrative history than literary history, however, because its theoretical underpinnings are weak. Jones's ideas about Romanticism, for instance, do not go beyond Lovejoy's of 50 years ago.

The book deals with both the French and American Revolutions, with what Jones posits as their cultural causes and aftermaths. He tries to show in each case how classical and neoclassical attitudes led to the various revolutions, and his historical erudition is impressive. Jones's culture heroes, conventionally enough, are Wordsworth (in

The Prelude) and Goethe (in *Faust*). He would obviously like to contribute a new historical overview, but his synthesis is not terribly
original. On the subject of the revolutions he is not as interesting as
either Crane Brinton or Hannah Arendt. On Romanticism, as I have
said, he does not seem to have read any recent critics. This book will
not satisfy the specialist and is probably too difficult for the beginner.

Another study of 19th-century Romantic culture is Walter L.
Reed's *Meditations on the Hero: A Study of the Romantic Hero in
Nineteenth-Century Fiction* (New Haven, Conn.: Yale Univ. Press).
This literate study unfortunately does not add a great deal to what
we already know about either the hero or Romantic fiction. The
book is heavily influenced by Kierkegaard and the categories he developed in a whole series of works. Within that context, Reed goes on
to discuss works by Emily Brontë, Lermontov, and Melville. There
is some discussion of Carlyle, but not nearly enough, given the immense influence on the concept of the hero Carlyle had during that
time. The short section on Byron is barely adequate for the same
reasons. In a book that dwells so heavily on Kierkegaard there should
be some mention of Murray Krieger's treatment of that writer in *The
Tragic Vision*. Reed is also as out of date in his concepts of Romanticism as was Jones. Again, what we have here is another book that is
pleasant to read but not finally original enough for the specialist.
Much better than the average Ph.D. thesis, it still betrays its origins.

A more interesting thematic study, largely concerned with modern literature and the arts, is John Fraser's *Violence in the Arts* (London: Cambridge Univ. Press). This wide-ranging, erudite book draws
on many sources from the popular arts, such as detective novels and
films. The theoretical orientation is heavily psychological. Fraser has
convincing insights into why we feel violated by particular forms of
violence in the arts, and he is acute in pointing out how the various
media bring about different responses in the perceiver. While Fraser's
tone is moral, he is not moralistic. Some of the chapter titles give
an insight into the combined moral-psychological focus of this work:
"Ambivalences," "Revolt," "Victims," "Violators," "Responsibilities."
This is a thoughtful, *engagé*, somewhat politically conservative work.
Fraser does not try to be hip about violence or sophisticated about
fascistic tendencies in the arts. He is concerned, and he makes the
reader concerned, about current trends toward the philosophical and

artistic validation of violence. The stubborn integrity of this short book has much to commend it.

Also among the thematically oriented books is another work with a grumble against the modern age. *Modern Dogma and the Rhetoric of Assent* (South Bend, Ind.: Notre Dame Univ. Press), by Wayne Booth, was originally presented as the Ward-Phillips Lectures in English Language and Literature. It is an examination of the rhetoric connected with what Booth calls "modernism." He discusses the reasons why we assent to ideas that are assumed to be "obvious," in an effort to examine the "rhetorical community" where certain ideas are simply taken for granted. The book still has the informal tone of the lectures, although in writing the final version Booth has added a number of long, discursive footnotes.

Booth's moral imperative is clearly fortified by his experience as dean at the University of Chicago in the late 1960s and early 1970s during the student revolt. He feels that our rhetoric and therefore our culture is in crisis, and he sees as the cause behind this the rhetoric of certain strains of Modernist thought of which Bertrand Russell is Booth's chief bête noire. His discussion of Russell is full of intelligent, well-informed ambivalence. The English philosopher is for Booth an unmitigated relativist, forced into self-contradiction by a moral stance characteristic of modern thought. As an enterprise to shore against the ruins of modernist chaos, Booth proposes literature, which he claims can teach better than a direct statement. To some extent this is just an old-fashioned aesthete's point of view, the sensitive English professor's plea for Art. And while Booth does make his point with utter conviction, he often lapses into some strangely modernistic contradictions. Still, he is always witty and impressively learned. I find myself always agreeing with him up to a point and then parting company, but he is a challenging author with whom to quarrel.

Almost as interesting a book is A. D. Nuttall's *A Common Sky: Philosophy and the Literary Imagination* (Berkeley and Los Angeles: Univ. of Calif. Press), a first-rate study of "solipsistic fear" in English philosophy and poetry from Locke, Hume, and Berkeley through T. S. Eliot. Nuttall seems equally at home in both philosophy and literature, and he shows quite convincingly how the concept of solipsism that developed in 18th-century English philosophy was also reflected in the fiction of the time and has continued as a tradition into the 20th century. His reading of *Tristram Shandy* is equally as good as his treatment of Hume, and he makes a good case for the continuity of his theme of solipsism in all of T. S. Eliot's poetry. The only problem I have with Nuttall is that his English common-sense attitude sometimes causes him to keep too loose a rein on his thesis. Otherwise, this is a well-written sophisticated book that treats effectively and without distortion both philosophical and literary works.

My favorite polemical text of the year is Richard Lanham's *Style: An Anti-Textbook* (New Haven, Conn.: Yale Univ. Press), which mercilessly attacks the handbook teaching of composition. Lanham opposes with wit and style the idea that "clarity" is the highest attainment of discursive prose, that transparency of style is a moral virtue. He argues for a concept of style as being sensuous and self-consciously pleasurable. One applauds such sentiments in the abstract, although with specific students in mind one shudders. Lanham insists that we recognize how different styles are useful in different situations. In this regard he is utterly pragmatic. This is a tonic book, although since it is a polemic it does lack a specific program. Perhaps Lanham will now give us his own composition handbook—nonprescriptive and nonmoralistic, of course.

iii. Theory of Literature

In the theory of literature there were a number of interesting though not always successful books. Typical of this judgment is John M. Ellis's *The Theory of Criticism: A Logical Analysis* (Berkeley and Los Angeles: Univ. of Calif. Press), which begins with promise and ends in serious disappointment. Ellis would like us to have a logical, systematic approach to the study of literature, an aim propounded by many theoreticians, both American and European. He claims rightly that we lack such an approach now and also claims rightly that Wellek's and Warren's *Theory of Literature* is outdated.

Ellis's orientation is that of the philosophy of ordinary language. He wishes us to establish what kinds of statements are valid in particular contexts. In opposing the reference theory of language he has the later Wittgenstein as his hero, for Ellis suggests that we distinguish between kinds of statements rather than claim that words refer directly to entities. He attacks biographical and intentionalist criticism very well, and here he puts forth some new arguments, not just those of Wimsatt and Beardsley. But why beat such a dead horse?

Ellis's criterion for defining a literary work is that it fits the community's categorizing of certain objects as literary. There are possibilities in this approach, but they were explored with much greater sophistication a decade ago by Morse Peckham in *Man's Rage for Chaos*, a book and an author I find mentioned nowhere in Ellis. This is not the only area where Ellis does not seem to have done his homework. In a work like this such omissions are a serious flaw. In addition, the book is written in such a dry, matter-of-fact style that it is difficult to follow the argument, especially with such a paucity of direct literary examples to back up the abstractions.

Another work with somewhat the same general concerns is *The Literary Text: An Examination of Critical Methods* (Berkeley and Los Angeles: Univ. of Calif. Press), by P. M. Wetherill. This too is a somewhat dry work, although I find it more useful because it systematically attempts to survey the various ways in which we examine literary texts both to interpret and evaluate them. Wetherill's chapter titles give a sense of his concerns: "Sounds," "Grammar," "Meaning I: Words," "Meaning II: Style," "Counting," "Construction," "Sequence." The book hangs between being an introductory text and an advanced survey, although I think it is more of the latter. Wetherill's critical approach is eclectic. In "Construction" he deals with Structuralism as a literary movement, seemingly favoring its program, although he suggests that when rigidly applied it is reductionistic. His plea for the sequential analyses of certain literary texts suggests that he finds the purely synchronic emphasis of Structuralism a problem. The bibliography, although selective, is still quite extensive, although any reader will quibble about some of the omissions.

Still another book published by the University of California Press concerns itself with literary theory. This one, *Literary Criticism: Idea and Act*, is a collection of major papers given at the English Institute meetings between 1939 and 1972, and is edited by W. K. Wimsatt. It is over 600 pages long and contains more than 30 essays. In a way it is like a survey of American criticism of the past three and a half decades, and the selections contain some of the most distinguished work produced in our universities during that time. Books such as this are often amorphous and inconsistent, but one cannot make such an accusation here. A number of these essays have been reprinted elsewhere or were the germ of longer works by such distinguished critics as Meyer Abrams, Geoffrey Hartman, George Steiner, Lionel Trilling, Francis Fergusson, and Harold Bloom. To single out any of the essays would do an injustice to almost all the others. I recommend the book highly, in spite of its inflated price ($18.50).

Wayne Booth is represented by yet another book, this one a more serious work of scholarship, *A Rhetoric of Irony* (Chicago: Univ. of Chicago Press). Like his celebrated *Rhetoric of Fiction* this book attempts systematically to survey and create a set of critical tools for discussing a major literary genre. With its publication this work becomes the major critical statement on irony, and yet it is not the work we might have hoped for. Booth opposes the "modern" theory that all good literature is by definition ironic. In developing his argument Booth contrasts two types of irony which he calls "stable" and "unstable." By the former he means an irony that comes out of a definite social value base and that is indisputable in both intent and reference to those who can understand it. His exemplary authors here are Jane Austen and Jonathan Swift. "Unstable" irony has a kind of infinite regress of values so that it is impossible to point exactly to what the author finally stands for—only to what he or she opposes. As a prime example of this Booth cites Samuel Beckett.

The problem is that Booth goes over familiar ground in a somewhat individual but not finally systematic way. He is most at home with 18th-century irony in which he finds a fairly well-accepted set of social values out of which ironists can operate. But as in *The Rhetoric of Fiction* Booth does not do nearly as well with the relativistic 20th century. He would like to find "rational" grounds for agreeing on value judgments, but he—though an absolutist of sorts—is trapped by his own intellectual honesty. He always implies the exception to his rules. This urbane, witty, and "ironic" book is quite useful, but it does not finally provide us with a transmittable critical tool. Perhaps irony defies definition beyond our own sensibilities, but I should like to see someone more sophisticated in the techniques of linguistic and semiological analysis explore the problem.

Another well-known writer, Jacques Barzun, has produced a set of lectures that present a theory of art in *The Use and Abuse of Art*

(Princeton, N.J.: Princeton Univ. Press), originally the Mellon Lectures, 1973. Barzun's echoing of one of Nietzsche's titles signals his intention to treat Art as a subversive force. In trying to establish his case, Barzun explores a series of modern attitudes toward art. Again the chapter titles are quite descriptive: "Why Art Must Be Challenged," "The Rise of Art as Religion," "Art the Destroyer," "Art the Redeemer," "Art and Its Tempter, Science," "Art in the Vacuum of Belief." Barzun accepts art as a potentially dangerous force in a series of witty *aperçus*. But this is not a heavyweight book. There is little here that we have not heard before, although perhaps not always so gracefully said, which may be the problem, for Barzun has obviously succumbed to crowd-pleasing. In that sense the lecture format works to the book's disadvantage.

I shall conclude this section with two books on the theory of Comparative Literature. The first is *Introduction to Comparative Literature* (Indianapolis and New York: Bobbs-Merrill), by François Jost, which is designed to be an introductory handbook. Jost proposes four basic approaches to Comparative Literature: 1) analogies and influences; 2) movements and trends; 3) genres and forms; 4) motifs, types, and themes. The author is a literary historian and philologist who emphasizes solid scholarship, but although an excellent philologist he is not an exciting critic, and I do not think his statements would stimulate much student interest. He also works too hard to legitimize his discipline, and his apologies for Comparative Literature (is this really necessary anymore?) are dull and methodical. I do not recommend this book as a textbook, and I think its level of sophistication would only intermittently prove interesting to the specialist. It is useful primarily as a book that covers the territory with some modicum of completeness.

A more sophisticated work on the same subject is Ulrich Weisstein's *Comparative Literature and Literary Theory: Survey and Introduction* (Bloomington: Indiana Univ. Press—paperback and hardbound), translated from the German by William Riggan in collaboration with the author. First published in 1968, it attempts to be a Wellek and Warren for Comparative Literature, as it deals with such basic problems as the distinction between comparative, world, and general literatures. Weisstein discusses a number of terms crucial to the discipline, such as influence, genre, and thematology, and although he is basically dependent on the ideas of others, this may not

be a serious criticism in such a book. This is a competent introductory
survey for graduate students, but I do not recommend it for under-
graduates. Because it is comprehensive, however, it is a rich but not
original source of information for specialists.

iv. Phenomenology and Structuralism

It is by now a commonplace to say that the American critical scene
is increasingly influenced by European philosophical and critical
movements. This trend is made even more apparent by the number
of books now appearing for the first time in English translation that
many years ago were crucial to Phenomenology. I refer in particular
to three works I received too late to review last year. The first two
are by Roman Ingarden, a Polish philosopher and student of Husserl
who was a leading figure in European philosophy from the 1930s
through the 1960s. *The Literary Work of Art*, translated from the
German and introduced by George C. Grabowicz (Evanston, Ill.:
Northwestern Univ. Press, 1973), was first published in 1931.

Ingarden establishes the ontology of the literary work of art by
analyzing the various levels (strata) on which we perceive it—i.e.,
the phonetic, the semantic, the representational, the sequential. He
discusses three further levels in our cognition of literature: artistic
creativeness, language, and universals, and he makes careful, logical
distinctions among these. The argument throughout this long, difficult, and fascinating book is heavily logical, complex, and idealistic,
in the tradition of continental philosophy and very much, I am afraid,
not in our own pragmatic tradition. It is not easy reading, but it is
worth the effort.

The same could also be said of Ingarden's companion work, *The
Cognition of the Literary Work of Art*, trans. Ruth Ann Crowley and
Kenneth R. Olson (Evanston, Ill.: Northwestern Univ. Press, 1973),
first published in 1937. Written from within the tradition of Hus-
serlian idealism, this book's focus is epistemological rather than ontological. Ingarden is concerned with the varieties of the reader's response and with the processes involved in the cognition of literary
works, a concern that is shared by many recent critics who make this
older work seem very up to date. This is really a book about how to
read, and it is well worth the trouble it takes for an American reader
unschooled in the idealist tradition to learn the terminology in order

to read it. Ingarden discusses how we apprehend verbal signs, how we perceive works of literature as wholes, and how we apprehend the literary work in the act of reading it (one of Georges Poulet's concerns). I am sure that we shall see Ingarden's name mentioned more and more frequently now that his books are available in English.

I think this will also be true of Mikel Dufrenne, whose major work, *The Phenomenology of Aesthetic Experience*, trans. Edward S. Casey et al. (Evanston, Ill.: Northwestern Univ. Press, 1973), was first published in French in 1953. Dufrenne's scope is larger than Ingarden's, for his is a comprehensive aesthetic theory presented in phenomenological terms. This massive, closely reasoned work is more difficult than either of Ingarden's. Dufrenne's point of view is that of the art perceiver or spectator. He divides the territory into three parts: 1) the spectator, 2) the aesthetic object, and 3) the ways in which the preceding two come together. Dufrenne claims that it is the aesthetic *experience* which establishes the unique ontology of the work of art by combining both perceiver and object. The argument proceeds not only with a heavy reliance on abstract ideas but with a marked lack of psychologizing. This kind of reasoning will not be widely accepted in this country without some kind of transformation.

Structuralism is represented by two interesting works, one a work of serious criticism and the other an introductory handbook. Frederic Jameson's *The Prison-House of Language* (Princeton, N.J.: Princeton Univ. Press) was originally published in 1972 but has been reprinted in 1974, thus giving me the excuse to talk about it in these pages. Since it is an analysis of Russian Formalism and French Structuralism rather than a summary of the two movements, it assumes that the reader knows something about the people of whom Jameson writes. The author is an acute dialectician with an excellent grasp of philosophical implications, although I think he is more informative on the Formalists than on the Structuralists. Jameson's Marxist point of view is never an ideological trap, although it does give him some trouble in handling the diachronic limitations of Structuralism. Jameson is a fine linguist and thinker, and I recommend this book as a necessary companion piece to his earlier important book, *Marxism and Form* (Princeton, N.J.: Princeton Univ. Press, 1971).

The tireless Robert Scholes has prepared an introductory summary of Structuralism for American audiences, *Structuralism in Literature: An Introduction* (New Haven, Conn.: Yale Univ. Press). For

beginners this is as good a place as any to start, with the possible
exception of Howard Gardner's *The Search for Mind* (New York:
Random House, 1972), a book that focuses less on literature. Scholes
is lucid and systematic, although somewhat lightweight. He talks not
just about Lévi-Strauss, but also about the linguistics of Roman
Jakobson and about the Russian formalists, particularly Vladimir
Propp, the folk-tale theorist. He also discusses Roland Barthes, although he stops short of such au courant French figures as Gilles
Deleuze and Jacques Derrida (by the time this goes to press they
will, no doubt, have gone out of date). For Scholes, as for this reviewer, Structuralism's major contribution to literary theory has been
in genre theory. The book is a good piece of high-level popularization, but it is not an original contribution, and Scholes's exemplary
structuralist readings of *Ulysses* and other 20th-century works are
not as useful as his summation of other theorists.

v. Post-Structuralism and Semiology

There are of course Post-Structuralist critical movements, although
because they are all arriving on the American scene so quickly, it is
difficult to maintain a sense of their developmental chronology. One
of the major figures involved in the critique of both Phenomenology
and Structuralism is Jacques Derrida, whose *Speech and Phenomena*, trans., introd. David B. Allison (Evanston, Ill.: Northwestern
Univ. Press, 1973), first published in 1967, is considered one of the
important philosophical works published in France during the past
decade. This brilliant critique of Husserl's theory of signs is almost
opaque to someone not familiar either with Husserl's works or with
the general program of Phenomenology. Nonetheless it contains some
key concepts that are increasingly being used in American criticism.
These concepts are "differance" (with an *a*) and "deconstruction." In
the preface Newton Garver explains the concept of "differance" by
suggesting that speech and writing are for Derrida essentially "in
harmony" because the concept of "differance" is essential to both.
In order for a vocal sign to emerge it has to exist in a state of differ-
entiation from everything else and yet also be within a system in
which the instituted difference systematically appears. This is another
way of dealing with Ferdinand de Saussure's distinction between
langue and *parole*, the former referring to a system of language that

exists independent of individual acts of speech and the latter to individual speech acts that can be understood only within the context
of the individual's language system. It is through a process of "deconstruction" that Derrida attempts to take us back to the essential
"differance" that constitutes the emergent being of an individual utterance and that is distorted by the act of putting it into words.

That this difficult concept can be applied to criticism is excitingly
demonstrated by Joseph Riddel's *The Inverted Bell: Modernism and
the Counterpoetics of William Carlos Williams* (Baton Rouge: La.
State Univ. Press). This is the first full-length treatment of an American poet that I know of that employs either Structuralist or Post-
Structuralist techniques. Riddel is influenced by both Heidegger and
Derrida, whose technique of deconstruction is Riddel's major critical
instrument. For Riddel, as for Heidegger, the "Fall" lies in our attempt to state the unstatable. Williams's poetry, in Riddel's view, attempts to recapture the primary essence lost when humankind made
its first statements and became differentiated into being. It is from this
point of view that he explains Williams's famous line, "no ideas but in
things." Riddel's nonchronological reading of Williams attempts to
show how he deconstructs language back to the essential "differance."
This is a radically new technique for American criticism, in line perhaps only with the work of J. Hillis Miller and, to some extent, Harold
Bloom. Riddel's book will be important to American criticism not
just as a reading of Williams but as the forerunner of a new technique
of reading we shall see much more of during the next decade.

A lot of European critical thought has recently been concerned
with the developing discipline of semiotics, which sees all human
communication, whether in narrative, discourse, myth, film, fashion,
or gesture as part of a comprehensive system of signs. Roland Barthes's
Elements of Semiology is the key document in this field, but there are
other writers whose ideas have spread to this country largely through
the work of linguists. Two recent texts are worth mentioning. Cesare
Segre's *Semiotics and Literary Criticism*, trans. (from Italian) John
Meddemmen (The Hague: Mouton, 1973) is a mixed book, with a
few good essays. The first half focuses on modern literary trends,
particularly Structuralism, but what Segre has to say about that
movement is no better than competent journalism. What he writes,
however, about semiotics is very good, particularly in relation to
film. The key essay here is "Between Structuralism and Semiotics," an

excellent discussion not only of the relationship of the two disciplines but also of the historical transition between them.

A more substantial though not quite distinguished collection of essays is by William O. Hendricks: *Essays on Semiolinguistics and Verbal Art* (The Hague: Mouton, 1973). Hendricks's definition serves as the underlying theme behind this fairly unified collection: "It [semiotics] differs from linguistics in that it takes as the basic unit, not the sentence, but the text. Its primary concern is with the compositional principles underlying texts" (p. 7). Hendricks is influenced primarily by Chomsky, Saussure, Barthes, and Lévi-Strauss in combining semiotics and linguistics. The strength of his essays lies in their developing a systematic way of discussing narrative continuity, a theme central to a number of this year's books. In his later essays Hendricks uses Vladimir Propp on the folk tale as a theoretical base for discussing narrative texts. When he develops his own analyses, however, he is much less convincing than when he theorizes. Like most linguists and many Structuralists he falls back on graphs and semimathematical formulae. There must be some way for linguists and critics to find a common language without resorting to flow charts.

vi. Theory of Fiction

As I have already suggested, much critical interest was expressed this year in fictional theory and the theory of narrative. The following books reflect and demonstrate that interest. The general level of competence is relatively high, and yet I find myself disappointed by them as a group.

The most sociologically oriented is Alan Kennedy's *The Protean Self: Dramatic Action in Contemporary Fiction* (New York: Columbia Univ. Press). The book opens with a well-informed discussion of current sociological theory relevant to the author's concerns. Kennedy's definition of action is dramatic, sociological, and existentialist. Because he is explicitly interested in the relation of fiction to life, he uses his sociological and philosophical orientations to define human beings as role-players; his focus on dramatic action is thus more on the actor than on the act. His general discussion of Modernism is quite suggestive, but his specific practical readings of some contemporary English novels are not as interesting. Still, the opening few chapters contain an excellent and useful discussion of sociological theory in relation to the novel.

Arnold L. Weinstein's *Vision and Response in Modern Fiction* (Ithaca, N.Y.: Cornell Univ. Press) is more disappointing. Perhaps the problem is that the author never really develops his thesis enough for the book to take coherent shape. Early on Weinstein draws an analogy between vision and response and our "perception of the world and our reaction to it." He suggests that novels both "*depict* an education" and "constitute an education," and that "to analyze the ways in which specific novels achieve their meaning and posit their reality is the goal of this study" (p. 15). It is a thin thesis and the choice of novels to exemplify it is too random, ranging as it does from Balzac and Dickens through Borges and Robbe-Grillet.

This is basically a conservative book that laments the loss by modern novelists of interest and belief in interpersonal relationships. While the breadth of Weinstein's selections does gives an illusory sense of literary history, the theory behind the individual analyses is insufficient. As a result, although the book is well written and erudite, it leaves an impression of intellectual thinness.

Bernard Paris's *A Psychological Approach to Fiction* (Blooming-ton: Indiana Univ. Press) has a much stronger thesis, and within its self-imposed limitations it is more successful. Paris bases his theory on "Third Force" psychologists Abraham Maslow and Karen Horney, emphasizing, accordingly, the human need for self-realization. In his emphasis on character and personality Paris focuses more on "realistic" fiction and fictional characters than on action or setting. He claims that critics like Booth and Frye undervalue the mimetic goals of fiction. To this reader's taste, at any rate, Paris tries too hard to make sense of what he sees as thematic inconsistencies in the novels he treats. Although it is not wholly successful, this thoughtful book takes its place alongside, but does not replace, Simon O. Lesser's *Fiction and the Unconscious.*

Another work whose subject is narrative is Boris Uspensky's *A Poetics of Composition,* trans. (from Russian) Valentina Zavarin and Susan Wittig (Berkeley and Los Angeles: Univ. of Calif. Press). This book contains the most thorough discussion of point of view that I know. Uspensky establishes many categories for describing fictional point of view, among them the compositional, ideological, phraseological, spatial and temporal, and psychological. His critical technique is the antithesis of European idealist theorizing, but Uspensky carries almost to absurdity his tendency to describe without generalizing. The book's basic dialectic is the contrast between the internal description of the fictional character and the point of view from which the character is presented. Uspensky's major examples are drawn from Tolstoy and Dostoevsky, particularly *War and Peace*, *The Brothers Karamazov*, *Crime and Punishment*, *The Idiot*, and *The Possessed*, and so the book is quite accessible to the American reader.

The most important work on narrative published during 1974 is Harold Toliver's *Animate Illusions: Explorations of Narrative Structure* (Lincoln: Univ. of Nebr. Press). Toliver's orientation is philosophical, initially Kantian, and his technique tends toward the phenomenological; but he is not ideologically bound. His point of view reflects the fact that he sees narrative as a psychological need.

The opening chapter contains a historical survey of "consequential narrative" that is highly influenced by Vaihinger's philosophy of "as if." The author is also influenced by Kenneth Burke's ideas of symbolic form and of literature as equipment for living as well as by Kermode's *Sense of an Ending*. "Chaos is inimitable," says Toliver; "one cannot even make a statement about it without violating its nature. Hence, wherever the modernist begins in a theory of fictions, he is brought back sooner or later to the basic principle of the philosophy of 'as if': fictions cannot avoid either mirroring or remaking reality according to their own predispositions" (p. 66). Toliver is much concerned with the difference between fictional and historiographical narrative, and a great deal of his book discusses history and the demands of retelling it.

In an interesting chapter called "Narrative Stress Systems" he discusses the various types of breaks in narrative continuity—e.g., digressions and allegories—and the ways in which these function in different types of narrative. His somewhat modish use of systems-analysis terminology adds a touch of sophistication to the book. *Animate Illusions* is a comprehensive compendium of ideas on the subject of narrative, but it is finally too casual in both tone and structure to be a major statement.

vii. Modern Poetry and Poetics

In these related areas there were a number of interesting and even a few distinguished texts published during 1974. Justus Buchler's *The Main of Light: On the Concept of Poetry* (New York: Oxford Univ. Press) is actually more a work of philosophical inquiry than of literary criticism. What the author wishes to do in this book is to arrive at a legitimate philosophical definition of poetry. To explore the problem, Buchler chooses some fairly familiar quotations from critics and philosophers who have made statements about the nature of poetry. In analyzing these statements Buchler uses philosophical rather than critical or linguistic techniques, but while he easily pokes holes in Shelley, Wordsworth, and Mill for their imprecise thinking, Buchler does stack the deck by choosing vulnerable quotations.

When he gets around to his own definition of poetry, Buchler suggests in a chapter by the same name that its defining characteristics are "Ontological Parity and the Sense of Prevalence." The latter he defines in language that sounds like a mixture of Aristotle, Aquinas, and Stephen Dedalus on the subject of *quidditas*. I must confess that I do not quite know what to make of the following passage: "[Prevalence] occurs as a characteristic whole, and is repeatedly identifiable; but it is not simple, not instantaneous, not isolated in consciousness, not analyzed, not unanalyzable, and not unrelated to other complexes" (p. 130). This book finally strikes me more as an intellectual exercise than as a useful work for students of literature. Buchler's style is dull, and he leaves no room whatever for definitions of poetry or statements about it that lack philosophical rigor.

But just when I become impatient with Buchler's insistence on definitional exactitude, I read M. L. Rosenthal's *Poetry and the Common Life* (New York: Oxford Univ. Press) and feel that maybe Buchler has a point. Rosenthal's book is a highly impressionistic work written to show that poetry "is the province of everyone's thought, not just that of literary specialists" (p. ix). To be fair to Rosenthal, I should stress that he is not just writing an apology for the kind of common verse immediately apprehendable by everyone. He does not shrink from talking about difficult modern poets. Rather his book is an attempt to show that—even when difficult—poetry does deal with subjects that are common to all humanity. His chapter titles give a clue to his concerns: "Poetry and Ordinary Experience," "Memory and the Sources of Poetry," "Musics of Awareness: Time and Space," "Musics of Awareness: Association and Feeling," "Politics," "Love and Death and Private Things." Rosenthal is frankly attempting to be a cheerleader for poetry. The book reads like a set of lectures to a fairly bright Introduction-to-Poetry course or perhaps to an Adult Education Society. Rosenthal does not write down to his audience, but at times he comes close. This ought to be a text rather than a trade book.

A much more sophisticated work is Hugo Friedrich's *The Structure of Modern Poetry*, trans. (from German) Joachim Neugroschel (Evanston, Ill.: Northwestern Univ. Press), and one of the best-selling books in Europe on modern poetry. From this, the first translation into English (it was originally published in 1956), it is apparent why. Not exactly a history of poetry of the past 130 or 140 years, it is nonetheless historical in its presentation and philosophical in its orientation. Friedrich's subject is those structures he thinks basic to modern poetry.

He begins by discussing Rousseau and develops a concept of the Void which he defines as "moral vacuity" and which he sees as an inescapable perception underlying almost all the work of poets we consider the chief modern figures. After an inconsequential discussion of Romanticism Friedrich gives us excellent chapters on Baudelaire, Rimbaud, and Mallarmé, establishing the roots of 20th-century verse in these 19th-century predecessors. There are few better general discussions anywhere of these poets. Friedrich, like Heidegger, has an extraordinary ability to find connections between language and ontology. For him Modernist poetry is the calculated expression of chaos and the inexpressible, which, as in Derrida's view of language, is never able quite to say what it means but is condemned nonetheless to attempt to make a statement. Friedrich is excellent in connecting this attempt to the breakdown of form, or fragmentation, so characteristic of poetry in all languages during the early part of this century. Unfortunately, his final chapter, "European Poetry in the Twentieth Century," is not equal in quality to his earlier insights. It is too long and categorical, containing short squibs on individual poets that are often unsympathetic and judgmental. But this criticism should not deter any serious student of modern poetry from reading this book.

Nor should any such reader ignore *Modern Poetry and the Idea of Language: A Critical and Historical Study* (New Haven, Conn.: Yale Univ. Press), by Gerald L. Bruns, one of the most interesting books I have read this year. Bruns begins by distinguishing between what he calls the "hermetic" and "Orphic" attitudes toward language in both philosophy and poetry. In the first "the direction of the poet's activity is toward the literary work as such, that is, the work as a self-contained linguistic structure." In the second the poet is a "singer whose sphere of activity is governed by a mythical or ideal unity of word and being, and whose power extends therefore beyond the formation of a work toward the creation of the world" (p. 1). Bruns begins by tracing these attitudes through history up to the key modernist figures, Mallarmé, Joyce, and Beckett.

In the latter part of the book the author gets more involved in discussing theories of language, and here his main subjects are Saussure, Husserl, Heidegger, Ricoeur, and Barthes. His discussion leads gracefully into the topics of Phenomenology and Structuralism, at which point it becomes clear that the "Orphic" and "hermetic" have had their correspondences all along in these contemporary categories. Bruns is equally at home with both poetry and language theory. His orientation is neither phenomenological nor structuralist, but he uses both with real intelligence. This thoughtful, carefully written book contributes not only to the discussion of modern literature but also to the amalgamation of European and American critical techniques.

Conclusion

This was not an outstanding year either for books of literary theory or for comprehensive overviews of American literature. There were surprisingly few books on the subject of the latter and none, it seems to me, that will take their place as major statements. In literary theory the choice is a bit better. The trend continues of bringing into the mainstream of American criticism the basic schools of European critical and philosophical thought. Such a trend, given the competence of a number of the books, no longer seems in any way like a forced marriage. The relationship is developing naturally, and the direction of American criticism will therefore never again be the same.

The outlook for next year is more hopeful. New books have appeared in 1975 by such writers as Ihab Hassan, Harold Bloom, Edmund Wilson, George Steiner, and Hugh Kenner, to name a few of the prominent authors, and I look forward to reading them and reporting on the experience in these pages.

University of California, Davis

21. Foreign Scholarship

i. French Contributions

Jean Rivière

The year 1974 saw the publication in France of a steady flow of books and articles on American literature which we might, for clarity's sake, divide into pure academic scholarship on the one hand and popularization on the other.

Academic scholarship, first, confronts us with two heavy volumes, both the products of over ten years' research for the *doctorat d'état*. Professor Claude Pérotin's *Le courant abolitionniste dans la littérature américaine de 1808 à 1861* (Lille: Université de Lille III) is an analysis of the works of all American writers concerned with the abolitionist movement grouped in three major subdivisions: "Les précurseurs" is a thorough study of the main currents of thought both in America and in Europe that led to the formulation of a cross-Atlantic abolitionist movement. "Pionniers et prophètes de l'abolitionnisme" concentrates on an analysis of abolitionism on American soil with illuminating chapters on William Lloyd Garrison, William Ellery Channing, Wendell Phillips, and Theodore Parker. The third part is entirely devoted to the reactions of the major American writers of the period toward the problem of slavery: John Greenleaf Whittier, James Russell Lowell, Walt Whitman, Harriet Beecher Stowe, Melville, Emerson, and Thoreau. The writers most involved in the movement are not necessarily those who put forth the best literary achievements on the subject and H. B. Stowe's *Uncle Tom's Cabin* pales before Melville's "Benito Cereno." Pérotin's conclusion emphasizes the fact that "on the artistic plane, the abolitionists' achievements were rarely commensurate with their ambitions. Their fight probably took place in a nation too young to allow the blossoming of more elaborate and more perfect works of art" (p. 758). Still, the author thinks that they were forerunners in the constant fight of the best American writers for more human dignity.

Professor Georges-Albert Astre's *John Dos Passos: de l'Initiation d'un homme à U.S.A.* (Paris: Minard, Lettres Modernes) has come out in book form after its original publication in *Revue des Lettres Moderns* between 1956 and 1962. It is divided into two main parts: "Conflicts et contradictions" and "Présence de la ville" are studies of Dos Passos's personal and intellectual development from 1896 to 1926 with special emphasis on his rejection of old liberal America, his impossible adhesion to art for art's sake, and his timid approach toward Marxism, for which he could not forsake his old self based on ethical and spiritual references. "Procès d'une Amérique" traces his struggle as a writer and as a militant to find a new approach to the art of fiction that might express the most glaring contradictions and crimes of the postwar period that culminated with the execution of Sacco and Vanzetti. In fact, Dos Passos's indictment of the America of his time is that of the uprooted individual of the industrial Northeast with accents reminding us of the Bible, Whitman, and Marx. Astre closes his book with a study of *U.S.A.* and can therefore only suggest Dos Passos's later evolution toward some sort of nostalgic Goldwaterian conservatism. He concludes with a vivid image showing at the same time Dos Passos's ambition as a philosopher of history and his parochial outlook: "the author of *U.S.A.* sounds indeed like someone who reads [Montesquieu's] *L'esprit des lois* in a New York speakeasy with Louis Armstrong or Charlie Parker's blues as background music" (p. 534).

Two confirmed scholars in the field of American literature, Jean Béranger and Maurice Gonnaud, are responsible for *La littérature américaine jusqu'en 1865* (Paris: Armand Colin): their ambition is to present the French reader, and especially the student of English, with an evolutionary survey of American literature. It is to a large extent a bird's-eye view as far as Colonial literature is concerned (with analyses of judicious samplings) and coalesces into more structured literary movements on the European model for the study of antebellum literature: Romanticism, Transcendentalism, and the birth of American fiction. With the French public constantly in their minds, the authors are at pains to ascertain the position of the literary artist in American society, emphasizing his loneliness and the contradictions between his theories and his art. Béranger and Gonnaud sum up most convincingly the dilemma of the 19th-century American writer who wants to be both an American and an artist, and the slow evolution toward more genuine Americanness and more literary artistry.

The University of Bordeau III has just published the first issue of a new periodical: *Annales du centre de recherche sur l'Amérique anglophone*. It is entirely devoted to studies of colonial and revolutionary literature: traditional analyses of the *Federalist Papers* (by Daniel J. Koob) and education according to Benjamin Franklin (Christian Lerat) are to be found side by side with more modern approaches (mainly structuralist and linguistic) toward literature and politics in the studies of Mrs. Mercy Otis Warren (by Rolande Diot), Paine's *Common Sense* (André Ladousse), and Jonathan Mayhew (Jean Béranger).

The last two works to be examined have more to do with the popularization of American literature than with pure academic research. Yet they are perhaps even more potent appetizers for the lay reader. Philippe Mikriammos in his *William S. Burroughs* (Paris: Seghers) studies the work of the creator of *Naked Lunch* from a triple viewpoint: drugs, homosexuality, and exile. The long period of utter dejection that stretches from 1944 to 1956 is dominated by an ever-increasing drug addiction until his final recovery in the late 1950s. Mikriammos shows how, through the conquest of his addiction, Burroughs becomes an innovator in the field of literary art, particularly in his use of the "cutup," a technique akin to that of Tristan Tzara and dadaism. Burroughs finally thinks that his style can change the world. He remains, in spite of himself, the master of the Beat Generation, because he lived its dilemmas.

A little fresh air to put the finishing touch to this essay. Maurice E. Coindreau in his *Mémoires d'un traducteur* (Paris: Gallimard) explains the reasons for his kinship with American Southern literature and makes us understand his action in introducing Faulkner and Southern fiction to the French public. But, in the case of Coindreau's translations (especially those of Faulkner), the rendering in French is far more than a passage from one language to another; it is a re-creation through a perfect appreciation of the possibilities of French and occasionally an illumination of the English text. Coindreau had long interviews with Faulkner before translating his works and his interpretation is often considered, even by American scholars, as the authorized version. Coindreau's peasant ascent from Vendée (a section on the losing side during the French Revolution, like the South

in the American Civil War) put him from the start on an equal footing
with southern manners and sense of history. Faulkner and Coindreau
can deservedly be compared to Poe and Baudelaire.

Another book-length French study of an American author, Roger
Forclaz's *Le Monde d'Edgar Poe*, is reviewed in chapter 3.

Université Paris IX, Dauphine

ii. German Contributions

Hans Galinsky

The overall organization followed in 1973 has been maintained, but
a short section on the literary manifestations of "Popular and Youth
Culture" has been supplemented with "Literary Didactics." As to
the general characteristics of German contributions in 1974, three
deserve brief mention: (1) a gratifying rise in the number of such
useful tools of scholarship as bibliographies and state of research
reports, (2) a steady increase of festschriften and volumes of collected essays from several hands, covering the entire history of
American literature or special periods of a literary genre or combining studies in American and British literature, (3) a shift from
annual to biannual publication of *Amerikastudien,* formerly *Jahrbuch
für Amerikastudien,* the periodical sponsored by the German Association for American Studies. Thus opportunities for placing articles
have improved. The present chronicle omits unpublished doctoral
dissertations. Those that are published will be listed according to
years of publication.

a. **Literary History—General.** Monographs and articles with a
wider historical sweep have slightly increased, yet devotion to a
single period or author still prevails.

Contributions characterized by an extensive historical vista include vol. 2 of Rudolf Haas's *Amerikanische Literaturgeschichte*
(Heidelberg: Quelle & Meyer). It displays the qualities of vol. 1
(1972): a deliberate selectiveness, a blend of narration with interpretation and shrewd criticism, a firm grasp of the international literary
context. Likewise ranging from the 17th to the 20th century, *Die
amerikanische Lyrik,* ed. Klaus Lubbers (Düsseldorf: Bagel) offers,

by way of its interpretations of 36 poems and a competent introduction by the editor, a historic panorama of American poetry. The same four centuries are spanned by *Amerikanische Lyrik: Vom 17. Jahrhundert bis zur Gegenwart* (Stuttgart: Reclam). The joint work of Annemarie and Franz Link, it unites original texts with German translations and bio-bibliographies. Smaller in range and thematically confined to "nature in the New World" but still surveying almost three centuries of literary expression, Frieder Busch's *Natur in Neuer Welt: Bericht und Dichtung der amerikanischen Kolonialzeit, 1493–1776* (Munich: Fink) unfolds the history of discoverers', explorers', and settlers' reactions to the American natural environment. The racial, Afro-American, aspect of the New World receives bibliographical treatment in Werner Sollors's *Supplement One* to his *Bibliographical Guide to Afro-American Studies* (Berlin: J. F. Kennedy Institute). Two festschriften, which invited contributions from Americanists and Anglicists alike, also range across more than one period. *Studien zur englischen und amerikanischen Sprache und Literatur: Festschrift für Helmut Papajewski* (Neumünster: Wachholtz) was edited by Paul Buchloh et al.; *Miscellanea Anglo-Americana: Festschrift für Helmut Viebrock* was edited by Klaus Schuhmann et al. (Munich: Pressler). The 19th- and 20th-century novel is represented by a volume of interpretations, *Der amerikanische Roman im 19. und 20. Jahrhundert*, ed. Edgar Lohner (Berlin: Schmidt). The selection made by the 12 Germans on the 21-member team extends from Cooper through Updike. Of individual articles venturing farther afield than one period, Ursula Brumm's "Christ and Adam as 'Figures' in American Literature" in *The American Puritan Imagination: Recent Essays in Revaluation*, ed. Sacvan Bercovich (London and New York: Cambridge Univ. Press) testifies to her usual expertise on typology. Franz Link's "Die Fiktion der Gegenwart im Drama" (*DLVG* 48:417–31) explores time-treating devices of the dramatic genre. Comparatist interest marks Uwe Böker's affinity and impact study in James's and Graham Greene's concepts of literary form in "Henry James, Graham Greene und das Problem der Form" (*LWU* 7:180–90).

 Colonial and 19th Century. The sacred rage for only one literary period and for one, rarely two or more of its authors, produced studies of more than 120 subjects. The 16th and 17th centuries are visited preferably by senior tourists and "old hands at the game."

Gustav Blanke contributes "Early English Images of North America" to *Festschrift for Robert Falk*, ed. W. Matthews (Los Angeles: Univ. of So. Calif. Press), and sketches "Waldseemüllers Beitrag zur geistigen Entdeckung Amerikas" in *Festschrift für R. Brummer*, ed. D. Brisemeister (Bern and Frankfurt: Lang). Hans Galinsky opens the long series of interpretations collected in *Die amerikanische Lyrik* (pp. 21–31). He also analyzes "Bacon's Epitaph, Made by His Man," attributed to John Cotton of "Queen's Creek" (ibid., pp. 44–56), and applies to it Austin Warren's concept of "Colonial Baroque." Edward Taylor's "10. Meditation, John 6.55" finds a brilliant interpreter in Ursula Brumm (ibid., pp. 57–67). A young scholar, Renate Schmidt-v. Bardeleben, intelligently explicates Anne Bradstreet's "The Author to Her Book" (ibid., pp. 32–45).

The 18th century has but one attempt each at its prerevolutionary and postrevolutionary periods to its credit. Galinsky in "Amerikanische Hochschulkritik aus dem Jahre 1722: Eine Interpretation der Harvard-Satire des jungen Franklin" (*Papajewski Festschrift*, pp. 440–66) finds as much food for thought as reason for timely amusement in Silence Dogood's famous fourth letter. Frieder Busch has written a subtle analysis of Freneau's "The Indian Burying Ground" (*Die amerikanische Lyrik*, pp. 68–76). If they had not been included in *Die amerikanische Lyrik*, Bryant's "Thanatopsis" and Emerson's "The Snow-Storm," ably interpreted by Klaus Lubbers and Edith Mettke respectively, would hardly have been a part of German scholarship for 1974. The same may be said for Longfellow's "Seaweed," empathetically analyzed by Karl Schubert (ibid., pp. 95–102). It is all to the good that such collections of interpretations invite the modern reader to expose himself not only to the winds of fashion but also to climates of quite different taste. Among the other major poets of the earlier 19th century, Poe always stimulates both popular and academic interest. "Ulalume" is given a sensitive examination by Franz Link (ibid., pp. 103–14).

Aside from Edgar Lohner's collective enterprise, which includes a knowledgeable interpretation of "Coopers Lederstrumpf Saga" by Rudolf Sühnel (*Der amerikanische Roman*, pp. 23–35), German research on the American novel and the short story of the early and middle 19th century shrinks to an article on Hawthorne and a volume of selected contributions to Melville scholarship. Astrid Schmitt-v. Mühlenfels's "*The Scarlet Letter* as Fernsehfilm: Darstellung, Deutung und Umdeutung" (*LWU* 7:39–46) furnishes an instructive comparison of the romance with its TV movie version. The volume on Melville has been brought together by Paul Buchloh and Hartmut Krüger in *Herman Melville, Wege der Forschung* 294 (Darmstadt: Wissenschaftliche Buchgesellschaft). It limits itself to older and newer criticism, mainly American, of *Moby-Dick*, "Bartleby," "Benito Cereno," and *Billy Budd*. The emphasis is on variety of approach. Of the middle and later 19th-century poets Whitman and Dickinson occupy firm places in German literary criticism. "There Was a Child Went Forth" and "Song of Myself XXIV" receive interpretations, particularly enlightening for difference of method, from Karl Ortseifen and Armin Geraths (*Die amerikanische Lyrik*, pp. 115–30, 131–46). "Song of Myself" is also approached from the angle of "identity" and "identification" in Franz Link's "Identität und Identifizierung in Whitman's 'Song of Myself'" (*Papajewski Festschrift*, pp. 486–506). In "Walt Whitman und die Tradition der amerikanischen Verskunst" (*Viebrock Festschrift*, pp. 351–71) Link also comments upon contemporary attempts to define Whitman's place in the tradition of American poetry. Teut A. Riese takes a new look at Dickinson's "Like Some Old fashioned Miracle" and "As imperceptibly as Grief" (*Die amerikanische Lyrik*, pp. 147–56, 157–62). The same volume includes an analysis of a poem by Lanier, a rare phenomenon in German scholarship". It is due to Herwig Friedl's interest in "The Marshes of Glynn" (ibid., pp. 163–75).

Whereas in 1973 Hawthorne was "the man of the year" in German research on American fiction, in 1974 this honor went to James. A book, three articles, and a state of research report illustrate the change. Hildegard Domaniecki's *Zum Problem literarischer Ökonomie: Henry James' Erzählungen zwischen Markt und Kunst, Amerikastudien* 38 (Stuttgart: Metzler) opens a new direction in German James scholarship in two senses: hers is the first study of all of the tales, and hers is the first attempt to systematically apply the notion of "economy" to both the artist and the professional author dependent on a "market." The appeal of problems of form, and the fascination of ambiguity, two life lines of international James criticism, reassert themselves in German terms in Böker's abovementioned article on James and Greene, as well as in Christine Brinckmann's and Ulrich Keller's joint paper "Erzählen und Lügen: Zur Auslegung von Henry James's *The Turn of the Screw*" (*Viebrock*

Festschrift, pp. 26–77). Teut A. Riese provides readers of Lohner's *Der amerikanische Roman* (pp. 92–105) with a reliable introduction to *The Golden Bowl*. Friedl's "Henry James, 1968–1972" (*Amerikastudien* 19:334–47) has produced a useful state of research report. The "high" for James scholarship corresponds with a "low" for Twain. Interest in Twain would have dropped to zero if Karl Schubert had not written an illuminating interpretation of *The Adventures of Huck Finn* for *Der amerikanische Roman* (pp. 70–91). The same collection includes Klaus Poenicke's "Evolution als Erzahlstrategie: Frank Norris' *McTeague*" (ibid., pp. 126–37), and Dietmar Haack's investigation of *The Red Badge of Courage* (ibid., pp. 138–51). From the turn of the century the socioeconomic rather than the literary aspects of the muckrakers figure in Klaus-Bert Becker's *Die 'Muckrakers' und der Sozialismus: Eine Untersuchung zum politischen Bewusstsein in der Progressive Era*, Europäische Hochschulschriften, ser. 3, vol. 35 (Bern: Lang).

20th-Century Poetry. More purely literary interests converge on the early 20th century and the "between wars" period. Channeled into collective undertakings like *Die amerikanische Lyrik, Der amerikanische Roman*, and *Das amerikanische Drama*, ed. Paul Goetsch (Düsseldorf: Bagel), they revolve around most of the major figures of the three genres.

In the field of poetry the following are represented: Robinson's "Eros Turannos," Williams's "The Yachts," and Jeffers's "To the Rock that Will Be a Cornerstone of the House," analyzed by Horst Kruse, Dietrich Jäger, and Hans-Joachim Zimmermann (*Die amerikanische Lyrik*), Marianne Moore's "*Poetry*," attracting Alfred Weber's interest in "poetological" poems (ibid., pp. 251–58), Ransom's "Master's in the Garden Again" and "Conrad in Twilight," the youngest of its three previous versions, compared by Robert Weber (ibid., pp. 259–68), MacLeish's "You, Andrew Marvell," explicated by Gustav Blanke (ibid., pp. 269–77), Cummings's "pity this busy monster, manunkind," taxing Horst Meller's intelligence and sense of humor (ibid., pp. 394–405), Hart Crane's "The Broken Tower" and Richard Eberhart's "The Horse Chestnut Tree," finding congenial interpreters in Heinz Ickstadt and Roswith von Freydorf (ibid., pp. 306–16; 317–26). All these poems, most of them standard selection pieces, are represented in *Die amerikanische Lyrik* only once. The privilege of being included twice is enjoyed only by such poets as Frost, Stevens, and Pound. Whereas Rudolf Haas, examining "Mending Wall" (ibid., pp. 194–206), and Alfred Weber, investigating "The Idea of Order at Key West" (ibid., pp. 292–305) join an international host of previous interpreters, Hans Combecher, battling with Frost's "Come In" (ibid., pp. 187–93) and Fritz Schulze, wrestling with Stevens's "Note on Moonlight" (ibid., pp. 278–91), follow paths rarely trodden before. Pound explication, represented by Hans-Joachim Zimmerman (ibid., pp. 217–31) and Klaus Heinrich Köhring (ibid., pp. 232–42), has dealt with "E. P. Ode pour l'élection de son sépulchre" and "Canto I." Pound proves to be the only poet able to draw attention to himself outside a sheltering volume of collected essays. Manfred Pütz's "A Conversation with William C. Chace" (*Occident 8*, N.S. [Spring 1974]:51–65) elicits new information on Pound and Eliot. On the whole, these interpretations are more revealing by variety of method than choice of theme or form type.

20th-Century Drama and Fiction. Concentration on post–World War I works is more exclusive in *Das amerikanische Drama*. Paul Goetsch, its editor, frankly attributes only "literary-historical value" to the earlier specimens of the art. Naturally choices taken once again fall on major and minor classics of the period. O'Neill has retained his old attraction. He is the exceptional playwright for whom three articles are reserved. Ulrich Halfmann (ibid., pp. 27–49), Gerhard Hoffman (ibid., pp. 50–85), and Rudolf Haas (ibid., pp. 86–105) analyze three plays characteristic of O'Neill's development: *Beyond the Horizon, Mourning Becomes Electra,* and *The Iceman Cometh.* American Expressionism, however, is exemplified not by him but by Elmer Rice. His *Adding Machine* has found a knowledgeable spokesman in Hans Bungert (ibid., pp. 106–26). Anderson's *Winterset,* Odets's *Golden Boy,* and Wilder's *The Skin of Our Teeth,* all of them minor classics of the 1930s and early 1940s, form the subjects of special articles contributed by Christian Thomsen (ibid., pp. 127–48), Heinz Kosok (ibid., pp. 149–69), and Rudolf Germer (ibid., pp. 170–82). A rare procedure in 1974, Wilder's selected play is treated along comparative lines by Franz Link in "Zeit und Geschichte in Thornton Wilders *Wir sind noch einmal davongekommen* und Max Frisch's *Chinesische Mauer,*" *Festschrift für Clemens Bauer,* ed. Erich Hassinger et al. (Berlin: Duncker & Humblot), pp. 31–39. A less familiar figure in the German academic reception of American drama is Lillian Hellman. To the exclusion of her pre-

1945 plays, one of her later works, *The Autumn Garden*, is explored by Karl Schubert (*Das amerikanische Drama*, pp. 252–75). Like the poetry of the contemporary period, its drama has engaged the attention of a remarkable number of German Americanists different in age, outlook, and approach.

If the Lohner collection (*Der amerikanische Roman*) had not included Michael Hoenisch, Hans-Joachim Lang, Helmut Viebrock, and Jürgen Peper writing on Fitzgerald's *The Great Gatsby*, Santayana's *The Last Puritan*, Wilder's *The Eighth Day*, and Hemingway's *A Farewell to Arms*, the American novel of the 1920s and 1930s would have been slighted in 1974. Faulkner, however, received his usual attention with Ursula Brumm's perceptive "Geschichte als Geschehen und Erfahrung: Eine Analyse von William Faulkners *Absalom, Absalom!*," an essay contributed to *Der amerikanische Roman* (pp. 258–74), and Dieter Meindl's *Bewusstsein als Schicksal: Zu Struktur und Entwicklung von William Faulkners Generationenromanen*, Amerikastudien, 39 (Stuttgart: Metzler), which marks a decisive advance in the understanding of *Sartoris, Absalom, Absalom!*, and *Go Down, Moses*. Profiting from French structuralists like Roland Barthes, Meindl has skillfully blended an analytic with a historical and typological approach. In Steinbeck criticism in 1974 Christine Brinckmann's "Zitierte Dokumentarität: Überlegungen zur Verfilmung des Romans *The Grapes of Wrath*" (*Amerikastudien* 19:88–110) reinforces a trend toward the comparison of artistic media, a phenomenon already noticed in a German Hawthorne monograph. Horst Groene's "*The Grapes of Wrath*: Sozialkritische Studie und Kunstwerk" (*LWU* 7:47–63) furnishes an instructive state of research report on pertinent Steinbeck studies in English and German. Aside from Faulkner, Caldwell is the only writer of fiction to stimulate a German book-length treatment in 1974. Hartmut Heuermann's *Erskine Caldwell's Short Stories: Studien zum amerikanischen Neo-Naturalismus*, Mainzer Studien zur Amerikanistik 4 (Bern and Frankfurt: Lang) critically but sympathetically follows the rise of "America's best best-selling author" and the decline of the artist. Thanks to Olaf Hansen's "Henry Miller: der konservative Avantgardist und das Obszöne," Miller has found a niche in the study of literary sexuality erected by Horst A. Glaser, ed., in *Wollüstige Phantasie: Sexualästhetik der Literatur* (Munich: Hanser).

Fiction since 1945. Traditional interest, with fiction in the foreground, drama and poetry further back, is restored, with the post-1945 novel receiving primary attention. Authors already "established" in Germany like Ellison, Salinger, Updike, and Vonnegut have also become established in scholarly criticism, and this not only under the wings of *Der amerikanische Roman*, in which Peter Freese and Haas take good care of *The Catcher in the Rye* and *The Centaur* (pp. 320–36, 337–52). Hartmut Selke's "The Education at 'College of Fools': References to Emerson's 'Self-Reliance' in *Invisible Man*" (*NConL* 4,i:13–15), and a companion article, "An Allusion to Sartre's *The Flies* in Ralph Ellison's *Invisible Man*" (*NConL* 4,i:3–4) provides information on the origin and function of strands in the elaborate texture of a classic of the 1950s. Freese displays similar ingenuity in detecting references to Dickens and Lardner in yet another classic of the same decade: "Zwei unbekannte Verweise in J. D. Sallingers *The Catcher in the Rye*" (*Archiv* 211:68–72). Updike has been raised from article to book status by Richard W. Burr's *Puer Aeternus: An Examination of John Updike's "Rabbit, Run"* (Zurich: Juris Verlag). In "Who Am I This Time?: Die Romane von Kurt Vonnegut" (*Amerikastudien* 19:111–25) Manfred Pütz stresses Vonnegut's exposition of "the causes of a now familiar loss of identity" as an underlying principle of his fiction. Pütz has also made the novels of other, and in part more recent, experimenters his domain. Pynchon figures in two of his articles printed in American periodicals: "Science as Metaphor: Thomas Pynchon and *Gravity's Rainbow*" (*ConL* 15:345–59), and "Thomas Pynchon's *The Crying of Lot 49*: The World is a Tristero System" (*Mosaic* 7:125–37). In "Transcendentalism Revived: The Fiction of Richard Brautigan" (*Occident* 8:39–48) the title thesis seems debatable. Pütz's "Alternative Fictions: The Novels of Rudolph Wurlitzer" (*Fiction International* 2/3:134–40) maps out a terra incognita to most Germans. To the ones who know their own Handtkes, Artmanns, and Jandls, Donald Barthelme will strike a more familiar note. Freese's "Donald Barthelmes *fictions*: Fragmente aus Wörtern mit Würmern" (*Amerikastudien* 19:126–41) helps readers grasp such international affinities. Best-sellers easily lend themselves to sociological inquiry. An example is Lothar Bredella's "Ästhetische und soziale Kategorien bei der Analyse des Bestsellers *Valley of the Dolls* by Jacqueline Susann" (ibid., pp. 30–49). Foreshadowed by Vonnegut's success with scholars, science fiction emerges as the only theme-based narrative type that has earned itself book-length treatment: Dieter Wessels's *Welt in Chaos: Funktion und Struktur des Weltkatastrophenmotivs in der neueren Science Fiction* (Frankfurt: Athenaion). Of form-determined types of fiction the short story is unique in receiving the same honor. It is conferred by Peter Freese's *Die amerikanische Kurzgeschichte nach 1945: Salinger, Malamud, Baldwin, Purdy, Barth* (Frankfurt: Athenäum). Equally focusing on several authors, Dieter Meindl's "Zur Renaissance des amerikanischen Ich-Romans in den fünfziger Jahren" (*Amerikastudien* 19:201–18) illustrates the revival and function of the first-person mode in the 1950s, relating them to the "contemporaneous emergence of 'role theory' in sociology." A byway of post-1945 fiction, the " 'adult-fantasy' subspecies of science fiction": as cultivated by MacDonald, Baum, and Segal, is examined in Frank Bergmann's "Under the Sign of the Unicorn's Head: Adult Fantasy and Contemporary America" (ibid., pp. 50–57).

Drama since 1945. Research on the American post-1945 drama still concentrates on Williams. Two books and four articles furnish sufficient proof of his continuing popularity. Franz Link's *Tennessee Williams Dramen* (Darmstadt: Thesen Verlag) emphasizes universals like loneliness and love as recurrent themes of varying tension. Jürgen Koepsel in *Der amerikanische Suden und seine Funktionen im dramatischen Werk von Tennessee Williams*, Mainzer Studien zur Amerikanistik 5 (Bern and Frankfurt: Lang) explores a specific element, the South, and its dramatic uses. According to him, "the South has, in most cases, only exemplary functions, and its importance degenerates, especially in the later works, into that of mere theatrical scenery." Even the uses of the locale are disentangled in Horst Oppel's " 'Every Man is a King!' Zur Funktion der lokalhistorischen Elemente in *A Streetcar Named Desire*" (*Papajewski Festschrift*, pp. 507–22). Oppel also contributes an illuminating interpretation of the same play to *Das amerikanische Drama*, pp. 183–207, 365–68). Paul Buchloh returns to his favorite field with "Tennessee Williams: Assoziationschiffren, Zeichen der Verweisung und Akzentuierung—Versuch einer Systematisierung" (*Papajewski Festschrift*, pp. 405–39). His aim is to systematize Williams's uses of obvious and subtle cross-reference. The Williams not of the 1940s but the 1960s finds critical favor with Hartmut Heuermann, author of "Die Psychomachie in Tennessee Williams *The Milktrain Doesn't Stop Here Anymore*" (*Amerikastudien* 19:266-79). Extending our knowledge of Williams's links with psychoanalysis, the essay conceives of this play as "a crucial struggle—a psychomachia—for spiritual survival." Arthur Miller's popularity has not declined either. Paul Goetsch competently interprets *Death of a Salesman*, in "Evergreen" on the German stage, while Hans Itschert chooses *The Price* for his contribution to the same volume of explications (*Das amerikanische Drama*, pp. 208-33; 234-51). Albee's *Who's Afraid of Virginia Woolf?*, analyzed by Goetsch (ibid., pp. 295-318), Jack Gelber's *The Apple*, with Gerhard Stebner as reliable guide into the perplexing world of the American antitheatre (ibid., pp. 276-94), and Charles Gordone's *No Place to Be Somebody*, approached by Robert Taëni in the context of the Black Arts movement and its belief in the unity of ethics and esthetics (ibid., pp. 319-38) mark the non plus ultra of recent scholarly criticism of modern American drama in Germany.

Poetry since 1945. Interest in older authors and young experimenters as encountered in novel and drama criticism reveals itself in post-1945 poetry interpretation. Wilbur's "Juggler," explicated by Hans Combecher (*Die amerikanische Lyrik*, pp. 377-85), Roethke's "Orchids," presented by Horst Priessnitz (ibid., pp. 327-37), Lowell's "Mr. Edwards and the Spider," analyzed by Hans Borchers (ibid., 353-63) exemplify the appeal of the older poets, with Jarrell the only one receiving the double honor of essay and book-length study. The essay, Paul Buchloh's sensitive interpretation of "The Death of the Ball Turret Gunner," is contributed to *Die americanische Lyrik*, pp. 338-52. The book, *The Black Goddess: A Study of the Archetypal Feminine in the Poetry of Randall Jarrell*, Swiss Studies in English (Bern: Francke), comes from Helen Hagenbüchle-Imfeld, who applies the insights of Carl Jung's depth psychology to poetry. Ginsberg's "A supermarket in California," Mary Ellen Solt's "Geranium," and LeRoi Jones's "Preface to a Twenty Volume Suicide Note," chosen for close observation by Armin Geraths, Horst Priessnitz, and Hans Finger (ibid., pp. 364-76, 406-18, 386-93), wrestle with various degrees of modernity in American poetry.

Post-1945 literature as a whole finds few critical investigators. One of them is Paul Buchloh, whose "Tendenzen und Charakteristika der amerikanischen Literatur nach dem Zweiten Weltkrieg" (*LWU* 7:

180–90) defines major trends. Rudolf Haas's survey article, "Biblische und theologische Themen in der modernen englischen und amerikanischen Literatur" (*Viebrock Festschrift*, pp. 202–20), includes the period as part of the larger whole of 20th-century literature, both English and American. No German equivalent to Ihab Hassan's *Contemporary American Literature, 1945–1972* has emerged in 1974. The gap has been temporarily filled by Brigitte Scheer-Schäzler's translation of Hassan's book under the title *Die moderne amerikanische Literatur* (Stuttgart:Kröner).

As a timely reminder that a chronicle of German contributions to American literary scholarship is sadly incomplete without the ones published in the German Democratic Republic, Michael Hoenisch and Werner Sollors have compiled a *Bibliographie der amerikanistischen Veröffentlichungen in der DDR* (Berlin: J. F. Kennedy Institute).

b. **Literary Criticism, Didactics, and Theory.** Here the drought continues. A few short rainfalls can be registered, though. Brigitte Scheer-Schäzler appends an instructive essay, "Von der neuen Kritik zur Parakritik: Anmerkungen zum Werk Ihab Hassans," to her above-mentioned translation of Hassan's study as *Die moderne amerikanische Literatur* (pp. 227–51). Armin P. Frank keeps up his enthusiasm for Eliot's critical work. "Elliot on Babbitt: A Note on Influence" (*TSEN* 1, ii: 7–9), and "Eliot on Milton: Tone as Criticism" (*Viebrock Festschrift*, pp. 184–201) examine basic concepts of criticism. Problems in the teaching of American literature in German high schools and universities are treated in Berthold Schik's essay, "Thornton Wilder's *Our Town*: Eine exemplarische Deutung des Anfangs," in *Aspekte und Aufgaben der Literaturdidaktik in Hochschule und Schule*, ed. Hans Hunfeld and Gottfried Schröder (Kiel: Schmidt and Klaunig), pp. 57–66. As is evidenced by Peter Freese's "Eric Segal's *Love Story* als Herausforderung an die Literaturdidaktik" (*NS* 23:18–30), not even best-sellers escape the nets of didactics fishermen any longer. American literature as seen in the wider context of American studies figures in one article only: "American Studies in Germany: Their Growth, Variety and Prospects" (*American Studies: An International Newsletter*. 13, i:3–10). Here Hans Galinsky tries to systematize the checkered history of American literature, language, and culture in German universities after 1945.

c. **Popular and Youth Culture.** The literary manifestations of American popular and youth culture have met with devoted students and critics in Germany later than in their homeland. Walter Kühnel's "Amerikanische Comicbooks und das Problem einer Analyse populärkultureller Phänomene" (*Amerikastudien* 19:58–87) is informative and method-oriented. Jürgen Peper's "Der heruntergekommene Surrealismus oder Repression als Fortschritt" (ibid., pp. 9–29) offers a scathing critique of Abbie Hoffmann's *Revolution for the Hell of It* and Jerry Rubin's *Do It! Scenarios of the Revolution.* Peper is not slow in detecting "the dialectics which intimately link emancipatory and primitivist tendencies in the Counter Culture with contemporary civilization and its constructivist drive in administration and technology." The critic is challenged by Olaf Hansen (ibid., pp. 287–95), who is answered by Peper (ibid., pp. 296–306).

Thus the year has yielded an extraordinarily large crop of articles ranging from the 16th to the 20th century, with the usual heavy stress on the latter. Admittedly, a great many of them have come into being at the magic word of editors of festschriften and cooperative enterprises. Yet a healthy pluralism of outlook and method, and an indispensable historic dimension have been maintained. Books have been few in number. They include theme-related studies in American nature and "worlds to come," author-oriented research on James and Faulkner, Caldwell and Updike, Tennessee Williams and Jarrell, vol. 2 of an American literary history now completed, a survey of post-1945 short-story writing and a bilingual anthology of American poetry. It is these achievements in particular which stand out as major evidence of scholars' devotion to American literature in Germany in 1974.

Johannes Gutenberg Universität, Mainz

iii. Italian Contributions

Rolando Anzilotti

As was to be expected, the fields of interest of the young generation of Italian Americanists continued in 1974 to be mainly those of contemporary fiction and contemporary poetry, since the vital issues, tensions, and contradictions of our age are found by them to be directly reflected in the works of American contemporary writers. Much of this year's production covers those two fields. The tempo of scholarship on American literature in Italy remains brisk. This year's essay will review 9 books and 14 articles as opposed to 9 books and 13 articles discussed or cited last year. We must assume that it has been a fruitful year, especially in view of the lamentable postponement of the publication of a group of articles and essays in the long-awaited *Studi americani* because of unfortunate circumstances.

The book that has received the most attention, both on the part of the Americanists and Italian literary people in general, is Agostino Lombardo's *Il diavolo nel manoscritto* (Milano: Rizzoli). Lombardo, one of the chief promoters of American studies in Italy (he is the editor of the annual review *Studi americani*), has gathered into one volume the essays on the American literary tradition that he has published during the past 20 years, part of them in his *Realismo e simbolismo* (1957) and in *La ricerca del vero* (1961). With remarkable power of clarification and sound critical judgment he brings out the trends, the important themes and the stylistic achievements of the literature of the United States, investigating and analyzing particularly the works of a good many authors, from Hawthorne, Melville, Emerson, Twain, and Thoreau to Bellow and Salinger, from W. C. Williams to Roethke and Creeley. The image of American literature that successfully emerges from this extensive presentation is that of a literature that has reached maturity, stylistic complexity, and highly intellectual and moral texture.

Three works fall into the category of general studies of fiction. Ruggero Bianchi's *La dimensione narrativa: Ipotesi sul romanzo americano* (Ravenna: Longo) is a stimulating introduction to American fiction, especially the fiction of this century. In the five essays that make up the volume the author dwells on matters of both theoretical and historical import, such as the dialectic relationship between narrative structures and ideological contents, the inadequacy of "realistic" techniques in rendering an ever-changing reality, and the meaning of some recent antirealistic trends. A serious attempt at understanding the fiction of the last decade is Francesco Binni's *Narrativa americana degli anni sessanta* (Torino: E.R.I.). Binni intelligently examines the relation between literature and society, singles out the trends that distinguish such novelists as Bellow, Barth, Mailer, Vonnegut, Pynchon, Heller, Barthelme, and others, whom he sees immersed in a new sociopolitical culture, and basically accepts "exhaustion" and "anticipation" as fundamental characteristics of their fiction. In *Struttura e mito nella narrativa americana del '900* (Padova-Venezia: Marsilio) Franco La Polla deals somewhat journalistically with adolescent figures in the fiction of a group of 20th-century Southern writers (Faulkner, Wolfe, McCullers, Capote, Agee, Styron, Lee), but the ambition displayed in the title and the enthusiasm for the subject, shared by Gianni Celati, who writes an appendix to it, do not add much of significance to Leslie Fiedler's ideas, which were used as a starting point.

The theme of violence in the novels of Styron, Roth, Updike, and Morrell is discussed from a Marxist point of view by Antonio Donno in his article "I modi della violenza americana in alcuni romanzi dell' ultimo ventennio" (*Antologia Vieussieux* 35:24–36). Donno sees such violence as a symptom of capitalistic repression of the proletariat since the New Deal. Aggression by the system causes not only destruction of individuality and of the person's power to choose but also suicide and psychological disintegration, eventually resulting in atrophy of the human soul and of the capacity to communicate. "Nathanael West e l'industria culturale" (*AION-SG* 17,i:77–109) is a lively and detailed essay in which Alessandra Contenti places West within the context of American culture and describes him as a forerunner of the social critics of the 1960s for his indictment of the mass media as a conditioning agent. Contenti's close examination of images and techniques seeks rather successfully to establish how the feeling of dehumanization was achieved in the novels. Barth's *Giles Goat-Boy* was the subject of a perceptive and accurate exegesis by Guido Sommavilla: "Logica tragica e mistero nell' epica di John Barth" (*Letture* 1:3–26). With clearness and admirable understanding, Sommavilla investigates the metaphors, the philosophical implications, and the moral paradoxes of the writer's ambitious epic. He finds that the message of the book is "nothing less but the Gospel, sincerely and authentically (though not aways clearly or univocally) reinterpreted in favor of contemporary man." The Italian translation of Nabokov's early novel *Despair* gives Claudio Gorlier the opportunity of briefly assessing the writer's first fictional phase in "Nabokov, gioco e parodia" (*Approdo* 65:129–31). It is a phase in which on one side there is a character who builds himself up, while on the other the same character rejects a current dimension of reality. Gorlier also contributes an interesting discussion of the term *Gothic* in his article

"La trappola dell' 'American Gothic'" (*Approdo* 67–68:208–210). After expressing his reservations on the use of such an abstract label as "Northern Gothic," proposed by Frank Baldanza in a recent essay, he sees Purdy (the main example of Northern Gothic) and Brautigan (Western Gothic) as writers who break up old categories at the same moment they use them.

Coming to longer-established authors like Miller and Fitzgerald, we find Rosella Mangaroni's "L'utero di Henry Miller, o della sostituzione" (*Per la critica* 7–8:49–61), a longish article that tries to clarify the relation between Miller's conception of literature and his attraction toward "the darkness of the womb," both of which are seen as expressions of a violent prenatal longing. Some of the equations (e.g., word=sperm) are, however, too vague to be convincing, and the article gets lost somewhere between cosmology and psychology. Silvana Coccolini's "*Il Grande Gatsby*: tra sogno e realtà" (*Humanitas* 11:854–62) offers no new approach to Fitzgerald's major novel, but furnishes a correct appraisal of it.

Henry James alluded to six noble Venetians in his "Two Old Houses and Three Young Women" (*Italian Hours*), without mentioning their names. Were they real people? Marilla Battilana Shankosky in her "Sei personaggi in cerca di nome" (*Ateneo Veneto* 10, i–ii[1972]:217–30) relates the amusing story of her successful research into the identity of those six characters. We know now that the "three young women" were the three Mocenigo sisters. Poe's "The Masque of the Red Death" suggested Margherita Guidacci's article "Su un racconto di Poe" (*Humanitas* 10:721–30). Poe's literary craft, his metaphysical concern, his use of time as a supernatural presence, and the tale's affinities with Hawthorne's "Howe's Masquerade" are competently analyzed and described. Lina Unali's "Sulla *Divinity School Address* di Ralph Waldo Emerson e sull'uso della parola *Soul*" (*Annali della Facoltà di Lettere-Filosofia e Magistero* [Cagliari] 36[1973]:3–21) is a sound scholarly contribution that shows how in the "Divinity School Address" Emerson often used the word *soul* as antithetical to the idea of "church" and, when it realizes its full potential, analogous to the idea of God. Emerson's conception of the divine as embodied in the human spirit is therefore clarified. W. D. Howells's critical essay on the Italian poet Giusti and his remarkable ability as translator are briefly evaluated in Rolando Anzilotti's essay on the fortune of Giusti's work in

English-speaking countries contained in *Giuseppe Giusti e la Toscana del suo tempo* (Roma: Accademia Nazionale dei Lincei), pp. 83–85. The continuing interest in T. S. Eliot's poetry among Italian scholars was evidenced by *Rhapsody* (Milano: Bompiani), a 123-page book that includes three close analyses of "Rhapsody on a Windy Night," which are meant also to prove the fecundity of semiological methods. Marcello Pagnini's convincing "Sullo stile modulare del primo Eliot" ferrets out the structuring principle of the poem; Alessandro Serpieri sees the poem as a revealing moment of Eliot's metaphorical system, particularly as regards wet/dry and flesh/bones oppositions; Anthony Johnson, professedly indebted to the previous two contributions, offers a deeper and sometimes overingenious exposition of phanopoeic progression and sexual suggestions in the text. Another major figure of 20th-century poetry who received attention was Ezra Pound. Margherita Guidacci sympathetically reviewed most of his important critical statements in "Saggi letterari di Ezra Pound" (*Humanitas* 4:277–84). Girolamo Mancuso's *Pound e la Cina* (Milano: Feltrinelli) is certainly one of the best scholarly works that have appeared this year. It is a very able and comprehensive study, based on extensive reading, critically sound and penetrating. As a sinologist Mancuso proves competently how Pound's approach to the Chinese language, poetry, and thought—though marred by deficiencies in information, errors in understanding and idiosyncrasies—had an all-important influence on Pound's poetry and ideology. The ideographic method is accurately studied and defined; its basic features are found in juxtapositions, quotations, and recurring themes; its validity "is to be gauged by the poetical results it has brought about and not by the scientific precision of Pound's and Fenollosa's ideas on Chinese ideographs." The identification and analysis of one "ideographic constellation" in the *Cantos* proves the viability of the new way of reading that is proposed.

Thomas Merton, uomo e poeta (Pisa: Pacini) by Francesco M. Casotti is a well-balanced study, remarkable for scholarly accuracy, sympathetic understanding, and sober judgment. A detailed account of Merton's intellectual journey and literary development (particularly enlightening is the chapter on his encounter with Neotomistic Aesthetics) leads to an apt description of his major poetical themes—condemnation of materialistic, mundane, massified society and contemplation of nature as a way to God—and to the assessment of his representatives and validity not only as a 20th-century intellectual but also as a modernistic poet.

An essay in book form and an article were devoted this year to Sylvia Plath. Biancamaria Pisapia's *L'arte di Sylvia Plath* (Roma: Bulzoni) is a detailed comment on and appreciation of Plath's poetry, lacking perhaps in cultural density (one misses a discussion of the use of symbolic language, and also of the relationship with the cultural movements of the poet's time), but sensitive and clearly written. Bianca Tarozzi's "La nascita del mostro" (*Per la critica* 7–8:75–86) deals with Plath's obsession with death. The birth of the monster, the terrible event prefigured in the early poems, finally takes place in the revelation of the dry, biting verse of *Ariel*: it is the poet's surrender to her own voracious death-wish.

In "Marianne Moore, il Basilisco Piumato" (*Nuova Corrente* 63:178–80) Silvano Sabbadini opposes Eliot's view of Moore, maintaining that "she does not see the object as an objective correlative of the idea; she sees the idea as the correlative of an object." Moore's poetry, he argues, rejects the all-knowing ambition contained in traditional romanticism. Her abstract menagerie, her exquisite arabesques are ideas, not objects; they give expression to the contemporary view of the universe as fragmented and inhuman, bounded by death.

Interest in black literature this year was represented by the final chapter of Loretta Valtz Manucci's *I negri americani dalla Depressione al dopoguerra: Esperienze sociali e documenti letterari* (Milano: Feltrinelli). The author sees the works of black fiction writers of the 1940s (Wright, Himes, Yerby, and Ellison) as documents of the decline of the Uncle Tom self-image and the rise of a new self-awareness among black Americans.

University of Pisa

iv. Japanese Contributions

Keiko Beppu

A salient aspect of Japanese work on American literature published during the year 1974 is our scholars' interest in contemporary novels and novelists, enhanced (perhaps) by the visits of Ihab Hassan in July and of John Gardner in September. Giichi Ouchi's *America*

Kokujin Bungaku [*Afro-American Literature*] (Tokyo: Hyoronsha)
and *Gendai America Bungaku Nyumon* [*Contemporary American
Literature: An Introduction*] ed. Naotaro Takiguchi (Tokyo: Hyoronsha) are valuable student guides, which cover the subject extensively, though not in depth. More ambitious works on the same
subject are: Iwao Iwamoto's *Gendai no America Shosetsu: Tairitsu
to Mosaku* [*The Contemporary American Novel: Rebellion and
Quest*] (Tokyo: Eichosha) and Tetsuji Akasofu's *Logos no Yukue:
Gendai America Bungaku Ron* [*The Fate of Logos: A Study of Contemporary American Literature*] (Tokyo: Eichosha).

Iwamoto, prolific critic of American literature and translator of
Ihab Hassan's *Radical Innocence*, shows some insight into contemporary literature, both American and Japanese. The first part of Iwamoto's book is a succinct summary of literary trends in America since
the end of World War II; the third part is a valid, though already
familiar, analysis of contemporary literary scenes. In the second part
Iwamoto deals with individual novelists: Mailer, Capote, Malamud,
Styron, Updike, and Roth. Especially suggestive is his chapter on
John Updike. Iwamoto draws an interesting parallel between Updike's *Rabbit, Run* and Kobo Abe's *Woman of the Dunes*. In these
novels he sees the same leitmotif—the "strategy of escape"—but he
concludes that Abe's protagonist, who comes to see the futility of his
efforts to escape, is tragic, and that Updike's "hero," who never understands the meaning of his escapade, is comic. Tetsuji Akasofu,
author of *The Fate of Logos* is psycholinguistics oriented. He examines the possibilities of verbal expression in contemporary novels; he
regards John Barth's *The End of the Road* and Philip Roth's *The
Breast* as experiments in symbology. Like Iwamoto, Akasofu sees
both American and Japanese writers sharing a similar problem, and
devotes an entire chapter to a discussion of Japanese writers' concern
with their language.

Along with studies of contemporary novelists, there is continued
interest in 19th- and early 20th-century writers. Masao Takahashi's
Ushinawareta Jidai no Sakkatachi [*Writers of the Lost Generation:
F. Scott Fitzgerald, John Dos Passos, Ernest Hemingway, and William Faulkner*] (Tokyo: Toyamabo) is the second in a series of studies on 20th-century American literature.

In his *Nathaniel Hawthorne Ron: America Shinwa to Sozoryoku*
[*Nathaniel Hawthorne: American Imagination and Myth*] (Tokyo:

Nanundo), Koji Ohi takes the position of Leo Marx (and of David Noble) that the job of any serious writer is to debunk the American myth—either of the agrarian paradise or of the kingdom of God on earth—and he considers Hawthorne such a writer. Ohi's attempt to see the embodiment of the American "cultural symbol" in Hawthorne's major stories ("The Birthmark" and "Rappaccini's Daughter") and romances is valid and executed with competence. The best discussion is his chapter on *The Blithedale Romance*, but the application of his thesis to *The Scarlet Letter* is not convincing. The reader detects a note of strain in his comment that the letter *A* may represent the *A* in *American*! Yet, on the whole, Ohi's *Nathaniel Hawthorne* is a valuable study, which goes beyond literary criticism, establishing Hawthorne in a much wider scope of American studies.

The most unusual work among the books here surveyed is Masami Nishikawa's *Ambrose Bierce: Kozetsu no Fushika* [*Ambrose Bierce: A Lone Satirist*] (Tokyo: Shinchosha). This readable literary biography is the fruit of our senior scholar's long research on Bierce's writings. In the preface to his book, Nishikawa recalls his discovery in 1964 of a complete set of the first edition of *Collected Writings of Ambrose Bierce*, once owned by a Japanese genius of the short story, Ryunosuke Akutagawa. Akutagawa's article, written in 1921, is possibly, Mr. Nishikawa contends, the first to introduce Bierce to a Japanese audience. Nishikawa's twofold interest in Bierce and in Akutagawa is the embryo of his present work.

Nishikawa vividly reconstructs the life of the "dean of West Coast journalism" mostly from Bierce's articles, stories, and autobiographical sketches, and partly from Paul Fatout's biography and Robert Wiggins's study on Bierce. He admits the disadvantage in writing a biography based on insufficient materials, and leaves much to his (and our) speculation. For example, he attributes Bierce's prejudice against the Japanese people he encountered in California to his belief in the doctrine of "election" inherited from his puritan parents. Like Akutagawa's enjoyment of Bierce's bizarre tales, Mr. Nishikawa's interest in his subject is strongly personal. These three—Akutagawa, Bierce, and the biographer—seem to have their share of the "devil's delight."

Among the numerous articles published in various journals and English studies, Tsuguo Aoki's "Matsuei no Kokuhaku: the Revision of *The Aspern Papers*" ["The Confession of a Descendant of Puritans: on the Revision of *The Aspern Papers*"] in *The English Literary Quarterly* (12:49–69) deserves attention here. Aoki, a devoted James scholar, is thoroughgoing in his reading of James's revision of the nouvelle. The article throws light on a new aspect of the narrator, whom Wayne Booth has condemned as shameless and insensitive. The implied conclusion of Aoki's essay is that the "New England conscience" is not the monopoly of a Strether or a Fleda Vetch. The confession is James's and the commentator's own. Some other readable essays (Japanese titles omitted) are "Gertrude Stein and the Atomic Bomb" by Hisao Kanazeki in *The Rising Generation* (120: 418–19) and "Man and Woman in American literature" by Naotaro Takiguchi (ibid., pp. 54–57).

Kobe College

v. Scandinavian Contributions

Rolf Lundén

With few exceptions the Scandinavian contributions during 1974 were devoted to 19th-century fiction, and, in particular, to that of the American Renaissance.

Erik Ingvar Thurin's *The Universal Autobiography of Ralph Waldo Emerson* (Lund Studies in English, vol. 46) is a book whose value is diminished by being too thesis-ridden. Thurin leaves no reader in doubt of his own learning, and he produces a number of fresh and thoughtful insights into Emerson's works and character, and yet the book comes out all wrong. In an illuminating way the author draws our attention to the frustrations that undoubtedly existed under Emerson's "optimistic" surface, investigating the Transcendentalist in the light of sex. But Thurin is carried away by his subject. Emerson becomes a homosexual—at heart if not in practice —a woman-hater dreaming of sublime friendship with other men. What is least satisfactory is Thurin's way of proving his point. Too often he "assumes" what Emerson's opinions were on sex, friendship, women, family life; a page or two later these assumptions have become facts on which new assumptions are based. Thurin insists that his investigation is "not a search for 'low' motives in a Freudian sense," but all his scholarly discussions on philosophical "affinities" cannot free him from the suspicion that such is the case. He even implies (p. 217) that Emerson felt more than parental love for his own son, Waldo, II. One leaves the book with the feeling that not only Emerson but everybody else from Jesus to Thoreau were thwarted homosexuals.

Hawthorne was given a fairer deal by the Scandinavian scholars. Orm Överland's "The Unhumanizing Imagination: Hawthorne's *The Blithedale Romance*" (*SN* 46:370–81) tries to demonstrate on the one hand Coverdale's reluctance to become involved in life and on the other his "corresponding urge to approach life with the cold, dissecting and analytic intellect of the natural scientist." Parallel to the Theodore–Veiled Lady legend in the book, Coverdale isolates himself by turning down the love and affection of Priscilla, Zenobia, and Hollingworth. Överland also sees Coverdale as a detached scientist speculating in the feelings of others, a speculation which "unhumanizes" his heart. However, Coverdale learns to distrust the ability of the artist's imagination. The irony of the story is that his reluctance to embrace life and his attempt to remain true to his vocation as the calm observer make it impossible for him to recapture life in his art.

Arne Axelsson finds Överland's picture of Coverdale somewhat distorted. In a companion piece, "Witness for the Defense: Coverdale in Hawthorne's *Blithedale Romance*" (*SN* 46:382–90), he holds, using evidence from the text, that Coverdale's failure to become involved in life was "not so much [his] own reluctance to approach other people as their insensitivity and lack of response to [his] attempts." Nor is Coverdale, according to Axelsson, as cool an observer as Överland states, but rather a man who is capable of sympathy and who acts out of jealousy and a wish for revenge.

Axelsson has also proved his intimate knowledge of Hawthorne in a doctoral dissertation, *The Links in the Chain: Isolation and Interdependence in Nathaniel Hawthorne's Fictional Characters*, Studia Anglistica Upsaliensia, 17 (Uppsala: Universitets-Biblioteket). This study displays an admirable completeness in that it discusses the theme of isolation-interdependence in all the characters, thereby showing how truly predominant this motif is in Hawthorne's fiction. Axelsson even finds this theme so central that it could be considered the synthesis of all Hawthorne wanted to say, a statement open to discussion. Although Axelsson is aware of the arbitrariness of too rigid pigeon-holing, he distributes the characters into nine different categories. The isolatoes are divided into voluntary or involuntary, each of these main groups having subdivisions. Lady Eleanore Rochcliffe withdraws voluntarily from life because of her pride, whereas Chillingworth's isolation is designated involuntary because he too strongly desires revenge. Isn't Chillingworth rather taking the consequences of a deliberate choice? Axelsson considers Hilda's isolation in *The Marble Faun* involuntary (she is put into a subcategory called "Victims of Other People"), while characterizing Hepzibah Pyncheon's withdrawal in *The House of the Seven Gables* as voluntary. In what way is Hilda a victim and Hepzibah not? But in spite of such disputable classifications Axelsson's book gives many perceptive analyses of Hawthorne's characters and their roles.

Dorothy Burton Skårdal deals with an entirely different aspect of 19th-century fiction. *The Divided Heart: Scandinavian Immigrant Experience through Literary Sources* (Oslo: Universitetsforlaget) uses subliterary Scandinavian immigrant fiction published in the United States as a basis for a sociohistorical analysis. Conscious of the unreliability of the material, Skårdal gives a balanced picture of the Scandinavian-American immigrants: the cultural shock and the "dog years" they all experienced; the gradual change in their schools, churches, morals, and manners; the homesickness and the generation gap. In the preface Oscar Handlin correctly characterizes Skårdal's achievement when he concludes that "she has been able to tell us much about the character of immigrant literature and the character of immigration. On both accounts, she has made a valuable contribution to American social history."

In "Henry James ex Cathedra: The Performing Pedagog" (*American Studies in Scandinavia* 6:47–65), Thor Gabrielsen scrutinizes the prefaces to the New York edition. This study, which includes extraneous material and is somewhat disorganized, pays special attention to James's pedagogic gifts: his ability to keep the reader's interest, his method of establishing his own authority, his use of such rhetorical devices as repetition and imagery.

The long period from James to the 1950s received virtually no interest during 1974 from the Scandinavian scholars. Jan W. Dietrichson makes a general evaluation of "Theme and Technique in James Agee's *A Death in the Family*" (*American Studies in Scandinavia* 6:1–20). Drawing extensively on the judgment of other critics,

Dietrichson presents the two main themes of death and family as being equally important. He also studies the tripartite structure, the double time scheme, and Agee's descriptive impressionism.

Although Per Seyersted gives an outline of the early developments of black fiction, his main concern in "A Survey of Trends and Figures in Afro-American Fiction" (*American Studies in Scandinavia* 6:67–86) is the post-Wright period. Quite naturally, the focus is on Wright, Ellison, and Baldwin, but Hughes, John A. Williams, and Sam Greenlee are also discussed. Seyersted convincingly depicts the change towards greater militancy in Williams and Greenlee and the parallel shift from self-hatred to celebration of blackness that occurred after 1965. In the authors of the 1970s—George Cain, James Alan McPherson, Ernest J. Gaines—Seyersted finds a trend away from solidarity with the group toward a greater emphasis on common humanity. These writers look upon their fictional characters as individuals rather than representatives of a race, a development which of course does not exclude a political commitment as well.

This year only one study was devoted to poetry, none to drama. Brita Lindberg-Seyersted's "Notes on Three Poems by Sylvia Plath" (*Edda*, Hefte 1:47–54) draws attention to the ironic undercurrent in "Watercolor of Grantchester Meadows"; to the fact that wilderness leads to purification from the triviality of daily life and from the egocentricity of modern man as presented in "Two Campers in Cloud Country"; and to the common misreading of "Daddy" as an autobiographical poem, which should rather be read primarily as an allegory.

University of Uppsala

Author Index

Subject Index